Reminiscences of
Swami Vivekananda

By

His Eastern and Western Admirers

Advaita Ashrama
(Publication House of Ramakrishna Math)
5 Dehi Entally Road • Kolkata 700 014

Published by
Swami Muktidananda
Adhyaksha, Advaita Ashrama
Mayavati, Champawat, Uttarakhand, Himalayas
from its Publication Department, Kolkata
E-mail: mail@advaitaashrama.org
Web Site: www.advaitaashrama.org

First Edition, May 1961
Second Edition, March 1964
Third Edition, May 1983
Fourth Edition, May 2004
Fifth Edition, June 2017
2M2C

ISBN 978-81-85301-17-4

Printed in India at
Trio Process
Kolkata 700 014

PUBLISHER'S NOTE
TO THE FIFTH EDITION

We are pleased to present to our readers this new and enlarged edition of *Reminiscences of Swami Vivekananda*. Twenty-two new reminiscences have been added in this edition—reminiscences by Swamis Shivananda, Turiyananda, Saradananda, Akhandananda, Vijnanananda, Achalananda, Atulananda, Virajananda, and Sadananda, as also of Brajendranath Seal, C. Ramanujachari, Kumudbandhu Sen, Lillian Montgomery, Mohanlal Shah, Mary Tapan Wright, Sacchindranath Bose, Manmathanath Chowdhury, Harbilas Sarda, G. G. Narasimhachari, Ella Wheeler Wilcox, Shailendranath Bandopadhyay, and Alice Hansbrough. The source has been cited at the end of each reminiscence.

In addition, some short reminiscences have been given in a separate chapter. Swami Shuddhananda's reminiscences have been enlarged by adding hitherto untranslated portions. Again, reminiscences by Mary C. Funke have been enlarged by including relevant portions from *Inspired Talks*. The reminiscences by K. Sundararama Iyer, which had previously been divided into two chapters, have now been combined into one.

Swami Vimohananda of Advaita Ashrama, Kolkata, has compiled the new reminiscences and also translated the reminiscences of Swami Shivananda and the additional material by Swami Shuddhananda from the original Bengali. Some years ago the late Peter Schneider, known to all as Hiranyagarbha, a devotee of the Vedanta Society of Southern California, kindly revised the whole manuscript and gave us his valuable suggestions. It is a matter of regret that he is not with us now to see the result of his devoted labour.

We are also grateful to Arvind Nevatia for going over the final proofs.

We are certain that this new edition will be warmly received by all the admirers and followers of Swami Vivekananda.

—Publisher

1 April 2017

PUBLISHER'S NOTE
TO THE FIRST EDITION

Most of these reminiscences appeared in periodicals from time to time. They are reproduced with due permission and thanks. The memories of Sister Christine are copyrighted by Shri Boshishwar Sen of Almora. In the absence of a more comprehensive term for the contributors, we have styled them as "His Eastern and Western Admirers", though some of them are disciples, some friends, and some others admirers. The last writer is rather prejudiced.* His article, however, deserved inclusion as depicting a picture not generally known. The articles are printed almost as they appeared earlier. In Sundararama Iyer's second account, a few paragraphs summarising Swamiji's Chennai speeches have been omitted as these would have been superfluous.

A few more articles have been treated thus for similar reasons and the omitted portions have been marked with three dots.

Although these reminiscences are attractive, informative, and instructive, we must tell the readers that the publisher does not necessarily subscribe to all the opinions expressed in them. For instance, B. G. Tilak's belief that Swamiji agreed with him that the *Bhagavad Gita* does not speak of monasticism and Reeves Calkins's insinuation that in his talks Swamiji reproduced verbatim some of his set speeches are palpably wrong, and no student of Swamiji's life and works can be misled. Such errors, however, are not many. At some places we have added footnotes to rectify biographical inaccuracies.

We hope that the book will be received as a timely publication, coming as it does on the eve of Swamiji's birthday centenary celebrations.

Mayavati   —Publisher
1 May 1961

SWAMI VIVEKANANDA (1863 – 1902)

"My ideal indeed can be put into a few words, and that is: to preach unto mankind
their divinity, and how to make it manifest in every movement of life."

Contents

Swami Shivananda

There is no doubt that the more one studies the life of the world-famous Swami Vivekananda, foremost disciple of Sri Ramakrishna, the more will grow one's faith and devotion and the more will one progress along the path of service.

I first had the great good fortune of meeting Sri Ramakrishna and receiving his grace in 1879 or 1880. This was certainly due to some merit I may have acquired in my previous births. I first saw him at the house of his great householder devotee Ramachandra Dutta, a relative of Swamiji—then called Narendranath Dutta—who also lived nearby. On that day, Ramachandra had invited Sri Ramakrishna and many of his devotees to his house to celebrate a religious festival. That was probably also the first time I saw Swamiji among the devotees.

As I started to visit Dakshineshwar and got to know Sri Ramakrishna and his devotees, I became very friendly with Swamiji. In those days, the devotees used to meet regularly at Ramachandra's house and take part in discussions on the life and teachings of the Master while singing and taking part in other devotional activities. My hunger to associate closely with Sri Ramakrishna's devotees grew stronger. Noticing this, the Master said to Ramachandra in the presence of other devotees, "Tarak [Swami Shivananda's pre-monastic name] is very eager for close association with my devotees, so let him stay at your house." Ramachandra agreed, and that very day I accepted his invitation to stay at his house from then on.

SWAMI SHIVANANDA

When Swamiji was in Sri Ramakrishna's presence, I was struck to see the great love the Master had for him. Now that I had the opportunity to mix with Swamiji and talk to him, the more did I realize his greatness.

By the Master's grace I was able to renounce the world, and Swamiji too gradually cut off all worldly ties. However, the power and force of Swamiji's character shone so brightly that I felt like a faint star next to the full moon of Swamiji. When Sri Ramakrishna was lying ill at Cossipore, it was Swamiji who gathered us and engaged us in his service. It was also under his leadership that we wholeheartedly undertook spiritual practices and scriptural study.

Many incidents bear testimony to the fact that, from his very childhood Swamiji used to feel intensely for others. After the death of his father, his family was in dire straits. Swamiji's friends greatly appreciated his many good qualities and tried to help him financially, some of them even keeping it anonymous. But many times, returning home after somehow earning a little money, Swamiji would meet a needy friend on the way. Knowing fully well that what little he had in his pocket would provide his family's next meal, Swamiji would nevertheless give it to the friend and go home empty-handed. When his mother would ask whether he had gotten any money, he would say, "Not today—please manage somehow." But then, by the Lord's grace, some other acquaintance of Swamiji's would turn up with money, and Swamiji would immediately hand it over to his mother. Such incidents were frequent.

One day, at Cossipore, Swami Yogananda said to Swamiji: "A lady of our village is very poor and has become a widow. She has her children to look after and there's no one to support her. She'll be in big trouble if she doesn't get at least thirty rupees immediately." This pained Swamiji greatly. Most of us were students, and nobody had much money. However, Swamiji knew I had a savings account. He came to me and said: "Brother Tarak, you are a monk. What do you need money for? That poor lady has a great need for thirty rupees. Please take that much out of your account and send it to her. We'll certainly help her however we can." I withdrew the required amount and handed it over to Swamiji, who immediately sent it to Swami Yogananda for the lady.

These incidents illustrate Swamiji's great compassion while still a young man. And now, the people of India—nay, the whole world—are coming to see how, as time went by, his compassion embraced all of mankind.

During the time when we were engaged in the service of the Master at Cossipore, we were studying Vedanta intently, and at one point our spirit of renunciation grew so intense that suddenly Swamiji, along with Swami Abhedananda and myself, without mentioning it to Sri Ramakrishna, left for Bodha Gaya—the place where Lord Buddha performed austerities and attained illumination. Reaching the place, Swamiji sat under the sacred Bodhi tree and entered into deep meditation. We, too, sat in meditation next to him. After some time, Swamiji suddenly burst into tears like a child and embraced me, and then again entered into meditation. When I later asked him about it, he replied: "While meditating I recalled how that great soul, Lord Buddha, left his kingdom, parents, wife, and child in search of knowledge and engaged himself in severe austerities which culminated in samadhi. 'Where is he now? Where is that great soul? Why can't I see him?'—thinking in this way, I so keenly felt the absence of Lord Buddha that I couldn't control myself and burst into tears."

We spent three days in meditation and other spiritual practices as well as visiting other places near Bodha Gaya, bathing in the river Phalgu and so forth, and then returned to Cossipore. When we got back we found out that Sri Ramakrishna had become worried at Swamiji's going away without informing him, and our brother-disciples had also been filled with anxiety. When the young disciples, becoming distressed, had approached the Master, he had said: "Just like a bird who sits on the mast of a ship flies off in all directions but finally returns to the mast, Naren will come back here after all his wanderings. Don't worry." What the Master had said came to pass and all of us returned to Cossipore on the fourth day.

After the Master's passing away, Swamiji became very concerned for his brother-disciples. All of us were without any means of support, yet, having lived together and served the Master for so long, we were now united by a strong tie of brotherhood which would be difficult to break. Eleven or twelve days after the Master's passing away, I joined a party consisting of Holy Mother, two women devotees, and Swamis Adbhutananda and Yogananda on a pilgrimage to Vrindavan. We all stayed in a house belonging to Balaram Bose, a close devotee of the Master.

Meanwhile, back in Kolkata (then Calcutta), Swamiji was frantically searching for a place where all of us brother-disciples could take shelter, and, spending our time in spiritual practices and scriptural study in solitude, could attain the Self-knowledge which the Master had taught us to be the ultimate goal of human life. By the grace of the Master, one of his rich householder devotees, Surendranath Mitra, who lived near Swamiji, came to him suddenly one day and said, with tears in his eyes, "Naren, will you grant me a favour?" "Of course!" Swamiji replied, "How sincerely you've served the Master! We'll do anything for you." Surendranath then said: "Sri Ramakrishna appeared before me and said: 'Oh! what are you doing? My children are wandering in the streets. Look at their sad condition! Make some arrangement for them and help them to attain the goal of life.' So I'm asking you to gather all the disciples of the Master and rent a house in some secluded place between Kolkata and Dakshineshwar where you can all stay."

Swamiji replied: "I, too, have been wondering how to bring together all the young disciples of the Master. Now, by the will of the Lord, you come to show us the way. I'll set to work today itself." The next day, Swamiji called Bhavanath Chatterjee—his dear friend and a disciple of the Master—

and arranged to rent a house at Baranagore. The house was old and belonged to some zamindars of Taki. One of the rooms contained the library of a self-improvement association Bhavanath had formed, and meetings were occasionally held there. Our monastery was established in the remaining five or six rooms. A picture of Sri Ramakrishna was placed in one of the rooms, and many of his young disciples began to gather at the house. Swamiji didn't have to worry about us anymore, for here we could completely immerse ourselves in austerities and the study of the scriptures.

After a few days, Swamiji, along with myself and a few other brother-disciples, went to Varanasi for some days and practised austerities there. Swamiji lived alone in a garden-house, and we stayed in another spot. We would meet occasionally. Swamiji also visited Ghazipur to meet Pavhari Baba and stayed close to the saint's cottage. After some days, Swamiji set out for the Himalayas with some of his brother-disciples. However, a disciple who had set out with him from Hathras fell seriously ill on the way, and after getting as far as Rishikesh, Swamiji had to return to Hathras. Staying there with his disciple, Swamiji also fell ill.

I, too, had set out for the Himalayas after Swamiji. But on the way I decided to visit Vrindavan, and got down at Hathras to change trains. However, I happened to learn that Swamiji was also there and that he wasn't well. I cancelled my Vrindavan trip, and found Swamiji after a little searching. Seeing me, he said: "You have come, brother Tarak! I had thought of going to Haridwar, set up a hut, and ask you to join me there. Anyway, please come back here after visiting Vrindavan so that we can go to Rishikesh together."

But when I got back from Vrindavan I could see that he was very ill. I told him so, and added: "It's better if you don't go to the Himalayas now. I'll postpone my journey, too, and go back to the monastery with you." Swamiji replied: "No, you have set out with a noble purpose and shouldn't cancel your plans. Please go to Haridwar, and I'll go there after I recover." "This can never be," I said. "There's no way I can leave you in this condition. I'll go back with you to Kolkata. What—you're lying ill in a remote place like this and I will go away to practise austerities? Never!" Swamiji agreed to my plan, and we left for Kolkata the same day.

After spending some days in the monastery at Baranagore, Swamiji again wished to go to the Himalayas to practice austerities. He visited various places in the Himalayas with four brother-disciples, and finally settled down in Rishikesh. After spending some days joyfully in spiritual practices, he fell very ill, and at one point his life seemed to be in danger. However, he recovered and the group then descended to the plains. Swamiji then spent some time at Meerut and fully recovered his health. After this he set out alone in the direction of Rajputana. Before leaving, he said to his brother-disciples: "I'm now going to travel alone. You won't know my whereabouts for some years."

And in fact, we received very little news about Swamiji for the next three years. When we were at the Alambazar monastery, we occasionally received news of Swamiji being somewhere in the Kathiawar district. One day we suddenly received a long letter from him, about ten-twelve pages, written in Persian, and from this we learned that he was learning Persian. After this we received no news of him for quite some time. In May 1893, he left for America to attend the Parliament of Religions in Chicago.

In 1897 Swamiji returned to India, halting at Sri Lanka on the way. From there he went to Chennai. I, along with a few monks, went to receive him at Madurai. At Madurai he alighted from the stage coach of the raja of Ramnad and embraced us with great joy. Swamiji was accompanied by his disciples, Captain and Mrs. Sevier and Mr. Goodwin, and all of us took up our residence in the palace of the Raja of Ramnad. In the evening the educated community of Madurai presented Swamiji with an address of welcome at Madurai College. Here I experienced, for the first time, the force of Swamiji's lectures.

Never before had I been conscious of such power in his speech, though I had lived and travelled with him. He had acquired such a command of the English language that it now seemed to be his mother tongue. The college campus was filled to overflowing, and people were even standing outside—they, too, were listening to his lecture in mute wonder. That evening we boarded a train bound for Chennai (then Madras). On the way, Professor Rangachari, Swamiji's friend from his premonastic days, asked him to stay for a day at Kashi Kumbakonam (here the Sanskrit language is very popular, as in Kashi; thus this name. There is also a First Class college here). Swamiji couldn't ignore his request, and got down at Kumbakonam. In the evening, at the request of the professor, he gave a lecture at the college that lasted about two hours. The teachers and students as well as the scholars who were present were charmed by the lecture. Next morning, we left for Chennai. When the train arrived at the station we found the platform overflowing with so many people that we could not find a way out of the station. The police commissioner, along with a few sergeants, came to Swamiji and had to lead him by the hand out of the station to a chariot made specially for him.

Swamiji and the rest of us took our seats in the chariot. Outside the station the roads, the balconies, and the rooftops of the houses were full of people waiting to see Swamiji excitedly, as if he were a god. It took us about two hours to reach Castle Kernan, where Swamiji was supposed to stay. He stayed in Chennai for five or six days, and delivered as many lectures. Then, along with a few of his Chennai disciples, he travelled by steamer to Kolkata. We accompanied him, as did his foreign disciples. There, too, Swamiji discussed religious topics with some clergymen who happened to be aboard the steamer, and the clergymen learned many things from Swamiji. To hear Swamiji talk, almost all of the passengers would assemble on the deck of the steamer, making it look like a lecture hall.

When Swamiji reached Kolkata, he was welcomed on a grand scale. Here, too, he delivered a few lectures. We spent a few days with him in the monastery in great joy. The bliss we experienced in those days can never be described. Swamiji again visited America via England in the middle of 1899. He remained in the West for about a year and a half, spreading the message of Vedanta and establishing two Vedanta centres. Putting Swamis Abhedananda and Turiyananda in charge of the centres, he returned to India in December 1900. He suffered much from diabetes for about two or three years.

Swamiji's health had broken down due to his excessive labours in Europe and America, and he decided to go to Almora to rest with a few disciples. At the time I was staying there, and thus got the opportunity to be with him again. His talk was always pregnant with wisdom. A few days before Swamiji arrived at Almora, the monastery was transferred from Alambazar to a rented house near the present Belur Math.

While I was in Almora, Swamiji asked me to go to Sri Lanka and establish a Vedanta Society there. Accordingly, I stayed in Sri Lanka for about eight months and established the Colombo Vedanta Society. There also I would receive regular news of Swamiji, and of how his brother-disciples and disciples were spending their days joyfully in his company at Belur Math. My desire to be in his holy company again grew so strong that I, too, went to Belur Math.

Towards the end of 1901 or the beginning of 1902 I had gone to Kankhal, and there received the news that Swamiji's health being very bad, he would be going to Varanasi for rest and would stay there in the garden-house of Kalikrishna Thakur. I too went to Varanasi, but on arriving received the news that Swamiji hadn't arrived yet. Kalikrishna made his own room fit for Swamiji's stay and himself supervised all the arrangements. All his employees were asked to be in Swamiji's service as long as he stayed there. Swamiji looked very emaciated when he arrived, but his health slowly began

to improve after a few days due to the change of climate. While Swamiji was living in the garden-house, the abbot of the Kedarnath monastery came to meet him and also took him to visit his monastery. We also accompanied Swamiji. We went into the temple of Kedarnath to see the deity and were also fed sumptuously by the venerable abbot. The abbot worshipped Swamiji as he would worship Lord Shiva himself, and presented him with ochre clothes. We returned to the garden-house in the evening.

The raja of Bhinga was an important landlord who at the time was staying in his garden-house near the Durga temple in Varanasi. A graduate of Kolkata University and a renowned statesman, he was also a former member of the U.P. Council and the Imperial Council. When he learned of Swamiji's arrival in Varanasi, he sent him presents of fruit, flowers, and sweets. He also made the following request through the bearer of these presents: "I have taken a vow not to go out of the garden-house and will therefore be very grateful if you kindly come yourself to my humble abode. Please forgive me for all the trouble I am putting you to." To this Swamiji replied, "Though I am not keeping good health, I will certainly go to meet the raja." The next day the raja sent a vehicle for Swamiji and we went with him to the meeting. In the course of conversation the raja said to Swamiji: "I have been following your noble work since you left for America. It seems that you are a great soul—like Buddha and Shankaracharya—and have been born to establish religion in this age. For a long time I have been waiting to see you, and it is my good fortune to meet you today. I have seen many scholars and monks in Varanasi, but have not seen the spirit of true religion in anyone. It is my ardent request that you start a centre here for the propagation of the liberal principles of Vedanta. I will give a donation for this purpose." Saying this, the raja handed over some money to Swamiji. Swamiji replied, "I myself am not in good health right now, but I will engage one of my brother-disciples in this work. This is indeed a noble resolve."

While Swamiji was at Varanasi, a highly placed official of the Japanese government who wanted to take him to Japan for the propagation of Vedanta also stayed with him. However, Swamiji's poor health prevented him from visiting Japan.

In June 1902, Swamiji sent me to Varanasi to establish an Advaita Ashrama there. This could be said to be his last effort to spread the message of Vedanta. At his command, I stayed in Varanasi for five years. In due course, by the Lord's grace, a centre got established there on a stable basis.

While Swamiji was staying in Belur Math, many college students came to him to learn the fundamentals of religion and lead a pure life. Gradually his fame spread like a tidal wave through the length and breadth of India, and many centres were established for the propagation of Vedanta and the ideal of service.

Swamiji attained mahasamadhi on 4 July 1902.

There is no doubt that even a little study of the life of this great soul will be conducive to our spiritual progress.

(*Sandipan*, August 1963)

Swamiji stayed for a long time at the home of Chhavildas in Mumbai. It was then that he visited many places in this part of the country. Chhavildas belonged to the Arya Samaj and was against the worship of God with forms. He had much discussion with Swamiji concerning it. One day he said to Swamiji: "Well, Swamiji, you say that worship of God with forms, idol-worship and such other doctrines are true. If you can prove these doctrines by arguments quoted from the Vedas, I shall leave the Arya Samaj, I promise you."

Swamiji replied emphatically, "Yes, surely I can do that." He began explaining the Hindu doctrine of image-worship and such other doctrines in the light of the Vedas, until Chhavildas was convinced. Chhavildas made good his promise by leaving the Arya Samaj. Swamiji was such a genius that he could do that.

It was at this time that Swamiji visited Poona, Malabar, and other places. Usually he avoided travelling by train, but when he took the train, he would travel first-class. Ordinarily he did not accept money from anyone, but if a person insisted on giving him something, he would say, "You may buy me a first-class train ticket, if you wish." Because of his weak stomach he had to have the facilities of a lavatory, which are available in a first-class compartment.

Once, being invited, Swamiji was going to the Maharaja of Limbdi (who was then staying at Mahabaleswar). Plainly dressed, he was resting on a bench in a first-class compartment when some distinguished passengers entered by another door. Finding a sannyasi occupying an entire bench, they became very annoyed and gave vent to their feelings in English. "It is these sannyasis who have been responsible for the downfall of India," they said. Swamiji remained lying down and listened to their criticism unconcerned. But later, when they went to extremes, he lost his patience. He sat up and started arguing the issue with them. He said: "What are you saying! Instead of ruining India the sannyasis have kept her alive. Just think for a moment how great were Buddha, Shankara, Chaitanya and others! Think what they did for India!"

In this way Swamiji proved from history that it is the monks who have kept India alive. He answered these people's arguments so beautifully that they were very much surprised. The foremost of the critic was so pleased with Swamiji's flawless English and scholarly arguments that he invited him to his place. Of course, Swamiji could not accept his invitation at the time, because he was proceeding to the place of the Maharaja of Limbdi who had great regard for him.

Swamiji was fond of the *Nasadiya Sukta* and would chant it so rhythmically, in the right Vedic metre, that one would feel as if a Vedic seer were repeating his own spiritual experience.

> Darkness there was, and all at first was veiled
> In gloom profound—an ocean without light .

Swamiji would repeat this portion of the hymn and say that nowhere in any language would you come across such poetic beauty. In one of his writings he brought out this idea nicely.

Swamiji used to cook sometimes. He had a small water-pot such as the one used in northern India, and in it he would cook lentils and rice. He would offer all food to the Master first, and after distributing it amongst us, he himself would eat. He would say, "Narayana should be fed before one eats."

In the early days of the monastery the hymn "Om, Glory be unto Shiva! Worship Shiva" used to be chanted at the time of vespers. Swamiji composed the hymn to Sri Ramakrishna and put it to music, introducing it at the monastery. He himself would play the drums and lead the singing. That was a wonderful sight! He was so divinely handsome and would put so much spiritual fervour into his singing!

At that time Swamiji made a rule that all should get up at four o'clock in the morning, when the bell rang, and after finishing ablutions go to the chapel for meditation. Swamiji himself would also go there for meditation. If anyone missed it, he would not be allowed to have his meal at the monastery, but would have to beg for his food. Though all of us got up early and meditated, once in a while it so happened that we slept on and did not hear the bell. In the morning Swamiji would say, "If we ourselves do not abide by these rules, how can we expect the boys to do so?"

When Swamiji returned to this country from America after his triumphal preaching, one day Girish Babu said to him: "Well, Naren, you will have to do one thing in compliance with a special request of ours." Girish Babu was very fond of Swamiji, that is why he spoke that way. Swamiji with great earnestness said: "Why do you talk that way? Just tell me what you want me to do." Girish Babu replied, "You will have to write a biography of Sri Ramakrishna." Immediately Swamiji fell back several steps and said in a serious tone: "Well, Girish Babu, please never make such a request to me. I shall very gladly do whatever you ask me other than this. I would not even hesitate to revolutionize the world at your request; but I shall not be able to do the work you have suggested. He [the Master] was so profound, so great, that I have not understood him at all. I have not been able to know even a fraction of his life. Do you advise me to fashion a monkey while trying to mould an image of Shiva? I can't do it !"

At different times Swamiji would be in different moods and would inspire us accordingly. Sometimes we would discuss the path of knowledge, at other times the path of devotion, and so on. There were times when we would remain absorbed with one idea for a month at a stretch. We would be engrossed in the same mood day and night without interruption. While eating, lying down, or sitting—at all times we would have the same discussions and arguments, and we would also perform spiritual disciplines appropriate to those moods.

Swamiji was very fond of the ideas of Lord Buddha and he was well read in Buddhist philosophy. He was not one-sided in any way. From those days on, Swamiji had ideas, language, and reasoning of a unique kind. Even his ordinary conversation would be full of lofty ideas expressed in scholarly language. He liked the style of Milton, and he would carry on his discussion and arguments in that style. Before going to America, Swamiji wandered as an itinerant monk from one corner of India to another, and during those wanderings he met the Dewan of Junagad. By talking with Swamiji the Dewan was so impressed that he said to him, "Swamiji, you have a very bright future before you." His prediction came true. While in America, Swamiji became a little nervous at the Parliament of Religions in Chicago. It was but natural. It was such a huge gathering: thousands of people—the very best, the cream of society. Swamiji didn't know what he would say, because he hadn't gone there with a prepared lecture. Dr. Barrows called upon him to speak but he kept putting him off. Suddenly he was reminded of a certain verse: "I salute the all-blissful Krishna, by whose compassion the mute become eloquent and the cripple scale mountains." The moment this verse came to his mind, all nervousness left him. Saluting the Master mentally, he stood up; and what followed you must have read. The world heard a new message from his lips. His lecture was the very best. My child, it was all the play of the power of God! Swamiji was a direct instrument of the Master. All the scholarly speakers who came prepared to establish the greatness of their denominations paled into insignificance before Swamiji.

Noticing his success, the people of America collected large funds and sent Dr. Barrows to India and such other countries to preach Christianity. Dr. Barrows visited different places in India and gave lectures with very little result. Swamiji started preaching the message of Vedanta in the West and we received reports of his lectures here. At first we could hardly believe that these were lectures given by Swamiji. He didn't use the language nor the ideas we were familiar with. Everything had changed. He had a new message and a new language. Before going to America, he had a leaning towards the path of knowledge and his language was very philosophical and scholarly. But in the lectures which he gave in the West his language was simple and direct and his ideas were full of life and love. Returning to India, he remarked: "Do you think I gave those lectures? It was the Master who spoke through me." In reality it was so.

Swamiji would enter the shrine [for worship], take his seat and meditate for a long time. It would be a deep meditation. After meditating for about an hour and a half, he would begin the worship. Meditation was very important in his worship. He would then bathe the Master and, adding sandalwood paste in the tray of flowers, would offer those flowers with both hands at his blessed feet again and again. His worship was indeed a sight to see. Finally he would prostrate himself, get up, and leave the shrine. Someone else would go and offer the food. In his worship meditation was the major feature.

See how Swamiji had to depart prematurely owing to incessant strenuous work. Many a time did he go away to the Himalayas to practise intense austerities, but each time somebody dragged him down from the lap of the mountains. He started moving through Rajasthan and other places, and met many rajas and maharajas. In the course of his wanderings, he reached Porbandar. That princely state was then without a ruler and it was in a chaotic condition. So the British Government appointed Sri Shankara Rao administrator of the state. He was a very learned, intelligent, and honest man. He had travelled extensively in Europe, and had learnt French and German quite well. In his house he had a big library of his own; he was very studious by nature. This library attracted Swamiji very much. When he expressed his feelings to Sri Shankar Rao, the latter said with great delight, "You can stay here as long as you like and study".

So Swamiji stayed there for some time. Sri Shankar Rao was a master of Sanskrit. One day he said to Swamiji: "To tell you the truth, Swamiji, when I first read the scriptures, it seemed as though they contained no truth, as though it was all a figment of the brains of the writers of those books—as though they had written as and when the fancies fleeted across their minds. But after seeing and keeping company with you intimately, my idea has changed; now it strikes me that our religious literature is all true. I noticed in the

West that the thinking people there are very eager to be acquainted with our philosophies and scriptures. But they have not yet come across anyone who can explain our scriptures to them properly. It would be a real achievement if you could go to the West and explain to them our Vedic religion." Now, see how the Master's work starts.

In reply, Swamiji said: "That is a good proposal. I am a sannyasi, and to me there is no difference between this country and that. I shall go when the need arises." Sri Shankar Rao added: "If one wants to mix with the elite there, one has to learn the French language. Please learn it; I shall help you." And so Swamiji learnt that language well enough. I was then at the Alambazar Math. Swamiji had been travelling for about two years without giving any news about himself. Nobody knew his whereabouts, and he had not even seen the Alambazar Math. One day, all of a sudden, a letter of full four pages came from him. None of us could make out in what language it was written. Swami Ramakrishnananda and Swami Trigunatitananda knew a smattering of French. After a close examination, they said: "It seems to be a letter from Naren written in French." Then we had to go with that letter to Aghore Chatterjee in Kolkata. He had been the principal of the Hyderabad State College, and knew French very well. He read the letter and translated it into Bengali for us. Only then did we come to know Swamiji's whereabouts and that he had learnt French.

Well, I told you at the start that Swamiji had planned to spend his life in meditation, japa, and other spiritual practices. But the great power that descended as Sri Ramakrishna did not allow him to do so; it yoked him to the work of propagating the message of the age that would save the world. The master yogi that Swamiji was, he could easily have spent his days in samadhi, totally absorbed in God, if he had only wanted to do so; but the Master drew him into the midst of intense activity. He has engaged all of you as well to give shape to his message. Blessed are the men whom he has chosen.

This ceremony [Christmas Eve celebration] started from the old Baranagore days. A few days after the Master had passed away, the mother of Swami Premananda invited us to her village home at Antpur. Swamiji took us all there. Our hearts were then afire with renunciation; we felt great agony at the loss of our Master; and all were engaged in intense spiritual practices. The only thought we had during those days, and the only effort we made, was for the realization of God and the attainment of peace. When we were at Antpur, we applied ourselves much more intensely to spiritual practices. We would light a fire with logs under the open sky, and spend the nights there in japa and meditation. Swamiji would talk with us fervently about renunciation, and self-sacrifice. Sometimes, he would make us read the *Gita*, the *Bhagavata*, the Upanishads, etc. and hold discussions on them. Thus we spent some days.

One night we sat near the log-fire absorbed in meditation. After a long time Swamiji broke the silence all of a sudden; and, as though in an inspired mood, started talking about Jesus Christ with utmost devotion. He spoke about the intense spiritual practices, burning renunciation, and message of Jesus, and, above all, his realization of unity with God. This he did with such spirit, enthusiasm, and lucidity that we were all struck dumb. It seemed to us for the time being that it was none other than Christ himself who spoke to us through Swamiji. And as we heard, we floated on a current of bliss, as it were. The only idea that reigned supreme in our hearts was that we must realize God, however hard the struggle might be, and must become one with Him; for all else mattered little. It was Swamiji's habit that, whenever he took up a topic, he would follow its implications to their utmost.

We came to know later that it was the Christmas Eve, and yet we had no idea of it earlier. So we were convinced that it was none other than Christ himself who, through Swamiji, made us hear that glorious life and message of his, so as to intensify our spirit of renunciation and our quest for God-realization.

Well, a very strange phenomenon occurred while living with Swamiji at the garden-house [Cossipore]. In those days we all slept together side by side, in a room downstairs; for we had no beddings worth mentioning. We had a big mosquito-curtain which we put up, and all took shelter under it. One night I slept near Swamiji; there were Swami Ramakrishnananda and some others as well. Suddenly I woke up to find the inside of the whole curtain flooded with a brilliant light. Swamiji had been by my side; but now I could not find him there. Instead, there slept a number of Shivas—all of the age of seven or eight years, without clothes and white in colour, and their heads covered with matted hair. It was the light emanating from their bodies that lit up the place. As I looked on I was dumbfounded at the sight. I could not understand anything at first. I thought it was a hallucination; so I rubbed my eyes and again looked—there slept the Shivas, sure enough, just as before. So I was in a fix and sat up with wonder; I did not lie down again. Besides, I was afraid that I might touch them with my feet unconsciously during my sleep. So I spent the whole night in meditation. When the day dawned, I found Swamiji sleeping just as before. When I told him everything, he laughed heartily.

Long afterwards, while reading a hymn to Vireshvara Shiva, I discovered a mantra about meditation on him that coincided with my vision; and then I knew that my vision was quite true. Swamiji was nothing but that in reality. He was born as a part of Shiva, and that's why I saw like that.

(Culled from *For Seekers of God*)

SWAMI TURIYANANDA

Swami Turiyananda

We have seen with our own eyes and heard with our own ears. The tremendous yearning of Swami Vivekananda for God-realization used to surprise us and make us despair of ourselves, in spite of all encouragement and assurance from the Master. And we would think that this life would go in vain, without realizing God. But at last, favourable days came through the grace of the Master.

Swamiji used to say, "Since you have been born on earth, leave a lasting mark on it." At the Baranagore Math he said, "Let me tell you, our names will be recorded in history." Swami Yogananda ridiculed him. But Swamiji replied, "Well, well, you will see, I can convince every one of the truths of Vedanta. If you will not listen to me, I shall go to the Pariah villages and teach Vedanta to the villagers."

Whenever Swamiji said "I", he identified it with the all-comprehensive "I". When we say "I", we identify it with the body, the senses, and the mind. Hence we have to say "the servant I", "the devotee I". Swamiji would never identify his "I" with any adjunct of the Self—he would identify himself with Brahman and go beyond body, mind, and intellect. This was his central and normal mood, and in that he used to pass the greatest part of his time. But such a mood does not come to us. We are living separate from Him. Hence we have to say "Thou" and "Thine" in reference to God.

We saw Swamiij working hard till the end. During his last illness, he would press a pillow to his chest in order to relieve breathing difficulties, but he would still roar, "Arise! awake! What are you doing?"

—————

Swamiji used to tell us, "Do you think I only lecture? I know I give them something solid, and they know they receive something solid." In New York Swamiji was lecturing to a class. Oh, the tremendous effect of it! K. said that while listening to the lecture he felt as if some force was drawing the Kundalini up, as at the time of meditation. After the lecture was finished (it took an hour) K. announced that he would hold a question class. Most of the audience had gone after Swamiji's lecture. Swamiji rebuked him, saying: "A question class after this! Do you want to spoil the effect of my lecture?" Just see! Oh, what a power Sri Ramakrishna left for the world in Swamiji! Hasn't he changed the very thought-current of the world?

—————

Swamiji gave away everything not to his disciples but to his brother-disciples. ... He used to live upon a private fund, for as he said, "I have given away everything". Once he wrote to me, "Now that I have given everything to you, I am at peace." What a wonderful man! You could have seen his influence, had you been to the West. He himself used to say, "My work will be more in the West; thence it will react on India." One day he was very much annoyed and said, "I see I have to conduct the whole music single-handed—to sing and play the instruments and do everything myself, with none to help me!"

Swamiji used to bring with him all sorts of people to Sri Ramakrishna. At this the Master would say: "What worthless people do you bring—one-eyed, lame, and so forth? You don't know good people from bad people. Don't bring anyone and everyone."

Swamiji always used to help the weak. He would say: "The weaker the man, the more help should he get. If a Brahmana boy needs one teacher, engage four such for a Pariah." What a grand sentiment!

───

Once Sri Ramakrishna was very angry with a lady devotee. He asked all of us not to go to her house or eat from her hands. He also asked her not to come to Dakshineshwar. Against this serious injunction of his, who would dare visit her house? Swamiji, however, said to Swami Shivananda one day, "Come, let us have a walk." In the course of the walk he came to the lady's house and wanted something to eat. The lady was beside herself with joy and fed him heartily. After this Swamiji went to Sri Ramakrishna and told him what he had done. Sri Ramakrishna said, "Well, I forbade you and yet you went there and ate!" Swamiji replied: "Well, what harm was there? I have also invited her to come here."

───

Once Swamiji importuned the Master for the sake of Hazra. The Master was then at Cossipore. Swamiji would not leave him—his persistent demand was: "You must do something for him; must bless him." Sri Ramakrishna said, "He will have nothing now, but he will have it at the time of death." It actually came to pass. Swamiji was a believer at heart in grace and things of that sort.

L. used to fall asleep early, and once the Master was very much vexed at it. He wanted to remove him from Dakshineshwar. But Swamiji interceded and the matter ended peacefully. It was for this reason that L. used to say, "If anyone is really a brother-disciple, it is Vivekananda."

───

Once a boy came to the Math to stay. Everyone was against it. Swamiji said: "The Master could read a man's heart, so his opinion as to admitting a man or otherwise used

to be correct. But I do not have this power. So I am prepared
to give a chance to all. If you, like the Master, know how to
read one's mind, well, you may decline to admit the boy."
Then he asked everyone his opinion on the matter. When my
turn came I said: "I have marked this well that none can live
here whom the Master does not like to have. Those who are
to stay will stay, and those who are not, will go away." At this
Swamiji remarked, "Well said. It is an excellent plan." The
boy was admitted but left after a few days.

—

Swamiji had a great sense of humour. One day I was
working with a knife when its tip broke, and I was sad.
Seeing this Swamiji said: "Well, a knife has always an end
like that. It certainly won't have an attack of cholera or
typhoid!" At this I laughed out. Didn't he put it beautifully?

—

Swamiji really had the power to help others. He had no
jealousy. But that's where we are put into difficulties. We
are always afraid lest anybody excels us. But he was too
great for that sort of fear. He had not the least bit of jealousy. He used to say: "Help everyone forward from where
he is, and if you can, supply his particular deficiency. But if
you can't, don't try to drag him to your own level."

Swamiji used to say, "He who has seen even a ghost is
much greater than a mere book-learned pundit because he
has got an opportunity to form a conviction about the future
life."

—

When Swamiji went to America for the first time, I accompanied him from Mt. Abu to Mumbai. In the running
train, Swamiji said to me in all seriousness: "Well, all that
preparation that you see going on [in America] is for this
(pointing to his own body). My mind tells me so. You will see
it verified at no distant date."

Swamiji used to say: "Religion is the very life of India. Even now it is so. What has India been doing all this time if not producing saints? India will have to preach religion to the whole world." Swamiji's words cannot but turn out true. India will surely rise again. Swamiji once remarked, "This time I have left nothing unsaid." Yes, he has said everything, and his ideas are now being worked out. ... Swamiji prophesied many times about the future glorious mission of India in unmistakable terms, and his prophecy cannot prove false. There is already a good beginning.

———

Who was as sattvika as Swamiji? My impression of him is not derived from hearsay, but from constant companionship and ocular evidence. I have seen him sitting at meditation at nine in the evening, quite insensible to the bitter stings of swarms of mosquitoes, and rising from it at five in the morning to take an early bath. It seemed as if Shiva himself was meditating, so deeply absorbed and unconscious of the external he would be! Self-control and harmony—these are characteristics of sattva. Swamiji saw that India could not redeem herself unless she passed first through rajas or activity. That is why he preached the doctrine of selfless work, which is activity inspired and controlled by sattva, or mental poise and dispassionateness. ... Indians are going down in tamas under the pretext of sattva. Swamiji tried hard to whip them into activity.

———

Swamiji once told me: "From the very nature of things, it is difficult to understand anything of the world. And now after lifelong labour it seems that I have known a little and when I think of giving that knowledge to others, the call has come from Above: 'Come away, just come away. Don't bother yourself about teaching others. It is not the will of the Granny that the play should be over.'"

Once, one of Swamiji's brothers came to see him at the monastery at Baranagore. Swamiji abused him right and left and drove him off. At this I took the boy aside and comforted him. Then I asked Swamiji, "Why did you abuse the boy so much?" Swamiji replied, "You think I have no feeling, that I am heartless; is it not?" I was completely silenced. Then he said: "You see, if I show my love for them even to a little extent, it will not be possible for me to stay here; they will all come and give me all sorts of troubles."

(Culled from *Spiritual Talks*)

Let me tell you an incident that happened when I was in America. I was then staying in Montclair, New Jersey, at Mrs. Wheeler's residence. I heard that a middle-aged American was teaching pranayama [breathing exercises]. She would give two lessons and charge five dollars each. She introduced herself as Swami Vivekananda's student. Mrs. Wheeler invited her to her home to meet me. I talked to her on many subjects; she seemed to be a nice person. Later when I met Swamiji in New York, by the by I mentioned that woman to him. I asked him: "Is this women your student? Is it proper that she is charging money and doing business in your name?" Swamiji replied: "You have seen only one. There are many like her. It is not wrong for her to make a little money for her living. She might have attended my lectures or classes. I may recognize her face but I don't know her name. It is all right that she is making her living in this way." The way Swamiji expressed his compassion and sympathy for that women made me feel embarrassed for my narrow attitude. Swamiji's catholic feeling is unparalleled; that is why he is so great!

The sweet memory of Swamiji at Meerut [a place between Haridwar and Delhi] is still vivid in my mind. He was very sick at Rishikesh, then he was brought to Meerut for treatment, and we stayed with him for about six weeks until he recovered. I can't describe how blessed were those clays! Swamiji taught us everything—from mending shoes to studying the scriptures. On the one hand, he would read and explain to us Vedanta scriptures, Upanishads, Sanskrit dramas; and on the other, he taught us how to cook and many other things.

During this period an incident happened that left an everlasting impression on my mind. One day he cooked some fancy dishes for us. They were so delicious that I can't express it to you. While we praised his tasty cooking, he served everything on our plates and he himself did not take even a bite. When we objected, he said: "I have eaten these things many times. It is a great joy for me to feed you. Please eat everything."

Just imagine his attitude! It was an insignificant incident, but it is imprinted on our minds forever. How great were his love and care for us! We talked together; we walked together—the memory of those experiences is still vivid in my mind. From Meerut Swamiji began his journey alone. In Delhi we met Swamiji again and stayed with him for a month. Later, just before his departure for America, Swami Brahmananda and I met him briefly in Mumbai (then Bombay). We were virtually out of touch with him for eight years, until he returned to the Alambazar Monastery as a world figure. Now he is with the Master. But the immortal memory of our association with him is our lifelong companion. That is the subject of our meditation, our conversation, and our spiritual practice. ...

(Culled from *Spiritual Treasures*)

I vividly remember some remarks made by Swamiji at that time.[1] The exact words and accents, and the deep pathos with which they were uttered, still ring in my ears. He said, "Brother, I am still unable to understand anything of your so-

---

1. Before Swamiji left for America.

called religion." Then with an expression of deep sorrow on his countenance and intense emotion shaking his body, he placed his hand on his heart and added: "But my heart has expanded very much, and I have learnt to feel. Believe me, I feel intensely indeed." His voice was choked with feeling; he could say no more. For a time profound silence reigned, and tears rolled down his cheeks. Can you imagine what passed through my mind on hearing the Swami speak thus? "Are not these," I thought, "the very words and feelings of Buddha?" ... I could clearly perceive that the sufferings of humanity were pulsating in the heart of Swamiji: his heart was a huge cauldron in which the sufferings of mankind were being made into a healing balm.

I came to see Swamiji [at Balaram Bose's house] and found him walking alone on the veranda lost in such deep thought that he did not perceive my arrival. I kept quiet, lest I should interrupt his reverie. After some time Swamiji, with tears rolling down his cheeks, began to hum a well-known song of Mirabai. Then, with his face in his hands and leaning on the railings, he sang in anguished tones, "Oh, nobody understands my sorrow! Nobody understands my sorrow!" The sad strains, and Swamiji's dejection, seemed to affect even the objects around him! The whole atmosphere vibrated with the sad melody: "No one but the sufferer knows the pangs of sorrows." His voice pierced my heart like an arrow, moving me to tears. Not knowing the cause of Swamiji's sorrow I was very uneasy. But it soon flashed upon me that it was a tremendous universal sympathy for the suffering and the oppressed that was the cause of his mood.

(*Life*, Vol. 1, pp. 388-389)

Swami Saradananda

A few months before we heard the Master [Sri Ram-akrishna] describing Narendra's good qualities, we had the good fortune to meet him one day at the house of a friend. That day we only saw him, but did not talk with him on account of an erroneous impression. But the words he spoke that day were so deeply imprinted on our memory that even after the lapse of many decades, it seems that we have heard them but yesterday. Before describing them, the circumstances under which we heard those words should be narrated; otherwise one will fail to understand why we carried that wrong impression about Narendranath on that occasion.

The friend in whose house we saw him that day had hired a two-storeyed building in front of Narendra's dwelling house at Gaur Mohan Mukherjee's Lane in the Simla quarter. We had been fellow-pupils in the same school for four or five years. Two years before our friend was to appear for the Entrance Examination, he set out for England, but could not proceed farther than Mumbai. Failing in his ambition, he became the editor of a newspaper, wrote essays and poems in Bengali, and rose to be an author of a few books. He had been married a short time previously. After that event, we heard from many sources that he was living an indifferent moral life and that he did not hesitate to earn money by various dishonest means. It was only for the purpose of ascertaining the truth of this that we went without notice to his house that day.

Informing him of our arrival through a servant, we were sitting in a room of the outer apartment, when a young

SWAMI SARADANANDA

man entered the room, and lolling against a bolster, began humming a Hindi song in an absolutely nonchalant manner, which indicated his familiarity with the owner of the house. The songs, as far as we remember, related to Sri Krishna; for the two words, "Kanai" and "flute" distinctly fell on our ears. His song about the 'black one's flute', his meticulously clean, though not ultra-fashionable, dress, his well-tended hair, and his absent-mindedness verging on coldness—all these joined together to confirm the adverse impression we had of him from his familiarity with our unprincipled friend. Seeing him behave unabashedly in that manner and smoke tobacco afterwards, ignoring our presence altogether, we concluded that he was a faithful follower of our unprincipled friend and that the latter had acquired his evil ways by mixing with such young men. Anyway, we also did not try to get introduced to him, as he assumed an attitude of great indifference and continued to be in his own mood even though he noticed us.

Our boyhood friend came out shortly after. Though we were meeting each other after a long interval he spoke only a word or two to us. Leaving us aside, he began to talk delightfully on various subjects with the above-mentioned young man. Though we resented the indifference he showed to us, we thought it was against etiquette to take leave suddenly. So we sat there, listening to the conversation on English and Bengali literatures, which our friend, the litterateur, held with the young man. Although, when they began the conversation, they were to a great extent agreed as to the function of high class literature, namely, that it should correctly express human sentiments, there arose a difference of opinion between them regarding the question whether a composition expressing any and every kind of human sentiment should be called literature, only because it correctly represents it. Our friend, as far as we can remember, took up the affirmative position, whereas the young man held the contrary opinion. He refuted our friend's position and tried to convince him that no composition, simply by virtue of its expressing a sentiment, good or bad correctly, could be classed as a piece of high class literature, if it did not accord with good taste and establish a high ideal. In support of his own position, the young man mentioned the books of famous English and Bengali literary men beginning with Chaucer and showed how each of them gained immortality because he adhered to this high principle. The young man said in conclusion, "Although man feels all kinds of good and bad sentiments, he has always been straining to express some particular ideal in his mind. It is only in the realization and manifestation of that particular ideal that all the difference between man and man exists. Thinking that the enjoyment of sights, tastes, etc., is permanent and real, ordinary men make the realization of it the aim of their life. They idealize what is apparently real. There is little difference between such people and beasts. High class literature can never be created by men of this type. There is another class of men who, unable to remain satisfied with the realization of the pleasure of enjoying what is seemingly real, feel higher and higher ideals within and are anxious to mould all outward things after that pattern—they want to realize the ideal.

It is this class of men only who create real literature. Again, those among them who have recourse to the highest ideal and try to realize it in life, have generally to stand outside worldly life. I have seen the Paramahamsa of Dakshineswar alone to have realized that ideal in life. That is why I have reverence for him."

We were, of course, astonished with the scholarship of the young man and with his power of expression as evinced by his advocacy of those profound ideas. But we were disappointed to think that there was no agreement between his words and way of life; for how could he be otherwise so closely associated with a bad character like our friend? We then took leave of our friend. It was a few months after this event that we happened to hear the Master's encomiums of Narendra and the noble qualities of his head and heart, which prompted us to visit him at his home to get introduced to him. To our utter astonishment we then found that the much-praised Narendranath was none other than the young man we saw the other day at our old friend's house.

—~—

We remember that we went to Narendra's house at Gaur Mohan Mukherjee Street in Simla, a little before midday on that occasion and were with him till eleven at night. Swami Ramakrishnananda also was with us that day. The unearthly attraction that we felt for Narendra since we first met each other, became multiplied a thousand times that day by the dispensation of providence. The only opinion that we entertained about the Master before was that he was a perfected man, that is, a person who had known God. But that day the words of Narendra about the Master penetrated into our hearts and shed a new light on our minds. The extraordinary events, like those recorded in the biographies of great souls, the teachers of the world such as the holy and glorious Jesus, Chaitanya and others, which we had read about and had been disbelieving so long, were, we understood that day, taking place daily in the Master's life. He granted devotion to those who had taken refuge in him by a touch, or by his will he untied the knots of their heart and effaced its past impressions. He made them enter into ecstasy and realize divine Bliss. Or he changed the course of their lives into spiritual channels in such a way that the realization of God followed very soon and they were blessed for all eternity. Narendra, we remember, took us for a walk at dusk that day to the banks of the Hedua tank while relating the divine experiences he had had in his life by the grace of the Master. Immersed in his self, he remained silent for some time, and at last burst out in a song sung in his charming voice and pouring out the wonderful bliss of his heart:

> Gora Ray distributes the wealth of love.
> Nitai Chand calls 'come, come';
> Come, O you, who long to have it.

Jarfuls of love are being poured out,
Yet it does not get exhausted.
Shantipur is being flooded and
Nadia is swept off.
Nadia is swept off by the current of Gora's love.

The song came to an end. In a soliloquy, as it were, Narendra said gently, "He is actually distributing love. Gora Ray is bestowing love, devotion, divine knowledge, liberation and whatever else one may desire, on whomsoever he likes. Oh, the wonderful power! (He sat silent and motionless for a while.) I was lying on my bed at night with the door of my room bolted from within, when he suddenly attracted me and took me—the one that lives within this body—to Dakshineshwar. Giving a great deal of instruction to me and talking on various subjects, he allowed me to return. He can do anything he likes; this Gora Ray of Dakshineshwar can do anything."

The darkness of dusk had intensified into the jet-black of night. We could not see each other; nor was it necessary. For, the glowing mass of Narendra's spiritual emotion had entered deep into our heart and produced such an intoxication in our mind that even its frame, the body, was actually reeling and even the world whose palpable reality was evident to us so long, receded, as it were, into the realm of dream. Moreover, the truth, that under the impulse of pure and unalloyed grace, the infinite God appears as a finite human being, setting in motion the wheel of religion and destroying the bondage of the past impressions of thousands of jivas—this truth, which, according to the majority of the people of the world, is but a figment of the imagination— then stood revealed to us in its living, blazing form. How time slid away, we did not know. But suddenly we heard the clock strike nine. I was reluctantly thinking of taking leave of Narendra, when he said, "Come, let us go. I'll accompany you for a short distance." As we were going, similar interesting discussions were started, and we became soon

absorbed in them. It occured to us when we reached home
near Champatala, that it was foolish on our part to have let
Narendra come so far. Therefore, inviting him to the house,
we asked him to take a little refreshment, after which we
accompanied him up to his house, and returned. I remember
distinctly another incident of that day. As soon as he entered
our house, Narendra stood motionless, saying, "I feel I have
seen this house before. I find everything here is known to
me; all the rooms and the ways leading to them are all fully
known to me. Oh, how strange and wonderful."

[One night at Cossipore, Narendra went to bed,] but he
had no sleep. He got up in a short time. Seeing Gopal and
one or two others of us awake, he said, "Come, let us go
and stroll in the garden and have a smoke." He said, while
walking, "The Master is suffering from a fell disease. Who
can say if he has not made up his mind to give up his body?
While there is time yet, let us make as much of spiritual
progress as we can by service, meditation, and devotional
exercises. Otherwise, when he passes away, there will be no
limit to our repentance. To postpone calling on the Lord till
desires are fulfilled! This is exactly how our days are passing,
and we are getting more and more entangled in the net of
desires. It is these desires only that lead to destruction and
death. So let us give up desires; yes, let's give them all up."

The winter night of the month of Paush (Dec.-Jan.) was
drowsing away in utter silence. The infinite blue above was
looking steadfastly at the earth with a hundred thousand
starry eyes. Below, the ground under the garden trees was
now dry on account of the powerful rays of the sun, and was
well cleansed and fit to sit on. Narendra's mind, inclined to
dispassion and detachment and accustomed to meditation,
felt, as it were, within, that external silence merging in itself.
Instead of walking any more, he sat down under a tree.
Shortly afterwards he saw a dry heap of grass and broken
branches of trees and said, "Set fire to it. Holy men light

dhunis under trees at this time. Let us also light a dhuni and burn up our desires within." A fire was lighted. We pulled along similar heaps of dry fuel lying on all sides and offered them as oblations to that fire, thinking, all the while, that we were offering the desires of our minds as oblations and felt a wonderful bliss. We felt as if our worldly desires were burnt up and our minds grew pure and serene, and we were approaching God. We thought, "Ah, why did we not do this before? It has given us so much bliss!" We then resolved to light such dhunis whenever opportunities should occur. When two or three hours elapsed in that way and no more fuel could be found, we extinguished the fire, returned to our places and went to bed again. It was then past four in the morning. Those who could not join us in lighting the dhuni felt sorry when they woke up at daybreak and heard of it. They were grieved at not being called. Narendranath said by way of consolation to them, "The whole thing was not preplanned. And who could know beforehand that it would be so blissful an experience? We shall gather together from now on and light a dhuni whenever we find time. We need not worry on that account."

———

[At Cossipore] we were witnessing with our own eyes the intense eagerness of Naren for the realization of God—how spiritual awakening came on him when he was going to deposit the fee for his Law examination; how, goaded by intense zeal and oblivious of the world, he ran along the city road like one mad, bare-footed and covered with but a single piece of cloth, to the place where the Master was, and obtained his grace on laying bare to him the anguish of his heart; how, since then, he spent his time night and day in japa, meditation, devotional songs, and spiritual study; how on account of his boundless enthusiasm for sadhana, his usually tender heart turned adamant and remained quite indifferent to the sufferings of his mother and brothers; and how, advancing with single-minded devotion on the path of sadhana pointed out by his preceptor, he was having vision after vision, culminating at last in his first enjoyment of the bliss of the Nirvikalpa Samadhi in a short period of three or four months. All these things took place before our very eyes left us completely dumbstruck!

(Culled from *Sri Ramakrishna: The Great Master*)

SWAMI AKHANDANANDA

Swami Akhandananda

While I was in Kashmir, a desire arose in my mind to go to Turkistan. Swamiji was then at Ghazipur to see Pavhari Baba. As he knew of my whereabouts, he sent for me. He had many times made preparations to wander about in the Himalayas, but his attempts had failed. He now said: "Gangadhar is an experienced traveller in the Himalayas. So I shall go with him to the Himalayas."

I went to Ghazipur, only to learn that Swamiji was at Varanasi. I followed him there, but by that time he had reached Baranagore Math. So from Varanasi I returned to the Math via Ghazipur. After I had stayed there for two months, Swamiji took me with him on his journey to Western India. Before we started, the Holy Mother gave me this injunction: "My son, I hand over to you all that we have. You know every detail about the hills. See to it that Naren does not suffer for want of food." We went forth to Bhagalpur, Vaidyanath, Ghazipur, Varanasi, Ayodhya, Naini Tal and Almora.

One day, on our way to Almora, Swamiji became very hungry. There was no house nearby to take shelter in, only the grave of a Muslim saint. A Muslim fakir lived there. As I begged alms from him, he said, "Babaji, I can only spare a cucumber." Swamiji relished that cucumber.

At Almora we met Swami Saradananda and Vaikunthanath Sanyal. Swamiji started for Garhwal to practise austerities. ...

During this journey I was ill for the first time. On the way, Swamiji and I both had a fever. At Salarkar Chatti (inn) we were in bed for five or six days. At the next Chatti, too, we were feverish. But we were cured by some medicine administered by the Sadar Amin (surveyor) of Almora. We proceeded to Srinagar in Garhwal, and stayed there for a month and a half. On the way, we took lessons in the Upanishads from Swamiji. At Srinagar we spent our time in intense prayer and meditation. Swamiji was very eager to go to the Bhagirathi. We all went to Tihiri on foot.

We halted some twenty days at Tihiri, spending our time in prayer and meditation. As the Holy Mother had ordered, I begged alms daily for Swamiji.

Sri Raghunath Bhattacharya, brother of Sri Haraprasad Shastri, was the Dewan of the Raja of Tihiri. Swamiji consulted him and decided to have a hut made at Ganeshprayag, the junction of the rivers Bhagirathi and Bhilangana, and do tapasya there. As I had a bad cough, he sent me to the doctor for an examination of my chest.

"Your lungs are congested," said the doctor. "You must not live here in the hills. Go down to the plains and have proper treatment." Swamiji, as he heard this, gave up his idea of tapasya and hastened to Mussoorie with me. From Mussoorie we went to Rajpur where we were joined by Swami Turiyananda, and then proceeded to Dehra Dun.

At Dehra Dun we took shelter in a merchant's house. But as the floor of our room was very damp, Swamiji would not allow me to stay there.

The Civil Surgeon of Dehra Dun examined my chest. He asked me not to go up the Himalayas, and wanted me to provide myself with warm clothes and proper diet. Swamiji begged shelter from every rich man of Dehra Dun, but in vain. Just when he had given up all hope, he met a native Christian who had known him before—a teacher at the missionary school there. He had been a fellow student of Swamiji at the General Assembly College and now agreed to put me up for the time being, giving me a room.

Finally Pandit Anandanarayana, a pleader, agreed to take charge of my treatment and helped us in every way. I stayed with him while Swamiji, Saradananda, Sanyal and Turiyananda left for Rishikesh. ...

At Rishikesh, Swamiji, living in a hut, contracted a slow remittent fever. One day he broke down and lost his powers of speech. His brother-disciples gave up all hope, calling on God and weeping. Turiyananda was reciting the *Sankata Stotra.*

Suddenly a sannyasi wrapped in a blanket made his appearance and asked them in Hindi why they were weeping. He then gave a drug to be administered with honey. He left the place quickly and went away, nobody knew where. Some time after the medicine was administered, Swamiji regained consciousness. His body grew warm, and he regained his speech.

At this time Dewan Raghunath Bhattacharya was going to Mayo College at Ajmer in the company of the Raja of Tihiri. At Rishikesh he heard that a Bengali Swami with vast learning was lying mortally ill, and conjectured that it was none other than Swamiji. So he came with a letter of introduction and advised Swamiji to go to a doctor at Delhi. On the way, Swamiji stopped at Saharanpur and learnt from Banku Chatterji that I was at Meerut. Before this, he had met Swami Brahmananda at Hardwar. As he was eager to see me as well, the whole party came to Meerut, where we stayed for four or five months. Here Swamiji and I recovered our health, but Saradananda fell ill.

Swamiji left alone for Delhi. Ten days later, the rest of the party departed.

As Swamiji left for Delhi, I said, "It was at your bidding that I gave up the idea of a journey to Central Asia and went back to Baranagore—and you now leave me!" "The company of brother-disciples," said Swamiji, "is a great obstacle to the practice of tapasya. Don't you see, you fell ill at Tihiri and I could not undertake spiritual practices. I cannot undertake them unless I sever the tie of brother-disciples. Whenever I think of tapasya, the Master sends an obstacle. This time I shall move about by myself. Nobody will know my whereabouts."

"You may even go to the nether world," said I, "but nonethe-less I shall find you, or my name is not Gangadhar!" ...

At Gopinathji's temple at Jaipur, I met Sardar Chatur Singh. I learnt from him that Swamiji had stayed at Khetri for two or three months. After initiating the Raja of that place, he had left for Ajmer. I visited Jaipur and went on to Ajmer. At Ajmer I learnt that Swamiji had left for Ahmedabad. I went to Pushkar. There I met Swami Trigunatitananda, and we went back to Ajmer. ...

After I had given Trigunatitananda a send-off, I thought, "Travelling on foot, I cannot get hold of Swamiji. But how can I travel by rail?" Fortunately someone paid eight annas and I booked a ticket for Biawar. There I heard that Swamiji had come and left for Ajmer.

From Biawar I started for Abu. I had to travel according to what people paid for my railway fare. After I had visited the places of interest at Abu, I left for Ahmedabad. There I learnt that Swamiji had left for Oadhoan in Gujarat. A gentleman took me from Ahmedabad to Dakore. From there I went to the Bay of Cambay via Baroda and Broach, and had a dip in the confluence of the Narmada.

At Oadhoan junction I met a gentleman from whom, on enquiry, I learned that a sannyasi named Vivekananda was staying at Junagadh. So a sannyasi who was known to me got me booked for Junagadh.

At Junagadh I learnt that four or five days before, Swamiji had left Porbandar for Dwaraka. After I had seen the places of interest at Junagadh, I left for the holy place of Prabhas. From there I took the steamer at Verawal to go to Dwaraka. There I learnt that Swamiji had left for Bhetd-waraka. After spending the night at Dwaraka, I went there. Once there, I got the news that at Verawal, Swamiji had received an invitation from the Prince of Kutch-Bhuj, and had accordingly gone to Kutch-Mandavi. I immediately left for Kutch-Mandavi.

Even after such a long pursuit, I could not reach Swamiji. My eagerness rose to such a pitch that I left for Mandavi without caring to see objects of interest at these places. There I learnt that Swamiji had gone to Narayan Sarovar. Spending a night at Mandavi, I started on foot towards Narayan Sarovar.

At a village eight miles from Mandavi a householder said: "Swamiji, your path is infested with highwaymen. Swami Vivekananda has the Prince's men with him; but how can you go alone? "I have nothing with me, the robbers can expect nothing from me," I replied." Well, to move from village to village," said he, "you should at least have a bullock cart—I'll give you one. Why don't you take a guide also?" I did so. A boy was my guide. ...

Travelling sometimes by camel and sometimes by horse, I at last reached Mandavi. There I had the news that Swamiji was residing with a Bhatia (a man of Kutch). I lost no time in reaching there.

Swamiji's appearance had completely changed. His beauty illuminated the whole room. He was startled to see me there. He listened to all that I had experienced on the way. It filled him with apprehension, and he said: "You have braved all these dangers and pursued me even at the risk of your life. Surely you will never give up hunting for me. But I have a plan which I cannot put into effect if any of my brother-disciples is with me."

However, I was obstinate. At last Swamiji said: "Look here, I have become a bad man! Leave my company." I replied: "Who cares if you have become bad? I love you. I am not concerned with your conduct. But I won't stand in your way. I was so anxious to see you. My anxiety has been allayed. Now you may go alone."

Swamiji was glad to hear this. The very next day he left for Bhuj. I did not join him, but waited a day before starting on my own journey to Bhuj. Swamiji was now sure that I would not intrude upon his freedom.

At Bhuj, Swamiji said to me: "The Raja here is paying us too much attention, and that may be an annoyance to many if we stay here too long. Twenty-five years ago a Bengali sannyasi named Ananda Ashrama came to Bhuj and contributed much to the improvement of the State. In those days, it was the Prince's custom to lease out villages. The lessee would extort from the tenants several times the amount he paid the Prince as revenue. The tenants thus suffered greatly. On Ananda Ashrama's advice, the Prince abandoned that custom and introduced the good system that is now common in the British Raj. The State is still ruled in that way. But such reforms did not find favour in the eyes of the State Officers, and they considered Ananda Ashram to be a nuisance. His enemies mixed poison with his food, and killed him. We may share the same fate. Let us leave tomorrow."

From Bhuj, we two came back to Mandavi and stayed there a fortnight. Swamiji then started for Porbandar, and five or six days later, I followed. There we met again. Swamiji was a guest at the residence of Shankar Pandurang, governor of Porbandar (Sudamapuri). Swamiji said that in the whole of India he had not seen Pandurang's equal in Vedic learning. As a commentary on the Atharva Veda was not available, he compiled one himself. Swamiji used to speak with him in Sanskrit.

From Porbandar, Swamiji went to Junagadh, and I to Kathiawad. I passed through Jetpur, Gondal and Rajkot, and came to Jamnagar. A terrible storm overtook me on my way to Jamnagar. Once there, I stayed for a year.

Shashipada Banerjee, father of Rajkumar Banerjee, a civilian officer of Chennai, was the founder of the Widows' Home of Baranagore. Shashi Babu often visited the Math. He talked of Swamiji and enquired about him. I often went to his home. Many widows were being educated there, and did the work of the household. At the home there was a school for girls, who were taught by the widows. The tender-hearted Swamiji would send money from America to the destitute families he remembered there. He sent more than a thousand rupees to a householder to help pay off a mortgage. He gave help to various charitable institutions—and did not neglect to send a contribution to Shashi Babu for the

Widows' Home of Baranagore. We had plenty of proof from Shashi Babu that the liberal Swamiji spread real joy with his contributions, and made no invidious distinction between creeds. Few people realize how many were benefited by such help from Swamiji.

While arguing, Swamiji sometimes advanced views that made him rather mystifying. By turns he would be an atheist, an agnostic or a pyrrhonist, again a theist, a monist, a dualist or a nihilistic Buddhist. At one time he would be an upholder of Vedantic doctrine *naham, nedam* (Not I, nor this); and again he would be inebriated with the lover's attitude, like one of the gopis in the sport of Krishna. While he discussed the Buddha, he would be filled with a calm both inner and outer, and the sound of samkirtan to the accompaniment of musical instruments, which we had been singing a short while before, would immediately die down. Swamiji himself would, along with us, repeat, *Naham nedam, naham nedam.*

When Swamiji took a particular stand, nobody could move him from it. But the marvel is that his lectures contained doctrines supported by the three Prasthanas (Upanishads, *Brahma Sutras*, and the *Bhagavad Gita*) as in the case of the great teachers of different schools of philosophy. It is known to all how Shankara, Ramanuja, Madhvacharya, Nimbarka, and even Sri Chaitanya had to take their stand on the three prasthanas to establish their schools of Advaita, Vishishtadvaita, Dvaita, Dvaitadvaita, Achintyabhedabheda, etc.

The views of Western scholars about the Vedas and other scriptures were ignored by Swamiji, in his lectures, as simply the work of "many men, many minds."

In a speech in America he said, "Man progresses birth after birth; he has no retrogression such as being reborn as beasts and other creatures." Hearing about this, I was in a fix. "Alas! How is it that from Swamiji's lips should come out views not supported by scriptural texts?" I thought. ...

A few days after I became aware of this, I read in one of Swamiji's writings that the soul has both progress and retrogression. I was mystified, but I knew that Swamiji was coming, so I thought my difficulty would soon be solved. I thought no more about it. At this time news came that Swamiji had reached Sri Lanka. Swamis Shivananda and Niranjanananda left for Sri Lanka to fetch him. The news of Swamiji's return from America made us so joyous that we scarcely had any time to think of anything else. After a good deal of deliberation, a reception committee was formed with some of the elite of the city. It was arranged that from Budge Budge, Swamiji should be brought to Kolkata in a special train.

Ramakrishnananda and I waited at the Math. For the reception, we made a small gate, planted some banana trees, and placed jars of water with mango twigs on them.

At Sealdah station there assembled a varied crowd to see and receive him. When Swamiji got on the carriage, the horses were unharnessed, and college students pulled it up to Ripon College. So big was the crowd that within the college a man was nearly crushed to death. Swamiji attempted to say something at that place, but he was prevented from doing so by the excessive noise and jostling.

From Ripon College, Swamiji was taken to the palatial building of Nandalal Basu at Nebubagan, Baghbazar. He took his midday meal there and in the afternoon came to Alambazar Math in an ordinary carriage. We honoured him on arrival and took him into the Math.

Accompanying Swamiji to Kolkata were Captain Sevier, Mother Sevier, Miss Muller, the stenographer Goodwin and others from London, Mr. Harrison, a Buddhist from Colombo, and Alasinga Perumal, the first editor of the periodical *Brahmavadin*, as well as "G.G." and "Kidi" from Chennai. The reception committee lodged them at Gopal Seal's garden-house at Cossipore.

It was in that garden that people of various stations of life came to meet Swamiji. Almost every day he would come from the garden to Alambazar Math where he spent the night with us and returned to the garden the next day.

At the Math Swamiji gave us advice on various matters for the maintenance of our health. Asked if we boiled and filtered our drinking water, we showed him our filter, about which he said, "Whatever you do, never forget to purify the drinking water in this way."

He then taught us all a sort of physical exercise called "Delsart". It utilizes several manipulations requiring one to bend the body backward and forward, to lower the right and left hand so they touch the ground, and to turn the legs and head around. It would do much good to exercise the limbs in this manner for at least half an hour without undergoing any strain. This became the vogue in the Math.

At the Math Swamiji put up hammocks near the windows and read while swinging. On his arrival at the Math, the first thing I said to him was: "What a marvel, you are an absolutely changed person in your speeches. From your lips I have heard so many contradictory views, yet all the arguments you put forth are based on scriptures. But, my brother, in one speech you have gone against the scriptures by stating that man is never reborn as a beast. Elsewhere you have said that man in his successive births undergoes both progression and retrogression. I am in a fix over this, and it is you that will have to solve my problem now." At this he said: "You are right. The stenographer who took notes of my speech did the mischief. He acquiesced in all my views, but he would never admit that man is reborn as a beast. After that speech had been printed I detected the error." Then I called in Ramakrishnananda, and as I told Swamiji about our talk on the point, they began laughing. I, too, was relieved.

(Culled from *Service to God in Man*)

Work, work; serve others. It is something positive, something palpable. We know what you meditate on, and how much you meditate. I was travelling with Swamiji in the Himalayas. We found a sadhu apparently meditating with his whole body covered. But Swamiji cried out: "Oh, he is sleeping and snoring. Put him to the yoke; then perhaps he may attain spirituality some day."

Observing these things, Swamiji concluded, "With the highest ideals of sattva on the lips, the country is sinking into the abyss of tamas." That is why he said: "To recover from this, the whole body from head to foot must be electrified by rajas." Thus he laid much stress upon work.

Oh, so many things about Swamiji are coming to mind. When he would lay emphasis upon a certain idea, for the time being everyone present would feel that *that* idea was the whole truth and all else was nothing. In Belur Math by the Ganga, from day to day he would talk about so many kinds of ideas and the Math would be filled with each of them in turn. The day he talked about Shiva, we would feel that Swamiji was Shiva Himself. The Math would be surcharged with that idea. Another day he would be talking about Buddha, and we would feel that this was a Buddhist monastery—everything calm and quiet. Again, on another day, when he started talking about Radha, all barriers gave in. It seemed as if he were the divine gopi and the entire Math was full to the brim of the sweet love of the gopi. How many times he said that Radha was not of flesh and blood, but the essence of the ocean of love. Many times I have heard him say this. Perhaps he would be walking briskly to and fro and repeating this to himself. Ordinarily, he would stop any talk on Radha and Krishna and encourage talks on Shiva and the study of Shankara's works."

In our wandering days, at Bhagalpur in Bihar, Swamiji once sang, accompanied by tanpura[1], this song on the yearning of Radha to meet with Krishna:

Shyam (Krishna) has not yet come to me:
I am waiting for Him!
Night is passing and He has not yet come to me,
I am still waiting for Him.

---

1. A stringed instument.

Swamiji became merged in the feeling of Radha. The music went on from evening till midnight. There was no end in sight. The elite of the town had gathered; no one could get up. Dinner had been served long ago and was getting cold. At last Swamiji was called again and again, and his ecstasy broke.

One night, when the Math was located at Nilambar Babu's garden at Belur, there were discussions on Vedanta which continued until two in the morning. Towards the end, the debate centred on the question of whether the soul is reborn after death, and later, whether man can be reborn as one of the lower animals or not.

Swamiji had started the debate, and the brothers had taken whichever side they pleased. Swamiji remained neutral and generally silent, but at times he supplied arguments to whichever side was losing. At last he stopped it at two o'clock. Everybody went to sleep. But just at 4 a.m. Swamiji asked me to ring the rising bell. He was by then walking up and down, singing to himself, after his morning ablutions.

Seeing me hesitating, he said to me: "Ring the bell, let them all wake up. I cannot see them sleeping any more." I replied: "They all went to sleep only two hours ago. Let them sleep a little more." But in a firm voice Swamiji said: "They went to sleep at two, so they will get up at six—is that your plea? All right, give me the bell; I will ring it! Are we starting a monastery for sleeping?"

Then I rang the bell quite vigorously and everybody got up crying: "Who is that? Who are you?" If I were alone, perhaps they would have finished me off, but when they saw Swamiji smiling behind me, they one by one went to the adjoining rooms on the other side—yawning and rubbing their eyes.

Again, one day—perhaps a little later, at Belur Math—Swami Turiyananda could not come to the shrine for meditation, or perhaps he was a bit late. He had had an attack of cold and fever. On hearing this, Swamiji flared up and

exclaimed: "Still this body? Shame upon you!" Among us,
Turiyananda was the most austere. He hung his head. Then
Swamiji began to talk to him affectionately: "Do you know
why I rebuke all my brothers? You are all the children of
the Master. The world will learn from you. It hurts me very
much when I see in you anything short of the ideal. If the
newcomers see such laxity in us, they will become still more
lax in their behaviour. The Master used to say 'If I do the full
sixteen parts, you will do only one.' Now if you do that one
part, others will do only one-sixteenth of that. If you do not
do even that one part, where will they stand?"

Swamiji once told us at the Baranagore monastery: "You
see, we shall all be sincere; our dispassion will not be like
that of the householders. They also have a kind of dispassion
at the cremation ground, when they see the body of a loved
one burning to ashes. That dispassion is temporary. It is
common to all. But when they go back to their houses, they
forget everything due to maya. They merge in it. But we
have known what worldly life is. We are not going back to it.
It is very well if we can realize God; but even if we cannot,
we are not going back. We shall proceed slowly, sailing
onwards. When the wind is favourable, we shall unfurl the
sail; when it is against us, we shall stop; but never go back!"

Yes, I have seen Swamiji after his passing away, as clearly
as I see you now: otherwise I could not have lived. Separation from him was so painful that I was going to commit
suicide, but I was prevented by Swamiji. He caught my hand
as I was about to jump under a moving train.

(Culled from *The Call of the Spirit*)

Swami Vijnanananda

S hortly after Swamiji had renounced the world, somebody asked him: "Have you attained ultimate knowledge, Sir?" The reply was in the negative. The questioner then asked: "Then why have you renounced the world?" "Because I have realized that its value is negligible and it leads to sure death," came the emphatic reply.

Though Swamiji preached much jnana and karma, his heart was full of love. Behind a stern and forbidding exterior, he concealed the softness of a mother's heart. And what deep love he possessed for his brother-disciples! For Swami Brahmananda, especially, he bore a deep love mixed with respect—similar to what he felt for his guru. But at the same time, he was intolerant of any of their faults or defects. He did not even spare Maharaj[1], whom he loved so deeply. Once he scolded him so severely that the latter wept bitterly, though he was not to blame at all. In fact it was wholly my fault, and Maharaj had made himself the scapegoat in order to shield me.

Work on the embankment of the river at Belur Math was then in progress, for which Swamiji had asked me to draw up a plan and give a rough estimate of the cost. I gave the estimate, but out of fear of Swamiji I understated the cost and said it would be approximately three thousand rupees. This amount made Swamiji happy. He immediately consulted

---

1. Swami Brahmananda was called Maharaja, or Raja, meaning King.

SWAMI VIJNANANANDA

Maharaj, and when the latter assured him that it would not be difficult to secure that amount, Swamiji ordered that the project be started. I was in charge of the actual work, but Maharaj looked after the accounts and the collection of money for the purpose. As the work proceeded, I realized that the cost would far exceed the estimate. I expressed my concern to Maharaj, who, being the loving soul that he was, asked me to complete the project anyway. I heaved a sigh of relief, but knew very well that sooner or later I would have to face Swamiji's wrath.

Sometime later, Swamiji asked Maharaj for the accounts. When he discovered that the expenses had already exceeded the original estimate, with the work still unfinished, he became angry with Maharaj and scolded him vehemently. The latter endured it stoically, but was very hurt. When Swamiji returned to his room, Maharaj went to his own room and closed the door and windows.

After a while, Swamiji regretted his bad temper. I was aware of all of this and feeling bad, because it was due to me that Maharaj had been subject to so much grief. Swamiji then called me to him, and said: "Could you check on what Raja is doing?" I went to Maharaj's room and found the doors and windows closed. I called for him but got no response.

When I reported this to Swamiji, he became very excited and said: "You are a fool! I asked you to find out what Raja was doing, and you say, 'His door and windows are closed.' Go back again and tell me what he is doing." So I went back to his room. This time, once again getting no response to my call, I quietly opened the door and found Maharaj on his bed, weeping. I said apologetically, "Maharaj, I am sorry; today you have suffered terribly for me." Maharaj looked at me and said: "Brother, can you tell me what wrong I have done that Swamiji could scold me so harshly? Sometimes it becomes so unbearable that I feel I should leave everything and go away to some place in the mountains."

I returned to Swamiji and told him that Maharaj was crying. At this, Swamiji rushed to the room, embraced

Maharaj, and said tearfully: "Raja, brother, please forgive me. In a fit of anger I scolded you. Please pardon me." Meanwhile, Maharaj had regained his composure. Seeing Swamiji weep, he was also moved. Then he said: "What does it matter? You have scolded me because you love me—that is all." But Swamiji continued: "Brother, please forgive me. I know how much the Master loved you and never uttered a harsh word to you. And I, on the other hand, for the sake of this petty work, have verbally abused you and given you pain. I am not fit to live with you. I shall go away to the Himalayas and live alone in solitude." "Don't say that, Swamiji," said Maharaj. "Your scolding is a blessing. How can you leave us? You are our leader. How shall we function without you?" Gradually both of them became calm.

I shall never forget that scene in my life. I never saw Swamiji weep so bitterly. What a bond of love existed between them! Swamiji loved his brother-disciples like a mother, and that is why he could not bear any shortcoming in them. He wanted them to be as great as himself; nay, even greater. His love was incomparable.

One hot summer day, I was supervising the construction work of the embankment. I had become very thirsty, and I noticed that Swamiji was enjoying a cold drink on his upper veranda. Presently, one of Swamiji's attendants came with a glass in his hand and said to me, "Swamiji has sent this cold drink to you." On hearing this I was very happy, but I found only a few drops at the bottom of the glass. I was disappointed and piqued by Swamiji's practical joke. However, I drank those few drops as prasad and, strangely enough, my thirst was instantly quenched. I was dumbfounded. As I returned to my room after finishing the work, Swamiji asked me with a smile, "Did you drink the cold juice?" "Yes, I did," I replied, and described my experience after drinking it. Swamiji seemed pleased to hear it.

Swamiji had moved among, and lectured to, thousands of people in many parts of the world—associating closely with all sorts of people, including women. Some of his Western disciples were even staying with him at the time. I wondered whether all this was in agreement with the Master's ideas. "Why does he mix with so many women?" I thought. So it was that, seeing Swamiji alone in his room, I asked him: "Swamiji, while you were in the West you associated with the women there; but didn't the Master teach the contrary in this respect? He used to say, 'A monk should not even look at the portrait of a woman.' He emphatically told me not to be close to women, however devoted they might be. So I am wondering why you did so."

Immediately Swamiji became very grave and his face and eyes reddened with anger. I got scared and was sorry about what I had blurted out. After a while he said: "Well, Peshan,[2] do you think that what you have understood about the Master is all that he is? What do you know about the Master? Do you know that the Master eradicated the idea of the difference between male and female from my mind? Is there any distinction of sex in the Atman? Moreover, the Master came for the good of the entire world. Did he come to liberate only men? He will save all—both men and women. You people want to belittle the Master by measuring him with the yardstick of your own intellects. Whatever the Master told you is true; follow that implicitly. But to me, his instructions were different. He not only gave me instructions, he clearly showed me everything. He holds my hands—whatever he makes me do, I do."

Gradually Swamiji calmed down. I was struck with terror at the severity of his mood, and could not utter a word. I wanted to fly from there, when Swamiji, noticing my embarrassment, said with a smile: "Can a nation rise or become great unless the primordial energy that lies dormant in women is awakened? I have travelled all over

2. Swami Vijnanananda's pre-monastic name was Hari Prasanna. "Peshan", was an abbreviation of Prasanna.

the world and found that women are neglected more or less everywhere, but it is particularly deplorable in India. That is why our nation has become degraded to such an extent. As soon as there is an awakening in women, you will see that the whole nation will rise up in all its pristine glory. For that reason, Holy Mother has come. With her advent there has been a stir among the women of all countries. This is just a beginning; you will see many more things later."

Swamiji's words were interrupted by the entrance of a visitor, which gave me the opportunity to make my exit. He had been speaking with such conviction and force that any kind of contradiction was unthinkable. It's true that it would be proper for me to do only what the Master had instructed me to, but Swamiji's case was quite different. He was the Master's chief disciple, and none else was in a better position to understand the Master. The Master got his work done through him. Swamiji was a unique personality, and no one could afford to imitate him. There was one thing we noticed about him. Though he mixed with his western women disciples, he never allowed any young monastic to approach them. If they required anything, he would either take it himself or send someone among the senior monks. Even amongst his brother-disciples he would make a distinction in this respect.

I feared Swamiji as much as I loved him. When I found him in an unpleasant mood, I would simply avoid him. If he called me at such moments, I would simply make a pretence of being extremely busy, and escape.

As I was under the care of Rakhal Maharaj, I didn't receive much of Swamiji's scolding. Once, Swamiji said that from a particular standpoint, India's decadence was due to her sages. I thought that Swamiji was criticizing the sages and objected: "No, Sir, you are wrong about the sages." Swamiji's face turned red and he told Maharaj, who was also present, "See, Rakhal, Peshan says I do not know anything." Maharaj then comforted Swamiji, saying: "Why do you take him seriously? He is just a boy and understands very little." Swamiji at once cooled down like a child on hearing Maharaj's words.

To those who came to Swamiji for initiation, he would say: "Don't be deluded by only seeing me in my pleasant mood. If you feel like taking initiation from me even after seeing my violent temper, then only come to me." At this the boys would reply, "Yes Maharaj, we can put up with everything."

Swamiji was a very strict man. Even for a small lapse he would take someone to task. I, however, generally escaped his scolding. Once, at Belur Math, he asked Swami Shivananda to meditate through a whole night. One day he asked Maharaj to beg for his food. No meal was prepared for him at the Math that day. Maharaj went out to beg his food. Swamiji had just started taking his meal when Maharaj returned. "Let me see what you have brought today," said Swamiji in a joyous mood. "The food got by begging is very pure," he added. Swamiji took a little of what Maharaj had brought and ate it with relish.

During the course of conversation, Swamiji once said to me: "Peshan, it is time to write a new Smriti according to the need of the present age. The old Smritis are now obsolete." I asked: "Swamiji, why will the people accept your Smriti?" Immediately, Swamiji—like a querulous boy—complained to Brahmananda: "Rakhal, listen, Peshan says that the people won't accept my message." Maharaj pacified him, saying: "What does Peshan know? He is a mere boy. The people will definitely accept your message some day or other." Like a pacified child, Swamiji said joyfully: "Peshan, did you hear what Rakhal said? The people will positively accept my message."

One day Swamiji remarked: "I cannot say anything to Peshan because I see the Master in him." To this I responded:

"The Master dwells in every being. It is no wonder that you see the Master in me through your divine sight." "No, Peshan," said Swamiji. "It is not like that. I see distinctly that the Master has made his habitat in you nicely." I then replied, "Swamiji, you see whatever you want to; but I don't understand it."

I have seen Swamiji meditating at night. I used to sleep in the adjoining room, and once when I was passing by his room, I found his room bright with a dazzling light. Sometimes at night, he would sing in an absorbed mood. I remember a song he once sang: "Thou art the saviour, O Mother! Beyond the course of all things, Thou art the substratum of all the three gunas." With what absorption and depth of feeling he sang it!

In those days, while staying at the Math, I mostly occupied a small room. I rarely opened the door leading to the veranda, as Swamiji often used to pace up and down there. He used to be in different moods at different times. One incident of that period still lingers in my memory. Once he spent the whole night singing, in an exalted mood, a hymn to the Mother, all the while walking about in that veranda. He mostly sang only the first line of the song: "Thou art the saviour, O Mother!" While he was in this mood, no one dared to approach him. He went on singing only that first line and sometimes walked about and sometimes stood still, his face bathed in tears. This continued till morning.

Swamiji's lectures had a special characteristic. While speaking, he used to forget himself and become an entirely different person. His speeches touched the core of people's hearts. He had a wonderful personality, which used to overwhelm all who came in contact with him. I have myself seen, at Belur Math, distinguished Western disciples of Swamiji squatting on the floor all around his chair to hear his inspired words. And how forcefully he spoke! Now, things are being done according to what he said, and people are getting inspiration from his words.

One day I went to Balaram Babu's house in Kolkata while Holy Mother was staying there. Swamiji was also there. All were going to pay their respects to Holy Mother while I continued to sit by Swamiji's side. He told me that I should also go and pay my respects. Accordingly, I went to Holy Mother and bowed down to her from a distance, touching my head to the floor. However, unknown to me, Swamiji had followed me to Mother. Seeing me bowing down in this way, he said: "Does anybody salute Mother in this way?" Saying this, Swamiji prostrated himself before Mother, and I did likewise.

Once we were staying at the Nilambar Mukherjee's garden-house at Belur. It was the monastery then. Swamiji was in those days on a very high spiritual plane. One day when I touched his feet in obeisance, I received a strong shock—as if electricity were passing through me. Anyone going near such people feel as if a spiritual zone has formed around them. Anyone entering that zone feels as if an electric force is entering into him.

Once, while strolling in Belur Math, Swamiji told me, "The Master's temple will be constructed here." He pointed out the exact spot where the construction has now been started. Then he asked me: "Shall I live to see it?" I said, "Yes Swamiji, you will certainly see it." He was then silent for some time and then said, "Yes, I will see it, but from above." Now that the temple is being built, he is seeing it from above.

I was in Allahabad when Swamiji passed away. While meditating in the Brahmavadin club I saw, in a vision, Swamiji on the lap of the Master. I was puzzled by this. Then I got a wire from Belur Math that he had passed away.

Swamiji is not dead, but still alive and active here. When I pass by his room, I walk on tiptoe very quietly lest I should disturb him. I don't look into his room for fear of meeting him face to face.

(culled from *Swami Vijnanananda: A short life and spiritual discourses*)

Swamiji used to call me "Peshan". One day I was sitting on the upper veranda of Belur Math eating puffed rice. Swamiji was passing by. All of a sudden he grabbed a handful of puffed rice from my bowl and began to eat it like a boy. I remonstrated: "Swamiji, why don't you take another bowl of puffed rice? By eating the food that I have defiled, you are making me feel guilty." Laughing, Swamiji left[3].

I used to take snuff. Once Swamiji went to Kolkata and bought a pice worth of snuff in a packet. Handing it to me, he said, "Here is a wonderful present for you." I opened the packet and found the snuff. Seeing me happy, he was happy. But if he ever became grave, it was difficult to go near him. At times like that, only Raja Maharaj could bring him back to the normal plane.

(*God Lived with Them*, p. 600)

---

3. According to Hindu custom, a senior, or highly respected person, does not eat from the same plate with a junior person. A junior person would feel extremely ill at ease were this to happen.

Swami Achalananda

I first came to know of Sri Ramakrishna and Swami Vivekananda in 1899. Belur Math was dedicated by Swamiji in
the same year, but at that time I was not so anxious to meet
him. Towards the end of the year I went to Belur Math [from
Varanasi], but I could not meet Swamiji as he had already
left for Europe and America. In 1900 I finished some relief
work in Rajputana and then went to Vrindavan. While I
was there I heard that Swamiji had returned to Belur Math
from the West. At this time Swami Saradananda wrote to
Swami Kalyanananda [in Vrindavan], "Those who want to
meet Swamiji can come." But I decided to go to Varanasi first.
There I found that the sevashrama was in a rented house
and that Charu Babu [later Swami Shubhananda] was
managing everything by himself. I did not want to leave him
when he was so hard-pressed.

After Swamiji returned to India in December 1900 he
heard that some young devotees of Varanasi had established
an ashrama to help the poor. When one member of our
group met Swamiji at Belur Math, Swamiji inquired in detail
about the ashrama and encouraged our friend, saying, "Such
an ashrama should be established in every holy place in
India." He also initiated him and advised him to maintain
good health. He was very pleased to hear of our work. Soon
after, Swamiji asked Swami Nirmalananda to visit the Varanasi Ashrama and inform him of its activities.

Just before the Durga Puja celebration in 1901, I felt an
intense desire to see Swamiji, which I expressed to Charu
Babu. He gave me fifteen days' leave, and I left for Belur

SWAMI ACHALANANDA

Math. After arriving at the Howrah [railway] station, I went first to see Holy Mother at her residence in Bosepara Lane in Baghbazar. However, I found that she was then staying at Nilambar Mukherjee's garden house in Belur. From there I went to Belur Math. I arrived the day before Durga Puja, but I had not been aware that the Divine Mother would be worshipped at the Math. I noticed that a grand preparation for Durga Puja was going on and Swami Brahmananda was quite busy. As I was already acquainted with him, I bowed down to him, and as far as I remember, it was he who introduced me to Swamiji. I first saw Swamiji in his room. He was shaven-headed and wore only a loin-cloth. After I bowed down to him he inquired about the activities at Varanasi.

Saptami Puja[1] ended with great festivity. The resolution mantra was said in Holy Mother's name. Krishnalal Maharaj [Swami Dhirananda] was the worshipper and Swami Ramakrishnananda's father was the prompter. Swamiji enjoyed the first day's worship. But on the second day he had an attack of asthma. When he had these attacks, he would gasp and wouldn't speak, but as soon as the attack passed he would again become cheerful and jovial. On the evening of the third day there was a performance of the drama *Nala-Damayanti*. While watching the performance Swamiji looked very happy and even cut jokes. Physical sickness or suffering could not make him depressed, nor could it diminish his love and concern for his disciples. Once, when he was ill with a very high fever, one of his attendants became sick. He noticed that many people were in his room to serve him, so he asked some of them to go and serve his attendant.

On the fourth day the image of Mother Durga was carried to the Ganga for immersion. Swami Brahmananda danced in front of the Divine Mother to the accompaniment of music. We were deeply moved to see this sight. Swamiji also enjoyed Maharaj's beautiful dance from the upper veranda of the monastery.

---

1. The first day of the four-day worship of Mother Durga.

Swamiji's health improved after Durga Puja. He made arrangements at the Math for Lakshmi Puja, and after that for Kali Puja in an image. It is hard to describe the joy and festivity of Kali Puja. That night, before the worship, Swamiji began meditating in front of the image. He then went into samadhi and lost all outer consciousness. After some time Swami Premananda chanted Sri Ramakrishna's name in Swamiji's ear and slowly brought him back to normal consciousness. A few days later Jagaddhatri Puja was held at Swamiji's parental home in Simla, Kolkata. We were all invited. Swamiji himself made all the arrangements, and we had a wonderful time. Swamiji also started Saraswati Puja at the Math in an image. Previously Saraswati Puja had never been performed in an image at the Math.

I cannot describe what deep love Swamiji had for us. It would be foolish for me to attempt to measure Swamiji's love. Love is a matter of experience and cannot be expressed in words. Those who received Swamiji's love were blessed. Never before had I experienced such love. I had heard that two opposite moods or ideas often coexist in a great soul, and I witnessed this in Swamiji's life. On one side he was the embodiment of love, and on the other he was the embodiment of harshness. When he was in a loving mood he would make everyone happy, and we would be amazed to see his childlike and joyful nature. But when he was in an angry mood all would avoid him out of fear. Then no one—not even Swami Brahmananda—dared to go near him.

Swamiji's love was not confined to human beings. It also included cows, goats, and other animals. Let me give some examples. In spite of Swamiji's bad health his mind remained on an elevated level, and this worried the doctors. They suggested to Swami Brahmananda that he get some pets for Swamiji, so that Swamiji's mind would come down to a lower plane. Thus Swami Brahmananda bought a goat, a cow, a dog, a duck, and some other pets for the monastery. Swamiji called the goat 'Matru'. He was very fond of the goat and it also was so fond of Swamiji that it would keep looking intently at his face. Whenever Swamiji would call Matru it would run to him, even from far away. That goat was so blessed that it died with its head on Swamiji's lap. Swamiji also had two dogs—Bagha [literally, tiger] and Lion. They too would look at Swamiji intently. Once Bagha did something wrong, so Swamiji banished him to the other side of the river. But soon after, Bagha was able to return to Belur Math by jumping on a ferry-boat. Swamiji was equally affectionate to the cow, the sheep, and the duck. He treated them with such love that those animals became very devoted to him.

Swamiji's relationship with the porters, labourers, and servants was also full of love and kindness. Once some Santhal [tribal] labourers were levelling the ground of the monastery. Swamiji would mix with them freely, exchanging news, and he would also try to find out about their needs. He talked with them so intimately that they considered him to be their very own and unburdened their hearts to him.

Soon after I joined the monastery I became ill. One day Swamiji was eating a pomegranate when all of a sudden he remembered me. Immediately he sent the remaining part of the fruit to me. Whenever he enjoyed some good food, he would share it with his disciples.

He gave shelter to all who took refuge in him. He saw only their good qualities and not their faults. Whenever he saw a little goodness in a person, he would magnify it, and he would praise a person who had done something good. As a result, that person would work with great zeal and joy.

I am incapable of adequately describing Swamiji's love and greatness, but this much I can say—that he was the embodiment of love. Once Swami Nirbhayananda [Swamiji's attendant] fell asleep on Swamiji's chest while fanning him. Lest his sleep be disturbed, Swamiji lay for a long time without moving. He got up from his bed only after Nirbhayananda woke up. He used to address his disciples as "Baba"[2]. What great joy we felt living with Swamiji! Once he said

2. Literally, "father", but when used endearingly it also means "son".

to me: "My child, can you help me get some sleep? I shall give you whatever you ask for." At that time he could hardly sleep. Moreover, he was also suffering from some physical pain. He told me, "As an adult, I have never had more than four hours sleep in a day."

There was something attractive about Swamiji even when he lost his temper. But surprisingly, his anger would leave within a moment, and he would soon behave in his normal loving way. No one could tell that he had been angry a short while ago. Once, for some reason, Swamiji became very angry at Swami Nirbhayananda. Swamiji chased him with a stick in his hand until he got exhausted and sat down. Then suddenly Swamiji's anger melted. On another occasion we were collecting rain water in bottles for drinking. For some reason Swamiji began to scold two brahmacharis. I was so frightened that I began to shake and the water bottle fell from my hand. Immediately Swamiji's mood changed and he became calm. He said to me: "My boy, you have become nervous. Go to my room, take some medicine, and rest a while."

Swamiji trained his disciples and also prayed for their welfare. I shall mention an incident. I had come from the Varanasi Ashrama on fifteen days' leave. Since there was a scarcity of workers at the sevashrama I was being recalled. I was then recuperating from my illness, and when Swamiji heard about my returning to Varanasi, he said: "Let him get well first. Later he will be able to do a lot of work for the sevashrama." Swamiji wanted to keep me with him a little longer for my welfare.

Swamiji taught his disciples to pay particular respect to the direct disciples of Sri Ramakrishna. As he pointed out, the disciples of the Master belonged to "Sri Ramakrishna's family". Swamiji especially respected those disciples who were identified by the Master as "Ishvarakotis", or ever-free souls. Sri Ramakrishna's words were to him the final authority. He advised his disciples to serve the disciples of the Master as they would their own fathers or relatives. ...

Swamiji tried very hard to see that his brother-disciples and his own disciples assimilated the sublime teachings and ideals of Sri Ramakrishna. He was not very anxious to spread Sri Ramakrishna's name. Once the members of the Varanasi Sevashrama wrote to me to ask Swamiji to give a name to the institution. Swamiji suggested the name "Home of Service". Swami Brahmananda then said, "Let the name of the institution be 'Ramakrishna Home of Service'." At this Swamiji said: "You people are always trying to spread Sri Ramakrishna's name. What is important is to spread the Master's ideas and teachings. Why are you in such a hurry to spread his name?"

Before the Varanasi Sevashrama was handed over to the Ramakrishna Mission, Swamiji advised its members to maintain its accounts carefully. He said: "When a donor offers money for a specific purpose, that money should be used for that purpose only. It is not proper to spend 'spinach-money for fish and fish-money for spinach'."

Swamiji always held before us the highest spiritual ideals, and at the same time he taught us moral and ethical values and even other small things. He did not like someone reading another person's letter, or watching someone else write a letter, or overhearing other people's conversation. He would scold anyone he found doing such things. Once he was writing a letter and I was seated near him. I had no intention of reading his letter, but accidentally my eyes fell on it. Swamiji became angry and immediately said: "Be careful. Don't read others' letters. It is very bad." I heard from Swami Turiyananda that once Swamiji asked him to post a letter. When he noticed that Swami Turiyananda was reading the address Swamiji said to him: "Brother, I asked you to post the letter, and not to read the address. Why do you read the address of another's letter? It is not proper."

There is another incident about Swamiji that I heard from Swami Turiyananda. In 1899 Swamiji and Swami Turiyananda were going to America by ship. Now and then

Swami Turiyananda would leave his watch in his cabin and walk on the deck. Swamiji noticed this and said to Swami Turiyananda: "Brother, why do you tempt the cabin boy to steal the watch? He is poor. It is natural for him to be tempted to take it." This is how Swamiji taught people.

Swamiji had a sharp eye for cleanliness and could not bear the monastery being untidy. He would therefore keep watch over the monks so that they put things in their proper places and kept their clothes and beds clean. We had to put our bed-sheets and pillows in the sun every day and check the mattresses for bugs. From time to time Swamiji would lie on our mattresses and check them himself. Once when I was with him he saw some dirt in the monastery. Immediately he called Swami Brahmananda, who was then the President of the Order, and said: "Raja, why is this place so unclean? If you cannot keep the monastery clean, it is better that we live under trees. As we have established this monastery we will have to keep it clean." Swamiji would teach us the importance of cleanliness in this way.

Swamiji would not accept anything from a person who had dirty fingernails. He scolded me about this one day and said, "If your fingernails are dirty I shall not accept anything from your hands." He would also be angry if someone used the cloth he was wearing to dry his hands. Once I cut a pomegranate and served the inner portion to Swamiji. Then I washed my hands and dried them on the cloth I was wearing. Seeing that, Swamiji said: "What! Are you going to serve me food again with those hands? Be careful! Never do that again." He would even use harsh words to correct our bad habits. I heard that Sri Ramakrishna was also very particular about neatness and cleanliness, and he taught those things to his disciples. The Master wanted everything to be orderly and things kept in their proper places. Swami Turiyananda used to say, "He who is orderly inside is orderly outside, and vice versa."

I shall now relate how Swamiji would inspire the monastics with the ideal of renunciation. He wanted to form two groups of monastics—lifelong brahmacharis and sannyasis. The first group would practise hard austerities. They would not shave. They would cook their own meals, study the scriptures, teach them to others, and practise steadfast devotion. And the second group—that is, the sannyasis—would dedicate their lives for their own liberation and for the good of others. When a new brahmachari joined the monastery, Swamiji would ask him to beg food from Belur village or some other place nearby. The newcomer would then cook that food and eat it after offering it to Sri Ramakrishna. Sometimes Swamiji would ask the other monks also to beg their food. He would remind us, "The monastic spirit should always be maintained". In order to emphasize the importance of this tradition, a month before he passed away he sent Swamis Brahmananda, Shivananda, and Saradananda to beg for alms. When they brought the food, Swamiji joyfully partook of some of it. Swamiji then said to Swami Shivananda, "Whether you like it or not, never give up this monastic tradition of begging alms." Swami Shivananda was about to leave to start a centre at Varanasi; thus this reminder from Swamiji.

Swamiji also did not like monks to associate freely with women, nor did he approve of intimacy between monks and householders. He did not like householders to sit on the beds of monastics or eat with them. He asked each monastic to memorize the following verse: "As is the difference between Mount Meru and a mustard seed, between the sun and a firefly, and between the ocean and a pond, similar is the difference between a monk and a householder." Let me give an example of how strict Swamiji was about householders eating with monastics. The dining hall was then below Sri Ramakrishna's shrine at Belur Math. The monks would eat inside the room and the devotees on the veranda. Once Govinda Babu of Santragachi, a householder disciple of Swamiji, sat with the monks inside the room. Seeing this, Swamiji said to him: "Why are you sitting with the monks? Please sit with the devotees on the veranda." Govinda

Babu immediately obeyed. Thus Swamiji would maintain a distance between monastics and householders.

Swamiji asked us to practise meditation as well as karma yoga. He said: "You cannot mediate for long hours. Therefore, use the time which is left after meditation for performing karma yoga. Karma yoga purifies the mind." He did not like us to gossip and idle away our time, avoiding work or meditation. And he hated laziness. When there was nothing to do Swamiji would create some work for us to do. Idleness and gossip were contrary to his nature. Swamiji himself would study the scriptures and teach them to the monks, and he wanted this tradition to be continued at the monastery. During Swamiji's time there was a night class after supper when the monks would discuss what they had read in the scripture class.

At that time two mission centres had been started: an orphanage, under the direction of Swami Akhandananda, and the Varanasi Sevashrama. Swamiji had a soft corner in his heart for the Varanasi Sevashrama, and he always encouraged its members in their endeavours. He even wrote an appeal for it. Previously the name of the sevashrama was "Poor Men's Relief Association" and it was managed by householders. Swamiji said: "What do you mean by 'relief'? Can anybody give relief to others? Change the name to 'Home of Service' and hand it over to monks. Otherwise the institution will not last long." After Swamiji's passing away the name of the Varanasi Sevashrama was changed to 'Home of Service', and it was handed over to the Ramakrishna Mission.

Kalikrishna Tagore, a rich man of Kolkata, once said to Swami Niranjanananda, "I will finance all the activities of the Varanasi Ashrama." Hearing of this Swamiji wrote to Swami Niranjanananda, "If Kalikrishna Tagore helps the Varanasi Ashrama, he will get the result of worshipping Lord Shiva one thousand times." One day Swamiji decided to meet Kalikrishna Tagore. Swami Akhandananda then said to Swamiji: "Why should we take the whole amount from only one person? It would be better if everyone could contribute to this noble cause."

Swamiji visited the Varanasi Sevashrama in 1902, and he was very pleased. One day he said: "Call all the workers of the sevashrama. I will initiate them." He then initiated all of them.

In 1901, according to Swamiji's instructions, a sevashrama was opened at Kankhal [Haridwar]. Swami Akhandananda had much sympathy for this type of work, but he wanted to start a centre in Kolkata first. One day Swamiji said, "These boys [of Bengal] are not doing anything, but the boys of Varanasi are doing something in accordance with my ideals." He advised us to continue the work with bulldog tenacity. Once he told me: "Look, I moved around like a madman for twelve years in order to establish a place for the Master on the bank of the Ganga. You boys do not have the patience and perseverance to hold on to one particular work. Only the old Satchidananda had that capacity." He advised us to work in the proper spirit. One day he said to Swami Kalyanananda in my presence: "Look, Kalyan, do you know what I would like to see? On one side of the monastery there will be a temple of Sri Ramakrishna, and monks and brahmacharis will meditate there. Then they will use their concentration and meditation in the practical field." His intention was to make Vedanta practical. He did not care for mere theoretical discussions.

Swamiji had great reverence for the scriptures. He would study them himself, and also encourage others to do so. He said to me, "If you cannot read anything else, at least read the *Gita*." He had a desire to open a Sanskrit grammar school at Belur Math. Pandit Mokshada Charan Samadhyayi, a great scholar of Panini's grammar, was a devotee of the Math. Whenever he visited the monastery, Swamiji would encourage him to start a Sanskrit school there.

Swamiji also had a desire to see the spread of Vedic culture in Bengal. He encouraged Swami Shuddhananda to study the scriptures and to teach them to the monks. In fact, he entrusted this work to Swami Shuddhananda and blessed him saying, "You will be scholar." When I was with Swamiji, Swami Shuddhananda was working in the publication department of *Udbodhan*. Swamiji released him from that work and brought him to Belur Math to teach the scriptures to the monks. And what enthusiasm he had for preaching work! He once expressed a wish that the monks should go out in groups, carrying a banner of the Ramakrishna Order, and spread the ideas and teachings of the Master in all the villages.

Swamiji was very strict about meditation and japa. A bell was rung for meditation at four o'clock in the morning. One of his attendants would ring the bell in front of every room, including those of Sri Ramakrishna's disciples. Everyone had to go to the Master's shrine for meditation. Swamiji himself would check to see who had come and who was absent. If someone was absent, Swamiji would go to that person's room and call him: "Hello, sannyasi Babu. How long will you sleep?" He was so strict about meditation that he would not hesitate to punish the monks who were absent from the shrine. One day he saw only a few monks in the shrine. After meditation he came downstairs and expressed his displeasure. He then called the cook and told him: "Give me the key to the kitchen. The monks who did not go to the shrine this morning will not get their food in the monastery today. Let them go out and beg their food." Swami Vijnanananda had been present in the shrine, so Swamiji gave him the key and left for Kolkata. Later, after returning to the monastery, he inquired about the monks. He was informed that those who had been absent from the shrine had begged their food on that day.

Regarding the monks' going to the shrine for meditation, he was uncompromising. One day he said to Swami Shivananda in my presence, "Look, Shivananda, you may be a great soul, but for setting an example to others you should go to the shrine." After that, as long as Swami Shivananda's health permitted he would meditate in the shrine. Swamiji also encouraged the monks to practise more spiritual disci-

plines on auspicious days, such as the day of a solar eclipse.
Till the end of his life Swamiji was very regular about his
meditation, even when he was sick. He asked the monks to
perform their daily duties as well as to practise meditation
and japa twice a day.

It was fascinating to see Swamiji in the role of a teacher.
One day he said to Swami Swarupananda: "Look, Swarup,
he on whose head I have placed my hand will not have to
worry about anything. Know this for certain." Another time,
while talking about Swami Sadananda [Swamiji's disciple],
Swamiji said to Swami Premananda: "If my disciples go to
hell a thousand times, I shall lift them up a thousand times. If
this is not true, then know Sri Ramakrishna to be false."

One day Swami Premananda was performing the
worship of Sri Ramakrishna in the shrine. Swamiji went
there and told Premananda that he would perform the
worship himself. Swamiji offered flowers a couple of times at
Sri Ramakrishna's feet, and then he began to put flowers on
his own head. After this he became absorbed in deep meditation. What a sight it was when he came out of the shrine!
His face was shining with devotion. As soon as he came out,
everyone prostrated before him.

One day Swamiji said: "You will see, after two hundred
years people will desperately cry for a hair of Vivekananda."

Swamiji explained to us that the guru and the President
of the Order are not different. One day Swamiji was sitting
on the veranda below the shrine and Swami Brahmananda,
the then President of the Order, was standing behind him.
I was passing through the courtyard. Seeing me, Swamiji
said, "Come here, and bring some flowers." I brought some
flowers. Then he said to me, "Put the flowers at my feet and
worship me daily." After that he said, "Go and bring some
more flowers." When I returned with the flowers he said:
"Now worship the President of the Ramakrishna Order
[Swami Brahmananda]. Remember, the guru and the President are one. Henceforth worship the President every day."
Thus Swamiji taught us in various ways.

6

During a scripture class one day, a discussion was going on as to which is greater—work or meditation. Swamiji silently listened to the discussion, and at last he said: "My boys, follow either one whole-heartedly. Then this problem will be solved automatically." Another day Swami Swarupananda asked Swamiji: "What an austere life you led at the Baranagore monastery! Was that life better or is the way we are now living at Belur Math better? Some say that those days at Baranagore Math were wonderful." Swamiji replied: "Yes, it was necessary then to lead that kind of austere life. But it is not possible for the present generation to lead such a life, so this new lifestyle has been arranged for them."

Swamiji gave the highest place to sannyasa. While initiating a brahmachari into the vows of sannyasa, he would say, "I shall sacrifice you to the Master [as a goat is sacrificed to a Deity]." Before the ceremony he would meditate and create a spiritual atmosphere. Then he would recite the sannyasa mantras and others would repeat them. After that he would ask the monks to offer their sacred thread and hair into the fire. Then he would tell them, "From today you are beyond caste and you can accept alms from any person in the world."

One day, while I was staying at Belur Math with Swamiji, I expressed my desire to receive sannyasa from him. He said, "Will you be able to beg food from door to door?" I replied, "With your blessings, surely I can." He then said: "Stay here. You will get your final vows in time." At that time Swamiji had planned to visit Mayavati, but the visit was postponed. Then I again asked him to initiate me into sannyasa. Swamiji decided to initiate me on Lord Buddha's birthday and asked Swami Bodhananda to make all the necessary arrangements. The night before, I passed in great anxiety. I was supposed to get up early. I woke up at 2:20 a.m., and thinking that it was 4:10 a.m., I asked Swami Nishchayananda to ring the bell. When Swami Bodhananda started for the shrine on hearing the bell, Swamiji inquired, "Who is going to the shrine at this time of the night?" Bodhananda told him about the bell, and Swamiji remarked, "The boy has become very nervous." Some time later, however, Swamiji came to the shrine and performed the Viraja Homa. After pouring oblations, Swamiji said, "From today all your worldly duties are over." He gave me my monastic name "Achalananda". I was Swamiji's last monastic disciple.

Swamiji once said: "He who can perform his worldly duties perfectly can also attain the knowledge of Brahman."

Swamiji taught people in many ways. We are blessed that we got a chance to serve and work for him. If those who come in the future can mould their lives according to Swamiji's ideals, they also will be blessed and will attain the Supreme Reality.

(*Vedanta Kesari*, November-December 1989)

SWAMI ATULANANDA

Swami Atulananda

It was in 1899 that Swamiji visited America for the second time. He was to go to the Vedanta Society, New York. When I heard the news, I naturally became very happy. I was one of the members of the Vedanta Society. He came to the Vedanta Society, entered the room and sat down on the floor. There were chairs in the room; they were arranged for the purpose; so when I saw him sitting on the floor, I thought it somewhat strange and astonishing. Then he got up, walked up as a familiar person among the inmates, speaking to them in a personal way. The first thing to impress me was his eyes. They were bright and big. His eyes spoke of deep concentration. When he spoke, he gave his whole mind to that. He spoke with absolute conviction. He meant seriously what he said. This impressed me very much. He said that he came to America to give and to take. He would speak of spiritual ideals, and would also try to learn how the flourishing society of America was built. The Western people needed meditation. They needed to be more sattvic and the Hindus ought to be more rajasic.

Swamiji would always remain absorbed. Even in little matters he could concentrate his mind. I shall tell you an incident. Once he was with the family of a devotee of New York. Soon he charmed all by his presence and talks. The lady of the house became extremely devoted to him and wished to do something for him. One morning the lady knocked at the door of the room where Swamiji stayed. As

Swamiji did not respond, she went away. After some time she came back and entering the room, she cleaned it. She found Swamiji reading a book all the while. She was astonished to find that he did not notice her though she knocked at the door and entered the room. She thought Swamiji might have been absorbed in some serious philosophical studies. She questioned Swamiji about that. Swamiji laughed and said that he was reading jungle stories of Kipling. This is wonderful. He could so perfectly concentrate his mind even on small things. This incident made a lasting impression on her mind.

There is a little picture buried deep down in the folds of my memory that I may try to reconstruct as it appears to me today. The incident took place in New York, sometime in the year 1900, when Swamiji had come to America for the second time. The office where I was then employed closed at noon on Saturdays and it was my habit after office hours to visit the Vedanta Society on these days to find out if I could be of any service there. One Saturday afternoon when I came to the house I met some of the Vedanta students in the parlour busily engaged in trying to find a suitable place to hang a large picture of Jesus. The picture had just been presented to the Society by one of its devotees and it portrayed Jesus praying in agony at Gethsemane, a few days before the crucifixion: 'O my father, if it be possible, let this cup pass from me: nevertheless not as I will, but as thou wilt.'

As we were thus engaged Swamiji unexpectedly entered the room, and seeing us, called out: 'Hello, what are you doing?' We told him about the picture and showed it to him. The Swami then stood before it for sometime in the attitude of adoration, his palms joined and head bent forward. And then in a very low voice, almost a whisper, he uttered the name of Jesus and continued as if speaking to himself: "He is Jesus, the great renouncer, the Christian sannyasi. What magnanimity! What nobility of heart! Mocked by the rabble, bleeding on the cross, that great soul prayed for forgiveness for his enemies even: 'Father, forgive them, for they know not what they do.'"

Then he turned around and silently left the room. The little episode stamped itself on our minds. What we saw and felt was Holiness paying tribute to Holiness—and this gave us an insight into the devotional aspect of Swamiji's nature.

(*Sandipan*, August 1963)

Swamiji was so simple in his behaviour—so like one of the crowd—that he did not impress me too much when I first saw him. There was nothing about his ways that would mark him as the lion of New York society, as so often he had been. Simple in dress and behavior, he was just like one of us. He did not put himself aside on a pedestal as is so often the case with lionized personages. He walked about the room, sat on the floor, laughed, joked, chatted—nothing formal. Of course, I had noticed his magnificent, brilliant eyes, his beautiful features and majestic bearing, for these were parts of him that no circumstances could hide. But when I saw him for a few minutes standing on a platform surrounded by others, it flashed into my mind: "What a giant, what strength, what manliness, what a personality! Everyone near him looks so insignificant in comparison." It came to me almost as a shock and seemed to startle me. What was it that gave Swamiji this distinction? Was it his height? No, there were gentlemen there taller than he was. Was it his build? No, there were near him some very fine specimens of American manhood. It seemed to be more in the expression of the face than anything else. Was it his purity? What was it? I could not analyse it. I remembered what had been said of Lord Buddha—"a lion amongst men." I felt that Swamiji had unlimited power, that he could move heaven and earth if be willed it. This was my strongest and lasting impression of him.

When the Swami returned from California, I was no longer in New York so I never saw him again. But I am grateful that I have seen him and that during those two weeks he had sometimes been very kind to me. And even now as I read and reread the Swami's lectures, that picture of wonderful strength and purity comes before my mental vision. And in those printed lines there still seems to vibrate something of that great spirit that came to enlighten the Western world. "These great and peaceful teachers," says the sage Shankaracharya, "come to regenerate the world like the spring that brings forth new fruits and flowers. And after they themselves have crossed over the ocean of world-bondage, they help those who strive for liberation to reach the haven of peace and blessedness. And this they do from a purely unselfish motive."

(*With the Swamis in America and India,* pp. 59-60)

Swami Virajananda

His [Swamiji's] eyes were captivating, just as the American newspapers had said. Light appeared to emanate from his entire body. What a charming figure—combining beauty and power, a nonchalant air, and a dazzling personality! My first reactions were love, devotion, and a sense of awe.

At that time [in 1897] Swamiji's complexion was extremely fair. His face seemed filled with an extraordinary unworldliness and looked radiant and flushed. It was difficult to look at him for fear that, if my eyes met his, mine might indeed be scorched. When immersed in his own thoughts, he paced to and fro like a lion on the terrace of the house. Though he was clad only in a loin-cloth, he seemed a veritable Napoleon of the spiritual world. It was as if a tremendous power were intensely vibrating, and that the earth beneath his feet was, at every step, shaking and cracking.

(*Monastic Disciples*, p. 75)

At that time [in 1897] the colour of Swamiji's body was fair. There was a brilliant lustre on his face. ... During the day Swamiji used to be at Gopal Lal Seal's house at Cossipore, and in the evening he used to walk the whole distance to the Math with his friends and disciples. After coming to the Math, he would remove his clothing and wear only a loin-cloth. Sometimes if it was too late at night, he would spend

SWAMI VIRAJANANDA

the night at the Seals' house. There, many people would come to see and talk with Swamiji; and when he came to the Math, there was also no end of talking. He used to tell stories, and relate incidents of his life, or make fun with his brother-disciples.

... Goodwin and the Chennaii disciples always remained with the Swami. Goodwin used to serve the Swami day and night. Oh, what a wonderful spirit of service he had! ...

Mrs. Sevier used to serve Swamiji at the Seals' house. Swamiji would take his lunch and afternoon tea there. Mr. and Mrs. Sevier came to the Math as well, once or twice. Niranjan Maharaj and Gopal junior used to entertain them then. ... Mr. Turnbull of Chicago had come to India long before Swamiji's return to India. He stayed in Kolkata and would visit the Math frequently. ... After Swamiji had come to Kolkata, Mr. Turnbull would often see him. ...

From 8 to 9 in the morning there would be a *Gita* or Upanishad class, or a question-answer class. All the brahmacharis and sannyasis used to attend it. ...

(*Life*, Vol. 2, p. 235)

SWAMI SADANANDA

Swami Sadananda

Once in our wanderings in the outlying districts of the Himalayas, I fainted from hunger and thirst. How great was Swamiji's love for me! He carried me and thus saved me from certain death. Another time we had to cross a mountain river which was very dangerous to ford because of its swift current and slippery bed. At each step there was the possibility of slipping, and even one slip meant certain death. I was securely seated on the horse which someone had kindly lent for the journey, while Swamiji, endangering his own life, held its reins and like a syce led it across the hazardous river. At times it seemed as though it would not be possible to lead the horse further. But Swamiji's courage was amazing. Caring nothing for his own life, he led the horse and me across to safety. What love and compassion he bore in his heart! Can his love ever be described in words? He was love incarnate. … While in his company, my heart would be so full of strength and courage that even death appeared to be a trifling thing! Once, when we were moving through the jungle, we came across some bleached human bones, with pieces of rotting ochre cloth lying here and there. Pointing to them, Swamiji said: "See, a tiger has devoured a monk here. Are you afraid?" I promptly replied, "Not with you, Swamiji!"

Those were busy days [at the Baranagore Math]; there was not a moment's rest. Outsiders came and went, pundits argued and discussed. Swamiji was never for one moment idle, never dull. Sometimes he was left alone for a while and he would walk up and down, saying, "Hari bol! Hari bol!

Call on the Lord!", or "Oh Mother!" And I watched all the time from a distance and in some interval said, "Swamiji, will you not eat?"—always to be answered playfully. ... Swamiji would work twenty-four hours at a stretch. He was like a madman, he was so busy! Early in the morning, while it was still dark, he would rise and call the others, singing "Awake! Awake! All ye who would drink of the divine nectar." Then all would proceed for meditation, afterwards drifting almost unconsciously into singing and talking, which would last till noon or even later. It might perhaps be one or two o'clock when Swami Ramakrishnananda—the cook, housekeeper, and ritualist of the community—would drive them all with threats to bathe and eat. But after this, they would "regroup"—again the singing and talking would continue, till at last evening had come, bringing with it the time for the two hours of arati to Sri Ramakrishna. After this would follow some talk of the Master, and then would come the trances of meditation. Or, sitting on the roof, till long after midnight they would sit and chant "Hail Sita Rama!"

(*Monastic Disciples*, pp. 207-08, pg. 210)

Swami Shuddhananda

It was February 1897. Swami Vivekananda had just returned to India after his triumph in the West. From the moment Swamiji proved the superiority of the Hindu dharma at the Parliament of Religions in Chicago and left the banner of Hinduism flying victoriously in the West, I gathered every possible bit of information about him from newspapers, and read them with great interest. I had left college only two or three years before and had not settled down to earning. So I spent my time now visiting friends, now going to the office of the *Indian Mirror*, devouring the latest news about him and studying reports of his lectures. Thus I had read almost all that he had said in Sri Lanka and Chennai from the time he had set foot in India. Apart from this, I used to visit the Alambazar Math and hear from his brother-disciples, as well as from my own friends who used to go there, various things about Swamiji. Further, no comment on him that appeared in *Bangabasi, Amritabazar, Hope, Theosophist,* etc.—whether satirical, admonishing, or patronizing, according to the writer's outlook and temperament—escaped my notice.

Today *that* Swami Vivekananda alights at the Sealdah station and comes back to Kolkata, the city of his birth! My idea of him, formed through hearsay and the reports of others, must be confirmed by observing his personality. I reached the Sealdah station early in the morning. Many had come to welcome the Swami even at that early hour. I encountered many of my acquaintances and had many pleasant chats with them concerning him. I noticed that two leaflets printed

SWAMI SHUDDHANANDA

in English were being distributed freely. These were the farewell addresses which the Americans and Englishmen had presented to Swamiji on the eve of his departure from the West, expressing their feelings of gratitude for all he had done for them.

Gradually, the dense crowd of people eager to see him became a surging mass of humanity pouring into the station platform. All were anxiously asking one another, "How long will it be before Swamiji arrives?" Then we heard that Swamiji was coming in a special train, and that his arrival was imminent. There it is! The sound of the train is heard, and with its usual puff of smoke it heaves into the platform. As the carriage bringing Swamiji stopped, I was fortunate enough to be waiting in the very spot that overlooked it. Swamiji was standing up and saluting with folded palms all who had assembled to receive him. I only got a quick glimpse of him, but this small gesture was enough to win my heart.

The Reception Committee with Babu Narendranath Sen at its head approached Swamiji and brought him down from the train. Many crowded to take the dust of his feet. The anxious crowd was spontaneously shouting in joyous exultation—'Jai Swami Vivekanandaji Ki Jai! Jai Ramakrishna Paramahamsa Dev Ki Jai!" My voice too mingled with it and began to ring in tune with theirs.

When I came out of the platform, I found that Swamiji's carriage was already unhorsed and a band of young men were getting ready to draw it up themselves. I also tried to join them, but the crowd prevented my doing so. Giving up this attempt, I began to accompany the carriage at a distance. In the station a samkirtana party had come to receive him, and along the road a band was playing, ahead of the procession. The roads were decorated with flowers, festoons, and buntings. The carriage drew up in front of Ripon College.

This time, I got an opportunity to get a good look at Swamiji. He was leaning out of the carriage and talking with an old acquaintance. His face was extraordinarily bright and seemed to be emitting rays of brilliant light. Only, he looked a little tired by the fatigue of the journey. There were two carriages. In one were Swamiji and Mr. and Mrs. Sevier. The Hon. Babu Charuchandra Mitra was standing in this carriage and helping to control the crowd with hand gestures. In the other carriage were seated Mr. Goodwin, Mr. Harrison (a European Buddhist monk from Ceylon), G. G., Kidi, and Alasinga (three of Swamiji's Chennaii disciples), and Swami Trigunatitananda. Responding to many earnest entreaties, Swamiji got down from the carriage and addressed the crowd for two or three minutes, and then drove towards the house of Pashupati Babu in Baghbazar. I tendered my salutations mentally, and wended my way back home.

After my noonday meal I went to the house where Khagen (Swami Vimalananda) lived, and from there we drove together in a cab to Pashupati Babu's house. Swamiji was resting in a room upstairs. Many were turned away. Fortunately for us, many of Swamiji's brother-disciples, whom we knew well, were there. Swami Shivananda took us into the presence of Swamiji and introduced us with the words, "These young men are your ardent admirers." Swamiji and Swami Yogananda sat side-by-side on two easy chairs in a well-furnished room on the first floor of the house. The other Swamis were moving about, clad in their ochre robes. We bowed down to Swamiji and sat on the carpeted floor. He was talking to Swami Yogananda about his experiences in America and Europe. "Well, Yogin, do you know what I saw in the West? All over the world I was seeing only the play of the same great Shakti (divine energy). Our forefathers manifested that power in religion and philosophy, and the West is manifesting the selfsame energy in the modern age through dynamic activity. Truly, through the whole universe there are only different expressions of that same great Energy." Noticing Khagen's emaciated appearance, Swamiji said, "This boy looks very sickly." Swami Shivananda said, "He has been suffering for a long time from dyspepsia." Swamiji replied, "Is not our Bengal a sentimental country?

That is why there are so many cases of dyspepsia here." After awhile, tendering our obeisance, we went home.

Swamiji and his disciples, Mr. and Mrs. Sevier, stayed in the garden-house of the late Gopal Lal Seal in Cossipore. We went there frequently with our friends and relations to attend Swamiji's conversations. I shall try to put down here what little is left in my memory of those days.

It was in one of the rooms of this garden-house that I talked with Swamiji for the first time. I went and prostrated before him. There was nobody else in the room. Suddenly, I don't know why, Swamiji asked me, "Do you smoke?" I replied, "No", to which he replied, "Very well, smoking isn't good. I am also trying to give it up." Another day Swamiji was speaking with a Vaishnava who had come to see him. Swamiji was saying, "Babaji,[1] once in America I lectured to them on Sri Krishna. Captivated by that lecture, one exquisitely beautiful young lady, who was also a heiress to an immense fortune, renounced everything and retired to a solitary island to lose herself in the intoxication of meditation on the Lord." Afterwards, Swamiji began to talk about renunciation: "In all religious sects that do not keep aflame the fire of renunciation, degeneration quickly sets in."

"Another day, we found a large gathering sitting before him. His remarks were directed to a young gentleman who was staying in the quarters of the Bengal Theosophical Society. The young gentleman was saying, "I've been to many a sect and denomination, but I have yet to find Truth." Swamiji replied affectionately: "Well, my child, once I too was in the same disconsolate state of mind as you are. Why should you be so anxious on this score? Tell me what their advice was, and what you have been doing." The young man replied: "Sir, in our society there is a preacher, Bhavani Shankar by name, who is a Sanskrit scholar. He made me understand in a beautiful way the value of image worship in the scheme of spiritual development. Obeying him, I began to worship with the proper rituals for a time, but this did not

1. Lit. Revered Father. Vaishnava holy men are addressed thus.

give me the peace I was yearning for. At that time one gentleman told me, 'Try to make your mind void, and if you can
succeed in the attempt, you will get supreme peace.' I also
spent some days in following this advice, but to no purpose.
Sir, even now I sit in a closed room, and meditate as long as
I can. Yet peace is far, far away from me. How am I to gain
peace?"

Swamiji continued to speak to him in an affectionate
way: "My boy, if you have any respect for my words, the
first thing I will advise you to do is throw open all the doors
and windows of your room! In your quarter there are lots of
poor people sunk in poverty. You will have to go to them and
serve them with all enthusiasm. Arrange to distribute medicines to the sick and nurse them, provide food for anyone
who is starving, and teach the ignorant as much as you can.
If you care for my advice, I tell you, my child, you will surely
get peace if you begin to serve your brethren in this way."

The youth replied, "But sir, if I serve the poor and
thereby break the regularity of my life by keeping awake late
at night and not taking meals at the proper time, I might fall
ill, and then what shall become of me?"

Up to this point, Swamiji had spoken to the youth very
lovingly, sympathizing with all of his mental reservations;
but this remark seemed to vex him. He then said: "Now I
understand—and so does everyone here—that you are not
the kind of man who will exert so much in the service of the
sick that your own health and convenience are affected."
There was no more talk with that youth.

Another day, he was talking to Master Mahashaya,
author of The Gospel of Sri Ramakrishna. Master Mahashaya
asked Swamiji: "You speak of service, charity, and doing
good to the world; but they belong to the domain of maya.
When the goal of Vedanta is liberation, to cut at the root of
all maya, what will be the result of these teachings to people
who are already bound tight in the coils of maya?" Swamiji
immediately replied: "Does not the idea of liberation also lie
within the realm of maya? The Atman is ever-free, so what

need is there for you to try to be liberated?" Master Mahashaya remained silent on hearing this.

Next the conversation was diverted to Thomas à Kempis,
and his *Imitation of Christ*. Many of us know that before
Swamiji renounced the world, he was reading this book
avidly, and when the sannyasis moved to Baranagore, the
brother-disciples of Swamiji used to study its teachings as
special aids to their sadhana. Swamiji loved the book so
much that in those days he had contributed to a contem-
porary magazine, *Sahityakalpadruma*, an introduction to the
book, and had started to translate it in Bengali, with the plan
to publish it in instalments under the name *Ishanusarana*.

One of those present, curious to know Swamiji's current
opinion of the book, read aloud from it a teaching on
humility—and remarked that unless one considers oneself
the lowest of the low, it is impossible to develop spiritually.
Hearing this, Swamiji said, "Why should we consider ourselves to be low? Where is ignorance again for us? We have
enjoyed the bliss of Illumination—we are children of that
Illumination." From this reply, we could easily understand
that he had transcended the stages of preliminary sadhanas
mentioned in that book, and had reached great heights of
realization.

We especially noted that even trivial everyday occur-
rences of life did not escape his scrutiny, and he transmuted
them into aids to popularise high spiritual truths.

Once Ramlal Chatterjee, the nephew of Sri Ramakrishna,
known amongst the Ramakrishna Order as Ramlal Dada,
came from Dakshineshwar to meet Swamiji. Seeing him,
Swamiji got him a chair and asked him to sit while he
himself paced to and fro. "Dada" felt very embarrassed at
this respect shown to him and began to implore Swamiji to
take the seat, but—with much protestation—Dada was made
to occupy the chair after all. Swamiji continued to walk to
and fro repeating to himself, *guruvat guruputreshu*—that is,
one is to treat the descendants of the guru with the same
honour as one would treat the guru. Here we noticed that

though Swamiji was the recipient of such glory and honour, there wasn't the least trace of any conceit in him.

Later, many students came to see him. Swamiji was sitting in a chair. The boys were squatting around him, eagerly waiting to hear a few words. There were no seats left where they could sit and hear him, so they sat on the floor. Perhaps it struck Swamiji that it would have been better to give them seats, but then he thought otherwise, for he said: "Doesn't matter! You have done the right thing. It is good to practise a little austerity."

One day we took with us Sri Chandi Charan Vardhan, who lived in our quarter of the city. Chandi Babu was the manager of a small school named Hindu Boys' School where education was given up to the third class. From the beginning, he had been a great devotee. After reading the lectures of Swamiji, he developed great reverence for him. At one point he even thought of renouncing the world to facilitate his devotional practices, but he was not successful in the attempt. For a while he was an amateur actor in a theatre, and he even figured as a playwright. He was very emotional by temperament. He had made the acquaintance of Edward Carpenter, the famous reformer, whose book *Adam's Peak to Elephanta* includes an account of the author's meeting with Chandi Babu as well as his picture.

Chandi Babu came and with great reverence made his obeisance and asked Swamiji, "Swamiji, whom can we accept as our guru?"

Swamiji: "He who can understand and speak to you of your past and future can be recognized as your guru. My guru spoke all about my past and future."

Chandi Babu: "Well, Swamiji, does wearing a loincloth help in any way to control lust?"

Swamiji: "It might help a little. But when the passion gets strong, can it be checked, my child, with a loincloth? Unless and until the mind is completely given to God, no external check can completely obliterate lust. But then, you know, as long as the mind has not reached that stage, it tries to protect itself by external aids. Once the feeling of lust rose in me. I got so disgusted with myself that I sat on a pot of burning cinders, and it took a long time for the wound to heal."

Thus did Chandi Babu put to Swamiji many questions regarding continence, and Swamiji with utter frankness clearly expounded all its secrets to him. Chandi Babu was making severe attempts to practise sadhana, but being a householder he wasn't able at all times to do this to his entire satisfaction. He knew full well that continence was the prime necessity for all sadhanas, but he was not yet able to practise it to his entire satisfaction. And as he was spending his time in the management and education of young boys, he had occasion to notice how—in the absence of any moral and religious education, and under the influence of bad company—the boys lost their sexual purity even at a tender age; he was always wondering how to restore their lost purity. But how can one who has not attained something give it to others?

Thus, unable either to practise continence himself or teach it to his boys, he would become worried and even desperate. And now, hearing from the ideal brahmachari these straightforward counsels and energetic words, it struck him suddenly that this great soul, if he desired, could revive in him and his boys the ancient ideal of brahmacharya. I have mentioned earlier that Chandi Babu was very emotional by temperament. Suddenly, apparently fired by an uncontrollable enthusiasm, he shouted out in English, in great excitement, "Oh Great Teacher, tear up this evil of hypocrisy and teach the world the *one* thing needful—how to conquer lust". Swamiji pacified Chandi Babu.

The next topic of conversation was Edward Carpenter. Swamiji said: "In London, he often used to call on me. Many other Socialist Democrats also used to visit me. Finding in the religion of Vedanta a strong support for their ideals, they felt much attracted towards its teachings." Swamiji had read Edward Carpenter's book, *Adam's Peak to Elephanta*. Recalling the picture of Chandi Babu printed therein, he told him that he had already been familiar with his appearance.

The shadows of evening began to fall, and so Swamiji got up to go to his room for a little rest. Addressing Chandi Babu, he said, "Chandi Babu, you come across many boys; can you give me some beautiful boys?" Chandi Babu was a bit distracted when Swamiji said this and didn't quite understand the full bearing of his words, so he followed him and asked what he had said about some beautiful boys. Swamiji replied: "I do not want those whose appearance is beautiful. I want some strongly built, energetic boys of exalted character. I want to train them up so that they may get themselves ready for their own liberation as well as for the good and welfare of this world."

Another day we went and found Swamiji pacing to and fro and talking very familiarly with his disciple Sharatchandra Chakravarti. We were eagerly waiting to put to Swamiji one question. The problem was this—what is the difference between an Incarnation of God and a man who has attained liberation by his own efforts? We requested Sharat Babu to place the question before Swamiji, and he did so accordingly. But without giving a direct reply to this question, Swamiji said: "It is my firm belief that of all states, videhamukti (liberation after death) is the highest. When I was travelling in different parts of India during the days of my sadhana, how many days I spent in caves, how many times I even thought of giving up this body since liberation was not attained, what strenuous spiritual practices I underwent! But now I do not feel the same urge for liberation. My present mood is that so long as even a single individual remains in bondage, I do not want my own liberation."

Hearing these words of Swamiji, I began to wonder at his infinite kindness of heart, and I thought to myself: "Is he describing the characteristics of an Incarnation of God by giving expression to his own attitude? Is he also then a divine incarnation?" And I thought, "Maybe, he no longer aspires after liberation because he has already attained it."

On another day, Khagen and I went to him after dusk. In order for us to be noticed by Swamiji, Haramohan

Mitra (a devotee of Sri Ramakrishna) introduced us to him personally: "Swamiji, these are your ardent admirers and they zealously study Vedanta." Though the first portion of Haramohan Babu's words were literally true, the second part was overdoing it. For although we had studied something of the *Gita* and a few primers on Vedanta, we could be credited with no more than a superficial knowledge; we had not studied them with the thoroughness of a student nor had we recourse to their original texts and commentaries. But, hearing Vedanta mentioned, Swamiji asked us, "Have you studied the Upanishads?"

I replied, "Yes, a little."

Swamiji: "Which Upanishad?"

Searching my mind and finding nothing else to say, I replied, *Katha Upanishad.*

Swamiji: "Well, repeat a few lines. *Katha Upanishad* is very grand, very poetic."

What a catastrophe! Perhaps Swamiji thought that I knew the *Katha Upanishad* by heart, and was asking me to repeat a few verses. Though I had turned over the pages of this Upanishad, I had cared neither to grasp its meaning nor commit it to memory. So I was in a sad predicament. What to do? Suddenly I struck upon a plan. A few years before, I had made some regular attempts to read the *Gita*, and as a result I could remember most of the verses. I knew for certain that if I did not at least repeat from memory some scriptural texts, I could hardly show my face to him afterwards. Therefore I said: "I do not know by heart *Katha Upanishad*; but I can repeat a few verses from the *Gita*." Swamiji ordered me to do so. From the latter part of the eleventh chapter I repeated all the verses which Arjuna sang in praise of the Lord. To inspire us with enthusiasm, Swamiji was punctuating my recitation with his appreciative remarks.

The next day, taking with us our friend Rajendranath, we went to see Swamiji again. I told Rajen beforehand, "Brother, yesterday I was put in a very delicate position before Swamiji with my poor knowledge of the Upanishads.

If you have a copy of any Upanishad, take it with you so that if any occasion arises, we can read it out before him." Rajen had a pocket edition of the Upanishads by Prasanna Kumar Shastri with a commentary in Bengali. I put it in my pocket. That evening, we found Swamiji's room filled with visitors. What I had envisioned came to pass: somehow or other, the conversation turned to the *Katha Upanishad*. Taking the book out of my pocket, I immediately began to read the Upanishad from the beginning. As I read, Swamiji spoke of the faith of Nachiketa, that faith whereby he dared to go even to the house of Yama, god of Death. When I began to read of the second boon of Nachiketa, regarding the attainment of heaven, Swamiji asked me to read a few verses here and there and to begin the part about the third boon. There, Nachiketa asks Yama about the doubts of men regarding whether anyone survives bodily death. And Yama places temptations before him, but Nachiketa rejects them all.

After the reading was over, Swamiji spoke in praise of Nachiketa's character, in words full of celestial fire. But my weak memory retains but little of that day's talk.

But with these two days of talk on the Upanishads, Swamiji infused into my mind something of his own intense faith and his love of the Upanishads. From that day, whenever I got an opportunity, I studied the Upanishads with due reverence and am still doing the same. Even now, I seem to hear those Upanishadic verses which Swamiji would repeat at different times, in his own distinctively powerful, clear, and ringing tone. Whenever I forget the Self, carried away by criticisms and judgments of others, memory brings back to me that familiar Upanishadic text which Swamiji often used to repeat in his sweet and melodious tone: "Know that Atman alone and give up all other talk. He is the bridge to Immortality." On a day when the sky is dark and thick with clouds and flashes of lightning, I remember his familiar figure pointing to a flash of lightning in the sky and uttering the well-known verse: "There the sun shines not, nor the moon, nor the stars. This lightning also does not shine there;

He shining, all these shine; His light illumines all." Or whenever my heart gets filled with despondency thinking that
supreme knowledge is far from me, I seem to hear Swamiji,
his face suffused with bliss, repeating in a sonorous voice the
message of hope from the Upanishads: 'Hear, ye children of
immortal bliss! Even ye that reside in higher spheres! I have
found the Ancient One, who is beyond all darkness, all delusion; knowing Him alone you shall be saved from death over
again—there is no other way!'"

Another day, I came in the afternoon. I saw that many
Gujarati pundits were sitting in the room, and Swamiji was
discussing spiritual matters with them in fluent Sanskrit.
Various topics, like devotion and knowledge, were being
discussed. Suddenly there seemed to be some kind of
commotion. From what I heard, I understood that while
speaking in Sanskrit, Swamiji had made some grammatical
error. Abandoning their discussions on devotion, knowledge,
and so forth, the pundits now took this up as their main
topic of deliberation, apparently elated by the idea that
they had succeeded in defeating Swamiji in debate! At this
I remembered the saying of Sri Ramakrishna: "The vultures
soar very high in the sky, but their attention is fixed on the
carrion on the ground." However, Swamiji at once submitted
by saying: "I am but a servant of the pundits, please excuse
this mistake." After some time, Swamiji got up and the
pundits also went to perform ablutions with Ganga water. I,
too, went to the banks of the Ganga, where I overheard the
pundits saying: "Swamiji is not a great scholar. His eyes have
a hypnotic spell, and it is only by virtue of that power that he
always comes out victorious.' Hearing this remark, I thought
to myself that the pundits were certainly right about the
hypnotic spell in Swamiji's eyes. Otherwise how could he
gain the admiration of so many rich, learned, and prestigious
men and women in India and abroad? Not because of his
intellect, beauty or riches, but because of the hypnotic spell
in his eyes. O readers! If you wish to know the source of this
hypnotic spell, then you should establish a divine relation-

ship with my Master, and try with all humility to learn the details of his extraordinary spiritual practices.

It was the end of April 1897. Only five days before, I had left home to live with the sannyasis of the Alambazar Math. Swamis Premananda, Nirmalananda, and Subodhananda were then living there. Soon, Swamiji came back from his visit to Darjeeling. With him were Swamis Brahmananda and Yogananda, and some Chennai disciples of Swamiji— Alasinga, Kidi, G. G., and others.

Only a few days before, Swami Nityananda had taken sannyasa from Swamiji. He spoke to Swamiji one day about the need for systematic training in the Math, as a large number of young men had at that time joined to lead a life of renunciation. Swamiji readily agreed and asked him to gather all the inmates in the hall. "Let someone be writing as I dictate," said Swamiji. No one seemed to be prepared to come forward, and finally the task fell on me. It might be said in passing that at that time, with the inmates of the Math, literary education was out of favour, the prevailing notion being that to realize God by sadhana was the goal, while book knowledge, even though it might bring a little name and fame, was really useless for a spiritual aspirant. Only in the case of those who are chosen by God to carry His mission or message was the need for literary training recognized. When I came forward to take down Swamiji's dictation, Swamiji asked whether I had joined the Order as a brahmachari or I had simply come to visit the Math for a few days. Someone answered that I had come to join the Order. All the while I was getting the writing materials ready; and Swamiji, before dictating the rules, remarked as follows: "Look here, we are going to make rules, no doubt; but we must remember their main object—to transcend all rules and regulations. We naturally have some bad tendencies which are to be changed by observing rules and regulations; and finally we have to go beyond these too, just as we remove one thorn with another and throw both of them away." The course of discipline and routine decided upon: Both mornings and evenings should be devoted to meditation, while the afternoons, after a short rest period, should be utilized for individual studies. In the evenings, one particular religious book should be read and expounded. It was also provided that each member would take physical exercise both morning and evening. Another rule was to the effect that no intoxicant save tobacco should be allowed. Having dictated the rules, Swamiji asked me to make a fair copy of them. He also instructed me to phrase all the rules in a positive, rather than a negative, way.

I found some difficulty in carrying out this last instruction. Swamiji's central idea was that it does no good to men to point out their various defects and tell them, "You should not do this, or that", and so on. Rather, he believed that if the proper ideal was clearly placed before the aspirants, it would help them to progress, and defects would gradually fall off by themselves. I was at every turn reminded of this principle when I carried out his instruction to express the rules positively. And I was able to make them all positive, except one—the matter of the intoxicants. In its original form, it was that "in the Math, except tobacco, no intoxicants shall be allowed". My first attempt to cast it in non-negative form was, "Everyone in the Math shall use tobacco"! But seeing that this seemed to make it incumbent upon everyone to smoke—even those who were entirely free of the habit—after many futile attempts I finally gave it this form: "In the Math, tobacco alone—among the intoxicants—is allowed." Somehow I now find this to have been an awkward compromise. As a matter of fact, in any set of rules and regulations it is not possible to do away with the negative form altogether; but it must be remembered that the more the rules embody the positive aspect of the ideal, the more helpful they become. And this was Swamiji's main idea.

Another day Swamiji was sitting in the hall, his face radiating an unusual brilliance. A variety of topics were raised. In the audience was our friend Vijayakrishna Bose. In those days, Vijaya Babu used to ascend many a platform and speak before many associations. He had once even spoken before the Congress in English. Somebody let Swamiji know of his capacity to deliver lectures, and so Swamiji asked Vijaya Babu to deliver a lecture as there was quite a good audience. The subject suggested was "The Atman". But Vijaya Babu exhibited no signs of willingness to rise to the occasion; in vain did Swamiji and all the rest tried to set him upon his legs. After nearly fifteen minutes of ineffectual persuasion, their glance fell upon me.

Before coming to the Math I had occasionally delivered a few lectures in Bengali, and in our debating society I trained myself to speak in English as well. Someone present referred to this, and I was importuned to speak on the same subject. I have never been encumbered much with that inconvenient commodity called modesty. I at once stood up and held forth for nearly half an hour, giving out ideas about the Atman beginning with the conversation between Yajnavalkya and Maitreyi in the *Brihadaranyaka Upanishad*. I did not pay any heed whether there were grammatical mistakes or any incongruity of ideas in my speech. Our gracious Swamiji also, without caring for any of these, cheered me on enthusiastically.

After me, Swami Prakashananda, a new initiate into sannyasa, also spoke for about ten minutes on the Atman. He modelled his speech on that of Swamiji and spoke in a good, sonorous voice. Swamiji much extolled his speech also.

In fact, Swamiji never looked into man's failings and weaknesses. On the contrary, he used to encourage whatever was good in anyone—thereby giving him the proper surroundings and facility to manifest his latent possibilities. But our readers need not be under the impression that Swamiji used to praise one and all in every one of his doings—far from it. Many times we have seen him assume a severe expression and point out someone's shortcomings, especially those of his brother-disciples and disciples. But he did that to rid us of our faults, to sound a note of warning, and never to discourage us in any way. Where could we find another like him to fire us with such enthusiasm, courage, and hope? Where could we find such another to write to his disciples: "I want each one of you, my children, to be a hundred times greater than I could ever be. Every one of you must be a giant—must, that is my word."

At that time in the Math, we received, from Mr. E. T. Sturdy of London, copies of Swamiji's Jnana Yoga lectures printed in pamphlet form. Swamiji had not then returned from Darjeeling. We were reading with great enthusiasm the soul-stirring and inspiring interpretations of the Advaita Vedanta contained in those lectures. The old Swami Advaitananda did not know English well, but it was his special desire to hear how "Naren" captivated the heart of the West—what interpretation of the Vedanta brought out their admiration of him. At his request we used to read and explain the substance of those lectures before him. One day, Swami Premananda asked the new brahmacharis to translate Swamiji's lectures into Bengali. So we began the task.

Now that Swamiji had returned to the Math, Swami Premananda spoke of this to him and asked us to read out the translations before Swamiji. Swamiji, while commenting on the translations mentioned that certain words would sound better if put in a particular way, and so on.

One day I was alone in the presence of Swamiji. Suddenly he said to me, "Why don't you translate my *Raja Yoga*?" I wondered why he had chosen an unfit person like me for this work. Long before, I had tried to practise raja yoga. For some time I had such an attraction for this yoga that I even used to look down upon the other paths of jnana, karma, and bhakti. I was under the impression that the sadhus of the Math knew nothing of yogic practices, and hence they did not encourage them. My reading of *Raja Yoga* revealed to me that Swamiji not only had a thorough grasp of the truths of raja yoga—for therein I found a masterly exposition of all ideas I had already gathered on the subject—but had also brought out in a beautiful manner their true relations with other yogas. Another thing that increased my faith and devotion was realizing that perhaps, in asking me to translate *Raja Yoga*, Swamiji meant to help me in my spiritual growth by bringing about, in that way, my close consideration of the truths of this yoga. Or was it because the raja yoga practices are not much current in Bengal that he desired that their truths should be sown broadcast there? In a letter to Babu Pramadadas Mitra, he writes that the practice of raja yoga is completely ignored in Bengal and what little there is of it is only such as blowing through the nose and the like.

In any case, ignoring my own shortcomings, I immediately set at work to carry out Swamiji's order.

One afternoon Swamiji asked the *Gita* to be read out. A copy of it was brought. The room was full of people, and everyone eagerly listened to Swamiji's comments on the *Gita*. Two or three days later, at the request of Swami Premananda, I wrote down from memory what Swamiji had said that day about the *Gita*. It was later published in the Udbodhan as *Gitatattva* (Essence of the *Gita*) and was also included in the book *Bharate Vivekananda*.

When Swamiji used to examine anything critically, he could be a very severe critic. As he enumerated in great detail the grounds for doubting the historicity of Krishna, Arjuna, Vyasa, the battle of Kurukshetra, etc., one would feel that even the most severe critic could not be harsher. While thus questioning the historicity of these people and events with such harsh thoroughness, he would not express his own opinion in the matter. In fact, he explained to us that there was no connection between this type of historical research and true religion. Even if it were proved that the people and events mentioned in the scriptures were imaginary, it would not harm the Hindu religion in the least. But then, if there was no connection between with this type of research and religion, was the former absolutely useless? In answer to this question, Swamiji said that there was still a need to look fearlessly into the historical angle. There was no need to distort history—even to fulfil a noble purpose. On the contrary, if people held onto truth with all their might in all aspects of life, they could even realize God thereby, who is of the very nature of truth.

Then he briefly explained the main themes of the *Gita, viz.* the harmony of all creeds and selfless work, and then started reading out verses from the book. In the second chapter, he was reminded of his own way of teaching people when we came to the following verse in which Sri Krishna encourages Arjuna to fight: "O Partha, yield not to unmanliness. This does not befit you." This does not befit you—you are all-powerful, you are Brahman, all these weakening emotions do not befit you. When he explained this verse, like a prophet in his powerful language, the power which emanated from him was palpable. He also said: "When you try to see the Supreme Self in others, you must not hate even the worst sinner." His expression while uttering the words "must not hate even the worst sinner" is something I will treasure forever. It was as if love began to flow from him in hundreds of streams. His being seemed to be overflowing with love, and his beaming face bore not the slightest trace of harshness.

He concluded the discussion by saying: "In this one verse lies the essence of the whole *Gita*. One who can assimilate the teaching of this verse gets the fruit of reading the whole *Gita*."

One day he asked the *Brahma Sutras* to be recited. He said that rather than trying to understand them with help of any commentary, we should try to understand the sutras independently. The reading began from the first aphorism of the first chapter. While reading, he would insist on correct pronunciation. Next, he showed how the meaning of an aphorism could be understood by understanding its constituent words. He also said: "Who has told you that the aphorisms signify the views of the Advaita philosophy alone? Shankara was an Advaitin, so he tried to explain the aphorisms in the light of the Advaita philosophy. But you should try to understand what Vyasa really meant. Look, for example, at the commentary on the aphorism, *Asminnasya cha tadyogam shasti*—'the Vedas also teach of the absolute identity of this one (the individual soul) with this (the Supreme Self) [1.1.19].'" It appears to me that here both the Advaita and Vishishtadvaita views have been presented by Vyasa."

The reading continued, and we came to the following verse: *Shastradrishtya tu updesha vamadevavat* [1.1.30]. The aphorism says that one who had realized the truth "Thou art that," as declared in the scriptures, could identify himself with the supreme Brahman. After explaining this sutra, Swamiji turned to Swami Premananda and said: "See, Sri Ramakrishna used to call himself God from this standpoint." But after saying this, Swamiji turned in another direction and said as if to himself: "But to me he said in his dying moments, 'One who was Rama and one who was Krishna is Sri Ramakrishna in this body, but not from the standpoint of your Vedanta.'" Saying this, he again started reading the aphorisms.

Great was Swamiji's compassion. He never asked me to believe blindly. To me he said: "Try to analyse the extraordinary phenomenon which was Sri Ramakrishna with your intellect, even if it be a dull one. The more you do this, the more you will be engrossed in his thought, and the more you will be immersed in bliss. I haven't been able to understand even a millionth part of his unique character."

One day Swamiji instructed us in meditation in the shrine. He said: "Make your seat firm and think in this way: 'May my seat be firm and immovable; with its help I will cross over the ocean of this world.'" When all of us had thought in this way for a few minutes, he said: "Think that your body is extremely fit and free from disease, and with its help you will attain liberation." After some time he spoke again: "Think that from you love for all beings is flowing in all directions, and pray in this way: 'Let good befall everybody, let everybody be healthy and free from diseases.' After this do pranayama—only thrice—and then repeat your mantra and meditate on your chosen deity in your heart for about half an hour." All tried to follow Swamiji's instructions.

This type of collective instruction in spiritual practices was given in the Math over a long period. Swami
Turiyananda also gave us detailed instructions in meditation
at Swamiji's request.

One day I was in my room at about 9 a.m. when Swami
Nirmalananda suddenly came and asked: "Do you wish to
take initiation from Swamiji?" "Yes," I replied. I had not yet
been initiated by anyone. We both then proceeded towards
the shrine. I did not know that Swamiji was then initiating
Sharatchandra Chakravarty. Since the initiation was not yet
over, we had to wait outside the shrine for some time. As
soon as Sharat Babu came out Swami Nirmalananda took
me to Swamiji and said: "This boy wants to be initiated."
Swamiji asked me to sit down. He then asked: "Do you like
God with form or without form?" "Sometimes I like to think
of Him as with form and sometimes as without form," I
answered. At this, Swamiji said: "It should not be like that.
The guru knows which path is best for the disciple. Let me
see your hand." He held my right hand and meditated for
a while. Then he said, "This mantra will help you," and
imparted the holy name. After this he made a prediction
regarding me, and told me to give him some fried pieces of
bread which were kept near us as the offering to the teacher.
Swamiji had his meal after initiating me, and Sharat Babu
and I also partook of his prasad.

Later, I realized that the deity whose name Swamiji
had imparted to me was completely in agreement with my
spiritual disposition. I had heard that a true teacher gives the
mantra after understanding the disciple's tendencies, and in
Swamiji I found proof of this.

In those days, the newspaper *Indian Mirror*, edited by
Narendranath Sen, was supplied to Belur Math free of cost,
but because the Math could not afford to pay the postage
incurred, it had to be collected from a home for widows at
Baranagore, a few kilometres from the monastery. Swamiji
had great sympathy for this home—while in America, he
had given a lecture to support it, all proceeds being handed

over to the home's administrators. At that time, Swami Nirbhayananda did the marketing and other chores, and he had
also been given the responsibility of bringing the newspaper
every day. Though many of us had joined the Math at that
time, such duties had not yet been evenly distributed. Since
most of the work still fell to Swami Nirbhayananda, he was
hard pressed for time. Once, thinking that it would be good
if someone else saw the home and could bring the paper as
well, he told me: "I will show you where we get the newspaper. Please bring it every day." Thinking that this would
relieve Swami Nirbhayananda to some extent, I agreed to
his proposal. When we were starting out for the place one
afternoon, Swamiji called me to attend a class on Vedanta.
However, he let me go on learning that I was going to bring
the newspaper. However, when I returned to the monastery,
I came to know that Swamiji did not approve of my going to
a women's institution. I immediately said to Swami Nirbhayananda, "Brother, though I have seen the place, in no way
will it be possible for me to fetch the paper from there."

This shows how concerned Swamiji was about building
up the character of his disciples, especially the new entrants.
Unless it was specifically required, he did not like any monk
to spend the night in Kolkata, especially if it meant coming in
contact with persons of the opposite sex. I have seen a great
many examples of this.

The day Swamiji was to leave for Almora, he called all
the new brahmacharis to him. What he told us then about
the importance of continence is still ringing in my ears:

Look here, my sons, you will never achieve spiritual
progress without celibacy. In spiritual life there can never
be any compromise in this regard. Always keep away
from women. I do not mean to say that you should hate
them. They are but different forms of the Divine Mother.
But for your own protection, I ask you all to keep them
at a distance. I have sometimes said that even a householder may attain spirituality, but from this do not think

that in my view celibacy or complete renunciation is not absolutely indispensable for this attainment. The fact is that on such occasions most of my listeners were house-holders. I softened my own point of view and made a compromise so that they might gradually be inclined to tread the path of complete celibacy. But to you I am say-ing what I really feel. There can be no spiritual progress without celibacy. Strictly maintain the vows of celibacy with your body, mind, and speech.

Referring to a letter that he had received from abroad, Swamiji mentioned the qualities which a religious preacher should have in order to be successful: good intellect, good looks, a broad, catholic heart, a sweet tongue, and self-control—i.e., he should be absolutely chaste. With reference to a certain preacher, he said that he possessed all the other qualities and only required a liberal heart, which, he would develop gradually.

In the same letter was mentioned the fact that Miss Margaret Noble would soon come to India. Swamiji praised Miss Noble highly, saying, "There are very few women of such exalted character in the West. If I were to die tomorrow, she would keep my work alive." Swamiji's prediction proved to be true.

A letter informed Swamiji that Sri Rangacharya Tirtha, a very famous scholar of Chennai and the translator of Ramanuja's commentary on the *Brahma Sutras* in English, would be arriving in Kolkata shortly. He was one of the main contributors to the *Brahmavadin*, a magazine started under Swamiji's guidance. Swamiji wanted to dictate some letters, and asked me to fetch pen and paper. To Sri Rangacharya Tirtha he wrote, among other things: "Vedanta is not very popular in West Bengal, therefore when you come to here, give a rub to the people of Kolkata." How eager Swamiji was to popularise the study of Vedanta in West Bengal! Since his health had broken down, he did not deliver more than two lectures in Kolkata, but he nevertheless was always trying to awaken the religious feelings of the people of the city in other ways. Because of this request by Swamiji, the people of Kolkata got the opportunity to hear, at the Star Theatre, the learned scholar discourse profoundly on "The Priest and the Prophet."

One evening, sitting on the veranda, Swamiji was conducting a Vedanta class for us. It was dusk—time for the vesper service in the shrine. At that time, Swami Premananda conducted the vesper service, and those who usually helped him in this work were also in the class. When Swami Premananda came and asked the new entrants in the Math to go to the shrine for vespers, they were rather disconcerted. On one side was the attraction of listening to Vedanta from Swamiji, but on the other was the evening service in the shrine. Swamiji then said to Swami Premananda in an excited voice: "Is not the study of Vedanta also worship of the Master? Do you think that the only way to worship God is to wave a lamp in front of a picture to the accompaniment of deafening drums?" As he said this, Swamiji became more and more excited and began to scold Swami Premananda even more harshly for disrupting the Vedanta class. As a result of all the commotion, the class was adjourned. After the vesper service, Swami Premananda was nowhere to be found. Swamiji became extremely worried and began to say: "Where has he gone? Has he ended his life by jumping in the Ganga?" etc. At last Swami Premananda was discovered seated alone on the roof, morose and melancholy. When he was brought to Swamiji, in how many ways did the latter show his affection! We were charmed to see the extraordinary love which Swamiji had for his brother-disciples, and we understood how much faith he had in them and how much he cared for them. He scolded them only because he wanted them be perfect. Afterwards I often heard from Swamiji that he had the greatest affection for those he scolded the most.

Once Swamiji had instructed me: "Look, you must maintain a diary of the Math and prepare weekly reports of its activities." I have obeyed this command to the best of my ability.

(*Swami Shuddhananda: Jivani O Rachana*, pp. 25-34)

In the latter part of 1897, while I was at the Alambazar monastery, Swamiji asked Swami Vijnanananda and me to make a tour of western India. Since Swamiji was then travelling, we were not sure where we would meet him. As per Swamiji's instructions, we first went to Ambala and stayed there for a few days. After that, Swami Niranjanananda took Swami Vijnanananda to Dehradun to select a suitable site for a monastery. I stayed back at Ambala for a few days. Later, on receiving the news that Swamiji was to come to Lahore, I went to meet him there. But I did not know the exact date of his arrival there. Therefore, instead of waiting at the station, I went to the address which had been given to me. Later I came to know that Swamiji had reached Lahore only an hour after I had, and some Hindu societies had arranged a grand welcome for him. Swamiji had expected to see me at the station, but after failing to trace me he sent a pre-paid telegram to me at Ambala, in spite of being very busy with the reception. However, I met Swamiji the same night, and the love and affection he showered on me touched me to the core of my heart.

"The Great Indian Circus" was then performing in the town. Its proprietor happened to be a childhood friend of Swamiji; they used to wrestle with each other in their younger days. Seeing his friend after such a long time and in such different circumstances, the circus chief was completely overwhelmed, and could not decide how he should address Swamiji. He got over his hesitation when Swamiji called him by his childhood name.

From here the party left for Dehradun. Though Swamiji was keeping indifferent health, he would still conduct classes for us on Vedanta and some other subjects. He would say, "I still want to live the life which is most suited to a monk—eating only what can be got by begging—but my health will not permit it." On our return journey, he encouraged some of us to travel to Saharanpur on foot. He taught us many things regarding monastic life at this time. A local boy used to do the cleaning and laundry for us at Saharanpur. Learning that the boy belonged to a high caste, Swamiji took him to Khetri to arrange for his proper education. But due to the boy's ill luck, Swamiji's effort did not bear fruit.

From Saharanpur we visited Alwar and Jaipur via Delhi. We stayed at each place for a few days and then went to Khetri, which is ninety miles from Jaipur. The king of Khetri was a disciple of Swamiji. At these places Swamiji would encourage us to take vegetarian food. He would sometimes say: "If one can remain a strict vegetarian for twelve years, one can attain spiritual realization." At Delhi Swamiji stayed with a devotee of moderate means instead of going to the home of a rich acquaintance. He did the same thing at Alwar. While we were there, Swamiji also encouraged us to learn riding. In short, Swamiji wanted each one of us to undergo spiritual, physical, and mental training, and become perfect men in every sense of the term.

I have written all this to you because you were so keen to learn about my experiences while travelling with Swamiji. It is indeed impossible to write about it in detail in a letter.

(Excerpts from an unpublished letter, Belur Math, 14.1.38)

Swami Bodhananda

In 1890 when I was a student in the Ripon College, Kolkata, I had the greatest blessing of my life to know of Sri Ramakrishna. With some of my classmates and friends I attended the anniversary of the dedication of the temple at Kankurgachi (east Kolkata) in the month of August of that year. There we first heard of Sri Ramakrishna from one of his greatest devotees, the late Ramchandra Dutta. His devotion to Sri Ramakrishna is indescribable. Only those who knew him personally can appreciate it. We often chant the sacred verse, "Thou art our Mother; Thou art our Father; Thou art our Friend; Thou art our Companion; Thou art our Wisdom; Thou art our Wealth; Thou art our All in all", but Ram Babu was one of those who realized its true meaning. To him Sri Ramakrishna was really his "All in All". He worshipped no other God than Sri Ramakrishna; never visited any other temple than the one at Kankurgachi in which Sri Rama-krishna's ashes were interred; never read or preached any other religious doctrines or discourses than those he had heard from Sri Ramakrishna.

Master Mahashay (Mahendranath Gupta) was our professor. We heard that he was also a disciple of Sri Ramakrishna. One day we approached him and introduced ourselves to him. We had a little talk on Sri Ramakrishna. He recommended us to visit the monastery at Baranagore where Sri Ramakrishna's monastic disciples were then living. He was naturally a very reserved man, but was most cordial to us and candid in his opinion about a devotee who lives in his family and a disciple who has renounced the world to devote

SWAMI BODHANANDA

his whole life to the practise of religion. He used this simile: The former is like a sour mango, but quite ripe and the latter (a monk) is like a mango of the highest grade, but not yet ripe. Master Mahashay's illustrations were very much to the point. He further said that if we wished to see the living examples of the teachings of Sri Ramakrishna, we must go to the monastery.

Shortly afterwards, we visited the monastery. Our first visit was on a weekday, as we went directly from the college. It was about 3 o'clock in the afternoon when we reached there. We first met Swami Ramakrishnananda. He was delighted to see us and inquired about us. When he learnt that we were students, he asked us some questions and advised us not to neglect our studies. We stayed until 5 or 6 o'clock. He took us to the shrine when it was opened at 4 o'clock, gave us some flowers from the altar and also prasada, which we valued most. We prostrated ourselves before the picture of Sri Ramakrishna on the bed and the wooden receptacle on the altar in which his sacred remains were preserved. There were four or five other Swamis. We saluted them all, one after the other, and they also very kindly spoke to us and blessed us with their good wishes. When we parted, they invited us to come again. We walked back home, and all the time we talked of the wonderful visit—the renunciation of the Swamis and the peaceful atmosphere of the Math.

Master Mahashay then lived in Kambuliatolah (Kolkata). On our way home, we stopped at his house and told him of the visit to the monastery. He congratulated us and urged us to go there often and render personal service to the Swamis, such as massaging their feet, preparing tobacco for their smoking, etc. To see them and serve them, to him, was like seeing and serving Sri Ramakrishna himself.

Swamiji had just left the Math for a pilgrimage to the North-Western Provinces[1] of India. This time he wanted to live so exclusively that he very seldom wrote letters to the

---

1. Later renamed United Provinces and still later Uttar Pradesh.

brothers at the monastery. In fact, for a year or two nobody knew where he was.

Shashi Maharaj, Baburam Maharaj, Mahapurushji, Yogen Maharaj, Kali Maharaj, and Niranjan Maharaj were at the monastery then. They all told us about Swamiji and Sri Ramakrishna's love for him and his love for Sri Ramakrishna. Some of them even then assured us that Swamiji would be pleased to initiate us into sannyasa when he returned to the Math.

Strangely enough, several years before that time (most probably in 1887) when I was a student in the Metropolitan School, Bowbazar Branch, I had seen Swamiji, who was then headmaster of that School for a few weeks. I belonged to a lower grade and did not have the privilege and pleasure of being taught by him. But I used to watch him from our classroom window almost every day as he entered the school compound. I still remember the scene vividly. He was clothed in trousers and black coat with a white scarf about six feet long around his shoulders. In one hand he carried an umbrella and in the other a book, most probably the textbook of the Entrance Class. With sparkling eyes and a smiling face he looked so indrawn that some would be attracted to him due to his charming personality, and some would not dare approach him due to his extreme gravity and solemnity. However, it was not until I came to the Baranagore Math that I knew that the great headmaster who had impressed me so much had been Swamiji himself.

Swamiji returned to India in December 1896 from his mission in America and Europe. He landed in Colombo in January, and arrived in Kolkata in February 1897. I was then a teacher in a High School in a village near my home about twenty miles west of Kolkata. The anniversary of the birth of Sri Ramakrishna then used to be celebrated in the compound of the temple gardens at Dakshineshwar. The Swamis then lived in the Math at Alambazar, about two miles from Dakshineshwar. That year the anniversary took place as usual either in the last week of February or in the first week

of March, the day before I came to the Math. That was a
Saturday, as the public celebration was then held on that day,
as it is now held on the Sunday following the actual birthday.

Swamiji was then temporarily living in a house on the
bank of the Ganga about three miles from the Math. Early
in the morning on Sunday I met him there. It was about six
o'clock—still dark—when I arrived at the house. Swamiji
was an early riser. He first saw me from the window of his
room and came downstairs to open the door. I saluted him
and he received me very kindly, as if he had known me since
long before. He talked to me in a familiar way and asked
me to fetch him a glass of water. He was then washing his
mouth. When he learnt that I was preparing for an examination, he was pleased and gave me his blessing. Mahapurushji
was there too. He told Swamiji that I was one of the group
of young men who had been coming to the Math for several
years and that I was planning to join the Order. On hearing
this, Swamiji said he would initiate me into sannyasa in the
near future. Those words made the hope of the realization of
my dream brighter.

A few days before the public anniversary—most probably on the actual birthday of Sri Ramakrishna—Swamiji
initiated four brahmacharis into sannyasa, and on that day
also gave initiation to one or two devotees. At about 8 o'clock
he arrived at the Math. I came with him, by his permission,
in the same carriage. Shortly after arrival, he took his bath
and went to the shrine for meditation. We followed him. It
was a most inspiring occasion.

At about 11 o'clock he went to the Dakshineshwar temple
gardens where the public festival was being held. There was
a vast concourse of people at the gardens, and Swamiji's
presence was another reason for that great crowd. Many
requested him to deliver a lecture near the Panchavati. But
the crowd was so enthusiastic and noisy in their expression
of joy at his sight that he found it impossible to make a
speech. About 1 o'clock he returned to the Math for a rest. I
was with him all that day and had the privilege of rendering

him a little personal service as an attendant. That was the most glorious day of my life. Its impression is indelible in my memory. As I think of it now I still seem to feel the thrill of the joy I felt then.

The next day I had to return to my school duties with great reluctance. The sense of gratitude and exaltation of this unique occasion remained with me for several days. I longed to see Swamiji again and sit at his feet for his further grace and guidance.

(*Prabuddha Bharata*, October 1934)

Swami Vimalananda

Before I knew Swamiji personally, I had heard much about his greatness from persons who had moved and lived with him on the closest terms of intimacy. Therefore, when it was announced in the year 1893 that he had gone over to America to represent our religion at the Chicago Parliament of Religions, I started following his movements with the closest attention and the greatest interest. I was anxiously waiting to see if his achievements would not confirm me in my very high estimate of him. I need not tell you that every bit of my expectation was much more than satisfied. But till I saw him with my own eyes, the perfect satisfaction of knowing the man could not come. Till then I could not be quite free from the secret misgivings that I might be after all labouring under a delusion. So you see that I did not meet Swamiji as one in any way biased against him. The throbbing interest and convincingness which attach to the glowing description of the conquest of opponents of a great man of overmastering personality does not belong to my subject. I may say, I was already a great admirer of his. But I must say at the same time that it was not too late in the day to retrace my steps and give Swamiji up as one unworthy of my love and esteem if facts were found to give the lie. Perhaps, the shock which such a disclosure would have given my mind would be too painful; perhaps it would have cost a great wrenching of the heart. But I can assure you that the instinct of moral self-preservation was yet stronger than my admiration of Swamiji, and cost how much it would, the heart could not

SWAMI VIMALANANDA

long cling to him if reason and moral sense condemned him with one voice.

And what was the nature of the greatness I was expecting to see in Swamiji? It was not the dashing and daring spirit displayed by a heroic warrior on the battlefield, nor the fine ethereal vision and ecstasy of the poet, nor the vast erudition of a scholar, nor the dazzling intellectual flourish of the master controversialist, nor the quick penetration and the wide comprehension of the philosopher, nor the weeping heart of a true lover of humanity. It was not that I had not had enough testimony as to these qualities of head and heart being abundantly present in him, but because my conception of religion was not wide enough to include all these under it. His marvellous achievements in the West were bringing us overwhelming evidences of his wonderful intellectual powers. But either from some constitutional necessity or my extreme poverty in that direction I was always attributing the brightness of his intellect to his highly elevated religious life, and it was this religious life that I expected to see in him. My idea of religion was then confined to purity and meditation. Sitting at the feet of the holy and good disciples of Bhagavan Sri Ramakrishna, I had learnt that these two were the indispensable conditions of acquiring spirituality and are the sure marks by which a religious man can always be known. My debt of gratitude to the blessed Swamis, at whose feet I had learnt these great lessons, is too big to be repaid. Personal contact with Swamiji, instead of diminishing the value of purity and meditation in my eyes, has only enhanced it. At the same time it has heightened and intensified my conception of religion by adding new elements to it. Till I came in personal contact with Swamiji my temperament had led me to expect to see in him a man of intense purity and meditative inwardness. And I need not tell you that I was not disappointed. The first sight of Swamiji, the peculiar brightness of his face, his lustrous yet soft and sweet eyes, at once carried into my heart an overwhelming sense of satisfaction that I had come to a man the like of whom I had never seen before. Then, when he began to talk to us making personal inquiries and giving us words of hope and encouragement with the cordiality of one truly interested in our welfare, we felt that our hearts were being drawn closer to him. To us, who were very insignificant compared with his friends and visitors who were standing or sitting around him in large numbers, this kindness on his part filled us with great joy and gratitude. Then the wonderfully free and frank way in which he was talking to his visitors revealed to us a heart that knew nothing of guile or fear nor cared a bit for social conventionality. The transparently clear and pointed words that were shooting out of his lips like meteors gave us a peep into the keen penetration of his intellect and the breadth and profundity of his mental vision. We felt ourselves to be in the presence of an overpowering personality whose immensity was not possible for us to gauge, but which was drawing us to itself as by a tie of close personal relationship. There arose on the first day of our meeting an excellent opportunity of knowing something of his real humility. I say "real humility" because it had nothing to do with that sense of self-abasement with its external manifestation of facial contortions which so often pass for humility. It was self-effacement and was not therefore without the charming dignity of self-respect. A question from one of the visitors as to why Swamiji's lecture on his Master delivered in America had not seen the light of day, brought the bold confession: "I did not allow it to be published as I had done injustice to my Master. My Master never condemned anything or anybody. But while I was speaking of him I criticized the people of America for their dollar-worshipping spirit. That day I learnt the lesson that I am not yet fit to talk of him." These words were really startling to us for more than one reason. Here was a man who was being idolized, nay, actually worshipped by so many, and this man in their very presence confessing his inability to represent his guru! "What an unpretentious man is before us," said we to ourselves. "What a wonderful man his guru must have been to occupy such a high place in the heart of this great man!"

This, in short, was my impression of Swamiji on the first day of our meeting. As days went and I knew more and more of him, it gained greater and greater strength. I only saw on the first day the few sparks that shot forth into our range of vision from a soul aglow with the fire of divine love and wisdom. It was yet in store for me to see many more sparks from the same source that drew me near to it, gave me a closer view of it, and enabled even my icy cold heart to possess a little of its warmth. I have already told you that I had always thought that Swamiji's gigantic intellect was the result of his highly elevated life of purity. Greater acquaintance with him was making my belief stronger till one day his own words made it a settled conviction with me. It was a memorable evening in my life, which shall never be effaced from my mind, when a question from one of his would-be disciples brought forth an exhaustive and stirring discourse on brahmacharya or sexual purity. In the course of the discourse he was explaining to us the incalculable value of purity in religious life, how to practise it, how religious fervour, suddenly aroused by working on the emotional side of man to the utter neglect of the moral and intellectual, is apt to produce great reaction on the sexual desires, and so forth. Then at last when he came to talk of the infinite powers of strict sexual purity and how the animal propensity is converted into spiritual might, he warmed up to such a high pitch of earnestness that it seemed as if the transparent soul within was flowing out in torrents through his lips, bathing its listeners with its heavenly waters. The picture that was being drawn by his words in our minds saw its own prototype in the figure that stood before us. And I leave it to you, gentlemen, to imagine the effect of these concluding words of the discourse upon us:

"My Master had told me that if I could attain to the perfect state of purity I have just described, I would have spiritual insight. I ventured to stand before the world only when I had been satisfied that I had attained to it. I earnestly appeal to you, my boys, to keep to this ideal with adamantine firmness. Pray, do not be unworthy of me." On another occasion too I heard him speak of his spiritual insight which could at once see the end of a thing hidden in the womb of futurity, of which the beginning is only made. I must not be understood to mean that intellectual brightness is always a sign of spirituality. A man may have a great intellect without being in the least spiritual. On the other hand a man may be spiritual without having his mind stored with information, vast and varied, or without the power to put his words in a logical form. But truth will always be his and will flash upon his mind of itself. My present idea of Swamiji's intellect has undergone some modification from what it was before I knew him personally. He combined in him spiritual insight with an intellect of the highest order. Truth came to him by intuition. But he would press his intellect into its service by giving it a logical form and making it convincing by a rich supply of facts and analogies stored in his brain.

And the purity which gave Swamiji this spiritual insight was something extraordinary. It was not the fragile purity that can protect itself only by keeping away from all corrupting influences. It had long outgrown the need of the citadel of isolation. But that was not all. It became aggressive, taking a sort of delight in encountering its enemies on their own grounds and winning them over to its side. In other words, it could not only keep itself untouched amidst corrupting influences, but could turn them into positive powers for good. I cannot go into personal details on a subject like this. But my knowledge of Swamiji's marvellous achievements in this direction compels me to lay at his feet my deepest reverence; this one element of perfection in Swamiji would have been quite enough to compel me to give him the highest place in my heart.

There was one more prominent feature of Swamiji's life which speaks to me volumes about his renunciation. I mean his dealing with rich men. Many of you are aware that among his foreign disciples some are very wealthy and a few of them came to India to help Swamiji in his work. The treatment which he used to give them did not in the least differ from that given to his most insignificant Indian disciples. He was kind and loving by nature to all, but his love did not make him blind to their flaws and defects which needed mending.

Gentle speech would not always serve the purpose, and Swamiji would have to be at times harsh. And in this apparently unpleasant treatment, his wealthy disciples would have exactly the same fate as his begging sannyasis. At times, this would be too much for persons born and brought up in the lap of luxury and accustomed to hear words of praise and flattery. From a worldly point of view, Swamiji paid dear for it. But did he ever regret? Far from it. The perfect unconcern which he showed whether rich people would stick to him or give him up is truly unprecedented.

.Of the few pregnant proverbs and epigrammatical expressions which Swamiji would never be tired of repeating, one was "The giver of the head is alone the leader", that is, he alone can be a leader who is ready to die for others. And Swamiji's own life determines his place among his fellow beings. I have already told you that Swamiji was not only kind and soft but was very harsh also at times. He could not only lay down his life for others, but could take arms against others if needed. Whatever he would think or feel he would do so with wonderful vehemence and intensity. And this whole-souledness was another marked feature of Swamiji's life. One evening, in the course of a talk that Swamiji was giving to one of his disciples, opening his eyes to the fact that the disciple's inability to manage the servants of the Math (which was one of his duties then) and make them do their respective duties was a weakness and did not proceed from love, he said: "Don't think that your heart is full of love, because you cannot give them a little scolding now and then. Can you give your life for them? I know you can't, because you do not love them. This minute I can die for them; but also I can hang them on this tree this minute if need be. Can you do that? No, my boy, namby-pamby is not love. Remember the words of the poet, 'Harder than the thunderbolt and softer than the flower', this is the ideal. No, love is not weak sentimentality."

I have seen no man who could be so soft as Swamiji. The death of a brother-disciple or a disciple would rob him of rest and consolation for days together. Some time in the year 1898, it pleased the Lord to take away one of his brother-disciples. The pang of bereavement was so intense in Swamiji that for a week he remained exceedingly heavy-hearted and absent-minded keeping as much away from others as possible. On the evening of the seventh or eighth day he came to the shrine-room of the Math, and began to talk to those that were present there like a simple child: "I did not come to the shrine all these days because I was very angry with my Master for having deprived me of my dear brother. I love them so much because I have lived longer and more intimately with them than even with my own brothers. ... But why should I be angry with my Master? Why should I expect that all things will be ordained according to my wishes? And why should I be sad at all? Am I not a hero? My Master used to say laying his arm upon my shoulder: 'Naren, you are a hero; the very sight of you inspires me with courage.' Yes, I am a hero. Why should I then give way to grief?"

... Ask each one of his disciples, American or English, Bengali or Chennai, and you will hear the same thing from all that their hearts were won by Swamiji's wonderful love and sympathy. Swamiji's marvellous intellectual powers, no doubt, evoked the awe of all. But this awe would have kept at a distance all unintellectual people like myself and would have proved more a barrier than a help to them to come in direct touch with him and drink from the fountain of his soul. Heaps of instances could be cited to show Swamiji's wonderful heart.

And how can universal love be without the ever present consciousness of the closest kinship with the universe, without the realization that whatever is, is mine, nay, whatever is, is me? And this is Brahmajnana (knowledge of Self) as our holy books describe it. This is the very core of Swamiji's teaching—the Selfhood of all—the Divinity of man. And this is, I am fully convinced, the key to his wonderfully versatile nature. He was a lover of all, because he was a jnani. And here I must tell you that the fatal illusion under which I had long laboured that jnana and bhakti are destructive of each other, dispersed in the presence of Swamiji as darkness before the sun. Swamiji was a tremendous worker because he was a bhakta and jnani. The tremendous energy that shook the whole world and is still at work awakening many a slumbering soul to its innate Divinity, instilling life into dead bones, bringing sunshine in the darkness of despair and love in dry, arid souls—this tremendous energy owes its origin to his realization of brahman in all. Here too, I must tell you that the fatally-erroneous idea that karma is antagonistic to jnana and bhakti is dispelled at once by the life of Swamiji.

I told you at the outset that before I met Swamiji I did not, on account of my limited religious views, expect to see in him anything of the warrior, the poet, the philosopher, or the philanthropist. But I found that he was all these and more. He was as much a poet as a philosopher; as much a sentimental visionary as a man of action. And he was all these not in spite of his religion but on account of it.

I have learnt that a religion which does not call forth into vigorous activity and chasten and elevate the moral, intellectual, and aesthetic faculties of man, make him humane and self-sacrificing and at the same time self-absorbed and meditative is an imperfect religion. But I have also learnt that even such imperfect religions have their great purpose to serve in helping the growth of persons less evolved and that our attitude towards them all should be one of extreme sympathy and love. I have learnt that I should hesitate thrice before I condemn any form or religious faith, however repellent it may appear to me. For I have seen forms of worship, generally condemned as superstitious, yield treasurers of infinite beauty and holiness touched by the magic wand of Swamiji. I have learnt that every individual, however degraded he may appear in my eyes, is God involved, and therefore cannot be lost forever. We should look upon him with respect and if possible give him a lift Godward, not by condemning his perverted ideal and by cruelly tearing it away from his heart but by gently replacing it by a true one suited to his temperament and culture. I have learnt that under peculiar circumstances even harshess and cruelty become a virtue, stubborn resistance, an excellence, and that activity is as much a help to spiritual growth as contemplative calmness. I have learnt that God can be enjoyed both within ourselves and outside of ourselves; within ourselves by effacing completely from our consciousness all impression of the world of senses and making the Spirit touch Spirit, and outside ourselves by seeing God in everything and pouring out our hearts unto His feet in the shape of loving service. I have learnt the incalculable value of great personalities in the scheme of individual, national, and universal redemption. I have also learnt that I have learnt all these only intellectually and am yet far from getting them woven into my nature. And all these I have learnt from the life of Swamiji. One thing more: My conviction that Swamiji's spiritual realization was of the highest order came to me not only from his intense purity, fearlessness, love of truth, and universal sympathy, but also from those subtler personal manifestations described in our scriptures. I have seen him weep like a child and becoming disconsolate at the name of God. I have seen him go into such deep meditation that even the function of the lungs stopped. Last of all came his own words to give the finishing touch to my conception of his spiritual greatness. ...

(*Vedanta Kesari*, January-February 1923)

Swami Sadashivananda

I first heard the holy name of Swami Vivekananda from a lawyer practising in the district court of Arrah, a remote town in Bihar. He was telling some of his friends in a public library about the wonderful exploits of a Hindu monk who hailed from a Bengali family in Kolkata and had unfurled the banner of ancient Hindu philosophy in the Parliament of Religions at Chicago.

It was sometime after, in the month of July 1898, that the sudden death of my elder brother caused me to move to the holy city of Varanasi, where my old widowed mother was living alone in her bereavement. I had already been initiated by Swami Ram Swarupacharya, a disciple of Swami Bhagavatacharya and grand-disciple of Swami Rangacharya, the first abbot of the holy temple of Sri Ranganatha at Vrindavan and of Sri Dwarakadhish at Mathura. The Swami had accepted me as a Vaishnava brahmachari with all the formal rules of worship and strict discipline of brahmacharya. By this time *The Life and Teachings of Sri Ramakrishna* by Sureshchandra Dutta had greatly influenced me, and I was thus brought nearer to the source of the spring which was eventually destined to quench my thirst for a spiritual life as it had done for many others.

It was the day of Mahashtami in the month of Ashvina. I went to the Durga temple in Varanasi with Jagat Durlabh Ghosh, and went the next day with the same friend to pay my respects to His Holiness Swami Bhaskarananda, then residing in the garden-house of the Maharaja of Amithi. There, two sannyasis attracted my notice, standing among some other gentlemen. The taller of the two, a robust figure in ochre robes, suddenly put me in mind of Swami Vivekananda who, by this time, had returned to India.

Maybe he is that Swami, I thought, and waited to see if this was the case. The tall Swami accosted Swami Bhaskarananda with the greeting "Om Namo Narayanaya," as is the custom among the Sannyasis of this order, and "Namo Narayanaya" was returned at once. They talked intimately. Somehow the topic of Swami Vivekananda came up, and at once the austere face of Swami Bhaskarananda took on a mild expression of love and reverence as he said, "Brother, bring Swami Vivekananda to me somehow so that I may see him once." Though there were many others gathered around Bhaskarananda who held him in high esteem as a great and learned man of knowledge, he seemed indifferent to the impression that such an open expression of admiration for Swami Vivekananda would create.

The tall Swami replied, "I will surely write to him, sir; he is unwell and is now at Deoghar for a change." Swami Bhaskarananda said, "Then please come again after nightfall." With this they parted and the person I was so keenly observing was lost to my sight. But on inquiry I came to know his name: Swami Niranjanananda, Swami Vivekananda's brother-disciple. The Swami with him was Swami Shuddhananda.

One day in September 1898, as I was coming from my daily session of prayer and meditation, I met Charuchandra Das, who later became Swami Shubhananda of the Ramakrishna Order of monks and founder of the Ramakrishna Mission Home of Service in Varanasi. It didn't take long for us to become friends, and he lent me a few books published by the Mission, some of which were the works of Swami Vivekananda. A study circle was established in the house of my learned friend Kedarnath Moulik, later Swami Achalananda, and for about two years Charu Babu took great pains to convince us of the importance of karma yoga and its enhancement of spirituality. He also read to us other works of Swami Vivekananda which emphasized other aspects of yoga. We would meet sometimes in the houses of Kedar Babu and Charu Babu, and sometimes in our own family residence. In this way he collected a batch of young workers to start a very modest Home of Service.

Meanwhile, we learned that Swami Vivekananda was coming to Varanasi for a change. Arrangements were made for his stay at the garden-house of Raja Kali Krishna Thakur, well known to Swami Niranjanananda. The youths of our Home chose me to receive the Swami at the station with flowers and garlands. When the Swami alighted from the train on the platform, I put the garlands around his neck and the flowers at his feet—and then looked into his face. Suddenly, a face familiar to me from my dreams came to mind. The similarity between the two was so striking that I stood there in silent admiration and wonder. He asked about me very mildly—"Who is this boy?" and a few other questions. Flowers scattered on his lotus feet, falling from my half-conscious folded hands, as I saw the Swami turn his face to speak to some people next to him. Again he fixed his loving gaze in deep tenderness on my entranced eyes, and smiled. It took only a moment perhaps, but in that very instant, I heard him speak untold volumes of sermons which said, "Deny thy father, deny thy name, and for that which thou losest—take all myself"; and my soul answered back, "I take thee at thy word." This is not poetry or fable of bygone days, but the simple truth as I experienced it.

With the Swami came Mr. Okakura from Japan, whom we gave the nickname of Uncle Akrura[1], who wanted to take the Swami—our Krishna—to Mathura, i.e. Japan. Arriving with Swamiji were Swamis Nirbhayananda and Bodhananda, and two boys—Gour and Nadu. Swami Shivananda and Swami Niranjanananda were then at Varanasi, and all of them went to the "Sondhabas" to see Raja Kali Krishna Thakur.

---

1. Akrura was an uncle of Sri Krishna.

One evening, Charu Babu and I went there to find the entire group sitting in chairs and conversing with Mr. Okakura in English about the Swami's tour of India. I bowed down and took my seat humbly on the carpeted floor. The Swami stopped midway in his conversation and looked at me with loving eyes, which were even more expressive than spoken words. "Sit down my lad, here on the chair"—he repeated several times, so that it became impossible to disobey.

The "Sondhabas" was five miles from the Home, and daily we went to see Swamiji there and occasionally spent the night there and ate together. Swamiji would then distribute some delicious preparation to us and ask with a smile, "Do you relish it? Taste it, taste it. I give it to you, for it tasted good to me." But it was not possible for us to be there every day, however much we desired it. One day, in my absence, Swami Shivananda requested Swamiji to give us initiation, to which he consented, but for which he fixed no date. Charu Babu and Haridas Chatterji asked me to confirm it from Swamiji himself, and so I asked him. Smiling, he said in a pleasant voice: "Why, you are already initiated as a Ramanuja Vaishnava. The worship of Vishnu is very good. I don't see any reason to initiate you again."

"But," I entreated, "I wish to be initiated by a yogi like yourself," to which he smiled his consent.

After a few days, my elder brother, a physician only a little older than me, died suddenly. I was so shocked, I felt as if I had been shot at point-blank range. A few days after, Swamiji asked me: "I hear that you have lost your brother. How did you feel about it? What did you say to your mother to console her?" On being told all that I had to say, he exclaimed, "Had it been one of my brothers, I would have no doubt felt it very keenly." He was at that moment feeling the loss himself, and strangely enough, this sympathy removed all my pain then and there. I felt that he was my true friend and more than a brother, and I took a vow to surrender myself completely and irrevocably at his feet.

It is customary not to be initiated until the obsequies are over, but Swamiji made an exception in my case and asked me to stay the night, and the next day was fixed for initiation. In the morning we took our bath, prepared for the occasion and waited before his room. The doors opened even before we expected them to, and Swamiji appeared there with a face illumined with divine fire. In peculiar accents he asked us to come one by one, emphasizing it with a movement of his hand. Charu Babu pushed me to go first, and as soon as I went near Swamiji, he remarked: "Oh! You have come first! Well, well, come along with me, my boy." Then we moved on to another small room, where there were two small carpets on the floor. He took his seat on one and I on the other.

Within a few minutes, Swamiji entered into deep meditation—his body erect and stiff, all his limbs motionless, eyes half-closed and very bright; his face indicated divine emotion, power, and love. He was the very personification of bliss; but his austere calm had subdued all emotions, which remained there frozen and fixed, without a ripple or wave. It was one person who had beckoned me inside the room, with the charm of love and smiles; it was now another personality that sat before me, who had transcended love and every other emotion.

He sat that way, unmoving. Time was locked out. He seemed to fight against this manifestation and the emanation of divine Presence, and it was slowly subdued and remained controlled within his body. He took my hand in his, where it remained for a few moments. Then he spoke of a few events in my past and remarked, "How did you feel when you were going to Chapra by steamer, when somebody spoke to you?" I had forgotten about that incident, but he asked me to try to remember it. It was Swami Ram Swarupacharya, whom I met at Arrah, and who later gave me the Vaishnava mantra. He was a resident of Againgarh district. He belonged to the Ramanuja School of Vishishtadvaita philosophy. I was asked to think of him, and as I did so, he said, "Now think of Sri

Ramakrishna and transform me into him and then him into Ganesha. Ganesha is the ideal of sannyasa."

At his touch, all desires and thoughts evaporated from me. There was no attraction or repulsion, no desire or aspiration. I do not know how long I was in this state, but gradually I became conscious of my body and I could see the objects of the room in a slight haze. I stood there initiated, and the Swami asked me to send in the next aspirant. I went out and sent Charu Babu, who was initiated in the same way and next, Haridas Chatterji.

After the ceremony was over, we dined together, and then I had to leave, for work awaited me in the Sevashrama which had been started three years before, inspired by the ideal of service as infused by Swami Vivekananda. Most of the workers had renounced their homes and lived on charity. This taxed their energies to the limit, but the work of the Sevashrama could not be allowed to suffer—they did their utmost, which greatly told upon their health.

This greatly distressed Swamiji. One day he called all the sevashrama workers and asked us to eat properly and adopt a nourishing diet, for it was necessary to keep the body fit and strong to serve others. He used to say that in the selection of food, both the nature of the work and the constitution of the worker must be taken into consideration. Many of us were ascetics and would not even taste delicious sweets and so forth, but the Swami stressed the aim and purpose of service first and last. For the service of others the body must be fit and healthy. Thus asceticism and personal samskaras were of less importance to the true worker and karma yogi. He asked us to take our food with him, so that he could see us following him in letter and spirit. Some of us were dining with our own families, but still he asked us repeatedly to dine with him, which we did whenever possible.

Among us there was a young worker, very lean and thin, who attracted the Swami's notice. How kind the Swami was to us can best be illustrated by the instance of this boy. This youth had come from some interior part of Bengal and was stranded in Varanasi, so he had joined the Sevashrama as a worker out of necessity. He was very weak and sickly. One day he went to see the Swami, who inquired about him and asked him to dine daily with him: "My lad, you are not very strong, and you have to work, so you must eat well. You must come daily and dine with me—at least your noon meal."

The work of the Sevashrama often kept the boy beyond the fixed time for Swamiji's dinner hour, who was constantly beseeched to take his food on time, lest his fell disease, diabetes, be aggravated. The physicians and brother-disciples begged him to take particular care of his health, and so he agreed. But out of his motherly love for the boy, he forgot all their entreaties and his own health. Before dinner he would anxiously inquire about the boy and wait for him; he would pace the floor with impatient steps and look towards the road and the door expecting him to appear there any moment. If he met anyone, he would at once ask him: "Has he come? Poor boy! Why is he so late today? He is very weak and has not taken anything till now. So young and weak, and so much to do!"

When at last the boy came with hurried steps, Swamiji's face would change again, glowing with the happiness and contentment of a mother who meets her son after a long separation. Smiling, he asked the youth, "Why, my child! Why so late? I know you were very busy. But did you take your breakfast in the morning? See, I have not taken my meal, for I am waiting for you. Come! My son, wash your hands and feet, let us hurry to our dinner. It is already late and you know, my boy, I am not so well. Not taking my food on time will aggravate my illness, so try to come a little earlier. But what could you do, my child, the pressure of work has kept you so late; I know it, I know it."

The Swami was followed by the boy and they took their seats with others. But while eating, he kept a constant watch on the boy and whatever he thought to be good or tasty was given to the boy from his own plate. Others noticed that the

Swami was hardly eating anything, but watching with loving care as the boy took his meal. Then they entreated now and then, "Swamiji, kindly take something yourself, you are not eating anything today." But who would listen? The Swami had forgotten his self: to him, the boy was Gopala.

One evening, Swamiji sat on one cot and Swami Shivananda on another. Several other gentlemen in the room were silently enjoying the jokes and humour of the two. Swamiji was like a blooming cherub with a happy boyish face, aglow with merry laughter which sparkled through his eyes and continued around the room in eddies and whirlpools. Swamiji said, addressing Swami Shivananda: "What do you say, sir? Then in your opinion I am Shukracharya—the guru of the demons! Say, Mahapurush, is it not? Eh—eh—have I put it right?" And again he burst into laughter. He raised his pitch higher and higher, while making faces in so many ways, which made the air reel and resound, and we looked at this mood of mirth with awe and reverence. A nerve in Swamiji's eye had been injured somehow, affecting his eyesight—hence the allegory of Shukracharya, who had one eye! Moreover, the Swami preached in foreign countries and made alien disciples; therefore he made this comparison with the one-eyed guru of the demons.

Swami Shivananda fanned his jolly mood by saying, "Yes, it is undoubtedly true." It was an atmosphere of simple laughter and merriment. The laughter became contagious as it permeated us, steeping us in bliss.

Ordinarily, we understand by religion an unclean body and dirty countenance, morose and melancholy appearance, lean and thin body and a winter face that never smiles—one who is aloof with high sounding phrases from the great scriptures. But the Swami stressed that the jovial and jocular side of one's nature was no less important. "Wit is the sign of intelligence," he would often remark, and he proved it by demonstrating mirth and humour in his own actions. I was literally awed by this high mirth of the Swami, and as I went to touch his feet, he said with a splutter of laughter, "Ho!

Ho! So it is you [a Vaishnava]. Well, let me see how you bow down like a true Ramanujite." On any other day he would have said, "Oh! No, no, my lad—no need of this." But today he was in a different mood altogether. Swami Shivananda interposed, "No, Swami, he has rheumatism, and his joints are stiff—it will be cruel to the boy to ask him to prostrate like that." To this Swamiji replied: "No, that is nothing. It will do him good and cure him. Come, my lad, you can prostrate yourself without reserve." I did so, as this was a cherished desire of mine, which otherwise might never have been fulfilled for fear of his annoyance.

Into this atmosphere came a brahmachari who announced that the abbot of the Kedarnath temple had come for a personal interview. Swamiji's face instantly became sober, and his figure majestic. The abbot was in another room; the Swami entered it with Swami Shivananda, and we followed them. "Namo Narayanaya" came from the respectful abbot of the Kedarnath temple who sang a devotional hymn in Sanskrit. While he spoke in the Southern dialect, a Sinhalese sannyasi interpreted it in English, and the Swami responded. The abbot said: "Swamiji, you are Shiva incarnate. You have come for the salvation of mankind. Your wonderful power manifested in Europe and America is unique in the history of civilization. You have held the banner of the Orient high before the Western people, and every Hindu and each sannyasi feels himself glorified. Your interpretation and teachings of the great truths of the Vedas and their universal application shown by you have made us—the sannyasis and all the Hindus in general—very grateful to you." The hoary-headed eighty-year-old abbot, whose knowledge and spiritual enlightenment were as great as his years, went on thus. Swamiji was visibly moved with emotion and softly replied: "Maharaj, I have not been able to do much. The little work that has been done is all through the grace of the Lord. It was His will and His manifestation; the greatness, if any, does not belong to me in the least. This body only has become His instrument and vehicle; that is all. You represent the wisdom of the ancient times in your saintly life. You are illumined with the great Knowledge. If such as you bless me and cherish a kind thought for me, such works and many more will not be difficult at all. Moreover, you are the high priest of Kedarnath. It is you who are the incarnation of Shiva. I am nothing but a frail human being."

The abbot added: "When you were touring towards the North, leaving Rameshwaram, a palanquin was sent for you, to be at your disposal with men and monks from our principal centre there, for receiving you with honour in the Math. But you were weary and tired, as an ocean of men had come to get a holy glimpse of you, and so you could not accept our invitation. Therefore, the saints of our Math were very sorry, and to mitigate it, they have wired me to receive you here in the temple and Math at Varanasi and to request you to accept alms, at least one day, in the temple, with all your following." This humble petition from the old and venerable abbot transformed Swamiji into a young boy, as it were, and he answered very meekly: "If you wished so, you had only to ask me or could have sent someone with your request, and I would have gladly accepted your invitation without your taking all this trouble yourself. Anyway, I shall certainly go." Next morning at about ten or eleven, Swamiji, Swami Shivananda, and others went to the Math of the abbot of the Kedarnath temple.

A Buddhist monk who hailed from Sri Lanka was then living in the Math. He asked Swami Vivekananda, "Sir, do you think that all the religions of the world have produced perfect souls?" To this, Swamiji not only replied in the affirmative but emphasized this with many illustrations. He added: "Even in the condemned Vamachara Tantra there have been great souls. But you know, our Master (Sri Ramakrishna) used to say that that path is a dirty one." It seemed that the bhikshu was convinced of what Swamiji said. Then the revered abbot fed them all sumptuously.

In the afternoon, the abbot took Swamiji to another room where there were portraits of his guru and his predecessors, whose names and traits he enumerated. Then he brought two pieces of ochre cloth and wrapped one around Swamiji's body. The abbot was in a very happy mood, and he remarked, "Today I have fed a true Vedantist."

Then at the request of the abbot, Swamiji and others went into the temple of Kedarnath. Out of respect to Swamiji, arati of Sri Kedarnath was performed, although it was not the usual hour for it. But Swamiji, as soon as he entered the outer chamber of the temple where Nandi (the Bull) stands facing the Ganga, entered into samadhi and stood at the door, still and motionless, without any outer consciousness. He could not move even a step further and stood there as a statue. His socks were getting wet, but no one came forward to remove them, as everyone there had also entered into an inner realm where the outer world and its activities were automatically suspended. Sri Ramakrishna used to say, "Within Naren's body is Shiva." He also said that Swamiji was one of the seven sages who came down on earth at his behest. And we were privileged to see this inner personality manifested before us. Everyone there could feel the divine presence.

When we came out of the temple, Swamiji was still in a state of divine ecstasy. Slowly and softly we came out and Swami Shivananda made Swamiji sit in an open carriage with great care, lest he might slip and get hurt. The carriage moved slowly, and gradually the Swami came to himself. When it passed before an alms-house, he boyishly cried out, "Not-cot-Chetti" in broken Tamil.

A physician often came there to see Swamiji. This man had strong leanings towards a particular system of theology newly evolved in the country. He went on about its founder and how the philosophy was doing a great service to the country—going so far as to assert that it was the only right and logical institution in India. Swamiji listened without any comment or contradiction—which emboldened the physician to speak even more dogmatically in this vein.

Gradually Swamiji's face underwent a change and his features became hard and firm. Suddenly, a torrent of words came out of his mouth. His voice was serious and resounding and almost dictatorial. A new personality now spoke to the doctor, who listened in amazement: "The foreigners have become our teachers in every way—only religion remained, and you want to give them precedence even there! You have made Europe your guru, and have become its hypnotized slaves. Do you think India has fallen so low that you must import even religious preachers? Is it a thing to be proud of, or should you rather be ashamed? I have not come here to make orations and give lectures. I am ill and I want quiet and rest." A short time before, the doctor—who did not place Swamiji spiritually above the ordinary level—had remarked patronizingly, "So, sir, such-and-such has not come to you— it is a matter to be regretted, no doubt." This had annoyed Swamiji a little. And now came the correction—Swamiji raised his voice and, fixing his large eyes on his critic, said, "If I so wish, this very night I can have the founder of your pet sect and all Varanasi at my feet, but I do not want to use such divine power in this way unnecessarily."

The physician changed the subject, and in a moment Swamiji was calm again. Again we saw the composed sannyasi radiating peace around him, as if the whole episode had never taken place at all!

Mr. Kelkar, the well-known patriot, was in Varanasi at that time. One evening he came to meet the Swami, who lay on a bed quite ill. Mr. Kelkar entered the room with marked respect for the Swami, as one would do on approaching one's own guru or a great saint, and took his seat on a carpet on the matted floor. The conversation took place in English. We sat at a distance and could not hear all that was said; but we saw Swamiji talking mildly without getting up. Soon he warmed up, sat up on the cot, and began talking like a healthy person. Then he became emotional. His eyes widened, and his lips became severe. His brow was furrowed and his face flushed. The sweet melodious voice became more and more resonant and high-pitched as his dormant powers became thoroughly awakened. It was quite a new experience for Mr. Kelkar who, amazed at this transfiguration, sat as if hypnotized as Swamiji became more and more eloquent.

The topic was India and her distress. Politics, social reforms, and many other things were under discussion. "What is the good of India living in this degeneration and extreme poverty any longer?" Swamiji thundered. "Every moment she is suffering hell; no food and no clothes; dishonour and distress is her only lot; she breathes—that is her only sign of life. It is a veritable hellish fire in which she is being consumed slowly and certainly. Were it not far better to be extinct from the face of the earth?"

He went on in this strain, and we listened with bated breath and wondered at the terrible anguish he was suffering for the cause of India. He was a real patriot, a real saint. Did he not say, "Him I call a great soul, whose heart bleeds for the poor"? It was literally true in his case, for the pain he felt was so poignant, that it made him lose his poise and even forget his physical ailments. He told Mr. Kelkar that mere politics and copying foreign countries in such movements would not bear fruit, nor would the heartless foreign policy of other countries help us. Only a spontaneous development from inside, following the ancient traditions, could lift India. He stressed the last point greatly and enlarged upon it for Mr. Kelkar. He also said that only religion, not new experiments of trial and error, could effect social reforms and other developments in India. Politics and social reform divorced from religion would not benefit India lastingly or effectively. Mr. Kelkar, seemingly much impressed with what he heard, folded his hands in respect and took his leave.

Swamiji was a very powerful personality. On the one hand he would attack with all his vigour and might any wrong and injustice, pouncing upon and attempting to root out all the evil; on the other, his heart was very tender and soft. Once he said: "Is it possible to cut your finger on the soft bubbles of fresh-drawn milk? Well, the heart of Sri Radha was even softer."

One day he was walking along a road in Darjeeling, enjoying the beauty of the hills with a few others after breakfast. All of a sudden he saw, in a mental vision, a Bhutia woman with a heavy load on her back slip and fall, injuring herself. Others accompanying him did not see the incident. The attendants were young and inexperienced and did not know the moods of his superconscious state. Swamiji kept his eyes fixed on some distant object and could not move an inch further. His face became pale, and he cried in pain, "Oh! I feel great pain here, and I cannot walk any further." Someone asked, "Where do you feel the pain, Swamiji?" He pointed to his side, saying, "It is here; did you not see that woman fall?" The youth, who could not understand anything, thought it queer that the Swami should feel the pain at all, but none dared say anything. Time taught them the great significance of this episode, when they learnt that a great sympathetic relation exists between man and man, and with these Godmen who feel and visualize the feelings of others at a distance.

We had started a society in Varanasi with the help of Charu Babu and others, some three years before Swami Vivekananda came there. It was our aim to study and discuss the literature about Swamiji and Sri Ramakrishna, and work with special emphasis on karma yoga. A few young men among us assembled to meditate, worship, and mould our lives with noble ideals, while serving the poor and the distressed. By and by, many prominent men of Varanasi joined us and our work expanded. We called it the Poor Men's Relief Association.

We struggled for two years, and by the third year Swamiji's practical Vedanta had inspired us to reorganize it and rename it Daridra Narayana Seva Samiti. After another year of such service, Swamiji came to Varanasi and accepted us as his humble disciples. He transmitted his power to Charu

Babu and asked him to devote his energies particularly for this kind of service. Often he told us: "You should think that even a paisa of the poor public is a drop of your blood. How can you relieve the poor with relief societies? Do not march in false colours. Name the institution Sri Ramakrishna Home of Service and give it to the Mission for its complete management." We did so, and thus was established the sevashrama.

It is customary for elderly Hindus to retire to Varanasi with a vow not to leave the city till death. A small landlord of Bengal, named Pundit Shivananda, who was very learned in Sanskrit philosophy and had attained a high spiritual state, was living there under such a vow. He had a big heart and a wide outlook. He was acquainted with us from the very beginning of his arrival at Varanasi and he became a patron of our sevashrama from its inception.

He often quoted from the scriptures to support Swamiji's teachings, and said: "I have taken a vow not to go out of holy Varanasi, and Swamiji lives in Kolkata. Will he not come here once at least?" Swamiji did come there in early 1902, and Punditji went to see him. The very first meeting filled him with joy and happiness and Swamiji became his great friend. Often the subject of their talk would be Sri Ramakrishna and his wonderful spiritual life. While speaking about the spiritual moods of his Master, Swamiji would unconsciously manifest them!

Sometimes Punditji discussed various topics from the scriptures. The Swami would often turn to his favourite subjects—karma and service. He managed to impress his ideas firmly upon this staunch Brahmin, who represented the pundits of Varanasi and the exaggerated stress they placed on orthodox Hinduism.

Punditji had an address printed in Sanskrit from Kolkata; but he would always forget to take it with him, as he went to see the Swami in the exuberance of emotion. One day he took it with him and was on his way to see him, when Charu Babu and myself joined him. We asked him, "Punditji, what do you think of the Swami?" He at once replied: "He is a true yogi, and therefore I go to see him every day. I am fully convinced that the lectures and other preachings which have made him so renowned are but secondary to his soul-uplifting force. The divine power plays in him and very little of it is manifested. It is impossible to judge his greatness and power—he seems to be an ocean without shores."

On the way we saw Swamiji passing in another vehicle towards the palace of Bhinga Maharaj, accompanied by Swami Shivananda, Swami Govindananda, and another Swami. Both vehicles stopped and Punditji presented the address, with a little nervous agitation, to the Swami, who at a glance at the contents understood its purport and said with marked humility: "Punditji Maharaj, what have you done! I am a very ordinary person, and do not deserve such high praise and eulogy. I have done nothing. It is the will of God alone and He can make an ordinary soul His instrument to carry out whatever He wills."

After this, Pundit Shivananda would often speak about the Swami to prominent men of Sanskrit learning at Varanasi. Many orthodox pundits, such as Mahamahopadhyaya Rakhaldas Nyayaratna, were in this way convinced of the divinity in the person of Swami Vivekananda. Punditji was drawn to the Swami as if to a magnet, and they became close friends. It was his inner conviction that as he would not leave Varanasi, Swamiji himself had come there to bless him.

The Raja of Bhinga was an important landlord near Lucknow. Proficient in English and Sanskrit, he too had taken a vow to spend the rest of his life in Varanasi. Not only would he not go out of the city, but he would not even leave his garden-house. His aim was to end his days in the Bhinga palace near the Durga temple of Varanasi. He was a sadhaka and lived like a sannyasi. When he learnt about Swamiji's arrival, he sent Swami Govindananda to him with presents of fruits, flowers, and sweets. Swami Shivananda was also present there. Swami Govindananda addressed both of them with "Namo Narayanaya" and said: "The Maharaja desires to see you. If you permit him, he will come here in spite of his sacred vow not to come out of the garden." Swamiji was visibly moved and said at once: "No, no, that will never be. It is wrong to ask to break his vow. I shall go there myself; the Raja need not come here." A day or two later, he went with Swami Govindananda and Swami Shivananda to see the Raja in his garden.

The Raja discussed scriptural matters with the Swamiji, and in the course of conversation said to him, "You are a great soul—like Buddha and Shankara." The entire conversation was marked with this kind of high respect and devotion for Swamiji. The Raja had been an ardent worker in the earlier part of his life, and he entreated the Swami to start some mission of service in Varanasi and promised to bear its expense. Swamiji's health was not good; so he could not promise. He only said: "I am now going back to Belur Math, and I shall concentrate on work more when my health permits." After various other discussions, Swamiji and Swami Shivananda returned to the Sondhabas.

Next day the Raja of Bhinga sent an envelope containing a cheque for Rs.500/- and a letter through a courier as a mark of respect. Swamiji said to Swami Shivananda, "Mahapurush, you please start a Math of Shri Ramakrishna here with this money." A garden was rented in July, and the Ramakrishna Advaita Ashrama established there.

One day, Sri Kalidas Mitra, son of the late Pramadadas Mitra, came to see the Swami at about 5 p.m. His father had been a friend of the Swami. The Swami was quite pleased to meet the son of his old friend. Kalidas Babu took a seat on the carpet and listened intently to whatever fell from Swamiji's lips. Swami Shivananda, Charu Babu, myself, and others sat near him. I was then not more than twenty, and cannot remember everything that Swamiji said that day, but still the picture is fresh in my memory, though half a century has passed.

Great and pure souls often answer the questions in one's mind, even before a word is uttered. Once, in London, before he began his lecture, the Swami said: "Each of you may write a question on a slip of paper and keep it in your pocket. There is no need of passing them to me, and I shall answer each of them." When they did so, the Swami turned to the right and said, "Your question is this." Then seeing that a gentleman on his left waited eagerly to hear him address his question too, the Swami turned to the left and did the same and then went on giving the details of his house, what was in it, who lived there, what they were doing at that moment, and so on. The person in question, along with everybody else, was astounded at this miraculous vision. The Swami then repeated this demonstration as he answered the questions of about six or eight other people.

One day, in England, Swami Saradananda, who had been suffering from malaria for a long time and was much reduced and in a weakened state, sat at the Swami's feet, feeling like a child. In a calm and meek spirit of surrender to his brother-disciple—to him, none other than Sri Ramakrishna in another body—he asked for Swamiji's blessings and the promise of knowledge and salvation. He was in an inspiration of spiritual fervour. In a moment, through the will of Vivekananda, Saradananda became healthy and strong. Swami Saradananda testified to this psychic power of Swami Vivekananda, which had never been revealed to him before. There may be many others, some still living, who had the occasion to see this side of the Swami—the great powers that came to him but remained suppressed because he hated to demonstrate them.

Kalidas Mitra was a great lover of fine arts, and he had studied them profoundly. One day, as soon as he seated himself in the room with Swamiji, his thoughts and ideas began vibrating in Swamiji's mind. Swamiji's facial expressions, tone of voice, and body language changed altogether. After a glance at Kalidas, he began speaking on fine arts, painting and its allied branches, even costumes of different countries and their relation to nature and modes of expression.

It was as if he were delivering a very learned and interesting lecture to an assembly of artists and painters. No one could have guessed, hearing him speak, that he was anything but a painter and artist himself—someone who had given over his life to the subject. Colour harmony, the different combinations of colours and shades, grace, postures, and different angles and position of the eye, the waist, the bust, different poses and attitudes, etc.—these were his subjects. I was young and could not follow the subject in detail; but I had no doubt that it was a wonderful lecture on the arts and painting and crafts in general. Then the Swami compared and contrasted the different schools of painting in different countries—Italy, France, China, Persia, Japan, and Buddhist and Mogul India.

Once the Swami was invited to a famous theatrical hall in France whose backdrops had been painted by a renowned artist. At the time, both the artist and the theatre were foremost in Paris. Swamiji, who knew French and thus could follow the drama, noticed that part of the backdrop revealed some technical flaws. When the play was over, he called the manager, who hurried over with several of the company, all of whom were eager to learn the impressions of this honoured and renowned guest. When Swamiji pointed out the technical defect in the painted backdrop they were astonished, for it was considered a masterpiece, and the defect could not be detected even by trained eyes. The artist admitted that Swamiji was right, and was highly pleased to hear his suggestions regarding the harmony of expressions in the figures. He was convinced that the Swami was as much of an expert on painting techniques as on any other subject.

We heard of another, similar incident. In England, Swamiji went with Miss Muller and a few others to see Professor Venn. Miss Muller had been a student of logic under the professor, whose famous *Logic of Chance* documented his deep knowledge of the subject. He had spent his life studying logic and was considered an authority on the subject in

Europe. The professor had heard of the Swami, but as meta-physical problems did not interest him much, the discussion turned to the subject of logic. When Swamiji spoke on logic, the Professor thought that, like himself, he had dedicated himself to this subject alone, and remarked, "A logician of India has come today to meet another of the West."

To return to the art of painting, the root of the word "chitra" is chit (heart). Whatever manifests the chit before us is an image. As soon as the Swami turned inwards into the chidakasa, the space eternal, all the principles of art and its expression came to his vision. He would at once know all the intricacies of art, and all the pictures that he had ever seen would focus themselves in his mind. He would often say, "If I see a thing, it goes down into the subconscious region of the mind and again comes out on the conscious plane when it is needed." Also, "If I meditate on the brain of a Shankara, I become a Shankara; if I meditate on the brain of a Buddha, I become a Buddha. Even thoughts and subjects that have never occurred to me come before me when I concentrate on a particular subject. I can visualize all of them, and go on speaking whatever I feel, forgetting myself. As all of you know, I have no learning and am a simple man!" He demon-strated this facility while lecturing in England.

At the theatre that day, we all thought of this peculiarity of the Swami, and wondered at this philosopher who would only talk of painting and art and the technique of colours.

Another evening Kalidas Mitra came to see the Swami. With a woollen sweater and hoses on, Swamiji was sitting with his back arched over a pillow on which his hands rested. The Swami was ailing, with evident suffering, and breathing with some difficulty. We were sitting very near him on the carpeted floor. Mr. Mitra came and touched his feet and the Swami said, "My health is now broken down and it troubles me very much". Mr. Mitra asked what the disease was—to which he replied: "That I cannot say. I consulted some of the best physicians at Paris and also in America, but neither could they diagnose it nor effect any cure or relief." Then Mr. Mitra inquired: "Swamiji, we have heard that you are going to Japan. Is it true?" He replied: "Mr. Okakura has been sent by the government of Japan for this very purpose. Japan is a fine country. She has made industry an art and every home a centre of industry. I went to Japan on my way to America. They live in small cottages of bamboo, and every house has a fine flower garden and a few fruit trees. As a race they are very progressive. Eventually if I go to Japan by the will of Sri Ramakrishna, you must accompany me. The Japanese have acquired the Western culture (of science and industry). Formally they were Buddhists, but now they are rather spiritually indifferent. If Indian thoughts and ideals penetrated into Japan, she would become more religious. With a little injection of Vedanta she will progress marvellously." Mr. Mitra asked, "What good will it bring to India?" Swamiji replied, "By the interchange of ideas and culture between the two nations, they will be mutually helped and both will progress." He talked about the wonderful progress Japan has made, and in the course of the talk he came to the extreme poverty of India. He forgot everything about the state of his health and physical ailments. He was pained at India's low status and economic distress. His face became livid and sorrowful. Occasionally, he sang a devotional song of Ramprasad. This turned him into a different person altogether. We, too, visualized the sentiments and emotions of India in those songs and our hearts ached for our country.

Swamiji talked about the rapid progress of Japan and how she had raised herself from a simple state, not marked for culture and civilization, into a country of self-reliance. He spoke of the French Revolution and Napoleon. From an ordinary soldier, Napoleon raised himself to the pinnacle of glory through self-reliance and strong character. This topic again changed Swamiji's countenance and bearing completely. He had become another person, as if he had gone to the time of Napoleon in France. Now Swamiji was full of vigour and vitality. His face became set with a purpose, the voice assumed a strong volume and pitch, eyes large and shining with a glint of steel. He was so excited that sometimes he knelt on the pillow and again on the carpet, and sometimes leapt up even in that sitting posture. Speaking of Napoleon, he himself had become like Napoleon. It was as if he himself were directing the fight of Jena and Austerlitz. "There goes the enemy—far away—they are flying—stop them—forward the eastern brigade—do not let a soul leave the field alive." "We have won the battle— we have conquered," he cried in joy, and sometimes with one hand raised and sometimes two he exulted in the imaginary conquest and sang the French battle songs of victory.

Swamiji was so excited and transformed that we all—Charu Babu, Swami Shivananda, and others—were astounded. The servants, gardeners, and everyone else were pinned in place, unable to lift our hands or feet, as if we were under a hypnotic spell. A heat and a radiance emanated from the body of the Swami, and the air of the room became warm, and we all were carried to the battlefield of Austerlitz or Jena and saw Napoleon with keen bright eagle eyes and heard his firm orders to his army. A spirit of heroism and courage was infused in all of us and, under the leadership of Swamiji in the role of Napoleon, we ourselves became Marshal Ney, Soult, Victor, Marmont, MacDonald, etc. We were convinced of the Napoleonic power in us which could conquer the world against very heavy odds. Swami Shivananda told us, "This is Swamiji's inspired lecturing. All the lectures he delivered in Europe and America were like this—given in an inspired state."

Then the Swami recited from the *Lalita Vistara*, the famous vow of Buddha when he sat on the slab of stone before his illumination, and he invoked that spirit in himself: "Let the body be dried up here on this seat, the flesh and bones be destroyed; but without that knowledge difficult to attain even in many cycles, I shall not leave this seat."

There was in the heart of Swamiji a great love for his brother-disciples and the householders who were devoted to him. If anyone were ill or Swamiji heard bad news about him, he would be extremely anxious for that person. Until he heard that he was a little better, he would be restless. Many such incidents have already come out, and they need not be repeated here.

At last, Swamiji's health broke down completely. He used to say to Swami Shivananda: "This is a shattered body. How long can you keep it going? And supposing this body is no more, Nivedita, Shashi (Swami Ramakrishnananda), and others will obey me. They will die in harness and can never falter in carrying out my words. They are my only hope." In this way he would give us hope and benedictions.

His love and attracting power had increased so much during these days that his body seemed to us to be congealed emotions, love, and sympathy. From his lips flowed a constant stream of love and blessings.

When we used to go to Swamiji, we did not understand what knowledge and devotion were, or the distinction between meditation and work. We were young and inexperienced. But we could understand his love—it was not of this world. We were attracted by his great love. Whoever has seen Swamiji even once can testify that he has seen a man who could love and who came to teach love to the world. How many youths have renounced everything to join the order of monks only because of his divine love! Even to this day, this love compels them to sacrifice their own lives to serve others.

(Vedanta Kesari, January-November 1954,
July & August 1956)

BRAJENDRANATH SEAL

Brajendranàth Seal

When I first met Vivekananda in 1881, we were fellow-students of Principal William Hastie, scholar, metaphysician, and poet, at the General Assembly's College. He was my senior in age, though I was his senior in the college by one year. Undeniably a gifted youth, sociable, free, and unconventional in manners, a sweet singer, the soul of social circles, a brilliant conversationalist, somewhat bitter and caustic, piercing with the shafts of a keen wit the shows and mummeries of the world, sitting in the scorner's chair but hiding the tenderest of hearts under that garb of cynicism; altogether an inspired Bohemian but possessing what Bohemians lack, an iron will; somewhat premptory and absolute, speaking with accents of authority and withal possessing a strange power of the eye which could hold his listeners in thrall.

This was patent to all. But what was known to few was the inner man and his struggle—the *Sturm und Drang* of soul which expressed itself in his restless and Bohemian wanderings.

This was the beginning of a critical period in his mental history, during which he awoke to self-consciousness and laid the foundations of his future personality. John Stuart Mill's *Three Essays on Religion* had upset his first boyish theism and easy optimism which he had imbibed from the outer circles of the Brahmo Samaj. The arguments from causality and design were for him broken reeds to lean upon, and he was haunted by the problem of the Evil in Nature and Man which he, by no means, could reconcile with the

11

goodness of an All-wise and All-powerful Creator. A friend introduced him to the study of Hume's scepticism and Herbert Spencer's doctrine of the Unknowable, and his un-belief gradually assumed the form of a settled philosophical scepticism.

His first emotional freshness and *naïveté* were worn out. A certain dryness and incapacity for the old prayerful devotions, an ennui which he concealed under a nonchalant air of habitual mocking and scoffing, troubled his spirit. But music still stirred him as nothing else could, and gave him a weird unearthly sense of unseen realities which brought tears to his eyes.

It was at this time that he came to me, being brought by a common friend—the same friend who had introduced him to the study of Hume and Herbert Spencer. I had had a nodding acquaintance with him before, but now he opened himself to me and spoke of his harassing doubts and his despair of reaching certitude about the Ultimate Reality. He asked for a course of Theistic philosophic reading suited to a beginner in his situation. I named some authorities, but the stock arguments of the Intuitionists and the Scotch common sense school only confirmed him in his unbelief. Besides, he did not appear to me to have sufficient patience for humdrum reading; his faculty was to imbibe not so much from books as from living communion and personal experience. With him it was life kindling life and thought kindling thought.

I felt deeply drawn towards him, for I now knew that he would grapple with difficulties in earnest.

I gave him a course of readings in Shelley. Shelley's Hymn to the Spirit of Intellectual Beauty, his pantheism of impersonal love and his vision of a glorified millennial humanity moved him as the arguments of the philosophers had failed to move him. The universe was no longer a mere lifeless, loveless mechanism. It contained a spiritual principle of unity.

I spoke to him now of a higher unity than Shelley had conceived, the unity of the Supreme Brahman as the

Universal Reason. My own position at that time sought to fuse into one three essential elements: the pure monism of the Vedanta, the dialectics of the Absolute idea of Hegel, and the Gospel of Equality, Liberty, and Fraternity of the French Revolution. The principle of individuation was with me the principle of Evil. Universal Reason was all in all; nature, life, and history being the progressive unfolding of the Absolute idea. All ethical, social and political creeds and principles were to be tested by their conformity to Pure Reason. The element of feeling appeared to me merely pathological, a disturbance of sanity and order. How to overcome the resistance of matter, of individuality and of unreason, to the manifestation of the Pure Reason was the great problem of life and society, of education and legislation. I also held with the ardour of a young inexperienced visionary that the deliverance of the race from the bondage of unreason would come about through a new revolutionary polity of which the watchwords were Equality, Liberty, and Fraternity.

The sovereignty of Universal Reason, and the negation of the individual as the principle of morals, were ideas that soon came to satisfy Vivekananda's intellect and gave him an assured conquest over scepticism and materialism. What was more, they furnished him with the card and compass of life, as it were. But this brought him no peace. The conflict now entered deeper into his soul, for the creed of Universal Reason called on him to suppress the yearnings and susceptibilities of his artist nature and Bohemian temperament. His senses were keen and acute, his natural cravings and passions strong and imperious, his youthful susceptibilities tender, his conviviality free and merry. To suppress these was to kill his natural spontaneity—almost to suppress his self. The struggle soon took a seriously ethical turn—reason struggling for mastery with passion and sense. The fascinations of the sense and the cravings of a youthful nature now appeared to him as impure, as gross and carnal. This was the hour of darkest trial for him. His musical gifts brought him associates for whose manners and morals he had bitter and undisguised contempt. But his convivial temperament proved too strong for him. It was, therefore, some relief to him when I occasionally kept him company on an evening when he went out for a musical soiree.

I saw and recognized in him a high, ardent, and pure nature, vibrant and resonant with impassioned sensibilities. He was certainly no sour or cross-grained puritan, no normal hypochondriac; he would indulge cynically in unconventional language except when he would spare my innocence. He took an almost morbid delight in shocking conventionality in its tabernacles, respectability in its booths; and in the pursuit of his sport would appear other than he was, puzzling and mystifying those outside his inner circle of friends. But in the recesses of his soul he wrestled with the fierce and fell spirit of Desire, the subtle and illusive spirit of Fancy.

To his repeated quest for some power which would deliver him from bondage and unavailing struggle, I could only point to the sovereignty of Pure Reason and the ineffable peace that comes from identifying the self with the Reason in the Universe. Those were for me days of a victorious Platonic transcendentalism. The experience of a refractory fresh or rebellious temperament had not come to me. I had not sufficient patience for the mood or attitude of mind which surrenders the sovereign right of self-government to artificial props or outside help, such as grace or mediation. I felt no need of conciliating feeling and nature in the cult of Reason, nor had had any experience of a will divided in its allegiance to the Self. The experience of a discord between the Ideal and the Real, between Nature and Spirit, had indeed come to me already in an objective way as an outstanding reality and was to come afterwards in subjective fashion though in forms quite other than what obtained in Vivekananda's case. But at the time, his problems were not mine, nor were my difficulties his.

He confessed that though his intellect was conquered by the universal, his heart owned the allegiance of the individual Ego and complained that a pale bloodless reason, sovereign *de jure* but not *de facto*, could not hold out arms to save him in the hour of temptation. He wanted to know if my philosophy could satisfy his senses, could mediate bodily, as it were, for the soul's deliverance; in short, he wanted a flesh and blood reality visible in form and glory; above all, he cried out for a hand to save, to uplift, to protect, a Shakti or power outside himself which could cure him of his impotence and cover his nothingness with glory—a guru or master who by embodying perfection in the flesh would still the commotion in his soul.

At the time, this appeared to me a weakness born of unreason, this demand for perfection in the flesh and for a power out of ourselves to save—this sacrifice of reason to sense. My young inexperienced self, confronted with this demand of a soul striving with itself, knew not wherewith to satisfy it, and Vivekananda soon after betook himself to the ministers and missionaries of the Brahmo Samaj, asking Brahmos with an unconscious Socratic Irony for an ideal made real to sense, for truth made visible, for a power unto deliverance. Here he had enough, he bitterly complained, of moral disquisitions, principles, intuitions for pabulum which to him appeared tasteless and insipid. He tried diverse teachers, creeds, and cults, and it was this quest that brought him, though at first in a doubting spirit, to the Paramahamsa of Dakshineshwar, who spoke to him with an authority as none had spoken before, and by his Shakti brought peace into his soul and healed the wounds of his spirit. But his rebellious intellect scarcely yet owned the Master. His mind misgave him and he doubted if the peace which would possess his soul in the presence of the Master was not illusory. It was only gradually that the doubts of that keen intellect were vanquished by the calm assurance that belongs to ocular demonstration.

I watched with intense interest the transformation that went on before my eyes. The attitude of a young and rampant Vedantist-cum-Hegelian-cum-Revolutionary like myself towards the cult of religious ecstasy and Kali-worship, may be easily imagined; and the spectacle of a born iconoclast and free-thinker like Vivekananda, a creative and dominating intelligence, a tamer of souls, himself caught in the meshes of what appeared to me an uncouth, supernatural mysticism, was a riddle which my philosophy of the Pure Reason could scarcely read at the time. But Vivekananda, "the loved and lost" was loved, and mourned most in what I could not but then regard as his defection; and it was personal feeling, after all, the hated pathological element of individual preference and individual relationship, which most impelled me, when at last I went on what to a home-keeping recluse like myself was an adventurous journey to Dakshineshwar, to see and hear Vivekananda's Master, and spent the greater part of a long summer day in the shady and peaceful solitude of the Temple-garden, returning as the sun set amidst the whirl and rush and roar and the awful gloom of a blinding thunder-storm, with a sense of bewilderment as well moral as physical, and a lurking perception of the truth that the majesty of Law orders the apparently irregular and grotesque, that there may be self mastery in apparent self-alienation, that sense even in its errors is only incipient Reason and that faith in a Saving Power *ab extra* is but the dim reflex of an original act of self-determination. And a significant confirmation of all this came in the subsequent life-history of Vivekananda who, after he had found the firm assurance he sought in the saving Grace and Power of his Master, went about preaching and teaching the creed of the Universal Man, and the absolute and inalienable sovereignty of the Self.

(*Life*, Vol. 1, pp. 107-111)

Nagendranath Gupta

Nearly a quarter of a century has elapsed since Swami Vivekananda went to his rest; and every year that passes is bringing fresh recognition of his greatness and widening the circle of his admirers. But the generation that knew him personally and heard his voice is also disappearing with the years. Such of his contemporaries as are left owe it to his memory and to their countrymen to place on record their impressions of one who, by universal assent, was one of the greatest Indians as well as one of the world's great men. There is no need to repeat the story of his life, for that has been well and fully done by his disciples in the four volumes[1] compiled by them. But one who knew him, as I did, may endeavour to strike a personal and reminiscent note, and to recall, so far as memory may serve, some small details of great significance, and the traits of character and the bearing that distinguished him from the people around him. I knew him when he was an unknown and ordinary lad, for I was at college with him, and I also met him when he returned from America in the full blaze of fame and glory. He stayed with me for several days and told me without reservation everything that had happened in the years that we had lost sight of each other. Finally, I met him at the monastery at Belur near Kolkata shortly before his death. In whatever relates to him I shall speak of what I heard from himself and not from others.

The conditions in India were very peculiar when Swami Vivekananda first attracted public attention. The imposition

---

1. Now in two volumes.

of a foreign domination and the grafting of a foreign culture had produced a pernicious effect on Indian life and Indian thought. The ancient ideals were either forgotten or obscured by the meretricious glamour of Western materialism. There was an air of unreality about most of the progressive movements in India. In every field of activity a sort of smug unctuousness had replaced the single-minded earnestness and devotion of the ancient times. The old moorings of steadfast purpose had slipped and everything was adrift and at the mercy of every wind and wave from outside India. The ancient Aryan had realized that there could be no achievement without sacrifice and self-surrender. The modern Indian in his new environment fancied that surrender was not necessary for attaining anything. Following the example of the West, the Indian reformer did his work while living in comfort and ease. The method followed was that of the dilettante, touching the surface of great problems, but seldom attempting to probe deeper. Men with an eloquent tongue and the gift of persuasive speech stirred the emotions and feelings of their hearers, but the effect was more or less fleeting because of the lack of strength in the appeals. The conditions in India might be described as a flux, if there were any assurance of a return of the tide. Perhaps there was no conscious self-deception, but people were deceived and mistook the sham for the reality. The placid self-complacence noticeable everywhere was an unmistakable sign of growing weakness and inability to resist the inroads of habits of thought and ideals of life destructive of everything that is enduring and everything that is real in the long established order of things in India.

In the midst of these depressing surroundings was the quiet and scarcely noticed emergence of Ramakrishna Paramahamsa after a period of preparation and meditation unknown to the people around him. He was practically an unlettered man like some of the great prophets of old, and by occupation he was the priest of a temple, a vocation for which he became unfit later. Ignorant people thought he was getting deranged, but in reality it was a struggle of the spirit seeking true knowledge and finding its expression. And when this was attained, he no longer avoided men, and drew around him a small band of earnest young men who sought his guidance and endeavoured to follow his teachings. Many of his sayings have been collected and published, but these give only a faint indication of his individuality. It may be said with absolute truth that he was one of the elect who appear at long intervals in the world for some great purpose. It has been my privilege to hear him speak; and I felt then, as I feel now, that it is only rarely that men have the great good fortune of listening to such a man. The Paramahamsa's language was Bengali of a homely kind; he was not supple of speech as he spoke with a slight though delightful stammer, but his words held men enthralled by the wealth of spiritual experience, the inexhaustible store of simile and metaphor, the unequalled powers of observation, the bright and subtle humour, the wonderful catholicity of sympathy, and the ceaseless flow of wisdom.

Among the young men attracted by the magnetic personality of the Paramahamsa was Narendranath Dutta, afterwards known as Swami Vivekananda. There was nothing to distinguish him from other young men who used to visit Ramakrishna Paramahamsa. He was an average student with no promise of brilliance, because he was not destined to win any prize of the learned or unlearned professions, but the Master picked him out early from the rest and predicted a great future for him. "He is a thousand-petalled lotus," said the Paramahamsa, meaning that the lad was one of those who come to the world fully equipped for a great purpose and to be a leader of men. The reference was to the spiritual sphere, since the Paramahamsa took no account of worldly success. Ramakrishna Paramahamsa could not only read faces with unerring accuracy, but he also had extraordinary psychic powers, which was demonstrated in the case of Vivekananda himself. The young man was not very regular in his visits to the Paramahamsa. On one occasion he was absent for several weeks. The Paramahamsa made repeated inquiries about him and ultimately asked one of Vivekananda's friends to bring him. It may be mentioned that the Paramahamsa lived in the temple of Dakshineshwar, some miles to the north of Kolkata.

The Paramahamsa added that when Narendra came he wished to see him alone. Accordingly, there was no one else in the room when Narendra came to see the Paramahamsa. As soon as the boy entered the room the Paramahamsa left his seat and saying, "Why have you been staying away when I wanted to see you?", approached the lad and tapped him lightly on the chest with a finger. Instantly—these are Vivekananda's own words—the lad saw a flash of dazzling light and felt himself swept off his feet, and he cried out in alarm, "What are you doing to me? I have parents." The Paramahamsa patted him on the back and soothed him, saying, "There, there, that will do."

Shortly after this incident Vivekananda became an accepted disciple of Ramakrishna Paramahamsa. The number of these disciples was very small and the Paramahamsa was very careful in choosing them. Every one of these disciples was subjected to a constant and unrelaxing discipline more than Spartan in its severity. There was no spoon-feeding and coddling. The Paramahamsa's prediction about Vivekananda was not communicated to any publicity bureau, and he and his fellow-disciples were always under the vigilant eyes of the Master. Vows of great hardship were imposed upon the disciples, and the discipline was maintained unbroken even after the passing away of the Paramahamsa. Vivekananda went to Varanasi, and it was there that he acquired the correct enunciation and the sonorous chanting of the hymns and the mantras[2] which he often recited very impressively in a deep musical voice. I have heard him singing in a fine tenor voice at the request of

---

2. According to another version, he preferred and learnt the Maratha intonation.

friends, and as an orator there were both power and music in his voice.

Ramakrishna Paramahamsa frequently passed into a trance or samadhi. The exciting cause was invariably some spiritual experience or some new spiritual perception. On one occasion—it was in 1881—I formed one of a party that had gone with Keshabchandra Sen by river to see the Paramahamsa. He was brought on board our steamer, which belonged to Maharaja Nripendra Narayan Bhup of Cooch Behar, Keshab's son-in-law. The Paramahamsa, as is well-known, was a worshipper of the goddess Kali; but he was also an adept in the contemplation of the formless Brahman, and had some previous conversation with Keshab on this subject. He was sitting close to Keshab facing him, and the conversation was practically a monologue, for either Keshab or someone else would put a brief question and, in answer, the Paramahamsa with his marvellous gift of speech and illustration would hold his listeners entranced. All of us there hung breathless upon his words. And gradually the conversation came around to the formless Brahman, when the Paramahamsa, after repeating the word "formless" two or three times to himself, passed into a state of samadhi. Except the rigidity of the body there was no quivering of the muscles or nerves, no abrupt or convulsive movement of any kind. The fingers of the two hands as they lay in his lap were slightly curled. But a most wonderful change had come over his face. The lips were slightly parted as if in a smile, with the gleam of white teeth in between. The eyes were half closed with the balls and pupils partly visible, and over the whole countenance was an ineffable expression of the holiest and most ecstatic beatitude. We watched him in respectful silence for some minutes after which Trailokyanath Sanyal, known as the singing apostle in Keshabchandra Sen's sect, sang a hymn to the accompaniment of music, and the Paramahamsa slowly opened his eyes, looked inquiringly around him for a few seconds, and then resumed the conversation. No reference was made either by him or anyone else to his trance.

On another occasion the Paramahamsa wanted to see the Zoological Gardens of Kolkata. His eagerness was like a child's and would not brook any delay. There were times when his ways were strongly reminiscent of the saying in the *Srimad Bhagavata* that the free soul, the emancipated and the wise, is to be recognized by his childlike playfulness. A cab was sent for, and the Paramahamsa, accompanied by some disciples, was driven the long distance from Dakshineshwar to Alipur. When he entered the Gardens, the people with him began showing him the various animals and aquatic collections, but he would not even look at them. "Show me the lion," he insisted. Standing in front of the lion's cage he mused, "This is the Mother's mount"—the goddess Kali in the form of Durga or Parvati is represented as riding a lion—and immediately passed into samadhi. He would have fallen but for the supporting arms around him. On regaining consciousness, he was invited to stroll round the gardens and see the rest of the collection. "I have seen the king of the animals. What else is there to see?" replied the Paramahamsa. And he went back to the waiting carriage and drove home.

There seems to be an obvious incongruity between the predisposing causes of samadhi on these two occasions. On the first, it was the contemplation of the formless Brahman, a high and abstruse spiritual concept; on the second, it was merely the sight of a caged lion. But in both instances the process of concentration of the mind and the spirit is the same. In one, it is the intense realization of the supreme Brahman without form; in the other, it is a realization in the spirit of a visual symbolism inseparably associated with the goddess Kali. In both cases a single spiritual thought occupies the mind to the exclusion of everything else, obliterates the sense of the objective world, and leads to samadhi. No photograph taken of the Paramahamsa in samadhi ever succeeded in reproducing the inward glow and the expression of divine ecstasy stamped on his countenance.

As a young enthusiast passing through a probation of discipline Vivekananda desired that he should have the experience of continuous samadhi. The Paramahamsa explained to him that this was unlikely as he had to do important work in the cause of religion. But Vivekananda would not be dissuaded, and once, while sitting in meditation, he went into samadhi. The Paramahamsa, when apprised of it, said, "Let him enjoy it for a time." Vivekananda realized afterwards that the Master was right, and the time came when in fulfilment of the prophecy of the Master he held aloft the torch of Truth in distant lands and proclaimed that the light of knowledge comes from the East.

Under the vow of poverty and mendicancy Vivekananda travelled widely in northern and southern India for eight years,[3] and his experiences, as may be imagined, were varied. He spent a great deal of his time in the Chennai Presidency, and he had first hand knowledge of the evil influence of professional monks. He knew intimately the village life of the Telugu and Tamil-speaking peoples, and he found his earliest admirers in the Chennai Presidency. He was in Bihar when there was great excitement in that province on account of the marking of mango trees with lumps of mud mixed with vermilion and seed grain. In a number of districts in Bihar numerous mango topes were discovered marked in this fashion. The trustees of an empire, as the Government in this country somewhat theatrically call themselves, may have a lofty function; but they have an uneasy conscience; and the official mind was filled with forebodings of some impending grave peril. The wonderful secret police got busy at once, and it was shrewdly surmised that the marks on the mango trees bore a family resemblance to the mysterious chapatis which were circulated immediately before the outbreak of the Mutiny. The villagers, frightened out of their wits by the sudden incursion of armed and unarmed (but not the less terrible on that account) authority in their midst, denied all knowledge of the authorship of these sinister marks. Suspicion

3. Actually less, as his travelling started long after the passing away of the Master.

next rested upon the itinerant monks wandering all over the country and they were arrested wholesale for some time. But they had to be released for want of evidence, since the recent facilities of regulations and ordinances did not then exist. It was afterwards found that the marking of mango trees was merely by way of an agricultural mascot for a good mango or general crops. Vivekananda had to get up early in the morning and to trudge along the Grand Trunk Road or some village path until someone offered him food, or the heat of the sun compelled him to rest under a road-side tree. One morning as he was tramping along as usual, he heard a shout behind him asking him to halt. He turned around and saw a mounted police officer, bearded and in full panoply, swinging a switch and followed by some policemen. As he came up, he inquired in the well-known gentle voice affected by Indian policemen who Vivekananda was. "As you see, Khan Saheb," replied Vivekananda, "I am a monk." "All monks are rogues," sententiously growled the Sub-Inspector of Police. As policemen in India are known never to tell an untruth, such an obvious fact could not be disputed. "You come along with me, and I shall see that you are put in jail," boomed the police officer. "For how long?" softly asked Vivekananda. "Oh, it may be for a fortnight, or even a month." Vivekananda went nearer to him and in an ingratiating and appealing voice said: "Khan Saheb, only for a month? Can you not put me away for six months, or at least three or four months?" The police officer stared, and his face fell. "Why do you wish to stay in jail longer than a month?" he asked suspiciously. Vivekananda replied in a confidential tone: "Life in jail is much better than this life. The work there is not hard compared with this wearisome tramp from morning till night. My daily food is uncertain, and I have often to starve. In jail I shall have two square meals a day. I shall look upon you as my benefactor if you lock me up for several months." As he listened, a look of disappointment and disgust appeared on the Khan Saheb's face, and he abruptly ordered Vivekananda to go away.

The second encounter with the police took place in Kolkata itself. Vivekananda was living in a suburb of Kolkata with some of his fellow-disciples, quietly pursuing his studies and rendering small social service as came his way. One day he met a police officer who was a friend of Vivekananda's family. He was a Superintendent of Police in the Criminal Investigation Department, and had received a title and decoration for his services. He greeted Vivekananda cordially and invited him for dinner on the same evening. There were some other visitors when Vivekananda arrived. At length they left, but there were no signs of dinner. Instead, the host spoke about other matters until suddenly lowering his voice and assuming a menacing look he said: "Come, now, you had better make a clean breast of it and tell me the truth. You know you cannot fool me with your stories for I know your game. You and your gang pretend to be religious men, but I have positive information that you are conspiring against the Government." "What do you mean?" asked Vivekananda, amazed and indignant, "What conspiracies are you speaking of, and what have we to do with them?" "That is what I want to know," coolly replied the police officer. "I am convinced it is some nefarious plot, and you are the ringleader. Out with the whole truth, and then I shall arrange that you are made an approver." "If you know everything, why don't you come and arrest us and search our house?" said Vivekananda, and rising he quietly closed the door. Now, Vivekananda was an athletic young man of a powerful build, while the police officer was a puny, wizened creature. Turning round upon him Vivekananda said: "You have called me to your house on a false pretext and have made a false accusation against me and my companions. This is the way you have treated me. I, on the other hand, have been taught not to resent an insult. If I had been a criminal and a conspirator, there would be nothing to prevent me from wringing your neck before you could call out for help. As it is, I leave you in peace." And Vivekananda opened the door and went out, leaving the redoubtable police officer speechless with ill-concealed fright. Neither Vivekananda nor his companions were ever again troubled by this man.

Another experience that Swami Vivekananda related to me bordered on the tragic. The particular vow he had undertaken at that time was that he should steadily walk the whole day without either looking back or begging from any man. He was to halt only if accosted, and to accept food if it was offered to him unasked. Sometimes he had to go without any food for twenty-four and even forty-eight hours. One afternoon he was passing in front of a stable belonging to some wealthy person. One of the grooms was standing on the road. Vivekananda had not eaten for two days and was looking weak and weary. The groom saluted him and looking at him asked, "Holy Sir, have you eaten anything today?" "No," replied Vivekananda, "I have eaten nothing." The groom took him into the stable, offered him water to wash his hands and feet and placed his own food consisting of some chapatis and a little chutney,[4] before him. The chutney was hot, but in the course of his wanderings Vivekananda had got accustomed to eat chillies, which were often the only condiment he had with his food. I have seen him eating a handful of pungent, green chillies with evident relish. Vivekananda ate the chapatis and the chutney, but immediately afterwards felt a frightful burning sensation in his stomach and rolled on the ground in agony. The groom beat his head with his hands and wailed, "What have I done? I have killed a monk." The pain must have been due to eating the chutney on an empty stomach. Just about this time a man with a basket on his head, who happened to be passing by, halted on hearing the cries of the groom. Vivekananda asked him what he had in his basket, and the man replied it was tamarind. "Ah, that is just what I want," said Vivekananda, and taking some of the tamarind he mixed it with water and drank it. This had the effect of allaying the burning sensation and the pain, and after resting for a while Vivekananda resumed his journey.

---

4. A sweet pickle or sauce.

In the remote regions of the Himalayas Vivekananda met
with some perilous adventures, but nothing daunted him
and he went through the treadmill of discipline with great
courage and tireless energy. The vows imposed upon him
entailed prolonged trials of endurance, an unbroken course
of self-discipline, meditation, and communion. When he
arrived in America, without friends, without funds, he had
nothing beyond his intellectual and spiritual equipment, and
the indomitable courage and will that he had acquired in
the course of his purposeful wanderings in India. One of his
own countrymen, who had attained some fame and was a
man of considerable eminence, attempted to discredit him by
circulating unfounded calumnies against him. In spite of difficulties Vivekananda found his way to the Parliament of Religions at Chicago, and it was there that he gained recognition.
He was probably the youngest man in that memorable and
historical as well as unique gathering. Beyond the fact that
he was a Hindu he carried no other credentials. The name of
his guru was unknown in Europe and America. He was an
obscure young man unknown to fame, with no reputation
either in his own country or out of it for scholarship, holy
living, or leadership. It is impossible to conceive an assembly
more critical or less emotional than that gathering of learned
and pious men from all parts of the world representing all
the churches and creeds of the world. Men of great erudition
steeped in sacred lore, reverend and high dignitaries of many
churches, men who had left the seclusion of the cloister and
the peace of the monastery had met in solemn conclave in
a great city in the Far West. It was a Parliament not filled
from the hustings and polling booths, but from the temples
and pagodas, the synagogues and churches and mosques
of the world. They were mostly men well-advanced in life,
accustomed by years of discipline to self-control, engaged
in contemplation and meditation, and not likely to be easily
swayed by extraneous influences. Some of them were men
of international repute; all of them were men of distinction.
Obviously the least among them was this youthful stranger

from the East, of whom no one had ever heard and who was probably there more by sufferance than by the right of any achievement to his credit. How he took that grave assembly of religious men by storm; how pen-pictures of the young Hindu monk in the orange-coloured robe and turban filled the newspapers of America, and how the men and women of America crowded to see and hear him are now part of history. Slightly varying Caesar's laconic and exultant message it may be truthfully said of Swami Vivekananda that "he went, he was seen and heard, and he conquered". By a single bound, as it were, he reached from the depth of obscurity to the pinnacle of fame. Is it not remarkable, is it not significant, that of all the distinguished and famous men present at the Parliament of Religions only one name is remembered today, and that is the name of Vivekananda? There was, in sober fact, no other man like him in that assembly, composed though it was of distinguished representatives of all religions. Young in years, the Hindu monk had been disciplined with a thoroughness and severity beyond the experience of the other men who had gathered at the Parliament of Religions. He had had the inestimable advantage of having sat at the feet of a teacher the like of whom had not been seen in the world for many centuries. He had known poverty and hunger, and had moved among and sympathized with the poorest people in India, then one of the poorest countries in the world. He had drunk deep at the perennial fountain of the wisdom of the ancient Aryan rishis, and he was endowed with a courage which faced the world undismayed. When his voice rang out as a clarion in the Parliament of Religions, slow pulses quickened and thoughtful eyes brightened, for through him spoke voices that had long been silent but never stilled, and which awoke again to resonant life. Who in that assembly of the wise held higher credentials than this youthful monk from India with his commanding figure, strong, handsome face, large, flashing eyes, and the full voice with its deep cadences? In him was manifested the rejuvenescence of the wisdom and strength of ancient India, and the wide tolerance and sympathy characteristic of the ancient Aryans. The force and fire in him flashed out at every turn, and dominated and filled with amazement the people around him.

Other men from India had preceded him in the mission from the East to the West—men of culture, men of eloquence and religious convictions—but no other man created the profound impression that he did. These others assumed a tone which was either apologetic or deferential to the superiority of the West to the East. Some said they had come to learn and did not presume to teach, and all were more or less overawed by the dazzling magnificence of Western civilization. But Swami Vivekananda never had any doubts or misgivings, and he knew he came from a land which had produced most of the great and wise teachers of men. The glitter of the West held no lure for him, and his voice never lost the ring of authority. Besides the people anxious to profit by his teachings, there was a good deal of promiscuous admiration. There was the usual sheaf of romantic letters from gushing and impressionable young women, and well-meant offers of service from many quarters. A dentist offered to clean his teeth free of charge whenever necessary. A manicurist presented him with a set of his dainty instruments for which an Indian monk has no use. A more substantial offer was about a lecturing tour with a well-filled purse of shining dollars at the end of the tour. The money would have been useful for the monasteries afterwards established by Swami Vivekananda, but his vows precluded him from either earning or laying by any money.[5] Besides the open lectures that he delivered in America and England, he held what may be called informal classes attended by a small number of select people, usually earnest inquirers or people anxious to learn what the Swami had to teach. The actual number of his disciples in those countries was not large, but he set many

---

5. But he actually accepted the monetary offer of a lecture bureau and delivered lectures under it for some time in different cities of the U.S.A.

people thinking while his marvellous personality made itself felt wherever he went.

Swami Vivekananda had left India an obscure and unknown young man. On his return he was preceded by the fame he had won in America and England, and was acclaimed everywhere as an apostle and leader of the ancient Aryan faith. At Chennai he was given an enthusiastic reception. Some of the organizers of his public reception at Kolkata thoughtfully sent him a bill of expenses incurred. Swami Vivekananda mentioned this incident to me with indignation. "What have I to do with any reception?" he told me. "Those people fancied I have brought a great deal of money from America to be spent on demonstrations in my honour. Do they take me for a showman or a charlatan?" He felt humiliated as well as indignant.

On his return to India earnest young men came to him to join the Ramakrishna Mission founded by him. They took the vows of celibacy and poverty, and they established monasteries in various parts of India. There are some monasteries in America also so that Swami Vivekananda's work in that part of the world is still carried on, and his memory is held in great reverence. Swami Vivekananda told me that the Paramahamsa insisted on celibacy and moral purity as the essence of self-discipline, and this is equally noticeable among Swami Vivekananda's disciples and those who have joined the Brotherhood after his passing. Every member of the Ramakrishna Mission is pure of heart and pure in life, cultured and scholarly, and is engaged in serving his fellow men to the best of his ability, and society is the gainer by their example and their selfless and silent service.

The last time I met Swami Vivekananda before he left for the United States was in 1886. I happened to be in Kolkata on a brief visit and one afternoon I received intimation that Ramakrishna Paramahamsa had passed into the final and eternal samadhi. I immediately drove to the Cossipore garden-house in a northern suburb of Kolkata where the Paramahamsa had passed his last days on earth. He was lying on a clean white bed in front of the portico of the house, while his disciples, Vivekananda among them with his eyes veiled with unshed tears, and some other persons were seated on the ground surrounding the bedstead. The Paramahamsa was lying on his right side with the infinite peace and calm of death on his features. There was peace all around, in the silent trees and the waning afternoon, in the azure of the sky above with a few clouds passing overhead in silence. And as we sat in reverent silence, hushed in the presence of death, a few large drops of rain fell. This was the *pushpa vrishti*, or the rain of flowers of which the ancient Aryans wrote, the flowers showered by the gods as a homage at the passing away of some chosen mortal to rank thenceforth among the immortals. It was a great privilege to have seen Ramakrishna Paramahamsa while he was alive and also to have looked upon the serenity of his face in death.

It was not till eleven years later in 1897 that I met Vivekananda again. He was then famous alike in the East and the West. He had travelled widely, seen many countries and many peoples. I was at Lahore and I heard he was staying at the hill station of Dharamsala. Later he went to Jammu and next came down to Lahore. There was to be a reception and a house had been engaged for him. When the train came in at the railway station, I noticed an English military officer alighting from a first class compartment and respectfully holding the door open for someone else, and the next second out stepped Swami Vivekananda on the platform. The officer was about to move away after bowing to the Swami, but Vivekananda cordially shook hands with him and spoke one or two parting words. On inquiry Vivekananda told me that he did not know the officer personally. After entering the compartment he had informed Swami Vivekananda that he had heard some of the Swami's discourses in England and that he was a colonel in the Indian Army. Vivekananda had travelled first class because the people at Jammu had bought him a first class ticket. The same night Vivekananda came to my house with two of his disciples. That night and the following nights and during the day whenever I was free we talked for long hours, and what struck me most was the intensity of Vivekananda's feelings and his passionate devotion to the cause of his country. There was a perfect blending of his spiritual fervour with his intellectual keenness. He had in an unusual degree the prophetic vision, and he had grappled with many problems and had found a solution for most of them. "The middle classes in India," he said, "are a spent force. They don't have the stamina for a resolute and sustained endeavour. The future of India rests with the masses." One afternoon he slowly came near me with a thoughtful expression on his face and said, "If it would help the country in any way, I am quite prepared to go to prison." I looked at him and wondered. Instead of making the remotest reference to the laurels still green upon his brow, he was wistfully thinking of life in prison as a consummation to be wished, a service whereby his country might win some small profit. He was not bidding for the martyr's crown, for any sort of pose was utterly foreign to his nature, but his thoughts were undoubtedly tending towards finding redemption for his country through suffering. No one had then heard of Non-cooperation or Civil Disobedience, and yet Vivekananda, who had nothing to do with politics, was standing in the shadow of events still long in coming. His visit to Japan had filled him with enthusiastic admiration for the patriotism of the Japanese people. "Their country is their religion," he would declare, his face aglow with enthusiasm. "Their national cry is: *Dai Nippon, Banzai!*—Live long, great Japan! The country before and above everything else. No sacrifice is too great for maintaining the honour and integrity of the country."

One evening Vivekananda and myself were invited for dinner by a Punjabi gentleman (the late Bakshi Jaishi Ram), who had met Vivekananda at Dharamsala, a hill station in the Punjab. Vivekananda was offered a new and handsome hookah to smoke. Before doing so, he told his host, "If you have any prejudices of caste, you should not offer me your hookah, because if a sweeper were to offer me his hookah tomorrow, I would smoke it with pleasure, for I am outside the pale of caste." His host courteously replied that he would feel honoured if Swamiji smoked his hookah. The problem of untouchability had been solved for Swami Vivekananda during his wanderings in India. He had eaten the food of the poorest and humblest people whom no bigoted person would condescend to touch, and he had accepted their hospitality with thankfulness. And yet Swami Vivekananda was by no means a meek man. In the course of his lecture on the Vedanta at Lahore, one of the loftiest of his utterances, he declared with head uplifted and nostrils dilated, "I am one of the proudest men living." And it was not pride of the usual worthless variety but the noble pride of the consciousness of a great heritage, a revulsion of feeling against the false humility that had brought his country and his people so low.

I met Goodwin, the young Englishman who at one time was on the high road to become a wastrel, but fortunately came under Vivekananda's influence and became one of his staunchest and most devoted followers. Goodwin was a fast and accurate stenographer and most of Vivekananda's lectures were reported by him. He was simple as a child and wonderfully responsive to the slightest show of kindness. Later I met some of the lady disciples of Swami Vivekananda—Mrs. Ole Bull, Miss MacLeod, and Miss Margaret Noble, the gifted young Irishwoman to whom Vivekananda had given the beautifully appropriate name of Nivedita, the "offered one", one dedicated and consecrated to the service of India. I first met Sister Nivedita at Srinagar in Kashmir and next at Lahore where I saw a great deal of her, and again in Kolkata where she came to my house more than once. I took her through the slums of Lahore and showed her the Ramlila,[6] which greatly interested her. She made eager inquiries about everything relating to India. She was in splendid health when she first came to India, but the austerities which she practised affected her health, and she

6. A dramatic presentation of Shri Ramachandra's life.

rapidly spent herself and was spent in the service of India. Of her fine intellect and gift of literary expression she has left abiding evidence in her exquisite books.

In conversation Vivekananda was brilliant, illuminating, arresting, and the range of his knowledge was exceptionally wide. His country occupied a great deal of his thoughts and his conversation. His deep spiritual experiences were the bedrock of his faith and his luminous expositions are to be found in his lectures, but his patriotism was as deep as his religion. Except those who saw it, few can realize the ascendancy and influence of Swami Vivekananda over his American and English disciples. Even a simple Mohammedan cook who had served Sister Nivedita and other lady disciples at Almora was amazed by it. He told me at Lahore, "The respect and devotion which these Memsahebs (foreign ladies) show Swamiji are far greater than that which any disciple shows to his religious preceptor among us." At the sight of this Indian monk, wearing a single robe and a pair of rough Indian shoes, his disciples from the West, among whom were the Consul General for the United States living in Kolkata and his wife, would rise with every mark of respect; and when he spoke, he was heard with the closest and most respectful attention. His slightest wish was a command and was carried out forthwith. And Vivekananda was always his simple and great self, unassuming, straightforward, earnest, and grave. Once at Almora he was visited by a distinguished and famous Englishwoman whom he had criticized for her appearance in the role of a teacher of the Hindu religion. She wanted to know wherein she had given cause for offence. "You English people," replied Swami Vivekananda, "have taken our land. You have taken away our liberty and reduced us to a state of servility in our own homes. You are draining the country of its material resources. Not content with all this, you want to take our religion—which is all that we have left—in your keeping and to set up as teachers of our religion." His visitor earnestly explained that she was only a learner and did not presume to be a teacher. Vivekananda was mollified and afterwards presided at a lecture delivered by this lady.

The next year I met Swami Vivekananda in Kashmir, our houseboats being anchored near each other on the river Jhelum. On his way back to Kolkata he was my guest for a few days at Lahore. At this time he had a prescience of early death. "I have three years more to live," he told me with perfect unconcern, "and the only thought that disturbs me is whether I shall be able to give effect to all my ideas within this period." He died almost exactly three years later. The last time I saw him was at the monastery at Belur shortly before his death. It was the birth anniversary of Ramakrishna Paramahamsa, and I saw Swami Vivekananda when the samkirtana was at its height, rolling in the dust and heaping dust on his head in a paroxysm of frenzied grief.

His thoughts ranged over every phase of the future of India, and he gave all that was in him to his country and to the world. The world will rank him among the prophets and princes of peace, and his message has been heard in reverence in three continents. For his countrymen he has left a priceless heritage of virility, abounding vitality, and invincible strength of will. Swami Vivekananda stands on the threshold of the dawn of a new day for India, a heroic and dauntless figure, the herald and harbinger of the glorious hour when India shall, once again, sweep forward to the van of the nations.

(Prabuddha Bharata, March & April 1927)

BAL GANGADHAR TILAK

Bal Gangadhar Tilak

About year 1892, i.e., before the famous Parliament of Religions in the World's Fair at Chicago, I was once returning from Mumbai to Poona. At the Victoria Terminus a sannyasi entered the carriage I was in. A few Gujarati gentlemen were there to see him off. They made the formal introduction and asked the sannyasi to reside at my house during his stay at Poona. We reached Poona, and the sannyasi remained with me for eight or ten days. When asked about his name he only said he was a sannyasi. He made no public speeches here. At home he would often talk about the Advaita philosophy and Vedanta. The Swami avoided mixing with society. There was absolutely no money with him. A deerskin, one or two clothes and a kamandalu were his only possessions. In his travels someone would provide a railway ticket for the desired station.

The Swami happened to express a strong hope that as the women in Maharashtra were not handicapped by the purdah system, it was probable that some of the widows in the higher classes would devote their lives to the spread of spirituality and religion alone like the old yogis of the Buddhist period. The Swami also believed like me that the *Srimad Bhagavad Gita* did not preach renunciation but urged everyone to work unattached and without the desire for fruits of the work.

I was at that time a member of the Deccan Club in the Hirabag, which used to hold weekly meetings. The Swami accompanied me at one of these meetings. That evening the late Kashinath Govindanath made a fine speech on a philo-

187

sophical subject. No one had to say anything in reply. But the Swami rose and spoke in fluent English presenting the other aspect of the subject very lucidly. Every one present there was thus convinced of his great abilities. The Swami left Poona very soon after this.

Two or three years later Swami Vivekananda returned to India with world-wide fame owing to his grand success at the Parliament of Religions, and, after that, both in England and America. He received an address of welcome wherever he went and on every one of such occasions he made a thrilling reply. I happened to see his likeness in some of the newspapers, and from the similarity of features I thought that the same Swami had resided at my house. I wrote to him accordingly, inquiring if my inference was correct, and requesting him to kindly pay a visit to Poona on his way to Kolkata. I received a fervent reply in which the Swami admitted that he was the same sannyasi and expressed his regret at not being able to visit Poona then. This letter is not available. It must have been destroyed along with many others, public and private, after the close of the Kesari Prosecution of 1897.

Once after this, during one of the Congress sessions at Kolkata, I had gone with some friends to see the Belur Math of the Ramakrishna Mission. There Swami Vivekananda received us very cordially. We took tea. In the course of our conversation Swamiji happened to remark in a somewhat jocular spirit that it would be better if I renounced the world and took up his work in Bengal while he would go and continue the same in Maharashtra. "One does not carry," he said, "the same influence in one's own province as in a distant one."

(*Vedanta Kesari*, January 1934)

Haripada Mitra

Dear reader, if you wish to enjoy reading a few pages of my reminiscences of Swami Vivekananda, you must bear with me for a while till I have given you some idea about the sort of man I was before I met the Swami, the conceptions I had of religion, my education, and my nature in general. Unless you have this background, you will not understand what I gained from my contact with Swamiji. Before I passed the Entrance (High School) Examination, I had not the faintest idea about religion; but when I reached the fourth class, and had a smattering of English, I developed a great dislike for the Hinduism of our days, and this though I had not studied in any missionary school! After passing the Entrance Examination, it became quite impossible for me to subscribe to the Hinduism that I knew. Then during my college life, that is to say, when I was between nineteen and twenty-five, I read a little of physics, chemistry, botany, and other branches of science, and had a little acquaintance with Western thinkers like Darwin, Mill, Huxley, Tyndall, and Spencer. The result was what could be expected from ill-digested knowledge—I became an out and out atheist. I believed in nothing, and I knew nothing about devotion to God. I then condemned all religions, though mentally; and I thought that others were inferior to me intellectually.

At this time, the Christian missionaries began to visit me very often. While condemning other religions, they, with great intellectual acumen, argued for me that faith is the *sine qua non* of religion. In Christianity, one must start with faith, and then only one can appreciate its unique-ness, as well as its superiority to other religions. But such a queer approach and scholasticism could hardly convert me, a sworn atheist that I was then. Western education had taught me, "Do not believe in anything without evidence", whereas the missionaries said, "First faith and then proof". I remained unconvinced. Then they said, "You should read the Bible attentively, then you will have faith." I followed the advice, and it was my good fortune that I had quite a number of distinguished missionaries to help me. Still faith was far away from me. Nevertheless, some of them said that I had advanced considerably and had imbibed faith in Christianity, but that my orthodoxy was standing in the way of my conversion. The net result was that I began to doubt my doubt itself. As a way out of this impasse, they suggested that they would answer ten questions put by me; that as each question was answered satisfactorily, they would take my signature on it; and that when the last question would be answered to my satisfaction, I should embrace Christianity. It so happened that soon after finishing the third question, I left the college and entered the world. Even after this, I continued to read religious literature and visit places of worship—churches, temples, and Brahmo prayer halls. But I could not chalk out a path for myself. At last, I came to the conclusion that nobody really knew anything about the soul or its existence after death, that one can get some solace in this life by holding on to some religion, whatever it may be, and that faith in any particular religion comes as a matter of habit. As a matter of fact, nobody can convincingly prove or disprove religion with the help of reasoning.

Fortune was in my favour, and I got an employment with a high salary. I now led a comfortable life. Yet a strange want made me uneasy. Thus days, months, and years rolled on.

Belgaum, Tuesday, October 18, 1892: It was about two hours past evening, when a stout young monk with a cheerful countenance came to my house with a lawyer friend of mine of the same locality. The friend introduced him with the words, "Here is a learned Bengali monk who has come to meet you." I turned and found a serene figure with eyes flashing like lightning and a face clean-shaven. His body was covered with an ochre robe; on his feet he had strapped sandals of the Maharashtrian type; and on his head was an ochre turban. The figure was so impressive that it is still vivid in my memory. It pleased me and attracted me, though I did not realize then why it was so. After a while, I saluted him and said: "Sir, do you smoke? I am a kayastha, and I have but one hookah. If you have no objection to smoke from it, I can have some tobacco prepared for you." He replied: "I smoke whatever comes to hand—tobacco from a hookah or cigarette. And I have no objection in smoking from your hookah." I ordered for some tobacco.

My belief at that time was that all monks in ochre robes were cheats, and I naturally thought that this one, too, had come to me with some motive. Besides, my lawyer friend belonged to Maharashtra, while he was a Bengali. It was inconvenient for Bengalis to live with Maharashtrians: and that was why he had come to live with me. Despite all such thoughts passing through my mind, I invited him to stay with me and asked him whether his belongings should be brought to my house. He replied: "I am quite at home with the lawyer; and if I leave him just because I have found a Bengali, he will be hurt, for they all love and respect me. But I shall think about it and let you know later." We did not talk much that night. But the few words that he spoke convinced me that he was more learned and intelligent than myself. He could have earned a decent sum if he wanted, but he did not touch money. Although he had not the wherewithal to make himself happy, he was, in fact, a thousand times happier than I was. It struck me that he had no want, just because he had no thought for any personal gain. When I learnt that he would not come to my house, I said, "If you have no objection to take tea with me, I shall be happy to have you here in the morning." He agreed and went back with the lawyer. At night I was thinking about him for a long time—I had never before met a man so free from wants, so happy and content, and having such a smiling face. I believed that a man without wealth might as well depart from this world, and that a monk truly free from wants is an impossibility; but that belief got a shaking today, which left it rather weak.

October 19, 1892: I had been waiting for Swamiji from six o'clock in the morning. It struck eight. So without waiting any longer, I left for Swamiji's place with a friend. There we found him seated in the midst of a respectable gathering of lawyers and other learned men, and conversing with them. He answered their questions without the slightest hesitation, sometimes in English and sometimes in Hindi or Sanskrit. There were also people like myself who accepted Huxley's philosophy as their Bible, and started arguing with Swamiji on that basis. But he silenced them all either through repartees or serious dissertation. As I sat there after saluting him, I was thinking, "Is he a man or a god?" So I could not remember all that I heard. I write down only the few words that come to my mind.

A very respectable lawyer asked: "The mantras we chant in our morning and evening prayers are in Sanskrit, and we do not at all understand them. Is it of any use to go on uttering them?"

Swamiji replied: "They do have good results. Born in a Brahmin family as you are, you can easily learn the meaning of those few mantras. If you do not do so, who is to blame? Even if you do not understand the meaning, I hope, when you sit for prayer, you have the feeling that you are doing something virtuous and not sinful. If you have the belief that you are doing something meritorious, that in itself is enough to yield good results."

Just then somebody said, "Talks on religious matters should not be carried on in a foreign language, since it is prohibited in such-and-such a Purana." Swamiji replied, "It is good to talk of religious things, no matter what the language is." In support of this he quoted from the Vedas and added,

"A judgement passed by a High Court cannot be set at naught by a lower court."[1]

Thus it went on till it struck nine, when those who had to attend office or court left, while others still sat there. Swamiji's eyes now fell on me, and he said: "My son, I had not the heart to disappoint so many people and go to your place. Please don't mind." When I pressed him to come and stay with me, he replied at last, "I shall go if you can make my host agree to your proposal." So I persuaded the lawyer friend somehow and returned to my place with Swamiji. His belongings consisted only of a kamandalu and a book wrapped in a piece of ochre cloth. Swamiji was then studying French music. We had our tea at ten o'clock after reaching home. He understood my hesitation in expressing my own doubts, and so he himself gauged my intellectual make-up through a few words.

Some time earlier, somebody had published a poem in the *Times* asserting that it was extremely difficult to determine what is God, which religion is true, and such other abstruse questions. As that poem had much affinity to my religious ideas of those days, I preserved it carefully. I now produced it before him. He read it and remarked, "The man has become confused". Gradually I got over my hesitation. From the Christian missionaries I had not got any solution of the contradiction involved in holding that God is both just and merciful; and I feared that Swamiji, too, could throw no better light on the problem. When I put the question to him, he said: "I think you have read much of science. Do not two opposite forces, centripetal and centrifugal—act in each material substance? If such a contradiction can exist in matter, may not justice and mercy be reconciled in God? All I can say is that you have a poor idea of your God." I was silenced. Again, I believed that truth is absolute, and that all religions cannot be true at the same time. In answer to such questions he said:

---

1. The Vedas are more authoritative than the Puranas.

"All we know about things now or may know in future are but relative truths. It is impossible for our limited mind to grasp the absolute truth. Hence, though truth is absolute, it appears variously to diverse minds and intellects. All these facets or modes of truth belong to the same class as truth itself, they being based on the same absolute truth. This is like different photographs of the same sun taken from various distances. Each of them seems to represent a different sun. The diverse relative truths have the same kind of relation with the absolute truth. Each religion is thus true, just because it is a mode of presentation of the absolute religion."

When I said that faith is the basis of all religions, Swamiji smiled a little and said: "A man goes beyond all wants once he becomes a king; but the difficulty is how to become one. Can faith be infused from outside? Nobody can have real faith unless he has personal experience." When in the course of talk I called him a sadhu, he said: "Are we really so? There are holy men whose very sight or touch wakes up spirituality in others."

Again I asked: "Why do monks idle away their time in this way? Why do they depend on the charity of others? Why don't they undertake some work beneficial to society?" Swamiji said:

"Now, look here. You are earning this money with such struggle, of which only a little portion you spend on yourself; and some of it you spend for others who, you think, are your own. But they neither acknowledge any gratefulness for what you do for them, nor are they satisfied with what they get. The balance you save like the mythological yaksha[2] who never enjoys it. When you die, somebody else will enjoy it all; and perchance, he will abuse you for not having accumulated more. This is your condition. On the other hand, I do nothing. When I feel hungry, I let others know by gestures that I want food; and I eat whatever I get. Neither do I struggle nor do I save. Now, tell me who among us is the

_____

2. A kind of demigod.

wiser—you or I?" I was astonished, for before this nobody had dared to talk to me so boldly and frankly.

After lunch we had some rest. Then we went to the house of that lawyer friend, where we had more of such discussion. At nine o'clock at night we returned home. On the way I said, "Swamiji, you must have been greatly bored today by all this argumentation."

He replied: "My son, would you have offered me even a morsel of food if I had kept mum, the out and out utilitarians that you all are? I go on chattering like this. People get amused, and so they crowd around me. But know it for certain that people who argue, or put such questions before an assembly are not at all eager to know the truth. I also recognize their motives and answer accordingly."

"Swamiji," I put in, "how do you get such ready and pointed answers for all the questions?"

"These questions are new to you," he said, "but these have been put to me before and I had to answer them times without number."

The conversation continued during dinner. He told me of the many adventures he had during his travels through the country under a vow of not touching money. As I listened, it struck me that he must have endured great hardship and trouble; and yet he related them with a smile, as though it was all great fun! Sometimes he went without food; sometimes he ate so much chillies that for lessening the burning sensation in the stomach he had to drink a cupful of tamarind water! At some places he was curtly turned away with the remark, "monks have no place here." Sometimes he was shadowed by government spies. Many other incidents he related in great glee, which were great fun to him, but they made my blood curdle. As the night had advanced very far, I spread a bed for him and then retired for the night. But I had no sleep. I wondered how the deep-rooted doubts that had haunted me all these years took flight at the very sight of Swamiji. Now I had nothing more to ask. As days passed by, not only my family, but also our servants developed such love and respect for Swamiji, and they served him so meticulously, that he became rather embarrassed.

October 20, 1892: In the morning I saluted Swamiji. Now I had more boldness as also more devotion. Swamiji, too, was pleased to hear from me many accounts of forests, rivers, hills, and valleys. He had now been in this town for four days. On the fifth day he said: "A monk must not live in a town for more than three days, and in a village for more than four days. I want to leave soon." I would not listen to all that; I was determined to argue it all away. After a long discussion he said: "If one stays at one place for long, one develops attachment for others. We have left our home and friends. It is but proper for us to be away from all such sources of maya." I entreated him to stay on and argued that he would never fall into maya's snares. At last he agreed to stay for a couple of days more.

In the meantime I thought that if Swamiji addressed a public gathering, we would get the benefit of his wisdom and others also would gain thereby. I pressed him for this, but he would not agree on the plea that such platform speeches might generate in him a desire for name and fame. At the same time he intimated that he would have no objection to a public conversation.

One day, in the course of a talk, Swamiji quoted verbatim some two or three pages from the *The Pickwick Papers*. I wondered at this, not understanding how a monk could get by heart so much from a secular book. I thought that he must have read it quite a number of times before he took orders. When questioned he said, "I have read it twice—once when I was in school, and again some five or six months earlier." "Then how do you remember so much," I asked in wonder, "and why can we not remember thus?" "One has to read with full attention," he explained, "and one must not fritter away the energy one gets from food."

Another day, Swamiji was reading a book all by himself, reclining in his bed. I was in another room. Suddenly he laughed so loudly that I thought that there must be some

occasion for such a laughter, and so I advanced to his door
to find that nothing special had happened; he continued to
read as before. I stood there for some fifteen minutes; still he
did not notice me. His mind was completely riveted on the
book. Later, he noticed me and asked me to come in. When
he heard that I had been standing there for a pretty long
time, he said: "Whatever one has to do, one must apply to it
one's whole attention and energy for the time being. Pavhari
Baba of Ghazipur would clean his brass water vessel with
the same undivided attention with which he did meditation,
japa, worship, study, etc. He cleaned it so diligently that it
shone like gold."

Once I asked Swamiji: "Why is stealing considered to be
a sin? Why do all religions prohibit stealing? It seems to me
that to think that one thing belongs to me and another to
somebody else is only a figment of imagination. As a matter
of fact, if one of my relatives should take away one of my
things without informing me it is not called stealing. Besides,
we do not call it stealing when the birds or animals snatch
away anything."

"It is true," said Swamiji, "that no act can be regarded
as stealing at all times and under all circumstances. Again,
every act may be considered wrong or even sinful under
altered conditions. You should not do anything that brings
misery to others, or weakens you physically or morally.
That is sinful and its opposite is virtuous. Just think of this:
Don't you feel sorry when somebody steals something from
you? What is true for you, you should know, is true for the
whole world. If you can be so bad as to inflict some pain on
some being in this world, though you are fully aware that
everything here is evanescent, you will gradually come to
such a state that no sin will be too great for you. Again, social
life becomes impossible if there is no division of virtue and
vice. When you live in society, you have to comply with its
rules and regulations. If you retire to a forest, you can go
about dancing naked; that harms nobody, and none will stop
you. But should you behave in such a manner in a town,

the reasonable thing to do will be to get you arrested by the police and have you locked up in some solitary place!"

Swamiji sometimes imparted very valuable lessons through humour or ridicule. Though he was my guru, to sit by him was not just like sitting before a schoolmaster. He would be merry and full of fun, just like a boy, even when imparting instruction. He laughed and made others laugh with him. Then, suddenly, he would start explaining an intricate problem with such seriousness that people wondered at his mastery over the subject and over himself. They used to think, "Did we not find him just now as but one like ourselves?" People would come to him at all hours for learning from him, and his door was always open. They had diverse motives. Some came to test him, some to enjoy his humorous talks, some others to be in closer contact with the rich people of the town who came to Swamiji, and still others to get a few moments' respite from the worries of the world, to hear his spiritual talks, and to be enlightened thereby. Such was his power of diving into others' minds that he understood their motives at once and dealt with them accordingly. Nobody could hide anything from his penetrating eyes. Once a boy from a rich family began to visit Swamiji just for the sake of avoiding his university examination, and said that he would become a monk. He happened to be the son of a friend of mine. I asked Swamiji: "Why does that boy come to you so frequently? Will you advise him to become a monk? His father is a friend of mine." Swamiji replied, "His examination is near at hand, and he wants to become a monk just to avoid the examination. I told him, 'Come to embrace the monastic life after passing the M.A. examination. It is easier to get an M.A. degree than to lead the life of a monk.'"

During Swamiji's stay at my house, so many people used to gather there in the evenings that it all looked like a big meeting. I shall never forget what he once told me while reclining against a bolster under a sandal-tree. As that subject requires a long introduction, I reserve it for a future occasion. Here I would like to add a few more words about myself.

Some time earlier my wife had expressed a desire to take initiation from someone, and I had told her: "Choose a guru who will command my respect as well. You will derive no benefit if the very arrival of your guru in the house creates some adverse feeling in me. We shall both be initiated together only if we come across a holy man, otherwise not." She too agreed to this. When Swamiji was with us, I asked her, "Would you like to be Swamiji's disciple?" "Will he really agree to be our guru?" she asked eagerly, and added, "If he agrees, we shall be only too grateful."

With great hesitation, I asked Swamiji one day, "Swamiji, will you fulfil a desire of mine?" When he wanted to know what it was, I requested him to initiate both of us. "For a householder, it is best to have some householder as his guru," he said. "It is very difficult to be a guru. The guru has to take the responsibility of the disciple. Before initiation the disciple must meet the guru at least three times." With these and other arguments he wanted to discourage me. But when he found that I was not to be dissuaded, he agreed. He initiated us on 25 October 1892. Then I desired to take his photograph, but he would not agree. I persisted, and after a long-drawn tussle, he gave his consent and a photograph was taken on the 28th. As Swamiji had not agreed to be photographed on an earlier occasion, in spite of the earnest request of another gentleman, I had to send two copies of this photograph to him on request.

In the course of a talk Swamiji said: "I have a great desire to spend a few days with you in a forest under a camp. But they are holding a Parliament of Religions at Chicago, and I shall go there if I get an opportunity." When I proposed to raise money by subscription, he refused it for some reason best known to himself. At this time, he was under a vow of not accepting or touching any money. After great effort I persuaded him to accept a pair of shoes in place of his Maharashtrian sandals as also a cane walking stick. Before this, the Rani of Kolhapur had not succeeded in making him accept any gift, and so she had sent him a pair of ochre clothes.

Swamiji accepted these and left behind the clothes he had been wearing with the remark, "A monk must not have a burden about him."

Before my contact with Swamiji, I had tried to read the *Gita* more than once. As I could not understand it, I concluded that there was really nothing to know from it, and so I gave up the attempt. One day Swamiji began to explain the *Gita* to us, and then I discovered what a wonderful book it was. As I learnt from him to appreciate the teachings of the *Gita*, so also I learnt from him to read the scientific novels of Jules Verne, and Sartor Resartus of Carlyle.

At that time I used to take medicines rather liberally. Observing this, Swamiji said: "When you find that some disease has made you bed-ridden, then only you should take medicines, not otherwise. Ninety per cent of such diseases as nervous debility are mere figments of imagination. The physicians kill more people suffering from such diseases than they save. What do you gain by thinking only of diseases? Be cheerful as long as you live. Never indulge in pleasures which tax the body or which make you repent. As regards death, what does it matter if one or two like you or me die; that will not make the earth deviate from its axis. We should never consider ourselves so important as to think that the world cannot go on without us."

Just then, for some reason or other, I was not pulling on well with my superiors in my office. Any little remark from them would make me lose my balance. Though I had a lucrative job, I could not be happy even for a day. When I told Swamiji about my difficulty, he remarked:

"Why are you in service? Is it not for the salary you get? You are getting it regularly every month, so why should you be upset? When you are free to resign at any moment you like, and nobody binds you down to it, why should you add to your miseries by thinking, "Oh, in what bondage am I placed!" Another thing: will you tell me whether, apart from doing the work for which you draw the salary, you ever did anything just to please your superiors? You never did so, and yet you are angry with them that they are not satisfied with you. Is that wise on your part? Know for certain that the ideas we entertain about others express themselves through our conduct; and even though we may not express these in words, people react accordingly. We see in the external world the image that we carry in our hearts. Nobody realizes how true the saying 'The world is good when I am good' is. From today try to get rid of the habit of finding fault with others, and you will find that, to the extent you succeed in this, the attitudes and reactions of others will also change accordingly."

Needless to say that, from that day, I got rid of the habit of taking too many medicines; and a new chapter in my life opened from my effort to give up faultfinding.

When the question was raised as to what was the definition of good and bad, Swamiji said: "What is conducive to the goal aimed at is good and what impedes it is bad. Our ideas of good and bad are just like our ideas of elevation and depression. As you rise higher, the distinction becomes obliterated. It is said that the moon has mountains and plains; but we see it all as a flat surface. It is just like that." Swamiji had this peculiar power that, whatever might be the question, his answer was so apt and ready that the hearer stood convinced.

Words fail to express the sorrow that Swamiji felt another day on reading the news that a man had died of starvation in Kolkata. Repeatedly he said, "Now the country is about to go to rack and ruin!" Being asked to explain, he said: "Don't you see that in other countries hundreds of people die every year, in spite of their poor-houses, work-houses, charity funds, etc.? But in our country we never heard of death through starvation just because of the system of alms-giving in vogue here. This is the first time I am reading in a newspaper that a man has died of starvation in Kolkata even when there is no famine."

As a result of my English education, I thought it a wastage of money to offer a paisa or two to beggars. My idea was that such petty help not only did no good to the recipients, but it also brought about their ruin by enabling them to smoke hemp with it. The only gain was that the giver's bill of expenditure went up by that amount! So I concluded that, instead of giving trifling amounts to many people, it is better to give somebody a big amount. When I asked Swamiji, he said:

"If a beggar approaches you, it is better to give him something according to your capacity. After all you will give only a paisa or two; so why should you rack your brain about what the man will do with it—whether he will spend it well or waste it? Even if he wastes it on hemp, it is to the advantage of society that he gets those few paisas; for unless people like you offer it to him willingly, he will steal it from you. If instead of that, he buys hemp, smokes a little, and then sits quietly, is it not to your own advantage? So even this kind of charity does only good to the society."

From the very beginning I found that Swamiji was very much against the system of child marriage. He always advised all, and particularly young men, to protest boldly against this social evil. Such patriotism, too, I had never seen in any other person. Those who met Swamiji after he returned from the West for the first time never knew how he had travelled through the length and breadth of India, observing all the rigorous vows of a monk and not touching money at all. When somebody suggested that a man of such a strong will as he had no need of so many rules and vows, he replied:

"Look here, the mind is like a madman and a drunkard. It can never remain quiet. If it gets the least opportunity, it will drag you after itself. To keep control over that mind, even a monk must observe rules. All are under the delusion that they have the fullest control over their minds and that they allow it some freedom knowingly. When one sits for meditation, one can very well understand how much control one really has over the mind. Even when one wants to think on a certain subject for some time, one cannot keep the mind fixed on that subject for so long as ten minutes. All are under the delusion that they are not henpecked and that it is only out of love that they allow their wives to exercise some influence over them. The belief that one has controlled the mind is just like that. Never relax yourself under the false belief that you are the master of your mind."

In the course of a talk one day I said, "Swamiji, it seems one must be highly educated in order to understand religion." He said: "One does not require any high education to understand religion for oneself; but one must have it if one has to explain it to others. Paramahamsa Ramakrishna signed his name as 'Ramkeshto', but who indeed knew the essence of religion better than him?"

I had an idea that monks and holy men could never be stout and ever contented. One day, when I gave expression to this with a smile and a dig at him, he answered in a bantering tone: "This is my famine insurance fund! Even if I do not get food for days on end, my fat will keep me alive, whereas your vision will be blurred due to weakness if you do not get food for a day. And a religion that cannot bring peace to men must be shunned as a disease brought about by dyspepsia."

Swamiji was a master in music. One day he started singing. I had no training to appreciate it; besides, how could I have the time to listen to it? We were charmed by his talks and stories. He was well acquainted with several branches of modern science—chemistry, physics, geology, astronomy, mixed mathematics, and so on, and he was able to solve our problems on all these subjects in a few words. He would explain intricate religious questions with the help and analogy of science. I never knew anybody else who could prove so convincingly that science and religion had the same goal in view and that their progress was also along the same path.

He liked chillies, pepper, and such other pungent things. When I once asked the reason for this, he said: "During his wanderings a monk has to take all kinds of food and drink water from all sorts of places, and these affect his health adversely. To counteract their bad effect, many monks become addicted to hemp and other intoxicants. For the same reason I have taken to chilli."

Many princes, including those of Rajasthan and the Deccan, greatly respected Swamiji, and he too loved them sincerely. Many could not understand why a monk of such strong principles should mix so much with princes and Rajas. Some foolish people even made sarcastic remarks regarding this. Asked about the reason, Swamiji explained one day: "Just compare the results one can achieve by instructing thousands of poor people and inducing them to adopt a certain line of action on the one hand, and by converting a prince to that point of view on the other. Where will they get the means for accomplishing a good project even if the poor subjects have a will to do it? A prince already has the power of doing good to his subjects; he only he lacks the will to do it. If you can once wake up that will in him, then, along with it, the fortune of his subjects will take a turn for the better, and society will be immensely benefited thereby."

To explain that religion does not consist in learned discussion, but in realization, he would say: "The proof of the pudding is in the eating. Religion is realization. Without that you can understand nothing." He had no kind word for a hypocritical monk, and would say: "One should renounce only after one has controlled one's mind while still at home. Otherwise one gets mixed up with the hemp-smoking monks once the first charm wears away." "But it is most difficult to have this at home," I intervened. "For instance, if I start practising all those virtues like considering all to be equal, giving up likes and dislikes, and so on, which you say are the best means for becoming a man of realization, then from the very next day, my servants, my subordinates, and even the members of my family will not leave me in peace even for a moment." In reply he related the parable of the snake and the holy man,[3] as narrated by Sri Ramakrishna,

---

3. A poisonous snake in a meadow became a terror to the cowherds and passers-by who had to cross it. At last a monk came that way, and as usual, the snake attacked him also. But the monk was more than a

and then added: "Never give up hissing. Go on with your work, thinking it to be your duty. Punish others when you have to; but don't be angry when inflicting punishment." Then he resumed the earlier topic and said: "Once I was the guest of a police inspector in a place of pilgrimage. He was a devoted and religious man. His salary was only Rs. 125 per month, whereas his monthly expenditure was about three hundred rupees. When we became more intimate, I asked him: 'Your expenditure seems to exceed your income. How do you manage?' 'Men like you manage it, sir,' said he with a smile. 'Don't think that all the monks who come to this place of pilgrimage are as good as yourself. Whenever any suspicion arises, I search their belongings; and often enough, much money is found. When any one of them is suspected of stealing, he at once takes to his heels leaving behind everything, which then comes to my possession. I do not resort to any other illegal means of income like accepting bribes, etc.'"

One day I had a very beautiful talk with Swamiji about infinity. He said: "There cannot be two infinites." When I said that time is infinite and so also is space, he replied: "I can understand that space is infinite, but I don't understand how time can be infinite. In any case, I can understand that only one thing can be infinite. If there be two infinites, how would you demarcate their respective spheres? If you advance further, you will find that time and space get lost in each other. Still further advance will show you that all things

---

match for it. He not only subdued the snake, but also got a promise from it that it would not bite people any more. The monk made the snake his disciple, gave it a mantra, and departed. The snake became so harmless from that day that the cowherd boys began to take liberties with it, till at last they gave it such a beating that it was all but dead. Somehow it dragged itself into its hole and lay there for days together, till at last the monk came that way once again. He called for the snake and searched for it, but it was nowhere to be found. Yet he knew that it could not die, the mantra would keep it alive. At last the snake somehow wriggled out of the hole and related the whole incident. The monk said, "The fool that you are! I asked you not to bite, but you could have hissed just to scare away the boys."

are infinite, but those infinite things are one in essence and not two."

Thus Swamiji's stay in my house till the 26th October turned it into a mart of joy. On the 27th he said: "I won't stay any more. I have been moving southward with a view to reach Rameshwaram." My further entreaties for keeping him back proved to be futile. On the 27th he decided to take the mail train for Marmagaon. I purchased a ticket for him. After seating him in the train, I saluted him and said, "Swamiji, till now I have never saluted anybody with wholehearted devotion, but I do so now and feel blessed thereby."

I met Swamiji only three times. The first meeting was before he left for America, about which I have already narrated. The second meeting was some time before he left for the West the second time, and the third meeting was some six or seven months before he left this world. It is impossible to present a detailed account of all that I learnt from him during these meetings. Many events are so personal that they cannot be related, while others escape my memory. Of the few things that I still remember, I shall present only those that may be of interest to the average reader.

I thought that in his lectures at Chennai just after his return from the West, in which he dealt with caste system, he was rather bitter against certain sections of the Hindu society. When I told him so, he replied: "I spoke only the truth and nothing but the truth. Taking into account the prevailing situation, the language was not at all harsh. I find no reason why truth should be diluted or hidden. Just because I criticized those customs does not mean that I have any ill feeling towards these people, nor should one think that I am the least sorry for what I have done out of a sense of duty. Neither of the two positions is true. I did not speak out of anger, nor do I regret now. Should the occasion arise again for performing such an unpleasant duty, I shall still do so without the least hesitation."

In my previous account I said something about his opinion of hypocritical monks. When that topic cropped up another day, he said: "It is true that many rogues adopt the monk's garb for concealing their nefarious deeds or for avoiding detection after some serious crime; but society, too, has its own share of the blame. Society labours under the false belief that a man goes beyond all shortcomings as soon as he takes the monk's vow. In your estimation, it is bad for him to have a full meal, bad to lie down on a bed; he must not even use such a common thing as an umbrella or a pair of shoes! Why, are monks not men like yourselves? It is quite wrong to think that one has no right to wear the ochre robe unless one is already a Paramahamsa (a monk of the highest realization). Once, I met a monk who had a fancy for good dress. You would have mistaken him for a luxurious man, but in reality he was a true monk."

Swamiji used to say:

"The mental attitudes and feelings of men differ very much according to time, space, and circumstances. Same is the case with religion. Then, again, each man has some prejudices, and every one in this world thinks himself to be wiser than others. That really matters little, but the difficulty arises when a person begins to think that the truth lies with none other than himself. Each one wants that others should look at a thing from his own point of view and understand it accordingly. He is convinced that nothing else but what he has known can be true. But nobody should allow such an idea to get hold of him, be it in the field of religion or secular knowledge.

"A single rule cannot equally apply to people of this world in any field whatsoever. For instance, you can notice that moral principles and even an appreciation of beauty differ according to time, space, and circumstances. In Tibet polyandry is in vogue. I came across such a family during my sojourn in the Himalayas. The family had six male members who had but one wife. When we became more friendly, I pointed out to them the outrageousness of the custom, at which they took offence and said: 'You are a monk, and yet you preach this kind of selfishness to people! Is it not wrong to think that something is meant only for oneself and not for others?'

"Every one knows that beauty among the Chinese is judged in accordance with the shortness of the nose and the smallness of the feet. The same kind of peculiar judgement prevails in the field of food. The English do not like the sweet-smelling rice that we like so much. Once when a judge of a certain place was transferred, the members of the bar sent all kinds of excellent food to him. Among these was a quantity of sweet smelling rice. When this was served to the judge, he thought it was rotten; and when he next met the lawyers, he said, 'You ought not to have given me rotten rice.'"

Once while travelling in a train, I had in the same compartment some four or five Europeans as my fellow passengers. In the course of a talk, I remarked that the best way to enjoy tobacco is to smoke it from a hookah full of water at the bottom and having at its top a lump of flavoured tobacco prepared with spices and molasses. I had some such tobacco, and I showed it to them. They smelt it and said, 'It emits such a bad smell, and you call it good flavour!' Thus, opinions about smell, taste, beauty, etc. differ among men according to time, place, and social environment."

It did not take me long to appreciate these words of Swamiji. I remembered how I loved hunting in my earlier days. Whenever I saw any animal or bird, I used to become restless to kill it, and would feel miserable if I failed to do so. Now I do not like killing at all. So likes and dislikes are a matter of habit.

Each man has a tendency to stick to his own views dogmatically, and this is particularly true in religious matters. About this, Swamiji used to tell us a story:

Once a king advanced with his army against a smaller kingdom. Naturally, a big council was summoned in the small kingdom to devise ways and means for its protection from the enemy. All classes of people were represented—engineers, carpenters, cobblers, blacksmiths, pleaders, priests, etc. The engineers advised, "Put a barricade around the kingdom and dig a deep trench." The carpenters said, "Raise a wooden wall." The cobblers said, "There is nothing like leather; put a barricade of leather." The blacksmiths said, "All this will be of no avail. An iron wall is the best thing, for shots cannot penetrate through it." The pleaders said: "No such thing need be erected. Let us convince the enemy by arguments that he has no right to conquer our country." The priests said: "You are all raving like lunatics. Offer sacrifices and perform other rites for warding off this evil, and the enemy will be baffled in his attempt." The result was that the councillors went on debating and nothing was done to save the kingdom. This is human nature.

The story reminded me of another incident. I told this to Swamiji: "Swamiji, as a boy, I liked very much to talk with lunatics. Once I came across a madman who seemed to be very intelligent. He knew a little English, and all that he wanted was to drink water. He had a broken water pot with him, with which he used to drink water wherever he got it, no matter whether it was a ditch or a lake. When I asked him why he drank so much water, he replied, 'Nothing like water, sir.' I wanted to give him a good water pot, but he would not accept it. When asked for the reason, he explained that he had the broken one with him for so long just because it was broken. If it had been a good one, it would have been stolen long ago."

When I had finished, Swamiji remarked: "He must have been a very funny lunatic. They are called monomaniacs. Each one of us has such prejudices. Only, we have the power to conceal it, whereas the unbalanced man lacks that power. That's where we differ from the madmen. A man comes to grief once he loses that self-control through disease, sorrow, egotism, passion, anger, jealousy, or any kind of self-indulgence or oppression. Then he fails to suppress his feeling, and we say that he is off his head. That's all that it means."

I have mentioned earlier about Swamiji's great patriotism. Once somebody told him that though it was a duty for lay people leading a social life to have love for their country, a monk should be above any attachment for his own country and that he should rather love all countries and pray for the good of all. I shall never forget the burning reply that these words evoked from Swamiji. He said, "How can a man who does not feed his own mother look after other people's mothers?" Swamiji admitted that there were many defects in our current religious practices, habits, and social customs; and he would say: "It is our bounden duty to try to rectify them by all means; but that does not mean that it is necessary to tell the English people about all these things by publishing them in the newspapers. There is no greater fool than one who washes one's dirty linen in public."

One day we started talking about the Christian missionaries, and I happened to remark that they had done, and had been doing, a great deal of good to our country. At this he said: "But the amount of evil they have done is no less. They have done all in their power to make people lose the little faith they had in themselves and their own culture. Loss of faith means disintegration of the personality itself. Does anybody understand that? How can the missionaries prove the superiority of their own religion without decrying our deities, without condemning our religion? There is another point to consider. If anyone has to preach a particular religion, he must not only believe in it fully, but also practise it in life with full faith and sincerity. Most of the missionaries say one thing and do something else. I can never tolerate hypocrisy."

One day he said some very fine things about religion and yoga. I shall reproduce the substance of these as far as I can:

"All creatures are ever eager to get happiness. They are eternally engaged in this effort, but they are seldom seen to arrive at the goal. Yet most people do not stop to find out why they fail. That is why men suffer. Whatever ideas a man may have about religion, nobody should try to shake his faith so long as he himself sincerely believes that he is deriving real happiness thereby. Even if one tries to rectify another, it does not yield any good result unless the man himself cooperates willingly. Whatever one's profession may be, when you find that a man is eager merely to hear of religion, but not to practise it, you may at once conclude that he has no firm faith in anything.

"The basic aim of religion is to bring peace to man. It is not a wise thing for one to suffer in this life so that one can be happy in the next. One must be happy here and now. Any religion that can bring that about is the true religion for humanity. Sense-enjoyment is momentary, and it is inevitably mixed with sorrow. Only children, fools, and animals believe this transitory pleasure to be real bliss. Even so, I won't mind if anybody can have perpetual happiness and freedom from anxiety by regarding that pleasure as the be-all and end-all of life. But I have still to find such a man. Rather, in common experience, it is found that those who mistake sense-enjoyment for the highest bliss become jealous of others who happen to be richer or more luxurious than themselves. They suffer due to their hankering for more refined sense-enjoyment. After conquering the world, Alexander the Great felt miserable at the thought that he had no other country to conquer. That is why thoughtful men, after long experience and examination, have decided that men can be really happy and free from anxiety only when they have full faith in some religion or other.

"Men naturally differ in their intellects and attainments. So religion also must differ according to men's temperaments; else they will never get any satisfaction from it, nor will they derive the highest benefit from it. A person has to find out for himself the religion that will suit his nature through a process of careful thinking, testing, and experimentation. There is no other way. Study of religious literature, instructions of the guru, company of holy men, etc. can only help him in his quest.

"About work also, it should be understood that nobody can stay without doing any work, and no work can be either wholly good or wholly bad. If you do some good work, you are bound to do some amount of evil also. As a result, along with the happiness derived from the good work, some amount of unhappiness and dissatisfaction also will come inevitably. If you want to avoid that, you will have to give up the hope of deriving the apparent happiness from sense-enjoyment, that is to say, you will have to give up all selfish motives and go on doing your work out of a sense of duty. That is what is called 'work without motive' (selfless work). While instructing Arjuna about this in the *Gita*, Sri Krishna says, 'Work, but dedicate its fruit to Me', that is to say, 'Work for Me'."

I asked Swamiji one day whether Sri Krishna instructing Arjuna on the eve of the battle of Kurukshetra was a historical event. What he said in reply is very charming:

"The *Gita* is a very old book. In ancient times there was no fuss about writing history or getting books printed; so it is difficult to prove the historicity of the *Gita* to men like you. Still, I see no reason why you should rack your brains about the authenticity of the *Gita*. Even if somebody were to prove to you with incontrovertible facts that the *Gita* represents the actual words of Sri Krishna as told to Arjuna, will you really believe in all that is written in that book? Even if God Himself incarnates and comes to teach you, you will challenge Him to prove His divinity, and you will apply your own arguments to disprove His claim. So why should you be worried about the authenticity of the *Gita*? If you can, accept as far as lies in your power the teachings of the *Gita* and apply them in your life. That will be of real benefit to you. Sri Ramakrishna used to say, 'If you happen to be in a mango garden, eat as many of the luscious fruits as you can; what need have you to count the leaves?' It seems to me that any belief or disbelief in the events recorded in a religious book is determined by a personal equation. When somebody falls into certain circumstances and finds that his condition is similar to some incident mentioned in the book concerned, he believes that the incident must be true; and then he eagerly adopts the means prescribed by the book for tiding over the difficulty."

One day he explained to us in a very attractive way the need for conserving one's physical and mental energy for the adequate discharge of one's duty. He said, "One who wastes one's energy in interfering in other people's affairs and in other aimless activities can hardly have any energy left for performing a desirable duty. The sum total of the energy that can be exhibited by a person is a fixed quantity. As such, if it finds an outlet in a useless way, it can no further be used for any purposeful activity. One requires tremendous energy to realize the deeper truths of religion. That is why the religious books of all races advise the aspirants not to waste their energy in the enjoyment of sense-objects, but to preserve it through continence and other means."

Swamiji disliked some of the customs prevailing in the villages of Bengal. He was disgusted with the habit of using the same reservoir of water for drinking as for bathing and washing clothes. He often said, "What can you expect from those whose brains are filled with all the dirt in the world? And the rural habit of interfering in other people's affairs is extremely bad. Not that the urban people don't have that habit. But they don't have much time to spare, for urban life is costly and it means harder labour. After the day's hard labour, they do not have much time left for playing chess while smoking and gossiping about other people. Were it not so, the urban people would have outdone the rural people in such matters."

A volume could be filled if what Swamiji taught in a single day had been recorded. It was not his habit to give the same kind of reply to the same question or to repeat the same illustration. Whenever he had any occasion to deal with the same question he threw such new light on it and used such new similes and illustrations that it seemed altogether a fresh subject and a fresh way of explaining it. As a result, his talks never bored anyone; rather the interest increased and people sat spellbound. In his public speeches also he used the same method. It was not his habit to think over the whole matter earlier and jot down points on paper.

Even a minute before the speech he would be talking on all sorts of subjects, making fun, and cutting jokes—none of them having any connection with the subject of the speech. In fact, he himself would not know what he would say in his speech. However that may be, I shall put on record, as far as I can, the things he told us during the few days that we had the good fortune of coming in contact with him.

I stated earlier that I had not met anyone who could equal Swamiji in his brilliant exposition of religion in the light of science and his successful reconciliation of the two. A few of his words on this subject are presented here. It is to be understood, however, that it is all reproduced from memory, so that there are chances of inaccuracy. If anything in this account appears to be wrong, that is not the fault of Swamiji's exposition, but rather of my poor memory. Swamiji said:

"All things, sentient and insentient, are rushing helter-skelter towards unity. In the beginning, men gave different names to the diverse things on which their eyes fell. Then, after examination, they arrived at the conclusion that all things are derived from sixty-three primary elements. Now again, many suspect that those elements themselves are compounds of more basic materials. When chemistry will reach its goal, all things will be discovered as emerging out of unity, of which they are but so many states. At first people considered heat, light, and electricity to be different. Now it has been proved that they are but different states of the same energy. In early days men divided the things of this world into the sentient, the insentient, and plants. Then they discovered that just like other living creatures plants also have life and feeling, the only difference being that they cannot move. So we are now left with only two divisions—the sentient and the insentient. A day will soon come when it will be found that even that which is considered insentient has some sort of sentience.

"The undulated land that we see on the surface of the earth is also trying to become plane. Rain water is washing down the hills to fill up the valleys. A hot thing placed amidst other things tries to attain the same state of warmth through radiation of heat. Things are thus advancing towards unity through conduction, convection, and radiation.

"Although the flowers, fruits, leaves, and roots of a tree appear to be different to us, science has proved that they all are same. A ray of light is perceived to have seven colours when seen through a prism. What is seen with bare eyes as having one colour may be seen as blue or red when seen through blue or red glasses.

"Thus also, truth is but one; but through maya we see it diversely. It is in this way that people get all kinds of knowledge in and through the one, undivided Truth, which is beyond time and space. But people are neither aware of this one Truth, nor can they comprehend it."

When Swamiji had spoken thus, I said: "Can we really believe even our own eyes? If two rails are placed parallel to each other, they seem to meet at the furthest end. That is the vanishing point. Mistaking a rope for a snake is a matter of daily occurrence; and mirage is also an example of an optical illusion. John Stuart Mill said that though man is mad after Truth, yet he lacks the power to comprehend the absolute Truth; for should even the real Truth come to him, how can he know that it is really so? All our knowledge is relative; we have no capacity to grasp the Absolute."

Swamiji said: "It may be true that you, or people in general, do not have absolute knowledge; but how can you say that nobody can have it? What you call knowledge now is really a form of ignorance. When true knowledge dawns, this false knowledge disappears; then you see everything to be but One. The idea of duality arises from ignorance."

"Swamiji, that is a very precarious position", I protested. "If there are two kinds of knowledge, viz. true knowledge and false knowledge, then what you consider to be true knowledge may well be false, and the dualistic thought that you denounce to be false may very well be true."

"Quite so," said he. "That is why one has to believe in the Vedas. The Vedas contain the truths experienced by the sages and seers of old who went beyond the range of duality and perceived unity. Depending on mere reasoning, we cannot pass any judgement as to whether the waking state or the dream state is true. How can we know which of the two is true so long as we cannot take our stand on something beyond both, from where we can look at them objectively? All that we can say now is that two different states are experienced. When you are experiencing one, the other seems to be false. You might have been marketing in Kolkata in your dream, but you wake up to find yourself lying on your bed. When the knowledge of unity will dawn, you will see but One and nothing else. You will then understand that the earlier dualistic knowledge was false. But all that is a long way off. It won't do to aspire to read the *Ramayana* and the *Mahabharata* before one has hardly begun to learn the alphabets. Religion is a matter of experience and not of intellectual understanding. One must practise it in order to understand it. Such a position is corroborated by the sciences of chemistry, physics, geology, etc. It won't do to put together one bottle of oxygen and two bottles of hydrogen and then shout: 'Where is water?' They have to be placed in a closed container and an electric current should be passed through them, so that they can combine to form water. Then only you can see water, and you can understand that water is produced from a combination of hydrogen and oxygen. If you wish to have the unitive experience, you must have that kind of faith in religion, that kind of eagerness, diligence, and persistence; and then only you will succeed. When one can hardly get rid of the habit one has acquired a month ago, what to speak of the habits acquired ages earlier? Each man carries a huge burden of tendencies acquired through a series of past lives, which blur his vision. And yet all and sundry would have the absolute Truth here and now! One feels a momentary dislike for the world when one gets a hard knock, and then one cries out, 'Oh, why don't I realize unity?'"

"Swamiji, if what you say is true," I argued, "it will lead to fatalism. If the accumulated results of past lives cannot be wiped off in a single birth, then one may as well give up all attempts. I can wait for my liberation until all will have it."

"That is not exactly the case," he explained. "While it is true that one has to reap the consequences of one's past actions, it is also possible to exhaust those results very quickly through certain processes. You can display ten magic lantern pictures in ten minutes, or you can spend the whole night in showing them. That depends on your own earnestness."

Swamiji's explanation of the mystery of creation was very interesting: "All created things are divided into two classes—sentient and insentient—for the sake of convenience. Man belongs to the highest rank of created beings. According to some religions, God created man in His own image, while some people think that man is only a monkey without a tail. Still others assert that man alone has the power of thinking, since his brain has a greater proportion of grey matter. In any case, all agree that man is a creature and, as such, he is included in creation as a whole. Now to understand what creation is, the Western scholars have recourse to the processes of analysis and synthesis on the one hand, and they go on examining everything individually. On the other hand, our forefathers in India spent very little time for the maintenance of the body in this warm climate and fertile land, and then, clad only in a loin cloth and having only a dim lamp, they started in all earnestness to find an answer to their question, 'What is that by knowing which everything will be known?' Their ranks were made up of all kinds of people. So in our religion, we come across all shades of opinion ranging from the ultra-materialism of the Charvakas to the non-dualism of Shankaracharya. Both these groups of people (in the West and in the East) are now converging on the same point, and they are beginning to speak the same language. They now assert that all the things in the universe have evolved out of one basic Reality, which is infinite in time and space, and which defies all description. Time and space also are of that kind. Time, that is to say such conception of time as days, months, years, aeons, etc., is determined for us chiefly by the motion of the sun. Now, think of time seriously. What does it amount to? The sun is not without a beginning; there was a time when the sun did not exist, and it is certain that a time will again come when the sun will cease to exist. So undivided time comes to mean nothing more than an inexpressible idea or entity. By the term 'space' we understand the limited space delimited by the earth or the solar system, which is only an infinitesimal part of the infinite creation. It is quite possible that there is a space without any matter in it. So infinite space is also an inexpressible idea or entity like time. Now from where and how did the solar system and all this creation come? Generally we do not see any product where there is no producer, and so we conclude that this creation must have a creator. But then this creator may have another creator, which is absurd. So the first creator, or first source, or God, also comes to be an infinite and inexpressible idea or entity. That which is infinite cannot be many; and hence all these infinites are but the different expressions of a single entity, and they must be one."

Once, I asked him, "Swamiji, is the common belief in the mantra etc. true?" He replied: "I find no reason why it should not be true. You become pleased when somebody addresses you with soft, sweet words, and you fly into a rage when you are spoken to in a harsh, jarring tone. Then why should not the deities presiding over different things be pleased by sweet invocation?"

After all this discussion, I said, "Swamiji, now that you have fully gauged my intellectual capacity, will you kindly chalk out the path that I should follow?" Swamiji replied: "First, try to bring the mind under control by any means. Everything else will follow as a matter of course. And knowledge, the non-dualistic realization, is very hard to attain. Know that to be the highest human goal. But before one reaches there, one has to make a long preparation and a prolonged effort. The company of holy men and dispassion are the means to it. There is no other way."

(Translated from *Swamijir Katha* in Bengali)

G. S. Bhate

I had the rare privilege of having Swami Vivekananda as
our guest at Belgaum, I believe some time in 1892. I am
not sure of the date, but it was about six months before he
reached Chennai and there became better known than he
was before. If I remember correctly, it was his first visit to
Chennai that led to his selection as a representative of India
at the Congress of Religions held at Chicago. As very few
people in India had the advantage of knowing him before he
made a name for himself, I think it would be interesting to
set down a few reminiscences, however hazy, of his visit and
stay at Belgaum.

The Swami came to Belgaum from Kolhapur with a note
from Mr. Golvalkar, the Khangi Karbhari of the Maharaja.
He had reached Kolhapur with a note from the Durbar of
Bhavnagar to the Durbar of Kolhapur. I do not remember
whether the Swami had stayed in Mumbai or merely passed
through. I remember him appearing one morning at about
six o'clock with a note from Mr. Golvalkar who was my father's great friend. The Swami was rather striking in appearance and appeared to be even at first sight somewhat out of
the common run of men. But neither my father nor anyone
else in the family or even in our small town was prepared to
find in our guest the remarkable man that he turned out to
be.

From the very first day of the Swami's stay occured little
incidents which led us to revise our ideas about him. In
the first place, though he wore clothes bearing the familiar
colour of a monk's garments, he appeared to be dressed

differently from the familiar brotherhood of monks. He used to wear a banyan. Instead of the danda he carried a long stick, something like a walking-stick. His belongings consisted of the usual gourd, a pocket copy of the *Gita*, and one or two other books (the names of which I do not remember, possibly they were some Upanishads). We were not accustomed to see a monk using the English language as a medium of conversation, wearing a banyan instead of being bare-bodied, and showing a versatility of intellect and variety of information which would do credit to an accomplished man of the world. He used to speak Hindi quite fluently; but as our mother tongue was Marathi, often he found it more convenient to use English than Hindi.

The first day after the meal, the Swami made a request for betel-nut. Then either the same day or the day after, he wanted some tobacco for chewing. One can imagine the kind of horror which would be inspired by a monk, who is commonly regarded as having gone above these small creature comforts, showing a craving for these things. We had discovered by his own admission that he was a non-Brahmin and yet a monk, that he was a monk and yet craved for things which only householders are supposed to want. This was really topsy-turvydom, and yet he succeeded in changing our ideas. There was really nothing very wrong in a monk wanting betel-nut or tobacco for chewing, but the explanation he gave of his craving disarmed us completely. He said that he was a happy young man and a distinguished graduate of the Kolkata University and that his life before he met Sri Ramakrishna Paramahamsa was entirely different from what he became afterwards. As a result of the teachings of Sri Ramakrishna Paramahamsa he had changed his life and outlook, but some of these things he found impossible to get rid of, and he let them remain as being of no very great consequence. As regards food, when he was asked whether he was a vegetarian or a meat-eater, he said that as a man belonging not to the ordinary order of monks but to the order of the Paramahamsas, he had no option in the matter. The

Paramahamsa, by the rules of that order, was bound to eat whatever was offered, and in case nothing could be offered he had to go without food. And a Paramahamsa was not precluded from accepting food from any human being irrespective of his religious beliefs. When he was asked whether he would accept food from non-Hindus, he told us that he had several times been under the necessity of accepting food from Mohammedans.

The Swami appeared to be very well versed in the traditional method of studying Sanskrit. At the time of his arrival, I was memorizing the *Ashtadhyayi*,[1] and to my great surprise, his memory even in quoting portions of the *Ashtadhyayi* which I had been painfully trying to remember, was much superior to mine. If I remember correctly, when my father wanted me to repeat the portions that I had been preparing, I made some slips which to my embarrassment the Swami smilingly corrected. The effect of this was almost overwhelming as far as my feelings towards him were concerned. When there was another occasion for repeating some portions of the *Amarakosha*,[2] I thought it better to be prudent than clever; and as I felt doubtful about my ability to repeat the portion with accuracy, I frankly confessed that I was unable to do so without committing mistakes. My father was naturally annoyed at my failure to come up to his expectation; but I did not want to be caught once more, and I preferred the temporary annoyance of my father to what I regarded as a humiliation at the hand of our newly arrived guest.

For a day or two after his arrival my father was busy trying to take a measure of his guest. In that period he made up his mind that the guest was not only above the ordinary, but was an extraordinary personality. So he got a few of his personal friends together in order to fortify his own opinion of the Swami. They soon agreed that it was quite worthwhile to get all the local leaders and learned men together. What

1. The system of Sanskrit grammar laid down by Panini.
2. A Sanskrit lexicon.

struck us most in the crowded gatherings, which began to be held every day after the presence of the Swami became known to all in Belgaum, was the unfailing good humour which the Swami preserved in his conversations and even heated arguments. He was quick enough at retort, but the retort had no sting in it. One day we had a rather amusing illustration of the Swami's coolness in debate. There was at that time in Belgaum an Executive Engineer who was the best-informed man in our town. He was one of the not uncommon types among Hindus. He was in his everyday life an orthodox Hindu of the type that I believe Southern India alone can produce. But in his mental outlook he was not only a sceptic, but a very dogmatic adherent of what used to be then regarded as the scientific outlook. He almost appeared to argue in spite of his orthodox mode of life that there was practically no sanction for religion or belief in religion except that the people were for a long time accustomed to certain beliefs and practices. Holding these views he found the Swami rather an embarrassing opponent, because the Swami had larger experience, knew more philosophy and more science than this local luminary. Naturally, he more than once lost his temper in argument and was discourteous, if not positively rude, to the Swami. So my father protested, but the Swami smilingly intervened and said that he did not feel in any way disturbed by the show of temper by this Executive Engineer. He said that in such circumstances the best method to adopt was the one adopted by horse-trainers. He said that when a trainer wants to break a colt, he merely aims at first to get on its back, and having secured a hold there, limits his exertions to keeping his seat. He lets the colt try its best to throw him off and in that attempt to exhaust its untrained energies; but when the colt has done its best and failed, then begins the real task of the trainer. He becomes the master, and soon makes the colt feel that he means to be the master; and then the course of training is comparatively smooth. He said that in debates and conversations this was the best method to adopt. Let your opponent try his best or worst, let him exhaust himself; and then when he shows signs of fatigue, get control of him and make him do just what you wish him to do. In short, conviction rather than constraint or compulsion must be the aim of a man who wants something more than mere silence from an opponent. Willing consent on the part of the opponent must be the inevitable result of such a procedure.

The Swami was a most embarrassing opponent for an impatient and dogmatic reasoner. He soon nonplussed in argument all the available talent in this remote town. But his aim appeared to be not so much victory in debate and argumentation as a desire to create and spread the feeling that the time had come for demonstrating to the country and to the whole world that the Hindu religion was not in a moribund condition. The time had come, he used to say, for preaching to the world the priceless truths contained in Vedanta. His view of Vedanta was, it appears to me, a great deal different from the view that has become traditional. His complaint appeared to be that Vedanta had been treated too much as the possession of a sect competing for the loyalty of the Hindu along with other sects, and not as a life-giving perennial source of inspiration that it really was. He used to say that the particular danger of Vedanta was that its tenets and principles lent themselves easily to profession even by cowards. He used to say that the Vedanta may be professed by a coward, but it could be put into practice only by the most stout-hearted. The Vedanta was strong meat for weak stomachs. One of his favourite illustrations was that the doctrine of non-resistance necessarily involved the capacity and ability to resist and a conscious refraining from having recourse to resistance. If a strong man, he used to say, deliberately refrained from making use of his strength against either a rash or a weak opponent, then he could legitimately claim higher motives for his action. If, on the other hand, there was no obvious superiority of strength, or the strength really lay with the opponent, then the absence of the use of strength naturally raised the suspicion of cowardice. He used to say that that was the real essence of the advice given by Sri Krishna to Arjuna. The wavering of Arjuna's mind may easily have been due to other causes besides a genuine reluctance to use his undoubted and unfailing strength. Therefore the long and involved argument embodied in the eighteen chapters of the *Gita*.

(Prabuddha Bharata, July 1923)

K SUNDARARAMA IYER

K. Sundararama Iyer

I met Swami Vivekananda for the first time at Trivandrum in December 1892, and was thereafter privileged to see and know a good deal of him. He came to Trivandrum in the course of an extended Indian tour, fulfilling the time-honoured practice obtaining among Indian monks of paying a visit to, and practising austerities at the sacred shrines in the four corners of this sacred land, viz Badrinath, Kedarnath, Dwaraka, Puri, and Rameshwaram, and claiming the hospitality and obeisance due to his sacred order from the Hindu householder. He came to me accompanied by a Mohammedan guide. My second son—a little boy of twelve who has since passed away—took him for, and announced him to me as a Mohammedan too, as he well might from his costume which was quite unusual for a Hindu monk of Southern India. I took him upstairs, entered into conversation, and paid him due obeisance as soon as I learnt who he was. Almost the first thing he asked me to do was to arrange for his Mohammedan attendant's meals. His Mohammedan companion was a peon in the Cochin State service, and had been asked to accompany him to Trivandrum by the then Secretary to the Dewan, Mr. W. Ramaiyya, B.A., formerly Principal of the Vishakhapatnam College. For himself the Swami would take no introduction, or have any sort of arrangement previously made for his comfort while on the way or after reaching Trivandrum. The Swami had taken almost nothing except a little milk during the last two days, and only after his Mohammedan peon had been provided with meals and taken leave he bestowed any thought on himself.

Within a few minutes' conversation, I found that the Swami was a mighty man. Having ascertained from him that, since leaving Ernakulam he had eaten almost nothing, I asked him what food he was accustomed to. "Anything you like; we monks have no tastes", he replied. We talked a little, as there was yet an interval of a few minutes before dinner. On learning that the Swami was a Bengali, I observed that Bengalis had produced many great men—and, foremost of them all, was the Brahmo preacher, Keshabchandra Sen. It was then that the Swami mentioned to me the name of his guru Sri Ramakrishna, and expatiated briefly on his eminent spiritual endowments, and took my breath away by the remark that Keshab was a mere child when compared with Sri Ramakrishna, that not only he, but many eminent Bengalis of a generation past had been influenced by the sage, that Keshab had in later life received the benefit of his inspiration and had undergone considerable change for the better in his religious views, that many Europeans had sought the acquaintance of Sri Ramakrishna and regarded him as a semi-divine personage, and that no less a man than the late Director of Public Instruction in Bengal, Mr. C. H. Tawney, had written a paper on the character, genius, catholicity, and inspiring power of the great sage.

All this conversation had occupied us while the Swami's food was being prepared and during the time he was breaking his nearly two days' fast by a hearty dinner. The Swami's presence, his voice, the glitter in his eyes, and the flow of his words and ideas were so inspiring that I excused myself that day from attending at the palace of the late Martanda Varma, the First Prince of Travancore, who was pursuing his M.A. studies under my tuition—my services having been lent to the Travancore State by the Chennai government to prepare him first for the B.A. Degree and later for the M.A. Degree. The Swami having had some rest, I took him in the evening to the house of Prof. Rangacharya, who was then professor of chemistry in the Trivandrum College—his services, too, having then been lent to the Travancore State—and who was even then at the height of his reputation as a scholar and man of science not only in Travancore, but throughout Northern India. Not finding him at home, we drove to the Trivandrum Club. There I introduced the Swami to various gentlemen present, and to Prof. Rangacharya when he came later, to the late Prof. Sundaram Pillai, M.A., and others among whom I distinctly remember a late Brahmin Dewan Peshkar and my friend Narayana Menon—who, I believe, is one of the Dewan Peshkars today in Travancore—owing to an incident which, however trifling in itself, revealed a prominent characteristic of the Swami, how he was all eyes and noted closely all that was passing around him and could use them effectively, how he combined with his rare gentleness and sweetness of temper, the presence of mind and the power of retort which could quickly silence an opponent. Mr. Narayana Menon had, while leaving the Club earlier in the evening, saluted the Brahmin Dewan Peshkar and the latter had returned it in the time-honoured fashion in which Brahmins who maintain old forms of etiquette return the salute of Shudras, i.e., by raising the left hand a little higher than the right. Many members of the Club had come and gone, and at last five of us were left, the Swami, the Dewan Peshkar, his brother, Prof. Rangacharya, and myself. As we were dispersing, the Dewan Peshkar made his obeisance to the Swami which the latter returned in the manner usual with Hindu monks by simply uttering the name of Narayana. This roused the Peshkar's ire, for he wanted the Swami's obeisance, too, in the fashion in which he had made his own. The Swami then turned on him and said, "If you could exercise your customary form of etiquette in returning Narayana Menon's greeting, why should you resent my adopting a monk's customary mode of acknowledging your obeisance?" This reply had the desired effect, and next day the gentleman's brother came to us and conveyed some kind of apology for the awkward incident of the previous night.

During the evening, short as his stay had been at the Club premises, the Swami's personality had impressed every one. Hindu society in Trivandrum town presents a strikingly motley appearance, as all the race and caste varieties peculiar to Southern India commingle within its narrow limits. The Trivandrum Club, of which all the leading educated men are members, also presents every evening a similar motley gathering representative of all those varieties, or almost all. The Swami entered freely into conversation with all, but in Professor Rangacharya he found the man nearest to himself in all that he most valued in life—an almost encyclopaedic learning, a rare command of eloquent expression, the power to call up readily all his vast intellectual resources to point a moral or prick the bubble of a plausible argument and an emotional temperament which unerringly pointed to the love of whatever is good and noble in man and beautiful in nature and art. One remark of Professor Sundaram Pillai, that as a Dravidian, he considered himself entirely outside the Hindu polity, put him somewhat out of court with the Swami, who later remarked of him that eminent as he was as a scholar, he had thoughtlessly given himself away to the sway of race prejudice, which already during his travels the Swami had noted as an unpleasant characteristic of certain South Indian minds of the unbalanced or mediocre type.

The Swami paid a visit the next day to prince Martanda Varma, who, as already stated, was then under my tuition and studying for the M.A. Degree, and who, when informed by me of the remarkable intellectual and imposing presence of my visitor, communicated to the Swami his desire for an interview. Of course I accompanied the Swami and was present during the conversation between him and the prince. The Swami happened to mention his visits to various native princes and courts during his travels. This greatly interested the prince who asked him about his impressions. The Swami then told him that, of all the Hindu ruling princes he had met, he had been most impressed with the abilities, patriotism, energy, and foresight of H. H. the Gaekwad of Baroda, that he had also known and greatly admired the noble qualities of the small Rajput chief of Khetri, and that, as he came more and more south, he had found a growing deterioration in the character and capacity of Indian princes and chiefs. The prince then asked him if he had met his uncle, the ruler of Travancore. The Swami had not yet had time to arrange for a visit to His Highness. I may here mention that a visit was arranged two days later through the good offices of the then Dewan, Mr. Sankara Subbier. The Maharaja received the Swami, inquired of his welfare, and told him that the Dewan would provide him with every convenience during his stay both in Trivandrum and elsewhere within the State. The visit lasted only for two or three minutes, and so the Swami returned a little disappointed, though impressed with H. H.'s gracious and dignified deportment.

To return to the Swami's conversation with the prince. The prince inquired regarding his impression of the late Maharaja of Mysore, whose guest the Swami had been for several days. The gist of the Swami's view was that the Maharaja, like many other Indian rulers, was a good deal under leading strings, that he could not or would not assert himself, and that that had produced some undesirable results. One incident he mentioned may be of some interest. I cannot give names. The Swami ventured to advise the Maharaja to remove from his neighbourhood a man of some reputation, who was supposed to be a favourite of his and of whom there had prevailed, rightly or wrongly, possibly wrongly, an unfavourable impression in the public mind. To this request, the Maharaja made the strange reply that, as the Swami was one of the greatest men he had seen and destined to fulfil a great mission in the land, he should not expose his life to the risk there certainly existed in the Indian prince's palace for one who openly ventured to disparage, or to endeavour to secure the dismissal, of one of his favourites. This throws light on the way in which the Swami and the Maharaja understood each other. The Swami then made earnest inquiries regarding prince Martanda Varma's studies and his aims in life. The Prince replied that he had already taken some interest in the doings of the people of

Travancore and that he had resolved to do what he could, as a leading and loyal subject of the Maharaja and as a member of the ruling family, to advance their welfare. The prince was struck, like all others who had come in contact with him, with the Swami's striking figure and attractive features; and, being an amateur photographer, asked the Swami for a sitting and took a fine photograph which he skilfully developed into an impressive picture and later sent as an exhibit to the next Fine Arts Exhibition held in the Chennai Museum. On leaving the prince's presence, the Swami remarked to me that he thought there was plenty of promise in him, but that he hoped that the University education which he was receiving would not spoil him. He evidently meant that since the prince was already a graduate, he might be left more to himself rather than be further kept under my care and instruction. But, in fact, the prince was only being helped to think for himself and no longer kept under control and, after another year or so, discontinued his studies.

Throughout the second day and even during the greater part of the third, we were left a good deal to ourselves, except for a brief visit in the evening from Prof. Rangacharya. The Swami found me much inclined to orthodox Hindu modes of life and beliefs. Perhaps that was why he spoke a good deal in the vein suited to my tastes and views, though occasionally he burst out into spirited denunciation of the observance of mere deshachara, or formal customs. As I keep no diary and write only from the tattered remains of an impression left on the mind by events which took place twenty years ago, I cannot vouch for the exact order of topics as they arose on this and other days. I had occasional and deeply interesting conversations with the Swami, sometimes when we were left to ourselves, at other times when visitors, to whom the news had been taken that a highly learned and gifted sannyasi from the North was staying with me, called to see him and earn the spiritual merit of rendering him homage in due form.

The Swami once made a spirited attack on the extravagant claims put forth by science on men's allegiance. "If religion has its superstitions," the Swami remarked, "science has its superstitions too." Both the mechanical and evolutionary theories are, on examination, found inadequate and unsatisfying, and still there are large numbers of men who speak of the entire universe as an open secret. Agnosticism has also bulked large in men's esteem, but has only betrayed its ignorance and arrogance by ignoring the laws and truths of the Indian science of thought-control. Western psychology has miserably failed to cope with the superconscious aspects and laws of human nature. Where European science has stopped short, Indian psychology comes in and explains, illustrates, and teaches how to render real and practical laws appertaining to higher states of existence and experience. Religion alone—and especially the religion of the Indian sages—can understand the subtle and secret working of the human mind and conquer its unspiritual cravings so as to realize the one Existence and comprehend all else as its limitation and manifestation when under the bondage of matter. Another subject on which the Swami spoke was the distinction between the world of gross matter (laukika) and the world of fine matter (alaukika). The Swami explained how both kept man within the bondage of the senses, and only he who rose superior to both could attain to the freedom which is the aim of all life and raise himself above the petty vanities of the world, whether of men or gods. The Swami spoke to me of the institution of caste, and held that the Brahmin would continue to live as long as he found unselfish work to do and freely gave of his knowledge and all to the rest of the population. In the actual words of the Swami which are still ringing in my ears, "The Brahmin has done great things for India; he is doing great things for India, and he is destined to do still greater things for India in the future." The Swami also declared himself sternly against all interference against the scriptural usages and injunctions with regard to the status and marriage of women. Women as well as the lower classes and castes must receive Sanskrit education, imbibe the ancient spiritual culture, and realize in practice all the spiritual ideals of the rishis; and then they would take into their own hands all questions affecting their own status and solve them in the light thrown on them by their own knowledge of the truths of religion and the enlightened perception of their own needs and requirements. I also asked the Swami for his views on the question of sea-voyage. He replied that the social environment in Western countries must be better prepared than it was and is by the preaching the Vedanta before Brahmins and other caste Hindus could find it suitable for their accustomed life of ceremonial purity and those timeworn and time-honoured restrictions as regards food, drink, etc., which have made them for ages almost the sole champions of, and channels for, the gospel of mercy. There was not the least objection, however, in the case of Hindus who were already free from, or were prepared to throw aside, all such restrictions.

On the third and fourth day of the Swami's stay with me, I sent information to a valued friend of mine in Trivandrum, who is my senior in years and still living, a man for whom, on account of his character, culture, purity of life, and sincere devotion to the Lord, I felt then, and have continued to feel, attached by the ties of genuine regard and friendship, Mr. S. Rama Rao, the then Director of Vernacular Instruction in Travancore. Mr. Rama Rao felt infinitely attracted to the Swami by the power of his spirituality and devotional fervour and asked him for the favour of taking alms in his house, which the Swami graciously consented to do. After the bhiksha was over, they returned together, and the Swami continued his instructive and fervid discourses to us. I remember vividly how once Mr. Rama Rao wished the Swami to explain indriya-nigraha, the restraint of the senses. The Swami then launched forth into a vivid narration of a story very much like what is usually told of Lila-Shukha, the famous composer of *Krishna-Karnamrita*. The vivid picture he gave of the last stage in which the hero is taken to Vrindavan and puts out his own eyes when he gets severely handled for his amorous pursuit of a landlord's daughter there, and then proclaims his repentance and his resolve to end his days in unswerving meditation on the divine Sri Krishna at the scene of the Lord's sportive deeds in the days of His childhood on earth, bursts on my mind, even at this distance of twenty-one years, with somewhat of the effect of those irresistibly charming and undying notes on the flute by the late miraculous musician Sarabha Shastriar of Kumbakonam. The Swami's concluding words after mentioning the closing incident of putting out the eyes were: "Even this extreme step must, if necessary, be taken as a preliminary to the restraint of the wandering and unsubjugated senses and the consequent turning of the mind towards the Lord."

On the third or fourth day of his stay, I made inquiries, at the Swami's request, regarding the whereabouts of Mr. Manmathanath Bhattacharya—now deceased—who was then Assistant to the Accountant-General, Chennai, and who had come down to Trivandrum on official duty in connection with some defalcations alleged to have taken place at the Resident's Treasury. From that time the Swami daily used to spend his mornings with Mr. Bhattacharya and stay for dinner. One day, however, I complained, and unfortunately there was a visitor too, to detain him, as I shall presently have to state. The Swami made a characteristic reply on seeing how unwilling I was to part with him, "We, Bengalis, are a clannish people." He said also that Mr. Bhattacharya had been his school or college mate, and that he had an additional claim for consideration as he was the son of the late world-renowned scholar, Pundit Maheshchandra Nyayaratna, formerly the Principal of the Kolkata Sanskrit College. The Swami also told me that he had long taken no fish food, as the South Indian Brahmins whose guest he had been throughout his South Indian tour were forbidden both fish and flesh, and would fain avail himself of this opportunity to have his accustomed fare. I at once expressed my loathing for the taking of fish or flesh as food.

The Swami said in reply that the ancient Brahmins of India were accustomed to take meat and even beef and were called upon to kill cows and other animals in yajnas or for giving madhuparka to guests. He also held that the introduction and spread of Buddhism led to the gradual discontinuance of flesh as food, though the Hindu scriptures had always expressed a theoretical preference for those who avoided the use of flesh-foods, and that the disfavour into which animal food had fallen was one of the chief causes of the gradual decline of the national strength, and the final overthrow of the national independence of the united ancient Hindu races and states of India. He informed me, at the same time, that in recent years Bengalis had, as a community, begun to use freely animal food of several kinds and that they generally got a Brahmin to sprinkle a little water consecrated by the utterance of a few mantras over a whole flock of sheep and then, without any further qualms of religious conscience, proceeded to hand, draw, and quarter them. The Swami's opinion, at least as expressed in conversation with me, was that the Hindus must freely take to the use of animal food if India was at all to cope with the rest of the world in the present race for power and predominance among the world's communities, whether within the British empire, or beyond its limits. I, as a Brahmin of strong orthodox leanings, expressed my entire dissent from his views and held that the Vedic religion had alone taught man his kinship and unity with nature, that man should not yield to the play of sensuous cravings or the narrow passion for political dominance. The ennobling gospel of universal mercy which had been the unique possession of the Hindus, especially of the Brahmins of South India, should never be abandoned as mistaken, out of date, or uncivilized, and that the world can and ought to make a great ethical advance by adopting a humane diet, and also that no petty considerations of national strength or revival should prevail against the adoption of a policy of justice and humanity towards our dumb, brother-jivas of the brute creation. Knowing, as I fully did, the Swami's views on this question, I was not surprised to learn that, while in America he had been in the habit of taking animal food, and I think he treated with silent contempt the denunciations and calumnies directed against him on this account.

The Swami visited the Dewan by appointment one evening, when this same subject somehow cropped up, and the Dewan held views identical with mine and even went on to express his views that animals had never been killed, or flesh used in yajnas in ancient times. This led to some little controversy in which the Dewan's son-in-law, the late Mr. A. Ramier, who was then his secretary, took sides with the Swami, so far as the use of flesh in yajnas was concerned. The Swami had also some little talk with the Dewan on the subject of bhakti. How the subject came in or what were the details of the Swami's conversation has clean dropped out of my memory. Mr. Sankara Subbier, the Dewan, was one of the most learned men of his time and even at his advanced age—for he was then fifty-eight—was a voracious reader of all sorts of books, and daily adding to the vast stores of his knowledge. The Swami, however, was not much impressed, nor could the Dewan spare time for a prolonged meeting. So we took our leave. As the Swami parted, the Dewan assured him that every want or wish of his would be attended to, and every attention paid to him throughout the State, wherever he might go. The Swami, however, wanted nothing and asked for nothing.

I have above referred to a visitor detaining the Swami one morning from his usual visit to his Bengali countryman, Mr. Bhattacharya. This visitor was the Assistant Dewan or Peshkar in the Huzoor office, Trivandrum, one Mr. Piravi Perumal Pillay. He seemed to have come to ascertain what the Swami knew of various cults and religions in India and elsewhere, and began by putting forward various objections to the Advaita Vedanta. He soon found out that the Swami was a master from whose stores it was more important to draw what one could for inspiration without loss of time than to examine what were the depths and heights in which his mind could range. I have seen the Swami exhibit on this occasion (as on another during his famous sojourn of nine days at Castle Kernan on the Chennai Marina in March 1897) his rare power of gauging in a moment the mental reach of a self-confident visitor, and then turning him unconsciously away to a ground suitable to him and then giving him the benefit of his guidance and inspiration. On the present occasion, the Swami happened to quote from *Lalita Vistara* some verses descriptive of Buddha's dispassion, and in such an entrancingly melodious voice that the visitor's heart quite melted, and he speedily fell into a passive listening mood, which the Swami skilfully utilized to carry home to his mind a lasting impression of Buddha's great renunciation, his unflinching search after truth, his final discovery of it and his unwearied ministry of forty-five years among men and women of all castes, ranks, and conditions of life. The discourse occupied nearly an hour, and at its close the Swami's visitor was so visibly affected and acknowledged himself as feeling so much raised for the time being above the sordid reailities and vanities of life, that he made many devout prostrations at the Swami's feet and declared when leaving that he had never seen his like and would never forget the discourse which had impressed him greatly.

During this and the following days various topics came up, upon which I had the pleasure of knowing the Swami's views. Many of these have passed out of my recollection, but two of them come home to me with more or less vividness just at present. Once I happened to ask him to deliver a public lecture. The Swami said that he had never before spoken in public and would surely prove a lamentable and ludicrous failure. Upon this I inquired how, if this were true, he could face the august assembly of the Parliament of Religions at Chicago at which he told me he had been asked by the Maharaja of Mysore to be present as the representative of Hinduism. The Swami gave me a reply which at the time seemed to me decidedly evasive, namely, that if it was the will of the Supreme that he should be made His mouthpiece

and do a great service to the cause of truth and holy living,
He surely would endow him with the gifts and qualities
needed for it. I said I was incredulous as to the probability
or possibility of a special intervention of this kind, as, even
though I had at this time much faith in the central and
fundamental verities of Hinduism, I had not studied its
source-books and had not obtained an insight into their
rationale, nor even had so much of a practical realization
of those verities as would enable me to perceive the truth
underlying a statement like the one made by the Swami.
He at once came down on me with a sledgehammer stroke,
denouncing me as one who, in spite of my apparent Hindu
orthodoxy so far as my daily observances and verbal professions went, was at heart somewhat of a sceptic, because I
seemed to be prepared to set limits of my own to the extent
of the Lord's power of beneficent interposition in the affairs
of the universe.

On another occasion, too, some difference of opinion
existed in regard to a question of much importance in Indian
ethnology. The Swami held that wherever a Brahmin was
found with a dark skin, it was clearly a case of atavism,
demonstrating the descent of a characteristic due to Dravidian admixture. To this I replied that colour was essentially a
changeable feature in man and largely dependent on such
conditions as climate, food, the nature of the occupation as
entailing an outdoor or indoor life, and so on. The Swami
combated my view and maintained that the Brahmins were
as much a mixed race as the rest of mankind, and that their
belief in their racial purity was largely founded on fiction. I
quoted high authority—C. L. Brace and others—against him
in regard to the purity of Indian races, but the Swami was
obdurate and maintained his own view.

I must get on rapidly to the close. But I must not fail to
mention the fact that during the time the Swami stayed, he
captived every heart within the home. To every one of us he
was all sweetness, all tenderness, all grace. My sons were frequently in his company, and one of them still swears by him

and has the most vivid and endearing recollections of his visit and of his striking personality. The Swami learnt a number of Tamil words and took delight in conversing in Tamil with the Brahmin cook in our home. It hardly seemed as if there was a stranger moving in our midst. When he left, it seemed for a time as if the light had gone out of our home.

Just as he was about to leave, accompanied by his Bengali companion, Mr. Bhattacharya—it was on 22 December 1892—an incident happened which is worth recording. Pundit Vanchisvara Shastri—a master of that most difficult branch of learning, Sanskrit grammar, and highly honoured by all who knew him for his piety, learning, and modesty— was a dependent of the first Prince of Travancore, who, at my request, had secured his services as a teacher of Sanskrit to my son. During all these days of the Swami's stay he never came to my house. As the Swami was leaving, he made his appearance and implored me to arrange for an interview, however short, even if it be of a few minutes' duration. He had heard of the arrival and stay with me of a highly learned sannyasi from the North, but had been ill and could not come. He was anxious to have some conversation. The Swami and Mr. Bhattacharya were just then descending the stairs to get into their carriage and drive away. The Pundit entreated me in the most pressing manner to ask the Swami for at least a few minutes' delay. On being informed of this, the Swami entered into a brief conversation with him in Sanskrit, which lasted seven or eight minutes only. At that time I knew no Sanskrit, so I could not understand what they talked about. But the Pundit told me that it related to some knotty and controversial point in grammar and that, even during that brief conversation, the Swami displayed his accurate knowledge of Sanskrit grammar and his perfect mastery of the Sanskrit language.

With this the Swami's stay of nine days had come to a close. In my recollection of today, it seems to be somewhat of a nine days' wonder; the impression is one which can never be effaced. The Swami's towering personality and marvellous career must be said to mark an epoch in history whose full significance can become discernible only at some distant future. But to those who have had the privilege of knowing him intimately, he seems to be only comparable to some of those immortal spiritual personages who have shed an undying lustre on this holy land. It is very pleasant to have recorded these personal reminiscences, even though they are meagre, and can add little or nothing to our knowledge of the Master, who enchanted and captivated the heart of human society in the East and in the West in his time and generation.

(The Life of Swami Vivekananda, first edition, Volume IV, *Appendix I)*

I must first mention the name of Mr. M. C. Alasinga Perumal, late headmaster of the High School attached to Pacheyappa's College. From the time when the Swami first came to Chennai in December 1892 after his visit to Kanyakumari and Rameshwaram, he attached himself with adoring love and never-failing enthusiasm to the Swami's person and to his ministry in the world in all its phases and details—an adhesion and service to the Great Master which, to me at least, has always seemed a thing of beauty and brought to me a consolation and joy in many a dark hour of my heart's sinkings. That our degenerate Hindu society could still produce one who had in his nature so pure and perfect a passion of reverence and tender affection towards the Swami's prophetic soul was to me a discovery, and I have seen nothing like it at least in this southern peninsula of India. He was the life and soul of the work of all kinds done in South India in support of the Swami's ministry, or by his direction and suggestion. "Achinga"—as we familiarly used to call him—was hard at work and ever vigilant and got everything needed to be done in order

to make the Swami's reception at Chennai a success. He
first got up some sort of a reception committee—one not
of a formal character, but which was of use to him. Dr.
Subrahmanya Aiyar was its chief, and it included Messrs V.
Krishnaswami Aiyar, P. R. Sundara Aiyar, C. Nanjunda Rao;
V. C. Seshachari, Col. Olcott, Dr. Barrows of Chicago (who
had come to deliver a course of lectures on Christianity),
and others. The committee got ready two or three leaflets
for distribution everywhere in the town; the object was to
give our people some account of the Swami's memorable
work of preaching in the West, and contained chiefly extracts
from the opinions formed of him by leaders of thought and
the leading journals in the United States and Great Britain.
They also arranged to put a number of triumphal arches
from the Egmore railway station to Castle Kernan and to
stick placards regarding the Swami's arrival in all parts of the
city. Everywhere a wide interest had already been created
in consequence of the reports, daily received and published
in the papers, of the hearty welcome accorded to the Swami
in his progress from Colombo, through Rameshwaram,
Ramnad, and Shiva-ganga to Madura, Trichinopoly, and
Kumbakonam. Even in the small and insignificant intermediate rural railway stations men flocked to catch a glimpse of
the great man. Men came from the remote areas in large
numbers to Chennai to meet the Swami, or even to have
the inestimable privilege of looking at this new and world-
moving messenger of the Indian sages of yore. Lots of young
men who had come to Chennai for the university examinations remained to have his glimpse and to hear his voice and
to learn of his message to his countrymen. Everyone—in fact
men of all ages, classes, and sects—felt that the Swami had
done an everlasting service to the cause of the motherland
and its immortal prophets and gurus, past and present,
such as no one had ever done before—and that he was not
only a true saint and religious messenger from India to the
civilization of the West, but a patriot who had raised his
country and his compatriots in the estimation of the civilized

world. Everywhere the Swami's personality, mission, and achievements became the one topic of absorbing interest, and all awaited his arrival with eager interest and intense expectation. *The Hindu* published a leader extolling the Swami's work in the West in terms of the highest enthusiasm leading up towards its close to a white heat of passionate outburst. Indeed, one still remembers vividly how among its educated readers many here and there quoted its concluding sentences, asking who there could be who would not associate himself with the Swami's great work for humanity and advance it in all possible ways.

The morning previous to the Swami's arrival Mr. and Mrs. Sevier, two of his zealous Western disciples, accompanied by one Mr. Harrison—a Ceylonese Buddhist and an admirer and friend of the Swami—arrived at Chennai and were met at the railway station and taken to Castle Kernan. That same evening a public reception was arranged for them, and it was attended, among others, by Col. Olcott. I thought, from what Col. Olcott said to me, that he was a warm friend and sincere admirer of the Swami. I had also once read in *The Theosophist* that the Swami had, during his previous visit to Chennai in December 1892, gone to the Adyar headquarters and received a hearty welcome there from the Colonel and his associates. Hence what we heard from the Swami on his arrival the next day and his outburst against the Theosophical Society in his first Chennai lecture in a manner altogether unusual with him came to me as a surprise; but more of this later in its due place. We were all squatting on the floor in the temporary platform at one end of the canopy put up for the Swami's interviews and meetings at the Castle Kernan. Mrs. Sevier was saying something about the Swami's stay in London, and about one of his meetings or lectures at Mr. Sturdy's house. Colonel Olcott at once quoted the example of Mrs. Besant, and asked Mrs. Sevier to take a chair while we remained squatting, and tell us all she knew about the Swami and how she became his disciple. At once Mrs. Sevier replied that she was not Mrs.

Besant—that, while Mrs. Besant was a speaker and a scholar and could command every one's attention on any and every occasion to what fell from her lips, she (Mrs. Sevier) was only a plain woman and could say nothing which was of much interest or importance to them. Col. Olcott was nonplussed and became silent. After making their acquaintance with the visitors, all who had assembled lingered for a while and then dispersed.

The next morning was the long and eagerly expected day of the Swami's arrival. Enormous crowds wended their way to the railway station and also gathered together and kept waiting to have a glimpse at him while he passed through the streets in order to reach Castle Kernan. The station, inside and outside, was a veritable sea of heads and faces. The previous night my neighbour Mr. R. V. Srinivasa Iyer came to me and asked me to accompany him in his carriage to the Egmore railway station. I had known him for several years as a colleague of mine in the Kumbakonam College and had also frequently met him after his transfer to the revenue department. He had never felt much interest in religious problems or personalities, though he had been a diligent student of European philosophy. His offer to join in the welcome which the city of Chennai was offering to the Swami was to me a pleasant surprise. On our way he said he too was eager to see what the Swami was like after all the glory he had gained in his career as an Indian teacher and promulgator of our ancient philosophic religion. At last the train steamed into the station to the great delight of all who had gathered there and been kept waiting owing to the lateness of its arrival. The Swami alighted in company with two of his brother-disciples and another person who was his disciple and had been attracted to him while he was a station-master in some railway line in North India. They had gone to Colombo to meet him and to give him a new ochre cloth to wear in lieu of his European costume. The Swami was also accompanied by Mr. Goodwin, the Englishman who had been engaged to take down in shorthand his lectures in America and who had become his disciple and refused to accept any wages for his work and now had got himself attached to the Swami for the rest of his life. To our surprise he was attired in an Indian costume. A few introductions were made to the Swami at the station. As I had known the Swami at Trivandrum in December 1892 even before his first visit to Chennai, and as we had moved and conversed freely and intimately with each other, I was very eager to meet the Swami at once but owing to the enormous crowds, it was a pure chance, except in the case of a few big men, whether one got an opportunity or not to see the Swami at the station. I managed, however, to elbow my way through the crowd to where the Swami stood and to see and exchange a few words with him before he entered his carriage and the procession started. I prostrated at the Swami's feet, and asked whether he still remembered me. He replied that he never forgot a face and referred to his staying in my house at Trivandrum. It was then that my name was mentioned to him by Dr. Subrahmanya Aiyar. Professor M. Rangacharya, my old friend and colleague at the Kumbakonam College, had also accompanied the Swami from Kumbakonam, and both of us went together to Castle Kernan, following the procession. As we went, we found that at the beach some students had insisted on having the horses unharnessed, and dragged the carriage themselves for some distance. This idea of releasing the horses and of young men dragging the carriage was rather disgusting to our Indian ideas and tastes. Later in the day I mentioned the matter to the Swami himself, and he too seemed not to quite relish the idea. He told me that he had already mentioned it to the students who had made and carried out the proposal.

On the route from Kumbakonam, the Swami had been joined at the Chingleput railway station by the representative of *The Chennai Mail* who sought an interview. The interview, in the form of questions and answers, appeared that evening in that paper and gave a most interesting account of the Swami's observations and activities in

America and of his future aims during his stay in India. Later, Mr. Rangacharya told me that all the questions were his own and had elicited from the Swami his short, pithy, and ready replies. *The Chennai Mail*'s representative had only to take them down in shorthand. At this distance of time, however, I only remember that the Swami said that the American men were absorbed in business and money-making and so the women were the masters of the situation and availed themselves of every opportunity to improve their minds and culture, and that it was the women who largely attended his lectures and classes. The Swami expected that his labours would bear better fruit in England than in America; for though the English people were rather "thick-skulled" and therefore were slow to take in new ideas, they never flinched from carrying out their convictions into practice when once their minds had been influenced. The Swami arrived at Castle Kernan and met several of his brother-disciples and entered into close and familiar conversation with them. Their simple ways and hearty greetings, their easy manners and frank, unconventional behaviour towards each other, were very attractive to all who had the privilege to see them. The Swami and they soon sat for dinner, and when it was over, the Swami came up into the hall in the upper storey for rest after his hard labours during his journey in receiving deputations and replying to addresses and almost always in giving more or less formal discourses when the demands and importunities for them could not be put off.

The Swami's health had largely given way in the course of his unwearied labours in the West during three years of lecturing, teaching, and training of disciples in various courses of Vedic discipline and methods of meditation. Much anxiety was evinced by his associates and felt even by himself in regard to this matter. It was a wonder how he responded under these conditions to the demands made on his almost exhausted stock of energy, while on this return visit of his to the motherland and in the course of his energetic attempts to start his mission of India's spiritual renovation under his Great Master's banner and the influence of his own unique personality and enlightened guidance.

Professor Rangacharya and myself were invited by "Achinga" to interview the Swami and arrived at an arrangement with regard to his lecture programme during his Chennai sojourn to satisfy the public expectations and also to reveal to his countrymen his plans and hopes for the future. The Professor was returning to Kumbakonam the next day, and so the matter had to be settled at once. The Swami had taken some rest, and we found him seated on a carpet in a room upstairs. When we broached the topics, the Swami replied that we might settle between ourselves the topics of his discourses and simply inform him and leave them in his hands. His first public appearance was to be made in order to receive and reply to the address to be presented to him on behalf of the people of Chennai, then there were to be four public addresses, devoted to a comprehensive and detailed exposition of his ideas regarding India's mission to the world and the mission of her sages to their own children in the motherland. The Swami had also to reveal his means and methods for renovating the national and spiritual life of India in accordance with its altered conditions. We fixed the topics for Swami's lectures as follows: (1) My plan of campaign, (2) The Sages of India, (3) Vedanta in its relation to practical life, and (4) the Future of India. The Swami also had, at "Achinga's" special request, to deliver an address to the Triplicane Literary Society on "Some aspects of his work in India". This programme was actually carried out, and all the topics mentioned were fully treated by the Swami according to his own method and manner. The Swami also consented to have two morning sittings at the Castle to meet people who desired to ask questions and elicit answers on any topic they liked.

The same evening, or the next day's forenoon (I do not remember which, very likely the latter) Rangacharya and myself wished to listen to a little music of the Swami of which we had heard a great deal. We suggested the *Ashtapadi*. The Swami had no public engagements, and having had necessary rest, was in one of his sweetest and most serene moods and at once responded. He sang one of Jayadeva's songs in a most entrancing voice and in the appropriate raga (tune) which we had never heard before in this part of the country. The impression then created is one never to be effaced, and the Swami revealed himself to us in one of the lighter veins or aspects of his composite nature and his complex and soaring personality. I may also add that from the first day on which he reached the Castle Kernan, and up to the last, his residence was at all times crowded with visitors from all classes of the population and by the people of both sexes. Many delicate and retiring women of high and respectable families approached the Castle Kernan as if they were visiting a temple. Their devotional feeling reached its climax when they gained admission inside and prostrated themselves before the Swami as if he were one of our avataras or acharyas revisiting the scene of their labours. A crowd kept waiting in front of the Castle at all hours of the day and even for some time after it was dark. It had gone forth that he was an avatara of Sambandhaswami (a Shaiva saint) and the idea was taken up everywhere and with absolute trust among the common people. Whenever the people who kept watching and waiting caught a glimpse of him while he passed to and fro within the Castle grounds or when he passed by them to get into his coach on the way to one of his meetings, they prostrated *en masse* before him. The scene on such occasions was as impressive as it was unusual. Even when our heads of monasteries appeared in public on the rare occasions in which they went on a tour among their enrolled or avowed disciples, or paid a visit to a temple deity, or passed in procession through the streets of the place in which they had their monasteries, I had never witnessed this kind of collective worship and homage giving conspicuous vent to the popular emotions of love and reverence, and revealing to the world where the heart of the nation still lay. The renunciation of the world's pompous vanities, and its unsubstantial fleeting attachments was the sole means to the attainment of the lotus feet of the Supreme and the resulting liberation from the miseries of the samsarika (transmigrating) wanderings in the material universe.

When the appointed day, the third after his arrival, came for the Swami to receive the Chennai address, he left Castle Kernan at about 4 p.m. It was a day of universal and great expectations. The interest felt and evinced by the entire educated community and the student population of Chennai had reached heights and summits not easily imaginable. The scene in front of the Victoria Hall and the roads and by-lanes leading to it defies description. The Swami's carriage, as it passed, could not easily find the space it needed for reaching its destination. Professor Rangacharya and myself, at the Swami's gracious request, took our seats in his carriage. I enjoyed the infinite pleasure and privilege of once more looking directly at his wonderful eyes, recalling all he had achieved and mentally running over what his future career might be as the future minister of the Vedic religion. I could not but indulge in high hopes and aspirations regarding the future of this great land of India after it had yielded itself in faith and hope to this new heaven-sent messenger of our holy rishis. I must avow that so far a gaping width or chasm separates the expectations of that moment and the actualities of the quarter of a century that has since passed. There is, however, no need at all for despondency. I fully believe that the mission then started by the Swami will sooner or later attain developments which will command our confidence in the efficacy of the working constitution framed by him, even though its rate of progress towards the ultimate goal, namely, the spiritualization of all human nature and human institutions, must necessarily be slow.

As we alighted from the carriage, there were loud cries of "Open air meeting" from the vast crowds assembled in front of the Hall. It had been arranged that the address to the Swami should be presented inside the Hall. The Hall was filled to its utmost capacity. Sir V. Bhashyam Ayyangar had already occupied the chair. The Swami took his seat on the dais by his side, and Mr. M. O. Parthasarathy Ayyangar read the address. All eyes were fixed on Swamiji, and expectation was at its highest pitch. Every heart was receptive and ready to imbibe the sweet flow of melody from the voice and wisdom of the Great Master on whose every word his Western listeners had so long hung with delight and which had charmed all ranks and conditions of people of both sexes in the very life centres of the material civilization of the West. Meanwhile, loud and continuous shouts of "Open air meeting" breaking into the Hall interrupted the proceedings within. They issued from every part of the immense gathering of students and young people outside, so that the Swami's heart was touched and it became impossible for him to speak from the dais where he was standing. He said also that he could not disappoint the countless masses of the eager and enthusiastic young men assembled outside. The Swami and his crowded audience issued out to meet and mingle with the vast and seething mass of human faces and figures visible as far as the eye could reach and which rejoiced and broke into thundering shouts of joy when the Swami appeared before them. Soon, however, he found that the sounds and shouts from vast crowds made it impossible that his voice could be heard everywhere or even beyond the few who stood in his neighbourhood. The Swami's voice, too, in spite of its attractive sweetness and the even flow of its thrilling cadence, wanted those qualities of sonorousness and strength which, mounting to the swell of a trumpet blast, made a Gladstone, Bright, or O'Connel heard to the utmost limits of a vast concourse of fifty thousand people or more. The Swami spoke from the top of a Chennai coach—"in the *Gita* fashion" as he called it, to the amusement of all who heard him—meaning that there was some sort of distant analogy between himself speaking from a coach and imparting his counsel and inspiration to his people at the dawn of the new epoch he was inaugurating, and Sri Krishna redelivering his "lost message of yoga to a world which had allowed it to sink into oblivion owing to the steady decline of national spirituality during the great efflux of time" (*Gita*, 4.2). The huge crowd became so unmanageable, and their loud shouts and cheers swelled so much as to make the Swami's voice inaudible. So he spoke briefly, though he did not fail to clearly enunciate the central truths of Hinduism, how renunciation, love, and fearlessness were India's offering to humanity in order to help souls cross the ocean of samsara and the "Mystery of Life" into the Joy of Truth and the ever-present realization and illumination of the Self, the One without a second. ...

But the Swami found it impossible to proceed further and concluded by thanking all who had heard him asking them to "keep up" their enthusiasm and to give all the help he required from them, "to do great things for India" and carry out all his plans for the revival of this "big gigantic race".

The subject of his first lecture was "My plan of campaign". The Swami told me and others in the course of his conversation that he intended "to be out once for all" with the truth regarding what the Theosophical Society had done for him in America and elsewhere. Some friends had told the Swami that Colonel Olcott had been claiming that the Theosophical Society had paved the way for the Swami in America, that had it not been for the spade work done by the Society in its mission of spreading "occultism" or "ancient wisdom" everywhere, the Swami would not have been able to accomplish even the little he had been able to do in propagating the truths and ideals of the Vedantic religion and philosophy. The Swami had also heard from one of his brother-disciples on his arrival in Chennai, that a well-known Buddhist friend of his at Kolkata had received a letter from a prominent Chennai Theosophist in which that gentleman, on hearing that the Swami had from America once wired to his friends in Chennai that he had only a trifling sum left of the funds he had received when starting for the Parliament of Religions and would soon be nearing starvation and be without the warm clothing required for the approaching cold season, had written that "they would soon be rid of the devil [Swami Vivekananda]". This letter had been handed over for safe custody to the Belur Math. The Swami also told us that, wherever he had been invited to lecture in America, the Theosophists had tried to hinder his preaching Vedanta in various ways. Moreover, the prejudice which many leading Americans had everywhere contracted against the Mahatmic cranks of Theosophy and its puerile trumperies and monstrous fictions had made them imagine that the Swami's mission, too, was a kindred movement of obscurantism appealing similarly to the credulity imbedded in the innermost recesses of the minds of the common masses of men and must be similarly ostracized by all enlightened leaders and by all who care to base their beliefs and convictions regarding religion on sound methods of investigation and proof and on the experiences resulting from established and authoritative processes of meditation. The Swami had to remove mountains of unreasoning dislike and unfounded opposition which had been engendered everywhere owing to this circumstance. Moreover, the Christian missionaries also tried to prevent people everywhere from receiving him or even supporting his endeavours to enlist support and sympathy for the doctrines and spiritual methods of the Vedas and the Vedanta. The Swami told me that even Mr. Mazoomdar, who was a participant at the Parliament of Religions and a leader of the Brahmo Samaj and a man whom he had known and esteemed almost from his boyhood and student days, joined the missionaries in spreading false reports against him and discrediting his endeavours on behalf of the Vedic religion and went about saying that religion was receding and losing its hold on the Indian mind—on the cultured intellects of India as well as on the mind of the masses—and that therefore Christ had come to stay in India. The Swami also showed me two issues of a Christian weekly journal published in America—whose name I do not distinctly recollect at this distance of time, but perhaps its name was *The Witness*—in which the missionaries had published an appeal for funds in aid of Mazoomdar's propagandist work in India, pointing out how he too would preach Jesus Christ and help forward the ultimate triumph of the Christian religion. The Swami condemned in unmeasured terms this transaction as opposed to all recognized canons of honourable public life and the relations between leaders of opposing creeds or churches. It was Mazoomdar that the Swami had in view, when he referred in this first Chennai lecture to "one of my own countrymen", "the leader of a reform party in India", and so on) ... Some of the Swami's friends and supporters in Chennai tried to dissuade him from making these references to his detractors in America, and especially from attacking the Theosophical Society and its founder. They told him that several members of that Society entertained unlimited regard and reverence towards him and had gathered in large numbers from the mofussil to greet and honour him on his return from the West. The Swami was inexorable, and gave forcible expression to the facts as he knew them and the feelings evoked in him by the troubles he had to encounter from those who had ever been proclaiming from the housetops that they formed "the nucleus of universal brotherhood". ...

The first of the four lectures arranged for him was delivered on the evening of Tuesday, the 9th, the fourth day after his arrival. That same day he lectured in the morning at the Triplicane Literary Society. As I could not be present at that lecture, I can say nothing about it from my own impressions. Nor was I present at his visit to the Social Reform Association on Wednesday, the 10th. I however asked the Swami about what happened, and he replied that he said nothing of special interest, but gave little or no encouragement to the revolutionary views entertained by its chief members, though he "admitted the need for social reforms" such as the removal of untouchability, the restoration and redistribution of the caste system so as to recover its ancient basis, etc.

Before I pass on, I must go back and narrate some incidents of the 8th February. I have the dates, and will try to preserve the chronological order of the facts, so far as I can rely on my memory of them. At about noon, Prof. P. Lakshmi Narasu—whom I have always esteemed as a gentleman of great learning and high character—came to the Castle, accompanied by the late Mr. N. K. Ramaswami Iyer. Mr. Lakshmi Narasu was a student of science and an avowed Buddhist, but I did not know who his companion was. The latter gentleman I learnt was the publisher and the former editor and the leading contributor to a journal which was appearing somewhat irregularly and was abandoned after a few issues had been published, called *The Awakener of India*. It was so named in order to deny the impression conveyed by the title of another journal, a monthly, which had been started at Chennai some time previously at the suggestion of the Swami, viz. *The Awakened India* (or *Prabuddha Bharata*) which was later transferred to the Advaita Ashrama established by the Swami at Mayavati and is still published from there. These two visitors of the Swami were evidently of the opinion that his mission and labours in America and the missionary work started in Chennai at his instance by the publication of the *Brahmavadin* and *Prabuddha Bharata* had yet had no effect in imparting a new impulse of activity, and India remained sunk as deep as ever in her lethargic slumber of ages. Their own *Awakener of India*, however, was, on the whole, a bright and rousing performance while it lasted. I still remember some vitriolic contributions on what it called "Blavatskosophy", containing uncompromising attacks on the creed of Theosophy as formulated by M. Blavatsky in her writings. On entering the side-room upstairs, I saw the Swami's two visitors and others seated, and the Swami in front of them but close to one of the walls, though not leaning against it and sitting in his usual posture appropriate to an expounder of the scriptures. Mr. Lakshmi Narasu sat calm and silent like one confident of his own invincible position. As I entered the room, his companion, whom we all knew well during his subsequent career, was saying: "We want, Swami, to have a free talk on various problems of philosophy and religion, especially on the Vedanta to which we have strong objections. When will you be able to find the time for us?" I took my seat, when the Swami called me to his side. Soon he said, with his usual smile lightening up his face: "Here is my friend, Sundararaman; he has been a Vedantist all his life, and he will meet all your arguments. You can refer to him." This greatly enraged N. K. Ramaswami Iyer who turned at me with eyes betokening scorn, if not contempt, and then turned once more to the Swami, "We have come here to meet you, and not any other person." The Swami of course did not reply. Meanwhile, other persons and topics turned up. The Swami remained where he was for some time longer. I left the room, and do not know what passed there afterwards.

In the afternoon of the same day, the Swami, after a short nap, was seated in the back room upstairs in the Castle Kernan and I found him in one of those moods of sweet serenity when his face assumed the air both of a child and an angel from heaven, an appearance with which I had become familiar at Trivandrum and whose fascination was irresistible to all who had the fortune to meet and converse with him on such occasions or moments. I have just mentioned the Swami's afternoon nap, and I will now say what used to happen on such occasions. He was always having visitors and sat listening or speaking to them. Suddenly his eyes became still, though remaining open, and he seemed not to listen or even to be conscious of what was passing about him. When once more he became aware of the scene, it seemed as if he had been utterly insensible to it. He had been neither asleep nor awake. On one of such occasions during these nine days at the Castle, I asked the Swami what sort of mood it was. He only answered, "I can't say what." I did not wish to press the matter. I do not know if it was not a case of voluntary retirement for his outer to inner self as a sort of escape from the weariness of the busy scene and life about him. Some may think that it was simply a state of drowsiness preliminary to the regular slumber which the Swami fell into later. But I, who have seen him both while getting into, and getting out of, this condition, and remember, too, how long he remained in a sitting posture and how peculiar his eyes appeared while they remained fixed and without the least sign of movement, cannot help saying that he seemed to me like one who for a while had left his physical tenement and fled away to another state of existence, something like what is described in one of the many strange episodes narrated in the *Yogavasishtha Ramayana*.

Later, in the same afternoon at about 4 p.m., there came a deputation to the Swami from Tiruppattur in the Salem District, a place now transferred to the North Arcot District. The Swami was, I think, seated in the same room as before. The deputation consisted of five or six persons, all Shaivites. There was no Brahmin among them. This would be easily understood when one knows that they seemed—at least to me—to have been prepared and sent to meet the Swami by the then District Munsiff of the place; who was later in the same year to become the founder and editor of the *SiddhantaDeepika*, now for some years defunct, and also the founder and organizer of the movement known as the "Shaiva Siddhanta Mahasabha", which continues to hold a peripatetic annual gathering and has also given the inspiration for many local Shaiva Sabhas and their activities and annual festive gatherings. Mr. Nallaswami Pillai was well-known to me and even very friendly. Though he was a strong advocate of the Shaiva cult, he wanted to liberalize it and propagate its tenets so as to make it acceptable to all, not only in India, but all over the world. He seemed to me—and I still think so—to have been fired by the example of the Swami and his activities and triumphal progress in America, England, India, and elsewhere. He was anxious to maintain the traditions of Shaivism, and also to include the Brahmins among the believers and brethren of the Shaiva faith. As the Swami was an Advaitin, the deputation from Tiruppattur was, perhaps, expressly prepared and sent to beard the lion in his den and to tackle him on some fundamental points of the Advaita doctrine. The head of the deputation had a whole sheet filled with questions, and he told the Swami that he wanted answers. The Swami nodded assent, and wanted him to begin. The first question was, "How does the Unmanifested become the manifested?" The Swami's reply came at once without a moment's hesitation, but it fell like thunder from the blue vault of heaven, paralyzing its victims and stultifying their nervous system and its workings. The same question was put later at one of the Swami's meetings by a young Madhva Brahmin who was then, I think, a college student and is now an active member of the Chennai Corporation. He, too, got the same answer, couched in the same or similar terms, and with the same stunning and electrifying effect. The Swami's reply was: "Questions of how, why, or wherefore relate to the manifested world, and not to the Unmanifested which is above all change and causation and therefore above all relation to the changing universe and our samsarika (transmigrating) life in it. The question, therefore, is not one which can be reasonably put. Put a proper question—a more rational question—and I will answer." The reply brought about an *impasse*, and his interlocutors felt that they were face to face with one who could meet and solve philosophic puzzles and queries of all kinds, a master before whom they must need bow in humility and meekness rather than launch forth in a game of dialectics. They seemed at once to have forgotten their carefully prepared and transcribed scheme and synopsis of questions in the manuscript they had brought, and suddenly, felt the wand of the magician sitting in front of them, and his enchantment was stealing over their minds and hearts with its occult power and overpowering grasp. The Swami at once realized the situation. Then followed a scene which is not possible adequately to depict. This past master of the arts and weapons of Indian dialectics, this lion of the Vedanta with his conquering air and roar, the impetuous and rolling thunder of his voice, and his lower jaw symbolizing, as he once told me himself, his "combative temperament", all of a sudden became transformed into what seemed a long-lost comrade of one's youth or a tenderly-loved brother restored after a long separation and whole-heartedly interested in all that concerned one's welfare. The Swami began to address them in a strain and in tones captivating all his listeners and all who were present. He spoke somewhat as follows: "The best way to serve and seek God is to serve the needy, to feed the hungry, to console the stricken, to help the fallen and friendless, to attend upon and serve those who are ill and require service, and so on. The deputation kept listening while the Swami's heart went out to them in a fervour of passionate exhortation to serve their fellow-men. It seemed as if after all they had met the one messenger of joy and peace from heaven for whom they had been searching in vain, one in whom there was no doubt or equivocation, a master who had searched their hearts and finding the void in them, had supplied the pabulum they needed, had taught them the central truth of life and of deliverance from its troubles. The shades of evening fell, they offered their homage at the feet of the saint; and as they took their departure, their countenances showed traces of a new light having touched their hearts and given them a new impulse to life and work.

We now come on to the day of his second Chennai lecture. That morning I met the Swami at the house of Dr. Subrahmanya Iyer in the Luz Church Road at the latter's special invitation. We met in the room upstairs, and the Swami explained to us his plans for a vast religious reformation and revival in India which would serve to bring Hindus, Christians, Mohammedans, Buddhists, and all others under a common flag of brotherly union and serve as a star of hope and harmony, and a ceaseless incentive to the striving by men of all creeds and colours after a common goal of national aspiration. He wanted a new sort and style of temple with a hall in front containing statues of the sages and prophets of all great religions, and behind it an inner precinct containing a pillar with the letter (or letters) Om inscribed on it and underneath the open sky. Nothing else

worth chronicling occurred here, except that the kind host
had got ready for the Swami a lot of sweets and well-spiced
preparations of which he partook but in name. There was
also the inevitable coffee which the Swami barely tasted. The
Swami was, perhaps, never a good eater, at least was not one
such, to my knowledge. When he stayed with me at Trivandrum, he used to take but one light meal in the daytime, and
only a little milk at night. At the Castle itself, in course of the
day, I saw nothing noteworthy. There was the usual stream
of visitors steadily flowing, and among them also the usual
flow of lady-visitors of high family status come to worship
at the Swami's feet and receive his blessing. There was one
young man from Coimbatore who had read the Swami's
lectures on Raja Yoga, published by Longmans, and had
tried to practise yoga according to the instructions conveyed
therein. He related his experiences, and among them he
mentioned that he felt that his body was growing lighter and
lighter. He also informed the Swami that some of his friends,
and especially pundits, had warned him of the danger and
even certainty of becoming insane if he persisted in his yogic
practices without seeking a practical instructor to correct or
enlighten him wherever he went wrong or had a doubt as
to the next step in his course of yoga. The Swami told him
not to give ear to these men, but to persist in his resolve to
reach the goal of samadhi. Each step he won would lead him
onward and enable him to overcome obstacles. There was no
danger at all anywhere and he was always ready to help him
whenever he needed help. The young man was quite satisfied and left for his native place. He did not seem in the least
interested by the Swami's career as a prophet of Vedantism
in the West or in India at the time he met him in the Castle.

In the evening the Swami delivered his second lecture
on "The Sages of India". The Victoria Hall was crowded to
its utmost capacity. The one exceptional feature of this day's
gathering was that the editor of *The Chennai Mail*, the late
Mr. H. Beauchamp, was present on the platform. No other
European in Chennai was present at any of the Swami's

lectures or meetings. But he rose and left in the middle of the Swami's address. I noticed, but it might have been a mere accident, that, just as Mr. Beauchamp was leaving the Swami was saying of Sri Krishna the following, after quoting a well-known verse of the *Gopika Gita*: "One kiss of those divine lips, and all sorrow vanishes and the thirst for Thee increases for ever", etc. This was a free rendering of the verse quoted. I trust that Mr. Beauchamp's British sense of social propriety was not wounded, and the Swami's utterances regarding Sri Krishna was not the direct cause of his leaving the meeting. ...

On Friday, the 12th February, I met the Swami twice. In the morning, the space beneath the canopy at the Castle was overflowing and bubbling with enthusiasm when the Swami arrived and took his seat on the platform. We had read glowing accounts of the manner in which he had replied to questions put to him in America, how his replies came like "flashes of lightning" and revealed to his audiences the extraordinary force of his intellect and his grasp of the varieties of life and the universe, how his retorts to those who attempted to land him in a deadlock or discomfiture carried confusion into the ranks of his opponents or detractors! Here was the opportunity for all to witness his dialectical sword-play and his sympathetic response to an honest inquiry, and he had a large and admiring audience before him. He rose to the occasion, but I regret that my memory fails me, and most or all of what happened is obliterated and gone out of my mind altogether. There was a young European lady of high intelligence and attractive appearance and demeanour who put various questions on Vedanta: What is realization of the Atman? What is maya? What is the relation of the one existence to the universe? and so on. The Swami's resources of knowledge and argument were all brought out in full to the delight and enlightenment of the lady and the entire audience. She expressed her intense gratification and gratitude to the Swami, and told him that she would be leaving for London in a few days to resume her social work among the dwellers in its slums and how great a privilege it would be to her if she could ever meet him again, but doubted much whether it would be vouchsafed to her. The Swami replied that she might be rest assured as to that, as he intended to go back to London after taking some rest and starting the Ramakrishna Mission here. The Swami rose from his seat and advanced a few steps to see that way was made for her to leave the meeting, and remained standing till she bowed and retired. In the afternoon, she came back, I was told, with her father who was engaged in Christian missionary work in Chennai, and sought and obtained for him an interview which lasted nearly an hour. When I saw the Swami after his visitors had departed, I asked him how he found the strength and stamina needed for this incessant activity, and he gave me the following reply full of significance to those who can appreciate it: "Spiritual work never tires one in India." I have already referred above to the young Madhva student who put a question, the same as stood first in the long array with which the members of the deputation from Tiruppattur had hoped to confound and baffle the Swami. The whilom young questioner of the Swami has now, I believe, developed into an ardent and public-spirited citizen of Chennai and is active among its city-fathers who form the Corporation Assembly. I hope he will not misunderstand me if ever these pages or lines happen to attract his notice. The Swami's answer was given in the very words already quoted by me, of course so far as I remember them at this distance of time. The terms of the reply confounded him somewhat, as they did almost every one to whom I had seen them addressed. ... The point raised is one fundamental to the Vedanta and is perhaps met somewhat differently therein; but the Swami's manner of meeting was quite his own, though implied in the language of the great commentator, Sri Shankaracharya. As I have earlier given the exact terms of the Swami's reply, I shall not repeat them. But the young man who put the question felt somewhat stunned and confused, and replied, "What, Sir?" The audience murmured somewhat when he used the term, "Sir", in addressing the Swami. But the incident closed at that point, so far as I can recollect it now. Another interesting event then occurred. A Vaishnava pundit spoke to the Swami in Sanskrit and raised some knotty point in the Vedanta for discussion. As I had not studied Sanskrit at that time, I was not in a position to know what it exactly was, and I can now say nothing of it. The Swami patiently heard the pundit, but then began addressing the audience in English. He said he did not care to waste his time in fruitless wranglings on doctrinal details which had no practical value in life. The pundit then asked the Swami to tell him in precise language whether he was an Advaitin or a Dvaitin. The Swami replied again, in English and in a tone and voice still ringing in my ears: "Tell the pundit that so long as I have this body, I am a Dvaitin, but not afterwards. This incarnation of mine is to help to put an end to these useless and mischievous squabbles and puzzles which only serve to distract the mind and make men weary of life and even turn them into sceptics and atheists." The pundit then said in Tamil, "The Swami's statement is really an avowal that he is an Advaitin." The Swami rejoined, "Let it be so". The matter was then dropped.

Yet another incident occurred at this meeting, and it has a personal interest for me. I have mentioned the name of the late Mr. R. V. Srinivasa Iyer, secretary to the Board of Revenue, whom I accompanied to the Egmore railway station on the day the Swami arrived. Once we were conversing about the Swami and his career and ministry among men in the West and in India after his return from America. Mr. Srinivasa Iyer said that so long as no one remembered what occurred in previous births, no relation of cause and effect could be discovered between what then occurred and one's present experiences of life. What then was to be gained by the teachings of the Vedanta regarding liberation and the means to it? So long as there is no proof of karma and of reincarnation as its fruit, one can rest content with learning or endeavouring how to get on here, and there the matter ends.

The Vedanta has no practical value, and has only a speculative interest for students of philosophy and metaphysics. He
wanted me to put a question or two to the Swami and obtain
his reply. The questions were as follows, and I give also the
Swami's replies.

Q. 1. So long as we have no memory of previous births,
how can the doctrines of karma and reincarnation command
assent or have a practical bearing and significance in life?
How can they be effective as an impulse to purification in
thought and act and thereby lead to the attempt to realize
the Atman and gain liberation from samsara?

A. Even in this life we have no continuous memory of
events, and still we act as if they are related as cause and
effect and influence our life and fortunes. Why not we act
similarly in regard to the relation between the events of the
past and present lives, and follow the injunctions of the Veda
and of our guru in regard to the means of liberation from
samsara and its troubles, past and present?

Q. 2. In this life we have the continuing consciousness of
our personal identity as we pass through the various stages
and events of our life. We have no such consciousness of a
personal identity persisting in relation to our past and present births.

A. We can, by going through certain well-recognized
processes, gain such a consciousness of the persistence of our
personality in different births. Why don't you try?

This was in substance what I had myself told Mr.
Srinivasa Iyer from my study of the Swami's lectures and
writings in the West and of translations of Indian works in
English. So, I was quite satisfied. Some of the people whom
I met after the meeting was over expressed the opinion that
the Swami had not attempted to meet the question raised in
a serious manner and he only fenced about and parried what
was a home-thrust. I replied that I got exactly the answers I
had expected. The Vedanta was a *practical religion,* and not
mere dialectics. When I met Mr. Srinivasa Iyer later, and told
him all, he told me that he was sure that he had raised the

one question which needed an answer, and that no real reply had been given. It was no answer to say that our course of life must be changed so long as no attempt was made to carry conviction by argument and instruction. The practical Vedantin knows better, and there we let the matter rest.

I again met the Swami in the central hall upstairs at about 1 p.m. Visitors were coming as usual, but nothing of interest occurred. At last, there turned up the late Mr. K. P. Shankara Menon, then the lawyer of the High Court, Chennai, and who later became a Judge of the Travancore High Court. He seemed to have known the Swami before. He and the Swami were seated together on a sofa. I took a seat in front and kept watching what was going on. The Swami said something about the absurd lengths to which the Malabar people carried their ideas of pollution and purification and especially their cries and groans to warn or scare away untouchables while passing on the roads and lanes. Suddenly, the Swami turned to the question of castes and marriages in Malabar, and said that the Nairs had every right to claim the status of Brahmins as for several centuries or even yugas, the Nambudiri Brahmins had lived in sambandham (relation) with their women. The *Manu Smriti* insisted on seven successive generations marrying Brahmins in order that non-Brahmins may secure Brahminical status by birth. The spirit of Manu's ruling was fulfilled among the Nairs, for, even though there might be interruptions in the middle, there was a certainty that, on the whole, there must be at least seven times seven sambandhams, if the whole period of Malabar history and Malabar society were taken in consideration. Mr. Shankara Menon seemed to be much interested in the Swami's suggestion, and even seemed to think the attempt feasible and that an effort might be made to see if it could be materialized. Just at this moment, Mr. (now Sir) C. Shankaran Nair—even then famous as a Chennai lawyer and political leader—entered the hall, approached the Swami, and received a hearty welcome. Mr. Shankaran Nair told the Swami that he had called at his residence in London when he was last there, but left on learning that he was not at home. The Swami was about to say something when Mr. Shankara Menon, looking at Mr. Shankaran Nair, broke forth suddenly as follows: "The Swami thinks that we, Nairs, must all claim to be Brahmins, and gives a reason based on the *Manu Smriti* where the status of a Brahmin is said to have been earned by a Shudra who had been born to seven generations of Brahmin fathers in succession." Mr. Shankaran Nair understood the situation in the twinkling of an eye, but was clearly in no mood for entering into a discussion on so delicate a matter, especially when, as it seemed to me, he found a stranger and Brahmin like myself was present and when the whole discussion might generate mixed feelings. ...

The next day, Saturday, 13 February, the Swami delivered his lecture on "Vedanta in Indian life" at the Pacheyappa's Hall. The Hall was packed to its utmost capacity. I was on the platform, and just by my side sat Mr. G. Subrahmanya Iyer, who was later to become the editor of *The Hindu*. At one point of his address the Swami, addressing the students assembled before him, said something to the following effect: "Don't be constantly crying out, *Gita*, *Gita*, *Gita*. The teachings of the *Gita* cannot be truly understood or put into practice by those who, like you, are physically weak and whose vigour is decaying prematurely by the cramming of text-books for examinations. Go and play football, develop your biceps, and be strong, and you will then be fit to understand the teachings of the *Gita*." Here was the opportunity for Mr. G. Subrahmanya Iyer, and he exclaimed in Tamil to those who were near him, even while the Swami was on his legs, "I have said the same thing often, but none would give ear. The Swami says it now, and you all cheer."

Mr. G. Subrahmanya Iyer had once been a very orthodox Hindu, and rigidly addicted to Vedic rituals and observances. He changed to the opposite extreme of a social revolutionary after the virgin-widowhood of his young daughter had given him a rude and painful shock and made him realize the penalties and pains inevitably associated with

Hindu orthodoxy which men had long borne and still do bear with invincible strength and serenity of heart, simply because they believe that the shruti and smriti impose them on the faithful in order to qualify them for and raise them ultimately to the spiritual blessing and innermost joy of supreme liberation from samsara. Mr. Subrahmanya Iyer was in a mood of ecstasy as the Swami went on with his deliverances on this occasion on the topics of "strength" and "fearlessness", and said that without them no spiritual perfection was possible. His words came on the audience with telling effect. "Believe", he said, "that you are not the body or mind, but the soul, the Atman; and that is the first step to the gaining of strength and to uphold and realize the teaching of the Upanishads." He also dwelt at length on the organismal basis and value of caste. Caste was a natural order, the only natural way of solving the problem of life. Mr. G. Subrahmanya Iyer's enthusiasm and ecstasies had somewhat cooled when the Swami spoke on caste and said, too, that caste was not only found in India, but everywhere, and in every country he had seen.

On Sunday, 14 February, the Swami delivered his fourth and last lecture on the "Future of India". I never saw a more crowded scene or a more enthusiastic audience. The Swami's oratory was at its best. He seemed like a lion, traversing the platform to and fro. The roar of his voice reverberated everywhere, and with telling effect. One remarkable utterance which showed the Swami's powers of foresight and omniscience and which I can never forget, was: "Peace, religion, language, government—all together make a nation; but one of these is the basis and the rest we build on that one. Religion is the keynote of Indian life and Indian nationality can be built on that basis."

The next day, Monday, 15 February, the Swami left for Kolkata by steamer. Several of his admirers and followers and personal friends accompanied him in order to take leave when the steamer sailed. Mr. Tilak had invited the Swami to Poona, and he first thought of going there. But he wanted rest, and was ever pining for the Himalayan atmosphere. At the beach, several merchants of the caste of Arya-Vaishyas (known as Komattis) met him and presented a formal address of thanksgiving to him for his services to the holy motherland. The Hon. Mr. Subba Rao of Rajahmundry presented the address to the Swami on their behalf. The Swami simply bowed his acknowledgement, and made kind inquiries of them. Several boarded the steamer, and remained with the Swami to the last. I was one of them, and the pain of having to part from this heaven-sent mahapurusha (great soul) was felt by each and all of us, who kept crowding about him. I begged of the Swami the favour of a moment's interview apart, and he came. We walked a few steps, and then I asked and obtained permission to put two questions. First, "Swamiji, tell me, if indeed, you have done lasting good by your mission to so materialistic a people as the Americans and others in the West." He replied: "Not much. I hope that here and there I have sown a seed which in time might.grow and benefit some at least." The second query was, "When shall we see you again, and on your mission work in South India?" He replied: "Have no doubt about that. I shall take some rest in the Himalayan region, and then burst on the country everywhere like an avalanche." This was not to be, and I never saw the Swami again. I had looked for the last time on his fathomless and compelling eyes, and at the prophetic fire and glow in the face of him whom I consider the greatest man and teacher of the age, a true mahapurusha and messenger from heaven to the people of India and to all mankind. Glory to Swami Vivekananda for ever and ever!

(*Vedanta Kesari*, January-February 1923)

K. S. RAMASWAMI SHASTRI

K. S. Ramaswami Shastri

IT was given to me to meet Swami Vivekananda and spend many days with him at Trivandrum towards the close of 1892 before he went to Chicago to represent Hinduism at the Parliament of Religions in September 1893, and also at Madras after he returned from Chicago and landed at Colombo on 15 January 1897 and reached Madras a few days later. My entire life was transformed by those memorable and holy contacts. I shall briefly record my impressions here to the best of my memory. ...

From Cochin he came to Trivandrum where my father (Prof. K. Sundararama Iyer) and I were at that time. He brought with him a letter of introduction from Cochin to my father at Trivandrum. My father was then the tutor to prince Martanda Varma of Travancore at Trivandrum. I passed my Matriculation in 1892 and joined the Maharaja's College, Trivandrum, for the Intermediate class. It was at this juncture, towards the end of 1892, that fate threw me into Swamiji's holy company.

Swamiji was then unknown to fame but felt a great urge to spread Hinduism and spirituality all over the world. One morning, while I was in my house, he came unexpectedly. I found a person with a beaming face and a tall, commanding figure. He had an orange coloured turban on his head and wore a flowing orange coloured coat which reached down to his feet and round which he wore a girdle at the waist.

Swamiji asked me: "Is Professor Sundararaman here? I have brought a letter to be delivered to him." His voice was rich and full and sounded like a bell. Well does Romain

Rolland say about the voice: "He had a beautiful voice like a violincello, grave without violent contrasts, but with deep vibrations that filled both hall and hearts. Once his audience was held he could make it sink to an intense piano piercing his hearers to the soul." I looked up and saw him and somehow in my boyishness and innocence (I was only fourteen years old at that time) I felt that he was a Maharaja. I took the letter which he gave and ran up to my father who was upstairs and told him: "A Maharaja has come and is waiting below. He gave this letter to be given to you." My father laughed and said: "Ramaswami! What a naive and simple soul you are! Maharajas will not come to houses like ours." I replied: "Please come. I have no doubt that he is a Maharaja." My father came down, saluted Swamiji, and took him upstairs. After a pretty long conversation with Swamiji, my father came down and said to me: "He is no doubt a Maharaja, but not a king over a small territory. He is a king of the boundless and supreme domain of the soul."

Swamiji stayed in our house for nine days at that time. My father has described his impressions of that period in an article entitled "My first Navaratri with Swami Vivekananda".[1] I shall set down briefly the indelible impression left on my mind by Swamiji's words during that memorable visit of his to our house.

One morning as I was reading Kalidasa's Kumarasambhavam, which was one of my text-books in Sanskrit, Swamiji came in. He asked, "What is that book you are studying?" I replied, "It is Kumarasambhavam, Canto I." He asked, "Can you repeat the great poet's description of the Himalayas?" I repeated, in the usual musical mode current in South India, the beautiful and sonorous verses which constitute Kalidasa's description of the Himalayas. Swamiji smiled and looked pleased. He said, "Do you know that I am coming after a long stay amidst the sublimity of the Himalayan scenes and sights?" I felt elated and interested. He asked me to repeat again the opening stanza. I did so. He asked: "Do

1. See pg. 227 of this volume.

you know its meaning? Tell me." I did so. He said, "That is good, but not enough." He then repeated the stanza in his marvellous, musical, measured tones:

अस्त्युत्तरस्यां दिशि देवात्मा हिमालयो नाम नगाधिराज: ।
पूर्वापरौ तोयनिधावगाह्य स्थित: पृथिव्या इव मानदण्ड: ।।

He said: "The important words in this verse are devatat-ma (ensouled by Divinity) and manadanda (measuring-rod). The poet implies and suggests that the Himalaya is not a mere wall accidentally constructed by nature. It is ensouled by Divinity and is the protector of India and her civilization not only from the chill icy blasts blowing from the arctic region but also from the deadly and destructive incursions of invaders. The Himalaya further protects India by sending the great rivers Sindhu, Ganga, and Brahmaputra peren-nially fed by melted ice irrespective of the monsoon rains. Manadanda implies that the poet affirms that the Indian civilization is the best of all human civilizations and forms the standard by which all other human civilizations, past, present, and future, must be tested. Such was the poet's lofty patriotism." I felt thrilled by his words. I treasure them even to this day, and they shine in my heart even now with an undimmed and undiminished splendour.

On another day, he said to me and my father: "Practical patriotism means not a mere sentiment or even emotion of love of the motherland but a passion to serve our fellow-countrymen. I have gone all over India on foot and have seen with my own eyes the ignorance, misery, and squalor of our people. My whole soul is afire and I am burning with a fierce desire to change such evil conditions. Let no one talk of karma. If it was their karma to suffer, it is our karma to relieve the suffering. If you want to find God, serve man. To reach Narayana you must serve the daridra narayanas—the starving millions of India." That was the root from which came the great tree of the Ramakrishna Mission later. His words melted our hearts and kindled in our souls the flame of social service. Thus service was as dear to him as spirituality. In his later life, in a memorable letter he exclaimed, "May I be born again and again and suffer thousands of miseries so that I may worship the only God that exists, the only God I believe in, the sum total of all souls: and, above all, my God the wicked, my God the miserable, my God the poor of all races, of all species, is the special object of my worship."[2] We seem to hear in these passionate words the voice of Rantideva himself.

On yet another day Swamiji told me: "You are still a young boy. I hope and wish that some day you will reverentially study the Upanishads, the *Brahma Sutras*, and the *Bhagavad Gita* which are known as the prasthana-traya (the three supreme sources of Truth), as also the itihasas, the puranas, and the agamas. You will not find the like of all these anywhere else in the world. Man alone, of all living beings, has a hunger in his heart to know the whence and whither, the whys and wherefores of things. There are four key words which you must remember, viz. abhaya (fearlessness), ahimsa (non-injury), asanga (non-attachment), and ananda (bliss). These words really sum up the essence of all our sacred books. Remember them. Their implication will become clear to you later." I was too young then to grasp all these ideas in full. But I gladly laid those lessons to my heart and have tried all my life since then to learn them in their fullness.

During the nine days when Swamiji was in our house, I was near him often as he was gracious to me and also because something in him, like a magnet, drew me towards him. My father had many a discussion with Swamiji on recondite questions of philosophy and religion which were above and beyond my comprehension. But Swamiji's eyes were so magnetic—though full of kindness and love, his voice had such an unusual combination of sweetness and strength, and his gait was so majestic, that it was a great joy for me to be in his presence and bask in the sunshine of his smiles. He now and then told me many other things

2. To Mary Hale, written from Almora on 9 July 1897.

in brief. But at this distance of time—over sixty years since that event—the memorable utterances narrated above are the ones which stand out most prominently from among the memory-pictures of the past. ...

Swamiji reached Madras in the beginning of February 1897. Romain Rolland's description of the grand public recep-tion accorded to Swamiji at Madras is perfectly accurate and I can vouch for it as I myself was an eyewitness. He says: "Madras had been expecting him for weeks in a kind of passionate delirium. She erected for him seventeen triumphal arches, presented him with twenty-four addresses in various languages of Hindustan, and suspended her whole public life at his coming—nine days of roaring fetes.

"He replied to the frenzied expectancy of the people by his message to India, a conch sounding the resurrection of the land of Rama, of Shiva, of Krishna, and calling the heroic Spirit, the immortal Atman, to march to war. He was a general, explaining his 'Plan of Campaign' and calling his people to rise en masse."

I was one of the delirious listeners and admirers of Swamiji. I had by that time passed the B.A. Degree examination from the Kumbakonam College and had joined the Law College at Madras. At that time studies in the Law College were not heavy, the classes being held for two hours every evening, between 5 p.m. and 7 p.m., in the premises of the Presidency College, Madras. The Law students and the Medicos have always been a keen and valiant group. I and my friends went to the railway station at Egmore on the day Swami Vivekananda was expected to reach Madras. A carriage, to which two horses had been yoked, was kept waiting for the Swami. He was to be taken in procession to the Castle Kernan on the beach, where Swamiji stayed for nine days. We saw at the station a sea of human faces. Shouts of "Jai" rent the air when the train carrying Swamiji was sighted. He got down from the train and made his way slowly to the carriage. When the procession had wended its way for some time, I and some others insisted on unyoking the horses and dragging the carriage ourselves. The horses were unharnessed, and many of us started pulling Swamiji's carriage, and, walking slowly, we covered a long distance before reaching the destination. We were perfectly happy as we had achieved our hearts' desire. To us Swami Vivekananda was "India incarnate" and God's holy messenger.

During all the nine days of his stay at Madras I was with Swamiji for most of the time. Throughout all the days there was a never-ending stream of visitors. Many silently sat near him and listened to his words. Some discussed momentous matters with him. A few intimate persons, among whom were some of Swamiji's friends and admirers, discussed with him his plans for future Vedanta work in South India. I was constantly with Swamiji, who had recognized me and recalled his visit to our house at Trivandrum in 1892. I can never forget his eyes which brightened up with a new light and his mobile lips which shone with a divine smile whenever he saw me sitting in front of him. My father was also in Madras at that time and met Swamiji several times. He has left on record his memories of Swamiji, during the latter's stay for nine days at Madras, in a lengthy article entitled "My second Navaratri with Swamiji".

The difference that I noticed between the Vivekananda of 1892 and the Vivekananda of 1897 was what struck me most. In 1892 he looked like one who had a tryst with destiny and was not quite sure when or where or how he was to keep that tryst. But in 1897 he looked like one who had kept that tryst, who clearly knew his mission, and who was confident about its fulfilment. He walked with steady and unfaltering steps and went along his predestined path, issuing commands and being sure of loyal obedience.

One other experience which I had in 1897 was my hearing the songs sung by Swami Vivekananda. That he had a musical voice was already experienced by me in 1892. That his songs had the power of transporting Sri Ramakrishna Paramahamsa into ecstasy became known to me only much later. During the nine days of his stay at Castle Kernan we heard him sing a few of the Ashtapadi songs of Jayadeva, from the famous devotional lyric poem Gita-Govinda. The mode of singing these lyrics in Bengal was evidently different from that adopted in South India. Vivekananda's melodious voice left a lasting impression on my mind.

One evening a somewhat curious and unusual incident took place. An orthodox pundit, who was one among the visitors, suddenly got up and asked Swamiji a direct and unexpected question in Sanskrit: "I learn that you are not a Brahmin and that according to the scriptures you have no right to take sannyasa. How then does it happen that you have donned ochre-coloured robes and entered into the holy order of sannyasis?" Not wishing to discuss at length with such a person, Swami Vivekananda cut short the pundit's argument by pointedly saying: "I belong to the line of Chitragupta to whom every Brahmin prays during his sandhya worship. So, if Brahmins are entitled to sannyasa, much more so am I entitled." Swamiji then turned the tables on the questioner by telling him: "In your Sanskrit question there was an unpar-donable mispronunciation. Panini denounces such mispro-nunciation—"one should not degrade or mispronounce words." So you have no right to carry on this debate." The pundit was nonplussed and went away, especially when he understood that the audience revered Swamiji and resented the irrelevant question. ...

Swami Vivekananda's first public lecture in Madras was on "My plan of campaign" and made a profound and indelible impression on me. ... I felt thrilled to the innermost core of my being by his words and my eyes were wet with tears. Many others who heard the speech were in the same condition. Then and there some of us took a vow to do what we could to relieve the ignorance, poverty, and misery of the masses of India to the extent possible for each one of us.

I also attended Swamiji's lecture on "Vedanta in its application to Indian life". ...

Yet another lecture by Swamiji was on "The Sages of India". It also made a deep impression on my mind.

In conclusion, I wish to refer to the unique experience which I had in May 1952. I was then on a pilgrimage to holy places in North India. It was my privilege and happiness to spend some hours in the Ramakrishna Math at Belur, near Calcutta. The kind Swami who took me round the Belur Math led me eventually into the room where Swami Vivekananda spent his last days. Ordinarily no visitors are allowed inside the room. But the Swami who took me there said: "In your case we gladly made an exception as you met Swamiji early in your life and have been, like your honoured father, an admirer and follower of the Ramakrishna Mission all your life." I entered the holy room with deep devotion and bated breath. It overlooks the river Ganga. The room throbs with an atmosphere that is sacred, solemn, and serene. I drank with brimming eyes the beauty of the grand view from the room and deeply felt the holiness of the place. I sat there in meditation for a while, thinking of Swami Vivekananda and of his peerless services to India, to Hinduism, and to the cause of spirituality all over the world. While inside that room where Swami Vivekananda once lived, I felt that the divine flame of spiritual knowledge (jnana-dipa, as referred to by Sri Krishna in the *Gita*), was lighted in my heart.

(*Prabuddha Bharata*, September & October 1953)

A. Srinivasa Pai

I n the year 1893 while I was a student reading in the Presidency College, Chennai, I had the good fortune of coming into personal contact with Swami Vivekananda.[1] It was shortly before he left for America to attend the Parliament of Religions at Chicago. He was then unknown to fame but his unique personality attracted a considerable number of people—a good proportion among them being students—to his informal talks. I do not recollect seeing at these meetings any of the leaders of Hindu society in Chennai then, but there were students, teachers, second grade officials and lawyers. It was after the Swami returned from America in 1897 with a worldwide fame that the leaders and high-grade officials used to flock in hundreds to listen to his talks and lectures.

On his visit in 1893 he was residing with Mr. Bhattacharya (a Bengali gentleman, then Deputy Accountant General at Chennai) in a house situated at a short distance from the southern end of the Marina. I used to go to this house in the evenings with some fellow-students to listen to the Swami. We used to squat in the orthodox fashion very near the Swami on carpets spread on the floor. Vivekananda would smoke while talking. His talk covered a large variety of subjects, and it was delightful to listen to him.

In those days knowledge of ancient Hindu philosophy and doctrines was far less popular among the English-

---

1. These reminiscences are based on the recollections of myself and my younger brother with whom I compared notes before recording—*Author.*

educated Hindus in Chennai than now; and there were also fewer popular writings on the subject. Our great gods in those days were Mill, Herbert Spencer, Huxley, Leslie Stephen, and Haeckel. To us theirs was the last word in philosophy, politics, and sociology. And so, Vivekananda's expositions—logical and trenchant as they were—came as wonderful surprises. We had, however, no proper grounding to appreciate his expositions at their true worth. And the prejudices of some of us students in favour of the above-named European writers were hard to break through.

Once Vivekananda explained to us how the modern doctrine of evolution had been anticipated by our sage Kapila. On another occasion, speaking of a Personal God and Impersonal God, he tried to show how the position of an agnostic or even atheist was really not one of negation, as they had to believe in continuity—a continuous Principle running through all eternity. The position of the orthodox Christians, he said, was illogical and untenable. An arbitrary and sudden creation of a soul and then its eternal damnation or salvation—it was like "a stick with only one end."

There was plenty of talk on lighter subjects. His own college days and the pranks that he and his fellow-students played on some of their professors; how once they struck work and "went away and smoked". The stories of "the marvellous" which he told us I distinctly remember. One of these was of a blind man whose memory and sense of hearing were exceptionally acute. When the Swami was quite a young boy, this blind man had once heard him talk and sing. Years afterwards he came one night to a house where Vivekananda was staying. On hearing the Swami sing he at once recognized the voice and asked whether he was not the boy whom he had heard in such and such a year at such and such a place. This blind man while walking in the streets would clap his hands, and listening to the sound would say, "Here on my right is a vacant space," or "There on my left is tall building," and so on. The other story was of a "magician", a man (a Mussalman, if I recollect correctly) who had acquired certain siddhis or (so-called) supernatural powers. A European wanted to test his powers, and one evening they drove together in an open carriage of the European in a street of Kolkata. While they were driving the "magician" said to the European, "Now ask for anything you want and I shall give it to you." The European thought for a moment and then said, "Give me a bottle of champagne," knowing that no such thing was in the carriage or anywhere near at hand. The "magician" stretched out his arm, clutched at something in the air and brought in a bottle of champagne. Then saying "Now look," he waved his hand towards the right row of shops in the street and all the lights in that row were put out; while the lights in the opposite row were burning as before. Before the people in the street and shops could quite recover from their surprise, he waved his hand again and the lights in the right row were relit.

I am reminded of another story he told us while on the subject of the rude and at times insulting behaviour of Europeans in India towards "natives". Naturally, he spoke with much feeling on the subject as every self-respecting Indian would. Once, it seems, a solicitor in Kolkata was rude and insulting to an Indian barrister. The leading Indian clients and lawyers held a meeting and resolved to boycott that particular solicitor. "And from the next day," said Vivekananda, with an expressive gesture tilting his thumb towards his lips, "the solicitor had to suck his thumb."

The bareheaded photographs in the book *Swami Vivekananda's Speeches and Writings*, published by Messrs G. A. Natesan & Co., give a good idea of Swamiji's appearance. But no photograph or description can give a correct idea of the power of his eyes. They were wonderful. Like the "Ancient Mariner" in Coleridge's famous poem he "held you by the eye". His voice too had an indefinable attraction. Though not ringing and silvery like Mrs. Beasant's in her prime, but more soft and pleasant like Mr. Norton's, it attracted and held you. He could sing beautifully. One evening as we were sitting listening to him, a pretty little child—the daughter of Mr. Bhattacharya, I believe—toddled in. He took the child on his lap and sang a Punjabi song. He observed that the song was attributed to Guru Nanak and told us of its origin. One evening, at the time of arati, Nanak went to a temple. The Brahmin priests would not allow him to enter. So, he turned aside and sang this song in which he compares the sky to a silver plate, the stars to little lights—nirajans—in that plate used for arati, the perfumed evening breeze to incense, and so on, reminding us, students, of Moore's poem which we had read in one of the School Text Books of the time, beginning with the lines:

> The Turf shall be my fragrant shrine,
> My Temple, Lord, that arch of Thine.

In person Vivekananda was not flabby like many Bengalis whom we see, but was sturdy and somewhat thickset. His complexion was brown with a slight coppery hue.

In manners Vivekananda was natural, unaffected and unconventional. There was none of that solemn gravity, measured utterance, and even temper that we usually associate with a sage. At times his manners were somewhat Johnsonian and brusque when he wanted to put down one who had asked a silly question or a question intended to show off one's knowledge. One hot morning (this was after he returned from America to Chennai) at the end of a long sitting when many questions had been asked and answered, a somewhat conceited young man asked pompously, "What is the cause of misery in this world, Swami?" "Ignorance is the cause of misery", blurted out Vivekananda and rose and closed the interview. On another occasion someone in the audience pointed out to the Swami that the view expressed by him on some point of philosophy differed from that of Sri Shankaracharya. "Well", said the Swami, "Shankaracharya was a man, you are a man, and you can think for yourself." An orthodox pundit had an interview with the Swami in which he attempted to show off his learning. Speaking of that interview the Swami said, "The fellow who cannot pronounce 'jnana' properly has the cheek to criticize my pronunciation of Sanskrit."

On Vivekananda's return to Chennai from America in 1897, the public reception given to him was magnificent and the crowds which came to greet him were some of the largest. His first public lecture in Chennai cannot be called a success as a lecture. But that was due to the over enthusiasm of the crowds. It was arranged for, I believe, in a big circus-tent, but even that was found insufficient to hold the crowds, and the Swami had to come outside and mount a carriage to address the huge concourse in the "*Gita* fashion" as he said. He strained his voice to the utmost, gesticulated, but it was no good. The noise and disorder were great and the lecture had to be given up after a short time. The subsequent lecture in the Victoria Hall on "The Sages of India" was a grand success. It was a very impressive lecture marked by a flowing eloquence. When he dealt with the love of gopis towards Sri Krishna, and explained the true significance of that sublime love, the expression of his face and especially of his eyes was beatific and soul-stirring.

Informal talks in the mornings and answering of questions were arranged in a canopy put up on the Marina, near the old Capper-House Hotel, somewhere near the site of the present premises of Queen Mary's College. The leaders of Hindu society in Chennai, big officials and lawyers and other people came in hundreds on this occasion, and we students found it hard to go near the Swami. One morning a European lady (a Protestant missionary, I believe) came and spoke somewhat disparagingly of the enforced celibacy of a monk's life and of the harmful results of the starving of a noble instinct (noble, when rightly regulated). After a short psychological and philosophical explanation of the necessity of celibacy for monk (which perhaps was not quite appreciated or understood by the lady), he turned to her and said a little humorously: "In your country, madam, a bachelor is feared. But here you see they are worshipping me, a bachelor."

Here I may mention that once the Swami in a communicative mood made a personal confession, "I am thirty years old now and have never known a woman."

Once he said to a number of young students in the audience that it was their first duty to cultivate physical strength and health. "You will understand the *Gita* better by playing football." He expressed on one occasion the view that it was the physically weak who yielded to temptations easily, and that those with plenty of physical vigour and strength were far better able to resist temptations and exercise self-control than the former.

Once, referring to himself he said, "There is an ustad under these robes" (an ustad is an expert gymnast or a teacher of gymnastics).

At this time (1897, after his return from America) Vivekananda was residing in Castle Kernan, the well-known house on the Marina. When I first went to Chennai it was known as the Ice-House; then the late Mr. Biligiri Iyangar bought it and named it Castle Kernan after Mr. Justice Kernan.

During these memorable days some of us students were invited in Castle Kernan, and we ate with Vivekananda. The Swami's appetite was great and he ate heartily. Once, pointing humorously to a dish of ice-cream before him he said, "I can renounce everything except this." At times baskets of fruits used to sent to him by his friends from Bangalore. As soon as they would arrive, they would be opened and the contents distributed among those present and the Swami also ate.

Sometimes in the early mornings Vivekananda would bathe in the sea opposite Castle Kernan along with a number of students.

Informal talks were at times held in the rooms of the Triplicane Literary Society. The late Dewan Bahadur R. Raghunatha Rao and a number of other social reformers, including my old Assistant Professor of history, the late Mr. A. Subba Rao (a sturdy social reformer and agnostic) used

to attend. Some of the social reformers were snubbed by
the Swami and he criticized their views and methods. Once
when Mr. A. Subba Rao spoke rather disparagingly of the
thinking power and views of our old rishis, the Swami remarked that Mr. Subba Rao could have no idea of the power
of intense meditation which the rishis had acquired through
long self-discipline, and added, "You will be burnt to ashes if
you think for half a minute like them."

When one evening the Swami was discoursing on "Faith
in God" in the Triplicane Literary Society, Dewan Bahadur
Raghunatha Rao broke in in a solemn manner, "I have
always preached that no nation, no race, and no individual
who did not believe in God ever became great." At this
some of the irreverent young students smiled in an amused
manner.

The Swami spoke of his guru Sri Ramakrishna and some
of his apparently queer actions undertaken with a view to
killing the "self" in him, the significance of which many—
especially in Europe and America—could not understand.
With reference to ordinary American audiences he said, "If
I had spoken of these acts to them, they would have thrown
me and my guru into the nearest ditch."

When the effect of religious beliefs (Hindu and Christian)
on the masses came up for discussion, Vivekananda said, "If,
like me, you had visited the slums of Europe and America
and seen how similar to brutes the inhabitants of those slums
are, and then compared them with our masses in India, your
doubts regarding the effect of Hindu religious belief on the
masses would have vanished."

(*Vedanta Kesari*, May 1927)

Sarah Ellen Waldo

When Swami Vivekananda's Chennai disciples decided to raise a sum of money sufficient to send him to represent Hinduism at the World's Fair at Chicago in 1893, they were in ignorance of the exact date of the opening of the Parliament of Religions. Consequently the Swami reached Chicago in the spring, several months before the time set for the delegates to meet. At first, he was much disturbed when he learnt how long he would have to wait, because his funds, none too extensive to start with, were running low. They had been greatly depleted by the bad management of his travelling companions to whom he had entrusted them. It became a problem to him how to maintain himself in a strange land until the time should come for him to fulfil his mission in America. He found his way to Boston and nearly resolved to return at once to India; but his charming personality soon won him friends, and his confidence returned.

He was most hospitably entertained in the family of a Professor of Harvard College, who persuaded him to adhere to his original plan to speak at the approaching Religious Congress.[1] By the advice of this kind friend Swami Vivekananda returned to Chicago, and his brilliant success at the Parliament of Religions is still fresh in the minds of all who heard him there. His very first words in his melodious voice aroused a perfect storm of applause. It is doubtful if any one of the thousands who listened to those first eloquent utterances had the least idea that never before in his life had

---

1. Actually he lived elsewhere, but the professor helped him in his mission.

284

he stood before an audience. So ready was his speech, so excellent his mastery of English, so finished his language, so flashing his wit and repartee that every one supposed he was an experienced public speaker. Surely the spirit and power of his Master spoke through him that day!

After the close of the Parliament of Religions, Swami Vivekananda received many flattering offers to lecture in various parts of the United States. He was so desirous to send help to his fellow sannyasis in India that he accepted an engagement with a Lecture Bureau and delivered many lectures in the Western States. He soon found, however, that he was utterly unsuited for such a career. Naturally, he could not speak to promiscuous audiences on the topics nearest to his heart, and the life of ceaseless change was too strenuous for a contemplative nature like his own. He was at this time a far different being from what he afterwards developed into. He was dreamy and meditative, often so wrapped in his own thoughts as to be hardly conscious of his surroundings. The constant friction of alien thoughts, the endless questioning, the frequent sharp conflict of wits in this Western world awoke a different spirit, and he became as alert and wide awake as the world in which he found himself.

At great pecuniary sacrifice, the Swami severed his connection with the Lecture Bureau; but once more his own master, he turned his steps towards New York. A Chicago friend was instrumental in bringing him to this metropolis of the U.S., and he reached New York in the early part of 1894. His Western experiences had convinced him that there were many in America who would gladly learn of the ancient philosophy of India, and he hoped that in this city he would be able to come in contact with such inquiring minds.

He gave a few public lectures, but was not yet in a position to begin regular work, as he was a guest in the homes of his friends. In the summer of that year he went to New England, still as a visitor, and spent a week or two at Greenacre where Miss Farmer was inaugurating the "Greenacre Conferences", which in later years became so widely known through the school of Comparative Religions conducted there by the late Dr. Lewis G. Janes, who was long the gifted and liberal minded President of the Brooklyn Ethical Association.

From New England, Swami Vivekananda returned to New York in the autumn, and at a lecture he gave in the parlour of a friend he met Dr. Janes, who at once recognized the unusual character and attainments of the Swami and invited him to lecture before the Association in Brooklyn. The two men became warmly attached to each other and formed a friendship that lasted as long as they lived.

Swami Vivekananda lectured in Brooklyn for the first time on 30 December 1894 and his success was immediate. A large and enthusiastic audience greeted his appearance at the Pouch Mansion, and a course of lectures there and at other places in Brooklyn soon followed. From this time his public work in America really began. He established himself in quarters of his own, where he held several classes a week and came into more intimate relations with his students. Earnest people flocked to hear him and to learn the ancient teachings of India on the all-embracing character of her philosophy that every soul must be saved, that all religions were true, being steps in the progress of man toward a higher and ever higher spiritual realization—and above all to hear the constant lessons of the Swami on a world-wide, universal religious toleration.

At this time the Swami was living very simply in New York; and his earliest classes were held in the small room he occupied, and in the beginning were attended by only three or four persons. They grew with astonishing rapidity, and, as the little room filled to overflowing, became very picturesque. The Swami himself always sat on the floor, and most of his audience likewise. The marble-topped dresser, the arms of the sofa, and even the corner washstand helped to furnish seats for the constantly increasing numbers. The door was left open, and the overflow filled the hall and sat on the stairs. And those first classes! How intensely interesting they were! Who that was privileged to attend them can ever forget them? The Swami so dignified yet so simple, so gravely earnest, so eloquent, and the close ranks of students, forgetting all inconveniences, hanging breathless on his every word!

It was a fit beginning for a movement that has since grown to such grand proportions. In this unpretentious way did Swami Vivekananda inaugurate the work of teaching Vedanta philosophy in New York. The Swami gave his services free as air. The rent was paid by voluntary subscriptions, and when these were found insufficient, Swami hired a hall and gave secular lectures on India and devoted the proceeds to the maintenance of the classes. He said that Hindu teachers of religion felt it to be their duty to support their classes and the students too, if they were unable to care for themselves; and the teachers would willingly make any sacrifice they possibly could to assist a needy disciple.

The classes began in February 1895, and lasted until June. But long before that time, they had outgrown their small beginnings and had removed downstairs to occupy an entire parlour floor and extension. The classes were held nearly every morning and on several evenings in each week. Some Sunday lectures were also given, and there were "question" classes to help those to whom the teaching was so new and strange that they were desirous to have an opportunity for more extended explanation.

In June, after four months of constant lecturing and teaching, Swami Vivekananda accepted the invitation of one of his friends and went to Percy, N. H., for a period of rest in the silence of the pinewoods. Before he left New York, he promised to meet at Thousand Island Park any students who were sufficiently interested in Vedanta to follow him so far, and there give them more special instruction. One of the class members had a cottage there and had invited the Swami to be her guest for as long a period as he felt inclined to remain. Swami said that those students who were willing to put aside all other interests and devote themselves to studying Vedanta, travelling more than three hundred miles to a suitable spot, were the ones really in earnest, and he should recognize them as disciples. He did not expect many would take so much trouble; but if any responded, he would do his share of helping them on the path.

About the middle of June, six or eight students gathered in the little house at Thousand Island Park; and true to his promise, Swami Vivekananda came there on the 20th of the month and remained for seven blessed weeks. A few more students joined us, until we numbered twelve, including our hostess. To those who were fortunate enough to be there with the Swami, those are weeks of ever hallowed memory, so fraught were they with unusual opportunity for spiritual growth. No words can describe what that blissful period meant (and still means) to the devoted little band who followed the Swami from New York to the Island in the St. Lawrence, who daily served him with joy, and listened to him with heartfelt thankfulness. His whole heart was in his work, and he taught like one inspired. Every morning he could hardly wait for the household duties to be attended to, so eager was he to begin his work of teaching. As early as it could be managed, we gathered around him, and for two and sometimes three hours he would steadily expound the teachings of his Master, Sri Ramakrishna. These ideas were new and strange to us, and we were slow in assimilating them; but the Swami's patience never flagged, his enthusiasm never waned. In the afternoons, he talked to us more informally, and we took usually a long walk. Every evening we adjourned to an upstairs piazza that commanded a glorious view over the waters and islands of the broad river. It was an enchanting picture that our eyes rested upon. At our feet stretched a thick wood, the tops of its waving trees like a lake of vivid green, gradually lost themselves in the dancing blue waters of the St. Lawrence. Not one building of any kind was in sight, save a hotel on a distant island whose many gleaming lights were reflected on the shimmering waves. We were alone with nature, and it was a fitting scene in which to listen to the utterances of such a teacher. The Swami did not appear to address us directly, but rather seemed to be speaking to himself in words of fire, as it were, so intense were they, so eloquent and convincing, burning into the very hearts of his listeners and never to be forgotten. We listened in utter silence, almost holding our breath for fear of disturbing the current of his thoughts, or losing one of those inspired words.

As the days and weeks passed by, we began to really understand and grasp the meaning of what we heard, and we gladly accepted the teaching. Every one of the students there received initiation at the hands of the Swami, thus becoming disciples, the Swami assuming towards them the position of a guru, or spiritual father, as is done in India, where the tie uniting guru and disciple is the closest one known, outranking that of parent and child, or even husband and wife. It was purely a coincidence that there were just twelve of us!

The ceremony of initiation was impressive from its extreme simplicity. A small altar fire, beautiful flowers, and the earnest words of the teacher alone marked it as different from our daily lessons. It took place at sunrise of a beautiful summer day, and the scene still lives fresh in our memories. Of those who became brahmacharinis at Thousand Island Park, two are dead, and one is now in India helping to carry on the work nearest to Swami Vivekananda's heart, the uplifting of his fellow-countrymen. Most of the others have rendered faithful service in the cause of Vedanta during the ten years that have passed since then.

In August the Swami went to France and later to England to start there a centre for Vedanta work. At the earnest solicitation of his many friends and students in New York Swamiji returned to us in December of 1895 and opened classes once more. There were nine in each week and all were attended by large numbers, to the full capacity of the rooms. This time we were fortunate enough to secure the services of a good stenographer, who, to unusual abilities, later added the

service of a devoted adherent. He became strongly attached
to the Swami and his teaching and never spared himself in
his work for the cause. He subsequently accompanied the
Swami to England and to India, and it is entirely due to his
efforts that the Swami's utterances in those countries have
been preserved. The fruits of his labours in New York are
known to us in the books, *Raja Yoga, Bhakti Yoga,* and *Karma
Yoga,* besides several pamphlets of the Sunday lectures. The
New York lectures on Jnana Yoga have never been published, although they are among the finest the Swami ever
gave. Those in bock form that bear the name *Jnana Yoga* were
delivered in England and India.[2]

A few more students became disciples in New York, some
of them being initiated on the occasion of the celebration of
the birthday of Sri Ramakrishna in 1896. In March of this year
Swami Vivekananda went to Boston, Detroit, and Chicago to
lecture. He delivered several addresses in Cambridge, Massachusetts, and one of these, known as the "Harvard Address"
has been preserved in pamphlet form and became widely
known, both in the United States and in India.

In the middle of April, the Swami sailed for England
where he lectured for many months, being joined there first
by Swami Saradananda and later by Swami Abhedananda,
who is now the head of the Vedanta Society in New York.
From London Swami Vivekananda returned to India at the
close of 1896 accompanied by his ever faithful stenographer
and several of his English disciples. He did much public
work there and many of his lectures delivered in India are
now in print, both in book and in pamphlet form. After more
than two years of most arduous labour, the Swami's health
broke down, and he was forced to retire to the monastery
at Belur for a much-needed rest. In the autumn of 1899 he
sailed for England, accompanied by Swami Turiyananda. He
did not remain long in London, but came once more to the

2. This refers to the book published in New York in 1902. The *Jnana
Yoga* published by Advaita Ashrama contains the lectures delivered in
New York as well.

United States. He made only a brief stay in New York and then went to California. The climate there proved very beneficial to his health, and he was able to deliver many lectures, from Los Angeles to San Francisco. He thus made a successful beginning of Vedanta work on the Pacific Coast; and later, Swami Turiyananda went to California to carry on the work thus inaugurated. A friend of the cause presented a large tract of land in the California mountains to Swami Vivekananda. It is situated about twelve miles from the far-famed Lick Observatory on Mt. Hamilton. The Shanti Ashrama has been established there; and for a couple of months each year the Swami in charge of the Vedanta work in San Francisco establishes a retreat there, accompanied by those members of his classes who wish to enjoy a period of meditation. They mostly live in tents, although a few wooden cabins have been erected under the fine old trees.

In the summer of 1900, Swami Vivekananda returned to New York, making short stops *en route* at Chicago and Detroit to visit his old friends there. When he reached New York, he was much pleased to find that the Vedanta Society had at last succeeded in securing a home. This was in East 58th Street, and the Swami spent seven weeks there. He gave a few public lectures, but he did not care to do much work of this kind. He was chiefly desirous to meet his old friends and disciples; and as in the days at Thousand Island Park, he spent most of his time in teaching them and in conversation with them. It was a happy time apparently for both teacher and disciples. All too soon, it came to an end. The Swami had received an invitation to address the Religious Congress held that year at the Paris Exposition. So he sailed from New York in August, never to revisit the city where he had done so much work in teaching and lecturing. He might have returned had his life been prolonged, but it was not to be.

In Paris, Swamiji met many prominent people and made many warm friends. He mastered the French language sufficiently to converse with those who could not speak English. From France he started with a party of friends for Egypt to visit the Cataracts of the Nile. But at Alexandria he received news of the death of a friend in India, which necessitated his immediate return to that country. His many Western friends saw him no more, but his memory will never die in our hearts and our gratitude for his loving service to us can never fail. It is a priceless privilege to have known such a man. He was truly a mahatma and did a great work, work that will long be an influence in the lives of his own countrymen as well as in those of his European and American friends. May he be forever blessed!

(Prabuddha Bharata, January 1906)

A few of those who had heard Swami Vivekananda in Brooklyn began to go to the place where he lived in New York. It was just an ordinary room on the second-floor of a lodging house, and as the classes rapidly increased beyond the capacity of the chairs and one lounge, students sat on the dresser, on the corner marble wash-basin, and still others on the floor, like the Swami himself, who, thus seated cross-legged after the manner of his own country, taught his eager students the great truths of Vedanta.

At last he felt that he was fairly started on his mission, which was to deliver to the Western world the message of his Master, Sri Ramakrishna, which proclaimed the truth and fundamental unity of all religions. The classes grew so rapidly that they soon overflowed the small upstairs room, and the large double parlours below were engaged. In them the Swami taught until the end of the season. The teaching was entirely free, the necessary expenses being met by voluntary contributions. These proving insufficient to pay the rent and provide for the maintenance of the Swami, the classes came near ending for want of pecuniary support. At once the Swami announced a course of public lectures on secular subjects for which he could receive remuneration, and so earned the money to support the religious classes. ...

By this time some of the students had become so deeply interested in the Swami's teachings that they were desirous to have them continued through the summer. He, however, was tired after a hard season's work and at first demurred against prolonging his labours through the hot weather. Then, too, many of the students would be out of town at this time of year. The problem solved itself. One of our number owned a small cottage at Thousand Island Park, the largest island in the St. Lawrence River; and she offered the use of it to the Swami and as many of us as it would accommodate. This plan appealed to the Swami and he agreed to join us there after a brief visit to the Maine Camp of one of his friends.

Miss Dutcher, the student to whom the cottage belonged, feeling that a special sanctuary should be prepared for the occasion, built as a true love offering to her teacher, a new wing that was nearly as large as the original cottage. The place was ideally situated on high ground, overlooking a wide sweep of the beautiful river with many of its far famed Thousand Islands. Clayton could be dimly discerned in the distance, while the nearer and wider Canadian shores bounded the view to the north. The cottage stood on the side of a hill, which on the north and west sloped abruptly down towards the shores of the river and of a little inlet that like a small lake lay behind the house. The house itself was literally 'built upon a rock', and huge boulders lay all around it. The new wing stood on the steep slope of the rocks like a great lantern tower with windows on three sides, three storeys deep at the back, and only two in the front. The lower room was occupied by one of the students. The one over it opened out of the main part of the house by several doors, and being large and convenient, became our classroom, where for hours each day the Swami gave us familiar instruction. Over this room was the one devoted exclusively to the use of the Swami. In order that it might be perfectly secluded, Miss D. had supplied it with a separate outside staircase, although there was also a door opening upon the second storey of the piazza.

This upstairs piazza played an important part in our lives, as all the Swami's evening talks were given here. It was wide and roomy, roofed in, and extended along the south and west side of the cottage. Miss D. had the west side of it carefully screened off by a partition, so that none of the strangers who frequently visited the piazza to see the magnificent view it commanded could intrude upon our privacy. There, close by his own door, sat our beloved teacher every evening during our stay and communed with us who sat silent in the darkness, eagerly drinking in his inspired words. The place was a veritable sanctuary. At our feet, like a sea of green, waved the leaves of the tree tops; for the entire place was surrounded by thick woods. Not one house of the large village could be seen, it was as if we were in the heart of some dense forest, miles away from the haunts of men. Beyond the trees spread the wide expanse of the St. Lawrence, dotted here and there with islands, some of which gleamed bright with the lights of hotels and boardinghouses. All these were so far away that they seemed more like a pictured scene than a reality.

Not a human sound penetrated our seclusion; we heard but the murmur of the insects, the sweet songs of the birds, or the gentle sighing of the wind through the leaves. Part of the time the scene was illumined by the soft rays of the moon and her face was mirrored in the shining waters beneath. In this scene of enchantment, "the world forgetting, by the world forgot", we spent seven blessed weeks with our beloved teacher, listening to his words of inspiration. Immediately after our evening meal each day of our stay, we all repaired to the upper piazza and awaited the coming of our Master. Nor had we long to wait; for hardly had we assembled there, the door of his room would open and he would quietly step out and take his accustomed seat. He always spent two hours with us and more often much longer. One glorious night, when the moon was about the full, he talked to us until it set below the western horizon, apparently as unconscious as we were of the lapse of time.

Of these talks it was not possible to take notes. They are preserved only in the hearts of the listeners. None of us can ever forget the uplift, the intense spiritual life of those hallowed hours. The Swami poured out all his heart at those times; his own struggles were enacted again before us, the very spirit of his Master seemed to speak through his lips, to satisfy all doubts, to answer all questioning, to soothe every fear. Many times the Swami seemed hardly conscious of our presence, and then we almost held our breath for fear of disturbing him and checking the flow of his thoughts. He would rise from his seat and pace up and down the narrow limits of the piazza, pouring forth a perfect torrent of eloquence. Never was he more gentle, more lovable than during these hours. It may have been much like the way his own great Master taught his disciples, just allowing them to listen to the outpourings of his own spirit in communion with himself.

It was a perpetual inspiration to live with a man like Swami Vivekananda. From morning till night it was ever the same—we lived in a constant atmosphere of intense spirituality. Often playful and fun-loving, full of merry jest and quick repartee, he was never for a moment far from the dominating note of his life. Everything could furnish a text or an illustration, and in a moment we would find ourselves swept from amusing tales of Hindu mythology to the deepest philosophy. The Swami had an inexhaustible fund of mythological lore, and surely no race is more abundantly supplied with myths than those ancient Aryans. He loved to tell them to us and we delighted to listen, for he never failed to point out the reality hidden under myth and story and to draw from it valuable spiritual lessons. Never had fortunate students greater cause to congratulate themselves on having so gifted a teacher!

By a singular coincidence just twelve students followed the Swami to Thousand Island Park, and he told us that he accepted us as real disciples and that was why he so constantly and freely taught us, giving us his best. All the twelve were not together at once, ten being the largest number present at any one time. Two of our number subsequently became sannyasins, both being initiated at Thousand Island Park. On the occasion of the consecration of the second sannyasin the Swami initiated five of us brahmacharins, and later, in New York City, the rest of our number took initiation, together with several others of the Swami's disciples there.

It was decided, when we went to Thousand Island Park, that we should live as a community, each doing his or her share of the housework in order that no alien presence should mar the serenity of our household. The Swami himself was an accomplished cook and often prepared for us delicious dishes. He had learned how to cook when, after his Master's death, he had served his brethren, a band of young men, his brother-disciples, whom he held together and taught, continuing the training begun by his Master, in order to make them fit to spread abroad over the world the truths imparted by Sri Ramakrishna.

Every morning, just as soon as our various tasks were over (and often before), the Swami called us together in the large parlour that served us as classroom and began to teach us. Each day he took up some special subject, or expounded from some sacred book, as the *Bhagavad Gita*, the Upanishads, or *Vedanta Sutras* of Vyasa. The sutras are in the form of aphorisms, being the briefest possible statements of the great truths imbedded in the Vedas. They have neither nominative nor verb, and so intent were the writers of them on eliminating every unnecessary word, that a Hindu proverb says that 'a writer of sutras would rather give one of his sons than add a syllable to his sutra.'

Because of their almost enigmatical brevity the *Vedanta Sutras* offer a rich field for the commentator, and three great Hindu philosophers, Shankara, Ramanuja, and Madhva, wrote elaborate commentaries upon them. In his morning talks the Swami would take up first one of these commentaries, then another, showing how each commentator was guilty of twisting the meaning of the sutras to meet his own particular view, and would read in the aphorism whatever would best substantiate his own interpretation. The Swami often pointed out to us how old is the bad habit of "text torturing".

Thus it was that in these lessons the point of view presented was sometimes that of pure dualism as represented by Madhva, while on another day it was that of the qualified non-dualism taught by Ramanuja, known as Vishishtadvaita. Most frequently, however, the monistic commentary of Shankara was taken up; but because of his subtlety, he was more difficult to understand. So to the end Ramanuja remained the favourite among the students.

Sometime the Swami took up the Bhakti Sutras of Narada. They are a short exposition of devotion to God, which gives one some conception of the lofty Hindu ideal of real, all-absorbing love for the Lord, love that literally possesses the devotee to the exclusion of every other thought. Bhakti is the Hindu method of realizing union with the Divine, a method which naturally appeals to the devout, it is to love God and Him only.

In these talks the Swami for the first time spoke to us at length about his great Master, Sri Ramakrishna, of his daily life with him and of his struggles with his own tendency to disbelieve, which at times drew tears from his Master. The other disciples have often said that Sri Ramakrishna always told them that Swami Vivekananda was a great soul who had come especially to help his work, and that as soon as he knew who he really was, he would at once give up the body. But he added that before that time arrived, there was a certain mission which the Swami would have to accomplish, to help not only India but other lands as well. Frequently Sri Ramakrishna said, "I have other disciples far away, who speak a language I do not understand."

After seven weeks spent at Thousand Island Park the Swami returned to New York City and later went abroad. He lectured and held classes in England until the end of November, when he returned to New York and resumed his teaching there. On this occasion, his students secured a com-

petent stenographer and thus preserved the Swami's words.
The reports of the class lectures were soon after published in
book form, and these books, together with the pamphlets of
the public lectures, remain today as enduring monuments of
Swami Vivekananda's work in America. To those of us who
were privileged to hear the lectures given, the Swami's very
presence seems to live again and to speak to us from the
printed pages; so exactly and accurately were his utterances
transcribed by one, who subsequently became one of the
Swami's most devoted disciples. The work of both teacher
and taught was purely a labour of love, and so the blessing
of the Lord rested upon it.

*(*Inspired Talks*, pp. 7-18)

Sister Devamata

My first contact with the Ramakrishna Movement was through Swami Vivekananda. It occurred before the Mission had taken definite form, when all there was to tell of the far-spread work to be done later was a band of wandering sannyasis, waiting for the call, yet half unaware that they were waiting. One of the band said to me years after: "If we had dreamed of the labours that lay before us, we would not have spent our strength in severe austerities or taxed our bodies by privations and long wanderings. All that was asked of us, we thought, was a simple life of renunciation, obeying in humble spirit what our Master had taught us."

The first hint of anything beyond this, I learnt from the same source, was a quiet voice heard only by Swami Vivekananda as he lay at the point of death in a Himalayan glade under a rude thatch of dry branches. It said: "You will not die. You have a great work to do in the world." He told it to two brother-disciples with him, and one of them told it to me. But the voice came without a form to give it substance. How could they know that the words spoken were prophecy?

Time proved them to be such. Their fulfilment had just begun, when all unexpectedly I touched the Swami's orbit, now circling a world. My mother, sister, and I had spent the month of June at the Great Fair of 1893 in Chicago, and we were planning to return for the Congress of Religions in the autumn on our way to Japan and the Orient. A death in the family brought our journey to a halt in a little town in Ohio. Soon after our arrival there the Swedenborgian minister, as a

SISTER DEVAMATA

courtesy to strangers, invited us to dine with him. We went. The minister himself met us at the door, his face aglow with enthusiasm. He had just returned from the Congress of Religions and he could talk of nothing else.

He described at length the various sessions of the Congress, dwelling with emphasis on this delegate or that. "But," he continued, "there was one speaker who stood out above all others, because of his learning, his eloquence, and his impressive personality. No other could compare with him except two or three Roman Catholic prelates, and they had sent their best men." He paused, leaving his brilliant figure without name or nationality. "Who was he?" I asked eagerly. The minister replied quietly: "A Hindu—Swami Vivekananda."

I was prepared to be keenly interested, for the spiritual teachings of India were not unfamiliar to me. Edwin Arnold's *Light of Asia* had acquainted me with the exalted beauty of Lord Buddha's life and doctrine; I had read and reread Mohini Chatterjee's translation of *The Bhagavad Gita*, looking up all his references to parallel passages in the Bible; and long hours had been devoted through the previous winter to the study of Max Muller's English version of the Upanishads. I still have the copy, worn and marked, that I used at that time. Thus a gradual orientation had taken place in my mind.

Autumn brought our return to New York. Winter set in with its busy routine, but the memory of the conversation with the Swedenborgian minister still remained vivid. One day, as I was walking up Madison Avenue, I saw in the window of the Hall of the Universal Brotherhood a modest sign saying: "Next Sunday at 3 p.m. Swami Vivekananda will speak here on 'What is Vedanta?' and the following Sunday on 'What is Yoga?'." I reached the hall twenty minutes before the hour. It was already over half full. It was not large, however—a long, narrow room with a single aisle and benches reaching from it to the wall; a low platform holding reading-desk and chair at the far end; and a flight of stairs at

the back. The hall was on the second storey and these stairs
gave the only way of access to it—audience and speaker
both had to make use of them. By the time three o'clock
had arrived, hall, stairs, window-sills, and railings, all were
crowded to their utmost capacity. Many even were standing
below, hoping to catch a faint echo of the words spoken in
the hall above.

A sudden hush, a quiet step on the stairs, and Swami
Vivekananda passed in stately erectness up the aisle to the
platform. He began to speak; and memory, time, place,
people, all melted away. Nothing was left but a voice ringing
through the void. It was as if a gate had swung open and I
had passed out on a road leading to limitless attainment. The
end of it was not visible; but the promise of what it would
be shone through the thought and flashed through the
personality of the one who gave it. He stood there—prophet
of infinitude.

The silence of an empty hall recalled me to myself. Everyone was gone except the Swami and two others standing
near the platform. I learnt later that they were Mr. and Mrs.
Goodyear, ardent disciples of the Swami. Mr. Goodyear
made the announcements at the meetings. After that I attended all the classes and lectures during the Swami's two
seasons in New York, but I never came in close personal
touch with him. There seemed to be an intangible barrier.
Was it created by shyness or a sense of strangeness, or by
my elder sister's prejudice? She had no sympathy with my
Oriental studies and often said she wished I "could get
salvation nearer home".

The meetings began in an upper room; then because
of their increasing size they were transferred to the floor
below. Later they moved to another house—one in a
long monotonous row of dingy boarding houses. It was
a heterogeneous gathering at the classes in those shabby
lodgings—old and young, rich and poor, wise and foolish;
stingy ones who dropped a button in the collection basket,
and more generous ones who gave a dollar bill or even

two. We all met day after day and became friends without
words or association. Some of us never missed a meeting. We
followed the course on Bhakti Yoga and the course on Jnana
Yoga. We walked simultaneously along the paths of Raja
Yoga and Karma Yoga. We were almost sorry that there were
only four yogas. We would have liked to have six or eight,
that the number of classes might be multiplied.

We were insatiable knowledge-seekers. We did not
limit ourselves to any one doctrine or scripture. We went to
one lecture in the morning, a second one in the afternoon,
and sometimes to a third in the evening. Philosophy,
metaphysics, astrology, each had its turn. Yet although we
seemed to scatter our interest, our real loyalty belonged to
the Swami. We recognized in him a power that no other
teacher possessed. It was he alone who was shaping our
thought and conviction. Even my dog—an Irish setter—felt
this. He would stand perfectly still and a quiver would run
through his body whenever Swamiji would lay his hand on
his head and tell him he was a true yogi.

The faithful group that followed the Swami wherever
he spoke was as relentless as it was earnest. If he suggested
tentatively omitting a class because of a holiday or for some
other reason, there was a loud protest always. This one had
come to New York specially for the teaching and wished to
get all she could; another was leaving town soon and was
unwilling to lose a single opportunity of hearing the Swami.
They gave him no respite. He taught early and late. Among
the most eager were a number of teachers, each with a blank
book in hand; and the Swami's words were punctuated by
the tap of their pencils taking rapid notes. Not a sentence
went unrecorded; and I am sure that if later any one had
made the circuit of the New York Centres of New Thought,
Metaphysics, or Divine Science, they would have heard
everywhere Vedanta and yoga in more or less diluted form.

Through the late winter and spring of 1895 the work—
carried on without the intermittence of the earlier teaching—
gained tremendous momentum and fervour. We divided our

interest no longer. It was wholly focussed on the message the
Swami had to give. That had become the foundation of our
daily living, the stimulus that urged us onward. For several
consecutive months class followed class, lecture followed
lecture. Now there remained only a final class and a final
lecture. Then the last class was over and in a hush of sadness
we filed out from the shabby lodging-house, dropping our
farewell offering in the basket at the door.

There was still a final Sunday lecture. It took place in
the Madison Square Concert Hall—a fairly large hall on the
second floor behind the Madison Square Garden, a vast arena
used for automobile exhibitions, bicycle races, horse shows,
for anything that required space. The building seemed huge
at that time, but later New York outgrew it, and it was torn
down. The Concert Hall was much used by Glee Clubs, string
quartets, and lectures. I do not know how many it held, but it
was full to the uttermost at that closing lecture—every seat,
every foot of standing room was occupied.

I believe that was the day on which Swami Vivekananda
delivered the lecture on "My Master". As he entered the
hall from a door at the side of the platform, one sensed a
different mood in him. He seemed less confident, as if he
approached his task reluctantly. Years after in Chennai I
understood. He hesitated at all times to speak of his guru.
During his early wanderings through South India he refused
to reveal his name even, believing he represented him so
poorly. Only in Chennai, when he came unaware upon his
Master's picture, did the words burst from his lips, "That is
my guru, Sri Ramakrishna," and tears streamed down his
face. So now was he reluctant. He began his lecture with a
long preamble; but once in his subject, it swept him. The
force of it drove him from one end of the platform to the
other. It overflowed in a swift-running stream of eloquence
and feeling. The large audience listened in awed stillness
and at the close many left the hall without speaking. As for
myself, I was transfixed. The transcendent picture drawn
overwhelmed me. The call had come, and I answered.

It was on this Sunday that Swami's first volume appeared. For some time the lectures of one Sunday had been for sale on the book table, the next Sunday in pamphlet form. Now a whole collection of lectures on Karma Yoga was brought out in a large, thin, closely-printed volume—very different from the edition published later. It was not very beautiful, but the workers were extremely proud of it.

A supplementary meeting in a private house marked the close of the Swami's New York work. In June he went with a group of students to Thousand Island Park and in August he sailed for Europe. The time of hearing was over; the time of pondering and practising had come. As we dwelt in memory on the Swami's teachings and tried from day to day to put them into our life, we came to feel more and more that a mighty comet had swung into our hemisphere, shone for a season in our heavens, and swung out again, leaving a line of light behind it. Its radiance still lingers.

Those who attended Swami Vivekananda's classes and lectures in New York soon grew familiar with a tall, very portly figure who moved about doing everything. We learnt before long that it was Miss Ellen Waldo, a distant relative of Ralph Waldo Emerson, and a person of wide philosophic and general culture. The Swami had given her the Sanskrit name "Haridasi", and it was well chosen. She was truly a "Servant of the Lord"—her service was continuous and untiring. She cooked, edited, cleaned and took dictation, taught and managed, read proof and saw visitors.

When Swami Vivekananda came to New York, he encountered a strong racial prejudice, which created many hardships for him both in his public and in his private life. Among other things, it was extremely difficult for him to secure a proper lodging. Landladies invariably assured him that they had no feeling themselves, but they were afraid they would lose their boarders or lodgers if they took an Asiatic in the house. This forced the Swami to accept inferior living quarters. Neither environment nor association was what he should have had. One day, after he had been overnight in one of these dingy lodgings, he said to Miss Waldo: "The food here seems so unclean, would it be possible for you to cook for me?" She went at once to the landlady and obtained permission to use the kitchen. Then from her own store she gathered together cooking utensils and groceries. These she carried with her on the following morning.

She lived at the far end of Brooklyn. The only means of transportation was a jogging horse-car, and it required two hours to reach the Swami's lodging at 38th Street in New York. Undaunted, every morning found her on her way at eight o'clock or earlier; and at nine or ten at night she was on her way home again. When there came a free day, the journey was reversed. It was Swamiji who took the jogging horse-car, travelled the two hours and cooked the meals. He found genuine rest and relaxation in the freedom and quiet of Miss Waldo's simple home. The kitchen was on the top floor of the house, in front of it the dining-room full of sunshine and potted plants. As the Swami invented new dishes or tried experiments with Western provisions, he ran back and forth from one room to the other like a child at play.

"In all this close association with Swamiji," Miss Waldo said to me later, "it seems strange that the idea of renunciation never once occurred to me. Nor did I ever think seriously of following him to India. I seemed to belong in America. Yet there was nothing I would not have done for him. When he first came to New York, he insisted on wearing his orange robe everywhere. It required no little courage to walk up Broadway beside that flaming coat. As the Swami strode along in lordly indifference, with me just behind, half out of breath trying to keep up with him, every eye was turned upon us, and on every lip was the question: 'What are they?' Later I persuaded him to adopt more subdued clothing for the street."

One morning the Swami found Miss Waldo in tears. "What is the matter, Ellen?" he asked anxiously. "Has anything happened?" "I seem unable to please you," she replied. "Even when others annoy you, you scold me for it." The Swami said quickly, "I do not know those people well enough to scold them. I cannot rebuke them, so I come to you. Whom can I scold if I cannot scold my own?" Her tears dried at once, and after that she sought scoldings; they were a proof of nearness.

Miss Waldo herself told me of this experience as her own. Romain Rolland tells it of another disciple. Both can be true. The incident could easily repeat itself.

Miss Waldo had had wide experience of teachers. She had sat at the feet of many during her long pursuit of truth, but sooner or later they had all fallen short in some way. Now the fear was in her heart that this new Hindu Swami might prove wanting. She was always watching for a sign of weakness. It came. She and the Swami were together in a New York drawing-room. The New York Swami Vivekananda knew was very different from the New York of today. The streets then were lined with monotonous blocks of brown stone houses, one so completely like every other that a visiting artist of note once asked: "How do you know when you are at home? You could as well be in the house next door."

Each of these narrow, but deep houses held on the first floor a long narrow drawing-room, with high folding-doors at one end, two large windows at the other, and between them a mirror reaching from floor to ceiling. This mirror seemed to fascinate the Swami. He stood before it again and again, gazing at himself intently. In between he walked up and down the room, lost in thought. Miss Waldo's eyes followed him anxiously. "Now the bubble is going to burst," she thought. "He is full of personal vanity." Suddenly he turned to her and said: "Ellen, it is the strangest thing, I cannot remember how I look. I look and look at myself in the glass, but the moment I turn away I forget completely what I look like."

It was during this first visit to America that the Swami's *Raja Yoga* took form. The greater part was dictated to Miss

Waldo. She took it down in long hand. Those cherished hours of work on it were especially happy ones for her. She often spoke of them. Each day when the Swami's meal had been prepared and her tasks in the kitchen were done, she would come up to the back parlour where Swamiji lodged; take her seat at a table, on which stood an open ink-well; and dip her pen in the ink. From that moment until the work was laid aside for the day, her pen was kept wet, to catch the first rush of words that fell periodically from the Swami's lips. Sometimes in seeking for an English equivalent for the Sanskrit word in an aphorism, he would sit in concentrated silence for fifteen or twenty minutes—but the pen was not allowed to dry. The burst of dictation might come at any instant.

When the manuscript was completed, it was entrusted to Miss Waldo to put into print, but many distresses and heartaches lay in wait for her before publication was accomplished. Another devoted follower of the Swami borrowed the manuscript, carried it to London, and brought it out there, believing it was to the Swami's advantage to have it appear in England. For the time this blocked the American edition, and it was only possible to have an American edition by adding the glossary and other matter.

(*Prabuddha Bharata*, April & May 1932)

Cornelia Conger

Before the Congress (or Parliament) of Religions met in Chicago at the time of the Columbian Exposition in 1893, members of various Churches volunteered to ask into their homes as guests delegates to it. My grandmother, Mrs. John B. Lyon, was one of these, requesting, if possible, that a delegate who was broad-minded be sent to us, as my grandfather was much interested in philosophy but heartily disliked bigots. Our home was 262 Michigan Avenue, a pleasant, somewhat old-fashioned frame-house, painted olive green with boxes of red geraniums across the front. It was full of guests all that summer as my grandparents were naturally hospitable and this World's Fair was a very exciting and fascinating affair. So all our out-of-town relatives and friends were eager to come to Chicago to see it. When word came that our delegate was to arrive on a certain evening, the house was so crowded that my grandmother had to send her elder son to a friend's house to have his room for our guest. We had been given no idea who he would be, nor even what religion he was representing. A message came that a member of our Church—the First Presbyterian—would bring him after midnight. Everyone went to bed except my grandmother, who waited up to receive them. When she answered the doorbell, there stood Swami Vivekananda in a long yellow robe, a red sash, and a red turban—a very startling sight to her, because she had probably never seen an East Indian before. She welcomed him warmly and showed him to his room. When she went to bed, she was somewhat troubled. Some of our guests were Southerners, as we had

CORNELIA CONGER

many friends in the South, because we owned a sugar plantation on the Bayou Teche in Louisiana. Southerners have a strong dislike for associating with anyone but whites, because they stupidly think of all people who are darker as on a mental and social plane of their former negro slaves. My grandmother herself had no colour prejudice, and she was sufficiently intelligent any way to know that Indians are of the same Caucasian inheritance as we are.

When my grandfather woke up, she told him of the problem and said he must decide whether it would be uncomfortable for Swami and for our Southern friends to be together. If so, she said he could put Swami up as our guest at the new Auditorium Hotel near us. My grandfather was dressed about half an hour before breakfast and went into the library to read his morning paper. There he found Swami and, before breakfast was served, he came to my grand-mother and said: "I don't care a bit, Emily, if all our guests leave! This Indian is the most brilliant and interesting man who has ever been in our home, and he shall stay as long as he wishes." That began a warm friendship between them which was later summed up—much to my grandfather's embarrassment—by having Swami calmly remark to a group of my grandfather's friends one day at the Chicago Club, "I believe Mr. Lyon is the most Christlike man I ever met!"

He seemed to feel especially close to my grandmother, who reminded him of his own mother. She was short and very erect, with quiet dignity and assurance, excellent common sense, and a dry humour that he enjoyed. My mother, who was a pretty and charming young widow, and I—who was only six years old—lived with them. My grandmother and my mother attended most of the meetings of the Congress of Religions and heard Swamiji speak there and later at lectures he gave. I know he helped my sad young mother who missed her young husband so much. Mother read and studied Swamiji's books later and tried to follow his teachings.

My memories are simply of him as a guest in our home—of a great personality who is still vivid to me! His brilliant eyes, his charming voice with the lilt of a slight well-bred Irish brogue, his warm smile! He told me enchanting stories of India, of monkeys and peacocks, and flights of bright green parrots, of banyan trees and masses of flowers, and markets piled with all colours of fruits and vegetables. To me they sounded like fairy tales, but now that I have driven over many hundreds of miles of Indian roads, I realize that he was simply describing scenes from the memories of his own boyhood. I used to rush up to him when he came into the house and cry, "Tell me another story, Swami", and climb into his lap. Perhaps, so far from home and in so strange a country, he found comfort in the love and enthusiasm of a child. He was always wonderful to me. Yet—because a child is sensitive—I can remember times when I would run into his room and suddenly know he did not want to be disturbed—when he was in meditation. He asked me many questions about what I learnt in school and made me show him my school-books and pointed out India to me on the map—it was pink, I recall—and told me about his country. He seemed sad that little Indian girls did not have, in general, the chance to have as good an education as we American children. Imagine how interested I was when Swami Shankarananda, President, Belur Math, told me he founded a girls' school in Kolkata!

My grandmother was president of the Women's Hospital at home, and he visited it with lively interest and asked for all the figures in infant mortality etc. So again it showed how much he was learning in our country to be used in helping his own people, because I was told that a maternity hospital was also founded later. How very happy that would have made my grandmother!

I was fascinated by his turban which struck me as a very funny kind of a hat, especially as it had to be wound up afresh every time he put it on! I persuaded him to let me see him wrap it back and forth around his head.

As our American food is less highly seasoned than Indian, my grandmother was afraid he might find it flat. He told us, on arrival, that he had been told to conform to all the customs and the food of his hosts, so he ate as we did. My grandmother used to make a little ceremony of making salad dressing at the table, and one of the condiments she used was Tabasco Sauce, put up by some friends of hers, the Mrs. Ilhennys, in Louisiana. She handed him the bottle and said, "You might like a drop or two of this on your meat, Swami." He sprinkled it on with such a lavish hand that we all gasped and said: "But you can't do that! It's terribly hot!" He laughed and ate it with such enjoyment that a special bottle of the sauce was always put at his place after that.

My mother took him to hear his first Symphony Concert on a Friday afternoon. He listened with great attention but with his head a bit on one side and a slightly quizzical expression. "Did you enjoy it?" mother asked at the end. "Yes, it was very beautiful," he replied, but mother felt it was said with some reservation. "What are you thinking?" she asked. "I am puzzled by two things," he answered, "First, I do not understand why the programme says that this same programme will be repeated on Saturday evening. You see, in India, one type of music is played at dawn. The music for noontime is very different, and that for the evening is also of a special character. So I should think that what sounds suitable to your ears in the early afternoon would not sound harmonious to you at night. The other thing that seems strange to me is the lack of overtones in the music and the greater intervals between the notes. To my ears it has holes in it like that good Swiss cheese you give me."

When he began to give lectures, people offered him money for the work he hoped to do in India. He had no purse. So he used to tie it up in a handkerchief and bring it back—like a proud little boy—and pour it into my grandmother's lap to keep for him. She made him learn the different coins and to stack them up neatly to count them. She made him write down the amount each time, and she deposited it in her bank for him. He was overwhelmed by the generosity of his audience who seemed so happy to give to help people they had never seen so far away.

Once he said to my grandmother that he had had the greatest temptation of his life in America. She liked to tease him a bit and said, "Who is she, Swami?" He burst out laughing and said, "Oh, it is not a lady, it is Organization!" He explained how the followers of Ramakrishna had all gone out alone and when they reached a village, would just quietly sit under a tree and wait for those in trouble to come to consult them. But in the States he saw how much could be accomplished by organizing work. Yet he was doubtful about just what type of organization would be acceptable to the Indian character, and he gave a great deal of thought and study on how to adapt what seemed good to him in our Western World to the best advantage of his own people. I can see that Belur Math and his many charities are the result of this period in his life. I spoke earlier of his delightful slight Irish brogue. I recall that this came as a surprise to Swami Shankarananda. My grandfather used to tease him about it. But Swami said it was probably because his favourite professor was an Irish gentleman, a graduate of Trinity College, Dublin.

After Swami left us, my mother was eager to do some studying along the lines of Oriental philosophy, as she realized she had not enough background to understand his teachings as fully as she wished. A Mrs. Peake held some classes in Chicago that following winter and, in the course of them, mother discovered much to her surprise that if she held a letter torn up into fine bits between her hands, she received a brief but vivid impression of the writer, both physically and mentally. When Swamiji returned to Chicago a year or so later to give lectures, mother asked him about this strange gift, and he said he had it also, and that when he was young, he used to have fun doing it to show off, but that Ramakrishna had wrapped his knuckles and said: "Don't use this great gift except for the good of mankind. Hands that receive these impressions can also bring relief from pain. Use this gift to bring healing."

On this second visit, he only stayed with us for a short time. He knew he could teach better if he lived in his own regime of food and of many hours for meditation. It also left him free to receive many who came to him for help. So my grandmother helped him find a simple but comfortable little flat, but I do not recall that I ever saw it.

Swamiji was such a dynamic and attractive personality that many women were quite swept away by him and made every effort by flattery to gain his interest. He was still young and, in spite of his great spirituality and his brilliance of mind, seemed to be very unworldly. This used to trouble my grandmother who feared he might be put in a false or uncomfortable position, and she tried to caution him a little. Her concern touched and amused him, and he patted her hand and said: "Dear Mrs. Lyon, you dear American mother of mine, don't be afraid for me. It is true I often sleep under a banyan tree with a bowl of rice given to me by a kindly peasant, but it is equally true that I also am sometimes the guest in the palace of a great Maharaja and a slave girl is appointed to wave a peacock feather fan over me all night long! I am used to temptation, and you need not fear for me!"

After having talked with Swami Shankarananda and been encouraged by him, I wished I had talked to my mother's younger sister, Katharine (Mrs. Robert W. Hamill) about her recollections of Swamiji. So when I reached home I asked her what she could add to my scattered memories. She was a bride and had her own home. So she was not at her mother's and father's so very much. She recalled Swamiji much as I did, but never heard him lecture. However, she and her husband were "young intellectuals" and had a group of young professors from our university, young newspaper men, etc. around them. One Sunday evening she was telling them how remarkable Swamiji was, and they said that modern scientists and psychologists could "show up" his religious beliefs in no time! She said, "If I can persuade him to come here next Sunday evening, will you all come back and meet him?" They agreed, and Swamiji met them all at an informal supper party. My aunt does not recall just what subjects were brought up, but that the entire evening was a lively and interesting debate on all sorts of ideas—Aunt Katharine said that Swamiji's great knowledge of the Bible and the Koran as well as the various Oriental religions, his grasp of science and of psychology were astounding. Before the evening was over, the "doubting Thomases" threw up their hands and admitted that Swamiji had held his own on every point and that they parted from him with warmest admiration and affection.

When I was taken to meet Swami Shankarananda, I felt my memories were too childish and trivial to put down in black and white, and I felt very humble and apologetic for taking up others' time. But the Swami said something infinitely kind and gracious which I shall never forget: That every great man is like a jewel with many facets. That each facet is important as it reflects a different aspect of his character. That I had come to him to offer a facet that was lacking in his records of Swamiji—of the weeks he had spent in our home when he first left India. So here is my very tiny "facet" offered in memory of someone I have loved for all these 62 years—not as a teacher, nor a great religious leader—but as a wonderful and vivid friend who lived in our home.

(*Prabuddha Bharata*, May 1956)

Martha Browne Fincke

Early in November 1935, I landed in Kolkata and set foot for the first time on the soil of India. As I left my home in the United States of America journeying westward to encircle the globe, I thought of myself as a tourist in the different countries through which I passed. Only when I reached India did I in thought become a pilgrim. As a pilgrim I went the day after landing to the Belur Math on the farther side of the Ganga to bow my head in reverence before the tomb of the great Swami Vivekananda. In the upper room of the guesthouse I met Miss Josephine MacLeod, his devoted friend. I also met several of the resident Swamis. When to each of them I said that I had once known Swami Vivekananda, their eagerness to hear of that far-off meeting surprised me. It was indeed to me one of the most vital influences of my life, but could it mean anything to others? Since they assured me that it was so, I am setting down my recollections of those two days, now 42 years ago, when I came under the influence of that great man.

In September 1893, at the World's Fair held in Chicago to commemorate the 400th anniversary of the discovery of America by Columbus, a Parliament of Religions was a part of the programme. To this journeyed the then unknown young Hindu monk, Swami Vivekananda. His power over the audiences who heard him set forth his universal Gospel and the magic of his personality are common knowledge.

At the close of the Parliament, in order to be independent of the personal benefactions of his admirers, the Swami engaged with a Lecture Bureau to tour the States beginning

MARTHA BROWNE FINCKE

with the East, and early in November he came to the town of Northampton, Massachusetts. This charming old town, half-way between New York and Boston, and since prominent as the home of Calvin Coolidge, is situated on low hills in the Connecticut Valley just before the river plunges into the gap between Mt. Tom and Mt. Holyoke. In flood seasons the low-lying meadows about the town shine with the covering waters, and the purple outline of the Mt. Holyoke range forms the horizon to the south. Stately elm trees border the streets, and the place had then a slumberous aspect except when an eruption of students woke it to animation. For a women's college (Smith College, founded in 1875 by Sophia Smith for the higher education of women) formed the centre of its intellectual life.

To this college I went as a freshman in the fall of 1893, an immature girl of eighteen, undisciplined but reaching out eagerly for the things of the mind and spirit. Brought up in a sheltered atmosphere, in the strictest Protestant Christian orthodoxy, it was with some misgivings that my parents saw me leave the home and be exposed to the dangers of so-called "free-thinking". Had not one of my friends gone the year before to Vassar College and was rumoured to have "lost her faith"?

The college dormitories were not large enough to house all of the incoming class, so I, with three other freshmen, boarded in a square brown house near the campus. This was kept by a lady whose independent spirit and humor-ous outlook endeared her to us, despite her despotic rule. College lectures for the whole body of students with com-pulsory attendance were of frequent occurrence, and many well-known leaders of thought visited us.

On the Bulletin for November was the name of Swami Vivekananda who was to give two evening lectures. That he was a Hindu monk we knew, nothing more; for the fame he had won in the recent Parliament of Religions had not reached our ears. Then an exciting piece of news leaked out; he was to live at our house, to eat with us, and we

could ask him questions about India. Our hostess' breadth
of tolerance may be seen in receiving into her house a man
with dark skin, whom the hotel had doubtless refused to
admit. As late as 1912 the great poet Tagore with his companion wandered through the streets of New York looking
in vain for shelter.

The name of India was familiar to me from my earliest
childhood. Had not my mother almost decided to marry a
young man who went as a missionary to India, and did not a
box from our Church Missionary Association go each year to
the zenanas? India was a hot land where snakes abounded,
and "the heathen in his blindness bows down to wood and
stone". It is astonishing how little an eager reader like myself
knew about the history or literature of that great country.
The life of William Carey I had read, had heard of St. Francis
Xavier at Goa, but it was all from the missionary standpoint.
You must remember "Kim" had not yet appeared. To talk
with a real Indian would be a chance indeed.

The day came, the little guest-room was ready, and a
stately presence entered our home. The Swami's dress was
a black Prince Albert coat, dark trousers, and yellow turban
wound in intricate folds about a finely shaped head. But the
face with its inscrutable expression, the eyes so full of flashing light, and the whole emanation of power, are beyond
description. We were awed and silent. Our hostess, however,
was not one to be awed, and she led an animated conversation. I sat next to the Swami, and with my superfluity of
reverence found not a word to say.

Of the lecture that evening I can recall nothing. The
imposing figure on the platform in red robe, orange cord,
and yellow turban, I do remember, and the wonderful
mastery of the English language with its rich sonorous
tones, but the ideas did not take root in my mind, or else the
many years since then have obliterated them. But what I do
remember was the symposium that followed.

To our house came the college president, the head of the
philosophy department, and several other professors, the

ministers of the Northampton churches, and a well-known author. In a corner of the living-room we girls sat as quiet as mice and listened eagerly to the discussion which followed. To give a detailed account of this conversation is beyond me, though I have a strong impression that it dealt mainly with Christianity and why it is the only true religion. Not that the subject was the Swami's choosing. As his imposing presence faced the row of black-coated and somewhat austere gentlemen, one felt that he was being challenged. Surely these leaders of thought in our world had an unfair advantage. They knew their Bibles thoroughly and the European systems of philosophy, as well as the poets and commentators. How could one expect a Hindu from far-off India to hold his own with these, master though he might be of his own learning? The reaction to the surprising result that followed is my purely subjective one, but I cannot exaggerate its intensity.

To texts from the Bible, the Swami replied by other and more apposite ones from the same book. In upholding his side of the argument he quoted English philosophers and writers on religious subjects. Even the poets he seemed to know thoroughly, quoting Wordsworth and Thomas Gray (not from the well-known *Elegy*). Why were my sympathies not with those of my own world? Why did I exult in the air of freedom that blew through the room as the Swami broadened the scope of religion till it embraced all mankind? Was it that his words found an echo in my own longings, or was it merely the magic of his personality? I cannot tell, I only know that I felt triumphant with him.

In speaking with a Swami ... at the Belur Math, he said that to him Swami Vivekananda personified Love. To me that night he personified Power. I think that I can explain this from my later knowledge. No doubt these great men of our college-world were narrow-minded, of closed convictions, "wise in their own conceits". How could they accept the saying "Whosoever comes to Me through whatsoever form, I reach him"? At Chicago the Swami had recently felt the rancour of Christian missionaries, and undoubtedly his accents took on an austerity as he felt the same spirit in these representatives of Western learning. To them Love would not appeal, but Power can awe even when it does not force agreement. The discussion, beginning with the utmost courtesy, became less cordial, then bitterness crept in, a resentment on the part of the champions of Christianity as they felt that it was "thumbs down" for them. And truly it was. The repercussion of the triumph that filled me then is with me to this day.

Early the next morning loud splashings came from the bathroom, and mingling with them a deep voice chanting in an unknown tongue. I believe that a group of us huddled near the door to listen. At breakfast we asked him the meaning of the chant. He replied, "I first put the water on my forehead, then on my breast, and each time I chant a prayer for blessings on all creatures." This struck me forcibly. I was used to a morning prayer, but it was for myself first that I prayed, then for my family. It had never occurred to me to include all mankind in my family and to put them before myself.

After breakfast the Swami suggested a walk, and we four students, two on each side, escorted the majestic figure proudly through the streets. As we went, we shyly tried to open conversation. He was instantly responsive and smiled showing his beautiful teeth. I only remember one thing he said. Speaking of Christian doctrines, he remarked how abhorrent to him was the constant use of the term "the *blood* of Christ". That made me think. I had always hated the hymn "There is a fountain filled with blood, drawn from Emmanuel's veins", but what daring to criticize an accepted doctrine of the Church! My "free-thinking" certainly dates from the awakening given me by that freedom-loving soul. I led the conversation to the Vedas, those holy books of India he had mentioned in his lecture. He advised me to read them for myself, preferably in the original. I then and there made a resolve to learn

Sanskrit, a purpose which I regret to say I have never fulfilled. Indeed as far as outward result goes, I am a case of the good seed choked by thorns.

One rather humorous outcome of this advice about the Vedas should not be omitted. The following summer a pretty little Guernsey calf was added to the family livestock, and when my father gave it to me, I named it "Veda". Unfortunately the little one only lived a few months and my father said its name had killed it.

Of the succeeding lecture I can say nothing. The great Swami left us and I never saw him again. I even lost sight of his journeyings through our country and did not know that he made another visit to it two years later. And yet those two days of his mighty presence have certainly coloured all the rest of my life. I wrote to my family a detailed account of this visit, expressing myself so strongly that my devoted but over-solicitous father became alarmed. He pictured me leaving the faith of my fathers and becoming a disciple of the Swami. He used argument and ridicule, and to spare him further anxiety—for I adored my father—I stopped talking of my new thoughts, and kept them to myself.

I often think of the time I have lost, of the roundabout way I have come, groping my way, when under such guidance I might have aimed directly for the goal. But for an immortal soul it is wiser not to spend time in regrets, since to be on the way is the important thing.

One reads of the seeds found in Egyptian sarcophagi, buried thousands of years previously and yet retaining enough vitality to sprout when planted. Lying apparently lifeless in my mind and heart, the far-off memory of that great apostle from India has during the past year begun to send forth shoots. It has at last brought me to this country. During the intervening years—years of sorrow and responsibility and struggle mingled with joy—my innermost self has been trying out this and that doctrine to see if it was what I wanted to live by. Always some dissatisfaction resulted. Dogmas and rituals, made so important by orthodox believ-

ers, seemed to me so unimportant, so curbing that freedom
of the spirit that I longed for.

I find in the universal Gospel that Swamiji preached
the satisfaction of my longing. To believe that the Divine is
within us, that we are from the very first a part of God, and
that this is true of every man, what more can one ask? In
receiving this, as I have on the soil of India, I feel that I have
come Home.

(Prabuddha Bharata, September 1936)

Henry J. Van Haagen

When a man steps from darkness into a very bright light, his eyes are dazed for a while and refuse to work properly for the moment. And when we are asked to speak and describe that great joy which lights our very soul, our answer would be, as it were, but a mere groping in the darkness for words. One may perceive and feel most perfect joy, yet not be able to describe it. It is with such feeling that my thoughts wander back to the great impressions of my life, which I can never forget. Although a number of years have passed, these events live in my memory as if they had occurred but yesterday.

I well remember my first meeting with Swami Vivekananda, that great teacher whose nativity we are commemorating this evening. Though filled with prejudice by my friends, I went to one of the Swami's classes, not so much to hear his lecture as to see for the first time a native of India, the land which I had learnt to love through reading the *Bhagavad Gita*, the *Song Celestial*. I was seated in the classroom waiting for the Swami's appearance when soon a man came in—one whose walk expressed dignity and whose general bearing showed majesty, like one who owns everything and desires nothing. After a short observation I also saw that he was a very superior man, and withal, one who quickly disclosed a most lovable character. Now I became anxious to hear the words he would speak; and after I had done so but a few minutes, I firmly resolved to be a regular attendant at all his lectures and classes. That prejudice which was so strong within me when I entered, now seemed to be driven away by his profound knowledge and charming magnetism. It would be too long to describe the great treats that followed. As wholesome food satisfies the hungry and fresh water quenches the thirsty, so my longing for truth was satisfied through the teaching of this wonderful man. And to this very day I have found nothing that gives a better answer and a clearer explanation to the various vital questions which arise in a man's mind than the Vedanta philosophy so ably taught by Swami Vivekananda.

Not only were his words in the classroom and lecture-room those of instructive value, but his conversations also, as he walked on the street or through Central Park, always conveyed the one message. Many of our interesting little talks I can readily call to mind; for instance, on one occasion I expressed my regret to the Swami that his sublime teachings had no larger following, and his wise and fitting answer was: "I could have thousands more at my lectures if I wanted them. It is the sincere student who will help to make this work a success and not merely the large audiences. If I succeed in my whole life to help one man to reach freedom, I shall feel that my labours have not been in vain, but quite successful." This remark filled me with the desire to be one of his students.

The strong impression which this lovable teacher always gave to his students was that of causing them to feel that they alone, while with him, had his whole attention and sympathy. Always willing to devote his entire attention to heeding his students' most humble wants and queries, he, by this most pleasing attitude, made them most enthusiastic and faithful disciples. This created that enduring bond of love between teacher and disciple which is so necessary for any teacher's real success. And how glorious was his success! Today almost every intelligent person is more or less familiar with the literature which like a flower blossomed out of his work. And many are those—the professor, clergyman, and layman alike—who have been influenced to the better through acquaintance with these literary gems.

His teaching bore to us the peace of mind of the Aryan rishis of which we are so much in need. It is but recently that an American scientist pointed out how our fashionable and business life is a continuous nerve storm—a literal hurrying to the grave, speeding along every lifeway, exhausting energy, and inviting premature nervous and mental ruin. Through the strong desire for wealth and sense-gratification the nerve energy is exceedingly overtaxed, and no remedy is sought to restore it. What better cure for this evil could be conceived than the living of that life which the Vedanta philosophy teaches? Not the excessive nervous rushing hither and thither, nor inactive dullness, but sattva—equipoise and tranquillity—is what is offered by Vedanta, and this only can bring back to us the calm which Western nations have long lost.

In his teachings the Swami has admonished us not to direct the war-spirit in us to win the greatest victories, to the slaying of our fellow-man in anger and hatred when he differs from us, but to the transmuting of this energy into a strict practice of self-control. And what better teaching can a man spread than one which contains such original thoughts as: "He conquers all who conquers self; know this and never yield", or "In books and temples vain thy search. Thine only is the hand that holds the rope that drags thee on. Then cease lament, let go thy hold."

And now, though he has gone into the great Peace beyond, because his work was finished, he still lives in our memory and in his work, as he also lives in the message which he brought to us. He has done his duty as a great, good, and true teacher, and gave us the means, *That we may know the Truth.* But that is only one part, the other, without which all is in vain, is our duty, *That we may live the Truth,* and increased knowledge brings this additional duty with it. For that purpose, to help and assist us to better live the truth, Vedanta Societies have been formed, classes and lectures are being held, and his brother-swamis and sannyasi disciples have come to our shores. However mighty nation we may be, he did not seek us for anything but for giving Truth and Wisdom, of which we are surely in need. Let us, by living the Truth of Vedanta, prove that this great Master has not brought his wonderful message to us in vain.

(*Prabuddha Bharata*, June 1911)

Sister Christine

Now and then, at long intervals of time, a being finds his way to this planet who is unquestionably a wanderer from another sphere; who brings with him to this sorrowful world some of the glory, the power, the radiance of the far distant region from which he came. He walks among men, but he is not at home here. He is a pilgrim, a stranger, he tarries but a night.

He shares the life of those about him, enters into their joys and sorrows, rejoices with them, mourns with them, but through it all, he never forgets who he is, whence he came, or what the purpose of his coming is. He never forgets his divinity. He remembers that he is the great, the glorious, the majestic Self. He knows that he came from that ineffable, supernal region which has no need of the sun or moon, for it is illumined by the Light of lights. He knows that he *was*, long before the time when "all the sons of God sang together for joy".

Such a one, I have seen, I have heard, I have revered. At his feet I have laid my soul's devotion.

Such a being is beyond all comparison, for he transcends all ordinary standards and ideals. Others may be brilliant; his mind is luminous, for he had the power to put himself into immediate contact with the source of all knowledge. He is no longer limited to the slow processes to which ordinary human beings are confined. Others may be great, they are great only as compared with those in their own class. Others may be good, powerful, gifted, having more of goodness, more of power, more of genius than their fellow-men. It

SISTER CHRISTINE

is only a matter of comparison. A saint is more holy, more pure, and more single-minded than ordinary men. But with Swami Vivekananda, there could be no comparison. He was in a class by himself. He belonged to another order. He was not of this world. He was a radiant being who had descended from another, a higher sphere for a definite purpose. One might have known that he would not stay long.

Is it to be wondered at that nature itself rejoices in such a birth, that the heavens open and angels sing paeans of praise?

Blessed is the country in which he was born, blessed are they who lived on this earth at the same time, and blessed, thrice blessed are the few who sat his feet.

THE MASTER AND THE MESSAGE

There are times when life flows on in a steady deadly stream of monotony. Eating, sleeping, talking—the same weary round. Commonplace thoughts, stereotyped ideas, the eternal treadmill. Tragedy comes. For a moment it shocks us into stillness. But we cannot keep still. The merry-go-round stops neither for our sorrow nor our happiness. Surely this is not all there is to life. This is not what we are here for. Restlessness comes. What are we waiting for? Then one day it happens, the stupendous things for which we have been waiting—that which dispels the deadly monotony, which turns the whole of life into a new channel, which eventually takes one to a far away country and sets one among strange people with different customs and a different outlook upon life, to a people with whom from the very first we feel a strange kinship, a wonderful people who know what they are waiting for, who recognize the purpose of life. Our restlessness is stilled forever.

After many incarnations, after untold suffering, struggle, and conquest, comes fruition. But this one does not know until long, long after. A tiny seed grows into the mighty banyan. A few feet of elevation on a fairly level plain determine whether a river shall flow north and eventually reach the icy Arctic Ocean, or south, until it finds itself in the warm waters of the Black or Caspian Sea. Little did I think when I reluctantly set out one cold February night in 1894 to attend a lecture at the Unitarian Church in Detroit that I was doing something which would change the whole course of my life and be of such stupendous import that it could not be measured by previous standards I had known. Attending lectures had been part of the deadly monotony. How seldom did one hear anything new or uplifting! The lecturers who had come to Detroit that winter had been unusually dull. So unvarying had been the disillusion, that one had given up hope and with it the desire to hear more. So I went very unwillingly to this particular lecture to hear one "Vive Kananda, a monk from India", and only in response to the pleading of my friend Mrs. Mary C. Funke. With her beautifully optimistic nature, she had kept her illusions and still believed that some day she would find "That Something". We went to hear this "Man from India". Surely never in our countless incarnations had we taken a step so momentous! For before we had listened five minutes, we knew that we had found the touchstone for which we had searched so long. In one breath, we exclaimed—"If we had missed this…!"

To those who have heard much of the personal appearance of the Swami Vivekananda, it may seem strange that it was not this which made the first outstanding impression. The forceful virile figure which stepped upon the platform was unlike the emaciated, ascetic type which is generally associated with spirituality in the West. A sickly saint everyone understands, but who ever heard of a powerful saint? The power that emanated from this mysterious being was so great that one all but shrank from it. It was overwhelming. It threatened to sweep everything before it. This one sensed even in those first unforgettable moments. Later we were to see this power at work. It was the mind that made the first great appeal, that amazing mind! What can one say that will give even a faint idea of its majesty, its glory, its splendour? It was a mind so far transcending other minds, even of those who rank as geniuses, that it seemed different in its very nature. Its ideas were so clear, so powerful, and so transcendental that it seemed incredible that they could have emanated from the intellect of a limited human being. Yet, marvellous as the ideas were and wonderful as was that intangible something that flowed out from the mind, it was all strangely familiar. I found myself saying, *"I have known that mind before"*. He burst upon us in a blaze of reddish gold, which seemed to have caught and concentrated the sun's rays. He was barely thirty, this preacher from far away India. Young with an ageless youth and yet withal old with the wisdom of ancient times. For the first time we heard the age-old message of India, teaching of the Atman, the true Self.

The audience listened spellbound while he wove the fabric as glowing and full of colour as a beautiful Kashmir shawl. Now a thread of humour, now one of tragedy, many of serious thought, many of aspiration, of lofty idealism, of wisdom. Through it all ran the woof of India's most sacred teaching: the divinity of man, his innate and eternal perfection; that this perfection is not a growth, nor a gradual attainment, but a present reality. *"That thou art."* You are that now. There is nothing to do but to realize it. The realization may come now in the twinkling of an eye, or in a million years, but "All will reach the sunlit heights." This message has well been called, "The wondrous Evangel of the Self". We are not the helpless limited beings which we think ourselves to be, but birthless, deathless, glorious children of immortal bliss. Like the teachers of old he, too, spoke in parables. The theme was always the same—man's real nature. Not what we seem to be, but what we *are*. We are like men walking over a gold mine thinking we are poor. We are like the lion who was born in a sheepfold and thought he was a sheep. When the wolf came he bleated with fear, quite unaware of his nature. Then one day a lion came, and seeing him bleating among the sheep called out to him: "You are not a sheep. You are a lion. You have no fear." The lion at once became conscious of his nature and let out a mighty roar. He stood on the platform of the Unitarian Church pouring forth glorious truths in a voice unlike any voice one had ever heard before, a voice full of cadences, expressing every emotion, now with a pathos that stirred hitherto unknown deeps of tragedy, and then just as the pain was becoming unbearable, that same voice would move one to mirth only to check it in a midcourse with the thunder of an earnestness so intense that it left one awed, a trumpet call to awake. One felt that one never knew what music was until one heard that marvellous voice.

Which of us who heard him then can ever forget what soul memories were stirred within us when we heard the ancient message of India: "Hear ye, Children of Immortal Bliss, even ye who dwell in higher spheres, I have found the Ancient One, knowing whom alone ye shall be saved from death over again." Or the story of the lion and the sheep. Blessed Truth! In spite of your bleating, your timidity, your fear, you are not the sheep; you are and always have been the lion, powerful, fearless, the king of beasts. It is only an illusion that is to be overcome. You are THAT now. With these words came a subtle force or influence that lifted one into a purer and rarer atmosphere. Was it possible to hear and feel this and ever be the same again? All one's values were changed. The seed of spirituality was planted to grow and grow throughout the years until it inevitably reached fruition. True, this sublime teaching is hoary with age. It may even be true that every Hindu man and woman knows it, many may be able to formulate it clearly, but Vivekananda spoke with authority. To him, it was not a speculative philosophy but the *living Truth*. All else might be false; this alone was true. He realized it. After his own great realization, life held but one purpose—to give the message with which he was entrusted, to point out the path and to help others on the road to the same supreme goal. "Arise, awake, and stop not till the goal is reached."

All of this one sensed more or less dimly in that first unforgettable hour while our minds were lifted into his own radiant atmosphere. Later, slowly and sometimes painfully, after much effort and devotion, some of us found that our very minds were transformed. Great is the guru!

Those who came to the first lecture at the Unitarian Church came to the second and to the third, bringing others with them. "Come," they said, "hear this wonderful man. He is like no one we have ever heard," and they came until there was no place to hold them. They filled the room, stood in the aisles, peered in at the windows. Again and again he gave his message, now in this form, now in that, now illustrated with stories from the *Ramayana* and *Mahabharata*, now from the Puranas and folklore. From the Upanishads he quoted constantly, first chanting in the original Sanskrit, then giving a free poetic translation. Great as was the impression which his spoken words made, the chanting produced an even greater effect. Unplumbed deeps were stirred; and as the rhythm fell upon the ear, the audience sat rapt and breathless. Our love for India came to birth, I think, when we first heard him say the word, "India", in that marvellous voice of his. It seems incredible that so much could have been put into one small word of five letters. There was love, passion, pride, longing, adoration, tragedy, chivalry, *heimweh*, and again love. Whole volumes could not have produced such a feeling in others. It had the magic power of creating love in those who heard it. Ever after, India became the land of heart's desire. Everything concerning her became of interest—became living—her people, her history, architecture, her manners and customs, her rivers, mountains, plains, her culture, her great spiritual concepts, her scriptures. And so began a new life—a life of study, of meditation. The centre of interest was shifted.

After the Parliament of Religions, Swami Vivekananda was induced to place himself under the direction of Pond's Lecture Bureau[1] and make a lecture tour of the United States. As is the custom, the committee at each new place was

---

1. The actual name of the Bureau was Slayton Lyceum Bureau.

offered the choice of several lectures—"The Divinity of Man",
"Manners and Customs of India", 'The Women of India",
"Our Heritage"... Invariably, when the place was a mining
town, with no intellectual life whatever, the most abstruse
subjects were selected. He told us the difficulty of speaking
to an audience when he could see no ray of intelligence in
response. After some weeks of this, lecturing every evening
and travelling all night, the bondage became too irksome to
bear any longer. In Detroit he had friends who had known
him in Chicago and who loved and admired him. To them he
went, and begged, "Make me free! Make me free!" Being influential they were able to get him released from his contract,
though at a financial loss which seemed unfair. He had hoped
to begin his work in India with the money earned in this way,
but this was not the only reason for engaging in this public
work. The impulse which was urging him on and which
was never entirely absent from his mind was the mission
with which his Master had entrusted him. He had a work
to do, a message to give. It was a sacred message. How was
he to give it? By the time he reached Detroit, he knew that a
lecture tour was not the way, and not an hour longer would
he waste his time on what did not lead towards his object. For
six weeks he remained in Detroit, his mind intent upon his
purpose, and he would give an occasional lecture. We missed
no opportunity of hearing him. Again and again we heard
the "wondrous Evangel of the Self". Again and again we
heard the story of India, now from this angle, now from that.
We knew we had found our teacher. The word guru we did
not know then. Nor did we meet him personally, but what
matter? It would take years to assimilate what we had already
learnt. And then the Master would somehow, somewhere,
teach us again!

THE DISCIPLES AT THOUSAND ISLAND PARK

It happened sooner than we expected, for in a little more
than a year, we found ourselves in Thousand Island Park in

the very house with him. It must have been the 6th of July 1895, that we had the temerity to seek him out. We heard he was living with a group of students. The word "disciple" is not used very freely these days. It implies more than the average person is willing to give. We thought there would be some public teaching which we might attend. We dared not hope for more. Mrs. Funke has told of our quest in her preface to the *Inspired Talks* of Swami Vivekananda.

Of the wonderful weeks that followed, it is difficult to write. Only if one's mind were lifted to that high state of consciousness in which we lived for the time could one hope to recapture the experience. We were filled with joy. We did not know at that time that we were living in his radiance. On the wings of inspiration, he carried us to the height which was his natural abode. He himself, speaking of it later, said that he was at his best in Thousand Islands. Then he felt that he had found the channel through which his message might be spread, the way to fulfil his mission, for the guru had found his own disciples. His first overwhelming desire was to show us the path to mukti, to set us free. "Ah," he said with touching pathos, "if I could only set you free with a touch!" His second object, not so apparent perhaps, but always in the under-current, was to train this group to carry on the work in America. "This message must be preached by Indians in India, and by Americans in America", he said. On his own little veranda, overlooking the tree-tops and the beautiful St. Lawrence, he often called upon us to make speeches. His object was, as he said, to teach us to think upon our feet. Did he know that if we could conquer our self-consciousness in his presence, could speak before him who was considered one of the great orators of the world, no audience anywhere would dismay us? It was a trying ordeal. Each in turn was called upon to make an attempt. There was no escape. Perhaps that was why certain of our group failed to make an appearance at these intimate evening gatherings, although they knew that often he soared to the greatest heights as the night advanced. What if it was two o'clock in the morning? What if we had watched the moon rise and set? Time and space had vanished for us.

There was nothing set or formed about these nights on the upper veranda. He sat in his large chair at the end, near his door. Sometimes he went into a deep meditation. At such times we too meditated or sat in profound silence. Often it lasted for hours and one after the other slipped away. For we knew that after this he would not feel inclined to speak. Or again the meditation would be short, and he would encourage us to ask questions afterwards, often calling on one of us to answer. No matter how far wrong these answers were, he let us flounder about until we were near the truth, and then in a few words, he would clear up the difficulty. This was his invariable method in teaching. He knew how to stimulate the mind of the learner and make it do its own thinking. Did we go to him for confirmation of a new idea or point of view and begin, "I see it is thus and so", his "Yes?" with an upper inflection always sent us back for further thought. Again we would come with a more clarified understanding, and again the "Yes?" stimulated us to further thought. Perhaps after the third tune, when the capacity for further thought along that particular line was reached, he would point out the error—an error usually due to something in our Western mode of thought.

And so he trained us with such patience, such benignity. It was like a benediction. Later, after his return to India, he hoped to have a place in the Himalayas for further training of Eastern and Western disciples together.

It was a strange group—these people whom he had gathered around him that summer at Thousand Islands. No wonder the shopkeeper, to whom we went for direction upon our arrival, said, "Yes, there are some queer people living up on the hill, among whom is a foreign-looking gentleman." There were three friends who had come to the Swami's New York classes together—Miss S.F. Waldo, Miss Ruth Ellis, and Doctor Wight. For thirty years, they had attended every lecture on philosophy that they had heard of, but had never found anything that even remotely approached this. So Doctor Wight gravely assured us, the newcomers. Miss Waldo had, during these long years of attendance at lectures, acquired the gift of summarizing a whole lecture in a few words. It is to her that we owe *Inspired Talks*. When Swami Vivekananda went to England that same year, he gave her charge of some of the classes, and on his return she made herself invaluable. It was to her that he dictated his commentary on the Patanjali's Aphorisms. She assisted too in bringing out the different books: *Karma Yoga, Raja Yoga, Jnana Yoga,* and *Bhakti Yoga.* Her logical, trained mind and her complete devotion made her an ideal assistant. Ruth Ellis was on the staff of one of the New York newspapers. She was gentle and retiring and seldom spoke, yet one knew that her love and devotion were unbounded. She was like a daughter to "little old Docky Wight", as we all called him. He was well over seventy but as enthusiastic and full of interest as a boy. At the end of each class there was usually a pause, and the little old "Docky" would stoop down and rub his bald head and say, with the most pronounced nasal twang, "Well, Swami, then it all amounts to this: 'I am the Absolute!'" We always waited for that, and Swamiji would smile his most fatherly smile and agree. At times like this, the Swami's thirty years in the presence of seventy seemed older by countless years—ancient but not aged, rather ageless and wise with the wisdom of all times. Sometimes he said, "I feel three hundred years old." This, with a sigh.

In a room below lived Stella. It was several days before we saw her, for she seldom came up to the classes, being, as we were given to understand, too deeply engrossed in ascetic practices to break in upon them. Naturally our curiosity was excited. Later we came to understand much. She had been an actress. Past samskaras are not so easily wiped out. Was this only another play which would restore her fast fading beauty and bring back her lost youth? For strange as it may seem, the demonstration of youth, beauty, health, prosperity is considered the test of spirituality in America in these benighted days. How could Swami Vivekananda understand that anyone could put such an interpretation upon his lofty teaching? How much did he understand, we wondered. And then one day he said, "I like that Baby. She is so artless." This met with a dead silence. Instantly his whole manner changed, and he said very gravely, "I call her Baby hoping that it will make her childlike, free from art and guile." Perhaps for the same reason, for her chosen ideal, he gave her Gopala, the Baby Krishna. When we separated for the summer, she went to live on a small island in Orchard Lake. There she built a tiny one-roomed house and lived alone. Strange stories began to be circulated about her. She wore a turban; she practised uncanny rites, called yoga. No one knew the meaning of yoga. It was a strange foreign word that had to do with India—the mysterious, and with occultism. Newspaper men came to interview her. One well-known writer tells the story of his first success. He was a lad engaged in running an elevator for his living. He wrote the story of this young woman practising yoga on an island not far away. He sent it to the *Detroit Free Press* and to his astonishment it was accepted. Long afterwards when his position was assured, he said, "After that I expected that everything I wrote would be accepted at once. Alas, the road to fame is not so easy." It was a long up-hill struggle. It was years before his name became so well-known and his manuscripts received respectful attention. Since then he had learnt the true meaning of yoga, and India has become for him the "Holy Land" to which one goes, not as a tourist but as a pilgrim. The scene of his first novel was laid largely in India. With what feeling and what rare insight he depicted the Indian village to which his hero comes at dusk! The homesick wanderer who reads the book lives in India again for a few hours. Who shall say that this career was not inspired in part at least by Swami Vivekananda, especially since the writer came to know him personally? It was he who said, "There is a glow about everyone who was in any way associated with Vivekananda." Stella went back to live the ordinary human life, and none of us knew anything of her afterwards until news came of her death a few months ago. What life had held for her during those thirty years in which she voluntarily cut herself off from all connection with us, even from him who had planted and watered the seed, who can say? One can only believe that the seed so planted bore fruit worthy of the planting.

Of Mrs. Funke Swamiji said, "She gives me freedom." He was seldom more spontaneous than in her presence. "She is naive," he said on another occasion. This amused her, for she did not spare herself in her efforts to meet his moods. Perhaps more than any of us she realized how much he needed rest and relaxation. The body and mind should not be kept at so great a tension all the time. While others were afraid of losing even a word, she thought how she could amuse him. She would tell funny stories, often at her own expense, and talk lightly and entertainingly. "She rests me," he said to one. To the same one, she said, "I know he thinks I am a fool, but I don't care as long as it amuses him." Is it because of her attitude of not wanting to gather anything from one who had so much to give, that she most of all retains the impress of his personality undistorted? Her sunny disposition, her optimism, and her enthusiasm were refreshing. Nor was she less attractive in other ways, possessing beauty, grace, and charm to an unusual degree. Even today, in spite of her physical disability, the old charm is there. Nothing rekindles the flame and brings the fire of enthusiasm to such a glow as conversation about the Swami. He lives. One actually feels his presence. It is a blessed experience. Who can doubt that when the time comes for her to drop the body which has now become such a burden, she will find the darkness illumined and in that luminous atmosphere a radiant presence who will give her that great gift—*Freedom.*

The Swami's choice of two others grew out of the theory which he then held that fanaticism is power gone astray. If this force can be transmuted and turned into a higher channel, it becomes a great power for good. There must be power. That is essential. In Marie Louise and Leon Landsberg, he saw that there was fanaticism to a marked degree, and he believed that here was material which would be invaluable. Marie Louise was, in some respects, the outstanding personality in this small community. A tall, angular woman, about fifty years of age, so masculine in appearance that one looked twice before one could tell whether she was a man or a woman. The short, wiry hair, in the days before bobbed hair was in vogue, the masculine features, the large bones, the heavy voice and the robe, not unlike that worn by men in India, made one doubtful. Her path was the highest, she announced, that of philosophy—jnana. She had been the spokesman for ultra-radical groups and had learning and some degree of eloquence. "I have magnetism of the platform," she used to say. Her vanity and personal ambition made her unfit for discipleship, and useless as a worker in Swami Vivekananda's Movement. She left Thousand Islands before any of us, and soon after organized an independent centre of Vedanta in California, and later, one in Washington.

One of the most interesting, as well as the most learned of the group was Leon Landsberg, an American by citizenship and a Russian Jew by birth. He had all the great qualities of his race—emotion, imagination, a passion for learning, and a worship of genius. For three years, he was Swami Vivekananda's inseparable companion, friend, secretary, and attendant. His intimate knowledge of Europe, its philosophies, its languages, its culture, gave him a profundity and depth of mind which are rare. He was fiery and picturesque. His indifference to his personal appearance, his fanaticism, his pity for the poor, which amounted to a passion, drew Swamiji to him. He often gave his last penny to a beggar, and always he gave not out of his abundance, but out of a poverty almost as great as the recipient's. He had as well a position on a New York paper which required but little of his time and gave him a small income. While he and Swamiji lived together in 33rd Street in New York, they shared what they had. Sometimes there was sufficient for both and sometimes there was nothing. After the classes were over at night, they would go out for a walk, ending with a light meal which was inexpensive, as the common purse was often empty. This did not trouble either of them. They knew that when it was needed, money would find its way into the purse again.

Landsberg was an epitome of Europe, its philosophies, its literature, and its art. Swamiji found greater delight in reading a man, than a book. Then, too, he was a revelation of the Jewish race—its glory, its tragedy. In this companionship, two ancient races met and found a common basis.

Landsberg was one of the first to come to Thousand Islands and to be initiated. He was given a new name as was customary at that time. Because of his great compassion, he was named Kripananda. His path was bhakti, worship, devotion. In this his fiery emotional nature could most easily find its true expression. He was the first to be sent out to teach.

After leaving Detroit, Swamiji had gone to New York hoping that there, in the cultural metropolis of America, he might find an opening to begin the work he felt destined to do. He was soon taken up by a group of wealthy friends who loved and admired him and were attracted by his personality, but cared nothing for his message. He found himself in danger of becoming a social lion. He was fed, clothed, and housed in luxury. Again there came the cry for freedom: "Not this! Not this! I can never do my work under these conditions."

Then he thought the way might be found by living alone and teaching in classes, open to all. He asked Landsberg to find inexpensive rooms for both of them. The place which was found (64 West 33rd Street) was in a most undesirable locality, and it was hinted that the right sort of people, especially ladies, would not come to such a place; but they came—all sorts and conditions of men and women—to these squalid rooms. They sat on chairs, and when chairs were filled, anywhere—on tables, on washstands, on the stairs. Millionaires were glad to sit on the floor, literally at his feet. No charge was made for the teaching and often there was no money to pay the rent. Then Swamiji would give a secular lecture for which he felt he could accept a fee. All that winter, he worked as he could. Often the last penny was spent. It was a precarious way of carrying on the work and sometimes it seemed as if it would come to an end.

It was at this time that some of those with means offered to finance the undertaking. But they made conditions. The "right place" must be selected and the "right people" must be attracted. This was intolerable to his free sannyasi-spirit. Was it for this that he had renounced the world? Was it for this that he had cast aside name and fame? A little financial security was a small thing to give up. He would depend upon no human help. If the work was for him to do, ways and means would come. He refused to make a compromise with the conventional outlook and worldly methods. A letter written at this time is revealing:

"— wants me to be introduced to the 'right sort of people'. The only 'right sort of people' are those whom the Lord sends—that is what I understand in my life's experience. They alone can and will help me. As for the rest, Lord bless them in a mass and save me from them. ... Lord, how hard it is for man to believe in Thy mercies!!! Shiva! Shiva! Where is the right kind? And where is the bad? It is all *He*!! In the tiger and in the lamb, in the saint and in the sinner, all *He*!! In Him I have taken my refuge, body, soul, and Atman, will He leave me now after carrying me in His arms all my life? Not a drop will be in the ocean, not a twig in the deepest forest, not a crumb in the house of the God of wealth, if the Lord is not merciful. Streams will be in the desert and the beggar will have plenty if He wills it. He seeth the sparrow's fall—are these but words, or literal, actual life?

"Truce to this 'right sort of presentation'. Thou art my right, Thou my wrong, my Shiva. Lord, since a child, I have taken refuge in Thee. Thou wilt be with me in the tropics or at the poles, on the tops of mountains or in the depths of oceans. My stay—my guide in life—my refuge—my friend—my teacher—and my God—my real self—Thou wilt never leave me, never. ... My God, save Thou me for ever from these weaknesses, and may I never, never seek for help from any being but Thee. If a man puts his trust in another good man, he is never betrayed. Wilt Thou forsake me, Father of all good—Thou who knowest that *all* my life, I am Thy servant, and Thine alone? Wilt Thou give me over to be played upon by others or dragged down by evil? He will never leave me, I am sure."

After this, a few earnest students took the financial responsibility for the work, and there was no further difficulty. Again he wrote: "Was it ever in the history of the world that any great work was done by the rich? It is the heart and brains that do it, ever and ever, and not the purse."

All that winter the work went on and when the season came to an end, early in the summer, this devoted group was not willing to have the teaching discontinued. One of them owned a house in Thousand Island Park on the St. Lawrence River, and a proposal was made to the teacher that they all spend the summer there. He consented, much touched by their earnestness. He wrote to one of his friends that he wanted to manufacture a few "yogis" out of the materials of the classes. He felt that his work was now really started and that those who joined him at Thousand Islands were really disciples.

In May 1895, he writes to Mrs. Ole Bull:

"This week will be the last of my classes. I am going next Saturday with Mr. Leggett to Maine. He has a fine lake and a forest there. I shall be two or three weeks there. From thence, I go to Thousand Islands. Also I have an invitation to speak at a Parliament of Religions at Toronto, Canada, on July 18th. I shall go there from Thousand Islands and return back."

And on the 7th of June:

"I am here at last with Mr. Leggett. This is one of the most beautiful spots I ever saw. Imagine a lake surrounded with hills and covered with a huge forest, with nobody but ourselves. So lovely, so quiet, so restful. You may imagine how glad I am after the bustle of cities. It gives me a new lease of life to be here. I go into the forest alone and read my *Gita* and am quite happy. I shall leave this place in about ten days or so, and go to Thousand Islands. I shall meditate by the hour and day here and be all alone by myself. The very idea is ennobling."

Early in June three or four were gathered at Thousand Island Park with him and the teaching began without delay. He came on Saturday, 6 July1895. Swami Vivekananda had planned to initiate several of those already there on Monday. "I don't know you well enough yet to feel sure that you are ready for initiation," he said on Sunday afternoon. Then he added rather shyly, "I have a power which I seldom use—the power of reading the mind. If you will permit me, I should like to read your mind, as I wish to initiate you with the others tomorrow." We assented joyfully. Evidently he was satisfied with the result of the reading, for the next day, together with several others, he gave us a mantra and made us his disciples. Afterwards, questioned as to what he saw while he was reading our minds he told us a little. He saw that we should be faithful and that we should make progress in our spiritual life. He described something of what he saw, without giving the interpretation of every picture. In one case, scene after scene passed before his mental vision which meant that there would be extensive travel apparently in Oriental countries. He described the very houses in which we should live, the people who should surround us, the influences that would affect our lives. We questioned him about this. He told us it could be acquired by anyone. The method was simple at least in the telling. First, think of space—vast, blue, extending everywhere. In time, as one meditates upon this space intently, pictures appear. These pictures must be interpreted. Sometimes one sees the pictures but does not know the interpretation. He saw that one of us would be indissolubly connected with India. Important as well as minor events were foretold for us nearly all of which have come to pass. In this reading the quality of the personality was revealed—the mettle, the capacity, the character. Having passed this test, there can be no self-depreciation, no lack of faith in one's self. Every momentary doubt is replaced by a serene assurance. Has the personality not received the stamp of approval from the one being in the world...?

Thousand Island Park, nine miles long and a mile or two in width, is the largest of the Thousand Islands. The steamers land at the village on the river. At that time the remainder of the island was practically a solitude. The house to which we were directed was a mile above the village. It was built upon a rock. Was that symbolic? It was two storeys high in the front and three behind. A dense forest surrounded it. Here we were secluded and yet within the reach of supplies. We could walk in all directions and meet no one. Sometimes Swamiji went out only with Landsberg. Sometimes he asked one or two of us to accompany him. Occasionally the whole party went out together. As we walked, he talked, seldom of controversial subjects. The solitude, the woods, seemed to recall past experiences in Indian forests, and he told us of the inner experiences during the time he wandered there.

We in our retirement seldom saw anyone except now and then someone who came for the view. The conditions were ideal for our purpose. One could not have believed that such a spot could be found in America. What great ideas were voiced there! What an atmosphere was created, what power was generated! There the teacher reached some of his loftiest flights, there he showed us his heart and mind. We saw ideas unfold and flower. We saw the evolution of plans which grew into institutions in the years that followed. It was a blessed experience—an experience which made Miss Waldo exclaim, "What have we ever done to deserve this?" And so we all felt.

The original plan was that they should live as a community, without servants, each doing a share of the work. Nearly all of them were unaccustomed to housework and found it uncongenial. The result was amusing; as time went on it threatened to become disastrous. Some of us who had just been reading the story of Brook Farm felt that we saw it reenacted before our eyes. No wonder Emerson refused to join that community of transcendentalists. His serenity was evidently bought at a price. Some could only wash dishes. One whose work was to cut the bread, groaned and all but wept whenever she attempted the task. It is curious how character is tested in these little things. Weaknesses which might have been hidden for a lifetime in ordinary intercourse were exposed in a day of this community life. It was interesting. With Swamiji the effect was quite different. Although only one among them all was younger than himself, he seemed like a father or rather like a mother in patience and gentleness. When the tension became too great, he would say with the utmost sweetness, "Today, I shall cook for you." To this Landsberg would ejaculate in an aside, "Heaven save us!" By way of explanation he said that in New York when Swamiji cooked he, Landsberg, would tear his hair, because it meant that afterwards every dish in the house required washing. After several unhappy experiences in the community housekeeping, an outsider was engaged for help, and one or two of the more capable ones undertook certain responsibilities, and we had peace.

But once the necessary work was over and we had gathered in the classroom, the atmosphere was changed. There never was a disturbing element within those walls. It seemed as if we had left the body and the bodily consciousness outside. We sat in a semicircle and waited. Which gate to the Eternal would be opened for us today? What heavenly vision should meet our eyes? There was always the thrill of adventure. The Undiscovered Country, the Sorrowless Land opened up new vistas of hope and beauty. Even so, our expectations were always exceeded. Vivekananda's flights carried us with him to supernal heights. Whatever degree of realization may or may not have come to us since, one thing we can never forget: We saw the Promised Land. We, too, were taken to the top of Pisgah and the sorrow and trials of this world have never been quite real since.

He told us the story of the beautiful garden and of one who went to look over the wall and found it so alluring that he jumped over and never returned. And after him another and another. But we had the unique fortune of having for a teacher one who had looked over and found it no less entrancing; but out of his great compassion he returned to tell the story to those left behind and to help them over the wall. So it went on from morning until midnight. When he saw how deep the impression was which he had made, he would say with a smile: "The cobra has bitten you. You cannot escape." Or sometimes: "I have caught you in my net. You can never get out."

Miss Dutcher, our hostess, was a conscientious little woman, a devout Methodist. How she ever came to be associated with such a group as gathered in her house that summer would have been a mystery to anyone who did not know the power of Swami Vivekananda to attract and hold sincere souls. But having once seen and heard him, what could one do but follow? Was he not the incarnation of the Divine, the Divine which lures man on until he finds himself again in his lost kingdom? But the road was hard and often terrifying to one still bound by conventions and orthodoxy in religion. All her ideals, her values of life, her concepts of religion were, it seemed to her, destroyed. In reality, they were only modified. Sometimes she did not appear for two or three days. "Don't you see," Swami said, "this is not an ordinary illness? It is the reaction of the body against the chaos that is going on in her mind. She cannot bear it." The most violent attack came one day after a timid protest on her part against something he had said in the class. "The idea of duty is the midday sun of misery scorching the very soul," he had said. "Is it not our duty?" she began, but got no farther. For once that great free soul broke all bounds in his rebellion against the idea that anyone should dare bind with fetters the soul of man. Miss Dutcher was not seen for some days.

And so the process of education went on. It was not difficult if one's devotion to the guru was great enough, for then, like the snake, one dropped the old and put on the new. But where the old prejudices and conventions were stronger than one's faith, it was a terrifying, almost a devastating, process.

TEACHING AT THOUSAND ISLAND PARK

We all attended our class lectures. To a Hindu the teaching itself might have been familiar, but it was given with a fire, an authority, a realization which made it sound like something entirely new. He too "spake like one having authority". To us of the West to whom it was all new it was as if a being from some radiant sphere had come down with a gospel of hope, of joy, of life. Religion is not a matter of belief but of experience. One may read about a country, but until one has seen it, there can be no true idea. All is within. The divinity which we are seeking in heaven, in teachers, in temples is within us. If we see it outside, it is because we have it within. What is the means by which we come to realize this, by which we see God? *Concentration* is the lamp which lights the darkness.

There are different methods for different states of evolution. All paths lead to God. The guru will put you on the path best suited to your development. With what sense of release did we hear that we not only may, but *must* follow reason. Before that it had seemed that reason and intuition are generally opposed to each other. Now we are told that we must hold to reason until we reach something higher—and this something higher must never contradict reason.

The first morning we learnt that there is a state of consciousness higher than the surface consciousness—which is called samadhi. Instead of the two divisions we are accustomed to, the conscious and the unconscious—it would be more accurate to make the classification, the subconscious, the conscious, and the superconscious. This is where confusion arises in the Western way of thinking, which divides consciousness into the subconscious or unconscious and the conscious. They cognize only the normal state of mind, forgetting that there is a state beyond consciousness—a superconscious state, inspiration. How can we know that this is a higher state? To quote Swami literally: "In the one case a man goes in and comes out as a fool. In the other case he goes in a man and comes out a God." And he always said: "Remember the superconscious never contradicts reason. It transcends it, but contradicts it never. Faith is not belief, it is the grasp on the Ultimate, an illumination."

Truth is for all, for the good of all. Not secret but sacred. The steps are: hear, then reason about it, "let the flood of reason flow over it, then meditate upon it, concentrate your mind upon it, make yourself one with it." Accumulate power in silence and become a dynamo of spirituality. What can a beggar give? Only a king can give, and he only when he wants nothing himself.

"Hold your money merely as custodian for what is God's. Have no attachment for it. Let name and fame and money go; they are a terrible bondage. Feel the wonderful atmosphere of freedom. You are free, free, free! Oh blessed am I! Freedom am I! I am the Infinite! In my soul I can find no beginning and no end. All is my Self. Say this unceasingly."

He told us that God was real, a reality which could be experienced just as tangibly as any other reality; that there were methods by which these experiences could be made which were as exact as laboratory methods of experiment. The mind is the instrument. Sages, yogis, and saints from prehistoric times made discoveries in this science of the Self. They have left their knowledge as a precious legacy not only to their immediate disciples but to seekers of Truth in future times. This knowledge is in the first instance passed on from Master to disciple, but in a way very different from the method used by an ordinary teacher. The method of religious teaching to which we of the West have become accustomed is that we are told the results of the experiments, much as if a child were given a problem in arithmetic and were told its answer but given no instruction as how the result was reached. We have been told the results reached by the greatest spiritual geniuses known to humanity, the Buddha, the Christ, Zoroaster, Laotze, and we have been told to accept and believe the result of their great experiments. If we are sufficiently reverent and devotional, and if we have reached that stage of evolution where we know that there must be some Reality transcending reason, we may be able to accept and believe blindly, but even then it has but little power to change us. It does not make a god of man. Now we were told that there is a method by which the result may be obtained, a method never lost in India, passed on from guru to disciple.

For the first time we understood why all religions begin with ethics. For without truth, non-injury, continence, non-stealing, cleanliness, austerity, there can be no spirituality. For many of us in the West ethics and religion are almost synonymous. It is the one concrete thing we are taught to practise and there it generally ends. We were like the young man who went to Jesus and asked, "What shall I do to inherit eternal life?" Jesus said, "Thou hast read the prophets. Do not kill, do not steal, do not commit adultery." The young man said, "Lord, all these have I kept from my youth up." Now we wanted to hear about yoga, samadhi, and other mysteries. This emphasis upon things which were by no means new to us was something of a surprise. But soon we found it was not quite the same, for it was carried to an unthought of length. The ideal must be truth in thought, word, and deed. If this can be practised for twelve years, then every word that is said becomes true. If one perfect in this way says, "Be thou healed", healing comes instantaneously. Be blessed, he is blessed. Be freed, he is released. Stories were told of those who had this power, and who could not recall the word once spoken. To the father of Sri Ramakrishna this power had come. Would that explain why such a son was born to him? Then there was the life of Sri Ramakrishna himself. "Come again Monday," he said to a young man. "I cannot come on Monday, I have some work to do; may I come Tuesday?" "No," answered the Master, "these lips have said 'Monday'; they cannot say anything else now." "How can truth come unless the mind is perfected by the practice of truth? Truth comes to the true. Truth attracts truth. Every word, thought, and deed rebounds. Truth cannot come through untruth." ...

Non-injury in word, thought and deed. There are sects in India which apply this mainly to the taking of life. Not only are they vegetarians, but they try not to injure still lower forms of life. They put a cloth over their mouth to keep out microscopic creatures and sweep the path before them so as not to injure whatever life may be underfoot. But that does not go far, even so there remain infinitesimal forms of life which it is impossible to avoid injuring. Nor does it go far enough. Before one has attained perfection in non-injury he has lost the power to injure. "From me no danger be to aught that lives" becomes true for him, a living truth, reality. Before such a one the lion and the lamb lie down together. Pity and compassion have fulfilled the law and transcended it.

Continence—Chastity: This subject always stirred him deeply. Walking up and down the room, getting more and more excited, he would stop before someone, as if there were no one else in the room. "Don't you see," he would say eagerly, "there is a reason why chastity is insisted on in all monastic orders? Spiritual giants are produced only where the vow of chastity is observed. Don't you see there must be a reason? The Roman Catholic Church has produced great saints, St. Francis of Assisi, Ignatius Loyola, St. Teresa, the two Catherines, and many others. The Protestant Church has produced no one of spiritual rank equal to them. There is a connection between great spirituality and chastity. The explanation is that these men and women have through prayer and meditation transmuted the most powerful force in the body into spiritual energy. In India this is well understood and yogis do it consciously. The force so transmuted is called ojas and is stored up in the brain. It has been lifted from the lowest centre of the kundalini—the muladhara—to the highest." To us who listened the words came to our remembrance: "And I, if I be lifted up, will draw all men unto me."

In the same eager way he went on to explain that whenever there was any manifestation of power or genius, it was because a little of this power had escaped up the sushumna. And did he say it? Or did we come to see for ourselves the reason why the avataras and even lesser ones could inspire a love so great that it made the fishermen of Galilee leave their nets and follow the young Carpenter, made the princes of the clan of Shakya give up their robes, their jewels, their princely estates? It was the divine drawing. It was the lure of divinity.

How touchingly earnest Swami Vivekananda was as he proposed this subject! He seemed to plead with us as if to beg us to act upon this teaching as something most precious. More, we could not be the disciples he required if we were not established in this. He demanded a conscious transmutation. "The man who had no temper has nothing to control," he said. "I want a few, five or six who are in the flower of their youth."

Austerity! Why have the saints in all religions been given to fasting and self-denial, to mortification of the body? True, there have been those who foolishly regarded the body as an enemy which must be conquered and have used these methods to accomplish their end. The real purpose however is disciplining the will. No ordinary will-power will carry us through the great work before us. We must have nerves of steel and a will of iron, a will which is consciously disciplined and trained. Each act of restraint helps to strengthen the will. It is called tapas in India and means literally, to *heat*, the inner or the higher nature gets heated. How is it done? There are various practices of a voluntary nature, e.g. a vow of silence is kept for months, fasting for a fixed number of days, or eating only once a day. With children it is often the denial of some favourite article of food. The conditions seem to be that the vow must be taken voluntarily for a specific time. If the vow is not kept, it does more harm than good. If it is kept, it becomes a great factor in building up the character so necessary for the higher practices.

Beyond a few directions in meditation there was very little set instruction, yet in course of these few days our ideas were revolutionized, our outlook enormously enlarged, our values changed. It was a reeducation. We learnt to think clearly and fearlessly. Our conception of spirituality was not only clarified but transcended. Spirituality brings life, power, joy, fire, glow, enthusiasm—all the beautiful and positive things, never inertia, dullness, weakness. Then why should one have been so surprised to find a man of God with a power in an unusual degree? Why have we in the West always associated emaciation and anaemic weakness with spirituality? Looking back upon it now one wonders how one could ever have been so illogical. Spirit is life, shakti, the divine energy.

It is needless to repeat the formal teaching, the great central idea. These one can read for himself. But there was something else, an influence, an atmosphere charged with the desire to escape from bondage—call it what you will—that can never be put into words, and yet was more powerful than any words. It was this which made us realize that we were blessed beyond words. To hear him say, "This indecent clinging to life," drew aside the curtain for us into the region beyond life and death, and planted in our hearts the desire for that glorious freedom. We saw a soul struggling to escape the meshes of maya, one to whom the body was an intolerable bondage, not only a limitation, but a degrading humiliation. "Azad, Azad, the Free," he cried, pacing up and down like a caged lion. Yes, like the lion in the cage who found the bars not of iron but of bamboo. "Let us not be caught this time" would be his refrain another day. "So many times maya has caught us, so many times have we exchanged our freedom for sugar dolls which melted when the water touched them. Let us not be caught this time." So in us was planted the great desire for freedom. Two of the three requisites we already had—a human body and a guru, and now he was giving us the third, the desire to be free.

"Don't be deceived. Maya is a great cheat. Get out. Do not let her catch you this time," and so on and so on. "Do not sell your priceless heritage for such delusions. Arise, awake, stop not till the goal is reached." Then he would rush up to one of us with blazing eyes and fingers pointing and would exclaim, "Remember, God is the only Reality." Like a madman, but he was mad for God. For it was at this time that he wrote *The Song of the Sannyasin*. We have not only lost our divinity, we have forgotten that we ever had it. "Arise, awake, Ye Children of Immortal Bliss." Up and down, over and over again. "Don't let yourself be tempted by dolls. They are dolls of sugar, or dolls of salt, and they will melt and become nothing. Be a king and know you own the world. This never comes until you give it up and it ceases to bind. Give up, give up."

The struggle for existence, or the effort to acquire wealth and power, or the pursuit of pleasure, takes up the thought, energy, and time of human beings. We seemed to be in a different world. The end to be attained was Freedom—freedom from bondage in which maya has caught us, in which maya has enmeshed all mankind. Sooner or later the opportunity to escape will come to all. Ours had come. For these days every aspiration, every desire, every struggle was directed towards this one purpose—consciously by our teacher, blindly, unconsciously by us, following the influence he created.

With him it was a passion. Freedom not for himself alone, but for all—though he could help only those in whom he could light the fire to help them out of maya's chains:

> Strike off thy fetters!
> Bonds that bind thee down.
> Of shining gold, or darker, baser ore; ...
> Say—*Om Tat Sat, Om.*

IN LIGHTER VEIN

But it was not all Vedanta and deep serious thought. Sometimes after the classes were over, it was pure fun, such gaiety as we had never seen elsewhere. We had thought of religious men as grave all the time, but gradually we came to see that the power to throw off the burden of the world at will and live for a time in a state of childlike joy is a certain sign of detachment and comes only to those who have seen the Great Reality. For the time being, we were all light-hearted together.

Swamiji had a stock of funny stories, some of which he told again and again. One was about a missionary to the cannibal islands who, upon his arrival, asked the people there how they liked his predecessor and received the reply, "He was de-li-cious!" Another was about the Negro preacher, who in telling the story of the creation of Adam, said, "God made Adam and put him up against de fence to dry," when he was interrupted by a voice from the congregation: "Hold on dere, brudder. Who made dat fence?" At this, the Negro preacher leaned over the pulpit and said solemnly, "One more question like dat, and you smashes all teology!" Then Swamiji would tell about the woman who asked, "Swami, are you a Buddhist?" (pronounced like bud), and he would say wickedly but with a grave face, "No, Madam, I am a florist."

Again, he would tell of the young woman, cooking in the common kitchen of the lodging house in which he lived with Landsberg. She had frequent disputes with her husband, who was a spiritualistic medium, and gave public seances. Often she would turn to Swamiji for sympathy after one of these differences. "Is it fair for him to treat me like this," she would say, "when I make all the ghosts?"

He would tell about his first meeting with Landsberg. It was at a Theosophical meeting where Landsberg was giving a lecture on "The Devil". Just in front of him sat a woman who was wearing a scarlet blouse. Every now and then,

Landsberg said the word "devil" with great emphasis, and when he did, he invariably pointed a finger at the woman with the scarlet blouse.

But soon we found ourselves in an entirely different mood for he was telling the story of Shakuntala. With what poetic imagination! Did we think we knew something of romance before? It was but a pale, anaemic thing—a mere shadow of real romance. Nature became a living thing when the trees, flowers, birds, deer, all things lamented, "Shakuntala has departed!" "Shakuntala has departed!" We too were bereft. Then followed the story of Savitri, the wife whose faithfulness conquered even the dread of Lord of Death. Not "faithful unto death", but with a love so great that even death retreated before it. Then Sati, the wife, who fell dead when she inadvertently heard someone speak against her husband. Uma, who remembered even in another body. Of Sita, he never spoke at length at any one time. It seemed to touch him as not even the story of Savitri did. It was too deep and precious for expression. Only now and then, a phrase, or sentence, at most a paragraph. "Sita, the pure, the chaste." "Sita, the perfect wife. That character was depicted once for all time." "The future of the Indian woman must be built upon the ideal of Sita." And then he usually ended with "We are all the children of Sita," this, with a melting pathos. And so was built up in our minds the ideal of Indian womanhood.

Sometimes he would tell us of his life in India—how even when he was a little child the ochre cloth exercised upon him such a spell that he would give away everything he could lay hands on when a holy man came into the courtyard. His family would lock him up when one of these men appeared. Then he would throw things out of the window. There were times when he would sit in meditation until he was lost to all outer consciousness. But the other side was there too—when he was so naughty that his mother would hold him under the tap, saying, "I asked Shiva for a son and he has sent me one of his demons!" The power which was to shake India could not be so easily harnessed! When a tutor came and poured out his knowledge, he sat like an image with his eyes closed. The enraged teacher shouted, "How dare you go to sleep when I am instructing you?" at which he opened his eyes and, to the amazement of the man, recited everything that had been said. It was not difficult to believe this story, for his memory was phenomenal. Once when someone commented on it, he said, "Yes, and my mother has the same kind of memory. After she hears the *Ramayana*, she can recite what she has heard." One day, he was speaking on some point of Swedish history when a Swede, who was present, corrected him. Swamiji did not defend his position, so sure was he of the facts that he made no comment. The next day the Swede came looking rather shamefaced and said, "I looked up the matter and I find you are right, Swami." Time after time came such confirmation. He considered a good memory one of the signs of spirituality.

Many were the stories he told of his mother—the proud, little woman who tried so hard to hide her emotions and her pride in him. How she was torn between disapproval of the life he had chosen and her pride in the name he had made for himself. In the beginning she would have chosen a conventional life for him, perhaps marriage and worldly success, but she lived to see the beggar exalted and princes bowing before him. But in the meantime, hers was not an easy task. Asked, many years later, what kind of a child he was, she burst out with, "I had to have two nurses for him!"

Those of us who were privileged to see his mother, know that from her he inherited his regal bearing. This tiny woman carried herself like a queen. Many times did the American newspapers in later years refer to her son as "that lordly monk, Vivekananda". There was a virginal purity about her which it seems she was able to pass on, and which was perhaps her greatest gift. But could a soul so great find a perfect habitation? India and such parents gave him one that was a fairly satisfactory vehicle. How he loved his mother! Sometimes when he was in other parts of India the fear would come that something had happened to her, and he would send to inquire. Or perhaps he was in the monastery in Belur, in which case he would send a messenger post-haste. To the very end her comfort and her care was one of his chief considerations.

And so perhaps for days we relived his childhood in his father's house in the Simla quarter of Kolkata. His sisters for whom he had a special love and his father for whom he had a son's devotion, flitted across the picture. "To my father," he said, "I owe my intellect and my compassion." He would tell how his father would give money to a drunkard, knowing for what purpose it would be used. "This world is so terrible, let him forget it for a few minutes, if he can," the father would say, in self-defence. His father was lavish in his gifts. One day when he was more recklessly extravagant than usual, his youthful son said, "Father what are you going to leave me?" "Go, stand before a mirror," was the father's reply, "and you will see what I leave you."

As he grew to boyhood, his energy was turned into other directions. There came a time when he would gather his companions together and hold religious services in which preaching played an important part. "Coming events cast their shadows before." Years afterwards, Sri Ramakrishna said, that if he had not interfered, Naren would have become one of the great preachers of the world and the head of a sect of his own.

EARLY ADVENTURES OF THE SPIRIT

As he grew towards young manhood, he became an agnostic, reading Herbert Spencer with great enthusiasm, with whom he also carried on some correspondence. But agnostic or devotee, the search for God was always uppermost in his mind. It was touching to hear him tell how he went from one religious teacher to another, asking, "Sir, have you seen God?" and not receiving the answer he hoped for, until he found Sri Ramakrishna at Dakshineshwar. With that began a new chapter in his life, but that is a long story, often told.

He spoke of his struggles to accept this priest of Kali who worshipped the Terrible One. He, the unorthodox agnostic, product of Western education, to sit at the feet of a superstitious worshipper of idols! It was unthinkable! And yet, in this simple man and in him alone, he found what he had been seeking—living spirituality. If the worship of Kali could produce such purity, such truth, such flaming spirituality, one could only stand before it in reverence. One was compelled to reverse all one's former opinions. The intellect surrendered, but the instincts did not submit so easily. There was a long struggle and many arguments with Sri Ramakrishna after he had accepted him as his guru. At last, he was conquered by an experience of which he never spoke. It was too sacred!

His devotion to his Master was unique. Such words as love and loyalty acquired a new meaning. In him he saw the living embodiment of Divinity, whose very body changed with the realization of his ideas. Although he was illiterate, Vivekananda said of him, "He had the greatest intellect of anyone I ever met." This from one whose scintillating intellect amazed men of outstanding intellectual achievements.

The process of reeducation into Hinduism began. He was among those who had stormed against idol worship, but in this priest of Kali who worshipped the image of Dakshineshwar as his Mother, he found a character greater than any he had met before—a being of shining radiance, the very embodiment of love, of Divinity. "If idol worship can produce such a character," he thought, "I bow down before it." He saw one who practised each religion in turn and found that all led to the goal. He learnt the truth of the Sanskrit verse, "Many rivers flowing in various directions, all lead to the one ocean," or "Whether we call it water, aqua, pani, jal, it is all one water." Best of all, he learnt that religion may be experienced, not merely believed, and that there are methods which give this experience; that man may here and in this body become divine-transmuted, from the human

into the superhuman. In Sri Ramakrishna, he saw one who
lived "God is the only Reality".

The time with the Master was drawing to an end. All too
soon, this God-intoxicated one left a little band of disconsolate disciples who at first felt like sheep without a shepherd.
After a time, this feeling of helplessness and desolation
gradually gave way to the knowledge which amounted to
a certainty of the presence of the Master. From that time
on, there was always a centre, however humble, where the
Master was worshipped. However far many of them might
wander, one was there to keep the altar-fire burning.

SWAMI VIVEKANANDA'S WANDER-YEARS

And now began years of wandering for them. From
Dakshineshwar to the Himalayas, from the Himalayas to
Rameshwaram, they travelled: by foot, by bullock cart, by
camel, by elephant, by train, these children of Sri Ramakrishna would wander. Some went into Tibet, some lived in caves
in the Himalayas. The palaces of Rajas knew them as well as
the huts of peasants. It was not until many years had passed
that they were all gathered together again, in the monastery
on the other side of the Ganga from Dakshineshwar. Vivekananda too became a wanderer, driven by an overwhelming
desire to find some means of help for his country. It was not
strange that he went first to Bodha Gaya to worship under
the Bodhi tree where 2500 years ago the "Enlightened One"
in this jungle of the world had found the way out.

What Buddha meant to Swamiji, it would not be easy
to say. The very name stirred profound depths. For days
together this would be his theme. With his dramatic genius,
he was able to bring before us the story with such intimacy
that we not only saw it, but relived it as scene after scene was
depicted. It seemed as if it had happened to us—and that
only yesterday. We saw the young prince, his palaces, his
pleasure gardens, the beautiful Yashodhara with her wistful
intuition—"Coming events cast their shadows before!" Then

the birth of the child, and with it the hope that was born in her heart. Surely this son would hold him to the world and to her! But when Siddhartha named him Rahula, the fetter, what a sinking of the heart there must have been! Even this could not hold him, and the old fear came over her again. The shadow of the fear came over us too. We suffered as she suffered. Not until long afterwards did we remember that in the telling of this story never once did Swamiji suggest a struggle in Siddhartha's mind between his duty to father, kingdom, wife, and child and the ideal that was calling him. Never did he say to himself, "I am my father's only son. Who will succeed when he lays down the body?" Never once did such a thought seem to enter his mind. Did he not know that he was heir to a greater kingdom? Did he not know that he belonged to a race infinitely greater than the Shakyas? He knew—but they did not, and he had great compassion. In listening, one felt the pain of that compassion and through it all the unwavering resolution. And so he went forth, and Yashodhara, left behind, followed as she could. She too slept on the ground, wore the coarsest cloth, and ate only once a day. Siddhartha knew how great she was. Was she not the wife of the future Buddha? Was it not she who had walked the long, long road with him?

Then came the story of the years of heart-breaking struggle that followed. One teacher after the other Gautama followed, one method after the other he tried. He practised the greatest asceticism, spent long days in fasting and torturing the body to the point of death—only to find that this was not the way. At last rejecting all these methods he came to the pipal tree at Bodha Gaya and called to all the worlds: "In this seat let the body dry up—the skin, the bone, the flesh go in final dissolution. I move not until I get the knowledge which is rare, even in many rebirths." He found it there. And again, he lifted up his voice, this time in a shout of triumph:

> Many a house of life hath held me,
> Ever seeking him who wrought this
>   prison of the senses.

Sorrow-fraught, sore was my strife.
But now thou builder of this tabernacle—thou,
                              I know thee.
Never shalt thou build again
                              these walls of pain.
Nor raise the ridge-pole of deceit,
Nor lay fresh rafters on the beams.
Delusion fashioned thee.
Safe pass I thence, deliverance to obtain.

Then the return to his father's kingdom; the excitement
of the old king; the orders for the decorations to welcome
the wanderer; the capital in gala attire. All is expectancy—the
prince is coming! But it was a beggar who came, not a prince.
Yet such a beggar! At the head of the monks he came. Watching from her terrace Yashodhara saw him. "Go, ask your
father for your inheritance," she said to little Rahula at her
side. "Who is my father?" asked the child. "See you not the
lion coming along the road?" she announced in quick impa-
tience. Then we see the child running towards that majestic
figure and receiving his inheritance—the yellow cloth. Later,
we see the same Rahula walking behind his father and
saying to himself: "He is handsome, and I look like him. He
is majestic and I look like him," and so on until the Blessed
One, having read his thought, turns and rebukes him; and
Rahula, as a penance, does not go out to beg his food that
day, but sits under a tree and meditates upon the instructions he has received. But that first day the king and the
nobles of the Shakyas listened to the teaching of the Buddha
and one by one entered the path. Yashodhara, too, found
peace and blessedness. Scene after scene, day after day it
went on. We relived the life of the Buddha from before his
birth until the last hour at Kushinagara, when like the Mallas,
we, too, wept—"The Blessed One".

Swamiji spent long months in Varanasi in the company
of holy men and pundits, questioning, studying, learning.
Here one day, one of the best known and oldest of the
sadhus, enraged at what he thought the presumption of

a mere lad, all but cursed him, only to be met with the response, "I shall not return to Varanasi until I have shaken India with the thunder of my voice." And Varanasi knew him no more until 1902 when he had long made good his assertion.

He always thought of himself as a child of India, a descendant of the rishis. While he was a modern of the moderns, few Hindus have been able to bring back the Vedic days and the life of the sages in the forests of ancient India as he did. Indeed, sometimes he seemed to be one of the rishis of that far-off time come to life again, so living was his teaching of the ancient wisdom. Asked where he had learnt to chant with that marvellous intonation which never failed to thrill the listener, he shyly told of a dream or vision in which he saw himself in the forests of ancient India hearing a voice—his voice—chanting the sacred Sanskrit verses. Again, another dream or vision, of this same time in which he saw the sages gathered in the holy grove asking questions concerning the ultimate reality. A youth among them answered in a clarion voice, "Hear, ye children of immortal bliss, even ye who dwell in higher spheres, I have found the Ancient One, knowing whom alone ye shall be saved from death over again!"

He told of his struggle against caste prejudices in the early years of his wandering life. One day just after he had been thinking that he would like to smoke he passed a group of scavengers who were smoking. Instinctively, he passed on. Then, as he remembered that he and the lowest untouchable were one Self, he turned back and took the hookah from the hands of the untouchable. But he was no condemner of caste. He saw the part it had played in the evolution of the nation, the purpose it had served in its day. But when it hardens the heart of the observer towards his fellow-man, when it makes him forget that the untouchable as well as he is the one Self, it is time to break it—but never as a matter of mere indulgence. It was during these wanderings that Vivekananda made his first disciple. On the train that came to

Hathras one day, the young station-master of that place saw among the third class passengers, a sadhu of his own age with a marvellous pair of eyes. Only a few nights before, he had dreamt of these very eyes. They had haunted him ever since. He was startled and thrilled. Going up to the young sannyasi, he begged him to leave the train and go with him to his quarters. This the wanderer did.

Later, when the station-master's duties were finished, and he was free to sit at the feet of the stranger in devotion, he found him singing a Bengali song to the refrain of: "My beloved must come to me with ashes on his moon face." The young devotee disappeared—to return divested of his official clothes and with ashes on his face. The train which took the Swami Vivekananda from Hathras, carried with it the ex-station-master, who later became Swami Sadananda. In after years he often said that he did not follow Swami Vivekananda for religion, but followed "a devilish pair of eyes".

And now began for Sadananda the life of the wanderer. The hardships of the road might have made him miss the ease of his former life, but his travelling companion exercised such a spell that he forgot the body. The tender care of the guru made him forget how footsore he was. To the last day of his life, Sadananda could not speak of this time without emotion. "He carried my shoes on his head!" he cried.

They were blessed, never-to-be-forgotten days. Both were artistic, both were poets by nature, both were attractive in appearance. Artists raved about them.

Then he told of his life alone in the caves of the Himalayas trying to find the solution within. But he was not left in peace and undisturbed for long. The vicissitudes of life drove him forth once more to the deserts of Rajputana and the cities of Western India. During this time he had deliberately cut himself off from his brother-disciples, for he felt a great need to be alone. Once after long search, one of them saw him driving in a carriage somewhere in the Mumbai Presidency. "His face shone," he reported, "like the face of a god. It was the face of a knower of Brahman." This witness describes how he came before his adored brother-disciple, but, although kindly received, was sent away again at once.

Vivekananda stopped for some time in Khetri, at the court of the Maharaja who became his disciple. One day while he was sitting in Durbar, a nautch-girl made her appearance and was about to sing. He rose to leave the assembly. "Wait Swamiji," the Maharaja said, "you will find nothing to offend you in the singing of this girl. On the contrary you will be pleased." The Swami sat[2] down and the nautch-girl sang:

> O Lord, look not upon my evil qualities!
> Thy name, O Lord, is Same-sightedness,
> Make of us both the same Brahman!
> One piece of iron is in the Image in the Temple,
> And another the knife in the Wand of the butcher,
> But when they touch the philosophers' stone
> Both alike turn to gold!
> So Lord, look not upon my evil qualities!
> 　　　Thy name, O Lord, is Same-sightedness,
> Make of us both the same Brahman!
> One drop of water is in the sacred Yamuna,
> And another is foul in the ditch by the roadside,
> But when they fall into the Ganga,
> Both alike become holy. (So, Lord etc.)

The young sannyasi was inexpressibly touched. He blessed the singer who from that day gave up her profession and entered the path leading to perfection.

During these years when Vivekananda travelled from one end of India to the other as a mendicant monk, his constant thought was how to solve the problems of India. Problem after problem presented itself—the poverty, the condition of the masses and the depressed classes; the duties

---

2. Actually he left the place, but came back attracted by the appeal of the song.

of the privileged classes towards them; malaria, plague, cholera, and other diseases; early marriages, the condition of women, of widows, illiteracy, diet, caste, sanitation, the whole dark brood.

The value of pilgrimage grew upon him. "To help India, one must love her; to love her, one must know her." To this day groups of ardent young students, following in his footsteps, make pilgrimages all over India, often travelling hundreds of miles on foot. Not only did it foster spirituality, it made for the unity of India. Pilgrims came to know and love their Motherland. They came with one faith, one hope, one purpose. This vast country has one sacred language, from which all the northern languages are derived; one mythology, one set of religious ideas, one supreme goal. What the Holy Sepulchre was to the crusaders, what Rome is to the Catholic, what Mecca is to the Moslem, this and more is the pilgrimage to the Hindu. If one could draw a map showing the pilgrim routes, it would be seen that they cover the face of India, from the Himalayas to Rameshwaram, from Puri to Dwarka. What is it that these pilgrims seek? "Whither winds the bitter road?" Their faces are set to the eternal goal of humanity; they seek something we have lost, they go in quest of the Holy Grail.

Is it a wonder that men like these love India, understand her problems and needs, as no other can, and devote their lives to her service? These are men who do not make the mistakes of mere reformers. For the work that they do is born of reverence for all that has gone before, together with an understanding for the present need, and great faith and love. They realize that all growth is organic. They do not destroy; their work is constructive.

Swamiji himself was not a reformer. He believed in growth, not destruction. He studied the history of Indian institutions and found that in the beginning they invariably fulfilled a need. As time went on, the need passed away, the institutions remained, while evil after evil had been added to them. He saw poverty widespread and dire. He saw famine and pestilence. The ancient glories of India were only a memory. The race with its great heritage appeared to be passing. Out of the emotions stirred by these sights there grew up later a form of service which still persists. When there is an epidemic of cholera or any other disease, where plague decimates the population, there, serving the suffering, regardless of their own health or life, you will surely find the spiritual descendants of Vivekananda. In times of famine they are there to distribute food to the starving, clothing to the naked. In times of flood, they are there to administer relief. For these purposes money comes from all parts of the country, for it is now well-known that every paisa will be accounted for, and that the money will be spent to the best possible advantage.

It was while he was in the Mumbai Presidency that the Swami perfected his knowledge of Sanskrit, paying particular attention to pronunciation. He considered the accent of the Deccan particularly good. From there he wandered on from place to place, staying a night here, a few weeks there, until he finally reached Chennai, where he met the band of devoted young men who hailed him as a true mahatma. These orthodox Brahmins accepted him as their guru, feeling that he was one with authority from on high, which placed him beyond the limitations of caste or any human restrictions. Poor as they were, they raised a sum of money which was to help towards his passage to America.

Filled with the message that he had to give and the work he had set himself, his mind had turned to America. There he hoped to find the solution. There, in the richest country in the world, he hoped to find help for his needy people. "You cannot expect people to be spiritual," he said, "when they are hungry." Although he went with the purpose of asking help, yet when he found himself there, this royal soul could only give. What did he give? A mendicant—what had he to give? He gave regally the most precious thing he possessed, the one priceless gift which India still has to offer the world—the teaching of the Atman.

Alone, unheralded, he went to that distant continent. In telling of his experience at the Parliament of Religions, he said, "I had never given a lecture before. True, I had spoken to small groups of people sitting around me, but in an informal way, usually only answering questions. Moreover, I had not written out my speech as the others had done. I called upon my Master, and upon Saraswati, giver of the power of speech, and stood upon my feet. I began: 'Sisters and Brothers of America'—but I got no further. I was stopped by thunders of applause." It seems the audience broke all bounds. He described the emotions which this amazing reception stirred in him—the thrill amounting to awe. He felt as never before the power behind him. From that time not a shadow of doubt assailed his mind as to his commission from on high. He was the pioneer, the first preacher of Vedanta. His spirituality caused astonishment. People began to ask, "Why send missionaries to a country which produces men like this?"

SOME IPSE DIXITIS

Some great ideas stand out, not because they are the most important, but rather because they are new and startling. As when Swamiji told the story of Yajnavalkya and Maitreyi and ended with: "Verily it is not the husband who is loved, but the Self who is loved in the husband."

Love. It was a new idea that all love is one; that we love child, father, mother, husband, wife, friend, because in them we see the Self. It is the bliss shining through. The mother feels the divinity in her child, the wife sees it in the husband, and so in all other relations. We have put it into compartments and called it: mother's love, child's love, friend's love, lover's love, as if they were different kinds of love instead of one love manifesting in various forms.

Bliss—Joy. "In joy were we born, in joy do we live, and unto joy do we return." Not born and conceived in sin, but in joy. Joy is our nature, not something to be attained or acquired. "Thou art That." In the midst of sorrow, of tragedy, still it is true; still I must say: "I am the Blissful One, I am the Radiant One. It depends upon nothing. Nothing depends on It." It is at once a terrible and a beautiful Truth.

Growth. Hitherto we had believed that final emancipation and enlightenment were a matter of growth, a gradual advance towards something higher and better, until at last the goal was reached. But from this great Master of the Ancient Wisdom we learnt that the process is not one of growth but of uncovering, of realization. The real nature of man is perfection, divinity, *now.* Nothing to be attained. The Truth is only to be realized. It is a hallucination to think that we are imperfect, limited, helpless. We are perfect, omnipotent, divine. We are that *now.* Realize it and you are free at once.

Incarnations. He believed that Jesus Christ was the Son of God, a divine incarnation. He worshipped and adored him, but not as the only incarnation. In other ages and in other climes God had vouchsafed this mercy to others also.

The Parsees. He told the story of the Parsees, a remnant of the followers of Zoroaster, who were saved by flight to India when Mohammedan hordes overwhelmed Persia a thousand years ago. These children of fire are still faithful to their ancient rites, which they have practised in undisturbed freedom in the land of their adoption. Although a comparatively small community, they have made an honoured place for themselves and have produced great men.

Christianity. Christianity, he told us, was first introduced into India by the Apostle Thomas, about twenty-five years after the Crucifixion. There has never been any religious persecution in India, and there are even to this day descendants of the first converts to Christianity living in Southern India. Christianity in its purest form was practised in India at a time when Europe was in a state of savagery. They now number scarcely one million though at one time there were almost three times as many.

Sameness. At one time Swamiji's effort was to attain sameness, he told us, and often quoted: "He who sees the

Supreme Lord dwelling alike in all beings, the Imperishable in things that perish, sees indeed. For, seeing the Lord as the same, everywhere present, he destroys not the Self by the Self. He then goes to the highest goal." One was reminded of the lines he had lately written:

Love, hate—good, bad—and all the dual throng.
No praise or blame can be
Where praiser praised, and blamer blamed, are one.

It was given to us to see how he practised this in the little details of life. Not until long long afterwards did we understand how great was the sensitiveness and pride which made this practice for him particularly difficult. When asked why he did not defend himself against the machinations of a family of missionaries long connected with Kolkata, who threatened to "hound him out of Detroit", he said: "The dog barks at the elephant, is the elephant affected? What does the elephant care?" The one with whom he lived had a violent temper. "Why do you live with him?" someone asked, "Ah," he replied, "I bless him. He gives me the opportunity to practise self-control." What a revelation to us with the Western outlook demanding comfort at any cost! Thus daily, hourly, we saw the great ideals of the *Gita* put into practice in the actual experience of daily life. To see the Self in a foe as well as in a friend, in the one who blames as well as in the one who praises, to be unmoved by honour or dishonour, this was his constant sadhana.

Seldom has it fallen to the lot of one at his age, to achieve fame overnight, or rather in a few minutes, but this is what occurred to Vivekananda at the Parliament of Religions. It was not merely fame, but the enthusiasm he inspired rose at times to frantic adulation. In the midst of the wildest popular emotion, he remained as calm as if he were alone in a cave of the Himalayas. This, for which other men pay by a lifetime of struggle, he put aside and referred to as the "filthy rags of name and fame".

Sometimes he was in a prophetic mood, as on the day when he startled us by saying: "The next great upheaval which is to bring about a new epoch will come from Russia or China. I can't quite see which, but it will be either Russia or China." This he said thirty-two years ago, when China was still under the autocratic rule of the Manchu Emperors, from which there was no prospect of release for centuries to come, and when Czarist Russia was sending the noblest of her people to the Siberian mines. To the ordinary thinker those two countries seemed the most unlikely nations in the world to usher in a new era.

In answer to our questions, he explained that in the beginning society was a theocracy under the rule of the Brahmin, or priestly caste. This was followed by the military caste, the Kshatriya. Now we were under the sway of the Vaishya, and commercial interest ruled the world. Economic considerations are all important. This phase is nearing its end, and would be followed by the ascendancy of the Shudra, the labourer.

Still the question arose: how did he know that the commercial era was nearing its end? And, a still greater mystery, how could he foresee that Russia or China would be the countries that would bring it about? With him it was never an expression of opinion, begging with, "I think," but an authoritative statement about something he knew with certainty.

A little later he said: "Europe is on the edge of a volcano. Unless the fires are extinguished by a flood of spirituality, it will blow up." This of Europe in 1895, when it was prosperous and at peace. Twenty years later came the explosion!

THE MOGULS

The Moguls seemed to have cast a spell over Swami Vivekananda. He depicted this period of Indian history with such dramatic intensity, that the idea often came to us that he was perhaps telling the story of his own past. We often wondered whether we saw before us the reincarnation of the mighty Akbar. How else could he have known the thoughts, the hopes, the purposes of the greatest of the Moguls?

One of his beliefs was that, before one reached the life in which the enlightenment was to be achieved, one must have run the whole gamut of experiences—suffered every tragedy and the direst poverty, and enjoyed to the utmost all that the world has to offer—wealth, adulation, fame, power, ecstatic happiness, dominion. "Millions of times have I been emperor," he would say in his exuberant fashion. Another idea was that, after lives of effort in which complete success had not been reached, there came a final life of worldly attainment, in which the aspirant became a great emperor or empress. This precedes the last life in which the goal is reached. Akbar, it is believed in India, was a religious aspirant in the incarnation before he became emperor. He just failed to reach the highest and had to come back for one more life in which to fulfil his desires. There was only one more reincarnation for him.

So vividly did Swami depict these historic figures for us—rulers, queens, prime ministers, generals—that they seemed to become for us real men and women whom we had known. We saw Babar, the twelve-year old King of Ferghana (Central Asia), influenced by his Mongol grandmother, and living a hard, rough life with his mother. We watched him later as King of Samarkand for one hundred days, still a boy and delighted with his new possession as though it were some super-toy; his chagrin and dismay when he lost the city of his dreams; his struggles, defeats, and conquests. The time came when we saw him and his men booted and spurred, crossing the great mountain passes and descending on to the plains of India. Although an alien and an invader, as Emperor of India, he identified himself with the country, and began at once to make roads, plant trees, dig wells, build cities. But his heart was always amongst the highlands of the land from which he came and where he was buried. He was a lovable, romantic figure, founder of one of the greatest dynasties within the history of man.

After his death the kingdom fell into other hands and Babar's heir, Humayun, became a fugitive. In the deserts of Sind, with only a handful of followers, he fled from place to place, in danger of his life. Here he met the exquisite young Mohammedan girl Hamida, married her, and shared with her his most unhappy fate. We saw him giving up his own horse to her while he walked at her side. And in the deserts of Sind was born her only son, later to become the Emperor Akbar. So reduced in circumstances was Humayun at that time, that he had no gifts for his followers with which to celebrate the event, except a ped of musk. This he divided among them with the prayer: "May my son's glory spread to all parts of the earth, even as the odour of this musk goes forth!"

Humayun regained the empire, but he was not to enjoy it long; for in the forty-eighth year of his age he met with a fatal accident in his palace at Delhi and died, leaving his throne to his only son, Akbar, then little more than thirteen years old. From that time until his death at the age of sixty-three Akbar was the undisputed master of India. There have been few figures in history with such a combination of qualities. His nobility and magnanimity put even his great general, Bairam, to shame. While still a boy, when his enemy was brought before them, and Bairam, putting a sword into his hand, told the young King to kill him, he said, "I do not kill a fallen foe." His courage was unquestioned and won the admiration of all. Few excelled him in sports: no one was a better shot, a better polo player, or a better rider. But with it all, he was severely ascetic in his habits. He did not take meat, saying, "Why should I make a graveyard of my stomach?" He slept only a few hours every night, spending much time in philosophic and religious discussions. Mohammedan though he was, he listened to teachers of all religions—*listened* and questioned. Whole nights he spent in learning the secrets of Hindu yoga from the Brahmin who was pulled up to his *Kawa Khana (buzh)*.

In later years he conceived the idea of establishing a new religion of which he was to be the head—the Divine

Religion, to include Hindus, Christians, and Parsees as well
as Mohammedans.

King of kings though he was, he had the faculty of
making real friends. There were three who were worthy to
be the friends of this Shadow of God: Abul Fazi, his Prime
Minster; Faizi the poet laureate; Birbal the Brahmin minstrel;
and his brother-in-law and Commander-in-chief, Man
Singh. Two Hindus and two Mohammedans, for there were
two brothers FazI. His friends shared not only his lighter
moments but stood by his side in the Hall of Audience and
followed him into battle. We see them making a line of
swords for him when his life is in danger in a battle with the
Rajputs. They, Mohammedan and Hindu alike, became ad-
herents of the new religion and support him loyally in all his
undertakings. Never was a man blessed with truer friends.
This is rare enough in ordinary life, but almost unheard of
regarding one in so exalted a position. His empire extended
from Kabul to the extreme parts of Southern India. His genius
as an administrator enabled him to pass on a united empire
to his son Salim, later known as the Emperor Jehangir. Under
this "Magnificent son of Akbar" the Mogul court reached a
splendour before which all previous ideas of luxury paled.

Now appears the fascinating figure of Nur Jehan, the
Light of the World, Empress of Jehangir and, for twenty
years, the virtual ruler of India. The influence of this remarkable woman was unbounded. To her great gifts of wisdom
and tact were due the stability, prosperity, and power of the
empire, in no small degree. Her husband had coins struck
in her name bearing the inscription: "Gold has assumed a
new value since it bore the image of Nur Jehan." The Great
Mogul's trust and faith in her were unbounded. To the
protest of his relatives that he had delegated his power to
her, he replied, "Why not, since she uses it to much better
advantage than I could?" When he was ill, he preferred her
treatment to that of all his physicians. She was the only one
who had power to check his habits, limiting him to three
cups of wine a day.

It was during the supremacy of Nur Jehan that the new style of architecture was introduced, a feminine type of architecture in which the virile red sandstone of Akbar's buildings was supplanted by white marble inlaid with precious and semi-precious stones. Jewelled walls instead of rough stone ones. The delicacy and effeminacy of Persia replaced the vigour and strength of the Central Asian Highlands. Its gift to posterity was the Taj Mahal and the marble palaces of Agra, Delhi, and Lahore. The exquisite building known as the tomb of Itmad-ud-daulah on the other side of the Yamuna, was built by Nur Jehan in memory of her father, the Lord High Treasurer, and later Prime Minister to Jehangir. It was one of the first buildings in the new style of architecture. It is believed that the stones were inlaid by the slaves of Nur Jehan. It is interesting to compare this first imperfect attempt with the perfection attained in the Taj Mahal where forty-four stones of different shades of red are used to reproduce the delicate shades of one rose petal. The progress in efficiency is striking.

Nur Jehan's own apartments in the Agra Palace, the Saman Burg, were also decorated under her personal supervision. She was truly a great patroness of the arts, and her charity was boundless.

In a man like Vivekananda, with a genius for seeing only what was great in an individual or a race, such understanding of the Mussulman was nothing strange. To him India was not the land of the Hindu only; it included all. "My brother the Mohammedan" was a phrase he often used. For the culture, religious devotion, and virility of these Mohammedan brothers, he had an understanding, an admiration, a feeling of oneness which few Moslems could excel. One who accompanied him on one of his voyages tells how passionately thrilled Vivekananda was, when their ship touched at Gibralter, and the Mohammedan lascars threw themselves on the ground, crying: "The Din, the Din!"

For hours at a time his talk would be of the young camel driver of Arabia, who, in the sixth century after Christ attempted to raise his country from the degradation into which it had fallen. He told of the nights spent in prayer, and of the vision that came to him after one of his long fasts in the mountains of the desert. By his passion for God, and the revelation granted to him, he became one of the Illumined Ones, destined to rank for all time with the very elect of God. There have been few of these Great Ones; of each, one may say with truth, "Of his kingdom there shall be no end."

We realize that, whether in Arabia, in Palestine, or in India, the children of God speak one language when they are born into the new life. He felt the loneliness of the Prophet who, to the average person, seemed a madman. For years, a mere handful believed in him and his message. Little by little we understood the patience, the compassion, the burden of the mission laid upon this Prophet of Arabia.

"But he advocated polygamy!" protested one with a puritanical turn of mind. Vivekananda explained that what Mohammed did was to limit a man to four wives: polygamy in a far worse form was already practised in Arabia.

"He taught that women have no souls," said another with an edge to her voice. This called forth an explanation regarding the place of woman in Mohammedanism. The Americans who listened were somewhat chagrined to find that the Moslem woman had certain rights not enjoyed by the so-called free American woman.

From this trivial questioning we were again lifted into an atmosphere of wider sweep and more distant horizons. However limited and ignorant his outlook may seem, it cannot be denied that Mohammed was a world figure, and that the force which he set free has shaken this world and has not yet expended itself.

Did he deliberately found a new religion? It is easier to believe that the movement evolved without conscious thought on his part; that in the beginning he was absorbed in his great experience and burning with the desire to share this precious attainment with others. Was the form which it took during his lifetime in accordance with his wishes? It is certain that the conflicts which soon ensued were no part of his plan. When a great force is let loose, no man can harness it. The Moslem hordes swept over Asia and threatened to overrun Europe. After conquering Spain, they established there great universities which attracted scholars from all parts of the then known world. Here was taught the wisdom of India and the lore of the East. They brought refinement, courtliness, and beauty into the everyday life. They left behind them Saracenic buildings—structures of surpassing beauty—a tradition of learning, and no small part of the culture and wisdom of the East.

TRAINING A DISCIPLE

The training Swamiji gave was individualistic and unique. Unless the desire for discipleship was definitely expressed, and unless he was convinced that the aspirant was ready for the step, he left the personal life of those around him untouched. To some he gave absolute freedom and in that freedom they were caught. When speaking of some of those whom we did not know, he was careful to explain, "He is not a disciple; he is *a friend.*" It was an altogether different relation. Friends might have obvious faults and prejudices. Friends might have a narrow outlook, might be quite conventional, but it was not for him to interfere. It seemed as if even an opinion, where it touched the lives of others, was an unpardonable intrusion upon their privacy. But once having accepted him as their guru, all that was changed. He felt responsible. He deliberately attacked foibles, prejudices, valuations—in fact everything that went to make up the personal self. Did you, in your immature enthusiasm, see the world as beautiful, and believe in the reality of good and the unreality of evil? He was not long in destroying all your fine illusions. If good is real, so is evil. Both are different aspects of the same thing. Both good and evil are in maya. Do not hide your head in the sand and say, "All is good, there is no evil." Worship the terrible even as now you worship the good. Then get beyond both. Say, "God is the only Reality." Shall we have the courage to say that the world is beautiful when disaster comes upon us? Are not others the prey of disaster now? Is not the world full of sorrow? Are not thousands of lives overshadowed by tragedy? Are not disease, old age, and death rampant upon the earth? In the face of all this anyone who lightly says, "The world is beautiful", is either ignorant or indifferent to the sorrows of others—self-centred.

Terrible in its sternness was this teaching. But soon there came glimpses of something beyond, an unchanging Reality. Beyond birth and death is immortality; beyond pleasure and pain is that bliss which is man's true nature; beyond the vicissitudes of life is the changeless. The Self of man remains serene in its own glory. As these great ideas became part of our consciousness, we "saw a new heaven and a new earth", "For him, to whom the Self has become all things, what sorrow, what pain, can there be, once he has beheld that Unity?" Without once saying, "Be sincere, be true, be single-minded", he created in us the most intense desire to attain these qualities. How did he do it? Was it his own sincerity, his own truth, his own straightness which one sensed?

"This world is a mud puddle," was received with shocked protest, doubt, and a tinge of resentment. Years after, driving along the Dum Dum Road in the suburb of Kolkata one glorious Sunday morning, I saw some buffaloes wallowing in a pool of mire. The first reaction was a feeling of disgust. It seemed that even buffaloes should find delight in something more beautiful than mire. But now they felt physical pleasure in it. Then suddenly came a memory, "This world is a mud puddle." We are no better than these buffaloes. We wallow in the mire of this mud puddle of a world and we too find pleasure in it. We, who are meant for something better, the heirs of immortal glory.

He refused to solve our problems for us. Principles he laid down, but we ourselves must find the application. He encouraged no spineless dependence upon him in any form, no bid for sympathy. "Stand upon your own feet. You have the power within you!" he thundered. His whole purpose was—not to make things easy for us, but to teach us how to develop our innate strength. "Strength! Strength!" he cried, "I preach nothing but strength. That is why I preach the Upanishads." From men he demanded manliness and from women the corresponding quality for which there is no word. Whatever it is, it is the opposite of self-pity, the enemy of weakness and indulgence. This attitude had the effect of a tonic. Something long dormant was aroused and with it came strength and freedom.

His method was different with each disciple. With some, it was an incessant hammering. The severest asceticism was imposed with regard to diet, habits, even clothing and conversation. With others his method was not so easy to understand, for the habit of asceticism was not encouraged. Was it because in this case there was spiritual vanity to be overcome and because good had become a bondage? With one the method was ridicule—loving ridicule—with another it was sternness. We watched the transformation of those who put themselves into line with it. Nor were we ourselves spared. Our pet foibles were gently smiled out of existence. Our conventional ideas underwent a process of education. We were taught to think things through, to reject the false and hold to the true fearlessly, no matter what the cost. In this process much that had seemed worthwhile and of value was cast aside. Perhaps our purposes and aims had been small and scattered. In time we learnt to lift them into a higher, purer region, and to unite all little aims into the one great aim, the goal which is the real purpose of life, for which we come to this earth again and again. We learnt not to search for it in deserts, nor yet on mountain tops, but in our own hearts. By all these means the process of evolution was accelerated, and the whole nature was transmuted.

So is it any wonder that we shrank from the first impact of so unusual a power? Nor were we alone in this. Some time afterwards a brilliant American woman, in speaking of the different Swamis who had come to the United States, said, "I like Swami ... better than Swami Vivekananda." To the look of surprise which met this statement she answered, "Yes, I know Swami Vivekananda is infinitely greater, but he is so powerful he overwhelms me." Later almost the same words came from the lips of a well-known teacher of one of the new cults whose message was so obviously influenced by Vedanta that I asked him whether he had ever come under the influence of Swami Vivekananda. "Yes, I knew him and heard him," he said, "but his power overwhelmed me. I was much more attracted to Swami ...," mentioning a preacher of Vedanta from Northern India who had spent some time in the United States. What is the explanation? Is it that we are temperamentally attracted by certain qualities and personalities and repelled by others? Even for that there must be an explanation. Is it the fear that the little personal self will be overwhelmed and nothing will be left? "Verily, he that loseth his life shall find it." Still those who feared to be caught in the current of this great power were but few; the others by thousands were drawn with the irresistible force, even as iron filings to a magnet. He had a power of attraction so great that those who came near him, men and women alike, even children, fell under the magic spell he cast.

Far from trying to win us by expediency and by fitting into our conceptions of what the attitude of a religious teacher towards his disciples should be, he seemed bent upon offending our sensibilities and even shocking us. Others may try to hide their faults, may eat meat and smoke in secret, reasoning with themselves that there is nothing essentially wrong in doing these things, but that one must not offend a weaker brother and should hide these things for expediency's sake. He on the contrary said, "If I do a wrong, I shall not hide it but shout it from the house-tops."

It is true that we were conventional and proper to the point of prudishness. Still even one more Bohemian might have been disconcerted. He, in the days when men did not smoke before ladies, would approach, and blow the cigarette smoke deliberately into one's face. Had it been anyone else,

I should have turned my back and not spoken to him again. Even so for a moment I recoiled. I caught myself and remembered the reason for coming. I had come to one in whom I had seen such spirituality as I had never even dreamed of. From his lips I had heard truths unthought of before. He knew the way to attainment. He would show me the way. Did I intend to let a little whiff of smoke turn me back? It was all over in less time than it takes to tell it. I knew it was over in another sense as well. But more of that later.

Then we found that this man whom we had set up in our minds as an exalted being did not observe the conventions of our code. All fine men reverence womanhood; the higher the type, the greater the reverence. But here was one who gave no heed to the little attentions which ordinary men paid us. We were allowed to climb up and slide down the rocks without an extended arm to help us. When he sensed our feeling, he answered, as he so often did, our unspoken thought: "If you were old or weak or helpless, I should help you. But you are quite able to jump across this brook or climb this path without help. You are as able as I am. Why should I help you? Because you are a woman? That is chivalry, and don't you see that chivalry is only sex? Don't you see what is behind all these attentions from men to women?" Strange as it may seem, with these words came a new idea of what true reverence for womanhood means. And yet, he it was, who wishing to get the blessing of the one who is called the Holy Mother, the wife and disciple of Sri Ramakrishna, sprinkled Ganga water all the way so that he might be purified when he appeared in her presence. She was the only one to whom he revealed his intention: Without her blessing, he did not wish to go to the West. Never did he approach her without falling prostrate at her feet. Did he not worship God as Mother? Was not every woman to him a manifestation in one form or other of the Divine Mother? Yes, even those who had bartered their divinity for gold! ... Did he not see this divinity in the nautch-girl of Khetri, whereupon she, sensing his realization of her true nature, gave up her profession, lived a life of holiness, and herself came into the Great Realization? Knowing the criticism that awaited him in India, he still dared in America to initiate into sannyasa a woman, for he saw in her only the sexless Self.

Sannyasi and beggar though he was, never did he forget to be regal. He was generous to a fault, but never uncontrolled in his generosity. Needless to say, there was never a trace of display in any act which he did. If he was with those who had abundance of this world's goods, he accepted what was offered gladly and without protest, even with an alacrity which at times approached glee. But from those who had little, he would accept nothing. He was no longer the mendicant monk, but something so different that one asked, "Has he at one time been one of the Great Moguls?" Foolish thought! Was he not greater than the greatest of the Moguls, than all the Moguls combined? Was he not more than regal? Was he not *majestic*?

His compassion for the poor and downtrodden, the defeated, was a passion. One did not need be told, but seeing him one knew that he would willingly have offered his flesh for food and his blood for drink to the hungry. To this day his birthday is celebrated by feeding the poor. The downtrodden and the outcasts are on this day served by Brahmins and Kayasthas, young men of the highest castes. To those in the West it is impossible to convey the significance of such service. Caste and outcast! Who but a Vivekananda could bring about this relationship so unobtrusively? No arguments regarding caste and the depressed classes. Nothing but heart and devotion. So even in small things while he was still in America. Thus, when asked why he was taking French lessons, he said in confusion, "This is the only way M. L. can keep from starving." Thrusting a ten dollar bill into the hand of another he said, "Give this to S..., do not say it is from me." When one of the group, a weak brother, was accused of juggling with the Vedanta Society's money, he said, "I will make good any deficiency." Then the matter was dropped and he said to one of the others, "I do not know where I could have found the money to make up the loss, but I could not let the poor suffer."

Even after he left America, he still had great concern for those he left behind, who found life a great struggle. Especially did he feel for "women with men's responsibilities". Asked whether he endorsed a certain woman who was going about the country as a religious teacher and using his name and reputation to get a following, he said: "Poor thing! She has a husband to support, and she must get a certain amount every month." "But Swami," someone said, "she claims to be authorized by you to prepare students for your teaching. She says, if we go through her two preliminary classes, we will be ready to be taught by you. It is so absurd and unscrupulous. To the first class she gives a few gymnastic exercises, and to the second she dictates some quotations or gems which she has gathered from various books on occultism. Should she be allowed to mislead people, take their money, and use your name?" All that he said was: "Poor thing! Poor thing! Shiva! Shiva!" With this "Shiva! Shiva!" he put the matter out of his mind. Someone asked him once what he meant when he said "Shiva! Shiva!" and he answered with a mischievous twinkle in his eyes: "Shiver my timbers. Ho, ho, ho, and a bottle of rum." This was not flippancy. How could he answer a casual question otherwise? We had noticed that when something disturbed him, after allowing himself to be troubled by it for a few minutes, his "Shiva! Shiva!" seemed to end it. We knew that he had reminded himself of his true nature, in which everything of a disquieting nature was dissolved.

In New York once there was pitiful little group that clung to him with pathetic tenacity. In the course of a walk he had gathered up first one and then another. This ragged retinue returned with him to the house of 58th Street which was the home of the Vedanta Society. Walking up the flight of steps leading to the front door the one beside him thought, "Why does he attract such queer abnormal people?" Quick as a flash he turned and answered the unspoken thought, "You see, they are Shiva's demons."

25

Walking along Fifth Avenue one day, with two elderly forlorn devoted creatures walking in front, he said. "Don't you see, life has conquered them!" The pity, the compassion for the defeated in his tone! Yes, and something else—for then and there, the one who heard, prayed and vowed that never should life conquer her, not even when age, illness, and poverty should come. And so it has been. His silent blessing was fraught with power.

PLANNING THE WORK

In those early days we did not know the thoughts that were seething in Swamiji's mind, day and night. "The work! the work!" he cried. "How to begin the work in India! The way, the means!" The form it would take was evolved gradually. Certainly before he left America, the way, the means, and the method were clear in every detail. He knew then that the remedy was not money, not even education in the ordinary sense, but another kind of education. Let man remember his true nature, divinity. Let this become a living realization, and everything else will follow—power, strength, manhood. He will again become MAN. And this he proclaimed from Colombo to Almora.

First a large plot of land on the Ganga was to be acquired. On this was to be built a shrine for worship, and a monastery to give shelter to the brother-disciples and as a centre for the training of younger men. They were to be taught meditation and all subjects relating to the religious life, including the Upanishads, the *Bhagavad Gita*, Sanskrit, and science. After some years of training, whenever the head of the monastery considered them sufficiently prepared, they were to go out, to form new centres, to preach the message, to nurse the sick, to succour the needy, to work in times of famine and flood, to give relief in any form that was needed. How much of what he thought out at this time has been carried out! To this India can bear testimony.

It seemed almost madness for a mendicant monk to plan such an extensive work. In later years we were to see it carried out in every detail.

The summer before he had been at Greenacre, a place on the coast of Maine, where seekers of Truth gathered year after year to hear teachers of all religions and cults. There, under a tree which to this day is called "The Swami's Pine", he expounded the message of the East. Here he came in contact with a new phase of American life. These splendid young people, free and daring, not bound by foolish conventions, yet self -controlled, excited his imagination. He was much struck by the freedom in the relations between the sexes, a freedom with no taint of impurity. "I like their *bonne camaraderie*," he said. For days at a time his mind would be concerned with this problem. Pacing up and down, every now and then a few words would fall from his lips. He was not addressing anyone but thinking aloud. His soliloquy would take some such form:

Which is better, the social freedom of America, or the social system of India with all its restrictions? The American method is individualistic. It gives an opportunity to the lowest. There can be no growth except in freedom, but it also has obvious dangers. Still, the individual gets experience even through mistakes. Our Indian system is based entirely upon the good of the society. The individual must fit into the system at any cost. There is no freedom for the individual unless he renounces society and becomes a sannyasi. This system has produced towering individuals, spiritual giants. Has it been at the expense of those less spiritual than themselves? Which is better for the race? Which? The freedom of America gives opportunities to masses of people. It makes for breadth, whilst the intensity of India means depth. How to keep both, that is the problem. How to keep the Indian depth and at the same time add breadth?

It goes without saying that this was not merely a speculative problem, mental gymnastics. It was a question vital to the welfare of India. In America he saw the value and effect of social freedom, yet no one was more fully alive than he to the inestimable good produced by the system of India—a form of society which has kept the country alive throughout many ages which have witnessed the rise and fall of other countries equally great. His problem was to find out whether there was a way of adding to this structure the best of other countries, without endangering the structure itself.

For days he would speak out of the depths of his meditation on this part of the work. In this case, location, buildings, ways and means were all subordinate to the ideal. He was trying to see the woman of the future, the ideal for India. It was not a light task for even his luminous mind, which wrought it slowly, detail by detail. Like a great sculptor standing before a mass of splendid material, he was lost in the effort to bring to life an image, such as no artist had ever conceived before: an image which was to be an expression of the Divine Mother, through which the Light of spirituality shines. We watched fascinated as this perfection slowly took shape. So might some favoured one have watched. Michaelangelo at work with chisel and hammer, bringing into form the concept of power, strength, and majesty, which was to grow into his "Moses!"

What was the work for women which he had in mind? Certainly not merely a school for children. There were already thousands of these. One more or less would make no appreciable difference. Neither was it to be a boarding school, even if it supplied a need by providing a refuge for girls whose parents were unable to marry them off. Nor a widow's home, though that too would fill a useful purpose. It was not to be a duplication of any of the forms of work which had so far been attempted. Then what? To answer that question it is only necessary to ask: What is the significance of Sri Ramakrishna and Vivekananda to the world, and more especially to India at this time? The new power, the new life

that came with this influx of spirituality was not meant for
men alone, but how could it be brought to the women of
India? How could they be set on fire and become torches
from which millions of others might catch the flame? This
was one of his greatest concerns. "For this work a woman
is needed," he cried. "No man can do it. But where is the
woman?"

As far back as his wander-years, he consciously searched
for the woman who should be able to meet his need. One
after another was put to the test and failed. Of one in whom
he had had great hopes he said, in answer to the question:
why not she?—"You see she intends to do her own work."
There was no criticism in this, only a statement of fact.
Again and again it happened that those in whom he had attempted to rouse the latent power within, mistook the power
emanating from him for their own, and felt that under the
same circumstances they too could manifest greatness. They
wanted to do not his work but their own! It was not easy to
find someone who had the necessary qualifications, spiritual
and intellectual, who had the devotion of the disciple, who
was selfless, and who could pass on the living fire. Having
found such a one, and trained her, she in turn would have
to train others, from amongst whom five or six would be
capable of continuing and extending the work. These five or
six would have to be women of towering spirituality, women
of outstanding intellectual attainments, combining the finest
and noblest of the old and the new. This was the goal. How
was it to be accomplished? What kind of education would
produce them?

Purity, Discipleship, and *Devotion* were to him essential
for the one who was to do his work. "I love purity," he
often said, always with a touching pathos. "All attempts
must be based upon the ideal of Sita," he said, "Sita purer
than purity, chaster than chastity, all patience, all suffering,
the ideal of Indian womanhood. She is the very type of the
Indian woman as she should be, for all the Indian ideals of a
perfected woman have centred around that one life of Sita,

and here she stands, these thousands of years, commanding the worship of every man, woman, and child throughout the length and breadth of Aryavarta."

Of purity he spoke constantly; but there was a quality which he seldom named, a quality which is not directly associated with womanhood—yet from the stories he told, one knew that to him no type could be complete without it. Again and again he told the story of the Rajput wife who, whilst buckling on her husband's shield said, "Come back with your shield or on it." How graphically he pictured the story of Padmini, the Rajput queen! She stood before us in all her dazzling beauty, radiant, tender, lovely. Rather than permit the lustful gaze of the Mohammedan invader, every woman of that chivalrous race would rush to meet death. Instead of sympathizing with the trembling timid woman, full of fear for the one she loved, he said, "Be like the Rajput wife!"

Had it been merely a question of a college degree, were there not already numbers of women who had achieved that? The young men who came to him, many of them with degrees, needed training. Much that had been learnt must be unlearnt. New values must be substituted for old, new purposes and aims must be brought into focus. When the mind had been purified, then it was ready for the influx of spirituality, which was poured into it by teaching, conversation, and most of all by the living contact with those who could transmit it. In this way a gradual transformation could take place and they would be trained to give the message and continue the work. Intellectual attainments were but secondary, although he did not underestimate their value. Reading and writing must be the key which would unlock the door to the treasure-house of great ideals and wider outlook. For it was not merely a school which he had in mind, not an institution, but something much larger, something which cannot be easily labelled or defined, something which would make thousands and tens of thousands of institutions possible in the future. In short, it was to be an attempt to create the educators of a new order. The education must not be merely academic, but to meet the requirements of the time, it must be intellectual, national, and spiritual. Unless those who initiated it lighted their own torches at the altar where burns the fire that was brought from above, the work would be of little value. That is why discipleship is necessary. All cannot come to the altar, but one torch can light others, until hundreds, thousands are aflame. Spirituality must be transmitted. It cannot be acquired, although regular practices are necessary—meditation, association with those who have realized, the reading of scriptures and other holy books.

Not that it was ever stated that devotion was one of the qualifications. It is only now, after this lapse of time, that in looking back, one knows how necessary it is. Swamiji made no demands of any kind. His respect, nay reverence, for the divinity within was so sincere and so profound that his mental attitude was always: "Hands off." He did not ask for blind submission. He did not want slaves. He used to say: "I do not meddle with my workers at all. The man who can work has an individuality of his own, which resists against any pressure. This is my reason for leaving workers entirely free." Imperious though he was, he had something which held this quality in check—a reverence for the real nature of man. Not because he believed all men equal in the sense in which that phrase is often glibly repeated, but because in the language of his own great message, all men are potentially divine. In manifestation there are great differences. All should not have equal rights, but equal opportunities. With his great compassion he would have given the lowest, the most oppressed, more than those who manifested their divinity to a greater degree. Did they not need it more? Could such as he exact anything in the nature of control of the will of another? The devotion which he did not demand, but which was necessary nevertheless, lay in acceptance of him as a guru, a faith and love in him that would replace self-will.

India is passing through a transition, from the old order of things to the new, the modern. No matter how much we may deplore it, how much we may cling to the old and oppose the change, we cannot prevent it. It is upon us. The question is: how shall we meet it? Shall we let it overtake us unawares, or shall we meet it fearlessly and boldly, ready to do our part to shape it to the needs of the future? Some have met it by blindly accepting an alien culture, suited to the needs of the land from which it sprang, but unsuited for transplantation. Each country must evolve its own culture and the institutions necessary for its development. If India cannot escape the change, which is taking place all over the world, especially in Asia, she must control the situation. The new must grow out of the old, naturally and in harmony with the law of its growth. Shall the lotus become the primrose? Rather, let us create conditions by which the lotus can become a more beautiful, a more perfect lotus, which shall live forever as the symbol of a great race, and, which, although its roots be in the mud of the world, bears flowers in a rarer, purer atmosphere.

In some respects the transition which is upon us affects women particularly. With the growth of cities women are taken out of the free natural life of the village, and confined within brick walls in crowded towns. If they are poor but of high caste, as most of them are, they often do not escape from this confinement for months at a time. The economic pressure is incredibly severe. Anxiety, poor food, lack of air and exercise result in unhappiness, disease, and premature death. The lot of the widow is worse than that of the married woman. There is no place for her in the scheme of things. In the old village life she was part of the social order, a respected, useful asset. Now she is in danger of becoming the household drudge. She feels that the least she can do in return for food and shelter is to save the family the expense of a servant. When poverty becomes still more grinding, she is the first to know that in her absence the family would dispense with such help. In such a case there is feeling of humiliation for the less sensitive. For others it is much deeper. They feel that they are taking the bread out of the mouths of those around them. Their suffering is great, the more so in that they are helpless. There is nothing they can do to add to the family's income.

It was this class that Swamiji particularly wished to help. "They must be economically independent," he said. How this was to be done, it was not for him to say, so he implied. It was a problem to be worked out by the one who should undertake the work. "They must be educated," he said next. Here he was more explicit and laid down certain principles. Education should not be according to Western methods but according to the Indian ideal. Reading and writing are not ends in themselves. The teaching could be such that these achievements would be used for a noble purpose and for service, not for self-indulgence and not to add one more superficial weapon. If the woman who learns to read, uses the knowledge only for imbibing vulgar, frivolous, sensational stories, she had better be left illiterate. But if it becomes the key which opens the door to the literature of her own country, to history, to art, to science, it proves a blessing. The great ideals of the *Ramayana* and the *Mahabharata* were to be kept before their minds constantly, by stories, by readings, jatras, Kathakatas,[3] until the characters lived and moved among them, until these ideas became part of their very being, something living, vital, powerful, which would in time produce a race of superwomen.

There should be, to begin with, a thorough education in the vernacular, next Sanskrit, then English, science, history, mathematics, geography. And to this, work with the hands—sewing, embroidery, spinning, cooking, nursing—anything in the way of indigenous handicraft. While all Western knowledge, including science, must be given a place, Indian ideals and Indian traditions must always be held sacred. Education will come by the assimilation of the greatest ideas of the East and of the West. Any kind of education which undermines the faith of the Indian woman in the past culture of her race, its religion and traditions, is not only useless but detrimental. She had better be left as she is. Mathematics must become a discipline for the mind, a training in accuracy

---

3. Open-air theatres and oral elaboration of mythological events.

and truth, history a practise in tracing effects to their causes, a warning against repetition of the mistakes of the past. The emancipation of women meant to him a freedom from limitations, which should disclose their real power.

The old methods of education in the West concern themselves only with the mind, its training, its discipline. To this, certain facts relating to history, literature, science, geography, and languages were added. This is a very limited conception. Man is not a mind only. Why not build up a new education based upon the true nature of man? When a new Light comes into the world, it must illumine all aspects of life. If man is divine now, education must be an uncovering of the knowledge already in man. "Education is the manifestation of the perfection already in man," he said.

Let us try a new experiment. At this crucial time when it becomes necessary to review the whole subject, let us break away from some of the old traditions of education. Let us build upon a broader conception, larger aims. Not only must Indian women be highly educated, but a few at least should be of outstanding intellect—the intellectual peers of any women in the world—their flame of spirituality set aglow by the Great Light which has illumined the world in these modern times. They should be on fire; renunciation and service should be their watchwords. A few such women could solve the problems of the women of India. In the past, women made the supreme sacrifice for a personal end. Are there not a few now who will devote heart, mind, and body for the greater end? "Give me a few men and women who are pure and selfless," Swamiji would say, "and I shall shake the world!" No man can do this work. It must be done by women alone. On this point he was stern. "Am I a woman that I should solve the problems of women? Hands off! They can solve their own problems." This was consistent with his unbounded faith in the power and greatness latent in all women. "Every woman is part of the Divine Mother, the embodiment of Shakti," he believed. This Shakti must be roused. If woman's power is often for evil rather than for good, it is because she has been oppressed; but she will rouse the lion in her nature when her fetters drop. She has suffered throughout the ages. This has given her infinite patience, infinite perseverance.

Just as in theology, we no longer teach that man is a child of sin and sorrow, born and conceived in iniquity, but is a child of God, pure and perfect, why should we not change our attitude towards education, and look upon the student as a creature of light and knowledge, unfolding the leaves of his destiny in joy, freedom, and beauty? All religions have taught: "The Kingdom is within you."

For obvious reasons, a new experiment in education can be worked out more easily with women than with men. Women need not work for a degree, as for some time to come they will not attempt to get positions requiring one. In this respect they do not yet find it necessary to conform to accepted standards. Out of it will grow a new race, a race of supermen and superwomen—a new order. Schools for children? Yes, for education should be widespread. Widows' homes, nursing, all forms of service and activity. New life on all planes, the new intellectual outlook, full of new vigour. If the experiment fails, it will not be an entire loss. Power, initiative, self-responsibility will have been developed. If it succeeds, as it inevitably must, the gain will be incredibly great. Results can hardly be foreseen at this stage. The woman who is the product of such a system will at least approach the stature of a superwoman. A few such are urgently needed at the present critical time.

Some of us believe that if Swami Vivekananda's ideas regarding the education of women are carried out in the true spirit, a being will be evolved who will be unique in the history of the world. As the woman of ancient Greece was almost perfect physically, this one will be her complement intellectually and spiritually—a woman gracious, loving, tender, long-suffering, great in heart and intellect, but greatest of all in spirituality.

(*Prabuddha Bharata*, January-December 1931)

SOME PROBLEMS OF INDIA

It often seemed to us that Swami Vivekananda was not consistent. For days together he would inveigh passionately against child-marriage, caste, purdah, emotionalism in religion, or some other subject, until he made us believe that there was no other point of view. Then quite suddenly, perhaps in answer to a facile acceptance of all that he had said, he would turn and rend those who agreed with him, demolish all his previous contentions, and prove conclusively that the opposite was true. "But, Swamiji," someone said in distress, "you said just the opposite yesterday." "Yes, that was yesterday," he would reply, if at all. Neither did he try to reconcile the two points of view or make any explanation. If we did not think he was consistent, what was that to him? As Emerson says, "A foolish consistence is the hobgoblin of little minds." He was looking at all the problems of life from a different vantage point. From his observation tower, the surrounding country looked different from what it did to us who were a part of the landscape. The most he ever said was, "Don't you see, I am thinking aloud?"

We came to know long afterwards that after weighing all the pros and cons, he came to a conclusion. This did not mean that he thought that one side was altogether right and the other altogether wrong, but rather that the balance was slightly in favour of the one, and probably only so because of the needs of time. Having come to this decision, he no longer discussed the matter but thought of some way to put his conclusions into practice.

Criticism he considered detrimental. Reform, he thought, did more harm than good because it always begins with condemnation. This was disintegrating, especially in a country in the position of India where it is most important to restore the lost faith of the individual and the race. All change of value must be growth and could not be superimposed from outside. With his prophetic sense he could see the causes already at work bringing about the changes which so many felt to be necessary. Economic causes prevailed at this period. Very little thought was required to see how the growing poverty would affect purdah, caste, child-marriage as well as other customs.

Someone ventured to oppose him one day, and he turned swiftly saying, "What, you dare argue with me, a descendant of fifty generations of lawyers!" Then he marshalled his facts and arguments and spoke so brilliantly that some of us were convinced that black was white. But if one said to him, "I can't argue with you, Swamiji, but you know that thus and thus is true," to that he always yielded with amazing gentleness, "Yes, you are right." All of this was but a little fun, a little relief from the tension at which he and we with him were kept much of the time.

What amazed us was that he not only saw the problems clearly but found solutions for them—solutions that were quite unique. Every custom was traced back to its origin. In the beginning there was a reason for it; it filled a need. In time it became a custom, and, as is usual with customs, accretions like barnacles were added and militated against its usefulness. What was valuable and what was harmful in this or that custom was now the question. As certain conditions brought it into existence, were the present conditions such as to put an end to it? After all, these institutions are not peculiar to India, as most seem to think. The United States has been in existence as an independent nation not much more than one hundred and fifty years, yet there are already two distinct castes which are as rigid as it is possible to make them. A negro may be as blond as a Swede, but can never cross the barrier between the two races. And then India never lynched its depressed classes! Besides these two rigid castes, there are many subdivisions less rigid, generally based on money. Is it not nobler to place highest the caste that is rich only in spirituality, than to make money the standard? Child-marriage was practised in Europe until quite recently. We read again and again of princesses married at twelve and we know that what the royal families did, the subjects imitated. In *Romeo and Juliet* of Shakespeare, Juliet is stated to have been just under fourteen at the time her parents planned her marriage to Count Paris.

Is it not evident that these customs grow out of the limitations of human nature and out of certain conditions which made them necessary at the time? Instead of condemning, Swami Vivekananda, after tracing them back to their source, following their history, and seeing clearly what undesirable things had been incorporated, tried to find first of all the corrective idea. In some cases this in itself would be sufficient. In others, the forces at work in India today would bring about the change. But there are cases, in which without implying any condemnation of the old a new institution must be created, which will gently, almost imperceptibly, in time displace the old.

Marriage is a great austerity. It is not for self but for the society. There must be chastity in word, thought, and deed. Without a great ideal of faithfulness in monogamy there can be no true monasticism. There must be fidelity even when the emotion is no longer there. Chastity is the virtue which keeps a nation alive. To chastity he attributed the fact that India still lives while other nations no older than herself have sunk into oblivion.

Such an observation would lead to a recital of the rise and fall of the nations of antiquity. In the beginning of the national life, in its days of struggle, there was self-denial, restraint, austerity. As the nation grew prosperous, this was replaced by self-indulgence, laxity, luxury, resulting in decay, degeneration, destruction. Babylon, Assyria, Greece, Rome—this is the story of each and all. But India lives. However individuals may fail, India had never lowered the standard.

Then, thinking of the changes which will inevitably come soon, he questioned: "Which is better? The arranged marriage of India or the individual choice of the West? But our young men are even now demanding the right to choose their wives." Again: "Is intermarriage advisable? Heretofore, the worst of both races have produced an unfortunate breed.

What if the best of the two races unite? It might produce a race of supermen. Would it? Is it advisable?" His country, always Swami's country! How to preserve this great race which has given to the world some of its most transcendental ideas, and is still the custodian of spiritual treasures of which the world outside stands in need?

Or he would turn to the question of child-marriage. Was there any subject upon which he did not throw the rays of his luminous mind? It was a revelation to watch the concentration of this searchlight upon problems. A question or a chance remark was enough. He would jump up and walk rapidly to and fro while words poured forth like molten lava. His mind would seize upon a subject and he would not let it go until it had revealed its secret to him. It has been said that he upheld child-marriage, caste, purdah. He has been accused of being untrue to the great principle inherent in his message. Those of us who saw him wrestle with these problems, know how far from truth this is. He who was roused to a very passion of chivalry at the sight of injustice, of suffering due to man's cruel domination, was he the one to add another link to the fetters which bind the helpless? He "whose heart was like butter," whose feeling for the downtrodden was a passion, whose mission it was to help those in bondage to attain the Great Freedom, how could one think that he would not prove himself the Master of compassion, the Deliverer?

Yet he had but little sympathy with reform and reformers. How could he be in harmony with a method which, while it tore up the evil by the roots, destroyed so much that was beautiful and precious in the process, leaving ugly barren places behind? Whatever changes were to be made in his country, must not be brought about by the loss of her self-respect or by loss of faith in herself. Denunciation of her customs and institutions—no, that was not the way. What perversity was it that made so many of his own generation see only evil in the land of their birth and unalloyed good in everything Western? How had this hypnotism come about?

Could India have lived through the ages if this were true? The heart of India is sound. Evils there may be. Where are they not? Is the West free from them? Pacing back and forth, hour after hour, he would wrestle with the problems of India.

It is essential in all cases, but particularly in India at the present day, not to destroy faith and reverence. Can you eliminate the evil without bringing graver dangers into existence? There was neither child-marriage nor purdah in ancient India—nor do they exist in all parts of India today. They are only in the provinces which have been under Mohammedan domination. What has it done? It has preserved the chastity of the race. Not only must women be chaste but men as well. The chaste woman must not so much as look at another man nor must she allow her face to be seen.

To him it seemed incredible that any man should look with contempt upon the institutions of his country or upon past institutions of which they were the product. But he was not blind to the other side. "We are degenerating in physique. Is this the cause? What is the remedy?" Of the evils that followed in the wake of child-marriage, he said little. Were they not too well-known? He did not say that they must be ended, for he never gave expression to what to him was obvious. Here was an institution that entailed suffering, that made for weakness, that was evil in some of its aspects. One cannot believe that after having faced the facts he did not at once try to find some way to eliminate all the undesirable elements. But was there any reason why he should adopt methods which would result in still worse evils? His was no stereotyped mind: then why expect of him stereotyped methods? Some of us were later to know why this subject stirred him so deeply.

After perhaps hours of thought on the subject, he would heave a deep sigh and say: "Well, well, the economic pressure will bring about changes. This together with education will do much to end it. Education! We must educate our women! But not the kind of education that is open to them

now. Heaven forbid! That would be worse than the existing
evil."

(Prabuddha Bharata, Golden Jubilee Number, 1945)

KANHERI

While he (Swami Vivekananda) was at Thousand Islands
he made plans for future, not only for his disciples in India
and the work there, but also for those of his followers in
America, who were hoping some time to go to India. At that
time we thought these plans only daydreams. One day he
said: "We shall have a beautiful place in India, on an island
with the ocean on three sides. There will be small caves which
will accommodate two each, and between each cave there will
be a pool of water for bathing, and pipes carrying drinking
water will run up to each one. There will be a great hall with
carved pillars for the Assembly Hall, and a more elaborate
Chaitya Hall for worship. Oh! It will be luxury." It seemed as
if he were building castles in the air. None of us dreamed that
this was something which could ever be realized.

Of all that group I was the one who was privileged to
go to India, though it was not until several years later. After
I had been in India two or three years, I found myself alone
in Mumbai with two or three days at my disposal. For some
time, I had had a desire to visit Kanheri,[4] which I knew was
not far from Mumbai. I knew nothing of this place except
that there were some caves there, one of them a Chaitya
Hall, which Fergusson in his *History of Indian and Eastern Ar-*

---

4. According to the latest records of the Maharashtra Government,
Kanheri caves are forty-two kilometres from Mumbai. These caves are
one of the largest groups of Buddhist caves in Western India—more
than one hundred in number. Earlier caves belong to the Hinayana
phase of Buddhist architecture and are excavated in a huge circular
rock. The caves are built during the second to ninth century A.D. Caves
Nos. 1, 2, and 3 are noteworthy for their massive pillars, sculpture and
stupas. Cave No. 3 is known as 'Chaitya Hall'. Cave No. 10 appears to
be the Assembly Hall. The view of the Arabian Sea through Cave No.
56 is charming. Even to this day the caves are surrounded by a forest.)

chitecture has described as a bad imitation of the one at Karli. Surely there was nothing in this to attract one! I wondered at the intensity of my desire, the more so as there were other groups of caves within easy reach of Mumbai, but which I had no special desire to see. I wondered at it. ...

The road led first through a field of stubble and from that into a forest. This forest grew denser and darker the farther we penetrated into the interior. Behind trees, I could see the dark aboriginal people of the forest with bows and arrows peering at us. The road had become a mere cow-path and then even this track came to an end. ...

We went only a short distance [by foot] and then came to a stream which at that season was almost dried up. On the other side was a small hill. Here we found carved stone steps leading to the top. And what a view there was from the crest of the hill! The ocean on three sides, a forest leading down to the water, carved seats on which to rest, sculptured halls of magnificent proportions. Here it all was—the island with the ocean on three sides, a great sculptured Assembly Hall, the Chaitya Hall built in imitation of the one at Karli, the small cells, containing two stone beds each, pools of water between the cells, even the pipes to carry water! It was as if a dream had unexpectedly come true. The place was deserted, not even a caretaker. Coming upon this abandoned site, which answered in detail to the fairytale we had heard long before in America, I was profoundly affected. It was perhaps not strange then that I had a very vivid dream that night, in which it seemed that I was in the Durbar Hall with the great assembly of those who lived there in a time long past. I could see the gathering and the one who was instructing the assembled novitiates. I could even hear what was being said and recognized it as a teaching with which I was familiar, although it was different from the form to which I had been accustomed. The impression remained with me all through the next day and for many days to come. In fact, it proved to be indelible. But to my regret, I could not remember the words that were actually said.

I came back to Kolkata still full of this experience which had affected me so deeply. When I told Swami Sadananda the story of the finding of the deserted island with the 109 caves, and explained how Swamiji at Thousand Islands had described the place, he said: "Yes, Swamiji in his wanderings in western India before he went to America, found these caves. The place stirred him deeply; for it seems that he had a memory of a previous life in which he lived there. At that time, the place was unknown and forgotten. He hoped that some day he might acquire it and make it one of the centres for the work which he was planning for the future. Later, in my wanderings in western India, I too found it, and now you! We have all lived there in the past!" In later years, when he was in a position in which he might have acquired it, it was no longer available, for the government had taken it over. Now there is a caretaker at the place. A road has been built, the jungle cut down, and picnic parties may frequently be seen there. ...

SWAMIJI IN DETROIT—1896

Vivekananda was to visit Detroit once more (in July 1900), but this time for only a short farewell visit.

When asked what preparation he made for speaking, he told us none—but neither did he go unprepared. He said that usually before a lecture he heard a voice saying it all. The next day he repeated what he had heard. He did not say whose voice he heard. Whatever it was, it came as the expression of some great spiritual power, greater than his own normal power, released by the intensity of his concentration. This may have been quite unconscious. No written words can convey the vitality, the power, the majesty that came with his spoken words. What might happen to one's ideas, values, personality, if this current of power were let loose upon them! It was great enough to move the world, let alone one little human personality, which was but as a straw upon its mighty current. It was force that could sweep everything before it. Old ideas would change, the purposes and aims of life, its values would change, old tendencies would be directed into a new channel, the entire personality would be transmuted.

What was it which emanated from him which all felt and none could explain? Was it the ojas of which he so often spoke, that mysterious power which comes when the physical forces of the body are transmuted into spiritual power? When this happens, man has at his command a power so great that it can move the world. Every word that he utters is charged. One who possesses it may say only a few sentences, but they will be potent until the end of time, while the orator who lacks it may "speak with the tongue of men and of angels", but it is as nothing, "as sounding brass or a tinkling cymbal." This, according to Swami Vivekananda, explains why the few simple sayings of a humble carpenter are still a power in the world after two thousand years, while all that was said by the scholars and the learned of his time has been forgotten.

Something of this power is lost in the written word, as those know well who were fortunate enough to hear Vivekananda speak. The spiritual force generated at such times was so great that some in the audience were lifted above the normal state of consciousness, so that it was possible to remember only the beginning of a lecture. After a certain point, there seemed to be a blank. The normal mind was no longer functioning: a higher state of consciousness, beyond reason and memory, had taken its place. Long after, perhaps, it would be found that during that period when the mind seemed blank, an especially deep impression had been made.

So popular was he as a lecturer that no place could be found which was large enough to hold all who wished to come. The man who had in vain tried to find a hall large enough to hold the audiences for the lectures during Vivekananda's second visit to Detroit said, "He could fill a circus tent!" After giving this course of lectures, he was invited by his friend Rabbi Grossman to speak at the Temple Beth-El on the last Sunday of his stay in Detroit. An hour before the time appointed, the Temple was filled to its utmost capacity and it became necessary to close the doors. Hundreds were turned away. Others, refusing to be shut out, hammered on the doors and tried by every means to gain admittance. Just as the lecture was about to begin the clamour became so great that it seemed as if the mob would storm the place. But when he appeared on the platform a hush fell over the audience. I heard a foreign voice near me gasp, "How beautiful he is!" And indeed never was beauty more ethereal. At this time the power was not so obvious. It had been transformed into a diviner radiance and a deeper compassion for the world which he was soon to leave. So India often pictures her gods—robes and turbans of concentrated sunlight, complexion of gold, a divine radiance lighting the face, an inner stillness as of a deep pool. He rose and poured forth majestic truths in a voice which completed a beautiful harmony of appearance, voice, and message. Not a gesture was there to detract the mind from the intense concentration into which he had plunged his hearers.

THE GURU

In America he preached only Advaita. He seldom spoke of his guru. Few suspected the tremendous influence upon his life of the simple Brahmin of Dakshineshwar. Even to those who were most sympathetic, he approached the subject with shyness. But of the profundity of the relation there could be no doubt. Through it, there came to us our first glimpses of the meaning of "guru". To this he added all that the scriptures have said, together with the tradition built up by the holy men of India throughout the ages. Passing through the crucible of his mind, his loyalty and devotion carried a most profound meaning. It did more than that. It created in us a similar feeling and attitude, and brought to birth a similar relation between us and our guru. It set a lofty standard.

How new these ideas were at that time! The first great idea was that the guru must be a knower of Brahman. This is the most important qualification, for only the knower of Brahman has the power to transmit spirituality. The transmission of spirituality from guru to disciple was a startling and fascinating idea to the Protestant type of mind in the West. Spirituality can be transmitted! This, then, explains the doctrine of Apostolic Succession. This is why the Church of Rome still believes that the spiritual power of Peter has been transmitted from Pope to Pope. Be that as it may, today in India it is believed, nay, known with certainty, that the guru can transmit his spirituality to a disciple.

Again, "each has an individual path which is known to the guru"; and his tendencies indicate whether he should take the path of devotion or worship, or of psychic control, or the path of knowledge of the Real, or of unselfish work. All paths lead to the goal, but one of these will present fewer obstacles to the aspirant. Having set the disciple on the path, the guru, like a loving mother, warns him of dangers, explains experiences that might otherwise alarm or dismay. He is the Guardian of the Threshold, not to forbid entrance, but to protect the neophyte against groundless fears. To him the disciple goes for courage. To him the disciple pours out his confidences and tells his experiences. He must tell them to no one else. His mantra, his ishta, his experiences, must be, as Swamiji said, "not secret, but sacred." There must be the utmost devotion and unquestioning faith in the guru. "Would you jump out of window if I asked you to?" he once asked. He wanted a few disciples who had that kind of devotion. He needed that quality for his work. Again and again, he told the story of Guru Govind Singh who, putting his disciples to the supreme test, asked who would trust him even unto death. One came forward. He took him into his tent and in a few minutes the great leader came out, his sword dripping with blood. Again he put their faith in him to test, and again one went into the tent with him and did not come out again. This was repeated until five had gone

into the tent not to return. Then he threw open the tent-
flap, and they saw their companions unharmed in the tent,
and with them a goat which the Guru had killed. Is it to be
wondered at that with disciples whose devotion was unto
death it was possible for Guru Govind Singh to accomplish
the great work he did? For, as Swamiji so often said:

"The guru must be wonderful and the disciple must also
be wonderful."[5]

"Worship your guru as God. He will take you to the other
shore. Trust him through everything. 'Though my guru
should visit the tavern, my guru is holy Nityananda still.'
—Have that kind of faith in him."

"Only those who go through the Sushumna (the path of
yogis) reach the Atman."

"They must go to a guru to learn."

"The guru is the vehicle by which the spiritual influence
is brought to you."

Great as he himself was, one never felt inferior in his
presence. In some indefinable way he made all who came
into contact with him feel great. Was this because he had
trained himself to see only the best in others and to make
nothing of their faults and weaknesses? It was probably even
deeper than that. Realizing himself as the Atman, it was his
constant effort to see that Divine Self in others. Little faults
can drop away, but *That* remains and shines forth. He knew
us better than we knew ourselves. How constantly he voiced
the highest truth as: "The greatest sin is to think yourself
weak. No one is greater; realize you are Brahman. Nothing
has power except as you bestow it. We are beyond the sun,
the stars, the universe."

IMPRISONMENT IN FLESH

Up and down, up and down ceaselessly. "He (Swamiji)
is restless, so restless," some would say. But it was not the
restlessness of the man who does not know what is urging

---

5. *Katha Upanishad*, 1.2.7

him on, what it is he wants. Only too well did he understand what was actuating him. He could have explained it lucidly, logically. A great free soul, conscious of the reality of his being, of his divinity, felt himself imprisoned in a cage of flesh. The bondage of the body was torture. The lion brought from the jungle, where he roamed at will, never forgets the glory of freedom. Restlessly he paces the short distance allowed by his bars. Here was a mighty free soul caged in flesh. The imprisoned glory struggled to escape. True, we are all caught in this bondage, but there is hardly a human being who knows it. We cling to our captivity. We would not give it up. Few even understand that "shades of the prison house begin to close upon the growing Boy".

But here before our eyes we saw one who was fully conscious, who realized the Great Freedom beyond, to whom the bondage was torture, who was ceaselessly struggling to break through. For us who witnessed this struggle, no words were necessary. Without any teaching whatever, our eyes were opened. "I am not the body, I am not the mind." "So that is what it means," we thought, "I am beyond the body with its disabilities, beyond the mind with its limitations, for I am That, I am That."

In 1902, I saw him at Belur, a very different Vivekananda from the one whom I had known in America. Here I saw the lion in his natural surroundings. Here it was not necessary to wear the mask of conventions, nor to conform to man-made rules. He had a serenity here which was sometimes lacking in foreign countries. He was among his own. He could be himself and it was an even greater self than we had seen before. He was surrounded by young devotees and brother-disciples, those sons of Sri Ramakrishna, who were now gathered after long years of wandering. Much of his work was finished. He had given his message in America, in England, and to a lesser degree in Germany and France. In India the roar of the lion was heard from Colombo to Almora. Through the devotion of his young English disciple Goodwin, his message was put into permanent form. He had acquired the plot of land on the Ganga of which he had dreamed in America, and built a shrine for the worship of Sri Ramakrishna and a monastery which was to shelter the children of Sri Ramakrishna—his brother-disciples. He had organized teaching centres, educational institutions, orphanages, famine and flood relief. He was only thirty-nine, and he knew that his release was near. It came on July 4, 1902.

He shared the Hindu belief in the saying of the *Gita* that, "Whenever virtue subsides and vice prevails, then do I manifest Myself. For the protection of the good and the destruction of the evil and for the preservation of righteousness, I am born anew in every age."[6]

Whenever spirituality is at a low ebb and the need of the world is great, God comes in human form. With the advent of an Incarnation of God a great spiritual force comes into the world, a force which protects the good, destroys evil, preserves the dharma, revivifies religion, draws thousands into the current of living spirituality, and brings new life. This influence is felt not only on the spiritual plane, but on the intellectual and physical planes as well. In the realm of intellect, it expresses itself as a revival of art, literature and music, of learning in every field. Men of genius appear and become famous in these realms. There is new life. In the physical world the power is not so intense, but more widespread and apparent. It manifests itself in a greater prosperity, in a renewed love of freedom, and in a more virile national consciousness. The nation enters upon a Renaissance. This power, according to Swami Vivekananda, continues in force for nearly six hundred years, gradually expending itself until the world again sinks into a state in which its only hope is another manifestation of God—another Incarnation. While these are not all of equal rank, each brings an influx of spiritual power, revivifies life on all planes and moves the world. A few instances may illustrate this theory.

Before the coming of the Buddha, India had sunk into a state of materialism. All privileges were usurped by the Brah-

---

6. *Bhagavad Gita*, 4. 7-8

mins, who decreed that hot oil should be poured into the ear of shudras who so much as heard the secret teaching. The time was ripe for the advent of a new manifestation of God, and the Buddha was born. He came, the Compassionate One, who withheld nothing. "I have never had the closed fist," he said. "All that I know I have taught." The highest teaching was given equally to the Brahmin and the outcast, to the holy man and to the thief. All were equal in his sight, as they are in the sight of God. With him came a new influx of spirituality, a mighty force into which thousands upon thousands were caught. Its highest and greatest manifestation was in the realm of religion. There a great revival took place. Great numbers of all ranks gave up the world for the life of renunciation. Princes and barbers, masters and servants, alike entered upon the path. Once having renounced, all were equal. The prince bowed at the feet of his former barber, if it should be that the barber had been initiated first.

This incident is narrated in the Pali Canon: A number of the most powerful of the Shakya princes had decided to become monks of the Sangha of the Buddha. They were attended by their barber, who was to return to their homes the garments and jewels they had laid aside. As they went on, the barber too felt the impulse to join them in the new life. The princes encouraged him in this resolve, but asked him to go before them and receive initiation first, so that they would be obliged to do reverence to him. Caste restrictions and special privileges were put aside and only he was great, who was great in the "Kingdom of God".

The revival was felt on all planes of life, even politically, until under Ashoka, the first Buddhist Emperor, India was a great, united, prosperous empire. But after two or three hundred years the decline began, until at the time of Shankaracharya in the eighth century, Buddhism had reached such a state of degradation that it had to be destroyed.

Six hundred years after Buddha came Jesus of Nazareth. The Roman was master in the land of his birth. Oppression was rife. So desperate was the situation that all classes of people were expecting the coming of the Messiah to deliver them. But does an Incarnation ever come in the guise acceptable to the worldly-minded? This son of a carpenter of Nazareth was "despised and rejected of men". Only a few of the humblest followed him. But he was a mighty one, the son of God in very truth, destined to shake the world to its very foundations; for not long after his death, as time is reckoned in the history of nations, came the decline and fall of the Roman Empire, followed by the adoption of Christianity by the Emperor Constantine as the state religion.

Again six hundred years later in Arabia came the Prophet Mohammed who lifted his country out of the darkness and degradation into which it had fallen. With him began the rise of the Moslem power which was eventually to sweep over western Asia, northern Africa, and even into southern Europe, as also into India.

Shankaracharya in southern India was another great light who came "for the protection of the good and destruction of the evil and for the preservation of righteousness." By this time, about A.D. 800, Buddhism had become degraded. Many evil customs had been added by the depressed races who had adopted it. It was fit only for destruction. He brought back to India the pure lofty teaching of the Atman. Buddhism was driven out of India, the ancient wisdom reestablished, and the country entered upon a new chapter in its life.

The thirteenth century in Europe was the great creative period following the "Dark Ages". Then came St. Francis of Assisi, "the troubadour of God". A wave of spirituality swept the country, thousands embraced "Sister Poverty". In the wake of this power came, first Dante (1265-1321) and Giotto (1266-1336), then later Savonarola (1452-1498) and Michelangelo (1475-1564), Benevenuto Cellini (1500-1571), Bernini (1598-1680) and other great names. The Renaissance had come.

We come now to the twentieth century—with the greatest war in the history of the world waging, brother fighting against brother, millions of the earth's finest and best wiped out, nation against nation in Europe, the East against the West, in a death struggle, famine, pestilence, the downfall of religion, materialism rampant, Western civilization in danger of extinction. If ever there was need of an Incarnation, it is at this time. Will the need be met in this time of direst need? What are the signs of the times? During the nineteenth century several stars of greater or lesser magnitude appeared in various parts of the world, all of whom did their part, great or small, to save the world from the cataclysm which seems about to overtake it. Each has brought new spiritual light and power. Among the greatest of these are the Bab and Bahaullah, in Persia, and Sri Ramakrishna and Vivekananda in India. Which is the Incarnation of this age? We are perhaps too close to these luminaries to know which is the greatest. The Baha'ist will say it is the Bab and Bahaullah, while the followers of Ramakrishna will claim with equal certainty that it is Ramakrishna and Vivekananda. Are there signs by which we can tell? Which has given the message most needed at the present time? It must be a message not for any particular nation but for the world. Which has ushered in a new spiritual era, has brought a light which will never be extinguished, has let loose a power which will make a new heaven and a new earth? The future alone can tell.

(*Prabuddha Bharata*, March, 1978)

Josephine MacLeod

On the twenty-ninth of January 1895, I went with my sister to 54 West 33rd Street, New York, and heard the Swami Vivekananda in his sitting room where were assembled fifteen or twenty ladies and two or three gentlemen. The room was crowded. All the arm-chairs were taken; so I sat on the floor in the front row. Swami stood in the corner. He said something, the particular words of which I do not remember, but instantly to me that was truth, and the second sentence he spoke was truth, and the third sentence was truth. And I listened to him for seven years and whatever he uttered was to me truth. From that moment life had a different import. It was as if he made you realize that you were in eternity. It never altered. It never grew. It was like the sun that you will never forget once you have seen.

I heard him all that winter, three days a week, mornings at eleven o'clock. I never spoke to him, but as we were so regular in coming, two front seats were always kept for us in this sitting room of the Swamiji. One day he turned and said, "Are you sisters?" "Yes," we answered. Then he said, "Do you come very far?" We said, "No, not very far—about thirty miles up the Hudson." "So far? That is wonderful." Those were the first words I ever spoke to him.

I always felt that after Vivekananda, Mrs. Roethlisberger was the most spiritual person I ever met. It was she who took us to him. Swamiji had a great place for her also. One day she and I went to the Swami and said, "Swami, will you tell us how to meditate?" He said, "Meditate on the word Om for a week and come again and tell me." So after a week

JOSEPHINE MACLEOD

we went back and Mrs. Roethlisberger said, "I see a light." He said, "Good, keep on." "O no, it is more like a glow at the heart." And he said to me, "Good, keep on." That is all he ever taught me. But we had been meditating before we ever met him, and we knew the *Gita* by heart. I think that prepared us for recognition of this tremendous life force which he was. His power lay, perhaps, in the courage he gave others. He did not ever seem to be conscious of himself at all. It was the other man who interested him. "When the book of life begins to open, then the fun begins," he would say. He used to make us realize there was nothing secular in life; it was all holy. "Always remember, you are incidentally an American, and a woman, but always a child of God. Tell yourself day and night who you are. Never forget it." That is what he used to tell us. His presence, you see, was dynamic. You cannot pass that power on unless you have it, just as you cannot give money away unless you have it. You may imagine it, but you cannot do it.

We never spoke to him, had nothing much to do with him; but during that spring we were dining one night with Mr. Francis. H. Leggett, who later became my brother-in-law. "Yes, we can dine with you but we cannot spend the evening with you," we had told him. "Very well," he answered, "just dine with me." When dinner was over, he said, "Where are you going this evening?" We told him we were going to a lecture; and he asked, "Mayn I come?" We said, "Yes." He came, he listened; and when it was over, he went up to Swamiji, shook hands with him and said, "Swami, when will you dine with me?" And it was he who introduced us to Swami socially.

The Swami came to Ridgely Manor, Mr. Leggett's place in the Catskill Mountains, and spent some days there. At the time some of the students said: "But Swamiji, you can't go. The classes are going on." Swami turned with great dignity and answered: "Are they my classes? Yes, I will go." And he did. While he was there, he met my sister's children who were then twelve and fourteen years old. But when we came down to New York and the classes began again, he did not seem to remember them, and they, very much surprised, said, "Swami doesn't remember us." We said to them, "Wait until the class is over." While he was lecturing, he was always completely absorbed in what he was talking about. When he was through speaking, he came up and said, "Well children, how nice to see you again," showing he did remember them. They were very happy.

Perhaps it was during this period, when he was our guest in New York City, when one day he came home very quiet and subdued. He did not speak for hours, and finally we said to him, "Swami! What did you do today?" And he said: "I have seen a thing today that only America can show. I was in the streetcar. Helen Gould sat on one side and a negro washerwoman, with her washing on her lap, on the other. No place but America can show that."

In June of that year Swami went up to Camp Percy, Christine Lake, N. H., to be the guest of Mr. Leggett at his fishing camp. We also went. There my sister's engagement to Mr. Leggett was announced, and Swami was invited to go abroad and be the witness at the wedding. While he was at the Camp, Swami would go out under those beautiful white birch trees and meditate for hours. Without telling us anything about it he made two beautiful birch bark books, written in Sanskrit and English, which he gave to my sister and me.

Then when my sister and I went to Paris to buy her trousseau, Swami went to Thousand Island Park and for six weeks gave those wonderful talks called *Inspired Talks*, which to me are the most beautiful words that were written, because they were given to a group of intimate disciples. *They* were disciples, whereas I was never anything but a friend. But that quality that he gave them! Nothing I think revealed his heart as those days did.

He came over to Paris with Mr. Leggett in August. There, my sister and I stayed at the Holland House, and the Swami and Mr. Leggett stayed at a different hotel; but we saw them every day. At that time Mr. Leggett had a courier who always called Swami *'Mon Prince!'* And Swami said to him, "But I am not a prince. I am a Hindu monk." The courier answered, "You may call yourself that, but I am used to dealing with princes, and I know one when I see one." His dignity impressed everyone. Yet, when someone once said to him, "You are so dignified, Swami", he replied, "It isn't me, it's my walk."

On the ninth of September Mr. and Mrs. Leggett were married, and the next day Swami left for London to be the guest of Mr. E. T. Sturdy, who had already met some of the Ramakrishna monks in India and who was a Sanskrit scholar. After Swami had been there some time he wrote, "Come over and get up classes." But by the time we went over he was already lecturing. He lectured very eloquently at Princes' Hall, and the next day the papers were full of the news that a great Indian yogi had come to London. He was very honoured there. Until the fifteenth of December we stayed in London. Then Swami again came to America to continue his work here. In April of the following year he went back to London when he established classes and began a real definite work. That was in 1896. He worked there all summer until July when he went to Switzerland with the Seviers.

Swamiji's knowledge was prodigious. Once when my niece, Alberta Sturges, later Lady Sandwich, was with him in Rome, showing him the sights, she was amazed at his knowledge of where the great monuments were. And when she went to St. Peter's with him, she was still more amazed to see him so reverential to the symbols of the Roman Church—to all the jewels, all the beautiful draperies, put upon the saints. She said, "Swami, you don't believe in a Personal God; why do you honour this so much?" He answered, "But Alberta, if you do believe in a Personal God, surely you give it your best."

That autumn he went from Switzerland to India with Mr. and Mrs. Sevier and Mr. J. J. Goodwin, where a great ovation awaited him by the entire nation. This can be read about in the discourses called *Lectures from Colombo to Almora.*

Mr. Goodwin was the stenographer who had been engaged at 54 West 33rd Street to take down the lectures of Swami Vivekananda. Mr. Goodwin was a court-stenographer, which meant two hundred words a minute, and he was very expensive; but as we did not want to lose any of Vivekananda's words, we engaged him. After the first week Mr. Goodwin refused any money; when they said to him, "What do you mean?" he said, "If Vivekananda gives his life, the least I can do is to give my service." He followed Swami around the world, and we have his words hot from his lips that Mr. Goodwin took down.

I never wrote to Swami after he went to India, waiting to hear from him. Finally I had a letter, "Why don't you write?" Then I sent back, "Shall I come to India?" And his answer was: "Yes, come, if you want filth and degradation and poverty and many loin cloths talking religion. Don't come if you want anything else. We cannot bear one more criticism." Naturally I went over by the first ship; I sailed on the twelfth of January with Mrs. Ole Bull and Swami Saradananda. We stopped in London. Then on to Rome. We arrived in Mumbai on the twelfth of February where Mr. Alasinga met us, who wore the vertical red marks of the Vaishnavite sect. Later on, once when I was sitting with Swami on our way to Kashmir, I happened to make the remark, "What a pity that Mr. Alasinga wears those Vaishnavite marks on his forehead!" Instantly Swami turned and said with great sternness: "Hands off! What have you ever done?" I did not know what I had done then. Of course I never answered. Tears came to my eyes and I waited. I learnt later that Mr. Alasinga Perumal was a young Brahmin teaching philosophy in a college in Chennai earning 100 rupees a month, supporting his father, mother, wife, and four children, and who had gone from door to door to beg the money to send Vivekananda to the West. Perhaps without him we never would have met Vivekananda. Then one understood the anger with which Swamiji met the slightest attack on Mr. Alasinga.

When we arrived in Mumbai they were very keen that we stay there; but we took the first train to Kolkata, and at four o'clock on the second morning following Swamiji met us with a dozen disciples. There were a score of other distinguished Indians with purple and gold and crimson turbans, to whom Mrs. Ole Bull had offered hospitality when they were in America. They covered us with garlands. We were literally enwrapped with flowers. It is always frightening to me to have garlands put on. Mrs. Ole Bull and I went to a hotel and Mr. Mohini Chatterjee came and stayed there from five o'clock in the afternoon until ten at night. I happened to remark, "I hope your wife will not be worried?" He answered, "I will explain to mother when I get home." I did not understand what that meant. After I knew Mr. Chatterjee well enough, perhaps a year later, I said to him, "What did you mean that first day when you said you would explain to mother?" He answered, "O, I never go to my room for the night without first going to my mother's room and confiding to her everything that happened during the day." "But your wife?" I said, "Don't you confide to her?" He answered, "My wife? She gets that relation from her son." Then I realized that fundamental difference between the Indian and our Western civilizations. The Indian civilization is based upon motherhood, and our civilization is based upon wifehood, which makes a tremendous difference.

In a day or two we went up to see Swami at his temporary monastery at Belur, at Nilambar Mukherjee's garden-house. During the afternoon Swami said, "I must take you to the new monastery that we are buying." I said, "O, but Swami, isn't this big enough?" It was a lovely little villa he had, with perhaps an acre or two of land, a small lake and many flowers. I thought it was big enough for anyone. But he evidently saw things in a different scale. So he took us across little gullies to the place where is now the present monastery. Mrs. Ole Bull and I, finding this old riverside house empty, said, "Swami, can't we use this house?" "It isn't in order," he answered. "But we'll put it in order," we told him. With that he gave us permission. So we had it all newly whitewashed and went down to the bazars, bought old mahogany furniture and made a drawing-room half of which was Indian style and half of which was Western style. We had an outside dining room, our bedroom with an extra room for Sister Nivedita who was our guest until we went to Kashmir. We stayed there quite two months. It was perhaps the most beautiful time we ever had with Swamiji. He came every morning for early tea which he used to take under the great mango tree. That tree is still in existence. We never allowed them to cut it down, though they were keen to do it. He loved our living at that riverside cottage; and he would bring all those who came to visit him, to see what a charming home we had made of this house he had thought uninhabitable. In the afternoons we used to give tea parties in front of the house, in full view of the river, where always could be seen loads of boats going up-stream, we receiving as if we were in our own drawing-rooms. Swamiji loved all that intimate use we made of things which they took as a matter of course. One night there came one of those deluges of rain, like sheets of water. He paced up and down our outside dining room veranda, talking of Krishna and the love of Krishna and the power that love was in the world. He had a curious quality that when he was a bhakta, a lover, he brushed aside karma and raja and jnana yogas as if they were of no consequence whatever. And when he was a karma yogi, then he made that the great theme. Or equally so, the jnana. Sometimes, for weeks, he would fall in one particular mood and become utterly disregardful of what he had been just previous to that. He seemed to be filled with an amazing power of concentration; of opening up to the great Cosmic qualities that are all about us. It was probably that power of concentration that kept him so young and so fresh, he never seemed to repeat himself. There would be an incident of very little consequence which would illuminate a whole new passage for him. And he had such a place for us Westerners whom he called "Living Vedantins". He would say: "When you believe a thing is true, you do it, you do not dream about it. That is your power."

It was one rainy night that Swami brought the Ceylonese Buddhist monk, Anagarika Dharmapala, to visit us. Mrs. Ole Bull, Sister Nivedita, and I were so happily housed in this cottage, it gave Swami particular joy to show his guests how simply Western women could settle there and make a real home.

On the twelfth of May in 1898 we started *en route* to Kashmir. We stopped at Naini Tal, the summer residence of the U. P. Government, and there hundreds of Indians met Swami with a beautiful hill pony on which they put him. Then they scattered before him flowers and palms, exactly as they did before Christ when he went into Jerusalem. And I said at once, "So, this is an oriental custom."

He left us alone for three days. We did not see him at all. We stayed at a hotel. Finally he sent for us. We went into one of the little houses, and there I saw him sitting on his bed wreathed in smiles, so happy was he to see us again. We had given him utter freedom. We never paid any attention to him. He never felt the weight of us. There was never any feeling of the necessity of entertainment.

From there we started for Almora where he became the guest of Mr. and Mrs. Sevier. We took a bungalow of our own, and there we stayed a month. Swamiji always meant Almora to be the Himalayan home of his Western disciples and expected the monastery to be founded there. But Mr. Sevier, who took his vocation of founding a monastery very seriously, was so interrupted by people coming in to tea parties daily that he insisted on going forty miles farther into the Himalayas; so Mayavati Ashrama, when started, was eighty miles from a station—and there were no proper roads.

While we were there, word came that Mr. Goodwin had died at Ootacamund. When Swamiji learnt that Mr. Goodwin had died, he looked a long time out upon the snow-capped Himalayas without speaking and presently he said, "My last public utterance is over." And he seldom spoke in public again.

We left Almora on the twentieth of June for Kashmir. By train to Rawalpindi, where we got tongas with three horses abreast to drive us the two hundred miles up into Kashmir. There were relays of horses every five miles, so that we dashed through on top of this beautiful road, as perfect then as any road the Romans ever made. Then to Baramulla where we got four native houseboats. These boats called dungas are about seventy feet long and broad enough to have two single beds in them and a corridor between, covered with a matting house; so wherever we wanted a window we only had to roll up the matting. The whole roof could be lifted in the day time, and thus we lived in the open, yet knew there was always a roof over our heads. We had four of these dungas, one for Mrs. Ole Bull and me, one for Mrs. Paterson and Sister Nivedita, and one for Swami and one of his monks. Then a dining room boat where we all met to have our meals. We stayed in Kashmir four months, the first three in these simple little boats until after September, when it got so cold, we took an ordinary house boat with fire-places and there enjoyed the warmth of a real house. Sister Nivedita has written a good deal of the talks we had there. Swami would get up about half past five in the morning, and seeing him smoking and talking with the boatmen, we would get up too. Then there would be those long walks for a couple of hours until the sun came up warm; Swami talking about India, what its purpose in life was, what Mohammedanism had done and what it had not done. He talked, immersed in the history of India and in the architecture and in the habits of the people, and we walked on through fields of forget-me-nots, bursting into pink and blue blossoms, way above our heads.

Baramulla is something like Venice. So many of the streets are canals. We had our own little private boat in which we went to and from the main land. But the merchants would come in small crafts all about our boats. We did most of our shopping over the rails of the boat. Each of our boats cost thirty rupees a month, which included the boatmen who fed themselves. The boatmen consisted of father, mother, son, daughter, and tiny children. They had their own little place at the end of the boat, and many a time we begged them for a taste of their food, the aroma being so delicious. The manner of travelling in these boats is that the boat is punted up the river, or it is dragged, the boatmen walking along the shore, or it is rowed. There is nothing extra to pay regardless of how one is navigated. When we wanted to move up the Jhelum river to some of the lakes, we would tell our servants the night before; they would get in supplies of food including ducks or chickens, vegetables, eggs, butter, fruits, and milk. In the morning, when we awakened, we would feel the boat moving along, gliding so imperceptibly that we were scarcely conscious of the motion. Our servant who had walked ahead would then have a delicious meal waiting for us. This he made over a little trough long enough and narrow enough to hold three pans, one containing soup, one meat, and the other rice. The dexterity of these people was a wonder and something we never got over. As a chicken is not considered clean food by the orthodox Hindus, we never told the people we intended to eat the chickens we bought. But when we went up the river, the lower part of the boat held half a dozen clucking chickens. The pundits who could come to visit Swami would hear them and look around for them. Swami, who knew they were hidden underneath, had a twinkle in his eye, but he would never give us away. Then the pundits would say: "But Swami, why do you have to do with these ladies. They are mlechchhas. They are untouchables." Then the Westerners would come to us and say: "But don't you see? Swami is not treating you with respect. He meets you without his turban." So we had great fun laughing at the idiosyncrasies of each other's civilization.

Swamiji then sent for Swami Saradananda to come and travel with us, to show us the sights of India—Lahore, Delhi,

Agra, Kurukshetra, and so on, Swami going straight down to Kolkata. By the time we got down there, he had already founded the monastery in our little cottage at Belur. As we would not go back there, we took a small house about two miles up at Bally and stayed there until we left for the West.

Mrs. Ole Bull had given several thousand dollars to found the monastery. I having very little, it took me some years to have eight hundred dollars. One day I said to Swamiji, "Here is a little money you may be able to use." He said, "What? What?" I said, "Yes." "How much?" he asked. And I said, "Eight hundred dollars." Instantly he turned to Swami Trigunatita and said, "There, go and buy your press." He bought the press which started the *Udbodhan*, the Bengali magazine published by the Ramakrishna Mission.

In July 1899 Swami came to England again with Sister Nivedita, where Sister Christine and Mrs. Funke met him. From there he came to America and he came to us at Ridgely Manor in September of that year where we gave him his own cottage with two of his monks, Turiyananda and Abhedananda. Sister Nivedita was also there, and Mrs. Ole Bull. It was quite a community of people who loved and honoured the Swami. He used to call my Sister, Mrs. Leggett, "Mother", and always sat beside her at table. He particularly liked chocolate ice cream, because, "I too am chocolate and I like it," he would say. One day we were having strawberries, and someone said to him, "Swami, do you like strawberries?" He answered, "I never tasted them." "You never tasted them! Why, you eat them every day!" He said, "You have cream on them—pebbles with cream would be good."

In the evening, sitting around the great fire in the hall of Ridgely Manor, he would talk, and once after he came out with some of his thoughts a lady said, "Swami, I don't agree with you there." "No? Then it is not for you," he answered. Someone else said, "O, but that is where I find you true." "Ah, then it was for you," he said, showing that utter respect for the other man's views. One evening he was so eloquent, about a dozen people listening, his voice becoming so soft and seemingly far away; when the evening was over, we all separated without even saying goodnight to each other. Such a holy quality pervaded. My sister, Mrs. Leggett, had occasion to go to one of the rooms afterward. There she found one of the guests, an agnostic, weeping. "What do you mean?" my sister asked, and the lady said: "The man has given me eternal life. I never wish to hear him again."

It was while the Swami was at Ridgely Manor that a letter came from a lady unknown to us to say our only brother was very ill in Los Angeles and that she thought, he would die and we ought to know it. So my sister said to me, "I think you must go." And I said, "Of course." Within two hours I was packed, the horses were at the door, we had four miles to drive to a railway station, and as I went out Swami put up his hand and said some Sanskrit blessing and then he called out, "Get up some classes and I will come." I went straight to Los Angeles and in a small white cottage covered with roses, on the outskirts of the city, lay my brother, very ill. But over his bed was a life-size picture of Vivekananda. I had not seen my brother for ten years, so after I had an hour's talk with him and saw how very ill he was, I went out to see our hostess, Mrs. Blodgett, and said to her, "My brother is very ill." She said, "Yes." I said, "I think he will die." She said, "Yes." "May he die here?" I asked. She said, "O yes." Then I said, "Who is that man whose portrait is over my brother's bed?" She drew herself up with all the dignity of her seventy years and said, "If ever there was a God on earth, that is the man." I said, "What do you know about him?" She answered: "I was at the Parliament of Religions at Chicago in 1893, and when that young man got up and said, 'Sisters and Brothers of America', seven thousand people rose to their feet as a tribute to something they knew not what. And when it was over and I saw scores of women walking over the benches to get near him, I said to myself, 'Well, my lad, if you can resist that onslaught, you are indeed a God.'" Then I said to Mrs. Blodgett, "I know him." "You know him?" she asked. I said, "Yes, I left him in the little village of Stone Ridge, of two hundred people, in the Catskill Mountains in New York." She said, "You know him?" I said, "Why don't you ask him here?" She said, "To my cottage?" "He will come", I told her. In three weeks my brother was dead and in six weeks Swamiji was there and began his classes on the Pacific coast, in "Kalifornia".

We were Mrs. Blodgett's guests for months. This little cottage had three bedrooms, a kitchen, a dining room, and a sitting room. Every morning we would hear Swami chanting his Sanskrit from the bath, which was just off the kitchen. He would come out with tousled hair and get ready for breakfast. Mrs. Blodgett made delicious pancakes, and these we would eat at the kitchen. table, Swami sitting with us; and such discourses he would have with Mrs. Blodgett, such repartee and wit, she talking of the villainy of men and he talking of even the greater wickedness of women! Mrs. Blodgett seldom went to hear him lecture, saying her duty was to give us delicious meals when we got back. Swami lectured a great number of times at the Home of Truth and in various halls, but perhaps the most outstanding lecture I ever heard was his talk on "Jesus of Nazareth", when he seemed to radiate a white light from head to foot, so lost was he in the wonder and the power of Christ. I was so impressed with this obvious halo that I did not speak to him on the way back for fear of interrupting, as I thought, the great thoughts that were still in his mind. Suddenly he said to me, "I know how it is done." I said, "How what is done?" "How they make mulligatawny soup. They put a bay leaf in it," he told me. That utter lack of self-consciousness, of self-importance, was perhaps one of his outstanding characteristics. He seemed to see the strength and the glory and the power of the other man who felt that courage enter into him, until everyone who came near him went away refreshed and invigorated and sustained. So when people have said to me, "What is your test of spirituality?" I have always said, "It is the courage that is given by the presence of a holy man." Swamiji used to say: "The saviours should take on the sins and tribulations of their disciples and let the disciples go on their way rejoicing and free. There is the difference! The saviours should carry the burdens."

Another thing he once said to my niece at Ridgely Manor is, "Alberta, no fact in life will ever equal your imagination of it."

One day Mrs. Blodgett had three ladies come to call on the Swami. I left immediately, so he could be alone with them; and after half an hour he came to me and said, "These ladies are three sisters and they want me to come and make them a visit at Pasadena." I said, "Go." He said, "Shall I?" "Yes go," I told him. They were Mrs. Hansborough, Miss Mead, and Mrs. Wyckoff. Mrs. Wyckoff's house is now the Vivekananda House in Hollywood, and one of Swamiji's monks is there with her.

It was from Alameda, California, that he wrote me on 18 April 1900, the most beautiful letter I think he ever wrote.

Later in 1900 my sister and Mr. Leggett took a house in Paris for the Exposition. We went over in June, and Swami followed in August. He stayed some weeks with us until he went to stay with Mr. Gerald Nobel, a bachelor. Afterwards he said of Mr. Nobel: "It is worth having been born to have made one friend as Mr. Nobel." So greatly he honoured this friend of ours. We entertained largely during these six months, Swami coming nearly every day to luncheon.

One day at luncheon in Paris Madame Emma Calve, the singer, said she was going to Egypt for the winter. So as I suggested accompanying her, and she at once turned to Swami and said, "Will you come to Egypt with us as my guest?" He accepted. We started out via Vienna for two days, Constantinople for nine days, and four days in Athens, then to Egypt when after a few days Swami said, "I want to go." "Go where?" I asked. "Go back to India." I said, "Yes, go." "May I?" he asked. "Certainly," I said. So I went to Madame Calve and said, "Swami would like to go back to India." She said, "Certainly." She bought him a first class ticket and sent him back. He arrived there in time to hear of the death of Mr. Sevier, and he wrote me at once of the serenity and beauty of the way in which Mrs. Sevier had taken the death, she continuing the life at the Mayavati Ashrama as if her husband were there.

Going up the Nile and meeting some charming English people who begged me to go to Japan with them, I had occasion to pass again through India *en route*. Again I saw Swamiji, and he said he would go to Japan if I wrote for him. In Japan I made the acquaintance of Okakura Kakuzu who had founded the fine arts Bijutsuin school of painting in Tokyo. He was very anxious to have Swami come over and be his guest in Japan. But Swami refusing to come, Mr. Okakura accompanied me to India to meet him. One of the happy moments of my life was when after a few days at Belur, Mr. Okakura said to me rather fiercely: "Vivekananda is ours. He is an Oriental. He is not yours." Then I knew there was a real understanding between them. A day or two after, Swami said to me, "It seems as if a long lost brother has come." Then I knew there was a real understanding between these two men. And when Swami said to him, "Will you join us?" Mr. Okakura said, "No, I haven't finished with this world yet." Which was a very wise thing.

That summer General Paterson, the American Consul General, allowed me to have the Consulate, and there I had as guest Mr. Oda, who had been my host at the Asakusa temple in Tokyo.

I saw Swami off and on all that year. One day in April he said: "I have nothing in the world. I haven't a penny to myself. I have given away everything that has ever been given to me." I said, "Swami, I will give you fifty dollars a month as long as you live." He thought a minute and then he said, "Can I live on that?" "Yes, O yes," I said, "but perhaps you cannot have cream." I gave him then two hundred dollars, but before the four months were passed he had gone.

At Belur Math one day, while Sister Nivedita was distributing prizes for some athletics, I was standing in

Swamiji's bedroom at the Math, at the window, watching, and he said to me, "I shall never see forty." I, knowing he was thirty-nine, said to him, "But Swami, Buddha did not do his great work until between forty and eighty." But he said, "I delivered my message and I must go." I asked, "Why go?" and he said, "The shadow of a big tree will not let the smaller trees grow up. I must go to make room."

Afterwards I went again to the Himalayas. I did not see Swami again. I went back to Europe for the King's Jubilee. As I said, I never was a disciple, only a friend, but I remember in my last letter to him in April 1902, as I was leaving India—I was never to see him again—I distinctly remember writing in this good-bye letter the one sentence, "I swim or sink with you." I read that over three times and said, "Do I mean it?" And I did. And it went. And he received it, though I never had an answer. He died July 4, 1902.

On the second of July, Sister Nivedita saw him for the last time. She went to inquire whether she should teach a certain science in her school. Swami answered: "Perhaps you are right, but my mind is given to other things. I am preparing for death." So she thought he was indifferent. Then he said, "But you must have a meal." Sister Nivedita always ate with her fingers, *a la* Hindu; and after she had eaten, Swami poured water over her hands. She said, very much the disciple, "I cannot bear you to do this." He answered, "Jesus Christ washed the feet of his disciples." Sister Nivedita had it on the tip of her tongue to say, "But that was the last time they ever met." It was the last time she ever saw him. That last day he spoke to her of me and of many people, but when he spoke of me he said, "She is pure as purity, loving as love itself." So I always took that as Swamiji's last message to me. In two days he died having said: "The spiritual impact that has come here to Belur will last fifteen hundred years—and this will be a great university. Do not think I imagine it, I see it."

They cabled me on the fourth of July, "Swami attained nirvana." For days I was stunned. I never answered it. And then the desolation that seemed to fill my life made me weep for years and it was only after I read Maeterlinck who said, "If you have been greatly influenced by anyone, prove it in your life, and not by your tears", I never wept again; but went back to America and tried to follow the traces of where he had lived. I went to Thousand Island Park and became the guest of Miss Dutcher to whom the cottage belonged, who gave me the same room that Swami had used.

Fourteen years elapsed before I returned to India. Then I went accompanying Professor and Mrs. Geddes. I then found, instead of India being a place of desolation, all India was alive with Swamiji's ideas, with half a dozen monasteries, thousands of centres, hundreds of societies. Since that time I have been going frequently. They like to have me at the monastery guest-house, because I keep Vivekananda alive, as none of these young men have ever seen him. And I like to be in India, remembering once when I asked him, "Swamiji, how can I best help you?" his answer was, "Love India!" So the upper floor of the guest-house at the monastery is mine where I go and will probably go winters, until the end.

(*Prabuddha Bharata,* December 1949)

Constance Towne

Out of the Old World of India forty years ago came a young, courageous, and handsome man in whose face shone the light of triumph over self. He came to the New World of America uninvited, unheralded, unknown. ...

How Vivekananda proceeded serenely on his hazardous pilgrimage—though more than once lacking food and change of raiment; how he was admitted as a delegate at the final session of the Congress of Religions; how he electrified the assemblage with the simplicity and beauty of his message; how on the following morning the metropolitan press of three continents exhausted their powers in proclaiming his spiritual stature among the great teachers of the world—all of this is still remembered by generations now living.

My personal story of Vivekananda—hitherto unpublished—seems to stand alone. When I met him he was twenty-seven years old.[1] I thought him as handsome as a god of classic sculpture. He was dark of skin, of course, and had large eyes which gave one the impression of "midnight blue". He seemed larger than most of his race, who often to us appear slight of frame, because they are small-boned. He had a head heaped with short black curls. At our first meeting I was struck by the emphasis of our colour contrast. I was twenty-four, fair, tall, and slender, with golden hair and grey-blue eyes. Probably there could have been no greater contrast.

---

1. He was then actually thirty-one years old.

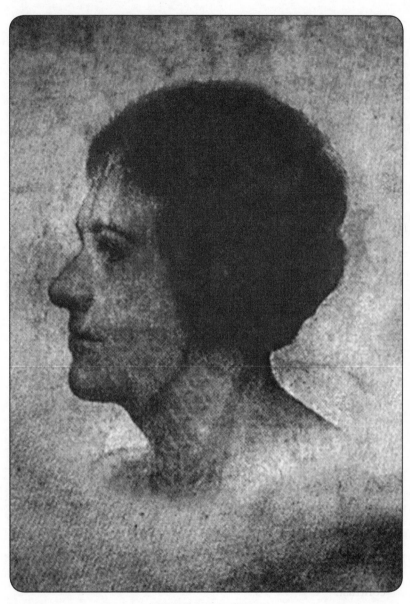

CONSTANCE TOWNE

Our meeting was rather unusual. After his triumph at Chicago he was, of course, showered with invitations to come to New York; where the great of all the world are entertained. Here lived at that time a very famous physician, Dr. Egbert Guernsey, genial, literary, and ideally hospitable, with a spacious and very handsome house on Fifth Avenue at Forty-fourth Street. It was Dr. Guernsey's pleasure, heartily endorsed by his charming wife and daughter, to introduce celebrated visitors from abroad to New York society. It was to be expected that he would pay special honour to the great Swami, whose ideal of closer relations between the East and the West in the interest of religion and world peace so strongly appealed to him.

Dr. Guernsey accordingly arranged to give a Sunday afternoon dinner party at which every guest should represent a different religious creed, he himself holding the viewpoint of Robert Ingersoll, who was absent from the city. His Grace the Cardinal was interested but declined to dine or to appoint a substitute from among his clergy. So it happened that I, being a Catholic and trained by the noted Jesuit Priest, William O'Brien Pardow, S.J., had the privilege of being a guest at that famous Sunday dinner. Dr. Guernsey, who was my physician, sent for me to uphold Catholicism. Dr. Parkhurst was there, and Minnie Maddern Fiske, the famous American actress, who was staying with the Guernseys at the time. I remember that there were fourteen at table.

There was, of course, a tacit understanding that everyone should be polite about his or her religious differences with the Swami and his so-called non-Christian ("Pagan" is a hard word!) attitude. Alas! As the dinner progressed, the most heated dispute was not with the Swami at all. All of the differences were confined to the Evangelical brethren!

I was seated beside the Swami. We looked on in amused silence at the almost comical intolerance of the Creeds. Now and again our host would adroitly make some wise or humorous remark that kept the conversation on a plane not actually injurious to the function of digestion. The Swami would make from time to time a little speech apparently in explanation of his native land and the customs of its people, so different from our own, but always to gain his point in philosophy and religion. A more broad-minded and tolerant man surely could not have been found anywhere in India to carry out the mission of founding Vedanta Centres in America.

He wore on that occasion his orange cassock, a tincture of deep rose-red silk, and his turban of white shot with threads of gold. His feet, otherwise bare, were covered by sandals of soft brown leather.

It was at this dinner that our friendship began. Afterwards, in the drawing-room, he said to me, "Miss Gibbons, your philosophy and mine are one; and the heart of our faiths is the same."

I then lived with my mother at the Beresford Apartments at 1 East Eighty-first Street, overlooking Central Park. My mother was Southern, of the royal French blood, from Charleston, South Carolina, and a famous beauty, dark of eyes and hair. She was a witty woman and delighted in the social pleasures centering about the Church of England, to which, she maintained, all the aristocratic world belonged. Thus the Swami and I were outside the fold. I told my mother of him on my return home from Dr. Guernsey's dinner party, and what a splendid mind he had. I dwelt on the great force which had come to us. To which she replied, "What a terrible dinner party, with all those Methodists, Baptists, and Presbyterians, and one black Pagan in orange cloths!" But she grew to like Vivekananda, to respect his viewpoint, and afterwards joined one of the Vedanta Centres. She was awfully amusing to him, and I can see him now, after all these years, laughing so gaily at her remarks about him.

On one occasion there was an all-star cast in "Faust" at the Metropolitan Opera, on a Monday night when all society appeared to sit in their boxes and show their anatomy covered with jewels; to gossip, to visit, to come in late and be observed of all observers, and to do everything but listen to the opera. There was Melba in her prime, and de Reszkes, and Bauermeister. The Swami had never been to the opera, and our subscription seats were in a conspicuous part of the orchestra. I had suggested that the Swami be invited to accompany us. Mama said to him, "But you are black. What will the world say?" To which he laughed and said, "I will sit beside my sister. She does not mind, I know." He never looked more handsome. Everyone about us was so wrapped up in him that I am sure they did not listen to the opera at all that night.

I tried to explain the story of "Faust" to Vivekananda. Mama, hearing me, said, "Heavens! you, a young girl, should not tell this awful story to a man."

"Then why do you make her come herself, if it is not good?" said the Swami.

"Well," replied Mama, "it is the thing to do to go to the opera. All the plots are bad; but one need not *discuss* the plot."

Alas for poor, vapid humanity and its foolishness! Later on during the performance the Swami said, "My sister, the gentleman who is making love to the beautiful lady in song, is he really in love with her?"

"Oh, yes, Swami."

"But he has wronged her, and makes her sad."

"Yes," I said humbly.

"Oh, now I see," said the Swami. "He is not in love with the handsome lady, he is in love with the handsome gentleman in red with the tail—what do you call him?—the Devil." Thus that pure mind reasoned out, weighed and found wanting both the opera and the audience.

One of society's pets, a very young girl, came down between the acts to Mama and said, "Mama is consumed with curiosity to know who the elegant man is in the yellow dressing gown."

Ours was a great friendship, and I fancy the only one that remains unpublished to the world. It was purely of the spirit, absolutely apart from the material loves and hates. He spoke always of when and what and where our souls would be ultimately, where in that other realm. He never spoke of me to anyone, nor mentioned my name. It was a friendship of spirit. It still is. He taught me much of the philosophy he preached and wrote about, how to meditate, and what a power it would be against the hurts of life; what force of purpose it would attain for the preservation of the body, for logical thought, for self-control, for ecstasy, for the attraction of others; its power for good, its knowing how to read others and their needs; not to dull the edge of your sword, to be moderate in one's consumption of food, to know what one's own body needs to make it live well; of chastity, tolerance, purity of thought, and love for the world—not of one person but of everyone and of all created things.

And now, forty years later, he has released me from the long silence and has demanded and commanded certain things he wishes done. ...

How liberal he was, how understanding of others' points of view! He went to Mass with me at St. Leo's Church, the little one on Twenty-eighth Street, where all was beauty, and the old priest, Father Ducey, such an artist. There he knelt at high noon at the canon of the Mass. A ray of light falling from the stained-glass window—blue, red, and gold—lit his white turban and outlined his beautiful profile against the marble walls. A great, gorgeous spot of living fire his orange robe made on the marble pavement, and the dear face was rapt in prayer. As the bell rang at the consecration and all heads were bowed in adoration of the presence of Christ on the altar, his hand touched mine, and he whispered, "It is the same God and Lord we both worship."

(Prabuddha Bharata, January 1934)

Mary C. Funke

Such a beautiful spot! There is a large classroom and a kitchen on the ground floor and a number of bedrooms on the second floor. The Swami has a private suite with a separate entrance by an outside stairway. There is a small veranda attached to his room to which he invites us every evening. The view is lovely, as we are higher up than any of the other cottages. We gaze over the treetops and for miles the beautiful St. Lawrence River winds its way.

We are deeply touched by the very cordial reception given to us who were strangers. Even the Swami had never met us personally, although we had attended all his lectures given in Detroit during the winter of 1894. The joy of it to be so sweetly received by him!

We were nearly frightened to death when we finally reached the cottage, for neither the Swami nor his followers at Thousand Island Park had the remotest idea of our existence and it seemed rather an impertinent thing for us to do, to travel seven hundred miles, follow him up, as it were, and ask him to accept us. But he did accept us—he did—the Blessed One!

It was a dark rainy night, but we could not wait. Every moment was precious, and our imagination was stirred up to the nth degree. We did not know a soul in the place, but finally we hit upon the plan of making inquiries at the various shops and thus find out where Miss Dutcher lived. At one place we were told that there was a cottage occupied by a Miss Dutcher and that a "foreign looking man who dressed queerly" was staying there.

Then we knew our quest was ended, and we found a man with a lantern who went ahead of us.

Up, up the wet and slippery path! It seemed as if we were taking one step up and two back, it was so slippery. The first thing we heard when we reached the house was the rich, beautiful voice of the Swami who was talking to those who had gathered on his porch. Our heartbeats could have been *heard*, I truly believe. His hostess asked him to come downstairs to see us as "two ladies from Detroit", and he greeted us so sweetly! It was like a benediction. "I like Detroit," he said. "I have many friends there, isn't it?" And what do you think? Instead of our staying at a hotel or boarding house, as we had expected, those dear people insisted upon our becoming members of the household. Our hearts sang paeans of praise.

So here we are—in the very house with *Vivekananda*, listening to him from 8 o'clock in the morning until late at night. Even in my wildest dreams I could not imagine anything so wonderful, so perfect. To be with Vivekananda! To be accepted by him! Surely we shall wake up and find it all a dream. For in our *dreams* we have sought the Swami, now, Reality! *Are* we "such stuff as dreams are made on?"

Oh, the sublime teaching of Vivekananda! No nonsense, no talk of "astrals", "imps", etc., but God, Jesus, Buddha. I feel that I shall never be quite the same again for I have caught a glimpse of the Real.

Just think what it means to listen to a Vivekananda at every meal, lessons each morning and the nights on the porch, the eternal stars shining like "patinas of bright gold"! In the afternoon, we take long walks and the Swami literally, and so simply, finds "books in the running brooks, sermons in stones, and good (God) in every thing". And this same Swami is so merry and fun-loving. We just go *mad* at times.

Later: We have been soaring on the Heights, since I last wrote to you. Swami tells us to forget that there is any Detroit for the present—that is, to allow no personal thoughts to occupy our minds while taking this instruction.

We are taught to see God in *everything* from the blade of grass to man—"even in the diabolical man".

Really, it is almost impossible to find time to write here. We put up with some inconveniences, as it is so crowded. There is no time to relax, to rest, for we feel the time is all too short, as the Swami leaves soon for England. We scarcely take time to array ourselves properly, so afraid are we of losing some of the precious jewels. His words *are* like jewels, and all that he says fits together like a wonderfully beautiful mosaic. In his talks he may go ever so far afield, but always he comes back to the one fundamental, vital thing—"Find God! Nothing else matters."

I especially like Miss Waldo and Miss Ellis, although the whole household is interesting. Some unique characters: One, a Dr. Wight of Cambridge, a very cultured man, creates much merriment at times. He becomes so absorbed in the teaching that he, invariably, at the end of each discourse ends up with asking Swamiji: "Well, Swami, it all amounts to this in the end, doesn't it? I *am* Brahman, I *am* the Absolute." If you could only see Swami's indulgent smile and hear him answer so gently, "Yes Dokie, you are Brahman, you are the Absolute, in the real essence of your being." Later, when the learned doctor comes to the table a trifle late, Swami, with the utmost gravity but with a merry twinkle in his eyes, will say, "Here comes Brahman" or "Here is the Absolute".

Swamiji's fun-making is of the merry type. Sometimes he will say, "Now I am going to cook for you!" He is a wonderful cook and delights in serving the "brithrin". The food he prepares is delicious but for "yours truly" too hot with various spices; but I made up my mind to eat it even if it strangled me, which it nearly did. If a *Vivekananda* can cook for me, I guess the least I can do is to eat it. Bless him!

At such times we have whirlwind of fun. Swamiji will stand on the floor with a white napkin draped over his arm, *à la* the waiters on the dining cars, and will in tone in perfect imitation then call for dinner—"Last call fo' the dining cah. Dinner served".—Irresistibly funny! And then, at table, such gales of laughter over some quip or jest, for he unfailingly discovers the little idiosyncrasies of each one—but never sarcasm or malice—just fun.

Since my last letter to you when I told you of Swamiji's capacity for merriment, so many little things have occurred to make one see how varied are the aspects of Vivekananda. We are trying to take notes of all that he says but I find myself lost in listening and forget the notes. His *voice* is wondrously beautiful. One might well lose oneself in its divine music. However, dear Miss Waldo is taking very full notes of the lessons and in that way they will be preserved.

Some good fairy must have presided at our birth—C's and mine. We do not, as yet, know much of *karma* and reincarnation but we are beginning to see that both are involved in our being brought into touch with Swamiji.

Sometimes I ask him rather daring questions, for I am so anxious to know just how he would react under certain conditions. He takes it so kindly when I in my impulsive way sometimes "rush in where angels fear to tread". Once he said to someone: "Mrs. Funke rests me, she is so naive." Wasn't that dear of him?

One evening, when it was raining and we were all sitting in the living room, the Swami was talking about pure womanhood and told us the story of Sita. How he can tell a story! You *see* it, and all the characters become real. I found myself wondering just how some of the beautiful society queens of the West would appear to him—especially those versed in the art of allurement—and before I took time to think, out popped the question, and immediately I was covered with confusion. The Swami, however, looked at me calmly with his big, serious eyes and gravely replied, "If the most beautiful woman in the world were to look at me in an immodest or unwomanly way she would immediately turn into a hideous, green frog, and one does not, of course, admire frogs!"

Apropos of my name, something so funny happened. One day, we all walked down to the village and passed a glass-blower's tent. Swami was much interested in this and held a whispered conversation with the glass-blower. Then he asked us to take a walk through the main street of the village and upon our return the glass-blower handed him sundry mysterious packages which proved to contain a gift for each of us, a large crystal ball, each one different with our names blown in the glass "With the love of Vivekananda". Upon reaching the house, we opened our packages. My name was spelled "Phunkey". We were convulsed with laughter but not where *he* could hear us. He never having seen my name written, "Phunkey" was the result.

And he was so sweet, so gentle and benign all that evening, just like an indulgent father who had given his children beautiful gifts, although many of us were much older than he.

The Swami has accepted C. as one fitted for his work in India. She is so happy. I was very disappointed, because he would not encourage me to go to India. I had a vague idea that to live in a cave and wear a yellow robe would be the proper thing to do if one wished to develop spiritually. How foolish of me and how wise Swamiji was! He said, "You are a householder. Go back to Detroit; find God in your husband and family. *That* is your path at present."

Later: This morning we went to the village and Swami had tin-types taken of himself at our request. He was so full of fun, so merry. I am trying to write you in class as there is literally no other time. I am sitting near the Swami, and he is saying these very words. "The guru is like a crystal. He reflects perfectly the consciousness of all who come to him. He thus understands how and in what way to help." He means by this that a guru must be able to see what each person needs and he must meet them on their own plane of consciousness.

Now he has closed the class for the morning, and he has turned to me: "Mrs. Funke, tell me a funny story. We are going to part soon, and we must talk funny things, isn't it?"...

We take long walks every afternoon, and our favourite walk is back of the cottage down a hill and then a rustic path to the river. One day there was olfactory evidence of a polecat in the vicinity, and ever since Swami will say, "Shall we walk down Skunk Avenue?"

Sometimes we stop several times and sit around on the grass and listen to Swami's wonderful talks. A bird, a flower, a butterfly, will start him off, and he will tell us stories from the Vedas or recite Indian poetry. I recall that one poem started with the line, "Her eyes are like the black bee on the lotus."

He considered most of our poetry to be obvious, banal, without the delicacy of that of his own country.

Wednesday, August 7th: Alas, he has departed! Swamiji left this evening at 9 o'clock on the steamer for Clayton where he will take the train for New York and from there sail for England.

The last day has been a very wonderful and precious one. This morning there was no class. He asked C. and me to take a walk, as he wished to be alone with us. (The others had been with him all summer, and he felt we should have a last talk.) We went up a hill about half a mile away. All was woods and solitude. Finally he selected a low-branched tree, and we sat under the low-spreading branches. Instead of the expected talk, he suddenly said, "Now we will meditate. We shall be like Buddha under the Bo tree." He seemed to turn to bronze, so still was he. Then a thunderstorm came up, and it poured. He never noticed it. I raised my umbrella and protected him as much as possible. Completely absorbed in his meditation, he was oblivious of everything. Soon we heard shouts in the distance. The others had come out after us with raincoats and umbrellas. Swamiji looked around regretfully, for we *had* to go, and said, "Once more am I in Kolkata in the rains."

He was so tender and sweet all this last day. As the steamer rounded the bend in the river, he boyishly and joyously waved his hat to us in farewell, and he had departed indeed!

As I finish these brief reminiscences, the calendar tells me that it is February 14, 1925—just thirty-one years almost to the very hour I first saw and heard Swamiji at the Unitarian Church.

Ah, those blessed, halcyon days at Thousand Island Park! The nights all glowing with the soft mystery of moonlight or golden starlight. And yet the Swami's arrival amongst us held no mystery, apparently. He came in simple guise.

We found later that anything which smacked of the mystery-monger was abhorrent to him. He came to make manifest the glory and radiance of the Self. Man's limitations' are of his own making. "Thine only is the hand that holds the rope that drags thee on"—this was the motif running through the Swami's teaching.

With infinite pains he tried to show us the path he himself had trod. After thirty-one years Swamiji stands out in my consciousness a colossal figure—a cleaver of bondage, knowing when and where not to spare. With his two-edged flaming sword came this Man "out of the East"—this Man of Fire and Flame, and some there were who received him, and to those who received him he gave Power.

Such was Vivekananda!

(*Prabuddha Bharata*, February 1927)

February 14th, 1894, stands out in my memory as a day apart, a sacred, holy day; for it was then that I first saw the form and listened to the voice of that great soul, that spiritual giant, the Swami Vivekananda, who, two years later, to my great joy and never-ceasing wonder, accepted me as a disciple.

He had been lecturing in the large cities of the country, and on the above date gave the first of a series of lectures in Detroit, in the Unitarian Church. The large edifice was literally packed and the Swami received an ovation. I can see him yet as he stepped upon the platform, a regal, majestic figure, vital, forceful, dominant, and at the first sound of the wonderful voice, a voice all music—now like the plaintive minor strain of an Eolian harp, again deep, vibrant, resonant—there was a hush, a stillness that could almost be felt, and the vast audience breathed as one man.

The Swami gave five public lectures and he held his audiences; for his was the grasp of the "master hand" and he spoke as one with authority. His arguments were logical, convincing, and in his most brilliant oratorical flights never once did he lose sight of the main issue—the truth he wished to drive home.

He fearlessly attacked principles, but in personal matters one felt that here was a man, whose great heart could take in all of humanity, seeing beyond their faults and foibles; one who would suffer and forgive to the uttermost. In fact, when it was given to me to know him more intimately, I found that he *did* forgive to the uttermost. With what infinite love and patience would he lead those who came to him, out of the labyrinth of their own frailties, and point out to them the way out of self to God. He knew no malice. Did one abuse him, he would look thoughtful and repeat, "Shiva, Shiva;" then his face would become illumined and he would say gently, "It is only the voice of the Beloved," or if we who loved him would become indignant, he would ask, "What difference can it make when one knows that blamer, blamed, and praiser, praised, are one?" Again, under like circumstances he would tell us some story of how Sri Ramakrishna would never recognize personal abuse or malice. Everything good or bad, "the dual throng", was from the "Beloved Mother."

It was given to me to know him in an intimate way for a period of several years, and never once did I find a flaw in his character. He was incapable of petty weakness, and had Vivekananda possessed faults they would have been generous ones. With all his greatness he was as simple as a child, equally at home among the rich and the great, or among the poor and the lowly.

While in Detroit, he was the guest of Mrs. John J. Bagley, the widow of the ex-Governor of Michigan and a lady of rare culture and unusual spirituality. She told me that never once during the time he was a guest in her house (about four weeks) did he fail to express the highest in word and action, and that his presence was a "continual benediction". After leaving Mrs. Bagley, Vivekananda spent two weeks as the guest of Hon. Thomas W. Palmer. Mr. Palmer was President of the World's Fair Commission; he had been formerly U.S. Minister to Spain and also U.S. Senator. This gentleman is still living and is over eighty years of age.

For myself, I can say that never in all the years I knew Vivekananda, did he fail to manifest the highest in life and purpose.

Blessed and beloved Swamiji, I never thought it possible for man to be so white, so chaste, as he was! It set him apart from other men. He was brought in contact with our most brilliant and beautiful women. Mere beauty did not attract him, but he would often say, "I like to cross swords with your bright intellectual women; it is a new experience for me, for in my country the women are more or less secluded."

His manner was that of boyish frankness and *naivete* and very winsome. I remember one evening after he had delivered a profoundly impressive lesson, scaling the very heights of realization, he was found standing at the foot of the stairs with a puzzled, almost disconsolate expression on his face. People were going up and down stairs putting on their wraps, etc. Suddenly his face lighted up and he said: "I have it! Going up the stairs, the gentleman precedes the lady, coming down, the lady precedes the gentleman; isn't it?" True to his Eastern training, he felt that a breach of etiquette was a breach of hospitality.

In speaking to me one day regarding those who wished to have a part in his life-work, he said, "They must be pure in heart". There was one disciple of whom he hoped much. He evidently saw in her great possibilities for renunciation and self-sacrifice. He found me alone one day and asked me many questions regarding her life and environment, and after I had answered them all, he looked at me so wistfully and said, "And she is pure, pure in soul, is it not?" I simply answered, "Yes Swami, she is absolutely pure in heart." His face lighted up and his eyes shone with divine fire. "I knew it, I felt it; I must have her for my work in Kolkata," he said with enthusiasm.

He then told me of his plans and hopes for the advancement of the women of India. "Education is what they need," he would say; "we must have a school in Kolkata." A school for girls has since been established there by the Sister Nivedita, and the above-mentioned disciple shares the work with her, living in a Kolkata lane and wearing the sari, doing the Mother's work as best she may. She shared all these experiences with me, for we together sought out the Master and asked him to teach us. He was the "man of the hour" in Detroit that winter. Society smiled upon him and he was much sought after. The daily papers recorded his comings and his goings; even his food was discussed, one paper gravely stating that his breakfast consisted of bread and butter thickly sprinkled with pepper! Letters and invitations came pouring in, and Detroit was at the feet of Vivekananda.

He always loved Detroit, and was grateful for all the kindness and courtesy shown to him. We had no chance to meet him in a personal way at the time, but we listened and pondered in our hearts over all that we heard him say, resolving to find him sometime, somewhere, even if we had to go across the world to do it. We lost trace of him completely for nearly two years and thought that probably he had returned to India, but one afternoon we were told by a friend that he was still in this country and that he was spending the summer at Thousand Island Park. We started the next morning, resolved to seek him out and ask him to teach us.

At last after a weary search, we found him. We were feeling very much frightened at our temerity in thus intruding upon his privacy, but he had lighted a fire in our souls that could not be quenched. We must know more of this

wonderful man and his teaching. It was a dark and rainy
night and we were weary after our long journey, but we
could not rest until we had seen him face to face. Would
he accept us? And if he did not, what then could we do? It
suddenly seemed to us that it might be a foolish thing to go
several hundred miles to find a man who did not even know
of our existence, but we plodded on up the hill in the rain
and darkness, with a man we had hired to show us the way
with his lantern. Speaking of this in after years, our guru
would refer to us as "my disciples, who travelled hundreds
of miles to find me and they came in the night and in the
rain". We had thought of what to say to him, but when we
realized that we had really found him, we instantly forgot
all our fine speeches, and one of us blurted out, "We came
from Detroit and Mrs. P. sent us to you." The other said, "We
have come to you just as we would go to Jesus if he were
still on the earth and ask him to teach us." He looked at us so
kindly and said gently, "If only I possessed the power of the
Christ to set you free now!" He stood for a moment looking
thoughtful, and then, turning to his hostess who was standing near, said, "These ladies are from Detroit; please show
them upstairs and allow them to spend the evening with
us." We remained until late, listening to the Master, who paid
no more attention to us; but as we bade them all good night
we were told to come the next morning at nine o'clock. We
arrived promptly, and to our great joy were accepted by the
Master and were cordially invited to become members of the
household.

Of our stay there, another disciple has written fully, and I
will only say that it was a most blessed summer. I have never
seen our Master quite as he was then. He was at his best
among those who loved him.

There were twelve of us and it seemed as if Pentecostal
fire descended and touched, the Master. One afternoon,
when he had been telling us of the glory of renunciation, of
the joy and freedom of those of the ochre robe, he suddenly
left us, and in a short time he had written his 'Song of the

Sannyasin', a very passion of sacrifice and renunciation. I think the thing which impressed me most in those days was his infinite patience and gentleness—as of a father with his children, though most of us were several years older than he. After a morning in the classroom, where it almost seemed as if he had gazed into the very face of the Infinite, he would leave the room, returning soon to say, "Now I am going to cook for you." And with what patience would he stand over the stove and prepare some Indian tit-bit for us! The last time he was with us in Detroit, he prepared for us the most delicious curries. What a lesson to his disciples—the brilliant, the great and learned Vivekananda ministering to their little wants! He was at those times so gentle, so benign! What a legacy of sacred tender memories has he left us!

One day Vivekananda related to us the story that had most impressed itself upon his life. It was told him over and over again in his babyhood by his nurse and he never wearied of hearing it repeated. I will give it as nearly as possible in his own words:

The widow of a Brahmin was left very, very poor, with one child, a little boy who was almost a baby. Because he was the son of a Brahmin, the boy had to be educated, but how to do it? In the village, where the poor widow lived, there was no teacher. So the boy had to go to the neighbouring village to be taught and because his mother was very, very poor he had to walk there. There was a small forest between the two villages, and through this the boy had to pass. In India, as in all hot countries, teaching is given very early in the morning and again towards evening. Through the heat of the day no work is done; so it was always dark when the little boy went to school and, also when he came home. In my country, instruction in religion is free to those who cannot pay; so the little boy could go to this teacher without charge, but he had to walk through the forest and he was alone and he was terribly afraid. He went to his mother and said: "I have always to go alone through that terrible forest and I am afraid. Other boys have servants to go with them and take care of them. Why cannot I have a servant to go with me?" But his mother replied: "Alas, my child! I am too poor, I cannot send a servant with you." "What can I do then?" asked the little boy. "I will tell you," said his mother, "do this. In the forest is your shepherd-brother Krishna,[1] call on him and he will come and take care of you and you will not be alone." So the next day the little boy went into the forest and called, "Brother-shepherd, brother-shepherd, are you there?" and he heard a voice say, "Yes, I am here", and the little boy was comforted and was no more afraid. By and by he used to meet, coming out of the forest, a boy of his own age, who played with him and walked with him, and the little boy was happy. After a while, the father of the teacher died, and there was a great ceremonial festival (as is common in India on such occasions), when all the scholars made presents to their teacher, and the poor little boy went to his mother and asked her to buy him a present to give like the rest. But his mother told him that she was too poor. Then he wept and said, "What shall I do?" And his mother said, "Go to brother-shepherd and ask him." So he went into the forest and called, "Brother-shepherd, brother-shepherd, can you give me a present to give to my teacher?" And there appeared before him a little pitcher of milk. The boy took the pitcher gratefully and went to the house of his teacher and stood in a corner waiting for the servants to take his gift to the teacher. But the other presents were so much grander and finer that the servants paid no attention to him. So he spoke and said, "Teacher, here is the present I have brought you." Still no one took any notice. Then the little boy spoke again from his corner and said, "Teacher, here is the present I have brought you," and the teacher looking over and seeing the pitiful little gift, scorned it, but said to the servant, "Since he makes so much fuss about it, take the pitcher and pour the milk into one of the glasses and let him go." So the servant took the pitcher and poured the milk into a cup, but just as soon as he poured out the milk, the pitcher filled right

---

1. Krishna is known in India as the 'shepherd god'.

up again and it could not be emptied. Then everybody was surprised and asked, "What is this? Where did you get this pitcher?" And the little boy said, "Brother-shepherd gave it to me in the forest." "What!" they all exclaimed, "you have seen Krishna and he gave you this?" "Yes," said the little boy, "and he plays with me every day and walks with me when I come to school." "What!" they all exclaimed: "You walk with Krishna! You play with Krishna!" And the teacher said, "Can you take us and show us this?" And the little boy said, "Yes, I can; come with me." Then the little boy and the teacher went into the forest, and the little boy began to call as usual, "Brother-shepherd, brother-shepherd, here is my teacher come to see you. Where are you?" But no answer came. The little boy called again and again, and no answer came. Then he wept and said, "Brother-shepherd, do come, or else they will call me a liar." Then from afar off a voice was heard saying, "I came to you because you are pure and your time has come, but your teacher has many many rounds to go through before he can see me."

After the summer at Thousand Island Park, Vivekananda sailed for England, and I did not see him until the following spring (1896), when he came to Detroit for two weeks. He was accompanied by his stenographer, the faithful Goodwin. They occupied a suite of rooms at *The Richelieu*, a small family hotel, and had the use of the large drawing room for class work and lectures. The room was not large enough to accommodate the crowds, and to our great regret many were turned away. The room, as also the hall, staircase, and library, was literally packed. At that time he was all bhakti—the love for God was a hunger and thirst. A kind of divine madness seemed to take possession of him, as if his heart would burst with longing for the Beloved Mother.

His last public appearance in Detroit was at the Temple Beth El, of which the Rabbi Louis Grossman, an ardent admirer of the Swami, was the pastor. It was Sunday evening and so great was the crowd that we almost feared a panic. There was a solid line reaching far out into the street and hundreds were turned away. Vivekananda held the large audience spellbound, his subject being, "India's Message to the West," and "The Ideal of a Universal Religion". He gave us a most brilliant and masterly discourse. Never had I seen the Master look as he looked that night. There was something in his beauty not of earth. It was as if the spirit had almost burst the bonds of flesh, and it was then that I first saw a foreshadowing of the end. He was much exhausted from years of over-work, and it was even then to be seen that he was not long for this world. I tried to close my eyes to it, but in my heart I knew the truth. He had needed rest but felt that he must go on.

The next time I saw him was in July 1899. He had been extremely ill, and it was thought that a long sea voyage would benefit him. So he sailed for England from Kolkata on the steamship *Golconda*. Much to his surprise, two of his American disciples were at the Tilbury Docks in London when the ship arrived. We had seen in an Indian magazine a notice that he would sail on a certain date, and we hastened over to the other side to meet him as we were very much alarmed at the reports we had heard regarding his health.

He had grown very slim, and looked and acted like a boy. He was so happy to find the voyage had brought back some of the old strength and vigour. Sister Nivedita and Swami Turiyananda accompanied him to England, and quarters were found for the two Swamis in a roomy old-fashioned house at Wimbledon not far from London. It was very quiet and restful, and we all spent a happy month there.

The Swami did no public work in England at that time, and soon sailed for America accompanied by Swami Turiyananda and his American friends. There were ten-never-to-be-forgotten days spent on the ocean. Reading and exposition of the *Gita* occupied every morning, also reciting and translating poems and stories from the Sanskrit and chanting old Vedic hymns. The sea was smooth and at night the moonlight was entrancing. Those were wonderful evenings. The Master paced up and down the deck, a majestic figure in the moonlight, stopping now and then to speak to us of the beauties of Nature. "And if all this Maya is so beautiful, think of the wondrous beauty of the Reality behind it!" he would exclaim.

One especially fine evening, when the moon was at the full and softly mellow and golden, a night of mystery and enchantment, he stood silently for a long time drinking in the beauty of the scene. Suddenly he turned to us and said, "Why recite poetry when there," pointing to sea and sky, "is the very essence of poetry?"

We reached New York all too soon, feeling that we never could be grateful enough for those blessed, intimate ten days with our guru. The next time I saw him was on July 4th, 1900, when he came to Detroit for a short visit among his friends.

He had grown so thin, almost ethereal; not long would that great spirit be imprisoned in clay. Once more we closed our eyes to the sad truth, hoping against hope.

I never saw him again but "that other disciple" was privileged to be with him in India for a few weeks before he left us forever. Of that time, I cannot bear to think. The sorrow and the heartbreak of it all still abide with me; but deep down underneath all the pain and grief is a great calm, a sweet and blessed consciousness that great souls do come to earth to point out to men "the way, the truth, and the life"; and when I realized that it was given to me to come under the influence of such a one, finding each day a new beauty, a deeper significance in his teaching, I can almost believe, as I meditate upon all this, that I hear a voice saying: "Take thy shoes from off thy feet; for the place whereon thou standest is holy ground."

(*Inspired Talks*, pp. 18-34)

Madame E. Calve

It has been my good fortune and my joy to know a man who truly "walked with God", a noble being, a saint, a philosopher, and a true friend. His influence upon my spiritual life was profound. He opened up new horizons before me; enlarging and vivifying my religious ideas and ideals; teaching me a broader understanding of truth. My soul will bear him eternal gratitude.

This extraordinary man was a Hindu monk of the order of the Vedantas. He was called the Swami Vivekananda, and was widely known in America for his religious teachings. He was lecturing in Chicago one year when I was there; and as I was at that time greatly depressed in mind and body, I decided to go to him, having seen how he had helped some of my friends.

An appointment was arranged for me; and when I arrived at his house, I was immediately ushered into his study. Before going I had been told not to speak until he addressed me. When I entered the room, therefore, I stood before him in silence for a moment. He was seated in a noble attitude of meditation, his robe of saffron yellow falling in straight lines to the floor, his head swathed in a turban bent forward, his eyes on the ground. After a brief pause he spoke without looking up.

"My child," he said, "what a troubled atmosphere you have about you! Be calm! It is essential!"

Then in quiet voice, untroubled and aloof, this man, who did not even know my name, talked to me of my secret problems and anxieties. He spoke of things that I thought were

MADAME E. CALVE

unknown even to my nearest friends. It seemed miraculous, supernatural!

"How do you know all this?" I asked at last. "Who has talked of me to you?"

He looked at me with his quiet smile as though I were a child who had asked a foolish question.

"No one has talked to me," he answered gently. "Do you think that is necessary? I read in you as in an open book."

Finally it was time for me to leave.

"You must forget," he said as I rose. "Become joyous and happy again. Build up your health. Do not dwell in silence upon your sorrows. Transmute your emotions into some form of external expression. Your spiritual health requires it. Your art demands it."

I left him, deeply impressed by his words and his personality. He seemed to have emptied my brain of all its feverish complexities and placed there instead his clear and calming thoughts.

I became once again vivacious and cheerful, thanks to the effect of his powerful will. He did not use any of the or- dinary hypnotic or mesmeric influences. It was the strength of his character, the purity and intensity of his purpose, that carried conviction. It seemed to me, when I came to know him better, that he lulled one's chaotic thoughts into a state of peaceful acquiescence, so that one could give complete and undivided attention to his words.

He often spoke in parables, answering our questions or making his points clear by means of a poetic analogy. One day we were discussing immortality and the survival of individual characteristics. He was expounding his belief in reincarnation, which was a fundamental part of his teaching.

"I cannot bear the idea!" I exclaimed. "I cling to my individuality, unimportant as it may be! I don't want to be absorbed into an eternal unity. The mere thought is terrible to me."

"One day a drop of water fell into the vast ocean," the Swami answered. "When it found itself there, it began to weep and complain just as you are doing. The great ocean laughed at the drop of water. "Why do you weep?" it asked. "I do not understand. When you join me, you join all your brothers and sisters, the other drops of water of which I am made. You become the ocean itself. If you wish to leave me, you have only to rise up on a sunbeam into the clouds. From there you can descend again, a little drop of water, a blessing and a benediction to the thirsty earth."

With the Swami and some of his friends and followers I went upon a most remarkable trip, through Turkey, Egypt, and Greece. Our party included the Swami; Father Hyacinthe Loyson; his wife, a Bostonian; Miss MacLeod of Chicago, an ardent Swamist and charming, enthusiastic woman; and myself, the song bird of the troupe.

What a pilgrimage it was! Science, philosophy, and history had no secrets from the Swami. I listened with all my ears to the wise and learned discourse that went on around me. I did not attempt to join in their arguments, but I sang on all occasions, as is my custom. The Swami would discuss all sorts of questions with Father Loyson, who was a scholar and a theologian of repute. It was interesting to see that the Swami was able to give the exact text of a document, the date of a Church Council, when Father Loyson himself was not certain.

When we were in Greece, we visited Eleusis. He explained its mysteries to us and led us from altar to altar, from temple to temple, describing the processions that were held in each place, intoning the ancient prayers, showing us the priestly rites.

Later, in Egypt, one unforgettable night, he led us again into the past, speaking to us in mystic, moving words, under the shadow of the silent sphinx.

The Swami was always absorbingly interesting, even under ordinary conditions. He fascinated his hearers with his magic tongue. Again and again we would miss our train, sitting calmly in a station waiting-room, enthralled by his discourse and quite oblivious of the lapse of time. Even Miss

MacLeod, the most sensible among us, would forget the hour, and we would in consequence find ourselves stranded far from our destination at the most inconvenient times and places.

One day we lost our way in Cairo. I suppose, we had been talking too intently. At any rate, we found ourselves in a squalid, ill-smelling street, where half-clad women lolled from windows and sprawled on doorsteps.

The Swami noticed nothing until a particularly noisy group of women on a bench in the shadow of a dilapidated building began laughing and calling to him. One of the ladies of our party tried to hurry us along, but the Swami detached himself gently from our group and approached the women on the bench.

"Poor children!" he said. "Poor creatures! They have put their divinity in their beauty. Look at them now!"

He began to weep. The women were silenced and abashed. One of them leaned forward and kissed the hem of the robe, murmuring brokenly in Spanish, "Humbre de Dios, humbre de Dios!" (Man of God!). Another, with a sudden gesture of modesty and fear, threw her arm in front of her face as though she would screen her shrinking soul from those pure eyes.

This marvellous journey proved to be almost the last occasion on which I was to see the Swami. Shortly afterward he announced that he was to return to his own country. He felt that his end was approaching, and he wished to go back to the community of which he was director and where he had spent his youth.

A year later we heard that he had died, after writing the book of his life, not one page of which was destroyed. He passed away in the state called samadhi, which means, in Sanskrit, to die voluntarily, from a will to die, without accident or sickness, saying to his disciples, "I will die on such a day."

Years later, when I was travelling in India, I wished to visit the convent where the Swami had spent his last days.

His mother took me there. I saw the beautiful marble tomb
that one of his American friends, Mrs. Leggett, had erected
over his grave. I noticed that there was no name upon it. I
asked his brother … the reason of this omission. He looked at
me in astonishment, and with a noble gesture that I remember to this day, "He has passed on," he answered.

The Vedantas believe that they have preserved, in their
original purity and simplicity, the teachings of Hinduism.
They have no temples, saying their prayers in a simple oratory, with no symbolic figures or pictures to stimulate their
piety. Their prayers are all addressed to the Unknown God.

"O, Thou who hast no name! O, Thou whom none dare
name! O, Thou the Great Unknown!" they say in their sup-
plications.

The Swami taught me a sort of respiratory prayer. He
used to say that the forces of the deity, being spread everywhere throughout the ether, could be received into the body
through the indrawn breath.

The monks of the Swami's brotherhood received us with
simple, kindly hospitality. They offered us flowers and fruits,
spreading a table for us on the lawn beneath a welcome
shade.

At our feet the mighty Ganga flowed. Musicians played
to us on strange instruments, weird, plaintive chants that
touched the very heart. A poet improvised a melancholy
recitative in praise of the departed Swami. The afternoon
passed in a peaceful, contemplative calm.

The hours that I spent with these gentle philosophers
have remained in my memory as a time apart. These beings,
pure, beautiful, and remote, seemed to belong to another
universe, a better and wiser world.

(*Prabuddha Bharata*, November 1922)

Maud Stumm

I T was in the fall of 1895 that I first saw him, sitting with his back to the light in Mrs. Leggett's sitting room in Paris.[1]

I did not catch his name, but presently found myself next to him, and being asked if I spoke French. He said he didn't either; when I asked him if in his opinion English would be the next dominant language of the world—as they seemed to be the coming race—"The next great leading force on the earth will be the Tartars or the Negroes"—was his astonishing reply; and he proceeded to give his reasons. I found that he dealt not with decades or even centuries but with vast ages and movements of races, as judged by his knowledge of the past.

Then I inquired who this deep-voiced man was, and was told he was a holy man from the East, Swami Vivekananda. It was long after this that the flower of the Italian army was destroyed utterly by the Negroes of Abyssinia, and I recalled the prophecy that sounded so unlikely!

Besides this wonderful guest were three others, one of them the young Boston woman who had taken the prize for the "Hymn of the Republic" sung at the World's Fair. She was little and sat very erect, with an alert expression. Swami was rolling out Sanskrit and translating the ancient glories of India, nobody *daring* to speak. He dwelt finally upon the spiritual superiority of the Hindu, even today. Thereupon the Boston lady interrupted: "But, Swami, you must admit that the common people of India are way below the cultivation

1. She saw him at a dinner given by Mrs. Francis Leggett at the Metropolitan Club, New York, in 1896.

of the same class in, say Massachusetts; why look at one item— the newspapers!" Swami, recalled from his poetic flight, raised his great eyes and regarded her silently. "Yes, Boston *is* a very civilized place," he said. "I landed there once, a stranger in a strange land. My coat was like this red one and I wore a turban. I was proceeding up a street in the busy part of the town when I became aware that I was followed by a great number of men and boys. I hastened my pace and they did too. Then something struck my shoulder and I began to run, dashing around a corner, and up a dark passage, just before the mob in full pursuit, swept past—and I was safe! Yes," he concluded, "Massachusetts is a *very* civilized place!" Even this did not silence the little woman, and with astonishing temerity she raised her voice again to say, "But, Swami, no doubt a Bostonian in Kolkata would have created just such a scene!" "That would be impossible," he replied, "for with us it is unpardonable to show even polite curiosity to the stranger within our gates, and *never* open hostility."

The next time I remember seeing Swami Vivekananda was when Mrs. Colston and I met him and ... Turiyananda, when they landed in New York in 1899. Tired and ill-looking, I saw them early on an August morning descend the gang-plank of the small steamer. I had telegraphed Sydney Clarke to help us by being at the pier to look after their baggage. He came, greeted them, claimed the curious foreign-looking boxes, had them checked, and was off to his work. The boat arrived ahead of time, and we happened to be the only three in town at that hour, the party from Ridgely arriving at 10 o'clock, and so disappointed! ... As Swami landed with Turi-yananda from the steamer, he was carrying most carefully a big bottle wrapped in papers that were torn and ragged; this precious bottle, which he refused to relinquish before reach-ing *Binne-water*, contained a wonderful kind of sauce like curry; brought thus by hand from India. "For Jo!" (Josephine MacLeod) he said. ...

Then we all went back together, and the days that fol-lowed! The air of freedom seemed to do him good—and such talks, such wonderful sermons! With his flame-coloured robes draped about him, what a figure he was as he strode the lawns of Ridgely! His stride came nearer to the poet's description of a "step that spurned the earth" than anything I ever expect to see again; and there was a compelling majesty in his presence and carriage that could not be imitated or described.

One day he told me that he wanted to undertake some sort of work that would keep his hands busy and prevent him from thinking of things that fretted him at that time—and would I give him drawing lessons? So materials were produced, and at an appointed hour he came, promptly, bringing to me, with a curious little air of submission, a huge red apple, which he laid in my hands, bowing gravely. I asked him the significance of this gift, and he said, "in token that the lessons may be fruitful"—and such a pupil as he proved to be! Once only did I have to tell him anything; his memory and concentration were marvellous, and his drawings strangely perfect and intelligent for a beginner. By the time he had taken his fourth lesson, he felt quite equal to a portrait; so Turiyanannda posed, like any bronze image, and was drawn capitally—all in the study of Mr. Leggett, with its divan for our seat, and its fine light to aid us. Many great ones may come to that room in its future years, and probably will, but never again that childlike man, toiling over his crayons, with as single a mind and heart as if that were his vocation. How often he thanked me for the pleasure it gave him, and for the joy of learning, even that!

Then one very warm day, in the morning-room, we asked him to show us how he wound his turban and he did, adding several other methods employed by different castes and tribes. When he arranged it as the desert people do, to keep the neck from the great heat, I asked him to pose, and he did, talking all the time. That was the day he talked to us of purity and truth.

There are many memories connected with those days at Ridgely. Nearly every day Swami was wonderful in a new way! Now it would be music that he dwelt upon, now art, and once he burst into the morning-room, declaring for "Liberty". "What do I care if Mohammed *was* a good man, or Buddha! Does that alter *my* own goodness or evil? Let us be good for our own sake on our own responsibility! Not because somebody way back there was good!" Another time he tried to teach me an ancient Indian love song:

> And the flower says, nodding, nodding,
> Come gather me, and make of me a garland
> For the neck of thy beloved!

I could learn the words, but the air was quite beyond me, so full of little half-tones, and curious runs and turns.

Soon after this, a very large and elaborate dinner was given at Ridgely—the flowers and lights on the table were wonderful and the ladies all in their loveliest gowns and jewels. At a moment when the talk and gaiety had reached its height, and I was observing it all without at that instant taking part, thinking of the good fortune that made such a thing possible and wondering if they all were as merry as they seemed, Swami was seated just obliquely opposite to me and all at once I heard his deep even tones, as if right at my ear, and through all the noise of other talk, "Don't let it fool you, Baby." And I saw he had been observing me, over the flowers and lights. ("Baby" was his nickname for me; why I do not know.)

"You never can hide your heart behind those eyes," he told me once, "for they speak before your lips." And then he added, "Don't try to. Keep the shell of pretence that everybody goes encased in off yourself; don't let it form. You will suffer, but you will feel more and do better work. Nearly all the world goes in a thick casing of convention and hpocrisy—like the two men in the fable, greeting each other with cheek pressed to cheek, each looking over the other's shoulder, meanwhile winking at the rest of the world."

One of the greatest things about Swami was his human side. Like a big lovable boy, he thoroughly enjoyed the things he liked: ice cream, for example. How many times I have seen him rise from the table after salad, excusing himself to smoke or walk, when a very quick word from Lady Betty (Mrs. Francis H. Leggett) that she believed there was to be ice-cream would turn him back instantly, and he would sink into his place with a smile of expectancy and pure delight seldom seen on the face of anybody over sixteen. He just loved it, and he had all he wanted too.

While I was there that autumn, I had a worriment that bothered me a good deal, and though I said nothing of it to anyone, it was constantly in my thoughts. Late one afternoon Swami asked me to take a little walk to see a threshing machine at work in a barnyard visible from the west windows of Ridgely. I had been staying in the village for a week, coming every day to the Manor House, and sharing in all its dear delights. All at once, as we went down the bill, he said, "Where were you last night? We missed you at the Ridgely party." I was perfectly amazed but managed to say I had not heard of it. "Wonderful affair," he continued, "stringed instruments and such a supper! Pheasants!" he added. "Ever taste pheasant?" "No," I faltered, "tell me who was there." "Oh everybody," he said, "and they danced and danced, not at the Casino but in the house, everything moved out. Wonderful party!" Why I had not been asked and what it all meant, how they could have managed not to speak of it to me before or after! Well, I gave it up, and did not learn until the next day that it was fable, told to change my line of thought and lift me out of the worry for a little while. And nothing could have been more convincing than his manner.

I can see him now, lying at full length on the green couch in the hall, sound asleep like a tired child. Once I tried to draw his features thus, in absolute repose; the lines of the mouth were so simple and lovely and yet so very difficult!

Once he asked me at the end of the drawing lessons, what he could do for me. And having heard that he was wonderful at reading the future, I begged him to do it for me. So he said he would when he felt "prophetic". A few days after he said, "Come!" and led the way to the library. We sat on the green divan, and asking me to open my hand flat, he laid his hand lightly upon it and turned his head away. He was absolutely silent and as nearly everyone had gone off to walk or read, I hoped for an uninterrupted reading. He took a deep breath or two and began to speak, "I see ..." when the door burst open and Alberta in her riding habit descended upon us and broke the spell. He never took it up again and I left shortly after.

Another time there were several lady guests, two of them were accompanied by daughters. We were in the hall, after dinner, and he was draped in his flame-coloured silks. Oh, how splendid a figure, enthralling to the heart and imagination. As he sat by the fire, his eyes slowly turned from one to the other, heavy, dark, liquid eyes, like the "thick clustering bees" in the Eastern simile. All at once he began to speak on marriage, and from the first word the depth of his great meaning was apparent. He spoke as I have never heard a man speak to women. Of the space that makes attraction felt" in that great bond; and while it seemed to cause some alarm at first to the two mothers, the dignity and nobility of his presentation soon enthralled them too. We shall none of us hear its like again. His views were those of a perfectly normal and natural being with a spiritual nature equal to the other. The words that he said were like a song, impossible to repeat, but of so clear a meaning that they were the very stuff or life itself. When he had finished he arose and amid perfect stillness took his departure; the ideal of a holy man.

(*Vedanta and the West*, November-December 1953)

Sister Nivedita

1. *Kolkata, February 15, 1899*: My lecture on Kali came off on Monday. The Albert Hall was crammed. ... Swami was greatly pleased about the lecture, and I trust that there is some reason, for I have several times since been inclined to think that I had done nothing but harm. ...

Anyway, the Kalighat people have asked me to speak on Kali worship there, at Kalighat. It may not come to anything, but Swami thinks that would be the greatest blow that could be struck against exclusiveness. ...

Yesterday morning two of us went early to be blessed by the old Devendranath Tagore. Swami sent word early that he was particularly pleased, and I told the old man this, and said I felt that I was making Swami's pranams as well as my own. He was quite touched, said he had met Swami once when wandering round in a boat, and would greatly like him to come to him once more. When I told Swami, he was wonderfully moved, and said, "Of course I'll go, and you can go with me, and fix a day as soon as you please!" It seems that as a boy he clambered up into Mr. T's boat and put anxious questions about Advaitism, and the old man paused and said gently at last, "The Lord has only shown me dualism." And then he had patted him and said he had the yogi's eyes.

2. *Kolkata, February 21, 1899*: My Kali lecture had been a good foundation for bringing Swami to an issue with some friends, whom we were visiting. And so the talk had been all of symbolism. He said: "Poor M. has never studied the history of symbolism. That is why he does not understand

465

SISTER NIVEDITA

that the natural symbols are no good. You see I had a curious education; I went to Sri Ramakrishna and I loved the man, but I hated all his ideas. And so for six years it was hard fighting all the time. I would say, 'I don't care in the least for this thing you want me to do', and he would say, 'Never mind, just do it, and you will see that certain results follow.' And all that time he gave me such love; no one has ever given me such love, and there was so much reverence with it. He used to think, 'This boy will be so-and-so', I suppose, and he would never let me do any menial service for him. He kept that up to the very moment of his death too. He wouldn't let me fan him, and many other things he would not let me do."

3. *Kolkata, March 12, 1899*: Last night a monk called, and when I said I wanted to interview Swami for *Awakened India*, offered to take me back at 6 in the house-boat, if I would drive home. S. came too, in order to bring me home, so we walked. We got there at 8 o'clock. Swami had been sitting beside the fire under the tree. ... When I had interviewed him, he said: "I say, Margot, I have been thinking for days about that line of least resistance, and it is a base fallacy. It is a comparative thing. As for me, I am never going to think of it again. The history of the world is the history of a few earnest men, and when one man is earnest the world must just come to his feet. I am not going to water down my ideals, I am going to dictate terms."

4. *Kolkata, April 9, 1899*: Swami says my great fault is attempting too much, in which he is emphatically right. I am to give up all thought of plague-nursing and throw my whole heart and soul still deeper into the sanitation that we have now on hand.

We have had two hundred and thirty-five rupees subscribed for sanitation. It seems a great success, though of course we could do with a great deal more. When the monk who has the work in hand went over on Saturday to report, he said Swami was so touched by the news, that they had two hours of everything, from the Upanishads onwards, "There could be no religion without that activity, that manhood and co-operation. There was Nivedita living in a corner and English people helping her. God bless them all!" But to my great amusement when I reported today, he just winked and said, "Plague, Margot, plague." He told me, "Our men might be rough and unpolished, but they were the manly men in Bengal. The manhood of Europe was kept up by the women, who hated unmanliness. When would Bengali girls play this part, and drench with merciless ridicule every display of feebleness on the part of man?"

5. *Kolkata, May 1, 1899*: ... At the Math Swami is lying ill with fever and bronchitis.

On Friday I went to lunch with Swami. ... His mood on Saturday was entirely different, however. His days were drawing to an end; but even if they were not, he was going to give up compromise. He would go to the Himalayas, and live there in meditation. He would go out into the world and preach *smashing* truths. It had been good for a while to go amongst men and tell them that they were in their right place, and so on. But he could do that no longer. Let them give up, give up, give up. Then he said very quietly, "You won't understand this now, Margot; but when you get further on you will."

I find there is money enough in Bengal for Swami, but people want to make their conditions, and so it never reaches him. This is his true attitude of staunchly refusing plum cake, and accepting starvation as the price of principle. Swami is right about the world being reached that way and no other. The world is something that overcomes the man who seeks it and crouches to him who renounces it. ...

6. *Kolkata, May 8, 1899*: I have seen Swami today. He told me how, as a child of thirteen, he came across a copy of Thomas à Kempis which contained in the preface an account of the author's monastery and its organization. And *that* was the abiding fascination of the book to him. Never thinking that he would have to work out something of the sort one day. "I love Thomas à Kempis, you know, and know it

almost off by heart. If only they had told what Jesus ate and drank, where he lived and slept, and how he passed the day, instead of all rushing to put down what he said! Those long lectures! Why, all that can be said in religion can be counted on a few fingers. That does not matter, it is the man that results that grows out of it. You take a lump of mist in your hand, and gradually, gradually, it develops into a man. Salvation is nothing in itself, it is only a *motive*. All those things are nothing, except as motives. It is the man they form, that is everything!" And now I remember he began this by saying: "It was not the words of Sri Ramakrishna but the life he lived that was wanted, and that is yet to be written. After all, this world is a series of pictures, and man-making is the great interest running through. We were all watching the making of men, and that alone. Sri Ramakrishna was always weeding out and rejecting the old, he always chose the young for the disciples."

7. *Coasting Ceylon, June 28, 1899*: It was quite exciting at Chennai. Crowds of people had an appeal to the Governor to let Swami land. But plague considerations prevailed, and we were kept on board, to my great relief, for the sea-voyage is doing him a world of good, and one day of crowds and lectures would be enough to cause him utter exhaustion. It was sufficiently tiring to have to look down and be polite to the constant succession of boat-loads who came to the ship's side with presents and addresses all day....

Swami had just been here for an hour, and somehow the talk drifted to the question of Love. Amongst other things he talked about the devotion of the English wife and the Bengali wife, of the suffering they would go through without a word. Then of the little gleam of sunshine and poetry, to which all human love must wade through oceans of tears. Then the tears of sorrow alone bring spiritual vision, never tears of joy. That dependence is fraught with misery, independence alone is happiness. That almost all human love, save sometimes a mother's, is full of dependence. It is for oneself, not for the happiness of the one loved, that it is sought. That the love on which he could most surely count, if he became a drunkard tomorrow, was not that of his disciples, they would kick him out in horror, but that of a few (not all) of his brother-disciples. To them he would be still the same. "And mind this, Margot," he said, "It is when half a dozen people learn to love like this that a new religion begins. Not till then. I always remember the woman who went to the sepulchre early in the morning, and as she stood there she heard a voice and she thought it was the gardener, and then Jesus touched her, and she turned round, and all she said was 'My Lord and my God!' That was all, 'My Lord and my God.' The person had gone. Love begins by being brutal, the faith, the body. Then it becomes intellectual, and last of all it reaches the spiritual. Only at the last, 'My Lord and My God.' Give me half a dozen disciples like that and I will conquer the world."

8. *America, October 9, 12 & 13, 1899*: Swami has been pacing up and down for an hour and a half, warning me against politeness, against this "Lovely" and "Beautiful", against this continual feeling of the external. "Come to the Himalayas," he would say every now and then. "Realize yourself without feeling; and when you have known that, you can fall upon the world like a bolt from the blue. I have no faith in those who ask, 'Will any listen to my preaching?' Never yet could the world refuse to hear the preaching of him who had anything to say. Stand up in your own might. Can you do that? Then come away to the Himalayas and learn." Then he broke into Shankaracharya's sixteen verses on Renunciation, ending always with a humming refrain "Therefore, you fool, go and worship the Lord". To get rid of all these petty relations of society and home, to hold the soul firm against the perpetual appeals of senses, to realize that the rapture of autumn trees is as truly sense-enjoyment as a comfortable bed or a table dainty, to hate the silly praise and blame of people—these things were the ideal that he was holding up. "Practise forbearance," he said again and again, that is, bearing the ills of the body without trying to remedy,

and without remembering them. The monk whose fingers were rotting away with leprosy and who stooped gently to replace the maggot that fell from the remaining joint, was the example he used. And he talked about loving misery and embracing death. Later he was pointing out how the only civilizations that were really stable were those that had been touched with vairagya.

Surely it cannot be that anyone of us fails to see that even the round of duties is merely a formula. It seems so clear that one is held by a chain that one has never yet been strong enough to break. Yesterday Swami talked of Shiva. "Let your life in the world be nothing but a thinking to yourself." Even meditation would be a bondage to the free soul, but Shiva goes on and on for the good of the world, the Eternal Incarnation, and Hindus believe that but for the prayers and meditations of these great souls, the world would fall to pieces (that is, others would find no chance of manifesting and so coming to freedom) at once. For meditation is the greatest service, the most direct, that can be rendered.

He was talking too of the Himalayan snows and the green of the forests melting into them. "Nature making eternal sacrifice on the body of Mahadeva," he quoted from Kalidasa.

9. *America, October 18, 1899*: At lunch on Friday, Swami talked about Sri Ramakrishna. He abused himself for being filled and poisoned with the Western reaction of those days, so that he was always looking and questioning whether this man was "Holy" or not. After six years he came to understand that he was not "Holy", because he had become *identified with holiness*. He was full of gaiety and merriment and he had expected the Holy to be so different! Later he began to talk of the functions of the nations, apropos, I suppose, of the Boer War. And as he passed to the problems of the Shudra, which would first be worked out here, his face took on a new light, as if he were actually seeing into the future; and he told of the mixture of races, and of the great tumults, the terrible tumults through which the next state of things

must be reached. "And these are the signs," he quoted from old books! "The Kali Yuga is about to thicken, when money comes to be worshipped as God, when might is right, and men oppress the weak."

At one of the meals, Mrs. B. turned and pointed out how his poetry had been the weak point on which he had been beguiled to the loss of honour. And she said her husband was never sensitive to criticism about his music. That he expected. He knew it was not perfect. But on road engineering he felt deeply, and could be flattered. Then, in our amusement, we all teased Swami for his carelessness about his religious teacherhood and his vanity about his portrait painting; and he suddenly said: "You see there is one thing called Love, and there is another thing called Union; and Union is greater than Love. I do not love religion, I have become identified with it. It is my life; so no man loves that thing in which his life has been spent, in which he really has accomplished something. That which we love is not yet oneself. Your husband did not love music for which he had always studied; he loved engineering, in which as yet he knew comparatively little. This is the difference between bhakti and jnana; and this is why jnana is greater than bhakti." All morning his talk of the great sweep of the Mogul hordes under Genghis Khan had been going on. It had begun in his talking about Law, the old Hindu conception of it as the King of kings who never slept and showing that the Hindu had in the Vedas the true notion of it, while other nations only knew it as regulations. On Sunday evening three of us accompanied a guest to her home. We had been reading Schopenhauer on "Women" aloud. Coming back it was wonderful moonlight, and we walked on up the avenue in silence; it seemed as if a sound would have been desecration. About it Swami said, "When a tiger in India is on the trail of prey at night, if its paw or tail makes the least sound in passing, it bites it till the blood comes." And he talked of the need we Western women had to absorb beauty quietly, and turn it over in the mind at another time.

One afternoon so quiet was everything, we might have
been in India. I had been feeling quite inferior to the people
who wanted Advaitism and the Vedic texts, but oh, what a
dose of the other was here.

It began with a song of Ramprasad, and I'll try to give
you the whole of that early talk.

From the land where there is no night
Has come unto me a man.
And night and day are now nothing to me,
Ritual-worship is become for ever barren.

My sleep is broken. Shall I sleep any more?
Call it what you will, I am awake.
Hush! I have given back sleep to Him whose it was. Sleep
have I put to sleep for ever.

The music has entered the instrument,
And of that mode I have learnt a song.
And that music is always playing before me,
And concentration is the great teacher thereof.

Prasad speaks, understand O Mind,
   these words of science,
The secret of Her whom I call my Mother. Shall I break
the pot before the market?[1]
Lo, the six philosophers[2] could not find out Kali.

The world hast thou charmed, Mother,
Charmer of Shiva.
Thou who playest on the vina,
Sitting on the huge lotus of muladhara.

This body is the great vina
And sushumna, ida and pingala

1. To make a public secret.
2. Six systems of Hindu philosophy.

are the strings thereof.
And thou playest on the three gamuts,
With the great secret of qualitative
differentiation.

Ramakrishna used to see a long white thread proceeding out of himself. At the end would be a mass of light. This mass would open, and within it he would see the Mother with a vina. Then She would begin to play; and as She played, he would see the music turning into birds and animals and worlds and arrange themselves. Then She would stop playing and they would all disappear. The light would grow less and less distinct till it was just a luminous mass, the string would grow shorter and shorter, and the whole would be absorbed into himself again. And as Swami told this, he said: "Oh, what weird scenes things bring before me, the weirdest scenes of my whole life! Perfect silence, broken only by the cries of the jackals, in the darkness under the great tree at Dakshineshwar. Night after night we sat there, the whole night through, and He talked to me, when I was a boy. The guru was always Shiva and was always to be worshipped as Shiva, because he sat under the tree to teach, and destroyed ignorance. One must offer all one's doings, or even merit would become a bondage and create karma; so Hindus getting you a cup of water will say, 'To the World' or may be 'To the Mother'. But there is one soul that can take it all without harm——One who is eternally protected, eternally the same, unspoilt—He who drank the poison of the world and only made Himself the blue-throated. Offer all you do to Shiva."

Then he talked of vairagya, how much grander to give one's youth, how miserable to have only age to offer. Those who come to it old attain their own salvation; but they cannot be gurus, they cannot show mercy. Those who come young shall carry many across without any benefit to themselves.

Then he talked of the school, "Give them all you like, Margot, never mind A B C. It matters nothing. Give as much Ramprasad and Ramakrishna and Shiva and Kali as you like. And do not cheat these Western people, do not pretend it is education and A B C you want money for. Say it is the old Indian spirituality that you want and demand help, do not beg it. Remember you are only the servant of Mother, and if She sends you nothing, be thankful that She lets you go free."

10. *America, October27, 1899*: Yesterday three of us were together when Swami came in, and said, "Let's have a chat." He talked about the *Ramayana*. I'll tell you a curious thing. When Sadananda talks about the *Ramayana*, I become convinced that Hanumana is really the hero; when Swami talks of it, Ravana is the central figure. So he told us: Rama was called "The Blue-lotus-eyed", and he trusted to Mother to help him to recover Sita.[3] But Ravana had prayed to Mother too, and Rama came and found him in her arms so he knew he must do something tremendous, and he vowed one hundred and eight blue lotuses to her image if she would help him. Hanuman went off and got the lotuses, and Rama began the great "Call upon the Mother". (It was autumn, and the time of Her worship was the spring, so it is in memory of that worship by Rama that the Great Mother Worship has ever since been held in September). Now he covered Her feet with blue lotuses till one hundred and seven were offered (and Mother had stolen one); and lo, the last was missing. But Rama was determined. He was not to be beaten, and calling for a knife, he was about to cut out his own eye that the number of blue lotuses might be complete. And that won the Mother; and She blessed the great hero, so that his arms prevailed. Though not indeed his arms altogether, for in the end Ravana was betrayed by his own brother, and the struggle was brought to an end. "But it was great about the traitor brother in one sense," said Swami. "For he was taken

---

3. The story is depicted in the *Ramayana* of Krittivasa—a Bengali recension.

away to reside at the court of Rama, and thither came the widow of Ravana to look upon the face of the warrior who had robbed her of her husband and son. Rama and his court stood prepared to receive the *cortège;* but to his amazement, he could see no great queen adorned in splendour, only a simple-looking woman attired in the simple garb of a Hindu widow. 'Who is this lady?' he asked the brother in bewilderment, and he replied, 'Behold, O King, the lioness whom thou hast robbed of her lion and whelps! She comes to gaze upon thy face.'"

What ideals of womanhood Swami holds! Surely not even Shakespeare or Aeschylus when he wrote Antigone, or Sophocles when he created Alcestis had such a tremendous conception. As I read over the things he has said to me of them, and as I realize that it is all, every word of it, a trust for the women of the whole world's future, but first and chiefly for them of his own land, it seems a trifling thing whether oneself should ever be worthy or not.

One night he was in a great mood of devotion, and told us of Rishikesh and the little hut that each sannyasi would make for himself and the blazing fire in the evening, and all the sannyasis sitting round it on their own little mats; talking in hushed tones of the Upanishads, "For a man is supposed to have got the truth before he becomes a sannyasi. He is at peace intellectually. All that remains is to realize it; so all need for discussion has passed away and at Rishikesh, in the darkest of the mountains, by the blazing fire, they may only talk of the Upanishads. Then by degrees, the voices die—silence! Each man sits bolt upright on his mat, and one by one they steal quietly off to their own huts." Another time he broke out with: "The great defect in Hinduism has been that it offered salvation only on the basis of renunciation. The householder was bound by his consciousness of an inferior lot. His part was karma. Renunciation was nothing to him. But renunciation is the whole law. It is an illusion that anyone has been trying to do anything else. We are all struggling to release this great

mass of energy. What does that mean but that we are hurrying towards death as fast as we can? The burly Englishman
who thinks he wants to possess the earth is really struggling
more than most of us to die. Self-preservation is only a
mode of renunciation. The desire for life is one method of
the love of death." Swami talked some time of the Sikhs,
and their ten Gurus, and he told us a story of Guru Nanak,
from the *Granth Sahib*: He had gone to Mecca, and lay with
his feet towards the Caaba Mosque. Then came angry
Mohammedans to waken, and if need be, to kill him, for
turning his feet towards the place where God was. He woke
up quietly, and said simply, "Show me, then, where God
is not, that I may turn my feet that way." And the gentle
answer was enough.

11. *America, November 4, 1899*: On Thursday evening,
Swami came in when two of us were talking earnestly; so he
joined in, of course. For the first time he talked of defection
and disease and treachery. Amongst other things, he said he
found himself still the sannyasi, he minded no loss, but he
could be hurt through defection. Treachery cut deep.

When Swami was talking of Krishna and Rukmini, he
said something of the double strain in us of preference and
approval. Of how often we give way to desire, and of how
our only guide should be the good. Therefore, the wise man
is he who likes nothing, and witnesses all. Men find it easy to
play their part of life, but something holds the heart captive,
and there they do not play. Let the whole be play; like
nothing; act a part all the time. Again he talked of Uma and
Shiva. As he says, "It beats all mythology hollow." Speaking
of Shiva he said, "Young is the guru, old is the disciple,"
because in India the man who gives his young life is the true
guru, but the time for learning religion is old age. And then
he commanded us to offer all we did to Shiva, the only protected soul in the universe. Uma, speaking to the Brahmin,
said, "Why should He, the Lord of the Universe, dwell in a
graveyard?"

At lunch time I laughed and said that your letter spoke of your wanting "nothing and nobody". Swami looked up and said: "No, she doesn't, that's right. It's the last stage one comes to. The beggar must look for alms and rebuffs; but for him who asks nothing, there are no rebuffs." He said he had been reciting the hatred of fame and wealth all his life, but he was only now beginning to understand what it really meant.

12. *Chicago, December 10, 1900:* "Somebody asked me, "How is it that Swami is so great, and yet today he says, 'Spirituality is the only thing for my country; I was wrong to desire material good,' and tomorrow he will be insisting the material benefits must be India's and so on?" "And his action remains constant both times," I said; then I went on, showing part of the great helpfulness of these contradictions to myself, how he dramatized for one absolute renunciation of the fruits of action. ... How true it is indeed that there is no peace without freedom!

13. *Chicago, January 26, 1900:* Did I tell you at the last centre how my most blessed helper was the thorniest of all thorns at the beginning of the week? And here it is just the same; two or three of the strongest workers are the most unspeakably unexpected. I find, too, that the marks of a great Renunciation are very different from those of a small, and I laugh daily at our mutual friend's blindness about Swami's. Why, that way he has of finding himself in any company, of hólding or withholding light indifferently, of caring nothing about people's opinions of him, are simply gigantic. I only realized, when, after all the love and warmth I had in one town, I reached another and found myself fuming and chafing against the artificiality of people about me, what Swami's greatness really was, in this respect. And it was these very people, from whom I would have escaped at once if I could, who proved Mother's appointed instruments— thus setting the seal on Swami's ways. That irresponsibility of his is so glorious too. Nothing is more enticing than to put oneself into the attitude of generalissimo of the forces, and

make splendid plans, compelling fortune; but Swami just waits, and drifts in on the wave. And so on. I am just beginning to understand his bigness.

14. *New York, June 4, 1900:* Swami has just lectured.

I went early and took the seat at the left end of the second row—always my place in London, though I never thought of it at the time.

Then as we sat and waited for him to come in, a great trembling came over me, for I realized that this was, simple as it seemed, one of the test-moments of my life. Since last I had done this thing, how much had come and gone! My own life—where was it? Lost—thrown away like a cast-off garment that I might kneel at the feet of this man. Would it prove a mistake; an illusion; or was it a triumph of choice; a few minutes would tell.

And then he came; his very entrance and his silence as he stood and waited to begin were like some great hymn. A whole worship in themselves.

At last he spoke—his face broke into fun, and he asked what was to be his subject. Someone suggested the Vedanta philosophy and he began.

Oneness—the Unity of all. ..."And so the final essence of things is this Unity. What we see as many—as good, love, sorrow, the world—is really God. ... We see many, yet there is but One Existence. ... These names differ only in the degrees of their expression. The matter of today is the spirit of the future. The worm of today—the God of tomorrow. These distinctions which we so love are all parts of one Infinite fact and that one Infinite fact is the attainment of Freedom. ...

"All our struggle is for Freedom—we seek neither misery nor happiness but Freedom. ... Man's burning unquenchable thirst—never satisfied—asking always for more and more. You Americans are seeking always for more and more. At bottom this desire is the sign of man's infinitude. For infinite man can only be satisfied when his desire is infinite and its fulfilment infinite also. ..."

And so the splendid sentences rolled on and on, and we, lifted into the Eternities, thought of our common selves as of babies stretching out their hands for the moon or the sun— thinking them as baby's toys. The wonderful voice went on:

"Who can help the Infinite. ... Even the hand that comes to you through the darkness will have to be your own."

And then with that lingering, heart-piercing pathos that no pen can even suggest, "We—infinite dreamers, dreaming finite dreams."

Ah, they are mistaken who say that a voice is nothing— that ideas are all. For this in its rise and fall was the only possible music to the poetry of the words—making the whole hour a pause, retreat, in the market place of life—as well as a song of praise in some dim cathedral aisle.

At last—the whole dying down and away in the thought—"I could not see *you* or speak to you for a moment—I who stand here seeing and talking—if this Infinite Unity were broken for a moment—if one little atom could be crushed and moved out of its place. ... Hari Om Tat Sat!"

And for me—I had found the infinitely deep things that life holds for us. To sit there and listen was all that it had ever been. Yet there was no struggle of intellectual unrest now—no tremor of novelty.

This man who stood there held my life in the hollow of his hand—and as he once in a while looked my way, I read in his glance what I too felt my own heart, complete faith and abiding comprehension of purpose—better than any feeling. ... Swami says, "All accumulations are for subsequent distribution, this is what the fool forgets."

16. *New York, July 15, 1900*: This morning the lesson on the *Gita* was grand. It began with a long talk on the fact that the highest ideals are not for all. Non-resistance is *not* for the man who thinks the replacing of the maggot in the wound, by the leprous saint, with "Eat, Brother!" disgusting and horrible. Non-resistance is practised by a mother's love towards

an angry child. It is a travesty in the mouth of a coward, or in the face of a lion.

Let us be true. Nine-tenths of our life's energy is spent in trying to make people *think* us that which we are not. That energy would be more rightly spent in *becoming* that which we would like to be. And so it went—beginning with the salutation to an incarnation:

> Salutation to thee—the guru of the universe,
> Whose footstool is worshipped by the gods.
> Thou one unbroken Soul,
>   Physician of the world's diseases.
> Guru of even the gods,
> To thee our salutation.

Thee we salute. Thee we salute. Thee we salute. In the Indian tones—by Swami himself.

There was an implication throughout the talk that Christ and Buddha were inferior to Krishna—in the grasp of problems—inasmuch as they preached the highest ethics as a world-path, whereas Krishna saw the right of the *whole,* in all its parts—to its own differing ideals. But perhaps no one not familiar with his thought would have realized that this lay behind his exclamation, "The *Sermon on the Mount* has only become another bondage for the soul of man!"

All through his lectures now, he shows this desire to understand life as it is, and to sympathize with it. He takes less of the "Not this, not this" attitude and more of the "Here comes and now follows" sort of tone. But I fear that people find him even more out of touch at a first hearing than ever used to be the case.

He talked after lunch about Bengali poetry, then about astronomy. He confessed to a whimsical doubt as to whether the stars were not merely an optical delusion, since amongst the million of man-bearing earths that must apparently exist, no beings of higher development than ours yet seemed to have attempted signalling to us.

And he suggested that Hindu painting and sculpture had been rendered grotesque by the national tendency to refuse psychic into physical conceptions. He said that he himself knew of his own experience that most physical or material things had psychic symbols, which were often to the material eye grotesquely unlike their physical counterparts. Yesterday he told me how, as a child, he hardly ever was conscious of going to sleep. A ball of coloured light came towards him and he seemed to play with it all night. Sometimes it touched him and burst into a blaze of light, and he passed off. One of the first questions Sri Ramakrishna put to him was about this, "Do you see a light when you sleep?" "Yes," he replied, "does not everyone sleep so?"

One of the Swamis says this was a psychic something which showed that concentration was a gift with which he started this life, not to be earned during its course. One thing I am sure of, that gift of Swami's, of never forgetting any step of his experience, is one of the signs of great souls. It must have been a part of that last vision of Buddha.

When *we* get to the end, we shall not want to know our past incarnations. Maria Theresa and Petrarch and Laura will have no meaning for us, but the steps of our realization will. *This* is what he shows. I sit and listen to him now, and all appears to the intellect so obvious, to the will so unattainable; and I say to myself, "What were the clouds of darkness that covered me in the old days? Surely no one was ever so blind or so ignorant!" You must have been right when you thought me hard and cold. I must have been so, and it must have been the result of the long effort to see things by the mind alone, without the feelings.

Swami is all against bhakti and emotion now—determined to banish it, he says. But how tremendous is that unity of mind and heart, from which he starts. He can afford to dispense with either—since both are fully developed, and the rest is merely discipline. I fancy most of us will do well to feel all we can.

17. *New York, June 24, 1900:* Swami is also a visitor in this house where I am staying.

I have just wound up my stay in America by writing a comforting letter to the Rev. Mother [Mrs. Ole Bull], telling the dear soul how all his luck has turned, and he is looking like a god, and leaving her to infer that all earth's crowns are at his feet.

But indeed it is all true! As he is now, nothing can resist him.

This morning at eleven, he is to lecture on "Mother Worship", and you shall have every word of that lecture, if I have to pay ten dollars to get it taken down. It was mentioned by someone yesterday to me, before him, and he turned and said, smiling, "Yes—'Mother Worship'—that's what I am going to lecture on, and that is what I *love.*"

The other morning I offered him advice that struck him as wrong. I wish you could have seen him! It was worth the offence to catch such a glimpse!

He said, "Remember that I am free—free—born free!" And then he talked of the Mother and of how he wished the work and the world would break to pieces that he might go and sit down in the Himalayas and meditate. That Europeans had never preached a religion, because they had always *planned;* that a few Catholic Saints alone had come near to this; that it was not *he but Mother* who did all, and *whatever* She might do was equally welcome to him. That once Shiva, sitting with Uma in Kailasa, arose to go, and when she asked him why, He said: "There, look, that servant of mine is being beaten. I must go to his aid." A moment later He came back and again She asked him why. "I am not needed. He is helping himself," was all the reply.

And then he blessed me, before he went, saying "Well! well! You are Mother's child." And I went away much moved, because the moment was somehow so great.

(*Prabuddha Bharata*, January-December 1935)

Eric Hammond

Whemn Swamiji came to London, he created considerable attention. Something of the wonder and admiration which had surrounded him during the Parliament of Religions at Chicago had anticipated his advent. His arresting appearance and even more arresting eloquence called many persons to his presence.

London is indeed a volcano of eruptions, sometimes pious, sometimes philosophical, sometimes pretentious, but mainly eager and earnest. Here, then, to London came Swamiji to place himself, among many conflicting elements, as the protagonist of Hinduism. No more fitting or outstanding person could have arrived at the centre of British thought. Fortified by his intimate acquaintance of, and his infinite belief in, Sri Ramakrishna, he brought the full force of that great soul to bear upon the minds of his hearers. The bedrock principle on which Sri Ramakrishna stood, and which Swamiji expounded, is stated by the latter in these few words:

"Do not care for doctrines, do not care for dogmas, or sects, or churches, or temples; they count for little compared with the essence of existence in each man which is spirituality; and the more this is developed in each man, the more powerful is he for good. Earn that first, acquire that, and criticize no one, for all doctrines and creeds have some good in them. Show by your lives that religion does not mean words, or names, or sects, but that it means spiritual realization. Only those can understand who have felt. Only those that have attained to spirituality can communicate it to others, can be great teachers of mankind. They alone are powers of light."

This essential doctrine of spirituality and its realization, preached as only Vivekananda could preach it, drew folks towards him from far and near. London quickly learnt that a striking personality had made his advent. Swamiji started a course of addresses, received visitors—in a word made himself known and felt. Among his earnest admirers was Miss Margaret Noble who was predestined subsequently to become his ardent follower, a resident in India, and a wonderfully vivid speaker and writer in defence of the Vedanta. It was indeed at her persistent urging that this present correspondent journeyed from an outlying district to Swamiji's lodging. There, on certain specified occasions, he might be seen and conversed with. A very uncomfortable evening, cheerless and dismal, found us at his door, where we were met, at first, by disappointment. Swamiji was not at home. However, a very kindly message awaited us. We were permitted—so the message ran—to follow him to the Sesame Club whither he had gone, at brief notice, to speak in place of a lecturer who was prevented from appearing. Obeying instructions with alacrity we sought the Club. We found ourselves in a big drawing room or hall, filled almost to overflowing by smart people in evening dress. Some courteous and obliging person ushered us close to a platform where one or two chairs were vacant. The position was conspicuous and so, alas! were we. Our overcoats were dripping with rain, nor were we otherwise clothed in fine raiment; not anticipating a summons to so distinguished a gathering. Most of those present were, we discovered, schoolmasters and schoolmistresses, tutors and the like. The subject announced for lecture was "Education". Soon he, Swamiji, appeared. He had little, if any notice, and his speech could not have been in any way prepared. Yet, then, as always, he proved himself more than equal to the occasion. Collected, calm, self-possessed, he stood forward. A Hindu, primed in heart and tongue with Hindu lore and Hindu faith, backed by the prestige of an ancient civilization and culture which inspired him! It was a novel sight, a memorable experience. His dark skin, his deep glowing eyes, even his costume, attracted and fascinated. Above all, eloquence acclaimed him, the eloquence of inspiration. Again, his surprising command of the English language delighted and held his audience, an audience it must be remembered which consisted largely, as we have said, of men and women whose profession it was to teach English students their mother tongue and through the medium of that tongue instruct them in other branches of knowledge. More, Swamiji soon showed that he was equally versed in history and political economy. He stood among these people on their own ground. Without fear, beseeching no favour, he dealt them blow upon blow enforcing the Hindu principle that the teacher who taught for money-making was a traitor to the highest and deepest truth. "Education is an integral part of religion and neither one nor the other should be bought or sold." His words, rapier-like, pierced the armour of scholastic convention; yet no bitterness spoilt his speech. This Hindu, cultured, gracious with his notable smile that disarmed unkindly criticism, held his own and made his mark. He had come sent by the spirit of Sri Ramakrishna, to make that mark; and he had succeeded at the first attempt. His idea was that teachers should work with their pupils for love, and not for the love of lucre, not even for the love of livelihood.

Discussion followed. Climatic and other reasons for charges for teaching were set forth, but Swamiji maintained his position.

Such then was our first meeting with him; a meeting which resulted in reverent friendship, in genuine admiration, and in most grateful remembrance.

(*Vedanta Kesari*, May 1922)

E. T. Sturdy

Although I am not to be present at your gathering in remembrance of your great predecessor, Swami Vivekananda, I think those present may like to have a pen-picture of him from one who was very closely associated with him.

It is now some forty years since Vivekananda left this country, but the impression that he left with me is as vivid now as on the day that I said farewell to him.

I think this is largely accounted for—for I am not strong in reminiscence—by a quality in him which is described by a Sanskrit word ojas: it signifies bodily strength, virility, and also vitality and splendour.

In fact he had a magnetic personality, associated with great tranquillity. Whether he was walking in the street or standing in a room, there was always the same dignity.

He had a great sense of humour, and as a natural correlative, much pathos and pity for affliction. He was a charming companion and entered with ease into any environment he found. And I found that all classes of educated persons that he was brought in contact with looked up to and admired the innate nobility that was in the man. One felt at all times that he was, to use a modern expression, "conscious of the presence of God". In walking, travelling, and leisure times, there constantly came from him some hardly formulated invocation or expression of devotion.

As a teacher he had a great capacity for perceiving the difficulty of an inquirer, and would elucidate it with great simplicity and point to its solution. At the same time he could enter into great intricacies of thought.

E. T. STURDY

I remember well his discussion with Dr. Paul Deussen, the then head of Kiel University. He pointed out where Schopenhauer and Von Hartmann were wrong in founding their philosophy upon the blind will, the Unconscious, as contrasted with Universal Thought, which must precede all desiring or willing. Unfortunately that error continues today and vitiates a great deal of Western psychology by its using a wrong terminology.

I will close this by remarking that, although if we were enlightened we should see Divinity in every manifestation, nevertheless it is a great boon when we can perceive it as patent in noble and holy men. One of such was the Swami Vivekananda.

(Vedanta Kesari, February 1937)

T. J. Desai

About this time (1895) I had an invitation from Miss Muller to attend the two public lectures delivered by Swami Vivekananda. I heard the first lecture at St. James' Hall with Mrs. Ingall. That was the first time I saw the commanding figure of the great Swami. He looked more like an Indian prince than a monk. He had an ochre coloured turban on his head. He electrified the audience by his grand and powerful oratory. The next day the report appeared in the papers that he was the next Indian after Keshabchandra Sen, who had surprised the English audience by his magnificent oratory. He spoke on the Vedanta. His large eyes were rolling like anything, and there was such an animation about him that it passeth description. After the meeting was over, the Swami took off his turban and put on a huge and deep Kashmiri cap looking like a big Persian hat.

The next time I heard him was at the Balloon Society. He spoke there for some time but not with his former fire. A clergyman got up after the lecture and attacked the Swami, and said that it would have been better if the Swami had taken the trouble of writing out his lecture at home and of reading it there, etc. The Swami got up to reply, and he was now on his mettle. He made such a fiery speech that the clergyman was nowhere. He said that some people had crude notions that the Vedanta could be learnt in a few days. The Swami further said that he had to devote about twelve long years of his life to the study of the Vedanta. He replied to the objections of the clergyman categorically one by one, recited the sonorous Vedic hymn beginning with *"Suparnam"*[1] and ended with a triumphant peroration that still rings in my ears.

In 1896 I became a member of the Royal Asiatic Society of Great Britain and Ireland. ... Once I remember that a paper was read by Prof. Bain on the Upanishads. Swami Vivekananda and Mr. Rameshchandra Dutta, C.I.E., were also there. Sir Raymond West had taken the chair. After the paper was finished, I made a vigorous and spirited speech.

Swami Vivekananda liked my speech very much, and he took me to his place, talking on various subjects on the way. Strange that the Swami had put on a top hat on that day. If I err not, it was on that day that he and some other Swami (Saradananda or Abhedananda) prepared khichudi, etc., at his place, and asked me to take supper with them.

Swami Vivekananda delivered a series of lectures in different places in London on Karma Yoga, Jnana Yoga, Bhakti Yoga, and Raja Yoga, during this year (i.e. 1896). He had also been invited to speak at the Blavatsky Lodge. I attended a good many of his lectures. The cream of the English society attended his lectures, and all were mad after him. The Swami used to take walks with me from the lecture-hall to his house, or from his house to some neighbouring places. I very often dined at his place of residence, at his own invitation, or that of my pupil—Miss Muller, and of Mr. Sturdy, who, I believe, paid for the household expenses after the Swami came to live in London from America. Mr. Sturdy was like a real yogi. Mr. Goodwin was another staunch adherent of the Swami, and he took down in shorthand the lectures of the Swami, which were afterwards published.

In July 1896, a conference of the London Hindu Association was held at the Montague Mansions. The chair was taken by Swami Vivekananda, the Hon. President of the Association. Mr. Dadabhai Naoroji was also present. ... Swami Vivekananda, as chairman of the conference, rose to speak, and he electrified the audience. Reporters of the press were also present. When he struck his hand on the table

---

1. *Taittiriya Aranyaka*, 3.11.1

during his speech, my watch bounded from the table and fell down on the ground, and created a visible sensation. He had a commanding figure, and my landlady, who had come to the meeting with me, was greatly impressed with his speech and personality. ...

Later on in the year, when I was living with the Owens for the second time, Swami Vivekananda had come to my house with another Swami (Saradananda or Abhedananda), as he was invited to take his dinner with us. It seemed from his conversation that he did not object to meat eating, although he and the other Swami took only the vegetarian dishes prepared for us. The Swami used to smoke cigars. The Owens were generally pleased by Swami Vivekananda's visit. They admired his personality and powers of conversation.

I came in close contact with the Swami during this year. Once he delivered a magnificent speech in a magnificent hall in the West End of London, wherein he narrated the story of a young sannyasi who accidentally happened to go to the palace of a Raja, holding a svayamvara[2] for his daughter. The princess, instead of throwing the garland round the neck of any of the princes present, took a fancy for the young sannyasi, and suddenly dropped it round his head. The sannyasi ran away, and she followed him wherever he went, but to no purpose, as he would not lay down his sannyasa and marry her. After the lecture was over, the Swami was surrounded by the best of the beauty of England, and they put questions after questions to him and asked for explanations. He somehow managed to extricate himself from them; and when he was alone, he heaved a sigh of relief, and asked me to go with him to his house.

On the way, in order to sound the mind of the Swami, I asked him whether it was not wrong on the part of the young sannyasi to break the heart of that young princess by not marrying her, on which he indignantly cried out, "Why should he desecrate himself?"

---

2. Choosing one's husband by a princess from among the assembled dignitaries at her father's house.

On another occasion, when Swami Vivekananda and myself were alone in his house, I put to him several knotty questions on Vedanta, and he explained them to me. One of them was about the unity of the individual soul with Brahman. As I had devoted much of my time to the study and realization of the nature of Brahman, I was looking for an answer in speechless silence, and at the same time was trying mentally to identify myself with the Universal Spirit. The Swami, on finding that at a particular moment at that time I was *en rapport* with Brahman, simply cried out, "Thou art That!" I wanted no further explanation. The Swami returned to India towards the end of this year (i.e. 1896).

I subsequently paid a visit to the learned Swami at his private residence. He kindly received me in a cordial manner. I had a talk with him on religious matters during which he repeated several verses from the *Bhagavad Gita*:

"Even in this life they have conquered the round of birth and death, whose minds are firmly-fixed on the sameness of everything, for God is pure, and the same to all, and therefore, such are said to be living in God.[3]

"O Arjuna, you and I have run the cycle of birth and death many times. I know them all, but you are not conscious of them.[4]

"Know them to be of demonical resolve, who, senseless as they are, torture all the organs of the body and Me dwelling within the body.[5]

"Cast off this mean faint-heartedness and arise, O scorcher of thine enemies."[6]

Thereupon, I naturally repeated within myself in an audible manner:

---

3. *Gita*, 5.9

4. *Gita*, 4.5

5. *Gita*, 17.6

6. *Gita*, 2.3

"Destroyed is my delusion, and I have gained my memory through thy grace, O Achyuta. I am firm; my doubts are gone. I shall do thy word."[7]

He said that "non-injury is the highest virtue" was a tenet of the Buddhists, and it had gone so far that it had enfeebled the people. He preached a bold and manly religion. He told me that when he had to speak before the Chicago Parliament of Religions for the first time, he felt a little nervous in the beginning, but the great Upanishadic saying "I am Brahman" at once flashed through his brain, and such a tremendous power entered his frame that he outdid himself. He electrified the American audience by his subsequent speeches, and the fact, no doubt, is testified by the reports of the American papers.

He, therefore, advised all men not to belittle themselves, but to realize their brahmanhood, their Divinity.

(*Vedanta Kesari*, January 1932)

---

7. *Gita*, 18.73

Kamakhyanath Mitra

It was in 1897, the year of my graduation, that I had the rare privilege of seeing at Kolkata the world-famous Hindu monk, the epoch-making Swami Vivekananda, in the house of the late Balaram Bose, a great devotee well-known to the disciples of Ramakrishna Paramahamsa. I went to see the Swami because I was profoundly interested in his message, though its significance was not yet quite clear to me.

A few words may be necessary to explain my interest. I was inquisitive from my boyhood, and the question of religion had a strange fascination for my mind. Just as in these days the predominant interest of my countrymen is politics, so in my boyhood their predominant interest was religion. It was a time of great religious movements and controversies. There was a constant play of action and reaction. On the one hand, there was the rising tide of Brahmoism with which most enlightened men were in sympathy. On the other, there was the frantic effort of the so-called orthodoxy with its pseudoscientific and fanciful interpretation of the religion of the Hindus. Then, again, there was Theosophy with its Mahatmas, occultism, and spirit-world to which many educated people were attracted because they did not like the Westernized outlook of the Brahmos, and further because they felt flattered by the uncritical eulogizing of everything Hindu by Colonel Olcott of America and Mrs. Annie Besant of England.

It must be said at the same time that a not inconsiderable number of university-bred young men were free-thinkers, rationalists or agnostics who swore by Mill, Comte, Spencer,

Huxley, and Haeckel and thought all religions equally false. Such was the intellectual milieu of my boyhood and youth as I listened to—and occasionally took part in—the discussions of my elders. Religion to me was not yet a craving of the soul; it was more a question of intellectual interest. Though born in an orthodox Hindu family, yet the influence that I felt most was that of the Brahmo Samaj and also a relative who was an out-and-out agnostic. With the social programme of the Brahmos I had every sympathy, but their theology I could not accept. I was swaying between two forces—Brahmoism and agnosticism.

It is in this state of mind that I finished my school education and entered college. In the first year class, if I remember rightly, I first heard of Ramakrishna—yet not from any fellow-countryman of mine, but a foreigner—no less a personage than Professor Max Muller himself. I happened to read two articles from his pen in The Nineteenth Century—one was 'Esoteric Buddhism', a scathing criticism of Madame Blavatsky and her theosophy, and the other was 'A Real Mahatman'. This Real Mahatman was no other than our Bhagavan Ramakrishna. A new horizon opened before me, a new light flashed forth. And all this happened at a mofussil town.

About a year after this, I read in the papers all about the famous Parliament of Religions at Chicago and the resounding triumph there of Swami Vivekananda. Who was this Vivekananda? I came to know soon after that he was the chief disciple of Ramakrishna, the Real Mahatman of Professor Max Muller. I was eager to know all about the man and his message. Unfortunately, I was not in Kolkata when the whole city turned out to receive him with the tremendous acclamation that signals the return of a conquering hero. But I read glowing accounts of the event and realized that honour such as this had never fallen to the lot of any man on Indian soil.

From then on, I read reports of all the speeches he delivered throughout India. I felt that the spirit of India herself breathed through his utterances. Such force, such fire was beyond the utmost stretch of my imagination. I had read several of the speeches of Keshabchandra Sen and had great admiration for his style, eloquence, and religious fervour, but here was a new atmosphere altogether—a new accent, a new emphasis, a new outlook at once national and universal. Here was Hinduism in all its phases, but how different from the Hinduism of the hide-bound Sanatanists, pseudorevivalists, the scribes and pharisees of India! I was under a spell. The two speeches that impressed me most were his Kolkata Town Hall speech and his Lahore address on Vedanta, which I read as a B.A. student in Kolkata.

I waited eagerly for an opportunity to see the man, and it came in 1897. I went to see Swami Vivekananda at the Kolkata residence of the late Balaram Bose in the company of a classmate of mine, Narendrakumar Bose.

We entered a hall which was full to overflowing. The people assembled there were for the most part students of the Kolkata colleges. They were all seated cross-legged on the floor, which was covered with mats. In the centre was the seat meant for Swamiji. I managed somehow to find a place in the hall, and we all eagerly waited for the arrival of Swamiji. Perfect silence prevailed. A few minutes passed and the Swami stepped in.

His gait was leonine and the dignity of his bearing simply royal. His frame was athletic and robust. He was wearing an ochre cloak, his feet were bare and his head, chin and lips clean-shaven—altogether a striking personality. He had the look of a man born to command. He was seated quickly, and then he looked around at us. His large eyes beamed with genius and spiritual fire. He spoke in Bengali mixed with English. Words flowed from his lips, and we listened with rapt attention. Each word was like a spark. His manner was impassioned. It was clear to all that here was a man with a message. His awakening power was wonderful; we heard him and felt aroused. A new spirit was breathed into us. Here was a man of faith in an age of doubt, sincere to the backbone, a dynamo of supernal force. To see him was an education. To hear him was an inspiration. It was the most memorable day in my life, and it is impossible for me to forget it.

What did he tell us all? To be strong and self-confident, to renounce and serve. Strength was his main message. He poured torrential scorn upon what he called "negative education" and spoke enthusiastically of man-making. He gave a vivid picture of our country's degradation and the misery of its masses. How he felt for the poor, the downtrodden, and the oppressed! If we had a millionth part of his feeling, the face of the country would change at once. He spoke of the greatness of Hinduism and proudly said, "It is my ambition to conquer the world by Hindu thought—to see Hindus everywhere from the North Pole to the South Pole." As he uttered these words I saw him as the veritable Napoleon of Religion. I saw the warrior's heart throb beneath the yellow robe of the sannyasi. Not a mild Hindu at all, this Swami Vivekananda, but the most aggressive Hindu I have ever seen in my life, made of the same stuff of which Alexander and Caesar were made—only his role was different.

Some of his words are still ringing in my ears: "You must have steel nerves and cast-iron muscles. A moment's vigorous life is better than years of jellyfish existence. Cowards die many time before their death. An honest atheist is a thousand times better than a hypocritical theist. Don't be jealous, for slaves are jealous. Virtue is heroism—from vir in Latin which means man and which again is the same word as vira in Sanskrit."

After about two hours the Swami left the hall and we dispersed in different directions. I returned to my lodgings but the Swami's words filled the air. I could think of nothing but Swami Vivekananda. There stood his heroic figure wherever I turned.

I could not resist the temptation to see him again, and so the next day I went once more to the house of the late Balaram Bose. On this day there was no great gathering.

Swamiji was seated in the veranda on a mat surrounded by his brother-disciples. The *Brahma Sutras* with Shankara's commentary was being read aloud by one of them, and Swamiji offered explanatory remarks here and there. Today's atmosphere was different altogether. It was all very quiet. Soon after the reading was finished, one of the Swami's brother-disciples spoke of the spirit world and read an extract from a theosophical book. Swamiji came down hard upon him, silencing him completely. I saw that the Swami was a hater of spookism. He made it clear that all this was weakening and debilitating and had nothing to do with true religion. After this, many lighter topics were introduced, and Swamiji laughed and joked like a child. Here was another mood altogether. I said to myself: Is it the same Swami I saw yesterday—the thundering Swami in dead earnest?

It was about a year after this that I saw the Swami once more—this time on the platform. Now I was face-to-face with Vivekananda the orator. The scene was the Star Theatre of Kolkata, the occasion the introduction of Sister Nivedita to the Kolkata public. The hall was crammed to the point of suffocation. On the dais were seated many distinguished persons, but of them I remember only Sir Jagadish Bose and Sir Ananda Charlu. Swami Vivekananda was at his best.

He wore an ochre turban and a long-flowing robe of the same colour. He introduced Sister Nivedita in a brief but moving speech, and the Sister addressed the meeting in her graceful style. Then Swami Vivekananda rose again and spoke on his foreign policy. He brought forward a scheme of his future missionary work in the West. The speech was full of fire. His voice thrilled with its rich intonation, variation of pitch, strong and sonorous accent and the occasional explosion, as of a bolt from heaven, such as I have never heard in my life nor am I likely to hear again. Sometimes he paced to and fro on the platform as he spoke, folding his arms across his chest; sometimes he faced the audience and waved his hand. His expressions flowed freely and quickly with the rush and impetuosity of a mountain torrent. His words were like the roaring of a waterfall. Well might *The New York Herald* say, "He is an orator by divine right." Altogether a more majestic, striking, and magnetic personality it is hard to conceive. We heard him spellbound, each word an arrow to the heart.

Such is my recollection of Swami Vivekananda. To fully understand his message, I subsequently read all of his speeches and writings and almost everything about his Master. There is not a single problem of our individual, social, and political life that he has not touched upon and illuminated. He has given a new impulse to the country. For me, he grows more and more vivid with the lapse of years, and I see his stature "dilated.../ like Tenerife or Atlas"[1], but with a message of freedom, strength, fearlessness, and self-confidence. It is the eternal truths of our religion that he has preached in a new way, in modern terms, and he has also shown how these truths are to be applied to the present conditions of India and the rest of the world. A more constructive thinker and inspiring teacher I have not seen in my life. I do not know a single self-sacrificing Indian worker of the present century who has not been influenced to some degree by his thoughts, words, and example. More than anyone else, he has made India respected abroad. Many a child of the West has found in his message the solace of his life and of his death. It is true that at the present moment the predominant interest of our country has become political, but the better minds believe with Swami Vivekananda that spirituality must be the basis of all our activities. It is difficult to say exactly what form our national reconstruction will take, and it is difficult to predict anything about the future of the world as a whole, but I sincerely believe that the ideas and ideals of Swami Vivekananda are destined to play a very important part in the history of the human race. May his influence grow and grow!

(*Prabuddha Bharata*, February 1930)

---

1. The author is quoting from John Milton's epic poem, "Paradise Lost."

Manmathanath Ganguli

In 1897, I heard that Swami Vivekananda had arrived in Kolkata and I went to see him. He was staying with Sri Balaram Bose in Baghbazar. On the first floor, facing the street, was a hall where a few people were waiting to see the great Swami, who was in an adjacent room. I took my seat in a corner, on the carpeted floor, and soon Miss Noble (Sister Nivedita) came through one of the doors inside the hall. She wore a robe of pale saffron which came almost to her ankles, and a necklace of holy rudraksha beads around her neck. Entering the room barefooted, she looked as pure as a goddess.

She went with slow strides straight to the threshold of the room where Swamiji was resting; but then she knelt down beside the door-frame and folded her hands; her fingers and palms joined as she offered obeisance to the Lord. She bowed down in this posture and then remained quietly sitting on her ankles with her palms together, as we do while praying. But she did not enter the room, in which Swamiji was sitting on a cot. Swamiji talked with her for a while, and she answered in a soft voice, reverentially—as if she were in church. Then she bowed down to the Swami again and went away as silently as she had come.

I'd heard much about Sister Nivedita, but this was the first time I saw her in person. Her face had the serenity and fullness one sees in the face of Madonna, indicating the direct personal vision of God. ...

After a while, Sri Vijayakrishna Goswami entered the hall with a few of his followers, who carried a drum and cymbals. They were seated at one corner of the hall, a little apart from the rest of the people who by this time had assembled there. As soon as Swamiji saw Sri Vijayakrishna, he left his room and came inside the hall and stood in the middle of the room. Seeing the Swami, Sri Vijayakrishna and his party stood up as a mark of respect. Then Sri Vijayakrishna Goswami advanced a step or two and tried to take the dust of Swamiji's feet. But Swamiji was alert, and he himself bent down to take the dust of Sri Goswami's feet. Simultaneously, both of them tried to avoid being touched by the other; again and again both of them tried to outdo the other in this form of homage. At last Swamiji took hold of Sri Goswami's hand and made him sit next to him on the carpet in the middle of the floor.

Sri Vijayakrishna was in a highly ecstatic mood and he looked like a man intoxicated with the love of God. A few minutes after, when he seemed normal, the Swami entreated him to speak a few words about Sri Ramakrishna. At this, Sri Vijayakrishna was again choked with emotion and he slowly repeated these words several times with great effort: "Sri Ramakrishna has kindly blessed me." But he could speak no further due to an immense surge of devotion. We saw divine grace in his flushed face and ecstatic mood. He sat quiet and motionless. Tears flowed from his eyes continuously for some time, wetting his cheeks. At this, the men who had come with him stood up and began samkirtana, surrounding him and the Swami. After some time, Sri Goswami was able to stand up. He seemed to be in a condition of half-awakened consciousness. His followers formed a circle around him as they all slowly moved out of the hall.

It was then that I bowed to the Swami from a distance. There was no one to introduce me to him, but I felt very happy to be able to see him face to face. I thought of my good fortune in being able to see this great Swami, lionized in America for his great learning and oratory. I was a petty clerk in government service at Allahabad, but when I heard about the Swami's return to India, I had taken leave from my office and gone to seek his blessings. So I had come to Kolkata, where my elder brother lived and practised as a lawyer. Two or three times a year I would come to Kolkata, and I never lost an opportunity to know at close quarters the sannyasis of the Math, and the disciples of Sri Ramakrishna, for my own spiritual benefit.

On a few occasions I had seen the Holy Mother, but never asked her for initiation. A Brahmo friend of mine, Sri Narendranath Basu, got a touch of divine intoxication at the very first sight of Mother's holy feet. By her grace, he and his wife soon got initiation. It is this friend who came to tell me that Swamiji was at Balaram Bose's house, so it is to his kindness that I own the good fortune of seeing the Swami in person for the first time.

I was born in an era which today's generation finds it difficult to understand, so far removed are they from the in-grained thoughts of those times—thoughts which may have become meaningless. But, at the time, I too was so heavily influenced by Brahminic ideas that prevented me from touching the feet of one born of the Kayastha caste—even if he was a sannyasi. I am not ashamed to confess today that to me, on that day, Swamiji was no exception to this rule. But as the Swami spoke a few words to me in a kind voice, my Brahminic barriers seemed to dissolve altogether.

One morning in the last week of December, I went to Belur. I found Swamiji standing near the open yard in front of the kitchen, an ochre woollen cap on his head. He wore a woollen dressing gown with a design of large black checks on a white background. His complexion was fair, but looked even fairer due to a peculiar brilliance and softness in it. The most attractive part of this fine personality were the eyes, large and expressive. I have never come across another pair so fine.

This time, I went up to him and bowed down—touching his feet with my fingertips. Nearby, in a small tent, were a small tea-table and a few stools. He asked a brahmachari to bring me a cup of tea. Tea and prasad were served, and then Swamiji fell into a conversational mood. He asked me where I lived and what I did, and I told him. Then he went elsewhere and I mingled with other Swamis of my acquaintance. Thus some time passed until about ten.

Inside the veranda, facing the courtyard of the Math, Swamiji was seated in a chair while Rakhal Maharaj, Mahapurushji, and Sharat Maharaj (Swamis Brahmananda, Shivananda, and Saradananda) occupied one of three benches. I was alone on another of the benches a short distance away. Swamiji was in the mood to talk, relating many of his experiences in America. In the course of the conversation he said:

"In Chicago it was proven that Hinduism was the greatest religion of the world, and the padres there got infuriated. They wanted to convene another Parliament of Religions in France. They had the idea of making it compulsory for the speakers to address the House in the French language. Since I didn't know French at the time, they imagined that my ignorance of the language would disqualify me from the Parliament. But I went to France and picked up the language in about six months and began to deliver some speeches in French. This damped the enthusiasm of the missionaries. Later on, the idea of having another Parliament was dropped.[1]

"In America, outside my room there was a private letter box. I used to lock it up. Occasionally, during the day, I opened it myself. Various were the letters that I used to get from all sorts of people. Many were threats from unknown persons. They asked me to stop preaching Hinduism. But sometimes I received letters of admiration and praise. Most of them were written by women. A few contained proposals of marriage. There had been other occasions when some influential ladies expressed a desire for me to get married to some rich woman and settle down in America. I had to explain to them that Indian monks do not marry. But it was difficult for them to be convinced, as some padres do marry in their country, and so they asked why I shouldn't."

---

1. Certain of the words attributed to Swamiji, both here and in other parts of this reminiscence, do not fully agree, in important details, with other records.

In the course of his conversation, Swamiji spoke of one peculiar incident which, to me, seemed very strange. Swamiji didn't try to explain it. He said, "I was then travelling from city to city and addressing many gatherings even in a single day. One day I was thinking that I had already spoken on all the topics that I knew about. I was to address a meeting the next day and it bothered me to think that I would be repeating some previous lecture. This I wanted to avoid. It was late at night. I was sitting on an easy chair, quite relaxed. In my mind I was accusing the Master of having caused this predicament. Suddenly I heard him speak to me. At that moment, I had closed my eyes and could not see him. I only heard his voice. He went on at some length and said, 'You should speak thus and thus, and not worry at all.' I was astonished. Still, I was glad enough to be informed of the topic of my next lecture! There was even more astonishment in store for me when the following morning a gentleman living in a room adjacent to mine asked me, 'Who was talking to you yesterday? I couldn't follow anything because the language was new to me.' Now, the language that I heard was Bengali. I wondered how this man also could hear it."

Swamiji continued, "Once, in America, I was asked to deliver a lecture on my guru. I told them that Sri Ramakrishna couldn't touch even a copper coin, what to say of gold or silver. It was true not only in the figurative sense but true literally—if he touched a metal coin inadvertently, his fingers cramped and the hand recoiled as if his nervous system rejected the touch instinctively. The contact would give him actual physical pain, and it was so intense that he would cry out even in sleep. One night the Master was asleep when I took a silver rupee and touched him with it. It had an instantaneous effect. Sri Ramakrishna woke up. It was evident that he was anguished with pain, and I was ashamed of my childish act."

Then Rakhal Maharaj requested Swamiji to write a life history of the Master. At this Swamiji winced and said, "I cannot do it. It is not for me to attempt such a difficult task. In the hand of a bad artist even the picture of Shiva may appear to be that of a monkey." At this, Rakhal Maharaj said, "If you say so, then the task will remain undone." But Swamiji answered, "If Thakur wishes it, someone else shall accomplish it."

For the time, his brother-disciples dispersed, leaving the Swami there alone. He now turned to me and started a casual conversation.

"So you live at Allahabad, isn't it? Do you know Doctor Nandi? When I was at Jhusi, I used to go to his house for receiving alms. I knew him very well." Dr. Nandi was a devotee of Sri Ramakrishna. We liked him and there was some acquaintance between us through this common bond. As far as I know, Dr. Nandi had seen Sri Ramakrishna. But I loved him because he had known Swami Vivekananda personally. He had told us that Swami Vivekananda, the chief disciple of Sri Ramakrishna, once stayed for some time on the other side of the Ganga where there were many huts for wandering monks. Swamiji at that time was an itinerant monk. It was summer and the days were very hot. Often there was a hot breeze, known locally as the loo. Swamiji, even in those hot days, wore half of a coarse blanket as an outer garment and half of it covered his upper body. He walked barefooted to and from the house of Dr. Nandi.

I went to Belur quite often. Many men, young and old, were coming to see Swamiji. But it was not so easy to see the Swami at all hours of the day. Mostly he remained in his own room, and he was seldom disturbed even by his brother-disciples. It was well-known that he was often absorbed in moods of tranquillity, and at those times it was painful for him to talk on affairs alien to his own mood. So the custom was that people saw him and could talk to him when he came down from the upper storey of his own accord, and then the visitors were allowed to approach him without any restriction.

One morning Swamiji's mother, Bhuvaneshwari Devi, came to see him. Her very appearance commanded respect.

She was a strongly built lady with fine large eyes and long lashes. She had a remarkably strong personality, and people obeyed her unquestioningly. No wonder Swamiji had these qualities! She went up to the veranda of the first storey and cried aloud "Viloo-oo", and her child came out of the room at once. The great Vivekananda was just like a teenaged son to his mother. He descended the stairs with her, and then they walked on the garden path together, conversing softly on personal matters.

During his last few years, whenever Swamiji was in Kolkata he would go himself to his mother. While at Belur he would occasionally visit her at Kolkata, but if for some reason he couldn't go to her for a week or two she would come down to Belur herself to see him and to ask his advice on family matters.

It was about four in the afternoon one day when the Japanese consul came to meet the Swami at Belur. He was asked to be seated on one of the benches inside the inner veranda where generally Swamiji received his guests. Though the Swami was informed of the honourable guest, the consul had to wait for some time before the Swami came down. Swamiji's mood determined whether he would meet a person immediately or at a more convenient time, no matter how important the visitor. On that occasion, the Consul had been kept waiting for quite a long time when Swamiji came down for his customary evening walk. He took a chair near the Consul and the conversation took place through an interpreter. After the formal greetings, the Consul came to the point: "Our Mikado is very keen to receive you in Japan. He has sent me to request that you visit Japan as early as may be convenient to you. Japan is eager to hear about Hindu religion from your lips."

Swamiji answered, "In my present state of health I think it will not be possible for me to visit Japan now."

The Consul said, "Then, may I with your permission inform the Mikado that you will go there some time in future when your health permits?"

Swamiji said, "It is very doubtful whether this body will ever be fit enough."

At the time, Swamiji was suffering from diabetes. His body was quite emaciated (he had not been so ill when I saw him the first time).

Shortly thereafter, I returned to Allahabad. But I soon availed myself of an opportunity to go to Kolkata and went to Belur in the hope of seeing the Swami. To my utter disappointment, he had gone elsewhere for awhile. But Rakhal Maharaj was there.

Next to Swamiji, Rakhal Maharaj was the head of the Order. I was well-known to him; yet I felt him at the time to be rather distant and aloof. He was often absorbed in his own spiritual moods and was not very open to easy conversation. I had heard about his great spiritual attainments. He often had samadhi, and he was beyond the reach of my understanding.

I sat near him. After we exchanged a few casual words of greeting, he remained quiet for some time. I was thinking of a few problems that I wanted to solve through his help, but I didn't speak—thinking that if he was a great divine soul, he would know my thoughts anyway. Suddenly he said to me, "Come with me, let us have a walk."

It was not yet dusk. The path led to one of the gates of the Math on one side and the river Ganga on the other. The temples were not yet built. There were only a few buildings. Most of the place was open. There were a few shrubs and trees. We went up to the gate leading to the jetty, and then turned back. We strolled for a little while, with Rakhal Maharaj doing all the talking. To my great wonder, he touched on all of my three problems one by one, and they were solved to my satisfaction.

Then Rakhal Maharaj took me to the ghat of the Ganga just facing the Math on one side and sat down on one of the steps, asking me to sit beside him. I sat on a step near his feet. At that moment, I was overwhelmed with a feeling of devotion and wished to surrender myself to him completely.

So I entreated him to give me initiation formally. He kept quiet for some time. Then he spoke slowly, "Your guru is Vivekananda, not I." It extinguished my hopes of ever being initiated, as I knew that Swamiji had initiated very few persons, and to be one among his disciples was a dream to me never to be realized. Completely disappointed, I returned to Allahabad in a few days.

The next time I went to Belur, Swamiji's health seemed to be a little improved and his mood was good. In the morning, someone told me that Swamiji was in the shrine. I went up the stairs and saw Swamiji in a divine ecstasy. He was pacing from one end to the other of the covered veranda just outside the worship room. His arms were now swinging, now crossed above his breast as was his custom. He paced rapidly, with a jerky gait. His face seemed red with an intense emotion which he was trying to suppress. ... I heard him constantly chanting the name of Sri Rama. Then, his entire mind seemed to turn inwards and he was very restless, as if keeping watch before his ideal Sri Rama and Sita, as Mahavira. It seemed as if he were a soul completely dedicated to Sri Ramakrishna, but one with a will that was full of explosive possibilities—and he was determined to do even the impossible for the sake of the service of the Lord.

That afternoon, about a dozen young men of college age had come to see Swamiji. They had assembled on the veranda facing the Ganga on the first floor in front of Swamiji's room. Swamiji came out after a short while and talked with them very freely. He was so jovial that he himself seemed to be one of them—quite young and enthusiastic. He talked to one, touched another on his back, or mildly slapped another's shoulder. It was a pleasing sight to see him in this mood, for usually when I saw him he was full of gravity and seriousness.

There was a solid gold chain around his neck, attached to a gold watch in his pocket, and it matched his fair complexion well. One of the young men touched the chain with his fingers and said, "It is very beautiful." At once Swamiji took watch and chain out of his pocket and dropped them both into the suddenly cupped hands of the amazed youth. He said: "You like it! Then it is yours. But my boy, don't sell it. Keep it with you as a souvenir." Needless to say, the young man was extremely happy. I marvelled at the ease with which Swamiji could part with such a valuable thing—not only valuable, now, for its cost but also invaluable for its association. Once I had heard him say: "Sacrifice means the sacrifice of something you possess. A man who has all things in his possession and yet is indifferent to them is a truly detached soul. The man who has nothing is only poor—what can he give?"

During the Christmas holidays, some scholars came from Agra. A few of them were professors. It was about nine o'clock in the morning. Inside the courtyard of the Math were a few ordinary benches on which the visitors sat while Swamiji took a chair near them. The college dons put their questions one by one, and Swamiji answered them with due gravity. The problems were various, some philosophical and some social or political. They seemed to be quite satisfied and after a while all went away.

I was sitting at a little distance and tried to follow the trend of the conversation. Swamiji would occasionally look at me, which made me feel at home. At about noon, the Swami suddenly asked me, "Sadhu Amulya lives at Allahabad. Do you know him? How is he doing? Tell me all about him." I said: "I've known him for many years. He used to serve all without any self-interest. His courage and spirit of service endeared him to all. Once, there was an epidemic of cholera and he nursed the helpless and the needy without the least fear for his own life. So he was loved by rich and poor alike, who considered him a congenial friend in times of distress."

Sadhuji was the name given to Amulya, who at the time wore white robes like those of a brahmachari. Later, he put on ochre clothes and some called him Guruji. Many of his devotees were addicted to intoxicants. They offered them to him, and when Guruji had smoked a little, they took the prasad. By and by he began to drink, and women of questionable character also visited him. After some time, he stopped wearing clothes and used to remain naked. When last I had seen him, he was a fully fallen man. On hearing this sorry tale, Swamiji was silent for some time. Then he said, "Ah! A great soul—a great soul!" He added: "For him, this life is lost. But he shall be free in his next birth. Amulya read with me in college. He was a good student. He had a wide vision and was a follower of the path of knowledge. ... Sadhu Amulya had no spiritual guru. When the disciple takes a wrong move and is about to fall, it is the spiritual guide who guards him so the disciple can regain his balance." I could see that Swamiji was visibly moved and very sympathetic. Though I knew him to be a great moralist, yet his love for the fallen made me wonder at his nature—stern on the outside but very tender within. He then addressed me: "Manmatha, this time when you go to Allahabad, go to Amulya and tell him I have sent you to ask what he wants. Whatever be the things that he asks of you, make it a point to supply him with them."

Accordingly, a few days later I went to Guruji and said: "Sir, Swamiji has asked me to come to you; otherwise I would not have. Please tell me what are the things that you need." He seemed not to mind my taunt, and exclaimed with a beaming face: "What! Swamiji has sent you—Swamiji? What did he say about me?" I reported all that I had heard him say. For some time he was silent, emotionally overwhelmed, and he tried to suppress it. Then he said, "Bring me about four seers of ghee from cows' milk, and some fruits." In a few days I brought these to him and he expressed his satisfaction. That was the last time I saw him. A few weeks later, I came to know of his death. Probably Sadhu Amulya had ended his life by not taking any food at all. He was a peculiar combination of a raja yogi and an aghori of the Tantrika school. Perhaps he took nothing after I saw him except the little present I had made to him in the name of Swamiji.

After telling me about Sadhu Amulya, Swamiji asked me: "What is it that you want to know from me? You may put any question you like." I said: "I have read your lectures on maya. They have appealed to me, but I have not understood them. Please let me know what maya is." For awhile, he was silent. Then he said, "If you have anything else to know, you can ask me." I said: "Sir, I have nothing more to ask. If a knower of Brahman like you cannot enlighten me, then it will remain a closed book to me during this life." At this Swamiji began a discourse on maya. He spoke quickly, and by and by, as I concentrated on his words and his logic, my mind lost its contact with my sense-organs. I experienced a subtle world around me, much finer than the gross world. With eyes open I could see the Math, the trees, and everything before me vibrating. If you look above a large fire you can see a vibration. Objects were oscillating and vibrating before my eyes just like that. Conscious that I was undergoing an uncommon experience, I asked myself, "What is this that I see?"

I looked around me and saw there was vibration everywhere. Slowly even Swamiji vanished from my eyes. Even then I could hear his voice, but not follow its meaning. Then suddenly I was aware of a vibration within my brain and there was only the void.

Again I could see and hear the Swami and follow his meaning. But my mind was conscious of my ego, and it no more asserted itself as it did before. I thought that I finally knew the meaning of maya.

I, who never had the courage to speak before the Swami, now considered myself a bubble in the ocean of maya in which the Swami was another bubble. The difference between us was lost to me for the moment. The giant personality of the Swami and his great spiritual power and everything else seemed to be something that was taking place in the ocean that Swamiji called maya. But it was nothing but undivided chit—the Cosmic Consciousness.

Then I said: "Swamiji, you are also in maya. Your activities of the Math, schools, service of God in the poor, hospitals, the Mission—everything is maya. What is the need of all this? You yourself are within the meshes of maya."

At this he smiled and kept quiet for some time. It was through his grace that I was considering myself to be one with the maya. And suddenly I reentered the little shell of my own self. I saw the Math, the Swami, and everything once again in its true perspective—or rather, the perspective that had been mine before this experience. Just before, I had spoken somewhat petulately in a high-pitched voice, and now I was ashamed. Swamiji and myself were no longer of the same substance, and I felt the vast difference.

Swamiji must have known that now I was normal once again. Then, he said: "Yes; you are correct. I am playing with maya. If you do not like this play of maya, you can go to a deep cave of the Himalayas. There you can lose yourself in spiritual practices."

It was high time for lunch, and everyone had been kept waiting. Swamiji stood up and I fell prostrate at his feet. He was Shiva in person, and I touched his feet.

It was then that I had the desire to have Swamiji's prasad. But I said nothing. He was pacing near the open veranda in front of the storeroom. He went to the room and took an apple and asked for a knife from a brahmachari. Slowly he peeled the apple and then cut a slice. He came near me and offered the slice to me. I was gratified. Then he took a piece himself. Then I wished to have anna-prasada from Swamiji. A little later when we were all seated for the midday meal. Swamiji asked a brahmachari to come to him and he said, "Take this cooked rice to Manmatha." It had been offered to Sri Ramakrishna.

When the midday meal was over everyone retired to his respective room and Swamiji also went to his own room. But he had little rest even then. He was very busy in framing the rules and regulations of the Math. Somehow he was apprehensive of his approaching death and wanted to lay down the principles for the future guidance of the sannyasis of the Order.

I stayed at the Math that day, and spent the night there as well. Next morning, I went to Swamiji to offer my obeisance. He was standing near the door of his room while I bowed down before him. He said, "Go to the Ganga and have a dip. Then come soon to me." His face was beaming with kind benediction, and I knew at once that he was in a mood to shower his grace. My heart beat fast as I understood this to be his permission to be initiated. I was as happy as a teen-aged boy and literally ran to have a dip, so impatient was I. Unless Swamiji was filled with gurubhava (attitude of the teacher) which they called the mood of Sri Ramakrishna himself, he would not initiate anyone. When I returned I found him lying on his back on a sofa. He let fall his right hand loosely and said, "Hold my hand." I sat down on the floor and held his wrist. His body was emaciated, yet his wrist was broad—when I tried to wrap my fingers around it, there was still a gap of about half a finger. Swamiji closed his eyes and lay motionless. Time passed and I held him as a young child would. It seemed to me that his personality engulfed me, but I tried to keep a hold of my consciousness. For a fraction of a second, it seemed to have vanished completely. Then he sat up.

Swamiji got off the sofa and stood up. He pointed to a carpet and asked me to sit on it. At a short distance there was another carpet and Swamiji took his seat on it. When I followed him, he said: "In dream you have seen the Mother as Kumari. But henceforth you should meditate on Her as Shodashi." As he said this I could vividly visualize the image, and at the time I didn't wonder at this at all. About the vision I had never spoken to any soul yet he knew it—and I marvelled not, for I had taken it for granted that he knew everything! In my dream, many years before, I had seen seven maids. The tallest was one of eleven, and the smallest and youngest was only five. The difference of age and height decreased in a graded manner and all were very beautiful divine persons. Each of them had a gold crown and they were dressed in very fine garments and ornaments. But they had all the brightness of goddesses. They emerged one by one from one side and moved forward on before me to vanish at a small distance. The vision was so vivid that the images left a permanent impression in my memory.

Swamiji went on: "After some time you saw Mahadeva in your vision. He had the trident in His hand and He gave you this mantra. ... From that time on you performed that japa." It was many years after the first one that I had this dream. He said, "But from now onwards your mantra is this." ... He repeated the bija mantra of the Mother thrice, aloud. And I saw before me a full-size divine figure of the classical image with the tongue lolling out. I asked him, "Shall I have to meditate on this form of Her's?" He said, "If you wish, you can think of Her with the tongue in." And he smiled.

After this he gave me certain hints about initiation and the process of sadhana that I was to practise. He gave me the mantra for the worship of the guru and showed me the centres for nyasa. He said, "First of all perform the mental obeisance, then visualize your guru as vividly as you can. For this, the sahasrara (the thousand-petalled lotus in the brain) is the best place. After this, the mantra of the chosen deity should be slowly repeated and Her image meditated upon in the heart.

"In offering the mental worship, first of all meditate on the feet, then slowly go upwards till you come to the face, and then meditate on the face. When meditation is deep, there will be no hands or feet. As long as you see the form, the nirvikalpa plane cannot be reached. But do not hurry. You must go slowly and cross the stages one by one. Otherwise it may take a much longer time."

When my initiation was over, he said: "Sit here, beside me, and meditate. Practise meditation every day without fail, however busy you may be. It must be done even for a short time, say for a few minutes. If you do not find time otherwise, you may do it in the bathroom. Even that will do."

The last time that I saw Swamiji was a few months before his passing away. There were many occasions when I went to Belur between my initiation and the beginning of January 1902. As I didn't record my impressions at the time, it isn't possible to give the exact dates now. But some of the things that I heard from him I shall try to present here.

Once he said: "This body will never be fit again. I shall have to leave it and bring another body to complete the work. There are many things that remain undone."

On a previous occasion he had said in a divine mood: "I do not want liberation. As long as there shall be one soul left, I have to come again and again."

The internal condition of China was politically very wretched. The European powers wanted to divide China among them. Japan also joined them in this exploitation and attacked China. One day I asked Swamiji: "China is such an old country. Do you think this ancient country with its civilization will die out?" He was silent for a while. Then he said: "I see before me the body of an elephant. There is a foal within. But it is a lion-cub that comes out of it. It will grow in the future, and China shall become great and powerful."

Of Indian freedom, he said: "Our country shall be free. But not with bloodshed. There is a great future for India after her independence." At the time he did not say when, but from another brother-disciple I later learned later that he predicted India would be free within 50 years.

Once I asked, "What will happen if I do not follow your behest and fall?" He said: "Go and fall to the very depth of abyss. It is I who shall raise you by the tuft of your hair. There is no power on this earth to keep you fallen."

At one time he remarked casually: "There are many souls that will come in future. They shall be free from birth and some shall become free just by hearing the name of Sri Ramakrishna."

He had said, "I want a band of sannyasis for my work. But some good parents must constitute the nucleus of a better order of things. From this shall originate the future society to outshine the past glory of India."

On the question of women's emancipation, he said, "There is no need of any set programme for uplifting women. Give them education and leave them free. They will work out the solution of their problems themselves."

Here are a few incidents that I heard from Swamiji which have been referred to by others. But I give the details as I heard them.

Swamiji said: "Then I used to beg my food from door to door in the Himalayas. Most of the time I spent in rigorous spiritual practices. The food that was available was very coarse, and often that too was insufficient to appease the hunger. One day I thought that my life was useless—these hill people were very poor themselves, and couldn't feed their own children and family properly. Yet they tried to save a little for me. Then what is the use of such a life? I stopped going out for food. Two days thus passed without any food. Whenever I was thirsty, I drank the water of the streams using my palms as a cup. Then I entered a deep jungle. There I meditated sitting on a piece of stone. My eyes were open, and suddenly I was aware of the presence of a large striped tiger. It looked at me with its shining eyes. I thought, 'At long last I shall find peace, and this animal shall find its food. It is enough that this body will be of some service to this creature.' I shut my eyes and waited for it, but a few seconds passed and I wasn't attacked. So, I opened my eyes and saw it going deeper into the forest. I was sorry for it and then smiled, for I knew it was the Master who was saving me till his work be done."

Here are a few of his remarks about the national traits of America and India. These were casual observations during his talks and discourses.

"I found the Americans to be full of rajas. They will now try to proceed to sattva. All Europe is predominantly active in achieving material success, but America leads them all in this respect."

"Indians had a preponderance of sattva guna during the days of rishis. Even now Indians have more sattva guna than people of any other country. India is still sattvika at heart, but it has an outer shell full of tamas. For a long time Indians have been passing through a great storm, and their bad days have not ended yet. It is hunger that is killing the nation, and the whole race is dying out slowly. Our duty is to give them food and education."

Once he said: "In America the beds are very soft and cozy. You do not even see such things here. But there have been many nights when I couldn't sleep in those soft beds, thinking of the extreme poverty of my own people. I have spent the night on the floor tossing and turning, without any sleep or rest.

"To change the condition of India, she must be fed and clothed properly. People must get education. The poor are our gods. They must be served with food and education.

"The Indians are religious at heart. For want of food and clothing the spiritual fire has become dimmed. When there will be no want and they get some education, the spiritual fire will blaze once more.

"Do not talk and think too much of child-marriage, widow-marriage, etc. When women get proper education and are enlightened, they will solve their problems themselves."

About brahmacharya and medha he seemed to hold the orthodox view. I heard him remark on his wonderful power of retentive memory in this manner: "If a man can be continent for twelve years, he can have extraordinary memory. One must be celibate and keep his brahmacharya intact even in his dreams."

He had once told me: "You must know that the sannyasi is the guru of the householders. Even if you but see the ochre cloth, bow down to it in reverence. Think of your own guru and pay your respect, whether the person is fit or unfit. Keep the ideal of renunciation before you, and the ochre cloth should remind you of the highest renunciation and knowledge."

To me he advised: "Choose one path. Do not keep your feet in two boats." He wanted me to become either a sannyasin or a householder. At that time was I unmarried. Later on, I chose to be a householder.

One day we were sitting in the room of the Math facing the Ganga. It was generally called the music-room. Nag Mahashaya entered the room. His dress was anything but neat. His hair was unkempt. His eyes were a little red as if he was intoxicated and his glance was rather vacant. He stood near the door within the room and with folded hands said to Swamiji: "You are Narayana—Narayana in a human form. The Master said so. My salutations to you." For some time he stood there as still as a statue.

Swamiji looked at us and said: "Look, engrave this scene in your memory. You will never see this again." Now I think it must have been a state of samadhi. When Nag Mahashaya opened his eyes again, Swamiji said, "Please, tell them something of the Master." Swamiji did not rise himself nor did he ask Nag Mahashaya to sit. Such an attempt would have jarred the ecstatic mood Nag Mahashaya was in at the time, and he would also have felt very uncomfortable.

Nag Mahashaya then suddenly smiled the heavenly smile of the gods who have the vision of Shiva's world. He half raised his right hand and said, "It is this, it is this." Every one felt a charge of spiritual energy and the atmosphere of the room was tense with awe and reverence. Then he went out as suddenly as he had come.

(*Vedanta Kesari*, January & April 1960)

S. K. Blodgett

I am ever recalling those swift, bright days in that never-to-be-forgotten winter, lived in simple freedom and kindliness. We could not choose but to be happy and good. And now while I share with all who knew and loved him a deep sense of loss, it would be an impertinence to measure your sorrow and loss by my own, so closely have you been associated with him in his intimate friendship with your family. I knew him personally but a short time, yet in that time I could but see in a hundred ways the child side of Swamiji's character, which was a constant appeal to the Mother quality in all good women. He depended upon those near him in a way which brought him very near one's heart. I think the Mead sisters must have marked this side of Swamiji.

Possessing as he did an almost inexhaustible knowledge of things old as the world—a sage and philosopher—he yet appeared to me to lack utterly the commercial knowledge which so distinguishes men of the Western world. You were constantly rendering him some apparently trifling service in the everyday homely happenings of our daily life, he in some small way requiring to be set right. That which we mother and care for in little, seemingly inconsequent ways must through the very nature of our care weave a world of tenderness around the object of our love—until in some sad day we are robbed of the divine privilege of loving service and are left like "Rachel mourning for her children because they are not". Thus I know, aside from the loss of a delightful and rare companion, the fact alone of your generous service brought him very near to you. One day busy with my work,

Swamiji absorbed with his curries and chapattis, I spoke to him of you, when he said: "Ah, yes! Jo is the sweetest spirit of us all"—He would come home from a lecture where he was compelled to break away from his audience, so eagerly would they gather around him—come rushing into the kitchen like a boy released from school, with, "Now we will cook". The prophet and sage would disappear, to reveal the child side or simplicity of character. Presently 'Jo' would appear and discover the culprit among pots and pans in his fine dress, who was by thrifty, watchful Jo admonished to change to his home garments.

Ah, those pleasant "Tea Party" days, as you termed them. How we used to laugh. Do you remember the time he was showing me how he wound his turban about his head and you were begging him to hasten as he was already due at the lecture room. I said: "Swami, don't hurry. You are like a man on his way to be hung. The crowd was jostling each other to reach the place of execution, when he called out, 'Don't hurry. There will be nothing interesting until I get there'. I assure you, Swami, there will be nothing interesting until you get there." This so pleased him that often afterwards he would say, "There will be nothing interesting till I get there," and laugh like a boy. Just now I recall a morning. Quite an audience had gathered at our house to listen to the learned Hindu, who sat with downcast eyes and impenetrable face while his audience waited. His meditations over, he raised his eyes to Mrs. Leggett's face and asked, like a simple child, "What shall I say?" This gifted man, possessing the subtle power of delighting an intellectual audience, to ask for a theme! There appeared to me in this question an exquisite touch of confidence in her judgement in suggesting a subject suitable to the occasion. A most interesting portion of the day you lost.

In the early morning when you and your sister would be sleeping, he would come in for his morning plunge in the bath. Soon his deep, rich voice would be heard in the something resembling a solemn chant. Though Sanskrit was an unknown tongue to me, I yet caught the spirit of it all, and these early morning devotions are among my sweetest recollections of the great Hindu. In the homely old-fashioned kitchen you and I have seen Swamiji at his best. He could let his thoughts have untrammelled sway.

Do you remember how interesting and instructive one morning he was in one of his inspirational moods? Something in the paper, an abused wife or maltreated child, had aroused my ire, when I vehemently protested against the utter abomination of a system of laws which permitted the indiscriminate production of a mongrel race of children who through heredity and environment were prenatally doomed to be paupers, lunatics, and criminals to prey upon the better born. My plea was for the enactment of a law to save the wretched from themselves by preventing worthless characters—boozy fathers and fool mothers—from forcing upon the world a blasphemy against God and a shameful profanation of His "image and likeness" in the shape of half-born children. Swamiji replied by taking us back to the time when a man's choice of a wife was emphasized with a club, step by step down through the ages showing the gradual amelioration of the condition of women. The evolution of thought had been broadening and developing for them greater freedom and happiness. The central idea in this morning's talk was that all great reforms had been developed slowly; otherwise, the order and equilibrium of the universe would be disturbed and result in chaos. Of course, I cannot follow him in detail or give his words. I can only give his idea. A curious thing to me, while I lost not a word nor failed to grasp the point he would make, I have yet found it impossible to repeat but fragmentary utterances of his. I question if one could repeat him in his inspirations. At such moments, one gave oneself up to the joy of listening.

I heard very few of Swamiji's public lectures. My age and household duties gave me no choice but like Martha to sit in the house. To follow in detail our pleasant hours at that time would be like one's repeating a dream from which one awoke too soon. Were you present at a lecture when one of those ladies who love to make themselves conspicuous by some ill-timed remark asked: "Swami, who is it who support the monks in your country? There are so many of them, you know." Like a flash Swami replied: "The same who support the clergy in your country, madam. The women!" The audience laughed. Madam was for the time effaced and Swamiji proceeded with his lecture.

Another time I was at a lecture of his in the Masonic Temple in Chicago. A noted clergyman present said, "You believe in creeds, do you not, monk?" "Oh, yes," said Swami, "while you need them. You plant an acorn for a tree and build around it a little fence to keep away the pigs and goats. But when your acorn has grown to a tall, spreading tree, you do not need your little fence." He was never at a loss—always equal to the occasion. And now "after life's fitful fever he sleeps well", never to be awakened to the discords and tumults of this life, or to be reclothed with an earthly body (in my belief), since this is true that we shall see him no more. Let us hope that in some distant star, above a world of separation and pain, his gentle spirit may again lead and influence the spirits of men. India has sustained a great loss in her Americanized son, who while he sacrificed no essential feature of their faith, yet saw things undreamed of by them, to their betterment and happiness. ... [1]

(*Prabuddha Bharata*, July 1963)

1. From a letter dated September 2, 1902, to Josephine MacLeod.

Ida Ansell

A ll the superlatives in the language couldn't convey one's impressions of Swami Vivekananda when he introduced us, early in 1900, to a completely new conception of life and religion. I have been requested, as one who took notes of his lectures for her own use, with no thought of their ever being published, to give my impressions of him. How to do it? He seemed like a radiant being from a higher plane, and yet so understanding of every phase of humanity. He appealed to every grade of intelligence by his oratory, his humour, his mimicry, his scornful denunciation of any form of pettiness or intolerance, and by his compassion for every human need.

Startled at the loftiness of his conception compared with our little ideals, we knew, as we left the hall with the Swami's vibrant chanting of a Sanskrit shloka still ringing within, that he was ushering us, in the beginning of this twentieth century, into a new and larger conception of the meaning of life.

It is interesting to look back on a long life and note the changes in one's sense of values, and also to note what tiny, insignificant events changed the whole course of life. If I had not accepted the offer of a course in stenography just before entering high school, and if, in the second year of high school I had not had a nervous breakdown and been forced to leave school, I might never have met Swamiji, although I probably would have heard some of his lectures. I had been studying the piano as well as going to school. The doctor, whose verdict was, "You must give up school or music, or you will not need either", sent me to Miss Lydia Bell for help. Miss Bell was the leader of the California Street Home of Truth in San Francisco. I was staying in the Home and taking notes of her morning classes and Sunday lectures.

In the morning classes we were studying Swami Vivekananda's *Raja Yoga* (it had been published in New York during his earlier visit to the West) when the Swami, then in Los Angeles, accepted an invitation from Rev. B. Fay Mills to give some lectures in the First Unitarian Church in Oakland. There I went with Miss Bell and other friends, early in February 1900, and we were startled and astonished at what we heard, amazed and enraptured at the Swami's appearance. He was surely a mahatma or a divine being, more than human. No one had ever been so sublimely eloquent or so deliciously humorous, such an entrancing story-teller, or such a perfect mimic. When I saw and heard him and thought of the interpretation we had been given of the civilization that had produced him, I felt almost ashamed that I was an American. I went to most of his lectures with Miss Bell and to some with other friends and met the same glowing enthusiasm in all, though with some it was the man rather than the doctrine that appealed most. I remember one very wealthy and aristocratic young lady, who was studying music with my teacher, saying ecstatically, "Oh, he is like a lovely golden statue!"

Besides the public lectures, Swamiji had some morning classes for earnest students, in meditation. They were held in the living room of an apartment on Turk Street where Mrs. Alice Hansborough (Shanti) and Mrs. Emily Aspinall (Kalyani) kept house for him. I was able to attend only a few of these classes and did not take any notes. First there would be a meditation and then a period of instruction, followed by questions and answers and practical suggestions as to exercise, rest, and diet. Swamiji stressed the importance of moderation in amount and mildness in quality of food. One suggestion I remember was that we refrain from eating salt for a week, thereby benefiting the nervous system, as salt is considered an irritant.

Many questions were answered in these classes. Also, for those who arrived before class time, there was a little opportunity for getting acquainted personally with the Swami. We were invited into the dining room, where we enjoyed some informal talks. He would make fun of our habit of rushing here and there. He never hurried. That majestic calmness never left him. It amused him to see someone run for a street car. "Won't there be another one?" he would ask. It did not trouble him at all if he was late in beginning a class or a lecture, and there was no set time for its ending. He would continue until he finished his subject, even if it took more than double the allotted time. These early morning visits previous to the class were completely informal. Swamiji would wear a grey flannel robe, sit cross-legged in an armchair, smoke, answer questions, and tell jokes. When it was time for the class, he would appear two minutes later in the living room, clad in his ochre robe, his hair smooth, and the pipe missing. But the jokes continued to be interspersed among the serious subjects.

The same was true in his public lectures. He playfully ridiculed the question: What becomes of one's individuality when one realizes his oneness with God? "You people in this country are so afraid of losing your in-di-vid-u-al-i-ty!" he would exclaim. "Why, you are not individuals yet. When you realize your whole nature, you will attain your true individuality, not before. In knowing God you cannot lose anything. There is another thing I am constantly hearing in this country, and that is that we should live in harmony with nature. Don't you know that all the progress ever made in the world was made by conquering nature? We are to resist nature at every point if we are to make any progress."

He encouraged questions at the end of each lecture, and once when someone suggested that they were tiring him with too many questions, he said: "Ask all the questions you like, the more the better. That is what I am here for and I won't leave you until you understand. In India they tell me, I ought not to teach Advaita Vedanta to the people at large, but I say I can make even a child understand it. You cannot begin too early to teach the highest spiritual truths."

Speaking of spiritual training for the mind, he said: "The less you read, the better. Read the *Gita* and other good works on Vedanta. That is all you need. The present system of education is all wrong. The mind is crammed with facts before it knows how to think. Control of the mind should be taught first. If I had my education to get over again and had any voice in the matter, I would learn to master my mind first, and then gather facts if I wanted them. It takes people a long time to learn things because they can't concentrate their minds at will. It took me three readings to memorize Macaulay's *History of England,* while my mother memorized any sacred book she wanted to in one reading. People are always suffering because they can't control their minds. To give an illustration, though rather a crude one, a man has trouble with his wife. She leaves him and goes off with another. She's a terror! But the poor fellow cannot take his mind away from her even so, and so he suffers."

One Sunday evening Swamiji was scheduled to give a lecture at the Home of Truth. "Come to my lecture tonight," he said to some friends. "I am going to throw some bombs. It will be interesting and it will do you good!" It was interesting and terribly convincing. He told us in plain and forceful language just what he thought of us and it was not flattering, but very wholesome if we could take it, and I think we could. I don't remember that anyone left. He stressed the idea of chastity as a means of strengthening the mind, and purity for the householder as well as for the monk. He told of a Hindu boy who had been in America for some time and was suffering from ill health. The boy told Swamiji that the Indian theory of chastity must be wrong because the doctors here had advised him against it. Swamiji said: "I told him to go back to India and listen to the teachings of his ancestors who had practised chastity for thousands of years." And then he severely rebuked the American doctors for giving such advice.

Mrs. Steele had prepared an excellent dinner which was served before the lecture, at which Swamiji was delightfully informal and jolly. We waited expectantly for him to say the usual grace, but to our surprise he immediately commenced to eat. He made some remark about saying grace after dinner rather than before, and he also said, addressing Mrs. Steele, "I will say grace to you, Madame; you have done all the work." She had some very fine dates for desert, which Swami evidently enjoyed, and when, after the lecture she expressed her appreciation of it, he replied, "It was your dates, Madame."

One evening Swamiji was talking of the different interpretations of heaven and hell presented in the Indian scriptures. He described several varieties of hell. Usually after a lecture some of the devotees would take him either to Mr. Louis Juhl's restaurant in the section of San Francisco known as Little Italy or to some uptown cafe, depending on whether his mood and the weather called for hot food or ice-cream. On this particular occasion it was a very cold night and Swamiji shivered in his overcoat, remarking, "If this isn't hell, I don't know what is." But, in spite of the hellishly cold weather, he chose ice-cream, which he liked very much. Just as it was time to leave the cafe the hostess had to go to the telephone and asked us to wait. As she left for that purpose, Swamiji called after her, "Well don't be long or when you come back you will find only a lump of chocolate ice-cream."

On another occasion a waitress made a mistake in the order and brought Swamiji an ice-cream soda, which he did not like. He asked her if she would change it. As she was on her way to do so Swamiji happened to see the annoyed manager, and called out loudly, not caring who heard him, "If you scold that girl I'll eat all the ice-cream sodas in the place."

Congregational singing in the Christian churches he referred to as "bottle-breaking business". He made all sorts of fun of "Beulah Land":

I've reached the land of corn and wine
And all its riches freely mine.

Another hymn that amused him was the "Missionary Hymn":
From Greenland's icy mountains
To India's coral strand. ...

He would sing it all through to the end, in his rich voice, and then pause, point dramatically at himself, and say, smilingly: "I am the heathen they came to save."

On March 30 Swamiji wrote to Swami Turiyananda, who was then in New York helping Swami Abhedananda, "I am leaving for Chicago next week." But more lectures followed and on April 23 he wrote to Mary Hale: "I ought to have started today, but cannot forego the temptation to be in a camp under the high redwood trees of California before I leave. Therefore I postpone it for three or four days." As it turned out he should have said "three or four weeks", for he did not leave the Bay district until May 26.

The invitation to be in such a camp had come to him from Miss Bell, to whom Mr. Juhl, the owner, offered it for a summer vacation. Miss Bell invited Mrs. Eloise Roorbach and me to accompany her. Various letters indicate that Swamiji remained in the Turk Street apartment until April 19, then worked and lived at Alameda on the other side of the Bay for some days, not actually reaching the redwood camp until May 2.

On April 22, Miss Bell, Mrs. Roorbach, and I were established at Camp Irving (the name of Mr. Juhl's camp at the outskirts of Camp Taylor, a rustic summer retreat in Mann County) a few miles north of San Francisco. The camp ground was a narrow strip of land between a railroad track and a creek. There was a circular clump of trees at one end which we used as a sort of chapel for classes and meditation. The kitchen was at the other end and its equipment consisted of a stove under a tree, a trunk for supplies, a rough board table with benches on either side, and some shelves built into the tree for dishes, the pots and pans being hung on nails driven into the tree. Between these two provisions for spiritual and material food there was room for four tents and an open space for a camp-fire.

When Swamiji did reach the camp, he arrived with Shanti after a series of efforts to get there which she related to me when I was in San Francisco a few years ago. She told me of her mental conflict in regard to going to the camp. She was torn between the desire to accompany Swamiji and the wish, after three months' absence, to get back to her daughter in Los Angeles. Swami said to her: "Don't go to Los Angeles. Come with me to the camp and I will teach you to meditate." In order to go from Alameda to Camp Irving it was necessary to take two ferry boats, one across the Bay to San Francisco and one north from there to Mann County. In Alameda there were two rail-road lines which carried passengers to the docks, one broad gauge and one narrow gauge, just a few blocks apart. Swamiji and Shanti missed the train at one of them and went to the other. Seated in the car, they discussed the matter of whether to have breakfast on the boat from Alameda to San Francisco or on the boat from San Francisco to Mann County, and then discovered that there was no engine attached to the car in which they were sitting. They returned to the Home and had breakfast there, and Swamiji said, "We missed the train because your heart was in Los Angeles and there is no force or power in the universe that can pull against the human heart."

Shanti told me of how, after reading Swamiji's books for two years, she had first heard him lecture in Los Angeles the winter of 1899-1900. At once she had been eager to help in his work. A society was organized of which Shanti was the first Secretary. Lectures were given at Blanchard Hall, the Los Angeles Home of Truth, the Shakespeare Club of Pasadena, and other places. Swami had been staying at the home of

Mrs. S. K. Blodgett. He was also the guest of the Mead sisters in South Pasadena, of whom Shanti was one. The other two were Mrs. Carrie Mead Wyckoff, who in later years gave her Hollywood home as the headquarters of the Vedanta Society of Southern California, and Helen Mead, who took some of Swamiji's Los Angeles lectures in shorthand. When Swamiji left for Oakland, he said, "You three sisters have become a part of my mind for ever."

Shanti told me: "Swamiji had such simplicity about him, he put one right on a level with himself. He said to me, 'You have no reverence.' When I told this to Swami Turiyananda, he remarked: 'Yes, he said that, but he was pleased that you did not have reverence. Where there is equality there is exchange of perfect love. Where there is no superior and inferior you have that perfect union.'"

When Swamiji received the invitation to lecture in the Unitarian Church in Oakland, he asked Shanti if she would like to accompany him north. He said, "If you want to go with me, don't let anybody keep you from coming." So Shanti went to San Francisco and at last to Camp Irving. There she was very active in caring for Swami's needs and comfort. One morning he found her in the kitchen preparing food when it was time for his morning class. "Aren't you coming in to meditate?" he asked. "Yes," she replied, "but I have to get this broth simmering first. Then I shall come in."

Then Swamiji said, "Well, never mind; our Master said you could leave meditation for service."

Two never-to-be-forgotten nights stand out in my long life. To think of either of them is a cure for any ill. One is the first night at Shanti Ashrama with Swami Turiyananda, about whom I have already written. The other is Swamiji's first night at Camp Taylor, May 2, 1900. I close my eyes and see him standing there in the soft blackness with sparks from the blazing log fire flying through it and a day-old moon above. He was weary after a long lecture season, but relaxed and happy to be there. "We end life in the forest," he said, "as we begin it, but with a world of experience between the two states." Later after a short talk, when we were about to have the usual meditation, he said: "You may meditate on whatever you like, but I shall meditate on the heart of a lion. That gives strength." The bliss and power and peace of the meditation that followed could never be described.

The next day it rained all day. In the morning after breakfast Swamiji sat on Miss Bell's cot and talked for a long time, although even then he had a fever. That night he was very ill, so ill that he made a will, leaving everything to his brother-disciples. Shanti and Kalyani took care of him. I can see Shanti now, in the pouring rain, heedless of getting drenched, spreading an extra piece of canvas over his tent directly opposite to the one I shared with Miss Bell.

The next day was Saturday and Miss Bell and I had to go to San Francisco. When we returned Sunday afternoon, Swamiji was better. He had been invited to the camp to rest, but every day after breakfast he would sit on Miss Bell's cot and talk to us for a long time, telling stories, answering questions. He told of his hopes for a better understanding of the East and the West and their mutual benefit thereby. He told of his love for Thomas à Kempis and how he had travelled all over India with two books, the *Gita* and *The Imitation of Christ*. In one of his lectures in San Francisco Swamiji closed with a quotation from the latter: "Silence all teachers, silence all books; do Thou only speak unto my soul."

After the morning talk and meditation, Swami would be interested in the preparations for dinner. Sometimes he helped. He made curry for us and showed us how they grind spices in India. He would sit on the floor in his tent with a hollow stone in his lap. With another smooth, round stone he would grind the spices much finer than we can do with a bowl and chopper. This would make the curry quite hot enough for us, but Swami would augment it by eating tiny red-hot peppers on the side. He would throw his head back and toss them into his mouth with a great circular movement of his arm. Once he handed me one of them, saying: "Eat it. It will do you good." One would eat poison if offered by Swamiji, so I obeyed, with agonizing result, to his great amusement. At intervals all the afternoon he kept asking, "How is your oven?" Another time he made rock candy for us, explaining how it is the purest kind of candy, all the impurities being removed by boiling and boiling.

The meals were jolly and informal, with no end of jokes and stories. Shanti had been to Alaska and was accustomed to roughing it, and her carefree spirit and indifference to conventions pleased Swamiji. At one breakfast he reached over and took a little food from her plate, saying, "It is fitting that we should eat from the same plate; we are two vagabonds." He also said to her again, "You have become part of my life for ever," and to Kalyani he remarked that even if she had lived on the highest mountain she would have had to come down to take care of him. "I know it, Swami," she replied.

Nothing escaped Swami's notice. Some work was being done on the place by a Mexican or American Indian, and Swami noticed that he watched us having breakfast. Later on he talked to the boy, who complained of not having been given any coffee. He said, "Black man like coffee; white man like coffee; red man like coffee." This amused Swami very much. He requested that the boy be given some coffee, and all the afternoon he kept repeating the boy's remark and laughing.

The afternoons were devoted to long walks. The grand climax of the day's activities was the evening fireside talk and the following meditation. After telling stories and answering questions Swamiji would give us a subject for meditation such as "Firm and Fearless" before beginning to chant. One morning he inspired us with a talk on "Absolute Truth, Unity, Freedom" and the subject for the evening meditation was "I am All Existence, Bliss, and Knowledge."

So the days went by all too fast, with serious mornings, merry afternoons, and sublime evenings.

When Miss Bell invited me to spend the summer with her at Camp Irving, it was agreed that I would go down to

San Francisco each Saturday morning, give a music lesson in the afternoon, and return Sunday after her lecture, which I was to try to take in shorthand. On the second week-end Miss Bell, for some reason that I have forgotten, went alone to San Francisco on Friday afternoon, with the understanding that I was to follow on Saturday.

When I was getting ready to take the train as usual, Swamiji said to me, "Why do you go?"

"I have to go, Swami," I replied. "I have to give a lesson." I have always regretted the answer, for the dollar I received for the lesson was not the motive for going. The real motive was Miss Bell's lecture.

Swamiji said, "Then go, and make half million dollars and send it to me for my work in India." He took me up the steep steps to the railroad track and flagged the train for me. There was no station and the train stopped only on signal. Swamiji's carriage was magnificent. His eyes were always turned skyward, never down. Someone said of him that he never saw anything lower than a telegraph pole.

When the engine passed us, as the train slowed down, I heard the fireman say to the engineer, "Hello! Who is this sky pilot?" I had never heard the expression and was puzzled at first as to its meaning. Then I realized that it must mean a religious leader, and that it was evident to any one who saw him that Swamiji was such a leader.

It has always been a matter of regret that I went to San Francisco that weekend, for soon after that Swami left Camp Irving. The half million dollars for his work in India has not been made, but I have never given up the childish hope that in some miraculous way it may yet be accomplished. Swami Turiyananda said many times, "Mother can make the impossible possible."

I do not know the exact date that Swamiji left Camp Irving, but various letters written by him indicate that he was still in San Francisco on the 26th of May and that he was under the care of Dr. M. H. Logan, at whose home he stayed, and gave three lectures on the *Gita* on May 26, 28, and 29. He wrote from Los Angeles on June 17, "Am leaving for Chicago in a few days," and he was in New York on July 11.

Tom Allan and his wife Edith (Ajoy and Viraja) are my oldest friends and they have told me many times of their first impressions of Swamiji and their experiences with him, and of the immense benefit they received from him. Edith was very ill when Swamiji first came to Oakland in 1900 and Tom went alone to hear the Hindu monk whose lecture was advertised in the paper. When he returned, he was very much excited and could scarcely contain his enthusiasm. He said: "I have met a man who is not a man; he is a god! And he spoke the truth!" Edith asked him to tell her what he had said that impressed him so much, and the two most startling ideas were these:

Good and evil are the obverse and reverse of the same coin; and you cannot have one without the other. We had been taught in the Home of Truth that all is good and there is no evil. The other idea that deeply impressed him was that a cow cannot tell a lie and a man can, but the cow will always be a cow, while a man can become divine.

Tom immediately began to give his services as usher in Swamiji's lectures, and as soon as she was able, Edith went to hear him. It was while she was standing near the entrance waiting for Tom to count the collection that Swamiji saw her, and called to her, "Madame, you come here." She went to him and he said: "If you would like to see me privately come to the flat. No collection is taken there; everything is free."

"When shall I come?" she asked.

"Tomorrow morning at nine o'clock."

She went to the flat the next morning and sat on one side of a bay window. Swamiji came in chanting and sat at the other side of the window. "Well, Madame," he said. Edith was so moved that she could not speak and could not stop crying for a long time. Then Swamiji said, "Come tomorrow morning at the same time." She went to him several times for spiritual instruction. He gave her some simple breathing exercises, warning her not to practise them except in his presence. He told her that he thought the work of the Home of Truth was the best then available in the West, and he appreciated the fact that the workers there did not charge for spiritual assistance, as some others did.

One time Swamiji said: "I am the disciple of a man who could not write his own name, but I am not worthy to unloose his shoes. How often I have wished that I could take this intellect and throw it in the Ganga."

"But Swami," protested one woman, "your intellect is what we like about you." "That is because you are a fool, Madame, as I am," was Swamiji's answer.

At the end of the last meeting of the class, Edith was departing quietly when Swamiji shouted: "Madame, you come back. Go into the dining room and sit down." When he finished saying good-bye to the others, he went in and asked her to stay for dinner. Then he began to cook and made her peel potatoes and onions. While working, he was chanting verses from the *Gita* and once he stopped and recited in English the sixty-first verse of the eighteenth chapter: "The Lord lives in the heart of every creature. He turns them round and round upon the wheel of his maya." "You see, Madame," he said, "he has us on the wheel. What can we do?"

When Swamiji was staying for a time at the Alameda Home of Truth, Edith had some wonderful times helping him cook. While the service was going on in the living room, they would be busy in the kitchen preparing the meal. There he was jolly and informal, but she was also given many incidental lessons. Once she was wearing a new green dress of which she was very proud. Suddenly some butter from the frying pan spattered on it. She was bemoaning the mishap and making a great tragedy of it, while Swami continued to chant and go about his work without taking the slightest notice of the incident.

Once they bought some pickles in a little wooden dish. Some of the pickle juice ran out on Swami's hand. He immediately put his fingers to his mouth and began to lick off the liquid. This seemed undignified, and Edith said, "Oh Swami!" in a shocked tone. "This little outside," Swami replied. "That's the trouble with you here; you always want this outside to be so nice."

Tom told me many of his experiences. He acted as usher at Swamiji's lectures and several times introduced him to the audience. The first time they stood together on the platform, Tom had the feeling that Swamiji's height was about forty feet and his about six inches. After that, when introducing him, he always stood at the foot of the platform. On one occasion Swamiji was speaking on India. Before beginning the lecture he said, "When I start on India I never know when to stop; so you attract my attention at ten o'clock." So Tom stood at the back of the hall and at ten o'clock took out his watch and swung it back and forth on the chain like a pendulum. After a time Swamiji noticed the signal and said: "I told them to stop me at ten o'clock. They are already swinging the watch and I haven't got started yet." But he stopped and, from that time on as long as he lived, Tom Allan always carried and used every day that same old watch.

On Easter Sunday night a group of friends were sitting on the porch of the Home of Truth, and Swamiji was telling some of his experiences in America. On one occasion he was advised to consult a lady chiropodist for some foot treatment. He evidently did not think very highly of her, for he always referred to her as the lady toe-doctor and said, "My toe hurts every time I think of her."

That evening someone asked Swamiji about renunciation. "Babies!" he answered, "what do you know of renunciation? If you want to be my disciples, you must face the cannon without a murmur."

Tom was English and had been an officer in the British Army. His speciality was naval engineering, and he had a stiff military bearing. Swamiji once said to him, as Tom stood up in his presence: "Mr. Allan, we are both in the same caste. We are in the military caste." When Tom asked him where he found his best disciples, Swamiji replied promptly: "In England. They are harder to get, but when you get them, you've got them.

Swamiji always attracted attention wherever he went. He had a majestic bearing which everybody recognized. As he would walk down Market Street, people would stand aside to let him pass or turn around and ask, "Who is the Hindu prince?" It was in this way that he was able to see a ship launched from the actual launching platform. Tom was working in one of the big iron works of San Francisco at the time, and when Swamiji expressed a wish to see a launching, he invited a little group to the shipyard. The launching platform was closed except to the invited guests of the management who had tickets, and the ramp leading to the platform was guarded by two attendants. Swamiji decided he would have a better view from the launching platform, so he just calmly walked past the guards, who made no protest. When he came down, after the launching, he said, "It is like the birth of a child."

Swamiji emphasized the fact that spiritual people are not fanatical or severe. "They are not long-faced and thin," he said. "They are fat, like me."

During one of the talks in Miss Bell's tent at Camp Irving, Miss Bell remarked that the world is a school where we come to learn our lesson. Swamiji asked, "Who told you that the world is a school?"

Miss Bell was silent. Swamiji went on, "This world is a circus, and we are clowns come to tumble." Miss Bell asked, "Why do we tumble, Swamiji?" Swamiji replied: "Because we like to tumble. When we get tired of tumbling, we quit."

Tom and Edith had an apartment in San Francisco which was permeated with the atmosphere of Swamiji. All the Swamis of the Ramakrishna Order in this country loved to visit them when they went to San Francisco, and some of them said or wrote, "You, more than anybody else in the West, are able to make Swamiji real to us." One of my friends said of them when she and her son visited the Allans a few years ago that their account of Swami Vivekananda was so full of joy and so vivid, it seemed as though he himself could walk into the room. There was a beautiful picture of him in the dining room, and the guests were always seated facing it. Chanting always preceded the meal, and there was little talk of anything during it other than of Swamiji, his Master, and his work. All his books were there, and the Allans had an enormous collection of pictures which they enjoyed showing to their guests. One particular favourite was taken in a garden. Swamiji was lying on the grass, enjoying a conversation with some friends, when someone came and wanted to take his picture. He did not want to get up but, urged by all to do so, he stood up, just as he was, without turban or robe, against a background of flowering vines, looking as if about to speak, and the result is one of his best portraits.

Edith had a nice contralto voice, and sometimes she would sing, with deep feeling, some of the songs associated with Swamiji. A favourite was the song of the nautch-girl, which she adapted from Swamiji's translation of a song sung by a courtesan in the palace of a Raja where he was staying just before leaving for America the first time. Although he left the room when he learnt that this girl was about to sing, he heard the song from outside and was so moved by the words and her manner of singing that he returned and spoke most beautifully to her, even thanking her for the lesson she had given him, thus removing the last vestige of a possible spiritual pride, and completing the preparation for his work in the West.

Never since the day Swamiji perceived Edith's need for help has he been out of her mind. Many times in the last fifty years she has remembered the words spoken at their last meeting: "If ever you are in trouble, you can call on me. No matter where I am, I'll hear you." Many ordeals she has met bravely, sustained by that promise.

In one of his lectures Swamiji said: "If a bad time comes, what of that? The pendulum must swing back to the other side. But that is no better. The thing to do is to stop it." Then he uttered an American expression which children used to use when swinging, when they would stop pumping and let the swing slow down to a halt: "Let the old cat die."

To have seen and heard Swamiji and to have *felt* his words of power flow through me on to paper and thence to print for many to read, thereby receiving courage and inspiration, is a rare privilege and is compensation for all ills of life. It makes me almost ready to let the old cat die.

(*Vedanta and the West*, May-June 1954)

Christina Albers

I met Swami Vivekananda in San Francisco in California. It was at a lecture in the year 1900.

The Swami arrived some twenty minutes before the lecture and was engaged in conversation with some friends. I sat at a short distance from him and was very deeply interested, for I felt he was one who had something to give to me. The conversation was of the ordinary nature, and yet I felt a peculiar force emanating from him.

His health was poor at the time, and when he rose to go to the platform, it seemed an effort on his part. He walked with a heavy gait. I noticed that his eyelids were swollen, and he looked like one who suffers pain.

He stood for a while in silence before he spoke, and I saw a change. His countenance brightened, and I thought his very features were different now.

He began to speak, and there was a transformation. The soul-force of the great man became visible. I felt the tremendous force of his speech—words that were felt more than they were heard. I was drawn into a sea of being, of feelings of a higher existence, from which it seemed almost like pain to emerge when the lecture was finished. And then those eyes, how wonderful! They were like shooting stars—lights shooting forth from them in constant flashes. Over thirty years have elapsed since the day, but the memory of it is evergreen in my heart and will remain so. His years on earth were not many. But, what are years when the value of a life is weighed? Unknown and ignored, he entered the lecture hall of the great metropolis of Chicago in 1893. He left that hall an adored hero. He spoke. It was enough. The depth of his great soul had sounded forth, and the world felt the vibration. One single man changed the current of thought of half the globe—that was his work.

The body is subject to decay. The great strain put upon him, weighed on the physical—his work was done. Scarcely forty years of life on earth, but they were forty years that outweighed centuries. He was sent from higher regions to fulfil a great mission, and that mission being fulfilled he returned to his seat among the gods, whence he had come.

> Great soul, thy work will live for evermore.
> We felt thy wondrous being from afar.
> Thou brought the whispers of the morning star,
> The murmur of the waves from greater shore.
> I heard thy voice in torrents bold and free,
> And yet the sweetness that flowed through it all
> Was like the song of sylvan water-fall,
> Like murmur round a cave in Southern Sea.
> Thou'st sent thy message thund'ring through the years.
> To hear thee was to blend the silver note,
> The mellow warble of the songbird's throat,
> With thunderbolt that comes from other spheres.
> And still we feel the pow'r of that great love,
> That noble spirit gently hover near,
> To give us courage in this darker Sphere,
> Blessings from realms of greater bliss above.

(*Prabuddha Bharata*, August 1938)

Isabel Margesson

I n response to your wish that I should write a few words recalling early memories of my friendship with and admiration for Swami Vivekananda, I find to my regret that they have grown faint after the lapse of nearly forty years.

Perhaps it is as it should be: The memories have become absorbed into his teaching, and they live as the inspiration of my deepest thoughts and are hardly to be separated from the undercurrent of my daily life. The main impression left on me is that I had been in touch with a truth that was so large and so *gründlich* that it contained in itself all that I had previously believed. It became a ground pattern, or a mosaic, capable of constant adjustment to fit the needs of my growing thought.

Let me quote some of those sayings of the Master that have moulded my character in the most positive way under the stress of joy and sorrow, of anxiety and illness, and of the many perplexities that invariably accompany us when we start the way.

I must put first that they are a key to all the rest. Without it, I can confidently affirm, there can be no real inner growth or progress of the soul in its search for Peace and for Reality.

The key lies in daily meditation. The Master's words on this subject can never be forgotten. I am well aware that of late years it has been recognized as the pearl of great price in almost all spiritual enlightenment, but when I first heard the Swami's lessons on it, it was new to me. The monkey mind, the charioteer who controls the horses (i.e., the senses), the silence of the Inner Self, the necessity of practise, the study of the teaching which teaches liberation of the Self, discrimina-

ISABEL MARGESSON

tion between the Real and the unreal, are thoughts and phrases that will at once recall the Swami to his disciples. Other words of practical wisdom, as I remember them in my own inadequate words are:

1. Grow up within the fold of your own particular church, but do not die in it. Let it gradually lead you into fresh pastures.
2. As scaffolding is an indispensable factor in material building, so is it in spiritual attainment. Do not destroy it either for yourself or for others (the Gospel says. "Let both grow until the harvest"), but wait for the inevitable moment of its automatic destruction.
3. Never debase your ethical standard by calling wrong right. If you know that an act of yours is wrong, do it if you wish, but do not call it right for that is a fatal self-deception.
4. Say to yourself when you repent of some small action: "I am glad I did that wrong, for now I see and I shall never do it again."
5. Unselfish work for other people must be regarded as beneficial to the doer, for it is the doer that gains in his character.
6. Do not identify your Self with any mental state. Perhaps this injunction is specially fundamental in sorrow or pity for the Self. Nothing leads so directly to wise judgement as holding the Real Self free from the unreal Self.
7. The greatest heresy is separation.
8. Unity is the Goal of Religion and of Science.
9. I am That.

I must add to these great sayings the stories told by the Swami—inimitable stories which illustrated the points in his teaching. They became like the parables in the Bible—marvellous "lamps of light unto our feet."

Disciples of the Swami will remember the story of the lion brought up as a sheep but awakening afterwards to its true nature; of the man who lost his wife and children and possessions in a flood, but when was himself cast up safely on a bank and came to himself, he found the disaster was all a dream and that he was now just as he was before the flood.

(*Prabuddha Bharata*, February 1939)

Viraja Devi

E arly in March 1900 the Swami Vivekananda gave a series
of three lectures on "Indian Ideals" in Redmen's Hall,
Union Square, San Francisco, and it was at the first lecture
of this series that I had the blessed privilege of hearing
him. Being in ill health, both mentally and physically, it
was a great effort to go to the lecture; and as I sat in the
hall waiting for the Swami to come, I began to wonder
whether I had not made a mistake in coming to hear him;
but all doubts vanished when the Swami's majestic figure
entered the hall. He talked for about two hours telling us
of India's ideals and taking us with him, as it were, to his
own country so that we might understand him a little and
be able to comprehend even in the least the great truths he
taught. After the lecture, I was introduced to the Swami;
but feeling overawed by his wonderful presence, I did not
speak, but sat down at a distance and watched him, while
waiting for friends who were busy settling up the business
connected with the lectures. After the second lecture, I was
again waiting, sitting at a distance watching the Swami,
when he looked across and beckoned to me to come to him.
I went and stood before him as he sat in a chair. He said,
"Madame, if you want to see me privately, you come to the
flat on Turk Street. No charge there, none of this botheration
about money."

I told him I should like very much to see him. He said,
"Come tomorrow morning", and I thanked him. Much of
the night was spent thinking of all the questions I should ask
him, as many questions had been troubling me for months

VIRAJA DEVI

and no one to whom I had gone was able to help me. On arriving at the flat next morning, I was told that the Swami was going out, so could not see any one. I said I knew he would see me because he had told me I might come, so I was allowed to go up the stairs and into the front sitting-room. In a little while the Swami came into the room, dressed in his long overcoat and little round hat, chanting softly. He sat on a chair on the opposite side of the room and continued chanting softly in his incomparable way. Presently he said "Well, Madame!" I could not speak but began to weep and kept on weeping as though the floodgates had been opened. The Swami continued chanting for a while, then said, "Come tomorrow about the same time."

Thus ended my first interview with the blessed Swami Vivekananda, and as I went from his presence, my problems were solved and my questions were answered, though he had not asked me anything. It is now over twenty-four years since that interview with the Swami, yet it stands out in memory as the greatest blessing of my life. I had the wonderful privilege of seeing Swamiji every day for a month, and was in the meditation class which he held in Turk Street.

I used to stay after the class and help him cook lunch etc., or rather, he allowed me to be in the kitchen with him and do odd jobs for him, while he talked Vedanta and chanted and cooked. One verse from the *Gita* he chanted a great deal is verse 61, Chapter 18: "The Lord dwells in the hearts of all beings, O Arjuna, by His illusive power, causing all beings to revolve as though mounted on a potter's wheel."

He chanted it in Sanskrit, and every now and then would stop and talk of it. He was so wonderful, his nature so many-sided, at times so childlike, at times the Vedanta Lion, but to me always the kind and loving parent. He told me not to call him Swami, but to call him "Babaji", as the children did in India. Once when walking along the street with Swamiji after a lecture, all at once he seemed to me so big, as though he towered above the ordinary mortals. The people on the street looked like pigmies, and he had such a majestic presence that people stepped aside to let him pass by. One evening after the lecture, Swamiji insisted upon taking a party of about ten or twelve of us to have ice-cream. Some ordered ice-cream and some ice-cream soda. Swamiji was fond of ice-cream but did not care for ice-cream soda. The waitress who took the order made a mistake and brought ice-cream soda for the Swami; she said she would change it for him. The proprietor spoke to the waitress about it, and when Swamiji heard him, he called out: "Don't you scold that poor girl. I'll take all the ice-cream soda if you are going to scold her."

After living in Turk Street for a month, Swamiji went to Alameda and stayed at the "Home of Truth". It was quite a large house and was surrounded by a beautiful garden, where the Swamiji used to walk about in smoking. There was quite a large porch on the house on which Swamiji sat sometimes talking to the few of us who gathered around him. The Easter Sunday night was the full moon, the wisteria was in full bloom and draped the porch like a curtain. Swamiji sat on the porch smoking and telling funny stories. He told of how his feet hurt him when he wore shoes in Chicago, and of his experience with a lady doctor who had undertaken to doctor his toe. He said: "Oh my toe, my toe! Whenever I think of that lady doctor, my toe hurts." Then one of the party asked him to talk on "Renunciation". "Renunciation?" said Swamiji, "Babies, what do you know of renunciation?" "Are we too young even to hear of it?" was asked. Swamiji was silent for a while and then gave a most illuminating and inspiring talk. He spoke of disciple-ship and of entire resignation to the guru, which was quite a new teaching to the Western world. While in Alameda Swamiji used to cook Hindu dishes for himself on Sunday afternoons, and I again had the privilege of being with him and partaking of his dishes; and although I attended all of Swamiji's public lectures both in San Francisco and Alameda, it was this close contact with the Swamiji that I most deeply cherish. Once after being quiet for some time Swamiji said:

"Madame, be broad-minded, always see two ways. When I am on the Heights I say 'I am He', and when I have a stomach-ache, I say 'Mother, have mercy on me'. Always see two ways." On another occasion he said: "Learn to be the witness. If there are two dogs fighting on the street and I go out there, I get mixed up in the fight but if I stay quietly in my room, I witness the fight from the window. So learn to be the witness." While in Alameda Swamiji gave public lectures in Tucker Hall. He finished one wonderful lecture, "The Ultimate Destiny of Man", by placing his hand on his chest and saying "I am God". A most awed silence fell upon the audience, and many people thought it blasphemy for Swamiji to say such a thing.

Once he did something in rather an unconventional way, and I was a little shocked at him. He said, "O Madame, you always want this little outside to be so nice. It is not the outside that matters, it is the inside."

How little we understood Swamiji. We had no knowledge of what he really was. Sometimes he would tell me things, and I in the abundance of my ignorance, would tell him I did not think that way, and he would laugh and say, "Don't you?" His love and toleration was wonderful. Swamiji was not in good health—much lecturing told upon him. He used to say he did not like platform work, "Public lecturing is killing. At eight o'clock I am to speak on 'Love'. At eight o'clock I do not feel like love!"

After he finished lecturing in Alameda, the Swami went to Camp Taylor and a little later started for the East and we in California never saw him again. Yet we who were blessed by his presence cannot feel he is entirely gone from us. He lives in our memories and in the teachings he gave us. Before he left, he told me if I ever got into psychic difficulty again to call on him and he would hear me wherever he was, even though hundreds of miles away, and it may be he can hear even now.

(Vedanta Kesari, September 1924)

C. Ramanujachari

My reminiscences of Swami Vivekananda must necessarily be fragmentary, but even fragments of Swamiji are too important to be forgotten.

I had three opportunities to meet Vivekananda during my life. The first was in February 1893, when he was in Chennai as a parivrajaka. He was a guest of one Mr. Bhattacharya, Accountant General of Chennai, who lived in a bungalow called Rahmat Bhag on the Beach Road, San Thome. Swamiji was given a suite of rooms in the western portion of the house. We, as students, had heard of a monk called Satchidananda Swami who had come from the North, was remarkably intelligent, and had an amazing personality. We had heard of his having met some young men at Chennai—Mr. M. C. Alasinga Perumal of the Pachaiyappa's College, G. Venkataranga Rao, D. R. Balaji Rao, latterly of the Indian Bank, G. G. Narasimhachari, and some members of the Triplicane Literary Society, a lively association of young men who had been active in inviting prominent men to speak at their Society's premises. The Swami must have been introduced to them through Mr. Bhattacharya.

The Swami first spoke at the Literary Society of Triplicane to a small audience. The impression he created then was that he was a remarkable speaker, and young men were first attracted to him chiefly for this. But immediately there followed the realization by the elders that within this magnificent personality were hoarded a prodigious intellect, profound learning, a fire of sincere patriotism, sparkling wit and, above all, an unbending spirit of renunciation. Soon Chennai came to know that here was a man who had a power that lifted him above all others, and everybody vied with each other to have a glimpse of him.

One morning, staff in hand, he walked majestically along the Luz Church Road followed by about fifteen or twenty young men. He was on his way to Mylapore, to the west, to Sir S. Subramania Iyer's house to see him and place before him a proposal that he—Swamiji—be sent to America for the Parliament of Religions. I followed him to the end of the road, but by the time we got there the crowd had grown so large that we had to be kept out when the main party entered Sir S. Subramania Iyer's house. I had no chance to see more of the Swami that year, but I heard that he was a great sadhu who was being sent to America for the Parliament of Religions.

At about this time, an important event occurred that captured the public attention: the complete transformation of Prof. Singaravelu Mudaliar of the Chennai Christian College. He was unorthodox and a declared agnostic and was one of the freethinking group. He wore a hat and adopted the ways of the Westerner and was creating a social revolution. This gentleman came in contact with the Swami when he was staying at Mr. Bhattacharya's house. At a mere touch by the Swami, Mr. Singaravelu Mudaliar was entirely transformed. He gave up his job, gave up his family, and became an ardent spiritual aspirant from that moment. Mudaliar eventually became a typical sadhu and lived alone in a hut opposite Dr. Nanjunda Rao's house in Mylapore, getting his noon and night meal from the doctor's house. This was the famous 'Kidi,' a name given to him by Swamiji. This news spread throughout Chennai and gave people an idea of the spiritual power that was in the Swami.

I was then eighteen years old. We had a small literary society in Mylapore, and we felt too small to invite the Swami to speak; nor had we any premises of our own. But I heard occasionally of the wonderful reception given to the Swami in America and of the great achievement he had made in securing a following for the Vedanta and for the spiritual teachings of India by his magnificent personality and his admirable presentation of the case of Indian religions.

In the beginning of 1897, news reached Chennai that this Swami who had gone to America and made such a name for himself—and for India—was coming home. People realized how greatly the country was indebted to him. There was a spontaneous enthusiasm throughout South India and especially in Chennai. Sir S. Subramania Iyer, Sir V. Bhashyam Iyengar, V. Krishnaswami Iyer, V. C. Seshachariar, Prof. M. Rangachariar, Prof. Sundararamayya, and Dr. Nanjunda Rao were among those responsible for arranging for a fitting reception to the Swami. They were happy that the Raja of Ramnad and the public at each important stop along the way had made suitable arrangements to welcome him. A few also went in advance to meet him at various stations on his route.

Never before and never since have I seen such a spontaneous outburst of gratitude and enthusiasm. There was no governmental or political whip behind it; the spontaneity was truly remarkable. All along his route were decorations and triumphal arches with blazing inscriptions such as 'Hail Harbinger of Peace', 'Hail Ramakrishna's worthy son', etc.

The day of the arrival was announced by posters and tom-tom and the whole route was studded with people. The Egmore Railway Station—a rickety tiled building then—was too small to hold the crowd. The route selected was from the station, through Chintadripet, coming out of Napier Park to Mount Road, and then proceeding along Pycrofts Road to the Beach Road and from there to Ice House. It was a sea of heads. The authorities of every temple on the way brought to the Swami Poornakumbham and temple honours with temple paraphernalia.

A month before, Swami Sadananda, Swamiji's first disciple—who, as a station-master, seeing Swamiji get down from the train and pass along to the Booking Office, dropped his keys and followed him, never to return to job or family—was now waiting in Mylapore to receive him. Krishnananda, a Swami not of the Ramakrishna Order, was also waiting to meet him at the station. An open landau belonging to Sir V. Bhashyam Iyengar, who had bought it from the Governor Lord Connemara, was made available and was waiting at the station—but Swamiji had trouble reaching it because of the immense crowd. It was Swami Sadananda who pushed his way through the crowd and was able to lead Swamiji out, holding him in his strong outstretched arms as they made their way slowly to the carriage.

All the formalities that had been arranged—the garlanding, the introductions and so forth—had to be abandoned. It was enough of an accomplishment for Swamiji to reach the carriage. In those days, railway and police arrangements were at a primitive stage. Along with Swami Sadananda, I carried baskets of garlands for Swamiji, which had to be put directly into the carriage and only then offered to Swamiji. As soon as Swamiji got into the carriage, there was a tremendous ovation; only a small number of the crowd had the privilege of actually seeing him. People began to move with the carriage, throwing garlands and flowers on him, and within minutes the garlands and flowers filled the carriage. I had a perch on the syce's step behind the landau, holding a silk umbrella of the Tanjore temple type over Swamiji's head. Along the route, temple honours were brought to the Swami; and at about 10 o'clock in the morning the carriage reached the Beach Road. There the horses were unyoked, and the enthusiastic young men drew the carriage themselves from the Presidency College up to the Ice House.

It was at the Ice House that Swamiji was accommodated. The property belonged to Mr. Biligiri Iyengar, who had just bought it and had it renovated. The whole hollow of the well, in which ice was formerly stored, was divided into flats, with the topmost of them reserved for Swamiji. From the moment of his arrival, he was so active that he never cared for any rest. He took a clean shave and, afterwards, looked like a prince of monks.

In the compound of the Ice House a big pandal was erected to accommodate the meetings which were held in the mornings. The day Swamiji arrived, it was proposed to present him formally with an address in the evening. Sir S. Subramania Iyer was the President of the Reception Committee. My brother-in-law Sri V. C. Seshachariar was one of the Secretaries of the Reception Committee. That was why I came in close contact with the Movement. To me was entrusted the duty of maintaining accounts, keeping the money and carrying out similar work. I had consequently to be always present there.

The formal reception meeting was to be held at the Victoria Public Hall—ground floor. The crowd around the hall was tremendous, and it was almost impossible for Swamiji to get into the hall. On the dais in the hall were seated Sir S. Subramania Iyer and Sir Bhashyam Iyengar. The address was read by Sir S. Subramania Iyer, but the crowd around the hall kept loudly clamouring to see Swamiji. Swamiji suddenly exclaimed: "I am a man of the people. The people are outside. I must go and meet them." Saying this, he rushed out. Then there was a regular stampede; and no arrangements having been made for his addressing the people in the compound of the Victoria Public Hail, the Swami got on a landau and tried to address the crowd. But that too was inadequate. He got into the coachman's seat. He was surrounded on all sides by people shouting "over here!" He began by saying: "Man proposes and God disposes. It was arranged that I should address you in an occidental fashion, but it was ordained by the Lord that I should address you in the *Gita* fashion, standing on the chariot." But the crowd and the noise around made it impossible for him to continue his speech. He finally said, "You have *seen* me today; you will *hear* me some other day," and got down.

I was all along following him as his valet. When we reached Ice House after this abortive meeting, Swamiji and important members of the reception committee were all seated on the open terrace, Swamiji with a wet towel on his head to keep cool. He was sitting in an easy chair, with Sir S. Subramania Iyer and others seated around him. The first point discussed was about the future action to be taken so far as Chennai was concerned. He definitely promised that a centre would be opened in Chennai, adding, "I will send you a Swami who will not smoke and who will be more orthodox than the orthodox people here." He meant Swami Ramakrishnananda, who was sent to Chennai in May 1897.

As regards the Chennai programme for Swamiji, it was decided that, since it was impossible to manage the big crowd, admission to his four Chennai lectures should be regulated by tickets to be charged at the rates of Rs. 3, Rs. 2, and Re. 1. One of my tasks was to keep an account of these tickets. My brother Ramu, Mr. Rangaswami of Bangalore, Sethuraman, and I helped make the arrangements for the meetings and other details. The first two lectures, held in the Victoria Hall, were "My Plan of Campaign" and "Vedanta in its application to Indian Life". The third was in the Pachaiyappa's College Hall, Esplanade, on the subject "Sages of India".

On the first day, speaking on "My Plan of Campaign," Swamiji had some unpleasant truths to reveal about his treatment by the Theosophical Society. It is known that before he sailed for America, he went to the Theosophical Society and asked its president, Col. Olcott, for some letters of introduction to the Branch Societies in America. Olcott refused, saying that the Swami would have to become a member of the Society first. Swamiji could not agree to this, and had to forego the introductions. But apparently this refusal wasn't the only thing that the Society passed on to America: Swamiji said that he had in his possession a letter which was not only unhelpful but was positively intended to obstruct his work. People who had till then known the Theosophical Society as the only organization in religion and had expected it to have been of help to the Swami were troubled to hear this. Swamiji premised this portion of his speech by saying "It is said that the Theosophical Society paved the way for me"; then, giving out the incident fully, he repeatedly asked, "Is this paving my way?" From that time on, Sir S. Subramania Iyer, who was president of the reception committee and cordially and actively devoted to the Swami, ceased to be so, for he himself was a prominent member of the Theosophical Society, and he was discomfited by Swamiji's making this incident public.

Swamiji's reference to Sri Ramakrishna in "Sages of India" was a most touching one. That was the only significant reference to Sri Ramakrishna in all the utterances of Swamiji in Chennai. The dazzle and brilliance of the Swami's personality fully possessed people's minds. His statement in the lecture that "If I have told you one word of truth it was his [Sri Ramakrishna's] and his alone, and if I have told you many things which were not true, which were not correct, and which were not beneficial to the human race, they were all mine, and on me is the responsibility" made people realise that some great power was responsible for the Swami's greatness. They seemed to have no inclination to probe further.

The fourth lecture, in the Harmstons's Circus Tent, was on "The Future of India". That was a wonderful lecture. Swamiji's voice could be heard distinctly in all parts of the tent, even the corners. In those days there were no loudspeakers. The effect of that speech was thrilling. In the mornings, large gatherings assembled in the pandal in the Ice House compound and Swamiji answered questions put to him. His answers were highly illuminating and inspiring. One day an English lady put some pertinent question to Swamiji and he asked, "Are you married?" When she replied "No," Swamiji immediately said, "God save you!" That provoked a tremendous round of laughter and produced a remarkable impression. There was another local pundit who, on the pretext of asking questions, began to make a speech in Sanskrit. The impatient Krishnaswami Iyer could not tolerate it. He at once appealed to Swamiji, "We have not come here to hear the pundit, but to hear you, Swamiji." Swamji smartly got out of the whole thing by putting a counter question to the pundit which collapsed him altogether.

These conversations left the indelible impression that Swamiji, the very embodiment of the spiritual lore of the country, was saturated not only with the living consciousness of Hindu spiritual experience, but also with the philosophical and scientific achievements of the West. From him one gained a lot of first-hand information about religious truths, spiritual discipline, and practical things as well.

Swamiji had dinner one day at Dr. Nanjunda Rao's at Mylapore. He also came to Sri V. C. Seshachariar's house, where I was staying. He went upstairs, and Seshachariar offered him ginger soaked in honey. Saying that such things were very good after a heavy dinner, Swamiji partook of it in large quantities. At night, after these meetings, my three associates and I used to bring the collection, walking the whole way to the Ice House and sleeping there. Whatever small errands needed to be done for Swamiji were done by us. I personally was attached to Swamiji. I used to help him dress and did other small tasks for him. I was in close contact with him for the entire nine days of his stay there. I was twenty-one years old and had just passed the B.A. degree examination.

The last day arrived, and Swamiji had to leave for Kolkata by steamer. The old Chennai Harbour had a pier, and Swamiji dressed up for the steamer journey in knicker and shorts. He asked me, "Don't I look like a wrestler?" He was towed in a railed wagon over the bridge and from there was taken to the steamer. We all stood on the shore gazing after him until the steamer had faded out of sight. For days after, having heard the brilliant addresses of Swamiji, we all felt as if we were in a dreamland.

The third time I saw Swamiji was in 1899 when he was to go to the West again. He travelled by steamer—a steamer that was under quarantine on account of plague. The steamer was in the middle of the harbour. Swami Ramakrishnananda, myself, and a few others went out by boat to see him. We were not allowed aboard the steamer, nor was the Swami allowed to get down from it. While he was on the deck and we were in the boat, Swamiji exchanged a few words with Swami Ramakrishnananda. But as he was ill and couldn't stand for long leaning on the railing, it was a very brief interview.

Though my personal contact with Swamiji was slight, it was enough: I served Sri Ramakrishna for the rest of my life. It was very largely due to Vivekananda's magnetic personality and its influence that I am here as a humble servant of the Ramakrishna Mission.

(Vedanta Kesari, May 1952)

K. S. Ghosh

At the request of the editor of the *Vedanta Kesari*, I venture with hesitation to relate an incident of my life which I have kept to myself now for about 40 years. ...

At this advanced age of mine, the diffidence of my early youth may be got over, and this momentary episode in the life of Swami Vivekananda may have its place in public print to show that he could be great even in small matters and that he could behave like a simple child of nature with schoolboys. These lines are jotted down in the hope that as full a narrative as my memory would now permit may be of interest to those who are eager to know all about the great Swamiji.

The art of writing a biography in this country is still in its infancy. Many good biographies have been written on some of our worthies. We come across in them a record of their achievements, but human touches and their failings, which give colour and flavour to their earthly lives, are in many cases conspicuous by their absence. This incident may be of interest to the readers as showing an interesting human side of the great Swamiji.

I was a student of the Matriculation class of Vaidyanath Deoghar High School in 1898. Once in the month of November of that year our Headmaster, the late lamented Kavibhushan Yogindranath Bose, the biographer of our poet Michael Madhusudan Dutta, told us that Swami Vivekananda of the Chicago Parliament of Religions fame had come to the town for a change of weather. The Swamiji, said our headmaster, was a classmate of his and if any of his boys cared to see this remarkable man, that was the time.

The great impression that Vivekananda made at the Parliament of Religions in America in 1893 produced quite a sensation in this country and considerably enhanced the self-respect of our people. This reputation of an Indian monk reached us, the veritable striplings in schools, and filled us with pride. The words Vedanta, the *Gita*, and Advaitavada, reached our ears, but their significance was beyond our comprehension. The thought that Swami Vivekananda had no time to waste with schoolboys did not deter us. My friend Satishchandra Mazumdar and I made up our minds to take our chance and wended our way one afternoon towards the hill stream Durwa which forms the western boundary of the beautiful town of Deoghar. Swamiji had taken up his residence in a house near by, lent to him by one of his Kolkata disciples.

With palpitating hearts, we entered the compound of the house and inquired of a man who looked like a helper in the household about Swamiji's whereabouts. He silently pointed to a majestic figure clad in a yellow robe which slowly emerged out of the western side of the house, with an umbrella in hand. We had no difficulty in knowing who it was, gathered courage, approached with hasty steps, and stooped low to touch the feet of Swamiji, for verily it was he. But he quickly stepped back and did not allow us to touch his feet and inquired who we were and what was the object of our visit.

We told him that we belonged to the local High School and had come to pay him our respects. He asked us to follow him and stepped into the public road in front of the house, leading to the stream Durwa. We felt proud to have the Swamiji all to ourselves and the privilege of being able to have a quiet walk with him.

The house was situated in a most beautiful quarter of the town. A well-laid road crossed the hill stream Durwa at a distance of half a mile from the place and traversed a high ridge beyond it and then disappeared in the midst of yonder hills. It was a lovely early winter afternoon; the sky was beautifully clear and the distant range of mountains clad in charming vegetation stood overlooking the plains below.

While we slowly walked with the Swamiji, he seemed to be troubled with hard breathing. On inquiry he replied he was not keeping good health and had come to rest for a few days in that health resort.

He thought his heart was sound, but there seemed to be some trouble with his lungs. We came with the idea that the moment the Swamiji would get an opportunity he would talk to us on the Vedanta philosophy. But we tried in vain to draw him out in that direction. He seemed to follow St. Paul and wanted to be all things unto all men. He reserved his Vedanta for those who were fit for it. He talked of health, hygiene, and sanitation to us, a couple of representatives of thousands of our schoolboys who are ruining their health over their studies, miscalled education. He turned his eyes towards a distant range of hills that stood majestically against the western horizon and inquired whether we had ever been to them. He expressed surprise at our answer that we had not the good fortune to go so far as yet. He then pointed out the utility of making long excursions occasionally for the benefit of our health, and told us that one of the best ways of utilizing Sunday noons was to take some refreshments with us, spend the whole day in communion with Nature on chosen spots in yonder hills, and to come back refreshed in the evening.

He inquired about our studies and the dietary arrangement in the hostels, and hearing that we took some amount of ghee regularly, told us, with a characteristic emphasis on the word "indigestible", not to take too much ghee because it is indigestible and it is better to take butter instead.

In the course of conversation, when he came to learn that we belonged to Eastern Bengal, he told us that he had been to our part of the country years ago and found that people there eat a good quantity of fish. This was all to the good. Common facts of life and living which escaped the notice of an ordinary monk had interest for him if they had anything to do with individual health and well-being.

After talking in this strain for a while, we reached the hill stream Durwa. Stopping on its bank for some time, we retraced our steps. While we walked silently, we noticed that continuous talk made him tired and the deep breathing caused discomfort. We realized to some extent that a mighty spirit was struggling with a physical frame that bore the impetuosity of a strenuous youth and was bending under it. But we did not know that it was to give way at no distant future and to liberate the spirit that could not be shut up within its confines.

Many thoughts, childlike and serious, were coursing through our youthful minds that seemed to be already under the fascination of a great soul. We inquired whether he was going to deliver any public discourses at the station and whether we could come to him occasionally. He replied to the effect that he was asked to take complete rest by his medical advisers and the period of his stay in the town was uncertain.

But Swamiji now stood in the middle of the road and we stopped with him not knowing the reason why. He stood—a stately figure his physical weakness not withstanding—just before me, looking in curiosity at my feet. In fact, he found fault with the way in which the laces of my shoes were tied, having both the ends of each lace turned one way. He asked me to tie them properly. Born and brought up in an out-of-the-way Eastern Bengal town, I failed to take the hint thus conveyed. I turned to my shoes, but could not detect the cause of Swamiji's uneasiness. His concern over the matter seemed to me to be inexplicable. His subtle perception of fitness of things in the matter of ordinary gear, showed not simply the keenness of his observation, but a high sense of propriety of the modern art of living. My friends have never complimented me on the neatness of my dress. At times indifference to these matters may have degenerated into slovenliness. But in the present instance my fault was that, though I had put on a new pair of shoes on this auspicious occasion, instead of tying the laces keeping the ends turned in opposite directions as the general custom is, I had tied them so that they were turned in one way. This did not escape the notice of the keen-witted, clear-sighted Swamiji. I stood still before him, almost stupefied, not knowing what to do. He asked me to tie them properly. This added further to my embarrassment. He then pointed one of his fingers to my shoes. This made the confusion worse confounded. Finding me irresponsive, he stooped low and blurted out, "Well, let me have it." This made me mechanically put forward my right leg towards the Swamiji, and in a couple of seconds he tied the lace properly keeping the two ends in two opposite directions and asked me to set right the other one. The whole behaviour seemed to be so natural, so instantaneous yet so significant, that sense seemed to be knocked out of me for the time being, and I failed to act up to his request. The thought that I failed at the moment to rise up to his expectation makes me uneasy even at this distance of time. A city-bred lad could have easily adapted himself to the situation, and would have gained approbation of Swamiji. Not knowing the disease, I could not apply Swamiji's suggested remedy. Fortunately for me he could easily understand that I was nervous and did not press the matter further. My wits returned and I atoned for my unconscious and seeming disobedience by trying to touch his feet, but he stepped back and did not allow me to take the dust of his feet in the orthodox Hindu fashion. The great Swamiji to tie shoelace of an ordinary schoolboy—what a great humanity and humility! How many educated men and women both here and abroad would have considered themselves fortunate to have the privilege of touching his feet. This utter self-forgetfulness on his part was so charming and so noble and compassionate that the matter needs no further comment. This momentary episode raised him immeasurably in our estimation and made his sacred name dear to us for life. Time came to bid him good-bye and we tried in vain for the third time to touch his feet.

We came back to the hostel after dark—the story got speedily circulated in our student world, and streams of friends came to examine the lace which was sanctified by the touch of the Swamiji; they would not allow me to untie the lace and take off the shoe. This was however done late at night not without some misgivings and with a heavy heart. The day has passed away, but its memory still clings to me and will do so as long as I live. The episode has revealed to me Swamiji's deep humanity and childlike simplicity that only a great man of his calibre could possess. While harbouring great thoughts in his mind and planning great schemes for social amelioration, he knew how to love children and lowly and simple folk. He was, in the language of Sri Chaitanya, "humbler than a blade of grass".

We saw him for the second and last time a few days after in a railway compartment at the Deoghar Station, by the side of Girishchandra Ghosh, the celebrated dramatist, on their way back to Kolkata. Swamiji was then dressed in what looked like his travelling gear—in half pants and coats, smoking his pipe in the right Indian fashion, and chewing betel-leaf. An ordinary monk would hesitate to appear in this way in public lest be might offend orthodox sentiments. But no monk had a scanter respect for social conventions than the Swamiji. This was a source of his strength and also the cause of his unpopularity with a certain section of his own people. He was indifferent to both as a selfless worker.

One thing more. Emerson has somewhere related the story of a nun who was reported to have performed miracles near Rome. This made the then Pope uneasy. His holiness deputed St. Philip of Neri to report on the matter. St. Philip went to the convent where the nun was staying and sought permission of the head for an interview with her. This was granted. He waited in a room for the nun and on her arrival put his dusty and heavy pair of boots on a chair near by and requested the nun to take them off his feet. The nun got offended and turned away. St. Philip left the room in a moment and came running to the Pope and reassured His

Holiness that there was no cause of apprehension. The nun was not humble and there can be no miracle where there is no humility.

Yes, the source of Swami Vivekananda's almost miraculous powers was in the hidden humility of his soul.

(*Vedanta Kesari*, January 1938)

FRANK RHODEHAMEL

Frank Rhodehamel

It is now more than ten years since the Swami Vivekanan-da lectured to California audiences; it seems but yesterday. It was here as elsewhere; the audiences were his from the outset and remained his to the end. They were swept along on the current of his thought without resistance. Many there were who did not want to resist: whose pleasure and novelty it was to have light thrown into the hidden recesses of their minds by the proximity of a luminous personality. There were a few who would have resisted if they could, but whose powers of resistance were neutralized by the irresistible logic, acumen, and childlike simplicity of the Great Teacher. Indeed, there were a few who arose to demur, but who resumed their seats either in smiling acquiescence or in bewildered impotency.

The Swamiji's personality impressed itself on the mind with visual intensity. The speaking eyes, the wealth of facial expression, and gesticulation; the wondrous Sanskrit chanting, sonorous, melodious, impressing one with the sense of mystic potency; the translations following in smiling confidence—all these, set off by the spectacular apparel of the Hindu sannyasi—who can forget them?

As a lecturer he was unique: never referring to notes, as most lecturers do; and though he repeated many discourses on request, they were never mere repetitions. He seemed to be giving something of himself, to be speaking from a super-experience. The most abstruse points of the Vedanta were retrieved from the domain of mere speculation by a vital something which seemed to emanate from him. It was his practice to look deliberately and leisurely over his audience before beginning a discourse. Then, beginning in a conversational tone and manner, his voice would run the gamut of impassioned modulation and impressive periods. That style of speaking was very effective for those within easy range of his voice, but it must have been an exasperation to those in the back of the hall, for cries of "louder!" were common from that quarter. His utterances were dynamic and constructive: arousing thought and directing it into synthetic process. Thus he was not only a lecturer but a teacher of the highest order as well.

He encouraged the asking of questions at the conclusion of every lecture, and would go to any length to make his questioners understand. On one occasion, after persistent queries by a number of persons, it occurred to someone that they were plying the Swami too insistently with questions, and he remarked to that effect. "Ask all the questions you like—the more the better", was the Swami's good-natured reply. "That is what I am here for, and I won't leave you till you understand." The applause was so prolonged that he was obliged to wait till it subsided before he could continue. At times he literally startled people into belief by his answers. To the question, after a lecture on Reincarnation, "Swami, do you remember your past life?" he answered quickly and seriously, "Yes, clearly, even when I was a little boy."

Quick and, when necessary, sharp at repartee, he met all opposition with the utmost good nature and even enjoyment. His business was to make his hearers understand, and he succeeded as, perhaps, no other lecturer on abstruse subjects ever did. To popularize abstractions, to place them within the mental grasp of even very ordinary intellects, was his achievement. He reached them all. "In India," he said, "they tell me that I ought not to teach Advaita Vedanta to the people at large. But I say that I can make even a child understand it. You cannot begin too early to teach the highest spiritual truths."

Once at the conclusion of a lecture he thus announced his next lecture: "Tomorrow night I shall lecture on 'The Mind: Its Powers and Possibilities'. Come to hear me. I have something to say to you, I shall do a little bomb-throwing." Here he glanced smilingly over the audience, and then with a wave of his hand added, "Come on! It will do you good." The next night there was barely standing-room. He kept his word. Bombs were thrown, and he, of all people, knew how to throw them with telling effect. In this lecture he devoted considerable time to the subject of chastity as a means of strengthening the mind. As a practice to develop purity, he expounded the theory of looking upon every woman as one's mother. When he had presented the idea, he paused and, as though in response to inarticulate questionings from the audience, said: "O yes, this is a theory. I stand up here to tell you about this beautiful theory; but, when I think of my own mother, I know that to me she is different to any other woman. There is a difference. We cannot deny it. But we see this difference because we think of ourselves as bodies. This theory is to be fully realized in meditation. These truths are first to be heard, then to be meditated upon."

He held purity to be for the householder as well as for the monk, and laid great stress on that point. "The other day, a young Hindu came to see me," he said. "He has been living in this country for about two years, and suffering from ill-health for some time. In the course of our talk, he said that the theory of chastity must be all wrong because the doctors in this country had advised him against it. They told him that it was against the law of nature. I told him to go back to India, where he belonged, and to listen to the teachings of his ancestors, who had practised chastity for thousands of years." Then, turning a face puckered into an expression of unutterable disgust, he thundered: "You doctors in this country, who hold that chastity is against the law of nature, don't know what you are talking about. You don't know the meaning of the word purity. You are beasts! beasts! I say, with the morals of a tomcat, if that is the best you have to say on that subject!" Here he glanced defiantly over the audience, challenging opposition by his very glance. No voice was raised, though there were several physicians present.

Bombs were thrown in all his lectures. Audiences were jolted out of hereditary ruts, and New Thought students, so-called, were subjected to scathing though constructive criticisms without mercy. Smilingly, he would announce the most stupendous Vedantic conceptions so opposed to Christian theologic dogma; then pause an instant—how many, many times, and with such winsome effect!—with his teeth pressed over his lower lip as though with bated breath observing the result. Imagine, if you can, greater violence done to the traditional teachings of Christendom than by his fiery injunction, "Don't repent! Don't repent! ... Spit, if you must, but go on! Don't hold yourselves down by repenting! Throw off the load of sin, if there is such a thing, by knowing your true selves—The Pure! The Ever Free! ... That man alone is blasphemous who tells you that you are sinners." And again: "This world is a superstition. We are hypnotized into believing it real. The process of salvation is the process of de-hypnotization. ... This universe is just the play of the Lord—that is all. It is all just for fun. There can be no reason for His doing anything. Know the Lord if you would understand His play. Be His play-fellow, and He will tell you all. ... And to you, who are philosophers, I say that to ask for a reason for the existence of the universe is illogical, because it implies limitation in God, which you do not admit." Then he entered into one of his wonderful expositions of the salient features of the Advaita Vedanta.

In the questions which usually followed a talk on this subject, there was almost sure to be the question: "But, Swami, what will become of one's individuality when one realizes one's oneness with God?" He would laugh at this question, and playfully ridicule it. He would say, "You people in this country are so afraid of losing your in-di-vid-u-al-i-ties," drawing out the word in laughing mockery. "Why, you are not individuals yet. When you know God, you will be.

When you realize your whole nature, you will attain your true individualities, not before. In knowing God you cannot lose anything worth having. ... There is another thing I am constantly hearing in this country and that is that we should "live in harmony with nature!" "Har-mo-ny with nature", he ridiculed. "Why, don't you know that all the progress ever made in the world was made by fighting nature, by conquering nature? There never has been an exception. Trees live in harmony with nature. Perfect harmony there; no opposition there—and no progress. We are to resist nature at every point if we are to make any progress. Something funny happens and nature says, 'laugh', and we laugh. Someone we love dies, and nature says, 'cry', and we cry—"

"But," interposed an old lady in the audience, "it would be very hard not to mourn for those we love, and I think we would be very hard-hearted if we did not mourn." "O yes, Madam," he replied, "it is hard, no doubt. But what of that? All great accomplishments are hard. Nothing worthwhile comes easy. But don't lower the ideal because it is difficult to attain. Hold the banner of freedom aloft! You do not weep, Madam, because you want to, but because nature forces you. When nature says, 'Weep!' say 'No! I shall not weep!' Strength! Strength! Strength!—say that to yourself day and night. You are the Strong! The Pure! The Free! No weakness in you; no sin; no misery!"

Such statements, vitalized by his tremendous personality, placed him in the same class with the world's greatest spiritual teachers. During these lectures, one was suspended in a spiritual firmament by the proximity of a soul to whom the world was really a joke, and to whom Consciousness, super-cosmic, was the One and only Reality.

The Swami was blessed with an irrepressible sense of humour, which enlivened his lectures and classes, and at times relieved the tenseness of embarrassing situations. Observe his parry to the question incredulously hurled at him at the close of a lecture which culminated in an impassioned outburst on the glory of God-consciousness: "Swami, have you seen God?" "What!" he returned, his face lighting up with a happy smile, "Do I look like it—a big fat man like me?"

On another occasion while he was expounding Advaita, an old man, sitting in the front row, arose deliberately, and with a look which said as plainly as words, "Let me get out of this place in hurry," hobbled down the aisle and out of the hall, pounding the floor with his cane at every step. The Swami apparently enjoyed the situation, for amusement overspread his features as he paused to watch him. The attention of the audience was divided between the Swami, smiling, fun-loving, and the disgusted old man who had had enough of him.

The whimsical, playful side of the Swami's character would break out at any moment. Certain Theosophic and New Thought students were interested primarily in occult phenomena. One such asked, "Swami, have you ever seen an elemental?" "O yes, we have them in India for breakfast," was the quick reply. Nor did he hesitate to joke about his own personality. At one time when looking at some works of art the Swami, surveying a painting of some corpulent monks, remarked: "Spiritual men are fat. See, how fat I am!" Again, speaking about the power of prophecy in the saints he said: "Once when I was a little boy playing in the streets, a sage passing by put his hand on my head and said, 'My boy, you will be a great man some day.' And now see where I am!" At this little conceit his face fairly beamed with fun. There was nothing egotistical in such statements. His simple fun-loving nature carried his hearers along with him in the spirit of his joke. At another time: "The Christian idea of hell is not at all terrifying to me. I have read Dante's *Inferno* three times, but I must say that I find nothing terrible in it. There are many kinds of Hindu hells. When a glutton dies, for instance, he is surrounded by great quantities of the very best kinds of food. He has a stomach a thousand miles long, and a mouth as small as a pin-head! Think of that!" During this lecture he got very warm owing to the poor ventilation. On leaving the hall after the lecture, he was met by a chill blast of north wind. Gathering his coat tightly about him he said vehemently, "Well, if this isn't hell, I don't know what is."

Dilating on the life of the monk as compared to that of the householder he said, "Someone asked me if I was ever married." Here he paused to glance smilingly over the audience. A multitudinous titter was the response. Then the smile giving place to a look of horror, he continued: "Why, I wouldn't be married for anything. It is the devil's own game." Here he paused as though to give his words effect. Then raising his hand to check the audible appreciation that had begun, he went on with a quite serious expression over-spreading his features, "There is one thing, however, that I have against the monastic system, and that is"—(another pause)—"that it takes the best men away from the community." He did not attempt to stem the outburst that followed. He had his little joke and enjoyed it. On another occasion, while speaking seriously, he suddenly broke out in merriment: "As soon as a man gets a little sense he dies. He begins by having a big stomach which sticks out farther than his head. When he gains wisdom, his stomach disappears and his head becomes prominent. Then he dies."

The Swami's assimilation of the world's maturest religious thought and his consummate power in expounding it, contrasted curiously with his youthful appearance, and much conjecture was rife as to his age. He must have known this, for he availed himself of an opportunity to have a little fun on this point at the expense of the audience. Alluding to his own age, which was apropos of the subject, he said, "I am only—" (breathless pause, anticipation)—"of a few years", he added mischievously. A sigh of disappointment ran over the audience. The Swami looked on waiting for the applause, which he knew was ready to break out. He enjoyed his own jokes as much as did the audience. Once he laughed outright at some particularly pointed joke which he just told. The house was in an uproar at once. The joke is irretrievably lost. What a pity! During his series of lectures on 'The Ideals of India', the fact was disclosed that he was a wonderful story-teller. Here, perhaps, he was at his best. He gave life to the ancient tales by telling them in his inimitable fashion, the subject giving full play to his unsurpassed power of interpretation, and to that wealth of facial expression which was his greatest personal charm. "I love to tell these stories," he said. "They are the life of India. I have heard them since babyhood. I never get tired of telling them."

The Swami commanded reverence when he revealed himself at times to his audience in one of those wonderful waves of transcendental feeling which he did not try to check. As when he said: "All faces are dear to me. ... As it is possible to 'see Helen in an Ethiop's face', so we must learn to see the Lord in all. All, even the very worst, are Mother's children. The universe, good and bad, is but the play of the Lord."

In private interviews he was the ideal host, entering into conversation, argument, or story-telling, not only without restraint, but with apparent enjoyment. His personal appearance on my first interview was a pleasurable shock from which I have never fully recovered. He had on a long grey dressing gown, and was sitting cross-legged on a chair, smoking a pipe, his long hair falling in wild disarray over his features. As I advanced, he extended a cordial hand and bade me be seated. Memory delivers but fragments of those interviews. What remains vivid is the contact with the great sannyasi—the impressions and impetus received—which refuses to be less than the greatest experience in life.

Speaking of spiritual training for the mind he said: "The less you read the better. What are books but the vomitings of other men's minds? Why fill your mind with a load of stuff you will have to get rid of? Read the *Gita* and other good works on Vedanta. That is all you need." Then again: "The present system of education is all wrong. The mind is crammed with facts before it knows how to think. Control of the mind should be taught first. If I had my education to get over again, and had any voice in the matter, I would learn to master my mind first, and then gather facts, if I wanted them. It takes people a long time to learn things, because they can't concentrate their minds at will. ... It took three readings for me to memorize Macaulay's History of England, while my mother memorized any sacred book in only one reading. ... People are always suffering because they can't control their minds. To give an illustration, though a rather crude one: A man has trouble with his wife. She leaves him and goes with other men. She's a terror! But, poor fellow, he can't take his mind away from her, and so he suffers."

I asked him to explain why the practice of begging, common among religious mendicants, was not opposed to renunciation. He replied: "It is a question of the mind. If the mind anticipates, and is affected by the results—that is bad, no doubt. The giving and receiving of alms should be free; otherwise it is not renunciation. If you should put a hundred dollars on that table for me, and should expect me to thank you for it, you could take it away again, I would not touch it. My living was provided for before I came here, before I was born. I have no concern about it. Whatever belongs to a man he will get. It was ready for him before he was born."

To the question: "What do you think about the Immaculate Conception of Jesus?" he replied: "That is an old claim. There have been many in India who have claimed that. I don't know anything about it. But for my part, I am glad that I had a natural father and mother." "But isn't such a theory opposed to the law of nature?" I ventured. "What is nature to the Lord? It is all His play," he replied as he knocked the ash from his pipe against the heel of his slipper, regardless of the carpeted floor. Then blowing through the stem to clear it, he continued: "We are slaves of nature. The Lord is the Master of nature. He can do as He pleases. He can take one or a dozen bodies at a time, if He chooses, and in any way He chooses. How can we limit Him?"

After answering at length various questions about Raja Yoga, he concluded with a friendly smile: "But why bother about Raja Yoga? There are other ways."

This interview was continued fifteen minutes beyond the time set for a class on Raja Yoga to be held in the front room of the house. We were interrupted by the lady in charge of affairs, rushing into the room and exclaiming: "Why, Swami! You have forgotten all about the Yoga class. It is fifteen minutes past time now, and the room is full of people." The Swami rose hastily to his feet, exclaiming to me: "Oh, excuse me! We will now go to the front room." I walked through the hall to the front room. He went through his bedroom, which was between the room we had been sitting in and the front room. Before I was seated, he emerged from his room with his hair (which I have said was in a state of wild disorder) neatly combed, and attired in his sannyasi robe! Not more than one minute had elapsed from the time he started from his room with dishevelled hair and in lounging attire, till he came leisurely out into the front room ready to lecture. Speed and precision of action were evidently at his command. It was difficult at times, however, to persuade him to stir beyond the pace he had set for himself. When late for a lecture, for instance, it was sometimes impossible to induce him to hurry for the street car. In response to entreaties to hurry, he would drawl: "Why do you hurry me? If we don't catch that car, we will catch the next."

At these yoga classes one came closer to the man and teacher than was possible in the lecture hall. The contact was more personal and the influence more direct. The embodiment of holiness, simplicity, and wisdom, he seemed speaking with incisive power, and drawing one's mind more to God and renunciation than to proficiency in Raja Yoga practices.

After delivering a short lecture, he would seat himself cross-legged on the divan and direct in meditation such of the audience as remained for that purpose. His talk was on Raja Yoga, and the practical instruction on simple breathing exercises. He said in part: "You must learn to sit correctly; then to breathe correctly. This develops concentration; then comes meditation. ... When practising breathing, think of your body as luminous. ... Try to look down the spinal cord from the base of the brain to the base of the spine. Imagine that you are looking through the hollow Sushumna to the Kundalini. Then imagine that you see this Kundalini rising upward to the brain. ... Have patience. Great patience is necessary."

Such as voiced doubts and fears, he reassured by saying: "I am with you now. Try to have a little faith in me." One was moved by his persuasive power when he said: "We learn to meditate that we may be able to think of the Lord. Raja Yoga is only the means to that end. The great Patanjali, author of the Raja Yoga, never missed an opportunity to impress that idea upon his students. Now is the time for you who are young. Don't wait till you are old before you think of the Lord, for then you will not be able to think of Him. The power to think of the Lord is developed when you are young."

Seated cross-legged on the divan, clothed in his sannyasi garb, with hands held one within the other on his lap, and with his eyes apparently closed, he might have been a statue in bronze, so immovable was he. A yogi, indeed! Awake only to transcendental thought, he was the ideal, compelling veneration, love, and devotion.

(*Prabuddha Bharata*, February-March 1915)

Swami Vivekananda frequently declared to his audiences while expounding the salient features of the Vedanta, "These truths have first to be heard, then thought about, then meditated upon." These three stages, hearing, thought, meditation, always succeed each other though when the last has made its appearance all three have concurrent activity.

The inspired utterances of the great Swamiji swept over the country like a tidal wave. Not only through the spoken word but by books and pamphlets the message of the Vedanta found lodgement in responsive minds. The silent work of assimilation and incorporation is going on and will continue to go on till the end of time, for Swami Vivekananda was a world-power, awakening the souls of mankind to the true import of life.

The right start had been made. Words fraught with supersensual power crashed into the inertia of materialism. Brains matured by experience gave efficient hearing, and the imperative demand for personal instruction gave rise to class-work.

Here the teacher of wisdom revealed himself as a power of love. The fiery aggressiveness of that mind, more than able to cope with all opposition, gave way to a gentle friendliness of demeanour which mirrored beneath his winsome, capricious temperament a depth of consciousness, remote and inaccessible. Here the undisguised admiration of audiences for the lecturer was transformed into devotion to the guru.

The second stage of spiritual culture was now under way—the absorption of what has been heard into thought. The conditions, physical and mental, necessary to efficient contemplation of the significance of spiritual teachings were patiently dwelt upon in detail. The difference between mere intellectual appreciation of spiritual ideals and the *desire to be spiritual* was sharply drawn.

He taught that in the attainment of the spiritual capacity, or the desire to be spiritual, nothing is arbitrary; that the whole process is one of natural development. There was nothing mystical about it. Practise, practise, practise, life-long practise, and if necessary, many lives of practise, was the one and only method to acquire the all-absorbing desire to be spiritual. And practise? Intensive contemplation of the significance of spiritual teachings and of the spiritual character. Hence the elimination of obstacles to deep contemplation and the employment of any accessories to that end was the scope of the Swami's efforts in his class-work.

The absorption of what has been heard into thought! Like babies learning to talk, that difficult task made delightful by the loving attentions of the mother, the Swami's spiritual babies dallied with his every word and drank in the sweetness of his badinage as he tried to teach them how to think.

In response to the mind's mysterious imagery, the atmospheric subtleness of the Swami's personality envelops and claims the present. Again we are seated in class about him. He is the orange-robed, the illuminated one, seated on the divan. His great, dark eyes searching the faces about him reveal no clue as to his findings. A few words of instruction as to posture, breathing, relaxation etc. follow, though without rigid conformity to the traditional teachings. His idea is apparently to make everyone feel at ease as if he would have the spirit of contemplation steal upon us unawares.

Two students, a man and a woman, squat on the floor in painful imitation of the Swami's posture. He looks at them a moment then looks at the rest and laughs. "You can't sit that way," he says. "Your legs are not trained to sit that way. In India we are trained to sit that way from babyhood, but you can't do it." Neither move. The woman replies, pressing her knees down: "Oh, this is easy for me. I am used to it. I always sit this way." The man laughs and hangs his head. Swami looks from one to the other and laughs again. "Come," he says, speaking to the man, "sit here beside me and let your feet rest on the floor." He is stubborn. "Come, come," he pleads, patting the divan beside him, "Come sit here by me. You can't meditate that way." But it is useless. Both remain on the floor. Swami laughs and abandons his efforts. Everyone laughs.

"All that is necessary," he continues, "is to sit comfortably with the body erect—that is all. Try to think of the body as luminous, full of light."

Now he chants. The rhythmic intonation of Sanskrit mantras stirs responsive chords. The result is emotional rather than intellectual. An intangible sweetness steals upon the senses, quieting them, and the mind reflects somewhat of that placid depth which is the Swami's habitual state.

Now he pauses to translate, weaving through the witchery of words an atmosphere of spiritual idealism. His personality becomes a magnet drawing one away from himself, and he feels as pleasurable those thought-flashes which, under ordinary circumstances, would have been resisted as inimical to personality. Something within leaps upward. Consciousness breaks through the incrustation of personal identity. One's life in the world fades into a mere tradition, unstable, unalluring.

A transitional period of spiritual probation is covered in a flash. The present consciousness becomes contemporaneous with that wisdom which is ever unsullied by the succession of events, but which, as it were, dips into the past, present, and future only to illuminate the mirage of time, and to lure the enslaved ones to break with themselves by giving the anaesthesia of joy in the breaking.

In him the life of renunciation is given the glint of romance. Now the sage-artist photographs upon the mind—screen the living pictures of the sannyasi, no longer traditional, but sensitized, pulsating with the passion of renunciation. Ah! What is this? The listener is himself that sannyasi, a wanderer on the arid plains of India, a pilgrim at holy shrines, a devotee at the feet of the Lord. The spell of that far-away punya bhumi is thrown up before the mind. This master of thought-forces, this weaver of sattvic maya, is planting within us the seeds of liberation.

Now, after the lapse of many years, this living past responds in proportion to the urgency of some condition calling it up. Thus by the moil of years one feels discouraged, all his efforts seem in vain. The mind reaches into itself for some means of support. A dark sannyasi-robed figure appears with arm uplifted and with face aflame with zeal, and the words, "Strength! Strength! Strength!" vibrate on the inner sense. The connection is made with a spiritual live-wire of unlimited power. One becomes surcharged with new-born hope, and he gets a glimpse of that truth that the mind is but a phase of life that is doomed to be displaced by the fullness of life. Again he feels the pressure of a friendly arm about him; and he knows, for the time being at least, that his efforts are not in vain.

That intimate touch, living in undying memory, brings to mind the lighter, whimsical side of this great personality. It contrasts as pleasurably to his deeper nature as spray on the seashore to the awe-inspiring presence of the sea.

One remembers that the Swami smoked, and at times he did so in jolly disregard of conventional time and place. Once while crossing the bay between San Francisco and Oakland, he took the notion to smoke. He was seated with some ladies on the upper deck of the ferry where smoking was prohibited. Drawing a pack of cigarettes from his pocket, he lit one and blew the smoke in playful defiance at the pro-hibitive sign, "No Smoking." One of his companions quickly warned him, "Swami! Swami! You can't smoke here!"

"Why not?" he drawled, encircling himself and his com-panions with wreaths of smoke.

"But don't you see that sign, Swami?"

"Yes, but what of that?" continuing to puff.

"Here comes the officer! Quick! put it out!"

"Why should I put it out?" he drawled in exasperating coolness.

The officer in question caught sight of the offender, and started for him. Swami continued to puff until the officer came up to him. Then he laughingly threw the half-smoked cigarette overboard. The officer looked at him a moment and slowly passed on.

The inmates of the "Home of Truth" had occasion to get used to the odour of tobacco while he lived there. He would usually be up in morning before the rest of the family, and lighting his pipe would walk through the unoccupied rooms, filling them with smoke. One imagines their efforts to rid the rooms of the odour of tobacco before time for their usual morning class.

Smoking was not his only offence in the "Home of Truth." The cream for breakfast was missing one morning.

It was a mystery, as they knew the milkman had left it. The event was discussed at breakfast. The Swami quietly listened until all had exhausted their wits in their efforts to solve the mystery. Then he coolly informed them that he had drunk it! I imagine that the more conservative members of the "Home of Truth" were shocked by his whimsical tendency.

This capricious temperament, viewed as the surface of his tremendous spirituality, was a refreshing departure from the traditional long-faced, unbending religious. To him the world was a joke at which he now frowned, now laughed, now jeered; with which he was now serious, now playful, now frivolous; but in relation to which he was at all times the witness, interiorly aloof and unmoved. The chief benefit derived from contemplating this side of his character was the practice it gave in viewing the contacts of life as a mere witness. The real genius of this great personality stood out the clearer thereby, for one felt the presence of an interior self-efficiency masquerading, as it were, in play of moods.

So the Swami, in whatever way one come into contact with him, was a constant incitement to think. His very presence compelled thought. The raw material of haphazard thinking he converted into orderly thought-processes, in which state alone it is possible to accomplish intensive mental work. Thus students were being qualified for meditation, the third stage of spiritual culture.

This stage of the development of the Vedanta in California was given an ideal setting in the establishment of the Shanti Ashrama in the San Antonio Valley among the Coast Range Mountains. The property on which the Ashrama was founded consists of one hundred and sixty acres of gently rolling hill-land, the gift of a Miss Book to Swami Vivekananda. She was actuated in this by her attention being attracted to a young Brahmachari who had taken his vows from the Swami Abhedananda. He had renounced the world and was homeless in a land where the homeless were in disrepute; so she conceived the idea of giving her place for him to go to, and for all other Vedantists who desired to retire for spiritual purposes either temporarily or permanently.

Just preceding the establishment of the ashrama Swami Vivekananda's labours terminated in California, and the Swami Turiyananda, by his request, came to continue his classes and to take possession of the ashrama. ...

India—the punya bhumi! By the world-witchery of the Swami Vivekananda and Turiyananda the psychological film of moving pictures unfolds a land of unfading glory—the land where the miracle of man rising and risen above himself is made inevitable. Himalayan snow-bound shrines, monasteries perched on those primeval slopes, way-houses for solitary sannyasis, holy rivers coursing their capricious ways to the sea, temple cities whose very existence is associated with the worship of God, are just so many settings in the consummation of human life.

To us of foreign mould, whose visions of India are creations of such thought-miracle-workers as Vivekananda and Turiyananda, India is a fair dream inhabiting the region of the mind where incongruous details are forever barred. Through the haze of remoteness we see the real India, intangible, paradoxical, philosophic, meditative—a dream spun of such ethereal texture that the light of Reality shimmers on its surface, and anon breaks through in blinding flashes when such master-minds have awakened from their world-dream and broken the figment through.

Om Tat Sat is the anthem of those Himalayas. It is the anthem of these ashrama hills. It breaks into eddies on a myriad lips and is born inward a mantra to the Real, the Deathless; and he who is able may follow its vibrations into sattvic consciousness, into peace, into liberation.

(*Prabuddha Bharata*, February-March 1916)

KATE SANBORN

Kate Sanborn

When I had the honour of entertaining a Hindu monk last summer, a man of wondrous learning, eloquence, and philanthropy, the excitement rose to fever height.

I had met him in the observation car of the Canadian Pacific, where even the gigantically grand scenery of mountains, canyons, glaciers, and the Great Divide could not take my eyes entirely from the cosmopolitan travellers, all *en route* for Chicago. Parsees from India, Canton merchant millionaires, New Zealanders, pretty women from the Philippine Isles married to Portuguese and Spanish traders, Japanese dignitaries with their cultivated wives and collegiate sons, high bred and well informed, etc.

I talked with all. They cordially invited me to visit them at their respective homes, and I, nothing abashed, spoke in rather glowing terms of my rural residence, and gave each my card, with 'Metcalf, Mass.' as permanent address.

I alluded to the distinguished men and women in Boston and vicinity who were frequently my guests, and assured all of a hearty welcome at my farm.

But most of all was I impressed by the monk, a magnificent specimen of manhood—six feet two, as handsome as Salvini at his best, with a lordly, imposing stride, as if he ruled the universe, and soft, dark eyes that could flash fire if roused or dance with merriment if the conversation amused him.

He wore a bright yellow turban many yards in length, a red ochre robe, the badge of his calling; this was tied with a pink sash, broad and heavily befringed. Snuff-brown trousers and russet shoes completed the outfit.

He spoke better English than I did, was conversant with ancient and modern literature, would quote easily and naturally from Shakespeare or Longfellow or Tennyson, Darwin, Muller, Tyndall; could repeat pages of our Bible, was familiar with and tolerant of all creeds. He was an education, an illumination, a revelation!

I told him, as we separated, I should be most pleased to present him to some men and women of learning and general culture, if by chance he should come to Boston.

We parted. I fatigued myself into positive illness by my pedestrian and cerebral exertions at the Exposition, and all that motley assemblage, with minds as diverse as their raiment, was only a highly coloured fantasy of the past.

Just risen from a sick bed, I received a telegram of forty-five words announcing that my reverend friend of the observation car was at the Quincy House, Boston, and awaiting my orders.

Then I remembered vividly. I had urged him to accept my hospitalities if he felt lonely or needed help. I had promised those introductions to Harvard professors, Concord philosophers, New York capitalists, women of fame, position, and means, with brilliant gifts in writing and conversation. It was mid-August. Not a soul was in town, and how could I entertain my gayly apparelled pundit? I was aghast, but telegraphed bravely: "Yours received. Come today: 4:20 train, Boston Albany."

As the cars stopped, even the piercing whistle had a derisive sound, and I trembled at the effect he might produce on the crowd gathered for the mail. But he was received in breathless silence. He was such a surprise!

If he had looked regal but bizarre among a group collected from all nations, he was simply amazing on the platform at Gooseville. His luggage was so considerable in amount that the train was ten minutes late at the next stopping place. He had brought almost a Bodleian Library with him of books recondite and rare, heavy in either sense.

The yellow headgear looked a brighter yellow than before.

The mulberry pink sash failed to harmonize at all with the red robe. He seemed slightly surprised by the simplicity and quiet of the place, but was too courteous to speak of it.

He never minded the stares and grins that were most evident to me. "Shall I give up the costume of my forefathers?" he sensibly inquired. "Shall you adopt the trailing robes of our women when you visit India?" It is only our bad manners and ignorance that make us think everything is queer, ludicrous, or wrong that differs from our own way. Rose Terry Cooke told me that in a little town where she once lived they spoke of every stranger as a "furriner", and there were dislike and a lurking contempt in the way the word was used. So with my "furriner".

But the climax was reached the next morning, when he was sitting on the porch wrapped in deepest thought or, rather, endeavoring to exclude all thought from his active mind, and thus give room for divine light and communications to flow in. As he sat there, immovable, with eyes vacant and fixed, striving for an approximate condition of Nirvana, Bill Hanson came round the back way, staring, half awestruck, half amused, and said to my man: "Gosh all hemlock![1] What has she got now, and how did she make it?"

He inclined to the theory that it was either a lifelike wax figure, or a rag doll, which I had built and painted and stationed there for effect and the wonderment of the public.

How could I imagine that? So, please, in future believe implicitly my truthful tales. It was trying and vastly embarrassing to have my Oriental visitor inquire in rotund but melancholy and doubting tones: "Where *are* those influential gentlemen, these women you promised me? I must see them, and begin my struggle for my poor people."

The mail bag was stuffed next morning with frantic appeals for help, and I am proud to say that my friends rallied nobly from their vacation haunts by seashore, lake,

---

1. A meaningless exclamation.

and mountain, and my careless promise was through them most gloriously fulfilled.

O dear: I cannot help laughing here all by myself at the remembrance of one evening when fully a dozen ladies were gathered around my honoured guest, looking at him admiringly and at each other with approving words as he explained at length his creed and philosophy and plans for bringing the wretched masses in India out of their poverty and suffering by introducing a little of our practical way of earning money. Then he told us that "the soul is a circle whose circumference is nowhere, and whose center can be everywhere, and that the universe is a power composed of the Great Infinite, and each separate world a distinct meter or rhythm."

My overstrained mind began to wobble, and I found I was sitting on the edge of my chair, with eyes aching from a prolonged stare of wonder, my mouth positively ajar... he talked on and on in glowing rhapsody, I... listening intently to the marvellous eloquence... I left the circle to indulge in immoderate, half-hysteric laughter all alone. I had achieved success, but I, too, had to "struggle". ...

He called me "mother" at parting—an especial tribute to any woman in India, as he explained. I appreciated the compliment. I was proud of such a son...

(*Samvit*, September 1992)

Kumudbandhu Sen

I officially met Swami Vivekananda for the first time in 1897, when he returned to Kolkata from the West. But I had seen him earlier, in 1890, near the twin temples of Sri Mani Gupta in Masjid Bari area.

On that occasion, I was talking to Mani Babu when suddenly a young man of bright brown complexion addressed him, saying, "Hello, young one![1] How are you?" Mani Gupta quickly took the dust of the young man's feet, saying, "As He, the Lord, has kept me. Are you going to Veni Ostad's?[2]" The young man answered in the affirmative, and continued on to his music lesson. When I asked Mani Babu about him, he replied, "He is that Narendranath, whom the Master used to describe as a thousand-petalled lotus and whom he used to address as 'One among the Seven Rishis'." From that point on, our conversation revolved around Swamiji. Though later—thanks to Mani Babu—I had the good fortune of being acquainted with Swamis Yogananda, Trigunatitananda, Saradananda and others, the monastic names of Swamiji and his brother-disciples were not yet publicly known.

In 1897, Vijaykrishna Goswami stayed for some days at the house of Gangaprasad Sen, the famous Ayurvedic physician of Kumartuli. At Vijaykrishna's behest, a small booklet containing Swamiji's addresses delivered at the Chicago Parliament of Religions and describing such things as Swamiji's oratorical powers and the unique spell he cast on

---

1. The word used, khoka, literally means 'baby'.
2. Ostad means an accomplished musician.

the Americans was being circulated there among the visitors. From that booklet I came to know that Swami Vivekananda was none other than Narendranath. In that booklet mention had also been made of the monasteries at Baranagar and Alambazar.

I became acquainted with the Swamis of Baranagore Math around the middle of 1893. We were young men then; when Swamiji returned to India, we had just passed the Entrance Examination and gotten ourselves admitted to college. At Balaram Mandir we used to hold discussions about Swamiji with Swami Brahmananda, Swami Yogananda, Girishchandra Ghosh, Purna, and other companions of the Master. When huge receptions were given to Swamiji at Ramnad and Chennai, descriptions of which appeared in the *Indian Mirror*, young men like us became charged with tremendous inspiration and I used to go often to Balaram Mandir for news relating to Swamiji.

One day, a discussion at Balaram Mandir centered around the fact that, although Swamiji was being received enthusiastically everywhere else, no reception committee had yet been formed in Kolkata. He whom the Master used to call Naren Junior,[3] who had meanwhile become an attorney, said: "Sri N. N. Ghosh has praised Swamiji in the highest terms in the Indian Nation. He exerts a great influence on Raja Benoy Krishna. Let's make a proposal to them about forming a Committee."

From then on, efforts to form a reception committee were made on all sides. The distinguished citizens of Kolkata and Sri Hiren Dutta took special interest in the matter. It was proposed to offer a certificate of honour to Swamiji in a meeting to be presided over by Maharaja Lakshminarayan Singh of Darbhanga.

When the reception committee was formed, I became a volunteer under the leadership of Sri Sachindranath Bose, a devotee. One day, when I went to Balram Mandir at 10 a.m., he gave me a letter to be delivered to Narendranath Mitra

3. Narendranath Mitra.

and said: "Swamiji is coming to Budge Budge. Narendra should send this letter [which mentioned this news] to Swami Trigunatitananda." Due to financial constraints, the reception committee reserved only a special first class compartment to bring Swamiji from Budge Budge to Sealdah Station.

Next morning, before daybreak, reaching the station at 5 a.m. as a volunteer, I found it difficult to enter the platform—so huge was the crowd assembled there. All the houses on Harrison Road had been decorated with flags, festoons, flowers, etc. On one side were samkirtan parties, hosts of monks and brahmacharis of various denominations and a vast assemblage of people. On account of our volunteers' badges, we somehow managed to stay, on the orders of Charuchunder Mitter, on the platform in front of the location where the special compartment was to halt.

When the special train carrying Swamiji arrived, there was so much jostling by the crowd that Ananda Charlu fell; volunteers had to lift him up and take him out. Then Charu Babu shouted, "Form a circle around Swamiji and guide him along the way we clear for him." This we did. When he stepped down from the compartment, I saluted him and he responded by saying, "That's all right."

As soon as Swamiji came outside, the public cheered him on all sides with victory chants. Charu Babu directed the coachman to unharness the horses and asked us to pull the carriage. Swamiji objected, but Charu Babu said: "We are welcoming you; your objection will not stand. They will gladly take you to Ripon College."

Then Swamiji, bedecked with garlands, remained standing and saluted all with folded hands. Captain and Mrs. Sevier and Mr. Goodwin were seated on the phaeton. Swami Trigunatitananda, who was standing at the back of the phaeton, cheered aloud in the names of the Master and Swamiji. Near the crossing of the Amherst Street, in front of the residence of Vijaykrishna Goswami, the phaeton came to a stop due to the huge crowd. From there we could see

Goswamiji saluting Swamiji with folded hands from his second floor veranda. Swamiji returned both Goswamiji's gaze and his salute.

With great difficulty, Swamiji was conducted to the narrow courtyard of the old Ripon College building. He was guided to a table and chair placed on a small, simple veranda. It was impossible to deliver a speech from there. He stood up and said simply, in English: "I have been fascinated and delighted by your enthusiasm and welcome. It is impossible to deliver a lecture here. With my conveying my thanks to you, let this meeting be dissolved."

As I turned back, I found that my friend, the well-known actor and playwright Aparesh Chandra, was about to be crushed by the crowd. In the nick of time he was somehow lifted up and deposited in a safer place. The young men, including us, were so charged with enthusiasm that we said, "Let's draw this phaeton up to the house of Pashupati Babu." As we thus went along, drawing Swamiji's carriage, slowly the crowd began to thin. Swami Subodhananda was standing on one side of the road and Latu Maharaj on the other, looking at Swamiji.

Swamiji asked us to stop the phaeton in front of Purna Babu's house on Cornwallis Street and told Swami Trigunatitananda, "Send word to brother Purna." Purna Babu, who had been bathing, came out wearing wet clothes. Prostrating himself before Swamiji, he said, "I saw you from a distance at the station earlier, and came away to avoid being late at the office." Swamiji said, "Come in the evening and see me."

Shouting exuberantly, we drew the carriage up to the house of Pashupati Bose. There, too, was a huge welcome arch decorated with flowers. Pashupati Bose and others saluted Swamiji in front of the gate and were leading him inside when Swamis Brahmananda and Yogananda garlanded him. Swamiji bowed to both and said, "The son of the guru should be treated as the guru himself." Swami Brahmananda replied, "The elder brother deserves the same respect as one's father." As Master Mahashaya came forward and saluted, Swamiji said, "Oh my girl comrade!" Then as Amrita Lal Bose, the master dramatist and actor, saluted him, he said, "Here is Vrinde,[4] the lady-messenger" and had all kinds of fun with him and the others. Hutko Gopal was seated on a bench below. Swamiji saw him and said" "Hello Hutko, I still remain the same Naren. Why do you hide there? Come here. I haven't forgotten the Bengali dialect." After ten minutes or so, Pashupati Bose and others came to take Swamiji inside.

As soon as Swamiji went upstairs, Girishchandra put a garland around his neck and was about to salute him when Swamiji held his hands and said: "What is this, G.C.?[5] That will bring me bad luck. I have carried your Ramakrishna across the seas with the shout of 'Jai Ram'."[6] Looking at Swamiji, Girish Babu beamed with an exuberance of joy. He was so overwhelmed that he could hardly utter a word.

Thereafter, Swamiji went to the adjoining room with Master Mahashaya and they began to converse. Swamiji said:

"Master Mahashaya, in all this [conquest of the West] that you witness, I am nothing but an instrument. It is he who sent me there. And as regards our Holy Mother—I apprised her that the Master had indicated to me [to go to the West] and asked her permission and command. Through the blessings of the Mother, I could cross all hurdles with ease and become the centre of attention among hosts of great scholars, people of wisdom, scientists, and thousands of men and women in that land [western countries]. I realize all these as the play of our Master. I have much to say; I'll tell you another time. However, I'm now convinced that in this country there has been enough religious preaching; what is wanted is education. What India badly needs at present is that her masses have clean clothes to wear, enough food

4. Vrinde was the companion of Radha and acted as her messenger.

5. Swamiji used to address Girish Ghosh as G.C.

6. Reference is to Hanuman's crossing the sea to Sri Lanka in one bound with the cry "Jai Ram".

to fill their stomachs, an education and a chance to earn their livelihood. Master Mahashaya, when I saw the riches of those countries, I thought about the wretched condition of our country and felt like weeping. I recalled the stanzas from Meghadutam: 'Well may the mansions of that city be compared with you, O cloud: while flashes of lightning play within you, they have charmingly attired damsels moving within; while you have the rainbow, they have their paintings; you have your deep rolling rumble, and they their drums sounding forth music; you contain pellucid water within you, they have their interior bedecked with transparent gems; you soar so high, their roofs kiss the sky.'[7]

"And in our country we have garbage and stench all around us, half-naked humans—lustreless, dim sighted, illiterate men and women. Seeing them, I thought that to serve them is the religion of the day for India. Did not the Master use to say one cannot have religion on an empty stomach? My aim is precisely to preach this religion of service.

"The Master protected me from all temptations in the West. And what a wonder: some of the people there had already come to know the ideas of the Master, some of them in dream. I looked upon the women there like mothers and sisters. And many of them treated me like their son or brother. In the West, the land of sense enjoyment, it is necessary to preach religion. Here, in this country, on the foundation of our religion, we have to spread their sciences, their high outlook and their social freedom."

Just then, Swami Brahmananda came in and said, "Arrangements have been made to serve you tea and refreshments." Swamiji said: "Raja, I saw Vijay Babu on the way. Could you not bring him and arrange for his stay at the Math?" Raja Maharaj said: "He now has many disciples, male and female. We don't have enough room to lay our own beds. If he lived alone, that would have been another matter." Swamiji said, "I will meet him soon."

---

7. Meghadutam, 66

Knowing the day Swamiji would go to the residence of Vijaykrishna Goswami, I went beforehand. A separate seat had been arranged in front of Goswamiji, who was waiting for the appointment time specified by Swamiji. Only about ten to fifteen other people were there when I arrived, but by the time Swamiji came upstairs, quite a crowd had assembled. Swamiji and Goswamiji made prostrations to each other for a long time. Finally Goswamiji said, "Glory to Ramakrishna! I saw that he was present by my side touching my body. When I go to Dakshineshwar, I get to see him at Panchavati and in his room. How marvellous it is! One day I went to him at Dakshineshwar; not many people were there at the time. He was alone in an ecstatic mood. As soon as I prostrated myself before him, he said, 'Are your worship, meditation and all that going on all right? The six passions associated with the body are great obstacles in the path of discrimination and renunciation.' In reply I said, 'But I have not been able to subjugate lust.' Then the Master said, 'What! You are taking God's name so much and yet lust has not come under control!'" Goswamiji said that Sri Ramakrishna then touched him, uttering the words, "Onwards ho! Be you immersed in the ocean of Existence-Knowledge-Bliss, plunged into samadhi." At this Goswamiji felt transmission of power like an electric current through his body. Swamiji replied, "That he used to transmit power through a mere touch, I have myself experienced first-hand."

"My intention," Swamiji continued, "is to establish some ashramas in India; presently, this is being done in Chennai, Kolkata and Varanasi. My English friends, the Sevier couple, want to start one at some secluded place in the Himalayas. They are on the lookout for a site, but as yet none has been decided upon. They intend to establish an ashrama in the sacred Himalayas and to pass their lives there in worship and meditation. A few monks and brahmacharis will also be there to assist them. Please give your blessings—you are my elder and worthy of respect like the guru—so that I can give practical shape to these intentions."

Goswamiji replied, "You are a person who is siddhasam-kalpa—one whose every intention shall be accomplished. And this intention is not yours; it is He who is rousing this intention within you."

Next, they started talking about the divine state of the Master and soon became overwhelmed with ecstasy. Later, they prostrated themselves before each other again and Swamiji took his leave.

That divine scene continues to shine vividly in my memory even now.

(*Prabuddha Bharata*, August 1997)

Lillian Montgomary

I would like to tell you my impression of Swamiji. My reaction to him was so spontaneous and unexpected.

The first thing I noticed was that his head was the most
perfect I had ever seen—no part over-developed or under-
developed apparently.

The distinctive feature of his voice was a wonderful
purity that was unique with a bell-like quality, full-toned and
melodious. It was free and flowed in an even rhythm—he
himself tuned to a perfect harmony—and every word was
luminous with new light and value.

Listening, veil after veil fell from your mind's eye—like
a miracle, your concept of the universe, personality, of the
relationship of the individual soul to God was changing.
There was a dawning vision of a new set of values and a
goal that would be the fulfilment of the heart's desire.

Most of all it was as if you had heard the term "soul"
all your life, then, there you were gazing into one highly
evolved for the first time, surprised by the full clearness of
its beauty, its limpid purity, its tremendous power in repose.
What you had imagined before to be "soul" was such a poor,
petty, insignificant thing.

Looking at him "being in his presence" was worth more
than hundreds of books—he, himself, was a light on the
scriptures. That is why you could never forget him.

But, with me, it has been something more than memory—a sort of drawing power—Oh! so faint, but steady, like
a magnet holding me even in my weakest, most bewildered
moments. And now I feel he may be drawing me closer to his

fold. From the first day I came to the Centre—I have told you this before—I felt it was home.

I am speaking the truth when I say that as I listened to Swamiji, hardly breathing, the thought came: if he would ask me to follow him barefoot I would do it. He held you charmed in the deepest sense of the word—spellbound.

For years, except now and then the Swamis, I couldn't listen to others speak on spiritual subjects. It was as if I asked for bread and they gave me something without substance, or a caricature of the real thing.

For months and months I read *Raja Yoga* with the rhythm, inflection, wonderful bell-like tone of his voice in my ear—timing the phrases by its accent—with its clear, pure, mellow fullness of sound. Its purity came from a plane crystal clear—that is why it shattered the clouds of your mind and distinguished it from others.

The very word "purity" took on a new significance. If, before, it had appeared something fragile that could be blown to smithereens, now you saw it as an element which nothing could shatter.

Listening to him one day the thought flashed: "He is so established in the realization that the Soul is eternal that he could face a cannon without fear."

But this is probably the most remarkable thing: I saw a sea of consciousness that filled space back of him. It was limpid and vibrant. And the flood of that light focussed and poured through his words. That is what gave the impression of the absence of ego. He was beyond "art"—he was "genius"... the divine glow. There seemed no break between him and an infinite intelligent light held by the voice that came from that altitude of light. Words such as "beauty," "harmony", "vision" came to mind and carried you to a realm intensely more vivid than any known before. And it all seemed so simple—so natural—as if it were the state we all should be enjoying.

But you see I was a weak character—a weak swimmer in the waves that tossed me about, but never losing the vision of what I had seen in him and sensing that life lived at his level would be a marvellous experience indeed. Still there was no aloofness about him, nor was there any feeling that he had denied his body—rather that he had transmuted the elements into their finest form. You saw fulfilment—attainment—a complete whole—and you said, so this is the meaning of *real culture*. What others talked about, he *was*. How sure I was at that moment—I had all the answers—a living ideal I had seen, and the path to follow. Life opened up as a wonderful adventure, with religion as the "open sesame" that would open the door to all its mysteries. ...

After the service there were always half a dozen or so who would linger to have a few last words with Swamiji. I always tagged on to look and listen, my one desire being to climb the golden path of awareness to the Ultimate Goal.

One day, finding myself at the side of Swami Turiyananda, I picked up courage and said, "I meditate but nothing happens." I remember his answer: "It comes in waves—each one carries you closer the shore."

Sister Nivedita was there—very smiling. One afternoon she spoke. I didn't go. I had heard the greatest of all voices. A lesser one had no attraction. It was much more impressive being in touch with Swamiji in the intimate surroundings of the Vedanta rooms than in a lecture hall. I have always been grateful for that. I understood two things—he spoke with authority from a realm of thought he was experiencing and there was nothing aggressive in that authority—it streamed from a source of pure knowledge.

About his poems, I still think, they compliment one other. By taking them as a whole you sense the magnitude of his personality. If we could sink into them to the depth of his realization we would all be Vivekanandas.

The first of Swamiji's that I learned years ago in Cannes was "The Song of the Sannyasin". I always said it in my walks and do still. It seems to call for the out-of-doors—wide spaces—the open road.

Do you know what his poems mean to me? I always drove my own car in Cannes. But on long trips I took a chauffeur. I'd write to Michalene for an itinerary and receive a typewritten manuscript covering the region I wanted to tour. It gave a detailed description of every turning to take for every detour to some hidden place of interest—a chapel, a shrine with a legend, a sight of beauty—and then the guide-book indicated the type of hotels and inns. I roamed about the whole of France, North Italy and the Tyrol, Bavarai and Switzerland in perfect confidence, knowing I could depend on the information given.

Well, I roam about the inner world through his poems with the same confidence. I can't penetrate to the depth of his vision. But I can glimpse it and know it is there. And life becomes more vivid in making a trip.

How India is drawing public interest. And when I discovered India through Swami Vivekananda, all we knew about it was that it was some far away country where we sent our missionaries. Now you can't pick up a paper that hasn't some mention of it. ...

Since my return last spring I have had very definite and unexpected "urges": One, suddenly, to say I surrendered myself completely to Sri Ramakrishna—lead me where he will.

The other is in regard to Swamiji's photograph. I have always turned to the one without the turban, seated in the high-backed chair, which is exactly as I saw him. Without warning I am drawn irresistibly to the one in meditation. It is as if that one is the medium through which something is pouring down from above. I offer no explanation. But that is the way it is.

[Extracts from a letter of Mrs. Lillian Montgomery to Swami Nikhilananda.]

Mohanlal Shah

I deem it a great good fortune that I am able to witness the birth centenary celebration of the world-adored Swami Vivekananda, whom I had the rare opportunity of seeing on four occasions.

I had his holy glimpse for the first time in 1890, when as a wandering monk he visited Almora. He was the guest of Lala Badrilal Shah. I had gone there just by chance and met him. I prostrated before him and then came away. Though I was only about twelve, that first glimpse is still vivid in my memory. I was taken aback by his radiant appearance. It looked as if a second Buddha had come in his form. To this day, I haven't seen another like him.

The second time I saw him was in 1897. He had come back to India after his triumph at the Parliament of Religions in America. Almora was affording him a big welcome—thousands of people greeted him and showered flowers on him. I can best describe the occasion by quoting Mr. Goodwin, who was with Swamiji at that time:

> At Lodea, close to Almora, there was a large crowd of citizens waiting in the afternoon to convey him along the final part of his journey, and at their request the Swami mounted a horse dressed in handsome trappings and headed a procession into the town. It seemed that, as the bazaar was reached, every citizen of the place joined the company. So dense was the crowd that some difficulty was experienced in leading the Swami's course through. Thousands of Hindu

ladies, from the tops of houses and from windows, showered flowers and rice on Swamiji, as he passed along. In the centre of the town, a section of the interesting old-fashioned bazaar street had been turned into a pandal capable of holding three thousand people; decorated cloths stretched across from side to side of the street forming the roof, and the ends being beautified with festoons of flowers, banners, etc. In addition, every house displayed lights till the town appeared to be a blaze of light, and the native music with the constant cheers of the crowd, made the entire scene most remarkable, even to those who had accompanied Swamiji through the whole of his journey from Colombo. ...

Naturally, with from four to five thousand persons crowding inside and outside the pandal, and with excitement in full play, the proceedings of the formal welcome were brief. Pandit Jwala Dutt Joshi read first a Hindi address of welcome on behalf of the Reception Committee. Pandit Hari Ram Pande followed, with a second address from the Swami's host, Lala Badri Sah, and a pandit read an equally appreciative address in Sanskrit.

Fortunately, I was one of those lucky citizens at the hill station and had the opportunity to participate in the functions.

The third time I saw Swamiji was in 1898, again in Almora. He had come there for a short change of scenery and there were some disciples—foreign and Indian—with him. At this time the *Prabuddha Bharata* press was started at the Thompson House, a spacious bungalow on the Mall at Almora. Swami Swarupananda, a disciple of Swami Vivekananda, was the editor, and one day I chanced to make his acquaintance. He was so kind to me and I was so charmed by his sweet behaviour that from the very next day I came to stay at Thompson House with him. It was perhaps sometimes in the month of October. From that day till now, the relationship between myself and the monks of the Ramakrishna Math is unbroken and becoming sweeter with the passage of time.

After about four months, in March 1899, the *Prabuddha Bharata* shifted to its permanent home at Mayavati, when Advaita Ashrama was started there by Capt. and Mrs. Sevier, two English disciples of Swami Vivekananda. I also came to Mayavati along with others. Swami Swarupananda became the first president of the Mayavati ashrama, and was succeeded, after his premature demise in 1906, by his brother-disciple Swami Virajananda. This was where I saw Swami Vivekananda for the fourth time.

In 1901, on January 3, Swamiji came to Mayavati with some of his brother-disciples and disciples. Though it was very cold and snowing rather heavily, Swamiji's fifteen-day stay was full of mirth and joy. It has proved to be the most memorable event in the history of this Himalayan monastery. Swamiji used to pass much of his time at Mayavati in reading and writing. I was working in the *Prabuddha Bharata* press and had occasion to show him some proofs. I was filled with awe to see him from close quarters. How kind was his heart! What feelings he had for the poor and the afflicted! He had infused this feeling for the poor among his disciples also; and I have seen some of them very closely. They looked upon the poor and the downtrodden as manifestations of God and used to serve them in that spirit. This has become the tradition behind all philanthropic activities of the Ramakrishna Mission.

I cannot adequately give expression to all the thoughts that come to my mind at the moment. My long association with the Advaita Ashrama of Mayavati, my personal contacts with many monks of the Ramakrishna Order, the happy incidents during my stay in the ashrama and the affection and kindness extended to me by the ashrama inmates—these and many more sweet moments of my life are crowding my memory, and I am overwhelmed with emotion. But

crowning them all are the precious memories of Swami
Vivekananda, which I hold very sacred. They are luminous
in the treasure-chest of my mind, and my heart is full. They
have been my most cherished possession till now, and will
continue to be so for the rest of my life.

(*Prabuddha Bharata*, January 1964)

Mary Tapan Wright

One day, at an unfashionable place by the sea, the professor [J. H. Wright] was seen crossing the lawn between
the boarding-house and his cottage accompanied by a man
[Swami Vivekananda] in a long red coat. The coat, which
had something of a priestly cut, descended far below the
man's knees, and was girded around his waist with a thick
cord of the same reddish orange tint. He walked with a
strange, shambling gait, and yet there was a commanding
dignity and impressiveness in the carriage of his neck and
bare head that caused everyone in sight to stop and look
at him. He moved slowly, with the swinging tread of one
who had never hastened, and in his great dark eyes was
the beauty of an alien civilization which might—should
time and circumstances turn it into opposition—become
intolerably repulsive. He was dark, about the colour of a light
quadroon, and his full lips, which in a man of Caucasian race
would have been brilliant scarlet, had a tint of bluish purple.
His teeth were regular, white and sometimes cruel, but his
beautiful expressive eyes and the proud wonderful carriage
of his head, the swing and grace of the heavy crimson tassels
that hung from the end of his sash, made one forget that he
was too heavy for so young a man, and that long sitting on
the floor had visited him with the fate of the tailor.
... He seemed very young, even younger than his
twenty-nine years, and as he seated himself he covered
his legs carefully with his flowing robe, like a woman or a
priest; but the hoary ancient turn of his thought belied his
childlike manner.... And then, having said his say, the Swami

was silent.... Occasionally he cast his eye up to the roof and repeated softly "Shiva, Shiva, Shiva!" ... And a current of powerful feeling seemed to be flowing like molten lava beneath the silent surface of this strange being. ...

He stayed among them, keenly interested in all practical things; his efforts to eat strange food were heroic and sometimes disastrous to himself. He was constantly looking about for something which would widen the possibilities of feeding his people in times of famine. Our ways seemed to inspire him with a sort of horror, meat-eating cannibals that we seemed to be! But he concealed it, either with absolute dumbness, or by a courteous flow of language which effectually hid his thoughts.

He had been brought up amidst polemics, and his habit of argument was mainly Socratic, beginning insidiously and simply by a story, or clear statement of some incontestable fact, and then from that deriving strange and unanswerable things. All through, his discourses abounded in picturesque illustrations and beautiful legends. To work, to get on in the world, in fact any measure of temporal success seemed to him entirely beside the subject. He had been trained to regard the spiritual life as the real thing of this world! Love of God and love of man! ... "The love of the Hindu," he told us, "goes further than the love of the Christians, for that stops at man; but the religion of Buddha goes on towards the beasts of the field and every creeping thing that has life."

At sixteen he had renounced the world and spent his time among men who rejoiced in these things and looked forward to spending day after day on the banks of the Ganga, talking of the higher life.

When someone suggested to him that Christianity was a saving power he opened his great dark eyes upon him and said, "If Christianity is a saving power in itself, why has it not saved the Ethiopians, the Abyssinians?" He also arraigned our own crimes, the horror of women on the stage, the frightful immorality in our streets, our drunkenness, our thieving, our political degeneracy, the murdering in our West, the lynching in our South, and we, remembering his own Thugs, were still too delicate to mention them. ...

He cared for Thomas à Kempis more than for any other writer and had translated a part of the *Imitation of Christ* into Bengali and written an introduction to it; as for receiving the Stigmata, he spoke of it as a natural result of an agonizing love of God. The teaching of the Vedas, constant and beautiful, he applied to every event in life, quoting a few verses and then translating, and with the translation of the story giving the meaning. His mouth, also, was full of wonderful proverbs. "Of what use is the knowledge that is locked away in books?" he said, in speaking of the memories of Hindu boys.

Himself a Hindu monk, he told, once, of a time when he turned into a forest, a trackless forest, because he felt that God was leading him, of how he went on for three days, starving and how he was more perfectly happy than he had ever been before because he felt that he was entirely in the hands of God. "When my time comes," he said, "I shall like to go up the mountain and there, by the Ganga, lay myself down, and with the water singing over me I shall go to sleep, and above me will tower the Himalayas—men have gone mad for those mountains!" There was once a monk, he told us, who went far up into the mountains and saw them everywhere around him; and above his head towered their great white crests. Far below, thousands of feet, was the Ganga—narrow stream at the foot of a precipice. "Shall I then like a dog die in my bed when all this beauty is around me?" the monk thought, and he plunged into the chasm. ...

All the people of that little place were moved and excited by this young man, in a manner beyond what might be accounted for by his coming from a strange country and a different people. He had another power, an unusual ability to bring his hearers into vivid sympathy with his own point of view. It repelled, in some cases, however, as strongly as it attracted, but whether in support or opposition, it was difficult to keep a cool head or a level judgement when confronted with him.

All the people of all degrees were interested; women's eyes blazed and their cheeks were red with excitement; even the children of the village talked of what he had said to them; all the idle summer boarders trooped to hear him, and all the artists longingly observed him and wanted to paint him.

He told strange stories as ordinary people would mention the wonders of electricity, curious feats of legerde-main, and tales of monks who had lived one hundred, or one hundred and thirty years; but so-called occult societies drew down his most magnificent contempt. ... He spoke of holy men who at a single glance converted hardened sinners and detected men's inmost thoughts. ... But these things were trifles; always his thoughts turned back to his people. He lived to raise them up and make them better and had come this long way in the hope of gaining help to teach them, to be practically more efficient. We hardly knew what he needed; money, if money would do it; tools, advice, new ideas. And for this he was willing to die to-morrow. ...

His great heroine was the dreadful Rani of the Indian Mutiny, who led her troops in person. ... Whenever he mentioned the Rani he would weep, with tears streaming down his face. "That woman was a goddess," he said, "a Devi. When overcome, she fell on her sword and died like a man."

In quoting from the Upanishads his voice was most musical. He would quote a verse in Sanskrit with intonations and then translate it into beautiful English, of which he had a wonderful command. And, in his mystical religion, he seemed perfectly and unquestionably happy.

... And yet, when they gave him money, it seemed as if some injury had been done to him and some disgrace put upon him. "Of all the worries I have ever had," he said, as he left us, "the greatest has been the care of this money!" His horrified reluctance to take it haunted us. He could not be made to see why he might not wander on in this country, as in his own, without touching a medium of exchange, which he considered disgraceful, and the pain he showed when it was made clear to him that without money he could not even move, hung round us for days after he left, as if we had hurt some innocent thing or had wounded a soul. ... And we saw him leave us after that one little week of knowing him, with fear that clutches the heart when a beloved, gifted, passionate child fares forth, unconscious, in an untried world.

(*Life*, Vol. 1, pp.406-409)

Sacchindranath Bose

Rented house, Belur, November 1898

Swamiji came downstairs. A few days before, he had returned from Kashmir. His complexion had darkened, and he looked tired. I bowed down to him, and he said to me with a smile: "Hello, Sachin. How are you?" His sweet voice sounded, to my ears, like a vina.[1]

Swamiji's aunt and an old maidservant who had raised him came to see him. He talked to them for awhile and then went to the main hall. We talked about the activities of the Varanasi Home of Service, and then he asked about me in detail. He also expressed a desire to visit East Bengal, Kamakhya (in Assam), and the Himalayan range along the Brahmaputra River. Swamiji treated me with love and affection. After awhile he said, "I shall not give any more lectures. Enough of it! I shall keep quiet and let the work continue steadily."

I asked Swamiji about his trip to Kashmir, and he spoke highly of that region's scenery and glaciers. When he described his experience at Amarnath, his eyes turned red with emotion. Then I mentioned Lord Lansdown's description of the beauty of Kashmir, and he said: "It is true. One will not have to cross Almora to see scenery as good as in Switzerland, but the panoramic scenery of Kashmir is unparalleled." He described the joy and spiritual experience he had got from seeing the snow-clad mountains of Kashmir. Then

---

1. An Indian lute.

he said, "I have experienced the existence of the formless Brahman and of the gods and goddesses." Just then an old servant of Swamiji's family, who used to walk him to school, came to see him. Swamiji gave him four rupees.

In the afternoon, we went for a walk in the new monastery grounds. A fence had been put up on the western boundary, and a couple of temporary sheds had been erected for the construction work. Swami Advaitananda had planted eggplant, okra, pumpkin, and other vegetables. The monastery building looked nice. Another two-storey building for the shrine and kitchen was under construction on the west side; Swami Vijnanananda was supervising the construction. I went upstairs with Swamiji. Looking at the Ganga, he sang from the *Vishvanathashtakam*: "The waves of the Ganga enhance the beauty of Lord Shiva's matted hair. Speech cannot express His glory—He who is the repository of all noble qualities. Worship Vishvanatha, the presiding deity of Varanasi." In the evening, I returned to Kolkata by boat with Sharatchandra Chakravarty.

Another day, I went to Balaram Bose's house in Baghbazar. Swamiji was walking on the roof with his cousin, Habul Dutta. Mr. Dutta was a flutist and used to play during the Ramakrishna festival at the Kankurgachi Yogodyan. Swamiji came downstairs to the hall, and a doctor arrived to examine him.

On the way home, I had a nice conversation with Habul. He said that Swamiji had brought about a change in his life. Swamiji had once asked him: "Brother, how can the Bengalis have renunciation? Neither have they enjoyed the world, nor do they have a million rupees. Renunciation comes after satisfying the desires for the world. Germany has finished enjoying the world, and now the Germans are ready for renunciation. Later it'll be America's and England's turn." Swamiji had also said to Habul: "Brother, Whatever Sri Ramakrishna advised you to do, please follow it implicitly. You will not have to practise various kinds of intricate yoga." Habul was doing this on his own. "The result of pranayama," the Swami told him, "will come to you automatically." When Habul asked Swamiji about his experiences during his trip to Amarnath, Swamiji replied: "It was a grand experience. Since visiting Amarnath, my mind is desperately seeking peace. I don't enjoy work anymore. I wish to be alone in a remote cave. Lord Shiva of Amarnath possessed me for eight days and eight nights. Sitting on my head, he would laugh a lot. I said to him, 'Father, I am suffering from physical ailments and you are laughing!' That form of Sri Ramakrishna which appeared to me before I left for America and asked me to go there—that same form appeared and advised me to visit Amarnath; so I went."

6 November 1898

I arrived at Baghbazar at 1:30 p.m. and learned from Swami Brahmananda that Swamiji had left for Belur Math a few minutes earlier with some foreign women devotees. I immediately went to the ferry ghat and hired a small boat, and reached Belur Math in an hour. Swamiji had arrived twenty minutes earlier. He showed the ladies the new site of the Math and they were very pleased. Mrs. Ole Bull and Miss Josephine MacLeod were going to leave for America on 2 December, and Swamiji planned to go there via London four or five months later. I returned to Kolkata with them, and on the way Swamiji talked to the ladies on various topics. Our boat reached Baghbazar in the evening. The ladies then boarded a tram bound for the Esplanade, and Swamiji and I went to Balaram Bose's house.

Swamiji's health was better. He was under Dr. R. L. Dutta's care and was on a restricted diet. In the hall of Balaram Bose's house, Rakhal Maharaj [Swami Brahmananda] and I sat in front of Swamiji. After a while, Sharat Chakravarty joined us. Soon thereafter Sarada Maharaj [Swami Trigunatitananda] joined us. His body was shaking; he had a high fever.

I should explain that when Swamiji was in Almora, Swami Trigunatitananda had written to him repeatedly asking for Rs. 2,000; he wanted to start a printing press. Swamiji gave him Rs. 1,000 and he took a loan of another Rs. 1,000, for which he has to pay Rs. 10 as monthly interest. He has bought two fairly good presses for Rs. 1,500, but as there are very few jobs, the machines are lying idle in a warehouse in Burra Bazar for which Rs. 8 per month has to be paid as rent. Swami Trigunatita has decided to print Swamiji's *Raja Yoga*, translated by Swami Shuddhananda, but there is no money to purchase paper for the book. ... Once I had told him: "Maharaj, this job of running a press is very mean work and not fit for a man like you. Let someone else do it!" At that time the Swami was in high spirits. He replied: "No! Every work is sacred. I will be happy with any work; I do not hesitate to do any kind of work!" I kept quiet. Nowadays, Swami Trigunatitananda goes to the press every day at six in the morning; he has his meal there, and comes back to his residence after seven in the evening. He has had a fever every evening for the last few days.

Swamiji and Rakhal Maharaj welcomed Swami Trigunatitananda, saying, "Come, what is today's news, Babaji [a nickname of Swami Trigunatitananda]? What progress have you made with the press work? Tell us! Sit down!"

Swami Trigunatitananda said in a distressed voice: "I am fed up. Does such work suit us? The whole day I have to sit quietly like a crow in a place of pilgrimage. There's neither work, nor anything else worthwhile. I have been given one job that will fetch eight annas at the most. What shall I do with that! I am now trying to sell the press."

Swamiji: What are you saying! Has your enthusiasm been dampened so soon! Try for some more days; then, think of giving it up. Bring your presses near Kumartuli, where we also can see them.

Trigunatitananda: No, brother, let them remain where they are. Let me wait a few more days. Then I shall sell them at a loss of Rs.10 or 15.

Swamiji: Oh, Rakhal, what is he saying! It seems he has undergone a severe trial. (To Swami Trigunatitananda:) How is it that all your hopes have been crushed already! You haven't a drop of patience left in you!

When Swamiji said these words, his eyes flashed. He sat up and roared like a lion: "What do you say! All right, sell the presses right now! I need money badly. Sell them now even if it means a loss of Rs. 100 or 150. I find their spirit of renunciation arises whenever they face a difficult situation; they say in a nasal voice, 'Well, I am fed up. Does such work suit us?' You fellow, you can only eat a sumptuous meal and lie on your belly. No patience for any useful work! Are they men who have no perseverance? Enough of it! Now I know your worth. You haven't worked for even three days in the press! Pooh! You thought you were big enough to do this work. Who asked you to start this press? You had great vanity. It is you who repeatedly pestered me to send you money to buy a press. Why don't you bring the machines here? What is the use of keeping them there? Besides, you are feverish every day. You're not taking care of your health!"

Trigunatitananda: I have to pay rent of Rs. 8 per month. I've already made an agreement for one month.

Swamiji: Fie on you! What does he say, Rakhal? Can such people do any work! You are staying there for the sake of Rs. 8 only! Can't you give up such small-mindedness? You and Haramohan are the same in this respect. You don't know how to do business. He, too, visits fifty shops to buy one paise's worth of potatoes and finally gets cheated. Send the printing press to Belur Math. We, too, need a press. Just see how many lectures I have delivered! How much I have written! Half of it has not been printed yet. Do you mean to say that I don't understand work? Rakhal, do you remember how, sitting on the bank of the Ganga, we wept in front of the Master's relics? I said: "We shall build a temple for the Master on the bank of the Ganga and install his relics there, because he was very fond of living near the Ganga." But he [Ramchandra Dutta] installed the relics in his garden at

Kankurgachi. It hurt me immensely. Rakhal, you remember how I made a firm resolve to build a temple for the Master on the bank of the Ganga. To fulfil this idea I have travelled for the last twelve years all over the world like a bulldog. I didn't get any rest. Look, today I have fulfilled that wish.

Trigunatitananda: Brother, how wonderful is your brain! Can you give me your brain?

At this, all burst into laughter. After a while Swami Trigunatitananda told the story of the rest of his day. With a high temperature in the morning, he had taken a small quantity of sago, but in the afternoon he had taken one seer of Rabri (a sweetmeat prepared by condensing milk), half a seer of Kachuri, and an equal quantity of curry. Hearing this, Swamiji laughed heartily and said: "You fellow! Give me your stomach. I shall change the face of this earth! Surajlal said to me at Lahore, 'Swamiji, you have Nanak's brain and Guru Govind's heart. All you need is the stomach of Jagmohan [the Dewan of Khetri].'"

Miss Margaret Noble [Sister Nivedita] left for England with Swamiji on 20 June 1899, by the S. S. Golconda. I was present at the Princep Ghat in Kolkata. Sister Nivedita gave her last lecture on Kali at the Kalighat temple in South Kolkata. It had been arranged that Swamiji would preside over the meeting, and the Halders [owners of the Kali temple] were very eager to receive him. A week earlier Swamiji had gone with a couple of monks and Nivedita to visit the Divine Mother at Kalighat. The Halders had paid their homage to Swamiji and opened the door of the temple for him. When he saw the Divine Mother's serene face he could not check his emotion. His love and devotion welled up, breaking through the outer shell of Vedanta. His large eyes became red, and tears began to flow. He chanted hymns to the Mother in his melodious voice. Then he offered a red hibiscus at the Mother's feet and asked others to do the same. The people at Kalighat were amazed to see Swamiji's devotional nature. ...

On 19 June, the day before Swamiji left for the West, he gave a talk at Belur Math. This lecture inspired all who were present and made them feel, at least for the time being, that they were "real human beings"—for Swamiji had said, with great zeal: "Brothers, I want you to be real human beings, strong as strength itself, yet possessing a woman's heart. If this 'man-making religion' is even partially successful, I shall consider that my life has not been in vain. What more shall I tell you? Please make a special effort to follow Sri Ramakrishna's footsteps, and combine action and renunciation in your lives."

The next day Swamiji came to Kolkata. It had been decided that he would leave for the Princep Ghat at 3.00 p.m. There was a discussion about his conveyance. I had arranged for the Raja of Mahisadal's brougham carriage. Swamiji changed his clothes for the sea voyage and put on an Assam silk coat, a pair of cabin shoes, and a night cap. Swami Turiyananda was dressed similarly.

Swamiji was not looking at all well. At the dock there was a strict health examination due to the epidemic of plague. Nearly fifty people were at the dock to see Swamiji off. The boat arrived at 5:00 p.m. and Swamiji boarded it, saying good-bye to everyone. They had first class tickets. Swami Turiyananda looked very grave. Almost all of the monks of Belur Math had come, and Swami Akhandananda had come from Mahula. When the boat was about to leave, tears came to everyone's eyes. Then fifty people bowed down to Swamiji, touching their heads to the ground. It was a sight to see on the bank of the Ganga. The other European passengers were amazed. Gradually the boat left the harbour and, as long as Swamiji was visible, people waved their handkerchiefs. When the boat was out of sight we returned with heavy hearts.

(*Vedanta Kesari*, Annual Number, 1987)

Manmathanath Chowdhury

One morning in August of the year 1890, Swami Vive-kananda with Swami Akhandananda came unexpected-ly to my house. Thinking them to be ordinary sadhus, I did not pay much attention to them. We were sitting together after our noonday meal; and believing them to be ignorant, I did not enter into conversation with them, but began to read an English translation of a work on Buddhism. After a while, Swamiji asked me what book I was reading. In reply, I told him the title of the book and asked, "Do you know English?" He replied, "Yes, a little." Then I conversed with him on Buddhism, but after a short time I found out that he was a thousand times more learned than I. He quoted from many English works, and Babu Mathuranath Sinha of Danapur and myself were astonished at his learning and listened to him with rapt attention. ...

One day Swamiji asked me if I practised any special sadhana, and we conversed on the practice of Yoga for a long time. From this I was convinced that he was not a common man, since what he said of Yoga was exactly the same as that which I had heard from Swami Dayananda Sarasvati. Besides, he gave out many other important things on the subject which I had not heard before.

Then, to test his knowledge of Sanskrit; I brought out all the Upanishads I had with me and questioned him on many abstruse passages from them. By his illuminating replies I found that his mastery of the scriptures was of an extraordinary kind. And the way in which he recited from the Upanishads was charming. Thus, being firmly convinced of his wonderful knowledge equally in English, Sanskrit and in Yoga, I was greatly drawn towards him. Though he stayed in my house for only seven days, I became so devoted to him that I resolved in my mind that by no means whatever would I let him go elsewhere. So I strongly urged him to live always at Bhagalpur.

Once I noticed him humming a tune to himself. So I asked him if he could sing. He replied, "Very little." Being pressed hard by us he sang, and what was my surprise to see that as in learning so in music he was wonderfully accomplished! Next day I asked him if he were willing that I invite some singers and musicians; he consented, and I asked many musicians, several of whom were ostads, or adepts in the art, to come. Believing that the music would end by nine or ten at the latest, I did not arrange supper for the guests. Swamiji sang without ceasing till two or three o'clock in the morning. All without exception were so charmed that they forgot hunger and thirst and all idea of time! None moved from his seat or thought of going home. Kailashbabu, who was accompanying the Swami on the drums, was forced to give up finally, for his fingers had become stiff and had lost all sensation. Such superhuman power I have never seen in anybody, nor do I expect to see it again. The next evening, all the guests of the previous night, and many others, presented themselves without any invitation. The player on the instrument also came, but Swamiji did not sing that evening; so everyone was disappointed.

Another day I proposed that I introduce him to all the rich men of Bhagalpur, and that I myself should take him to them in my carriage so that it would not be any trouble to him. But he declined and said, "It is not the sannyasi's dharma to visit the rich!" His fiery renunciation made a deep impression on me. Indeed, in his company I was taught many lessons which have always remained with me as spiritual ideals.

From my boyhood, I was inclined to live in some solitary place and engage in spiritual practices. When I met Swamiji, this desire grew strong. I often told him, "Let us both go to Vrindavan, and depositing three hundred rupees for each of us in the temple of Shri Govindaji we shall have Govindaji's prasad for the rest of our lives as food. Thus, without being a burden to anyone, we shall practise devotion day and night in a sequestered spot on the banks of the holy Yamuna!" In reply to this he said, "Yes, for a special temperament or nature, this scheme is no doubt good, but not for all", meaning not for himself, who had renounced everything. Amongst his many new ideas, the two most impressive to me were:

"Whatever of the ancient Aryan knowledge, intellect and genius is still left can be mostly found in those parts which lie near the banks of the Ganga. The further one goes from the Ganga, the less one sees them. This convinces one of the greatness of the Ganga as sung in our scriptures.

"The epithet mild Hindu, instead of being a word of reproach, ought really to point to our glory, as expressing greatness of character. For see how much moral and spiritual advancement, and how much development of the qualities of love and compassion, have to be acquired before one can get rid of the brutish force of one's nature, which actuates the ruining and the slaughter of one's brother-men for self aggrandizement!"

Swamiji visited only two places while staying at Bhagalpur. The first occasion was when we went to see the holy man of Barari, the late Parvaticharan Mukherjee; the second was when we paid a visit to the Temple of Nathanagar, one of the holy places of the Jaina community; and there Swamiji talked with the Jaina Acharyas on their religion. He was much pleased with his visits, and was also delighted to see the beauty of the scenery on the banks of the Ganga. He remarked, "These spots are very suitable for spiritual practices."

It used to pain me very much when certain detractors criticized him for taking sannyasa, because he had been born a Kayastha and not a Brahmana. They little knew what he was, and that birth had very little to do with the making of a saint. Of course, one has to look to the caste of a sadhu when his only qualification is the garb he wears; otherwise how can the Brahmanas reconcile themselves to offering worship to such a person, unless they have at least the consolation of knowing that the object of their veneration is a Brahmana by birth? The Swami was born with the Brahmanical conscious- ness, and thus is ten times more a Brahmana than he whose sole claim to Brahmanahood is the fact that he was born of Brahmana parents. And after all, who can resist worshipping what is of true worth and saintliness!

Swamiji well knew in his heart that I would not will- ingly or easily let him depart from Bhagalpur. So, one day when I was away on some important business, he grasped this opportunity of leaving, after taking farewell of those at home. When I came back I made a strenuous search for him, but could discover no clue of him anywhere. And yet, why should I have thought that my will should prevail? Why should Swamiji be like a frog in the well, when his field of work was the whole wide world?

He had expressed to me his intention of going to Badri- kashrama. Therefore, after he had left Bhagalpur, I even went up to Almora in the Himalayas in search of him. There Lala Badri Sah told me that he had left Almora some time before; and knowing that he must have already journeyed a long way in that direction, I was compelled to give up my idea of following him:

It was my heart's desire to bring him once more to Bhagalpur after his return from America, but he could not come, having then, perhaps, very little leisure or opportunity to do so.

(Life, Vol. 1, pp. 245-247)

Harbilas Sardar

I met Swami Vivekananda four times. The first time I met him was at Mount Abu. It was sometime in the year 1889 or 1890 [June 1891] in the month of May or June (I do not recollect which). I went to Mount Abu to stay with my friend T. [Thakur] Mukund Singh of Chhalasar [Jaleswar], Aligarh district, who was staying at Mount Abu for the hot season. When I reached there, I found Swami Vivekananda staying with T. Mukund Singh. T. Mukund Singh was an Arya Samajist and a follower of Swami Dayananda Saraswati. I stopped with my friend for about ten days and we, Swamiji and I, were together there and talked on various subjects. I was about 21 years old then and was impressed by Swami Vivekananda's personality. He was a most delightful talker and was very well informed. We used to go out for our afternoon walks. After dinner the first day, Swami Vivekananda sang a song at Thakur Sahib's request. He sang in a most melodious tone, which gave me great delight. I was charmed by his songs, and every day I begged him to sing a few songs. His musical voice and his manner have left a lasting impression on me. We sometimes talked about Vedanta, with which I had some acquaintance. ... Swami Vivekananda's talks on Vedanta greatly interested me. His views on various subjects were most welcome to me, as they were very patriotic. He was full of love of motherland and of Hindu culture. The time I passed in his company was one of the most pleasant times I have passed in my life. His independence of character particularly impressed me.

HARBILAS SARDAR

The next time I met him [the Swami] was at Ajmer. ... He was my guest, so far as I remember, for two or three days. I remember asking Him what his name was before he became a sannyasi, and this information he gave me. ... He left me and went away to Beawar. Shyam Krishna Varma, one of the most learned man I have met, lived in Ajmer in those days, but had gone to Mumbai, when the Swami was with me. On his return, I spoke to him about Swami Vivekananda's learning, eloquence, and patriotism, and told him that he had left only two or three days ago and was in Beawar. Shyam Krishna Varma had to go to Beawar the next day and promised to bring Swamiji with him back to Ajmer. The next day he returned to Ajmer with Swami Vivekananda. Swami Vivekananda was his guest for about fourteen or fifteen days and I met him every day at Mr. Varma's bungalow. We three used to go out together for our evening walk. I had the happiest time in the company of these two learned men. ... I remember well that we had most interesting talks with Swami Vivekananda. His eloquence, his nationalistic attitude of mind, and pleasant manner greatly impressed and delighted me. Very often I was a listener, when Mr. Varma and Swami Vivekananda discussed some literary or philosophic matters. ...

He [the Swami] had large luminous eyes and discoursed eloquently on religious and philosophical subjects. ... But what delighted me was Vivekananda's singing. He had a musical and melodious voice and I was entranced by his songs. [And in his diary Mr. Sarda wrote of the Swami:] His discourses are most interesting to me. I greatly like him. He is a most pleasant companion. He will be something in the world if I err not greatly.

(*Life*, Vol. 1, p 282, 286-87)

G. G. Narasimhachari

My first acquaintance with him [the Swami] began at the beginning of the year 1893 of Chicago Religious Parliament, when he came as a wandering sannyasi to Chennai, in the company of one Babu Manmathanath Bhattacharya, the then Deputy Accountant General of Chennai. Mr. Bhattacharya picked him up on his way to Rameshwaram as a beggarly sannyasi plodding on the road with a staff and kamandalu. Forewarned by a kind Mysore friend of ours of a remarkable English-speaking sannyasi travelling in the company of Mr. Bhattacharya at Pondicherry, half a dozen picked friends went to meet him at the Babu's on the day of his arrival at Chennai. Each one of my friends may be said to have represented a fair knowledge in a branch of modern Western culture, and shared my humble self's curiosity to see a modern sannyasi of a new type. The very fact that these young men were very good friends was a proof that they all possessed a decent amount of general culture. After we were welcomed by the Babu and left in the presence of the Swami with a bright smiling face and wonderful flashing, rolling eyes, my friends introduced themselves to the sannyasi through questions. After a few preliminary inquiries of ordinary etiquette, he was hemmed in with all sorts of questions—literary and scientific, historical and metaphysical. I was the wisest of the lot; I silently sat and enjoyed the fruits of their conversation. The Swami's pithy and melodious answers came like flashes silencing his questioners. Quotations were freely made from all sorts of classical authors, literary and scientific, historical and philosophical.

626

Late in the evening when my friends returned home, leaving the travel-worn sannyasi to rest, they began to indulge in all sorts of conjectures about his proficiency. ... From that day onward the house of Manmathanath Babu became a place of daily pilgrimage, to the young and old of the city, till the Swami left for America.

Swamiji was comfortably lodged in Mr. Bhattacharya's residence at St. Thome. Within a few days his intellectual attainments came to be known to all and his first introduction to the Chennai Public was in the Literary Society at Triplicane, where a conversazione was held. From that day, he became more and more known. Educated men of all ranks and position began to gather in his room and listen with enrapt attention to the mellifluous discourses of the Swami on all matters. His conversational power was marvellous. Even abstruse metaphysical subjects were handled by him in a very pleasing way and in simple language. ... Coming again to his discourses in Mr. Bhattacharya's residence, we used to gather there every evening. Even people whose minds were not settled and who were hating every form of religious faith began to take a peculiarly lively interest in his instructions—so much so that from 4 to 10 p.m. there would be quite a crowd at his residence. People who came to know him were unwilling to miss his company even for a day.

(*Life*, Vol. 1, pp. 361-62)

ELLA WHEELER WILCOX

Ella Wheeler Wilcox

I was listening to Vivekananda this morning an hour. How honoured by fate you must feel to have been allowed to be of service to this Great Soul. I believe him to be the reincarnation of some great Spirit—perhaps Buddha perhaps Christ. He is so simple, so sincere, so pure, so unselfish. To have listened to him all winter is the greatest privilege life has ever offered me. It would be surprising to me that people could misunderstand or malign such a soul if I did not know how Buddha and Christ were persecuted and lied about by small inferiors. His discourse this morning was most uplifting—his mere presence is that. His absolute sinking of self is what I like. I am so tired of people who place the capital "I" before truth and God. "To do good for good's sake, with no expectation or desire of reward, and never to speak of what we have done, but to keep on working for the love of doing God's work"—is Vivekananda's grand philosophy of life. He always makes me feel ashamed that I have ever thought for one moment I was burdened or that I ever spoke of any good act of my own.

(New Discoveries, Vol. 1, p. 44)

Twelve years ago I chanced one evening to hear that a certain teacher of philosophy from India, a man named Vivekananda, was to lecture a block from my home in New York.

We went out of curiosity (the man whose name I bear and I), and before we had been ten minutes in the audience, we felt ourselves lifted up into an atmosphere so rarefied, so vital, so wonderful, that we sat spellbound and almost breathless, to the end of the lecture.

When it was over we went out with new courage, new hope, new strength, new faith, to meet life's daily vicissitudes. "This is the philosophy, this is the idea of God, the religion which I have been seeking," said the man. And for months afterwards he went with me to hear Swami Vivekananda explain the old religion and to gather from his wonderful mind jewels of truth and thoughts of helpfulness and strength. It was that terrible winter of financial disasters, when banks failed and stocks went down like broken balloons and businessmen walked through the dark valleys of despair and the whole world seemed topsyturvy—just such an era as we are again approaching. Sometimes after sleepless nights of worry and anxiety, the man would go with me to hear the Swami lecture, and then he would come out into the winter gloom and walk down the street smiling and say: "It is all right. There is nothing to worry over." And I would go back to my own duties and pleasures with the same uplifted sense of soul and enlarged vision.

When any philosophy, any religion, can do this for human beings in this age of stress and strain, and when, added to that, it intensifies their faith in God and increases their sympathies for their kind and gives them a confident joy in the thought of other lives to come, it is good and great religion.

(*Life*, Vol. 2, pp. 10-11)

Shailendranath Bandopadhyay

Today at a mature age, I can only think of my meeting with Swamiji [Vivekananda] and Sister [Nivedita]. Till day, [many of my] friends and relatives have requested me to [record my] meeting [with them], but I really don't know why I never had the urge to pen down the experience earlier. Now as an ailing man waiting for death, I feel the need to write about those memories that are forever etched in my mind.

When Swamiji first came to our Darjeeling home (in Bolem Villa), then my age was either eleven or twelve. I did not pay attention to studies too much then; I only used to while away my time by playing with my friends.

Swamiji used to like us a lot. Brothers next to me were quite small (Dijendranath was 6 years younger while Rabindranath was only 4 years). Other brothers (elder brother Bolendranath and middle brother Bhupendranath) were involved in their respective work. I was the only one going to school. Thus I became Swamiji's constant companion during his morning and afternoon walk[s].

I used to call some of my friends as well. Swamiji used to walk dressed in hat-coat- boot with stick. He used to tell amusing tales which I still cherish. One such day, while on a stroll, we suddenly chanced upon an old woman porter who stumbled under the burden of the weight she was carrying. It was really painful. She was struggling to get up. Suddenly Swamiji sat down uttering 'ugh'. We thought that he was not feeling well. I asked, 'Are you feeling some pain? Then let's go back home'. Swamiji, after a moment, said to us, 'Cannot you see the plight of the old porter?' Today I can understand the significance of his condition. He was so sensitive to the suffering of others that he used to feel every sensation within his own body. Afterwards, people helped her [the porter] to reach home. My mother took responsibility of the porter when she heard of her plight.

When Swamiji came to our house for the second or third time, my mother asked, 'Nothing is happening to Shaila [referring to me]; what can be done about him?' Keeping quiet for some time, he said, 'Send him to Belur Math.' He further added, 'He will study there for some days, which will make him self-sufficient. It will help him in his life.' That day those words didn't mean much to me. However, his suggestion proved vital for me in future. From 1899 to 1902, I stayed at Belur Math, studying at Bally school and later at Presidency College.

While staying at our house, once Swamiji fell ill—with virulent diarrhea. His clothes were getting soaked regularly. My mother got very agitated. Swamiji became so frail that he could barely walk. I was then entrusted with the duty of changing his clothes, and cleaning his body. I used to provide him medication according to the instructions of the doctor. Under the guidance of doctor Davis, he recovered after six-seven days.

I used to meet Swamiji now and then at Belur Math—mostly in the afternoon. Then five- six boys used to reside at Belur Math. It was mandatory to play football and do extensive running in the afternoon. Sometimes, Swamiji used to inspect whether all the boys were present. If someone was absent deliberately, then he would scold him. We also learnt swimming from Swamiji. Swimming was a Sunday fixture.

Another detail that I remember is Swamiji's instruction to us regarding the preparation of watermelon 'sherbet'. One summer afternoon Swamiji called me. He enquired whether I knew how to make watermelon sherbet. When I replied in the negative, he wanted me to fetch a sieve. He also instructed me to bring a metal pitcher. When I brought them before him, he gave me the order to cut watermelon pieces. After scaling off the exterior, I kept the watermelon pieces in the metal pitcher. Then using a churning stick, the solid pieces of watermelon became liquid. After filtering it with the sieve, we added a pinch of salt. He ordered me to call others so that'they can share the sherbet as well. Drinking the watermelon sherbet, he certified it was excellent.

When Swamiji came to Darjeeling for the last time my mother said to him that my brothers had already taken 'Mahamantra', and requested Swamiji to give 'mantra' to me as well. Swamiji then said, 'Shaila, I will instruct you today only; come to my room.' Once inside Swamiji's room, he requested me to close the door. On the floor, he sat before me. Then he imparted the 'Mahamantra' into my ears by uttering it three times. I stuttered the first time and he corrected me. Then he assiduously taught me the way to take the Mahamantra. Afterwards, he gave me some money from the pocket and keeping it on the table said, 'Give me a paisa.' After doing so, I bowed down to take his blessing. He kept his hand on my head. At that very moment, a unique sensation went through my body—asensation that I cannot describe in words.

During the demise of Swamiji, I was not at Belur Math as I was engaged in some work at Darjeeling. However, I cried a lot that day. In fact, he came in [my] dreams afterwards—the image of Swamiji that lingered in my mind, that of him wearing hat-coat and boots. He seemed to say that I am with you only—ever present here, as long as you will live.

Mrs Alice M Hansbrough[1]

One bright Sunday morning in March 1941, Swami Ashokananda invited Mrs Alice M Hansbrough to drive home with him from his lecture at the Century Club in San Francisco. On the way, driving by a roundabout route over San Francisco's many hills to enjoy a sun made welcome by weeks of rain, the swami asked Mrs Hansbrough if she could give an account of her contacts with Swami Vivekananda during his visit to California in the winter of 1899 and 1900. Mrs Hansbrough had met Swamiji in Los Angeles a few days after his arrival there, and from the day of the meeting, had become a faithful follower. She served him devotedly during his stay in Los Angeles and San Francisco, and during her intimate contacts with him had many glimpses of Swamiji's spiritual greatness and of his human qualities as well.

Mrs Hansbrough readily agreed to give whatever recollections Swami Ashokananda desired. The swami evidently had already given considerable thought to the proposal, and ways and means were discussed. It was arranged that he should go to Mrs Hansbrough's home and that, through questions, he would suggest to her a direction of conversation which would bring out all that she could remember of her contacts with Swami Vivekananda; and that the swami would have someone (Mr A T Clifton) with him to take down the conversations. These talks covered several

---

1. In 1941 Mrs Alice Hansbrough gave these valuable reminiscences of Swami Vivekananda in a series of informal interviews with Swami Ashokananda in San Francisco. They were recorded by Mr A T Clifton (later Swami Chidrupananda), who was present at the interviews.

meetings, the first of which took place the day following Swami Ashokananda's first proposal of the subject to Mrs Hansbrough.

Monday Evening, March 3, 1941

Swami Ashokananda arrived at Mrs Hansbrough's home a little after eight o'clock in the evening. She was living with her daughter, Mrs Paul Cohn, at 451 Avila Street, near the broad Marina parkway on San Francisco Bay. As the swami walked to the door of the handsome Spanish-style residence, he caught a glimpse of Mrs Hansbrough reading beside the fire in the living room. In a moment she had greeted the swami at the door and escorted him to a seat before the fire.

The door to the spacious, high-ceilinged living room was across one corner; and across the corner to the right was the broad hearth of the fireplace, with a couch at right angles on the right, and comfortable chairs opposite. Another couch stood against the wall beyond, and in the far corner was a handsome old grand piano. The swami chose a chair, and Mrs Hansbrough sat on one couch in the light of a small table lamp.

Mrs Hansbrough was now well on in years [75 years old], but still was blessed with a keen intelligence and a ready humour, which must surely have endeared her to Swamiji. She was slight and below medium height, dignified and unvaryingly good natured in her manner, and possessed of a natural peacefulness which communicated itself to others. Her memory was clear and her conversation therefore filled with interesting details.

After inquiring about Mrs Hansbrough's daughter, Swami Ashokananda said: "Let us begin with your first acquaintance with Swamiji's work. How did you first hear about him?"

"I first learned of Swamiji in the spring of 1897 at a lecture in San Francisco about three years before he came to California," Mrs Hansbrough replied. "Two friends and

I went to hear a Mrs Annie Rix Militz speak on some meta-physical subject, and in the course of her talk she brought out some points from Swamiji's *Raja Yoga* and also quoted from the book. I was leaving not long after for Alaska, and my friends asked me what I would like for a steamer present. *Raja Yoga* was my answer. At the Emporium where they went to get it, the clerk inquired if it was for someone interested in such subjects. When they said it was, he recommended that they also get Swamiji's *Karma Yoga*, as the two were, as he said, 'parts of a set'. So I left for Alaska armed with the two books.

"Our ship was a steam schooner. The captain was not familiar with the course and we went far out of our way on the voyage. The result was four weeks en route, during which time I read from my books. I started with *Karma Yoga*, but found it a bit too high in thought for me, so put it aside and read *Raja Yoga* first. Then when I had finished it, I went back to *Karma Yoga* and read that. During the two years I was in Alaska I read both books over again many times.

"I remember that I used to read for a while, and the thought would come to me, "What marvellous thoughts these are!" I would hold the place with my finger, close the book and shut my eyes and think, "What a wonderful man he must be who wrote these words!" And I would try to form a picture in my mind of what he looked like.

"I met a man in Alaska who was interested in The-osophy. We used to talk about Swamiji's books and he looked through them; but he did not find anything interesting in them because he felt they were not Theosophy.'

"And after you returned from Alaska," Swami Asho-kananda asked, "did you go to Los Angeles?"

'Yes, Mrs Hansbrough replied. 'I came through San Francisco on the way, and arrived in Los Angeles on November 23, 1899. Swamiji had been in Los Angeles only a few days, I later learned.' [Swamiji arrived on December 3, 1899.]

'How did you first happen to meet him?' Swami Asho-kananda asked.

'Well, perhaps you would like to hear first what circumstances brought him to the West Coast,' Mrs Hansbrough suggested. 'The brother of Miss Josephine MacLeod at whose home Swamiji had been staying in New York, had been ill in Arizona with tuberculosis for some time. By the time November came, Mr MacLeod was not expected to live; and the wife of his business partner, a Mr Blodgett, wired Miss MacLeod to come west to see him, which she did. The brother died on November 2, 1899, however, and Miss MacLeod stayed on in Los Angeles, at Mrs Blodgett's house at 921 West 21st Street, where Swamiji later came.'

'Can you get a photograph of the house?' Swami Asho-kananda asked.

'I might be able to,' Mrs Hansbrough said. 'Well, when Miss MacLeod first entered her brother's bedroom at Mrs Blodgett's house, the first thing she saw was a full-page newspaper picture of Swamiji— you know that one that you have in your office in the Berkeley Temple, where he stands partly turned to the left—which Mrs Blodgett had taken from a Chicago paper and had framed. It hung above her brother's bed.

'"Where did you get that?" Miss MacLeod exclaimed. Mrs Blodgett told her she had heard Swami Vivekananda speak in Chicago and had cut the picture out of one of the papers at the time. "Well, Swami Vivekananda is our guest now in New York!" Miss MacLeod said.'

Swami Ashokananda then asked, 'Mrs Blodgett had some healing power, didn't she?'

'I never heard of it,' Mrs Hansbrough answered.

'Miss MacLeod said so some years ago at Mayavati,' the swami remarked. 'She said this was the reason it was suggested that Swamiji come to Los Angeles, as he had been unwell for a long time.' [Miss MacLeod took Swamiji to a healer named Mrs Melton.]

Mrs Hansbrough said she remembered that Mrs Leggett had come to Los Angeles for some such reason, and Swami Ashokananda was surprised to learn that Mrs Leggett had come west at all. After some discussion on this point, the conversation turned to Mrs Hansbrough's first hearing a lecture by Swami Vivekananda.

'It was on December 8, 1899,' she said. 'My sister Helen came home that evening and said: "Who do you think is going to speak in Los Angeles tonight? Swami Vivekananda!" All during the two years I had been reading his books in Alaska I had never expected to see him. Well, we rushed through dinner, made up a party, and went in. The lecture was at eight o'clock. Blanchard Hall was on Broadway between Eighth and Hill Streets. The audience was between six and eight hundred people, and everyone was enchanted with Swamiji. This was his first lecture in California and the subject was "The Vedanta Philosophy".

'He was introduced by a Professor Baumgardt, who had arranged for the hall and the lecture. Professor Baumgardt was connected with one of the Los Angeles newspapers in some business capacity. He was an astronomer. He had met Swamiji through the Academy of Sciences, which was a group of prominent scientists and scholars who had gathered together and called themselves by that name. Mrs Blodgett, with whom Swamiji was staying at the time, had introduced both Swamiji and Miss MacLeod to these men, and it was through these introductions that this first lecture came about. She also introduced him to a wealthy family called the Stimsons, with whom Swamiji later stayed for a week or so, but I don't think he enjoyed his visit with them.

'Professor Baumgardt had asked Swamiji to give the same lecture he had given at the Brooklyn Institute on the Vedanta Philosophy. When the lecture was over, the professor complained that it was not the same lecture at all; and Swamiji told him that it was impossible for him ever to give the same lecture twice: that he could talk on the same subject, but it would not be the same.'

'How was Swamiji dressed?' Swami Ashokananda asked.

'He wore a yellow robe and turban.'

'Yellow?'

'Well, a light orange, a little lighter than the robe you use,' Mrs Hansbrough replied.

'And how did he look?'

'His complexion was lighter than all the swamis here today, except Swami Devatmananda,' Mrs Hansbrough said. 'His hair was black—very black—with not one grey hair. A lady once asked him later on if Hindus' hair ever turned grey!'

'How did he impress you?' Swami Ashokananda then asked.

'I got the same impression I had previously had of him; that is, he was a most impressive personality. You know, you have told me that it is not possible to get an impression of a personality from the individual's writings; but I felt that I had sensed Swamiji's personality from his books, and the impression was verified when I heard him speak.

'His voice I should say was baritone—certainly nearer to bass than tenor; and it was the most musical voice I have ever heard. At the end of the lecture he closed with that chant, "I am Existence Absolute, Knowledge Absolute, Bliss Absolute." Everyone was enchanted with his talk.

'Whenever he quoted from Sanskrit he would chant the quotation—'

'He would actually chant?' Swami Ashokananda interrupted to ask.

'Yes,' Mrs Hansbrough replied. 'He would chant in Sanskrit and then translate. Once later on he apologized for quoting in Sanskrit, and explained that he still thought in that language and then had to translate his thoughts into English.

'When it was over, the rest of our party went up on the platform where a number of people had collected to speak to Swamiji. I sought out Professor Baumgardt, however, to find out when and where Swamiji was going to lecture again. When I asked him he inquired, "Are you interested in the swami's teachings?" I told him I had been studying them for two years, and he said, "Well, I will introduce you to the swami's hostess." He introduced me to Miss MacLeod, who, when I told her I had been studying Swamiji's works for so long, asked if I wouldn't like to go to call on him. Of course I said I would be delighted, and so it was arranged. It was not until after his second lecture, however, that we did meet him.'

'And what and where was his second lecture?' Swami Ashokananda asked.

'His second lecture [on December 12] was also arranged by the Academy of Sciences,' Mrs Hansbrough said. 'But this one was held in the Congregational Church and was free, whereas tickets had been required for the first one. The subject was, "The Building of the Cosmos", and it was equally as enchanting as the first one. I still have a copy of it, and often read it.'

'You have a copy of that lecture!' Swami Ashokananda exclaimed. 'Are you sure?'

Mrs Hansbrough assured the swami that she was. Here the talk turned for the moment to Mrs Hansbrough's collection of notes, early copies of the *Brahmavadin* and *Prabuddha Bharata*, and notes belonging to Dr M Logan on the founding of the San Francisco Vedanta Society. Then Mrs Hansbrough spoke again of the work in Southern California.

'Did you know that a Vedanta Society was actually established in Pasadena?' she asked. 'It was suggested to Swamiji that he visit Pasadena, which he did. There he met a Mrs Emeline Bowler, a wealthy woman who was president of the Shakespeare Club, and with whom Swamiji later spent a few days. During this visit, however, he wrote me that he was not happy there, and asked me to go and get him.'

Swami Ashokananda laughed at this.

'Why do you laugh?' Mrs Hansbrough asked him.

'Well, it is amusing that Swamiji had to ask you to go and get him,' the swami replied.

'He always did that,' Mrs Hansbrough said. 'Invariably he either phoned or wrote me whenever he wanted to leave any place. For instance, later in SanFrancisco he was the guest of some physician, and had expected to stay for some time. But the very day he went to the doctor's home he either phoned or wrote me—I forget now, which he did—to come for him. When I arrived, his hostess came in, introduced herself, and then withdrew again. Then Swamiji explained: "The trouble is, she is not a lady: she doesn't know what to do with me!"

'But to return to Pasadena,' Mrs Hansbrough continued. 'It was in the rooms of the Shakespeare Club that the Pasadena Society was formed. I had suggested it, but Swamiji had no interest in organizing. "It won't last," he said—and he said the same about the San Francisco Society later. Nevertheless, we went ahead with the project. He was present at the organization meeting, but as I say, he was not interested in the proceedings. I had drawn up a set of proposed bylaws, in which a proposal was included that each member pledge to contribute to the Society for a period of ten years.

Mrs Bowler objected to this, on the grounds that a member might die during the ten years. I said that would be all right: the deceased member would then be excused from further contributions. This amused Swamiji greatly. 'Mrs Bowler was perhaps overly interested in the financial affairs of Swamiji's lectures. Later, when I had begun to help Swamiji with arrangements for hall rentals, placing the newspaper advertisements, and so on, she once asked me, "How much are you getting for this?" I told her the truth: "The privilege of paying for the halls. And we are not wealthy people, Mrs Bowler."'

* * *

'I might mention here, speaking of the organization of the Pasadena centre, that it was I who suggested the founding of the San Francisco centre also. We held two meetings for the purpose, as the details were not completed at the first meeting. At this first meeting, I suggested to Swamiji that he leave before the meeting opened. He asked me why, and I told him that it was because I wanted to say some things about him that I would rather he did not hear. So he agreed, and went home with X. It was not that his staying would have made any difference to Swamiji; my reason for asking this was that I myself would have been embarrassed to speak as I wanted to about him in his presence. I then told the group about the arrangements which had been made in Los Angeles and Pasadena, and we proceeded with the organization here [in San Francisco].'

Here Swami Ashokananda asked about Mrs Hansbrough's first meeting with Swamiji.

'It was the day following his second lecture,' she told him. 'As I mentioned, Miss MacLeod had arranged for us to call on him at Mrs Blodgett's home, and my sister Helen and I went in the morning. He was dressed to receive us in the long, knee-length coat we see in the picture where he stands with Sister Lalita [Mrs Hansbrough's sister, Carrie Mead Wyckoff]. He wore a kind of minister's collar with what must have been a clerical vest; and his hair was covered by a black turban, which rolled back something like those the women wear here now. This was the dress he always wore on the street.'

'Was Miss MacLeod present at this first meeting?' Swami Ashokananda inquired.

'She was there at first,' Mrs Hansbrough said, 'but she went out after a few minutes. Later she told me that she always did this when visitors first called on the swami, because she felt the visitors liked it better.'

'And how did you feel about Swamiji when you met him?'

'I can only describe myself as enchanted by him,' Mrs Hansbrough answered. 'As I mentioned, this was my feeling from his books before I ever saw him, and the feeling has stayed with me throughout my life.'

'And what did he talk about with you at this first meeting?'

'The conversation was only general. He was rather shy and reserved in manner, as I remember. He said he was very glad we were interested in his lectures. We asked how long he expected to stay in Los Angeles, and he replied that he did not know, but that if we cared to arrange a class, he would be glad to address the group.

'Naturally, with such an offer, we eagerly went about getting a class together, and the first meeting was in the Blanchard Building, December 19. There were three meetings over a period of a week [December 19, 21, and 22] in this first series of classes, for which each person paid a dollar for every meeting.

'We had three rooms in the Blanchard Building, which opened into one another. The arrangement was not very satisfactory, especially since the attendance was running between 150 and 200. So when Mr J Ransome Bransby suggested moving to a nice chapel, which he could arrange for at the Home of Truth, it was decided to follow his suggestion. Accordingly, Swamiji moved there, and gave two more series of classes.'

'Now, tell me,' Swami Ashokananda asked, 'what disposition was made of the money taken in from these classes?'

'We gave it all to Swamiji,' Mrs Hansbrough replied.

'Was there no printing of leaflets or anything of the sort?'

'I don't think so, although there may have been.'

'Did Swamiji keep any account of the money?'

'Never. He never knew anything about the financial details connected with the work.'

'And was this true of San Francisco, too?'

'Yes.'

'Now, there I have you,' Swami Ashokananda said with a playful smile, 'for I have documentary proof that he did. When I was in India in 1934 and 1935, I was allowed to go through all the papers in his room, and among his things I found a notebook in which there were accounts, in Swamiji's own handwriting, of income and expenditures in connection with his lectures and classes.'

'Oh yes, afterward Swamiji may have made such records,' Mrs Hansbrough replied. 'But if he did, they were made from statements I gave him, for he never paid any attention to the money at the time.'

'Do you remember the topics of the classes, or the name of any book he used?' the swami asked.

'No,' Mrs Hansbrough replied, 'but the classes were all taken down in shorthand, and some were later printed in *Prabuddha Bharata*. Sister Nivedita sent for them. In all, she got some forty lectures and class notes of Swamiji's work. At first we had Mr Bagley, the nephew of Mrs John J Bagley with whom Swamiji had stayed in Detroit in 1894, to take the notes. I remember that he said Swamiji was "very hard to follow". Later we had Miss McClary, who followed Swamiji everywhere.

'This same Miss McClary on another occasion asked Swamiji if it were true that Hindu mothers threw their babies into the Ganges because they did not want them. He answered, "Yes, Madam, but I was one who escaped." After a moment he added, "Nowadays all the babies are born of men." Miss McClary then realized her own stupidity and hid herself behind her chair. Swamiji said, "I don't blame you. I would, too, if I had asked such a question!"

Swami Ashokananda asked if there was anyone still living who had copies of all these notes, but Mrs Hansbrough could think of no one. She said that one copy of each had been sent to Sister Nivedita and a copy to each of the magazines in India.

The Swami then asked about Mrs Hansbrough's close contacts with Swamiji after the lectures and classes had begun.

'In connection with the work, I always saw him before and after the lectures and classes.

'During questions after one of the classes, Mr Bransby asked Swamiji what difference there was between a cabbage and a man, if all things are one. Swamiji could be sharp on occasion. His answer was: "Stick a knife into your leg and you will see the line of demarcation."

'On another occasion, a woman asked who supported all the monks in India. "The women, Madam," Swamiji replied, "the same as in your country!"'

'And when was it that you asked him to visit you?'

'I think it was at Mrs Blodgett's home, once when Helen and I were there together.' Mrs Hansbrough smiled. 'Sometime before—as a matter of fact, before we had even met Swamiji, though it was after his second lecture—I one day said to my sisters, "Do you know, I think Swami Vivekananda wants to come to visit us." My sisters thought I was crazy. However, I defended my thought by pointing out that the swami was not well and that he might find our home restful. We were then living [at 309 Monterey Road] in Lincoln Park, which is now called South Pasadena, in a rented house. The property and the house are still standing, and the room still intact in which Swamiji slept (for he did come later to stay with us).'

'Of course we know that Swamiji was not well, but how did he look at that time?' Swami Ashokananda asked. 'Did he look unwell? Would anyone know from his appearance that he was ill?'

'Oh no,' Mrs Hansbrough told him. 'He always looked bright, especially when he was particularly interested in something. Then his eyes actually sparkled.

'When he declined my invitation to visit us, he was very gracious. I had explained that our home was very unpretentious, but that we would be very happy to have him with us. He smiled and said, "I do not need luxury", and explained that he was comfortably situated at Mrs Blodgett's.

'Later on [in late December] I asked him to come for Sunday dinner [probably on Christmas Eve]. He readily accepted, and asked me to invite Miss MacLeod also. When I asked Miss MacLeod, she wouldn't believe Swamiji had accepted my invitation. She herself went to ask him about it, and he told her, "Yes, and you are to come too."

'It was about an hour's ride on the electric train for them to reach our house. The train stopped just at the corner, and then they had only a few steps to our door.

'I can see the picture of them now, standing at the front door, so I must have met them when they arrived. After speaking to each of us as he came in, Swamiji turned and walked into the living room. The tall windows looked out through the trees in our garden. Swamiji walked to one of them and stood for some minutes looking out, the white curtains framing him against the sunlight.

Then he turned and spoke, answering again the question I had asked him at Mrs Blodgett's: "Yes," he said, "I will come to visit you!" 'Then he wanted to come right away, and he soon did. He had but one trunk, but he had many clothes, for he was always well dressed when he went out or met strangers. At home he cared little for his dress; he was most casual about it. Once while my nephew Ralph was blacking his shoes, he remarked, "You know, Ralph, this fine lady business is a nuisance!" He knew what was expected of him in public. When Mrs Bowler had invited him to speak in Pasadena, she had specifically asked that he wear his turban.

'"Do you *have* to wear the turban?" I asked him, for by that time he had given it up. "Don't you understand?" he said. "She wants the whole show!"'

Swami Ashokananda then asked about Mrs Hansbrough's closer contacts with Swamiji after the lectures and classes had begun.

'In connection with the work, I always saw him before and after the lectures and classes. I remember one evening when we were going home after a lecture he asked me how I had liked it. He had been very outspoken that evening in criticism of the West, and I said that I had enjoyed the lecture but feared that he sometimes antagonized his audience. He smiled as if that meant nothing to him. "Madam," he said, "I have cleared whole halls in New York!"

'I think the finest gesture I ever saw him make,' Mrs Hansbrough went on, 'was in connection with a rumour of scandal which arose about him while he was in Los Angeles. Professor and Mrs Baumgardt came to see Swamiji one morning and the subject came up in conversation. They had heard of it but thought nothing of it. We were all seated in the dining room except Swamiji, who was walking slowly up and down the room. Finally he said, "Well, what I am is written on my brow. If you can read it, you are blessed. If you cannot, the loss is yours, not mine."'

The conversation then turned once more to Swami Vivekananda's lectures, and Swami Ashokananda asked where Swamiji gave 'Christ the Messenger'.

'It was at Payne's Hall,' Mrs Hansbrough told him. 'We had moved from the chapel in the Home of Truth, because Swamiji did not feel free to speak critically of metaphysical ideas from their platform. The original title of that lecture, you know, was 'The Message of Christ to the World'; it was changed after it was sent to India.

'Swamiji was introduced by a Dr John Smith, a physician who greatly admired Swamiji. The lecture drew a tremendous crowd: more than a hundred people were turned away. The Mr Blanchard for whom the hall where Swamiji gave his first lecture was named, was present at this one, and the size of the audience was not lost on him.[2]

When Swamiji had finished, Mr Blanchard came up to me on the platform, where Swamiji was talking to some people. 'I would like to make some money out of this man—for him as well as for myself,' he said. 'Could I announce to the audience now that he will speak next Sunday at Blanchard Hall?' I told him I could not give him such permission. He then went to Miss MacLeod, who did give him permission. So while Swamiji was still there, Mr Blanchard announced from the platform that Swami Vivekananda would speak the following Sunday at Blanchard Hall, and

---

2. In addition to his five morning classes in the first week of 1900, Swamiji gave two evening lectures in the auditorium of the Blanchard Building.

that the admission would be ten cents. Mind you, there had been no admission charge at this lecture.

'When Swamiji heard this announcement, he turned and asked who gave the man permission to make it. Somehow Miss MacLeod crawled out of it, and Swamiji turned on me. He was thoroughly annoyed and looked quite angry. He said the man should not have been allowed to make such an announcement. And he could not be persuaded to give the lecture at Blanchard Hall. He pointed out that he had had no end of trouble trying to get rid of people who wanted to make money out of him. We learned later that [on the following Sunday] more than one hundred people went to Blanchard Hall nevertheless, and waited on the steps.

'This episode almost broke up the lecture series, but it was after this that he lectured at the Shakespeare Club in Pasadena. After one of the lectures at the Shakespeare Club I said to the swami, "Swamiji, I think you would like me to go on to San Francisco." His eyes lighted up as they always did when he was particularly interested in something and he answered, "Yes, of course I would."

'My sisters, Helen and Carrie, did not think much of the idea and discouraged it from the beginning. They did not feel that I was a "big" enough person to do what was necessary. They also felt that I was not "socially inclined" enough, and they never did think I was very bright.' Mrs Hansbrough's eyes twinkled. 'At any rate, Swamiji brought the matter up again himself one morning after breakfast, when he and I were sitting alone at the table. "Well, when are you going to San Francisco?" he asked.

'I was taken a little by surprise, as I had more or less abandoned the thought. "Why, I could go, if you wanted me to," I answered. He seemed to have sensed that I had been discouraged from the plan by my sisters' opposition. "When once you consider an action," he said, "do not let anything dissuade you. Consult your heart, not others, and then follow its dictates."

'Not long afterward a letter came from Dr B Fay Mills of the Unitarian Church in Oakland, inviting Swamiji to go there. So I said to Swamiji, "Well, I needn't go now." However, Swamiji wanted to give his first lecture independently, and was unwilling to start any San Francisco work with a lecture at the Unitarian Church. "We will support our own work," he said. "I am willing to trust an American woman. I will trust an American man sometimes. But an American minister—never!" He gave his first lecture in San Francisco on February 23 at Golden Gate Hall, on "The Ideal of a Universal Religion".

'Speaking of San Francisco reminds me of a remark he made to me one evening after one of his lectures here. Several of us were walking home with him. I was in front with someone, and he behind with some others. Apropos of something he had been discussing, he said, "You have heard that Christ said, 'My words are spirit and they are life'." He pointed his finger at me and declared, "So are my words spirit and life; and they will burn their way into your brain and you will never get away from them."'

It was now late in the evening. The talk turned to Swamiji's actual coming to San Francisco, so it was decided to continue the discussion on another evening. Swami Ashokananda said goodnight to Mrs Hansbrough and returned to the Temple.

Sunday, March 23, 1941

Sunday, March 23 was bright and cloudless, with a spring-like breeze that tempered the warm sun. After his morning lecture in the Century Club Building, Swami Ashokananda invited Mrs Hansbrough to drive home with him. On the way, the swami asked Mrs Hansbrough for further details regarding Swami Vivekananda's stay in Los Angeles. After driving to the ocean beach and then through Golden Gate Park, the swami ordered the car to be parked overlooking the waters of Lake Merced.

'Tell me now,' Swami Ashokananda began, 'how long Swamiji stayed at your home in Los Angeles.'

'It must have been all of four weeks,' Mrs Hansbrough replied. 'He came in late January 1900 and it was on February 21 when he left to come to San Francisco.'

'Did he ever express any opinion about Los Angeles?'

'Yes, he said, "It has an atmosphere like India: it is restful."' 'And did you have many conversations with him while he was in your home?' the swami asked.

'Oh yes. Usually they were in the evening. Every night we would sit after dinner was over, and he would talk on many subjects: philosophy, science, our national development—'

'You mean development of the United States?' the swami put in.

'Yes,' Mrs Hansbrough answered. 'He was very much interested in all phases of our national life. But he did not like to see the great concentration on material affairs. Swamiji said that our civilization would fall within fifty years if we did not spiritualize it.' 'He did say that?' the swami asked.

'Did he ever say that from the platform, or only in private conversation?'

'Oh, only in private conversation. He said we were deifying material values, and that we could never build anything lasting on such a basis.'

'How long would these conversations last in the evening? About what time would Swamiji retire?'

'He would talk as long as we wanted him to,' Mrs Hansbrough said, 'though actually it was never later than around ten or eleven o'clock.'

'And did he have a room to himself in your house?'

'Oh yes.'

'I have a picture of your house here,' Swami Ashokananda said. 'Can you point out his room to me in the picture?'

'No,' said Mrs Hansbrough, examining the photo. 'This shows only the front of the house, and his room was in the back, on the second floor. We all moved to bedrooms in the front of the second floor of the house so that Swamiji could be alone.'

'Well, now, let us see how he spent his day,' the swami said. 'At what time would he come down from his room? What time would he take breakfast?'

'He usually came down about seven o'clock. There was a bathroom on the second floor where his room was, and I presume he would bathe in the morning, but he didn't comb his hair.'

'He didn't!' Swami Ashokananda exclaimed.

Mrs Hansbrough smiled. 'No,' she replied. 'Though he was very careful about his dress when he went out, he was very careless about it at home. I remember that he himself remarked about it one Sunday morning: "Why should I be careful of my dress at home? I don't want to get married!" You see, where we think there is a "proper" dress for the dining room, just as for other times and places, he put all this down as show.

'This reminds me of Frank Alexander's writings about Swamiji. You know, he tried to paint Swamiji as a great man in every little detail. My inclination has always been to do just the opposite: that is, to remember him as the real human being he was—to take off any paint of artificiality others tried to apply to him. For he was so great in himself that no paint was ever needed to make him so.

'As I say, he would come down about seven in the morning, in his bathrobe and slippers and his long black hair not yet combed. He would have some kind of undergarment under his robe, which showed a bit at the neck. I remember that his robe had seen many winters. It was a black and white tweed of some kind, probably with a herringbone pattern in it, and with a cord around the waist.'

'You said his hair was black, as we know. How did he wear it at this time? Was it long?' Swami Ashokananda queried.

'Yes, when Swamiji first came to Los Angeles, his hair had grown long, and it was beautifully wavy. In fact it was so beautiful, and it set off his features so well, that we would not let him cut it again.'

'So you were responsible for the long hair!' Swami Asho-kananda exclaimed, half jokingly. 'And you liked it because it was beautiful!'

Mrs Hansbrough smiled assent. 'Swamiji himself did not object. In fact he appreciated the value that its beauty lent to his appearance. He actually remarked once when we were discussing it, "Beauty has its value." He was wholly devoid of self-consciousness.'

'Now, you were saying that he would come downstairs in the morning at about seven o'clock. What time would you have breakfast?'

'Breakfast would be at about seven thirty, in order to accommodate Helen, who was working, and Ralph, who had to get to school. Swamiji would pass the half hour walking outside.'

'In his bathrobe?'

'Yes. You see, at that time that part of town was not very closely built up. There were no houses across the street and the neighbours on either side were separated from our house by trees and shrubs. Swamiji would walk in the garden behind the house, or along the driveway at one side, and no one could see him there.'

'And what would he usually take for breakfast?'

'He always had fruit, usually an orange or grapefruit, and he liked poached eggs. He would have toast, and coffee usually.'

'Did he like his coffee with cream?'

'Yes, he took cream and I think he took sugar also.'

'And how big a breakfast would he eat?'

'Swamiji was a moderate eater. Usually he took two eggs, two pieces of toast, and two cups of coffee. Once I offered him a third cup of coffee. At first he declined, but when I urged him he finally yielded and said: "All right. Woman's business is to tempt man."

'Breakfast would usually last about an hour, for we never hurried. Ralph had to be at school at eight or eight-thirty, and Helen would leave for work, but the rest of us were not occupied. After breakfast Swamiji would stroll in the garden again or browse through the library. Often he would play with the children in the yard. Dorothy [Hansbrough, who was four years old] had several friends who would come, and Swamiji would hold hands with them and play ring-around-the-rosy and other games. He used to like to talk with them, and would ask them many questions about their activities, why they played this game or that, and so on.

'He was much interested in the problem of child training, and we often talked of it. He did not believe in punishment. It had never helped him, he said. "And I would never do anything to make a child afraid," he declared.'

'Well now, would Swamiji have any classes or meetings in the morning?' Swami Ashokananda asked.

'Yes, he was having both morning lectures and classes in Los Angeles and Pasadena while he was with us,' Mrs Hansbrough replied. 'They would start usually at ten-thirty or eleven, and we would leave the house at about ten.'

'What would Swamiji wear to the meetings? Would he wear his robe?'

'No, he wore the black garment we see in several of the pictures of him, something like a clerical frock, but looser. Sometimes if it was not too warm he would wear his overcoat over this. He would take his gerua robe and turban in a suit-case, and put them on when he arrived at the meeting place.'

'Do you remember any incidents in connection with any of these meetings?' the swami asked.

'I remember that on one occasion when Swamiji was going to speak at the Green Hotel, Professor Baumgardt was talking with some other gentlemen on the platform before the lecture began. One of them asked him, regarding Swamiji, "He is a Christianized Hindu, I suppose?" And Professor Baumgardt replied, "No, he is an unconverted Hindu. You will hear about Hinduism from a real Hindu."

'On another occasion, Swamiji was speaking in some church. I do not remember now why, but he did not have a previously announced subject on that occasion. So when he came on the platform he asked the audience what they would like to have him speak on. I noticed several women and a man conferring together, and the man finally stood up and asked if Swamiji would speak on Hindu women. So Swamiji took this as his subject, and spoke principally about Sita and one other woman (was it Mirabai?).'

'Yes, I know of that lecture,' Swami Ashokananda said.

'Do you know about the questions at the close of the talk?' Mrs Hansbrough asked.

'No.'

'Well, it was clear afterward that the group who had asked for this subject had done so in an attempt to trap Swamiji into saying something that would discredit him. We learned later that they belonged to some group who had missionaries in India. The questions they asked were along the line always taken by those trying to discredit India: the claim of abuse of Indian women, child marriages, early motherhood, and so on.

'Swamiji answered several of the questions directly; then when he saw the direction the questioner was taking, he said that the relationship between the husband and wife in India, where the basis of marriage was not physical enjoyment, was so entirely different from that of a married couple in the West that he did not think Western people could understand it. As the questioner continued to press him, Swamiji really became angry. It was the only time I ever saw him angry on the platform. At one point, to emphasize a statement, he hit his knuckles on the table so hard that I really feared he would break the skin. "No, Madam," he burst out, "that relationship in which children creep into life amidst lust, at night and in darkness, does not exist in India!"

'Finally, the woman openly called him a liar. "Madam," Swamiji replied, "you evidently know more about India than I do. I am leaving the platform; please take it yourself!"

He was thoroughly aroused. We had already gotten up, for we feared anything might happen now, and our only thought was to see him safely out of the building and home. He started up the middle aisle, but the woman with her friends blocked him and tried to continue her argument. Again he told her to take the platform herself. At last we got through, but as I passed her the woman turned on me and exclaimed: "You little fool! Don't you know he hates you?" I said no, I hadn't found that out yet. One woman in particular set out to corner him. She started talking about how the English were trying to reform India, and Swamiji simply said: "Madam, I am a monk. What do I know about politics?"

'Swamiji spoke more than once of the indignities to which he had been subjected in the West. It was because of the constant possibility of some unpleasant occurrence that he always preferred to have a woman escort. He said that people would respect the woman where they would not respect him. Once in San Francisco, when I was taking him somewhere into a rather rough part of the city on some call which escapes my memory now, some rowdies made some slighting remarks about him which he overheard. He said nothing, but after we had gone he remarked, "If you had not been along, they would have thrown things at me."

'He mentioned that well-known incident in Chicago when a man came up and pulled his robe and asked him why he wore his nightgown in public. He was deeply offended by such rudeness on the part of the American public. "A man could walk the length of India (in any costume) and such a thing would not happen to him," he said.

'He also spoke of the missionaries and their activities. He once said of Mr Leggett, "When I exposed the missionaries, he stopped giving his ten thousand dollars a year to them—but he did not then give it to me!"'

'Well, now let us pick up the routine of his day again,' Swami Ashokananda said. 'What would he do in the morning when he did not have any lecture or class?'

'It seems as if there was always something going on,' Mrs Hansbrough said. 'This was always true on Sunday mornings. But during the week, if he did not have a formal meeting somewhere, we would often go for a picnic lunch to the top of a hill about four city blocks' distance from our house.

'The weather was especially pleasant that winter; in fact they said it was the pleasantest winter in five years. You have seen that photo of Swamiji in a picnic group; that was taken on top of that hill. We would make up a party of people who were attending his meetings more or less regularly—or Swamiji would even hold some of his smaller class groups there. Naturally the talk was always on spiritual subjects.

'I remember that on one of these picnics a young woman Christian Scientist, Lillian Davis, was arguing with him that we should teach people to be good. Swamiji smiled and waved his hand to indicate the trees and the countryside. "Why should I desire to be 'good'?" he asked. "All this is His handiwork. Shall I apologize for His handiwork? If you want to reform John Doe, go and live with him; don't try to reform him. If you have any of the divine fire, he will catch it."'

'Was he a heavy smoker?'

'No. He would smoke after breakfast, lunch, and dinner, but never to excess.

'Sometime before he left for San Francisco he said one day, "I always leave something wherever I go. I am going to leave this pipe when I go to San Francisco." He left it on the mantelpiece in the living room, and we kept it there for a long time as an ornament. Then one day Mrs Carrie Wyckoff saw it. For some time she had been suffering a good deal from some nervous ailment. For some days the pain of her illness had been almost unbearable, and this, added to her other troubles, made her feel extremely depressed. She went to the mantelpiece and picked up Swamiji's pipe. No sooner did she have it in her hand than she heard Swamiji's voice, saying, "Is it so hard, Madam?" For some reason she rubbed the pipe across her forehead, and instantly the suffering left her and a feeling of well-being came over her. After that we felt that the pipe should belong to her; and she still has it today.'

'That is most interesting,' Swami Ashokananda said. 'Did you ever have any such experience?'

Mrs Hansbrough was thoughtful for a moment. 'Well, isn't it the same kind of experience when he talks to us all the time?' she asked.

'Oh yes,' the swami replied.

After a minute or two he returned to the routine of Swamiji's day. 'Now, what would he do after lunch? Would he go to his room for rest?' he asked.

'No, he very rarely went to his room after lunch. He would usually recline on the couch in the living room and read there, or talk, or do some such thing.

'It was probably during an after-lunch conversation when he was walking up and down the living room, that Swamiji told us: "The Master said he would come again in about two hundred years— and I will come with him. When a Master comes," he said, "he brings his own people."

'I had the feeling that by "his own people" he meant Sri Ramakrishna would bring with him a spiritual host to help him; that it would not necessarily include all the disciples who had been with him in this incarnation, but that Swamiji definitely would be one of them.

'I always felt, however, that whereas the rest of us were going up in our successive incarnations, Swamiji had come down to meet us on our level.

'Miss MacLeod said that she brought him West "for his health", but he never complained of it while he was with us.'

'He was never sick or tired or any such thing?'

'No, he never missed a meal or showed in any other way at that time that he was unwell.'

'Was he at all susceptible to heat or cold?'

'Cold did not bother him, but he was sensitive to heat. We always had a fire in the grate after dinner in the evening, and once when it had gone out, he exclaimed, "Praise the Lord, that fire's out!"

'Did you ever have guests for meals?'

'Yes, often there would be luncheon guests. We would go to class or lecture in the morning, and Swamiji would ask some to come for lunch afterward. Mrs Leggett and Miss MacLeod especially were frequent luncheon guests. Miss MacLeod was also a house guest for a few days. She asked Helen one day, "Can you put me up for a few days?" Helen told her she was welcome, provided she didn't mind "hospital style accommodations". As I said before, we had all moved to two front rooms of the second floor to let Swamiji be alone in the back of the second floor, so Miss MacLeod came and slept on a couch in the front room with the rest of us. She stayed several days and I think enjoyed it.

'Miss MacLeod set aside her superior airs when she was with us. It was principally with people who affected the same airs that she put them on. And she never made the mistake of putting on airs with Swamiji. He often told her "where to get off" when she had a tendency to be too high-toned. But the only time I ever heard him speak sharply to her was before class in the ballroom of the Green Hotel. She was expressing an opinion as to what should be done about some phase of Swamiji's work, and he suddenly turned on her. "Keep quiet about what should be done!" he said. "We will do whatever has to be done." But he also said of her, "Jo has a very sweet nature." He always called her "Jo".'

'Now let us go back once more and finish his day,' Swami Ashokananda said. 'Tell me about the evening meal. What time would you sit down to dinner?'

'Dinner would be about six-thirty. We would usually have soup, and either fish or meat, vegetables, and dessert— pie, perhaps, which Swamiji sometimes liked, or something else. Usually he did not take coffee in the evening.

'It is Lent now, and this reminds me of one evening when Swamiji was walking up and down in the dining room while the table was being set for dinner. We always had a plate of spring fruit on the table, and on this evening there were some guavas among the others. We were speaking of Lent and the custom of giving up some favourite food or pleasure during the forty days. Swamiji said that a similar custom existed in India which was always observed by the monks. "All but the wicked fellows like me renounce something," he said. "Now I, for example, will renounce these guavas!" We took the hint and did not have guavas anymore after that!

'When the evening meal was over, instead of going into the living room we would clear the dining room table and sit there, where we could light a fire in the open grate. Some would sit at the table, others would sit in easy chairs. We had an easy chair for Swamiji, which was large enough for him to sit cross-legged in, which he used to do. He usually wore either what you would call a dinner jacket or smoking jacket or his robe.'

'Did Swamiji ever read to you from any of his books?' Swami Ashokananda asked.

'Yes, he often read to us, and he was an excellent reader. People used to ask where he got his fine pronunciation of English. He himself used to say that it came after he reached the United States. He said that until he came to the United States he had a "bookish accent". Well, he read from various things. Once he was talking about Advaita and asked for his "Song of the Sannyasin", which he read to us. On another occasion late one evening as we sat by the fire, he asked for "The Need of a Guru". He had been talking to Helen, and then he began to read from this. For some reason, after he had read for some time, Helen got up, lit his bedroom candle and offered it to him. By now it was about eleven o'clock. "Does that mean I must go to bed?" Swamiji asked. "Well, it is eleven o'clock," Helen said, so the conversation closed.

'Long afterward, we were talking of the incident and all three of us felt that indirectly Swamiji had been inviting Helen to ask for discipleship.'

'Why didn't your sister take it?' Swami Ashokananda asked.

'She said she herself didn't know,' Mrs Hansbrough replied. 'She said she just didn't feel impelled to at the time.'

'Did you ever hear Swamiji sing?'

'Yes. He would usually sing when he was on the way somewhere. He would sing a song in Sanskrit or Bengali or whatever it might be, and then ask, "Do you know the meaning of the song?" Then he would explain it. Of course he would also sing or chant on the platform, too.

'At home he would sometimes sing that old hymn, "The heathen in his blindness bows down to wood and stone". I had taught it to him and it used to amuse him.

'Sometimes he would ask Lalita [Carrie Wyckoff] to stroll with him in the garden, and he would sing songs and explain them in a much more personal way than from the platform.

'Once while Lalita was preparing something in the kitchen for Swamiji, he was walking to and fro across the room as he often used to do. Suddenly he asked her, "Were you happily married?" For a moment she hesitated, then answered, "Yes, Swamiji." He left the kitchen for a moment, and then came back. "I am glad", he said dryly, "that there was one!"

'At another time, Swamiji had prepared some dish for Lalita to try. When he asked her whether she liked it she said that she did. After a moment's pause, Swamiji inquired, "Was it true, or just for friendship's sake?" Then Lalita confessed, "I am afraid it was for friendship's sake."'

'Tell me,' Swami Ashokananda asked, 'did Swamiji ever use slang?'

'He did occasionally, but not in public. Once, however, he did in a lecture at the Shakespeare Club in Pasadena. He was speaking of the Christian missionaries in India and their attitude toward the Hindus. He said their teachings amounted to saying, "Here, take my tomfool tin pot, and be happy! That is all you need."

'And regarding missionaries, he was once speaking of their antagonism toward him, and he told of a dinner to which he had been invited in Detroit. For some reason he suspected that his coffee had been poisoned. He was debating whether or not he should drink it, when Sri Ramakrishna stepped to his side, and said, "Do not drink—it is poisoned." He always spoke of his Master as "Atmaram". Whenever there were difficulties he would say, "Well, if things do not go well, we will wake up Atmaram."

'The missionaries were not the only ones who opposed Swamiji. There were many teachers of metaphysics, and many pseudo-teachers, who resented him or maliciously condemned him either because he was so far superior to them or because he exposed their shallowness and "spoiled their business" by teaching true metaphysics. Mr Bransby was one of these, more or less. He was constantly finding fault with Swamiji. One of his criticisms was that Swamiji was breaking the rules of his Order by taking money. I later told this to Swamiji. He was chanting something at the time, and he stopped, smiled, and said, "Yes, it is true; but when the rules don't suit me, I change them!"

'Mrs Allan has told me of another occasion when Bransby had been to see Swamiji while he was in Alameda. When he returned, he said, "How do you think I found the great man? Sitting on the floor, eating peanuts!"

'On another occasion in a conversation at home when Mrs Leggett was there, he was talking of the English in India. He said that actually, "the English did not come to India to conquer us, but to teach us." The great misfortune however was, he said, that the English soldiers—even the officers— were of such low caste. And he told of a time when he was sitting on the lawn in a park close to a footpath. Two soldiers passed by and one of them kicked him. Surprised, Swamiji said, "Why did you do that?" "Because I like to, you dirty something-or-other!" "Oh, we go much further than that," Swamiji retorted. "We call you 'dirty mlecchas'!" He spoke of the raping of lowcaste Hindu women by the English soldiers.

"If anyone despoiled the Englishman's home," he said, "the Englishman would kill him, and rightly so—but the damned Hindu just sits and whines!" he exclaimed.

At this, Mrs Leggett, who always agreed with everything Swamiji said, remarked, "How very nice!"

"'Do you think," he went on, "that a handful of Englishmen could rule India if we had a militant spirit? I teach meat-eating throughout the length and breadth of India in the hope that we can build a militant spirit."

'And that reminds me of a remark a Miss Blanche Partington once made about Swamiji later in San Francisco. She had been talking to Swamiji at the 1719 Turk Street flat. In answer to something she had said, Swamiji, bowing, had replied, "I am a loyal subject of Her Majesty [the Empress of India]!" Speaking of it afterward, Miss Partington said, "But it seemed to me he bowed almost too low!"'

'Did Swamiji laugh and joke very much?' Swami Ashokananda asked.

'Not much,' Mrs Hansbrough replied, 'though he always told some story on the lecture platform. He said he gathered his mind in this way.'

'Did you ever find him aloof, or did he make himself one with all?'

'I never found him aloof, though some said that he was. I felt as though he were someone to whom I was closely related, whom I had not seen for a long, long time, and who had been a long time coming.

'And indeed, Swamiji himself once said to Lalita, Helen, and me, "I have known all three of you before!" I think it was once when we were standing waiting for a train in San Francisco.

'Do you remember speaking the other day of the Christian in "Pilgrim's Progress" and the burden he carried on his back? Well, I felt that mine was on my chest—that is, after I met Swamiji, I felt the lifting of a burden which had been on my chest for so long that I had ceased to be conscious of it.

'When I returned to Los Angeles from San Francisco, after Swamiji had returned to the East, someone asked me how I felt about my brother [William Mead]. I replied that I did not know how I felt toward my brother, but that I felt much closer to the man I had been assisting in San Francisco than any other person I had ever known.'

'Did you ever see Swamiji in any especially exalted mood?'

'No, not particularly, though sometimes when he had talked for some time, the air would become surcharged with a spiritual atmosphere. There was one occasion in particular: we had gone to the hill near our home where we used to have the picnics. Swamiji became absorbed in some subject he was discussing, and he talked for six hours without interruption—from ten in the morning until four in the afternoon! The air was just vibrant with spirituality by the time it was over.

'At another time in Alameda, I was upset or depressed about something, and he said to me, "Come, sit down and we will meditate." "Oh, I never meditate, Swami," I told him. "Well, come and sit by me, and I will meditate," he replied. So I sat down and closed my eyes. In a moment I felt as though I were going to float away, and I quickly opened my eyes to look at Swamiji. He had the appearance of a statue, as though there were not a spark of life in his body. He must have meditated for fifteen or twenty minutes, and then opened his eyes again.'

'Do you think that when Swamiji came to San Francisco he felt as free as he did in your home?'

'Not while he was in the Home of Truth. This was natural, for quite a number of people were living there and he could not feel as free or at home as he had in our house. After some time there he told me one day, "I must get out of here." It was then that Mrs Aspinall and I took the apartment on Turk Street, and Swamiji came.

'But if he found it difficult to live in the Home of Truth, imagine his having a spiritualist for a travelling companion.'

'What do you mean?' Swami Ashokananda asked.

'Didn't you know that he travelled with a spiritualist when he was on a lecture tour through the Eastern States?'

'No!'

'Oh yes. While he was under contract to that lecture bureau during his first visit to the West, he travelled with a very well-known spiritualist named Colville, who apparently was also under contract to the same bureau. Swamiji used to say, "If you think X is hard to live with, you should have travelled with Colville." The man seems to have had a nurse to look after him all the time.'

'Did you find Swamiji at all abstracted and apparently not much interested in his activities toward the end of his stay?' Swami Ashokananda asked.

'No indeed,' Mrs Hansbrough replied. 'Probably you are thinking of that mood which later came over him, when in India he was asked by some of the monks about something and he told them they would have to decide it, that his work was done.

'This was never apparent here, nor even in June of that year when he wrote me from New York City. No, he took the greatest interest in people and in "the Movement", and in whom he would send to carry on after he left the Pacific Coast. I am sure that if his health had permitted, he would have come to the West a third time.

'Swami Abhedananda was having trouble with the Leggetts in New York during the period when Swamiji was staying with us in Los Angeles. Mr Leggett expected to run the Society there in his capacity as president and expected Swami Abhedananda to acquiesce in this. One day Swamiji remarked about this situation. "You people think the head of a society can run things," he said. "You know, my boys can't work under those conditions."'

The conversation had now lasted well over an hour and it was almost two o'clock. The Swami therefore directed that Mrs Hansbrough be driven home, and from there he returned to the Temple.

Sunday, March 30, 1941

On Sunday, March 30, 1941, Mrs Hansbrough was again invited by Swami Ashokananda to drive home with him after his morning lecture in the Century Club Building. The day, however, was windy and rainy, and the drive was therefore a short one.

There was some conversation about the attendance at the swami's lecture that morning, and this led the swami to ask if Swami Vivekananda's lectures in San Francisco were well attended.

'His Sunday morning audience usually ran from five to six hundred people,' Mrs Hansbrough said. 'At evening lectures there were not so many, but usually he did not lecture in the evening on Sunday.'

'And classes?' the swami asked.

'Class attendance averaged from one hundred fifty to two hundred—which was not bad, considering that there was a charge of fifty cents for each class. That is, the charge was a dollar and a half for a series of three. The lectures were free. We followed the custom of the day.

'If I were to have the work to do over again with my present perspective, I would do it much differently,' Mrs Hansbrough went on. 'I would get the Academy of Science to sponsor the first lecture, and have it free. If we had done this, it would have given Swamiji at the start a group of intellectual people, and then he could have chosen from there on what he wanted to do. As it was, Miss MacLeod was very determined in the view that his first lecture should be charged for. Swamiji usually let us decide these things as he was unfamiliar with the country. I did not have the temerity and outspokenness that I have now, or I would have ridiculed Miss MacLeod into agreeing that it should be a free first lecture. As it was, we charged a dollar admission.'

'Once after we had moved to the Turk Street flat a woman said something to Swamiji about his teaching religion. He looked at her and replied: "Madam, I am not teaching religion. I am selling my brain for money to help my people. If you get some benefit from it, that is good; but I am not teaching religion!"'

'Where do you think Swamiji showed the greater power in his lectures, here or in Los Angeles?' Swami Ashokananda asked.

'I think he showed greater power here,' Mrs Hansbrough replied. 'He seemed to get greater satisfaction from his work here.

'Swamiji said many seemingly contradictory things. For example, he said of his lectures and work, "I have been saying these things before, over and over again." In the Turk Street flat one day he said, "There is no Vivekananda", and again, "Do not ask these questions while you have this maya mixed up with your understanding."'

'Did he ever express any opinion about San Francisco?'

'No, not that I remember. He seemed to be like a bird in flight: he would stop here, then there, with no great concern for liking or disliking the places where he stopped.'

'Now, what instructions did Swamiji give you before you came to San Francisco from Los Angeles?'

'Well, I gave him the instructions,' Mrs Hansbrough said with a smile. 'I told him to give me a week and then to come on, and that I would get a place for him to stay so he would not have to be in a hotel. I got in touch with all my old friends and acquaintances, mostly those who were interested in so-called "new thought", and found nearly all of them readily agreeable to helping arrange plans for Swamiji's lectures. Later I found that their motives were largely to publicize themselves through publicizing Swamiji, though it did not occur to me then because I was so absorbed in working for him. I arranged for him to stay at the Home of Truth centre at 1231 Pine Street. (The building is still standing today, though it is no longer the Home of Truth.) They were delighted to have him, and provided him, free of charge, with a room and his board. You see, the Home of Truth centres were supported by public subscriptions: the idea was started by Emma Curtis Hopkins, who branched off from Mary Baker Eddy and Christian Science.'

'And did you make arrangements for the lectures and classes?'

'Yes, I selected a hall—Washington Hall it was— for the first Sunday morning lecture, and another smaller hall across Post Street for the classes. I had come north about the middle of February, and this first lecture of Swamiji's was near the end of the month. The attendance was very disappointing from the standpoint of numbers: there were probably less than one hundred and fifty.[3]

'I remember that Swamiji was seated down in the front row in the audience before the lecture began, and when I went to sit by him, he

made a sign to ask how many I thought there were. When I estimated one hundred and fifty, he wrote in the palm of one hand with his finger 100 as his estimate. He did not say anything, but he seemed disappointed. If we had had the first lecture free I am sure we would have had a better attendance. As it was, we charged a dollar per person.'

'Oh my!' Swami Ashokananda exclaimed. 'And one hundred came at a dollar each? Well, that shows that there was real interest.'

'How did Swamiji come from Los Angeles? Did he come alone?'

'Yes, he came alone, by train. It must have been the day train, because I remember that we met him at the Oakland Mole, came across on the ferry, and had dinner at the Home of Truth.'

'And how was he dressed when he arrived?'

'He had on that black loose-fitting suit which he usually wore, and the black silk turban.'

---

3. Swamiji's first lecture was held at Golden Gate Hall, San Francisco, on Friday evening, February 23, 1900. The subject: The Ideal of a Universal Religion.

'When was it that Swamiji spoke in Dr B Fay Mills' Unitarian Church in Oakland?'

'It was soon after he arrived in San Francisco [Sunday, February 25].'

'Did Swamiji know Dr Mills intimately?'

'No, as a matter of fact, although B Fay Mills had been at the Parliament of Religions in Chicago in 1893 and had heard Swamiji there, Swamiji did not remember him. At the time of the Parliament Dr Mills had been a Presbyterian minister. But he himself told me about Swamiji, "This man altered my life"; and he later became a Unitarian. Yet, in spite of his saying this about Swamiji, when I went to see him while he was lecturing in Metropolitan Temple to ask if he would announce a course of lectures by Swami Vivekananda, he refused! And he had wanted to manage Swamiji's whole visit in San Francisco; he had written Swamiji and asked to do so. This was after Swamiji's first lecture, and we felt that if he could obtain some announcements of this type it would help increase the attendance. I did not have the temerity then that I have now, or I would have told Dr Mills plainly what I thought of him!

'He was an astute man of business. His plan for introducing Swamiji in San Francisco had been to have him speak first outside of San Francisco—that is, in his own church in Oakland. Then he would advertise here that "many hundreds had been turned away"—which we used to do quite truthfully in Los Angeles—in first introducing him here. He did this when he advertised the lecture Swamiji did give at his church, and with good effect.

'I never could figure why Swamiji was unwilling to allow B Fay Mills to handle his arrangements here unless it was because of the trouble he had had [in 1894] with the lecture bureau and others seeking to gain a commission from whatever income he realized from his lectures and classes.'

'Was Swamiji comfortable in the Home of Truth in San Francisco?' Swami Ashokananda asked.

'No, he wasn't,' Mrs Hansbrough replied. 'So I took him to the home of a friend of mine. He was not comfortable there either; and it was then that Mrs Aspinall—she and her husband were heads of the Home of Truth on Pine Street—said, "See here, we must find a place where this man can be comfortable." So she and I took the flat then on Turk Street, and she explained to her husband that it was in order to make a comfortable place for Swamiji to stay. It was a poor sort of place, but the best we could do for the money we could afford to spend. When I told Swamiji this, he said, "That is because I am a sannyasin and can't get anything good."

'Mr Aspinall did not like the idea of Mrs Aspinall's leaving the Pine Street Home of Truth to set up the Turk Street flat with me so that Swamiji could have a quiet place to stay. At the time he objected strongly to it, but Mrs Aspinall told him, "Benjamin, you know that we do not have any truth; we just talk." She meant that in Swamiji she felt she had found someone who really had found the truth and could give it to others.'

'Did Swamiji speak in the Pine Street Home of Truth?' Swami Ashokananda asked.

'He spoke there once, probably in the evening. He also spoke one morning in another Home of Truth in San Francisco where a Miss Lydia Bell was head. In the Alameda Home of Truth he spoke at least twice.'

'When did he go to the Alameda Home?'

'After the lectures closed here on April 14. [He actually moved on April 11.] His idea was to go there to rest for a few days. He wanted, before he left for the East, to accumulate a certain sum of money for some purpose. I don't remember the amount, but I remember that one woman in Oakland gave him a thousand dollars. And someone introduced Mrs Collis P Huntington to him, and she gave him six thousand dollars for Sister Nivedita's girls' school. The money from the lectures and classes, I used to keep in a teapot when we were in the flat. In those days gold coins circulated freely, and I had several pots half full of twentydollar gold pieces. One day Swamiji wanted to figure out how much he had accumulated to date, so I got my notebook and pencil and brought the pots and dumped the coins out on the table. After counting the money, Swamiji found he needed more than he had so he said we would open some more courses. When he had the sum he wanted, he opened a bank account and deposited the money in it.

'One woman told someone that she did not like Swami Vivekananda because of the thin little woman who was always running along behind him with the black case. It was I, and the black case held my notebooks, advertising matter, and other things connected with the work—and the collections. Once Swamiji and I stopped in a market to do some shopping, and when we had gone out I discovered I had left the case. I said, "Just a minute, I forgot something!" and rushed back. There was the case, sitting on the counter. It had three hundred dollars in it!

'There was one conversation at the Alameda Home of Truth which reminds me of your question last week as to whether I had ever seen Swamiji in any particularly exalted mood. I think this was the most inspiring instance except at Camp Taylor. We were seated at the breakfast table in the Alameda Home. Mrs Aspinall, the two Roorbachs, Mr Pingree, the two housekeepers, the two gardeners, and myself. (Those who worked in the Home of Truth centres were all members, who gave their services according to their talents. Mr Pingree, for example, was a teacher, and the only member, incidentally, who demanded any pay: he asked for and got his board and room and fifteen dollars a month.) It was Mr Pingree with whom Swamiji used to walk in the garden of the Alameda Home, and who Swamiji said had an intuition of the conversation of the trees. He used to say the trees talked: he would put his hands on them and say he could understand what they were saying.

'Well, Swamiji began to talk as we all sat there at the breakfast table. Then someone suggested we go into the front room so that the housekeepers could clear the table. The two rooms were separated only by an archway with curtains hung in them. So five of us went into the front room and the rest went about their affairs: Swamiji, Mrs Aspinall, the Roorbachs, and I took our seats, Swamiji sitting on a chair facing the rest of us. He talked a great deal of his Master that day. Two stories which he said were his Master's I remember, because he directed them at me.

'The first was a story of an old water-demon who lived in a pool. She had long hair, which was capable of infinite extension. When people would come to bathe in the pool, sometimes she would devour them if she was hungry. With others, however, she would twine a hair around one of their toes. When they went home, the hair, invisible, would just stretch and stretch; and when the old demon became hungry she would just start pulling on the hair until the victim came back to the pool once more, to be eaten up.

'"You have bathed in the pool where my Mother dwells," Swamiji said to me at the end. "Go back home if you wish; but her hair is twined round your toe and you will have to come back to the pool in the end."

'The other story was of a man who was wading down a stream. Suddenly he was bitten by a snake. He looked down, and thought the snake was a harmless water snake and that he was safe. Actually it was a cobra. Swamiji then said to me: "You have been bitten by the cobra. Don't ever think you can escape!"

'Swamiji did not move from his seat once during the whole conversation. None of us moved from our seats. Yet when he finished it was five o'clock in the afternoon. Later the two housekeepers told us they had tried twice to open the door from the kitchen into the dining room to clear the table, but could not get it open. They thought we had locked it so we would not be disturbed. Even when Swamiji had finished, Mrs Aspinall was the only one who thought of taking any food. After talking with Swamiji for a few minutes in his room I put on my coat and came back to San Francisco. As we went up the stairs to his room, Swamiji said: "They think I have driven them crazy. Well, I shall drive them crazier yet!"'

'My, my,' murmured Swami Ashokananda. 'Did Swamiji talk in a loud tone, or quietly?'

'No, he talked in a low tone of voice,' Mrs Hansbrough said. 'Even in private conversation he was always a calm man, except when he was giving someone a dressing down. (This he never did to Helen or Carrie.) The only time I ever saw him get excited was when the missionary woman called him a liar.

'He used to talk often to my nephew, Ralph, when he was in our home in Los Angeles. Ralph was then a boy of about seventeen, and used to wait on Swamiji: he shined his shoes and did other little things for him. He would say, "Ralph, my tobacco", and Ralph would go up to his room and bring it down. Once he asked him, "Can you see your own eyes?" Ralph answered no, except in a mirror. "God is like that," Swamiji told him. "He is as close as your own eyes. He is your own, even though you can't see him."

'It must have been one morning in our home in Los Angeles that Swamiji gave what I call "baptism" to Dorothy and Ralph. I remember he laid his pipe aside and called Dorothy to him, and he only smoked after breakfast and dinner. Dorothy was four years old at the time. She went and stood between his knees, with her hands on his thighs. Swamiji put his hands at the back of her head where the hair joins the neck, and tapped up and over the top of her head to the eyebrows. Then he called Ralph and did the same thing. Ralph must have knelt, because I remember that Swamiji did not leave his seat. My two sisters may have been there too; I am not sure.

'"What is the meaning of this, Swami?" I asked. Usually I never questioned him, but I did ask him this.

'"Oh, it is just a custom we have in India", was all he would tell me.'

'Did Swamiji give any interviews to any newspapers while he was in Los Angeles?' Swami Ashokananda asked.

'Yes, there was an interview published under the title "A Prince from India". It appeared in some paper, probably a weekly, the name of which I have forgotten. I may be able to get the name of it from Mrs John Schmitz, the doctor's wife who was our first president in Los Angeles. She is still living there.'

'Did Swamiji ever tell you anything directly about Divine Mother?' Swami Ashokananda asked Mrs Hansbrough.

'Oh yes, he talked a great deal of Divine Mother,' she replied. 'He said that she was the receptacle of every germ of religion, and that she was here as a form, but was not tied to that form. She had her desires, he said, but they were related to people. She would reach for people, though they did not know it, and gradually she would draw them to her.'

Swami Ashokananda remarked in the course of the conversation on how gracious Swamiji was. 'He would not have held on to me as he did if he had not been,' she remarked. It reminded her of an episode indicative of the way Swamiji had held her in spite of her best efforts to leave him.

'One day while we were in San Francisco, I finally decided that I was going back to Los Angeles. I chose the day, and had all my bags packed, ready to leave for the train. All at once I heard a voice say: "You can't go. You might just as well not try." And for some reason I became completely exhausted— so exhausted that I had to lie down on the floor. I thought of getting some food, but I couldn't move. And I couldn't bear to look at the suitcases. So I had to make up my mind not to go.'

'Did Swamiji say anything to you?' Swami Ashokananda asked.

'No, he said nothing. I don't know whose was the voice I heard speaking to me.'

Sunday, April 6, 1941

Sunday morning, April 6, was bright with the spring sun when Swami Ashokananda left the Century Club Building after his lecture, accompanied by Mrs Hansbrough. The drive home this morning was through Golden Gate Park, and the swami had the car parked beside a lake, where ducks and swans swam about on the quiet water.

Swami Ashokananda asked Mrs Hansbrough to tell him about Swamiji's stay in the flat she had taken with Mrs Aspinall on Turk Street while he had been in San Francisco.

'We were in the flat on Turk Street for about a month,' Mrs Hansbrough said. 'There were two rooms which might have been called "parlours", with a sliding door between them. Next behind was the dining room, then Mrs Aspinall's room, then the kitchen. There was a kind of hall bedroom at the top of the stairs which was meant, I suppose, for a servant, and I occupied that.

'Swamiji's room was the second of the two parlour rooms. The classes were held in the front parlour, and if there were too many for the single room we would put a screen before the couch Swamiji used as a bed, open the doors into his room, and use both rooms. I think Mrs Aspinall and I paid about forty dollars a month for the flat.

'There was one item about the Turk Street flat which was distinctly different from our home in Los Angeles, and which had its amusing side as I look back. This was the bathtub, which was one of those old-fashioned things built of zinc. Porcelain tubs were still not in use everywhere, and I had to go over the tub carefully every day with a stone they called a bath brick. Swamiji would ask me regularly if I had washed the tub. He was most particular and exacting about it; and as I recall it now, I think the goings-over that I got about that tub were more for my benefit than the tub's. Swamiji would go on at great length about it.

'One day I scrubbed it three times. After the third time, when he still complained that it was not clean, I said, "Well, I have scrubbed that tub three times, and if you can't bathe in it now, I guess you will have to go without a bath!" So then he let it go and took his bath.

'Both here and before we came north, Swamiji liked to prepare one meal of the day himself, and he often helped with meals. He cooked curries, and especially chapatis, of which Ralph and Dorothy used to be very fond. He liked the way I cooked rice—in fact, he told me I was the only woman in America who knew how to cook it! In the Turk Street flat he often cooked pulao, that rich dessert made with [rice and ghee]. Sometimes he would cook breakfast; he used to like potatoes cooked in butter with a little curry powder.

'As I have mentioned before, Swamiji used to like to prepare one meal every day while he was at our home in Lincoln Park. Several of the ingredients he used had to be ground, and since he did not like to stand beside a table, he would sit cross-legged on the floor with a wooden butter bowl on the floor in front of him. One day during this ceremony we were talking about his health. Someone suggested that he had a weak heart. "There is nothing wrong with your heart," I told him. "If you mean that," he answered, "I have the heart of a lion!"'

'And how did he spend his day while he was in San Francisco? Was his routine about the same as in Los Angeles?' Swami Ashokananda asked.

'Yes, it was just about the same while we were at Turk Street,' Mrs Hansbrough replied. 'When he had no class in the morning we would often go out during the day. Swamiji liked to go to the market with me, and sometimes we would go out for lunch or go for a ride here in Golden Gate Park which he liked. I remember that once Mr Aspinall brought us out in a carriage and we were strolling along. We crossed a bridge onto what proved to be a fairly sizeable island in the midst of a rather swift stream. When we had left the bridge some distance behind and tried to discover some means of recrossing the stream, Swamiji realized we were on an island, and without thinking to use just that word he tried to indicate the fact to me as he looked about for a means of crossing. Finally when he saw that I had neither caught his meaning nor perceived that the land was an island he remarked, "Well, Madam, I am glad I haven't your brain!"

'Sometimes when he was not lecturing in the evening we would go out to dinner too. He never ate dinner before a lecture; he said it slowed his thinking. He was a hearty eater; in fact, Molly Rankin, one of the housekeepers at the Alameda Home of Truth, said that no person could eat as much as Swamiji did and be spiritual! Lucy Beckham and George Roorbach were quite agreeable, though. And Swamiji demanded what he felt he needed. Once, for example, he said: "See here, I must have meat. I cannot live on potatoes and asparagus with the work I am doing!" So they got meat for him, although they themselves were vegetarians.'

'About how many used to attend Swamiji's classes in the Turk Street flat?' Swami Ashokananda asked.

'I should say they numbered about thirty or forty,' Mrs Hansbrough replied. 'They were held three times a week, the same as his other classes. Swamiji would open the class at ten-thirty, usually with meditation, which often lasted for some time. Then he would speak or discourse on some sacred book. Sometimes he would ask the class what they would like for a subject.

'Swamiji always sat cross-legged on the couch in the front parlour, and when all the chairs were taken people often sat cross-legged on the floor. There was a Mr Wiseman who came to the classes. He was a devoted follower of Miss Bell. He came late once to the class when all the seats were taken, and he had to sit on the floor. In those days the style of men's trousers did not provide the generous leg-room they do nowadays, and Mr Wiseman's trousers were so tight he could not sit cross-legged. Swamiji noticed him sitting with his knees up under his chin and suddenly exclaimed: "Don't look like a fool! Come and sit by me!" Mr Wiseman was a quiet, unassuming sort of man and he would have felt it presumptuous to sit on the same couch with Swamiji. But he accepted the invitation and took a seat on the end of the couch.'

'Was any charge made for the classes at Turk Street?' Swami Ashokananda asked.

'No, the classes at Turk Street were free,' Mrs Hansbrough replied. 'We made a charge of one dollar and a half for a series of three classes downtown, however, and had small cards printed.

'Sometimes in these Turk Street classes Swamiji could be very sharp. Once when he was talking of renunciation, a woman asked him, "Well, Swami, what would become of the world if everyone renounced?" His answer was: "Madam, why do you come to me with that lie on your lips? You have never considered anything in this world but your own pleasure!" He told us at another time of a woman in Chicago who had asked him after a class or lecture, "Swami, do you hate all women?" It revealed a characteristic of many of his questioners, that they identified themselves with their question, but couched the question in general terms. I don't remember what Swamiji's answer was.

'Stupid and emotional people apparently gave the Christian ministers excuses for not a little criticism of Swamiji in the Eastern States. The ministers accused him of "separating families". It seems that there was at least one instance, in Detroit, in which a woman divorced her husband and left her children with him in order to "renounce the world".

'Swamiji often was asked questions about going to India, especially by women students. He used to tell them: "If you are going to India to see great yogis, don't go. You will see only poverty, filth, and misery."

'Swamiji was a great one to think out loud when he was at home. That is, as he would talk casually, one had the feeling that this was what he was doing. He liked a listener, however. He would ask us many questions about our family lives, and then would tell us about family life in India.

'One day when he and I were alone in the Turk Street flat he said: "I have in mind to send my mother a thousand dollars." I do not remember the details now, but it seems that his mother was involved in some litigation in connection with his father's estate, and she had appealed to Swamiji's brother disciple Swami Saradananda, who had written to Swamiji. "Saradananda is an impractical fellow like me," Swamiji remarked, "but I have written him what to do. In your country a man is allowed to have a mother; in my country I am not allowed. Do you think that is bad?" He was asking if I thought it wrong under these circumstances for him to send his mother money. I replied that it certainly did not seem bad to me, and I believe he did send the money later.'

'Did Swamiji ever scold you?' Swami Ashokananda asked.

'Oh yes, often. He was constantly finding fault and sometimes could be very rough. "Mother brings me fools to work with!" he would say. Or, "I have to associate with fools!" This was a favourite word in his vocabulary of scolding. And though he himself said, "I never apologize", he would nevertheless come after the scolding was over to find me, and say in a voice so gentle and with a manner so cool that butter and honey would not melt in his mouth, "What are you doing?" It was clear that he was seeking to make amends for the scolding. He used to say, "The people I love most, I scold most", and I remember thinking he was making a poor kind of apology!

'Going up the steps of a hall in San Francisco before one of his lectures, Swamiji asked me about something I had told him I was going to do. I had neglected to take care of it, and told him I had intended to do it, but had not. "Your intentions are good," he remarked, "but how like devils you sometimes act!"

'Once while we were in the Turk Street flat I questioned something about the way Swamiji was handling the work. He did not answer, but simply said, "Within ten years of my death, I will be worshipped as a god!"

'Once in the Turk Street flat I was dusting after breakfast in the dining room. As I worked, Swamiji was talking about something. I do not remember now what it was. "You are a silly, brainless fool, that's what you are!" he exclaimed. He continued to scold me heatedly until suddenly Mrs Aspinall appeared and he stopped. I said to him: "Never mind Mrs Aspinall. Swami, if you're not through, just keep right on!"

'Somehow, I never felt hurt by his scoldings. I would often get angry and sometimes would walk out of the room, but usually I was able to hear him through. He used to complain of everything. But he used to say, "If you think I am hard to get along with, you should have travelled with Colville!" Colville was a spiritualist with whom Swamiji travelled when on tour for a lecture bureau during his first visit to the West.

'There was the other side, however. As I have said, after a severe scolding, he would come back and speak in the gentlest of voices. And he could give credit, too, when he chose. On the evening we left the Turk Street flat to go to the Alameda Home of Truth, he was helping me on with my overcoat, and remarked, "Well, you have worked like a demon." I always felt as if he were my very own, a very close relation for whom I had been waiting a long, long time.

'Once at the Turk Street flat Swamiji asked me, "Why can't you join our Order?" He never asked me directly to join, but he did put this question. My answer was that I had my own little world that I had to go back and take care of.'

'Well, how did you go to Alameda that night [Wednesday, April 11, 1900] when you moved from Turk Street?' Swami Ashokananda asked.

'We took the streetcar and then the ferry across the Bay, and probably took the streetcar again on the other side. The three of us went together— Swamiji, Mrs Aspinall, and I—and we probably had dinner before we left San Francisco. Mrs Aspinall and I each had a small suitcase, and Swamiji probably had the same. His trunk with his many clothes in it, I sent by express. I may have packed it for him too, as I often did. About his clothes, he used to say, "In India I can exist on hips and haws and live in rags, but here I want to meet your demands."

'On the streetcar, Swamiji would always sit very straight with his hands, one on top of the other, on the walking stick he carried. He would often sing in a low tone of voice on the car, after he came north from Los Angeles. It was quite a trip across to Alameda, and as I say, I think the last part was on the streetcar too, as there was nothing like a cab service then such as there is now. When we arrived at the Home of Truth we were met in the hall by the teachers, George Roorbach and his wife, Eloise (both of whom were artists), and Miss Lucy Beckham. George Roorbach took Swamiji up to his room on the second floor. It was a fine, big room: the house was a mansion which had been loaned to the Home of Truth by a wealthy family while they were away in Europe. Swamiji was quite comfortable and did get some rest while he was there.'

'How many of our present members who knew Swamiji ever attended the Turk Street classes or visited Swamiji there?' Swami Ashokananda asked.

'I can remember only Mrs Allan at Turk Street,' Mrs Hansbrough said. 'She came for dinner once or twice. The Wollbergs, as I remember, came usually to the Sunday evening lectures downtown.'

'Did Swamiji ever express any opinion about San Francisco and his work here?'

'He thought that he got a better response here than he did in Los Angeles. And he was much more jolly here: he could see the end of his work after he had come here and had succeeded in collecting some of the funds he sought, and I think this helped to lighten his heart. Personally, I think he would have had even better response if B Fay Mills had managed his visit for him. Mills was an astute businessman. Sometime later he went to Los Angeles and founded a group he called [?] Fellowship. The membership at one time rose to three thousand members, and he actually persuaded the businessmen to close their offices not only on Sunday but on Wednesday in addition!'

'How did Dr Logan come into the work?'

'I don't remember just when he first became interested, but he was present the night the San Francisco lectures closed. The Wollbergs were there, but I don't remember whether the Allans were or not. We had asked a Mr Chambers to invite any to stay at the close of the lecture who would be interested in continuing the study of Swamiji's teachings. He did this, and when the others had left he asked me to tell about the organization of the Los Angeles and Pasadena centres. Then we discussed the or ganization of a centre here, but did not complete the arrangements that night. Dr Logan then suggested that we meet the next night in his office at 770 Oak Street, which we did, and it was on that night, April 14, 1900, that the organization of the Society was completed. Swamiji later held some classes there, and he also held some there after he returned from Camp Taylor [in mid-May].'

'That means, just before he returned to the eastern states?'

'Yes, we went to Camp Taylor from Alameda; then Swamiji spent a few days [two weeks] in San Francisco, at Dr Milburn Logan's home, 770 Oak Street, before he took the train on May 30 to Chicago and New York.

'Well now, did Swamiji express any opinion about the proposed organization [of a Vedanta Society] in San Francisco?'

'No, he didn't. The object of the Society was simply to keep in touch with his work, and the money which came in was to go to his work. He simply suggested that meetings should be held in someone's office.'

'What sort of man was Dr Logan?'

'He was a man of middle age at that time, and apparently devoted to Swamiji. He was very helpful to him. But when Swami Trigunatita came to take charge of the Society, he forced Dr Logan out of the work, because he said the doctor was in it for "name and fame". Swamiji seemed to like all people. He was most compassionate; it seemed as if he never saw distinctions between people—almost as if he didn't see the difference between a duck and a man! He felt that he had come to the West for two purposes: to deliver a message and to get help for India. But he was terribly disappointed in the amount of help he got.'

'Well now, you spoke of Swamiji's going out during the day in San Francisco. What places did he visit besides Golden Gate Park?' Swami Ashokananda asked.

'There were not a great many, but I think he visited the Cliff House, and he often went to Chinatown. For some reason, incidentally, he had a fascination for the Chinese. They would just flock after him, "shaking themselves by the hand" as the saying went, to express their pleasure at his presence. Mr Charles Neilson, a well-known artist who lived in Alameda and who became an admirer of Swamiji, invited us to have dinner one evening in Chinatown. We sat down and ordered, but the food had no sooner been put on the table than Swamiji said he could not eat it,

and rose from the table. Of course we went home. Mr Neilsen was very disappointed because he knew the Chinese who owned the restaurant; but Swamiji later explained that it was because of the character of the cook that he was unable to eat the food. One other such occurrence took place when we had had fried shrimps somewhere. When we got home Swamiji vomited his dinner. I said fried shrimps were always hard to digest and probably these were not good, but he insisted that it was the bad character of the cook that was responsible. "I'm getting like my Master," he said. "I shall have to live in a glass cage."'

'Did he ever seek any amusement? For example, did he ever go to the theatre?'

'He went to the theatre once in Los Angeles to a play, but generally speaking he never sought entertainment, such as playing cards. He did enjoy going out to dinner. He went out to dinner several times with Mr Neilson, the artist, who also took Swamiji to an exhibition of his paintings at the Hopkins Art Gallery, where the Hotel Mark Hopkins now stands on Nob Hill.

'Speaking of dinner reminds me of an incident one evening just as we were preparing dinner in the Turk Street flat. A Mrs Wilmot, a Theosophist who had been coming to Swamiji's lectures, phoned and asked Swamiji if he could come to see her. She said she felt she was losing her mind, that she was having trouble with the "elementals", whatever they were. She was very anxious for Swamiji to go right over to her home. "No," Swamiji said, "we are just preparing dinner. You come over here. Bring the 'elementals' and we will fry them for dinner!'"

'What was the play that Swamiji went to see?'

'It was a comedy which was a great hit at the time, called "My Friend from India". It was written, as a matter of fact, as a result of Swamiji's visit to the United States, though it had no real bearing on his actual activities here. The plot revolved around a wealthy family consisting of a man and his wife, their son and two daughters, and an unmarried sister. They became interested in a man from India, a "wearer of the yellow robe" as he was called, who had come to the West to teach Indian religion; and the whole family took to wearing yellow robes. The play was concerned chiefly with the night of a party to which the family had been invited. At the last minute the women discovered that they had all bought the same model yellow gown for the party. When they came home afterwards, the son tried to sneak a tipsy friend quietly to his room to put him to bed, by disguising the friend in his yellow robe and introducing him as the "friend from India", a bit wobbly from too much meditation! A Christian minister who was trying to make love to the maiden aunt also tried to get into the house disguised as the "friend from India", and the father finally concluded that he had lost his mind because he was sure he saw too many yellow robes and too many "friends from India".

'It was Professor Baumgardt who invited Swamiji, and a party of us went together. The play was really very funny, and Swamiji enjoyed it hugely. Professor Baumgardt said he had never seen anyone laugh so hard or so much as Swamiji did.'

May 4, 1941

Several weeks passed before Swami Ashokananda again had an opportunity to talk with Mrs Hansbrough of her days with Swamiji. However, on the fourth of May, Sunday, she once more accompanied him on a drive en route from his morning lecture at the Century Club Building. The talk turned to the emphasis some preachers put upon sin and the devil, rather than upon God, and Mrs Hansbrough said that Swamiji had told those in his meditation class that they should try to think of themselves as related closely to Kali or Shiva, or to whomever they meditated upon.

'Did Swamiji hold a meditation class?' Swami Ashokananda asked.

'He always held a meditation period at the beginning of his classes,' Mrs Hansbrough replied, 'but I wouldn't call that exactly a meditation class.'

'Well, how long would he meditate? Very long?'

'No, I should say fifteen minutes or half an hour. I remember one class particularly. When we were in the Turk Street flat, I used to prepare a lamb broth for Swamiji every day. I would cook it very slowly for three or four hours, and it was very nourishing because every bit of food value would be cooked out of the meat. One day for some reason I had not been able to get the broth made by the time the class was to start at ten-thirty. Swamiji looked into the kitchen before going to the class. "Aren't you going to the class?" he asked. I told him that because I had neglected to plan my work properly, now I had to stay in the kitchen and miss the class. "Well, that's all right," he said. "I will meditate for you." All through the class I felt that he really was meditating for me. And do you know, I have always had the feeling that he still does meditate for me.'

'Did Swamiji ever rest during the daytime while he was in the Turk Street flat?' Swami Ashokananda asked.

'Yes, when he did not have a lecture or some engagement in the afternoon he took a nap after lunch every day. He would sleep for about two hours.'

Swami Ashokananda's eyes twinkled. 'And did he ever snore?' he asked.

'No,' Mrs Hansbrough answered with amusement, 'I never heard him snore.'

'Now, when was it that Swamiji went to Camp Taylor?'

'It was about the first of May 1900. The lectures and classes closed in San Francisco on April 14, but on April 11 Swamiji moved to the Home of Truth in Alameda. It was Mrs Aspinall who suggested his going to Camp Taylor. She and Mr Aspinall had already arranged to go there, and one Sunday evening [April 22] when we were all sitting in the Home of Truth, she was conjecturing where each of us would be a week hence: Swamiji in Chicago (I had already bought his ticket for him), I in Los Angeles, and they at Camp Taylor. Then, turning to Swamiji, she said, "You had better change your mind and go with us." And Swamiji replied, "Very well. And madam (indicating me) will go with us."

'We set out the next morning. When I went to his room, Swamiji had on the English hunting suit which someone had given him in the East. He was just putting on the detachable cuffs, which men wore in those days. I had not intended to go to Camp Taylor, but was planning to return then to Los Angeles. I told Swamiji that I would go with

him on the ferry to Sausalito and say goodbye to him there.

'He took off his cuffs and dropped them in the bureau drawer. "Then," he said, "I go to Chicago." Of course I at once said that I would certainly go to Camp Taylor, and we started off shortly afterward.

'In the party were Mr and Mrs Aspinall, Mr and Mrs Roorbach, Miss Ansell and Miss Bell besides Swamiji and myself. I had packed Swamiji's things in two big wicker hampers, and Mr Roorbach undertook to handle them for Swamiji. When we got to the ferry, Mr Roorbach walked on ahead with his bulky load. As I mentioned before, he and all the others in the Home of Truth were vegetarians; and as Swamiji saw him struggling with the big baskets he said, "Boiled potatoes and asparagus can't stand up under that."

'In San Francisco we took another ferry to Sausalito, where we were to get the train for Camp Taylor. But the brief discussion I had had with Swamiji about leaving him at Sausalito had been just enough to make us miss the ferry that would have connected comfortably with the Camp Taylor train. The result was that we arrived just in time to see the train pull out. Mr Roorbach said there was a narrow-gauge train that also went there, and we found that that was just ready to leave. We hurried to the proper platform. This train was just getting under way. I called to the conductor on the back platform, who called back, "If you'll run, I'll wait for you." I looked at Swamiji. He simply said, "I will not run." Even though the train was there within a few yards of him, he would not hurry to catch it.

'Well, there were no more trains that day, so we had to go all the way back to the Home of Truth in Alameda. On the way back I remarked that we had missed the train because there was no engine hitched to our cars. Swamiji turned to me and said: "We couldn't go because your heart was in Los Angeles. There is no engine that can pull against a heart— there is no force in the world which can pull against a heart. Put your heart into your work and nothing can stop you." It was a tremendously significant statement, and it has been vivid in my memory all these years.

'The Aspinalls had gone on ahead of us to Camp Taylor, and I had discovered when we missed the train that my baggage was missing. Later I found they had taken it up with them. After all the missed trains and the loss of time, I had once more decided to go back to Los Angeles, but the next day I had to go up to Camp Taylor to recover my luggage. Mrs Aspinall tried to make me promise that I would not go to say goodbye to Swamiji when I got back to the city: she said I would surely prevent him from getting there [to camp] a second time. When I had told Swamiji I would have to go up [to the camp] for my baggage, he remarked, "Strange, Mother's dragging you up there, when you tried your best not to go." And when I returned with the baggage, he said, "Well, come up there for a week and we won't stay longer." (When I finally had departed for the south [several weeks later], he told someone, "She had to go back because the babe (Dorothy) wanted her.")

'So I went [to Camp Taylor]—and we stayed two weeks. On May 2 when we got on the train at Sausalito, we were soon travelling through wooded country, along the bank of the stream, and in the peaceful atmosphere Swamiji began to relax almost at once. He was sitting next to the window so that he could look out, and he began to sing softly to himself. "Here in the country I'm beginning to feel like myself, " he said. That first night Swamiji built a fire on a spit of sand that ran out into the stream. We all sat around the fire in the quiet night and Swamiji sang for us and told stories, such as those about Shukadeva and Vyasa. This was to be our custom on most nights. We would often cook chapatis, too, in pans over the coals.'

'How was Swamiji's voice?' Swami Ashokananda inquired. 'Was it a powerful voice?'

'No, it was not a powerful voice, but it had great depth. The manager of Washington Hall in San Francisco once told me he had never heard so sweet a voice.'

'What was the usual routine of Swamiji's day at Camp Taylor?'

'We would usually have breakfast sometime between seven-thirty and eight. Then about ten or ten-thirty Swamiji would hold a meditation, which took place in Miss Bell's tent, as she had requested it. We were located about a mile upstream from the old hotel, in a quiet, windless spot on the east side of the stream called Juhl Camp. The railroad ran by on the opposite bank. Mr Juhl was an admirer of Miss Bell and had arranged the location for us. We had five tents: one for Swamiji and one each for Mrs Aspinall, Miss Bell, Miss Ansell, and Mrs Roorbach. I slept outside Mrs Aspinall's tent until the rain drove me inside. She had some printed mottoes such as the Home of Truth people often put up, and she had pinned some of these to the sloping roof of the tent. Of course, wherever the pins were, the tent leaked; and one night I found the water dripping steadily on my forehead from "Love never faileth"! There was a delightful pool in the stream for bathing, which all of us used except Swamiji, who found the water too cold. Water for cooking and washing was piped to the camp, and we did our cooking outside. Swamiji really enjoyed his stay at Camp Taylor.

'After two weeks there, Swamiji returned to San Francisco [in mid-May] and was the guest of Dr Logan for a time. I stayed with a brother-in-law of mine, Jack Hansbrough, for about three days and then went back to Los Angeles. After I had left, Swamiji took another brief vacation trip somewhere outside of San Francisco with a Dr Miller [Hiller?] before he left for the Eastern States.

'In addition to Swamiji's one-night visit to Dr Miller's home in San Francisco, another doctor took him after he had been to Camp Taylor, to another resort outside of San Francisco for a rest.

'I saw him every day before I left, and twice the last day. Then he was ill in bed. I stood at the foot of the bed and said good-bye to him. "Come and shake hands," he said. "I never make a fuss over people even when I have known them many years." I assured him that I had certainly not expected him to make any fuss over me. "The Lord bless you and keep you," he said, and I departed. Later I discovered that I had left a handbag there. But after all the false starts for Camp Taylor I was not going back for that, so I asked Mrs Aspinall to get it when she had an opportunity and send it on to me. She told me later that when she went for it, Swamiji remarked:

"So she left that, did she? Take it out of here!"

'I did not hear from him until he reached Chicago and New York.'

June 22, 1941

Driving home from the Sunday lecture at the Century Club.

'Swamiji had marvellous patience with all of us,' Mrs Hansbrough declared. 'He made a great effort to do something for us. He took away any feeling on our part that he was superior to us.

'He paid a good deal of attention to children when he met them privately,' she continued. 'There was an old stable in the vacant lot next to our home in Los Angeles, where Swamiji used to sit with the children and look at their picture books. He particularly enjoyed Alice in Wonderland and Through the Looking Glass. He said they were absolutely typical in their portrayal of the processes of the human mind. He said that Lewis Carroll had some kind of intuition, that his was not an ordinary mind, to have written these books.'

Later Mrs Hansbrough spoke of an episode, also in their home in Los Angeles, involving a woman portrait painter, who was determined to do a portrait of Swamiji. She had approached him several times after meetings, but Swamiji had always declined.

'One day the woman came to our home,' Mrs Hansbrough said, 'and asked me if I would help her by letting her sketch him unawares. Somehow Swamiji sensed her presence and called me. "You get that woman out of here or I'll leave!" he told me. Needless to say, I saw her to the door.'

(*Prabuddha Bharata*, February-July, 1907)

Reeves Calkins

My first impression of the Swami was not a happy one. He had come to the World's Fair as India's representative at the Chicago Parliament of Religions, and I, a young preacher fresh from the University, did not greatly admire the magnificent ease with which he waved aside Christian history and announced a new Star in the East. I think it was his lordly manner that disturbed, somewhat, my American sense of democracy. He did not argue that he was a superior person; he admitted it. Afterwards, when I learnt that several cities, notably Boston, had formed Vivekananda Clubs, I was prepared to credit the report that, not his ideals, but his eyes, were leading captive silly American women, which was manifestly unfair. Then, for several years, I heard nothing further of him.

I reached India in December 1900, embarking at Naples on the *Rubattino* of the old Italian Line. It chanced that my seat in the saloon was at the end of one of the centre tables—which has considerable to do with my story. Mr. Drake Brockman, I.C.S., of the Central Provinces, occupied the first seat on the right, and another English Civilian whose name has escaped my memory sat opposite him. At Suez there was a shift at table, some of the passengers having left the vessel, and our first meal in the Red Sea saw a strange gentleman, in Indian habit, seated next to Mr. Drake Brockman. He was silent at that first meal, taking only a ship's biscuit and soda water, and leaving before the meal was finished. There was some question up and down the board as to the identity of the distinguished stranger, for, as was quite evident, he was no mean personage; whereupon a rough and ready traveller, disdaining delicacy, called to the chief steward to bring him the wine orders. Ostensibly looking for his own wine card, he drew forth a modest soda water slip which was handed round the table. "Vivekananda", in pencil, was what passed across my plate. In a moment I remembered the furore he had created at the Parliament of Religions, and looked forward with some interest to the coming days at sea.

My earlier impression of the Swami was still strong upon me, so I did not immediately seek his acquaintance; a bow at table answered every requirement. But I chanced to overhear one of the passengers speak his name, and add, "We'll draw him!" I suppose my instinct for fair play pulled me toward Vivekananda as his unconscious ally in the intellectual recounters of the next ten days. Perhaps he discerned my unspoken friendliness, for almost immediately, he sought me out.

"You are an American?"

"Yes."

"A missionary?"

"Yes."

"Why do you teach religion in my country?" he demanded. "Why do you teach religion in my country?" I countered. The least quiver of an eyelash was enough to throw down our guards. We both burst out laughing, and were friends.

For a day or two, at table, one or other of the passengers proceeded to "draw" the Swami—only he refused to be drawn! His answers were ready and usually sufficient; but, more than that, they were brilliant. They sparkled with epigrams and apt quotations. Presently the lesser wits learnt the valour of putting up their swords, all excepting Mr. Drake Brockman; his keen and analytic mind constantly cut across Vivekananda's epigrams and held him close to the logic of admitted facts. It worried the Swami a lot! The rest of the company soon lost interest and permitted our little group at the end of the table to hold uninterrupted forum, breakfast, tiffin, and dinner.

One night I participated in a discovery. Vivekananda had been particularly brilliant. His conversation was like Ganga at high flood. There was really no interrupting him. A question might deflect him for a moment, but presently he was moving again on the main current of his speech. At the close of an unusually eloquent period he bowed slightly to each of us, then arose and quietly left the saloon. The civilian sitting opposite Mr. Drake Brockman leaned across the table.

"Have you noticed that when the Indian gentleman is interrupted, he begins again where he left off?"

"Yes, we both had noticed it."

"He is repeating one of his lectures for our private benefit."

And so it was. But even so, it was an amazingly interesting performance, many leagues beyond the ordinary chitchat on board ship.

Vivekananda was a patriot much more than philosopher. I think his passion for the Vedantic propaganda was because this seemed to him the surest way of fostering Indian nationhood. I believe in this he was mistaken;[1] nevertheless, my recognition of his patriotism washed away completely my first unhappy impression of him and enabled me to know him as I think he would be glad to be remembered by his

---

1. The Swami's Vedantic mission served a twofold purpose as Sister Nivedita says: "One of the world-moving, and another, of nation-making." The function of the Swami's movement as regards India to quote his own words, was: "To find the common bases of Hinduism and awaken the national consciousness to them." The object of his carrying the spiritual message of India to the West he clearly stated in the following terms: "To give and take is the law of nature. Any individual or class or nation that does not obey this law, never prospers in life. We must follow the law. That is why I went to America. ... They have been for a long time giving you of what wealth they possess, and now is the time for you to share your priceless treasures with them. And you will see how the feelings of hatred will be quickly replaced by those of faith, devotion, and reverence towards you, and how they will do good to our country even unasked." That the Swami was right in the choice of his plan of campaign is borne out by the fruits of his labour in India and abroad.)

countrymen—not as a religionist propagating an ancient creed, but as a lover of his own land seeking to promote her good in the society of modern nations.

It was this passion for his country, short-circuited by a misapprehension of the purpose of Christian missions, that brought on an explosion. One evening, over the nuts and coffee, the conversation had turned on India's preparedness for self-government. (By the way, the conversation took place more than twenty-two years ago, when as yet the Montagu-Chelmsford Reform Bill was nebulous and far away; similar conversations may logically continue for one hundred and twenty-two years to come, for no nation ever yet as "prepared" for self-government.)

Suddenly Vivekananda blazed.

"Let England teach us the fine art of government," he burst forth, "for in that art Britain is the leader of the nations;" then, turning to me, "let America teach us agriculture and science and your wonderful knack of doing things, for here we sit at your feet; but"—and Vivekananda's pleasant voice grew harsh with bitterness—"let no nation presume to teach India religion, for here India shall teach the world."

That night we walked over the deck together and talked of the deeper things where there are no Britons, no Americans, no Indians, but only our hungry humankind and of one Son of Man whose sacrificial blood, somewhere in the shifting sands of Asia, still abides. I think I helped the Swami to understand that no missionary in his senses is seeking to teach "religion" in India, but only to help India know and love that Man.

During the last day or two of the voyage our understanding of each other increased greatly, and, as I believe, our mutual respect. The mysticism of Vivekananda was a fascination and wonder. For it was not affected. When our conversation touched, as it was bound to, on the hidden things of the spirit, his heavy eyelids would droop slowly and he wandered, even in my presence, into some mystic realm where

I was not invited. When, on one such occasion, I remarked that a Christian's conscious fellowship with the Supreme Person must be alert and awake (as all personal fellowships must be), and therefore is essentially and necessarily different from a Hindu's immersion in the all-pervading Brahman, he looked at me with a quick glance of scrutiny but made no reply. The last night, before the *Rubattino* reached Mumbai, we were standing on the forward deck. Vivekananda was smoking a short sweet-briar pipe—the one "English vice", he said, which he was fond of. The wash of the sea and the unknown life which would begin on the morrow invited quietness. For a long time no word was spoken. Then, as though he had made up his mind I would do India no harm, he laid his hand on my shoulder.

"Sir," he said, "they may talk about their Buddhas, their Krishnas, and their Christs, but we understand, you and I; we are segments of the All-One."

His hand remained upon my shoulder. It was such a friendly hand, I could not rudely remove it. Then he withdrew it himself, and I offered him my own.

"Swami," I said, "you will have to speak for yourself and not for me. The All-One of which you speak is impersonal, and therefore must remain unknowable, even though we be immersed in it as this ship is immersed in the Indian Ocean; He whom I know, whom I love, is personal and very very real—and, Swami, in Him all fullness dwells.

The sweet-briar went swiftly to his lips, and the drooping eyelids as he leaned against the rail gave token that Vivekananda had gone forth on a far quest.

Was it the All-One, or the One in all, the Swami sought the night?

(*Prabuddha Bharata*, March 1923)

Short Reminiscences

Swami Kalyanananda

Look, what can I say about Swamiji? What he was cannot be expressed in words. I could never look at him in the face. His eyes were simply dazzling, as if they were radiant! If my eyes ever happened to meet his, my head would immediately bow down and I would look away. It was truly a sight to see him meditate. He would become a statue carved out of stone, as it were! We too meditated in the shrine and would breathe very cautiously lest the sound of our breath disturb his meditation. Ah! What a sight! Just as you see in the photograph; one hand placed over the other. Every morning he would sit in the shrine and meditate for three to four hours at a stretch.

(Monastic Disciples, pp. 251-52)

Mahendranath Gupta

It was morning. The devotees went to the shrine room [of the Baranagore monastery], prostrated themselves before the Deity, and gradually assembled in the big hall. Narendra was clad in a new ochre cloth. The bright orange colour of his apparel blended with the celestial lustre of his face and body, every pore of which radiated a divine light. His countenance was filled with fiery brilliance and yet touched with the tenderness of love. He appeared to all as a bubble that had risen up in the Ocean of Absolute Existence and Bliss and assumed a human body to help in the propagation of his

Master's message. All eyes were fixed on him. Narendra was then just twenty-four years old, the very age at which the great Chaitanya had renounced the world.

Balaram had sent fruits and sweets to the monastery for the devotees' breakfast. Rakhal, Narendra, and a few others partook of the refreshments....

Narendra now began to joke like a child. He was imitating Sri Ramakrishna. He put a sweet into his mouth and stood still, as if in samadhi. His eyes remained unblinking. A devotee stepped forward and pretended to hold him up by the hand lest he should drop to the ground. Narendra closed his eyes. A few minutes later, with the sweetmeat still in his mouth, he opened his eyes and drawled out, "I—am—all—right." All laughed loudly.

(The Gospel of Sri Ramakrishna, p. 979)

Dr. Logan

Many are the moments of sadness since Swamiji has gone away. It seems that all the gods had left us, for his Divine presence spread peace and tranquillity wherever he went; the tumult of uncertainty departed from my soul at the sound of his magic voice. His very form and every mood were those of tender compassion and sympathy. None knew him but to love him; those of us who have had the royal good fortune to have met him in the flesh will some day realize that we have met the true Incarnation of the divine One.

To me he is "The Christ", than whom a greater one has never come; his great and liberal soul outshines all other things; his mighty spirit was as free and liberal as the great sun, or the air of heaven.

No being lived so mean or low, be it a man or a beast, that he would not salute. His was not only an appeal to the poor and lowly but to kings and princes and mighty rulers of the earth, to grand masters of learning, of finances, of art and of the sciences, to leaders of thought on all its higher lines. Great teachers bowed reverently at his feet, the humble followed reverently to kiss the hem of his garments; no other single human being was reverenced more during his life than was Vivekananda.

In the few short weeks that I was with him few could know him better than I. At first I attended him through a severe spell of sickness, then he sat with me partly through a paralytic stroke; he would charm me to sleep and enchant me awake. So passed the most sublime part of my life, and now that sweet memory lingers and sustains me ever and always.

(New Discoveries, Vol. 6, pp. 172-173)

Harriet Monroe

The Congress of Religions was a triumph for all concerned, especially for its generalissimo, the Reverend John H. Barrows, of Chicago's First Presbyterian Church, who had been preparing it for two years. When he brought down his gavel upon the "world's first parliament of religions" a wave of breathless silence swept over the audience—it seemed a great moment in human history, prophetic of the promised new era of tolerance and peace. On the stage with him, at his left, was a black-coated array of bishops and ministers representing the various familiar Protestant sects and the Russian Orthodox and Roman Catholic Churches; at his right a brilliant group of strangely costumed dignitaries from afar—a Confucian from China, a Jain from India, a theosophist from Allahabad, a white-robed Shinto priest and four Buddhists from Japan, and a monk of the orange robe from Mumbai.

It was the last of these, Swami Vivekananda, the magnificent, who stole the whole show and captured the town. Others of the foreign groups spoke well—the Greek, the Russian, the Armenian, Mazoomdar of Kolkata, Dharmapala of Sri Lanka—leaning, some of these upon interpreters. Shibata, the Shintu, bowed his wired white headdress to the ground, spread his delicate hands in suave gestures, and uttered gravely with serene politeness his incomprehensible words. But the handsome monk in the orange robe gave us in perfect English a masterpiece. His personality, dominant, magnetic; his voice, rich as a bronze bell; the controlled fervor of his feeling; the beauty of his message to the Western world he was facing for the first time—these combined to give us a rare and perfect moment of supreme emotion. It was human eloquence at its highest pitch.

(*New Discoveries* Vol. 1, p. 86)

Mrs. J. J. Bagley

You write of my dear friend, Vivekananda. I am glad of an opportunity to express my admiration of his character and it makes me most indignant that anyone should call him in question. He has given us in America higher ideas of life than we have ever had before. In Detroit, an old conservative city, in all the Clubs he is honoured as no one has ever been, and I only feel that all who say one word against him are jealous of his greatness and his fine spiritual perceptions; and yet how can they be? He does nothing to make them so.

He has been a revelation to Christians, ... he has made possible for all of us a diviner and more noble practical life. As a religious teacher and an example to all I do not know his equal. It is so wrong and so untrue to say that he is intemperate. All who have been brought in contact with him day by day, speak enthusiastically of his sterling qualities of character, and men in Detroit who judge most critically, and who are unsparing, admire and respect him.... He has been a guest in my house more than three weeks, and my sons as well as my son-in-law and entire family found Swami Vivekananda a gentleman always, most courteous and polite, a charming companion and an ever-welcome guest. I have invited him to visit us at my summer-home here at Annisquam, and in my family he will always be honoured and unwilling to part with him. They are Presbyterians; ...

cultivated and refined people, and they admire, respect, and love Vivekananda. He is a strong, noble human being, one who walks with God. He is simple and trustful as a child. In Detroit I gave him an evening reception, inviting ladies and gentlemen, and two weeks afterwards he lectured to invited guests in my parlour.... I had included lawyers, judges, ministers, army-officers, physicians, and businessmen with their wives and daughters. Vivekananda talked two hours on "The Ancient Hindu Philosophers and what they Taught." All listened with intense interest to the end. Wherever he spoke people listened gladly and said, "I never heard man speak like that". He does not antagonize, but lifts people up to a higher level—they see something beyond man-made creeds and denominational names, and they feel one with him in their religious beliefs.

Every human being would be made better by knowing him and living in the same house with him.... I want every one in America to know Vivekananda, and if India has more such let her send them to us.

(*New Discoveries*, Vol. 1, pp. 452-53)

Malvina Hoffman

One of my vivid memories of childhood [is] an exciting evening spent with a relative of my father's who lived in a modest boarding-house in West Thirty-eighth Street. In the midst of this group of old-fashioned city boarders was introduced suddenly a newcomer—the oriental philosopher and teacher, Swami Vivekananda. When he entered the dining room there was a hush. His dark, bronzed countenance and hands were in sharp contrast to the voluminous, light folds of his turban and robe.

His dark eyes hardly glanced up to notice his neighbours, but there was a sense of tranquillity and power about him that made an imperishable impression upon me. He seemed to personify the mystery and religious "aloofness" of all true teachers of Brahma, and combined with this a kindly and gentle attitude of simplicity towards his fellow men.

(New Discoveries, Vol. 3, p. 184)

Thomas J. Allen

Having heard of Swami Vivekananda and what a wonderful man he was and what a stir he made at the Parliament of Religions in Chicago in 1893, also having read his book *Raja Yoga*, it was with great joy that I learned of his coming from Los Angeles to this section of the State. He came to San Francisco in February, 1900, and his first [actually his second] public lecture in Oakland was given on 28 February 1900, in the Unitarian Church, Oakland, of which Church the Reverend Benjamin Fay Mills was the Pastor. The subject of this lecture was "Similarity between the Vedanta Philosophy and Christianity." He told us always to look for similarities, for common points of interest, and never to look for differences. I was at that lecture, and the impression he made on me was: "Here is a man who knows what he is talking about. He is not repeating what some other person told him. He is not relating what he thinks, he is telling what he knows." Going home from the lecture I was walking on air. When I got home I was still acting like a crazy man. When I was asked what sort of a man he was, I replied, "He is not a man, he is a god." I can never forget the impression he produced on me. To me he was a wonder, and I followed him to any of the Bay cities where he spoke.

(New Discoveries, Vol. 5, p. 342)

Sarah Fox

The lecture was scheduled for eight o'clock on a Sunday night in the spring of 1900, at the First Unitarian Church in Oakland. Everyone was on time except the Swami, and the minister was entertaining the congregation with stories to keep them from going away. In the middle of these tales we all became aware that the Swami had arrived. He entered the Church auditorium from the street entrance and without any ado walked down the aisle nearest the wall to the front of the church in long, slow, measured steps. This wonderful man, clad in an ochre robe and wearing a turban, looked as if he feared nothing and cared for nothing. He seemed like an immense wave going along; his back was straight as a rod, yet his entire bearing was a perfect blending of dignity and grace. He reached the pulpit and stood there for a long time just looking out over the congregation. Then after what seemed like an hour, he said, "Ladies and gentlemen ... " We were seated too far away to see his face closely, but how we enjoyed his discourse! He did not seem old, as indeed he was not, but tremendously wise and experienced.

(New Discoveries, Vol. 5, pp. 326-7)

Annie Besant

A striking figure, clad in yellow and orange, shining like the sun of India in the midst of the heavy atmosphere of Chicago, a lion head, piercing eyes, mobile lips, movements swift and abrupt—such was my first impression of Swami Vivekananda, as I met him in one of the rooms set apart for the use of the delegates to the Parliament of Religions. Monk, they called him, not unwarrantably, warrior-monk was he, and the first impression was of the warrior rather than of the monk, for he was off the platform, and his figure was instinct with pride of country, pride of race—the representative of the oldest of living religions, surrounded by curious gazers of nearly the youngest, and by no means inclined to give step, as though the hoary faith he embodied was in aught inferior to the noblest there. India was not to be shamed before the hurrying arrogant West by this her envoy and her son. He brought her message, he spoke in her name, and the herald remembered the dignity of the royal land whence he came. Purposeful, virile, strong, he stood out, a man among men, able to hold his own.

On the platform another side came out. The dignity and the inborn sense of worth and power still were there, but all was subdued to the exquisite beauty of the spiritual message which he had brought, to the sublimity of that matchless evangel of the East which is the heart, the life of India, the wondrous teaching of the Self. Enraptured, the huge multitude hung upon his words; not a syllable must be lost, not a cadence missed! "That man a heathen!" said one, as he came out of the great hall, "and we send missionaries to his people! It would be more fitting that they should send missionaries to us."

(Life, Vol. 1, p. 429)

Mr. Vijapurkar

In 1892, when he [the Swami] visited our holy place, each of us felt at the time that he would be a great orator in the future. Not only was he well read, but he had mastered the art of putting his subject in such a manner that it would impress the mind of the hearer. We had invited him to speak in our Rajaramiya Parishad. Had I not had the good fortune of spending about an hour and a half in his company, I would not have understood his power of fascinating his hearers. Before he spoke, we asked him whether he would need any help from our side. He did not take any notes for his lecture. We no doubt knew in general what he said, but when it came through his mouth, it had a unique power of attraction.

Raosaheb Lakshman Rao Golwalkar was the Private Secretary of the Maharaja. He had arranged for the Swami's stay at the Khasbag. We had learnt that a great sannyasi had come, and that he could speak English. On the way back from our evening walk, we went to see him. When we heard his voice from a distance, we could understand that he had a wonderful personality. When we approached and saluted him, he did not bless us by saying "Narayana" or anything else. He continued his talk without stopping.

He would reply promptly when anyone asked a question. We then invited him to come to our Rajaramiya Parishad the next day. There also I witnessed the same thing. ... I remember two sentences which he spoke on that occasion. He said, "My religion is that of which Buddhism is a rebel child, and Christianity but a far-fetched imitation. ... How will the Europeans understand religion? They are running after luxury." Someone interrupted, saying, "How can flesh-eaters understand religion?" The Swami immediately reacted saying: "No, no; your ancient sages were flesh-eaters. Have you not read that in your *Uttara Ramacharita*?" Then he quoted some verses from that epic, in which there are clear references to flesh-eating. After hearing this statement, some doubted his caste; but who would dare to ask him about it?

(*Life*, Vol 1, pp 307-08)

K. Vaysa Rao

A graduate of the Kolkata University, with a shaven head, a prepossessing appearance, wearing the garb of renunciation, fluent in English and Sanskrit, with uncommon powers of repartee, who sang "with full-throated ease" as though he was attuning himself to the Spirit of the universe, and withal a wanderer on the face of the earth! The man was sound and stalwart, full of sparkling wit, with nothing but a scathing contempt for miracle-working agencies...; one who enjoyed good dishes, knew how to appreciate the hookah and the pipe, yet harped on renunciation with an ability that called forth admiration and a sincerity that commanded respect. The young Bachelor and Masters of Arts were at their wits' end at the sight of such a phenomenon. There, they saw the man and saw how well he could stand his ground in wrestling and fencing in the arena of the Universal Soul; and when the hour of discussion gave way to lighter moods, they found that he could indulge in fun and frolic, in uncompromising denunciation and in startling *bons mots*. But everything else apart, what endeared him to all was the unalloyed fervour of his patriotism. The young man, who had renounced all worldly ties and freed himself from bondage, had but one love, his country, and one grief, its downfall. These sent him into reveries which held his hearers spellbound. Such was the man who travelled from Hooghly to Tamraparny, who bewailed and denounced in unmeasured terms the imbecility of our young men, whose words flashed as lightning and cut as steel, who impressed all, communicated his enthusiasm to some, and lighted the spark of undying faith in a chosen few.

(*Life*, Vol. 1, pp. 369-70)

Helen Huntington

But it has pleased God to send to us out of India ◆ ◆ ◆ a spiritual guide—a teacher whose sublime philosophy is slowly and surely permeating the ethical atmosphere of our country; a man of extraordinary power and purity, who has demonstrated to us a very high plane of spiritual living, a religion of universal, unfailing charity, self-renunciation, and the purest sentiments conceivable by the human intellect. The Swami Vivekananda has preached to us a religion that knows no bonds of creeds and dogmas, is uplifting, purifying, infinitely comforting, and altogether without blemish—based on the love of God and man and on absolute chastity. ...

Swami Vivekananda has made many friends outside the circle of his followers; he has met all phases of society on equal terms of friendship and brotherhood; his classes and lectures have been attended by the most intellectual people and advanced thinkers of our cities, and his influence has already grown into a deep, strong undercurrent of spiritual awakening. No praise or blame has moved him to either ap-probation or expostulation; neither money nor position has influenced or prejudiced him. Towards demonstrations of undue favouritism, he has invariably maintained a priestly at-titude of inattention, checking foolish advances with a dignity impossible to resist, blaming not any but wrong-doers and evil-thinkers, exhorting only to purity and right living. He is altogether such a man as "kings delight to honour".

(Life, Vol. 2, pp. 66-67)

William Ernest Hocking

I was a casual visitor at the Fair.... There were to be speakers from other traditions.... I didn't know the programme. It happened to be Vivekananda's period.

... He spoke not as arguing from a tradition, or from a book, but as from an experience and certitude of his own. I do not recall the steps of his address. But there was a passage toward the end, in which I can still hear the ring of his voice, and feel the silence of the crowd—almost as if shocked. The audience was well-mixed, but could be taken as one in assuming that there had been a "Fall of man" resulting in a state of "original sin", such that "All men have sinned and come short of the glory of God." But what is the speaker saying? I hear his emphatic rebuke: "Call men sinners?? It is a SIN to call men sinners!"

... Through the silence I felt something like a gasp running through the hall as the audience waited for the affirmation which must follow this blow. What his following words were, I cannot recall with the same verbal clarity: they carried the message that in all men there is that divine essence, undivided and eternal: reality is One, and that One, which is Brahman, constitutes the central being of each one of us.

For me, this doctrine was a startling departure from anything which my scientific psychology could then recognize. One must live with these ideas and consider how one's inner experience could entertain them. But what I could feel and understand was that this man was speaking from what he knew, not from what he had been told. He was well aware of the books; but he was more immediately aware of his own experience and his own status in the world; and what he said would have to be taken into account in any final world-view.

(New Discoveries, Vol 1, pp. 117-118)

Appendix

A GLANCE THROUGH
JOSEPHINE MACLEOD'S LETTERS

Miss Josephine MacLeod is well known to the students of Swami Vivekananda's life. Swamiji used to call her "Joe", and his disciples and admirers addressed her as "Yum", "Jaya" or "Tantine".

Josephine's father, John David MacLeod, married Mary Ann Lennon in 1845, and had two sons and three daughters. He was an American of Scottish descent and stayed at various places in the United States before permanently settling at Chicago. Among the daughters, Besse or Betty (1852-1931) and Josephine (1858-1949) came in intimate contact with Swami Vivekananda and the Ramakrishna-Vedanta Movement. Betty married Mr. William Sturges of Chicago in the year 1876. Josephine always stayed with Betty even after the latter's marriage. After the death of Mr. William Sturges in the year 1894, Betty married Mr. Francis Leggett, a business magnate of New York, in the September of 1895; and as Swamiji was by that time known to them, he attended their marriage at Paris. Josephine, Hollister and Alberta naturally became part of Betty's new household at New York and Ridgely, near Stone Ridge, in Ulster County, New York.

January 29, 1895, was a memorable day for Josephine, because on this day she and Betty attended Swamiji's Vedanta class at New York for the first time. Both sisters were very much impressed by the personality and teachings of Swamiji, and through them Mr. Francis Leggett, Alberta and Hollister became Swamiji's close friends and admirers. The

707

whole family loved Swamiji and helped in their own way in propagating his message and work.

Right from the first day of their meeting, Josephine accepted Swamiji as a prophet; and although she disclaimed formal discipleship, she became his ardent admirer and friend, so much so that Swamiji used to call her a "lady missionary" of the Ramakrishna Order. Even after Swamiji's death, Josephine continued to be an admirer of the Ramakrishna Order and often came and stayed at the Belur Math, headquarters of the Order, for many days.

Josephine had strong attachment for India as well, and on occasion she tried to do what was within her power for the betterment of India and her people.

In spite of her roving habits, Josephine maintained a regular correspondence with her niece Alberta Sturges, who was married to George Montagu, the Eighth Earl of Sandwich, in 1905. As Josephine was charged with love for Swamiji, the Ramakrishna Order and India, we find in these letters many of her reminiscences about Swamiji, his brother-disciples and other members of the Order, and the expression of her love for India and the work she did for the country. She lived for about half a century after the demise of Swamiji, and her letters written to Alberta are naturally very informative and interesting. Alberta left this valuable treasure with her daughter Lady Faith Culme-Seymour of Bridport, Dorset, England, who very kindly loaned those belonging to 1911-1946 period, to the Ramakrishna Vedanta Centre of England. Swami Bhavyananda, the Minister in charge of the Centre, and Swami Yogeshananda, then his assistant, worked hard on these letters and took relevant extracts from them. They prepared cyclostyled copies of these extracts and sent them, a few years ago, to some monks and devotees of the Ramakrishna Order. One of these sets was sent to the President of the Advaita Ashrama, Mayavati, in case he would be interested in publishing them in the Prabuddha Bharata.

At the request of the Editor, Prabuddha Bharata, I studied these extracts and tried my best to arrange them topic wise for the information of the devotees and admirers of Swami Vivekananda. These letters bring to light some hitherto unknown facts about Swamiji's personality and the activities of the Ramakrishna Movement in the East as well as the West. The matter under quotes has been taken verbatim from the aforesaid letters to maintain the originality; and I have introduced the various topics in my words to keep the continuity. The dates of the letters are mentioned in parentheses after the quotation marks.

Miss Josephine MacLeod first met Swami Vivekananda in New York on January 29,1895. About this she writes: "Every phase of the Swamiji epoch is clear, as it is the foundation of my life since forty-eight years. We were living with Mrs. Davidson at Dobbsferry; and coming one day to lunch with aunt Dora Roethlesberger in N.Y. [New York], we found a note from her—'Do come to 54 West 33rd St. and hear the Swami Vivekananda, after which we will return to luncheon'—so Mother[1] and I went to his parlour-sitting room, where twenty ladies and two or three men were, Swamiji sitting on the floor. His first sentence made me know I had heard the Truth—the truth that sets one free" (December 9, 1943). "I think that is what happened to me forty-one years ago, January 29, when I saw and heard Swamiji. Somehow one was lifted above the body and time and space" (January 2, 1936).

Afterwards Josephine used to consider January 29, 1895, as her spiritual birthday—the day on which "she found her own soul". Thus she wrote: "I'll be forty-eight—next January 29th! At the same time, eighty-four in my physical birthday!" (January 21, 1943). "It seems as if all my life dated from that event. As if I'd fulfilled the mission I was born for—recognition of the new Buddha" (May 9, 1922). Ruminating on that

---

1. Mrs. Betty Leggett, the mother of Alberta Sturges by her first marriage. During this period she was the widow of Mr. William Sturges.

day, in later life she never failed to wonder about that first meeting. She believed that the meeting was preordained: "Oh, the wonder of my having recognized Swamiji instantly and irrevocably; on that recognition the past forty-four years of my life has been built" (March 13, 1939). "It isn't chance that you at fifteen and I at thirty-five should come under the influence of Swamiji—as Nivedita said, 'Representing the next 3,000 years as Ramakrishna did the last 3,000 years'" (October 4, 1923).

After the first meeting Josephine and her sister began to attend Swamiji's lectures regularly, but they kept these visits secret from their friends for a few weeks. About this she wrote: "Mother and I came down to N.Y. three times a week and we brought you and Holly[2] on Saturdays. We never mentioned him [Swamiji] to anybody, for to us, he was holy. Some weeks after, Pater[3] invited us to dine at the Waldorf-Astoria (just opposite to where Swamiji had his classes). So we accepted his invitation to dinner, but said we could not spend the evening with him. When at 8 p.m. we rose to go to the lecture, Mr. Leggett said, 'Where are you going?' We said, 'To a lecture'; he said, 'May I not come?' We said, 'Yes, do come.' At once the lecture was over Pater went up to Swamiji and invited him to dine; there, at that dinner, we met Swamiji socially and not many weeks after, we all, including you two children and Swamiji, went to Ridgely Manor for a six-day visit!... Then Mother and I went to visit Pater with Swamiji at Lake Christine, Percy Coos Co., New Hampshire, and when they [Betty and Mr. Francis Leggett] became engaged to be married, Pater asked Swamiji to be his witness at the honeymoon and the next day Swamiji went to stay with Mr. Sturdy in England, and Swamiji began a series of big lectures in London (St. James Hall)[4], all the London

---

2. Hollister Sturges, the son of Mrs. Betty Leggett by her first marriage.

3. Mr. Francis Leggett, Betty's second husband.

4. Miss MacLeod perhaps means the Princes' Hall where Swamiji gave some lectures during his first visit to England.

papers quoting him as a 'Yogi'. Isabel[5] read this and went to call on him and later let her house in London to the Vedanta Society, having her two children Kitty and David blessed by Swamiji" (December 9, 1943).

We find in these letters how Josephine and her relations got on with Swamiji: "It was that attitude [of giving perfect liberty] in our family towards Swamiji that kept him with and near us. Days without speaking, days and nights continuous speaking! We followed his moods and kept ourselves busy in our own lives and happy when he wasn't about, so that there was no sort of weight put upon him" (December 19, 1913).

Love and admiration for Swamiji was common to them all: "We all recognized and loved Swamiji—you and Holly quite as much as Mother and Big Francy[6] and me. Perhaps on no other point did we all so heartily agree! ... Mother has gone on one line, you another, I a third, according to our talents. None of us could exhaust that spiritual force, nor come to its limitations" (November 15, 1926).

Josephine's attitude towards Swamiji is well revealed in her letters. To her Swamiji was unique: "I believe Swamiji to have been the biggest spiritual force that ever came to earth" [7](February 25, 1913). He was to her the prophet of the present age: "And we have known the new Buddha!" (June 22, 1939). "I'm deep in reading the Gospel of St. John—thrilling! So like the influence of Swamiji and his miracle of changing lives by his very presence, not by changing water into wine or healings. New prophets bring new gifts, don't they?" (June 11, 1941). She was amazed and held by his unlimitedness: "The thing that held me

---

5. Lady Isabel Margesson, an educationist English friend of Miss MacLeod. She became an admirer of Swami Vivekananda, and the Swami stayed at her London residence during his second visit to England.

6. Mr. Francis Leggett.

7. This line is from Miss MacLeod's letter to Alberta's husband Mr. George Montagu, the Eighth Earl of Sandwich.

in Swamiji was his unlimitedness! I never could touch the bottom—or top—or sides! The amazing size of him, and I think Nivedita's hold was that too" (March 12, 1923). Occasionally, her feeling towards Swamiji was intensely personal. She claimed to have a right on him: "It was to set me free that Swamiji came and that was as much part of his mission as it was to give renunciation to Nivedita—or unity to dear Mrs. Sevier" (March 12, 1923). "Swamiji was only a friend, but a friend who knew God, and so passed him on to me. Meeting Swamiji changed my life, in a twinkling!" (July 2, 1941).

But Josephine never failed to wonder at the immensity of Swamiji and to appreciate his role in her life in particular and in the world at large: "The Vivekananda episode in our life is of the Eternity quality! So let's play that game" (October 4, 1923). "I've known and lived for seven years with a world force. I'm charged through and through with it" (October 23, 1923). "To have known and assimilated even a little of Swamiji is no small inheritance!" (April 7, 1924).

Swamiji gave her a sense of security: "Somehow Swamiji is back of us one and all" (March 5, 1914). "Our lives are not left to blind chance. We are directed and protected. In a way we believe that, but if we realized it we could never have another moment's anxiety" (July 12, 1916). "I feel that Swamiji was a rock for us to stand upon—that was His function in my life. Not worship, nor glory, but a steadiness under one's feet for experiments!" (March 12, 1923).

He gave her faith: "Our great role is yet to be played. How? Where? I don't know nor really care—but we've not lived with and loved Swamiji for nothing. It's bound to work out gloriously; but even if it didn't, knowing Him was worth this and other worlds!" (June 15, 1914).

Josephine had many an occasion to know how Swamiji influenced the lives of others. To some of these instances she referred in her letters: "Mr. (Homer) Lane says what Swamiji has done for him is to make everything holy—all life, effort, work, play, prayer—equally holy, all complement parts and necessary parts of life" (February 11, 1913). "Yesterday Mrs. Hansbrough,[8] who is one of the three sisters who have always been devoted to Swamiji these fourteen years, said that after one of Swami's brilliant lectures here (Los Angeles) a man got up and said, 'Then, Swami, what you claim is that all is good?' 'By no means,' Swamiji answered. 'My claim is that all is not—only God is! That makes all the difference.'... And Mrs. Hansbrough says that that one sentence has been the rock on which she has lived all these years" (March 16, 1914). "As Swamiji said to you at Rome, of the gorgeousness of the religious ceremonies at St. Peter's, 'If you do believe in a personal God, surely you would give your best to Him!'" (November 5, 1923). "Today I've written (again) to the Maharaja of Alwar, asking him to come to the Birthday Celebration of Swamiji on January 17th....It seems he's 'on fire' with Swamiji. It was his father that asked Swamiji 'What's the use of all these images and idols?', and Swamiji, turning to the Prime-Minister said, 'Take that picture of His Highness and spit on it.' And he said, 'How can I? With His Highness sitting there?' But Swamiji insisted several times, the Prime Minister refusing. Then Swamiji said, 'It isn't His Highness, it is only a picture-image of him—not he'. Then His Highness saw. The image is sacred because it reminds one of God" (December 9, 1924). "It is Swamiji, bringing back to his race the great sustaining traditions of Hinduism, as lived by Ramakrishna, that is the new leaven pervading India and overflowing to the whole world. 'Eternal, pervading, sustaining', as the *Gita* puts it. I can even see it in your letter this week: 'Swamiji didn't bless me for nothing, or train me to sit down and cry. I may be lying down, but I will deal with this'" (November 15, 1926). "A young Parsee, K—, given a mantra years ago by Shivanandaji, has told me such a lovely story of Swamiji, told him a month ago in Ajmer by two Americans who were sent out to India by missionaries to

---

8. Mrs. Alice Mead Hansbrough, one of the Mead sisters of South Pasadena, California, who helped Swami Vivekananda during his visit to the West Coast by arranging lectures and keeping house for him.

offset Swamiji's influence. When they arrived, Swamiji was deep in meditation but when he finally appeared, his face radiating the light his meditation had given him, they were so overcome, that they turned to Swamiji asking, 'Where shall we find Truth?' Swamiji's answer: 'But It is with you always'—turned them into disciples: these two old men now, never leaving India" (February 9, 1939).

Anyone who had served or even had contact with Swamiji at any time had a special place in Josephine's heart: "Today Mrs. Wright comes to see me, widow of the Harvard professor who sent Swamiji to the World's Parliament. I am finally to begin my quest of his staff and drinking bowl" (February 20, 1912). "I've written to Mary Hale Matteini[9] that if she has anyone to take her a Swamiji crystal from England, I'd gladly give her one for the Hale Family. Without them to have nourished and protected him that long year, we might never have had him in our midst. It is interesting to see how each plays a different part in Swamiji's scheme, isn't it? The Hales had him for a whole year and always gave to him, I feel, that admiration and respect for American womanhood that was so fundamental in his life—them after that, he rarely saw or heard from. Then 'We' came along and remained to the end, seven years" (April 24, 1922). "Mary Hale Matteini is living her own loving life, gentle, considerate, faithful to mother, sister, husband. Deep down, there is the big note that Swamiji brought to them all, but no inclination to help his work. However she gave me £5 for the Math and £5 to buy his books.." (December 15, 1925). "David Margesson's appointment will please dear Isabel[10], to whom I owe much, perhaps most in her recognition of Swamiji!" (December 25, 1940). "She [Malvina Hoffman] saw Swamiji

---

9. Mary Hale, the daughter of Mr. and Mrs. G. W. Hale of Chicago, in whose house Swami Vivekananda stayed for a long time during his first visit to the United States. Swamiji called her sister, and wrote many letters to her. She was later married to Mr. Matteini, an Italian Tycoon.

10. Mrs. Isabel Margesson.

when eight or nine years old in a boarding-house in 38th Street. So we formed a real relationship. How curious!" (May 9, 1941).

Anyone who appreciated Swamiji struck a responsive cord in her: "I miss your personal letters dreadfully—but one from F—three days ago tells of her full life....and her having, at last, at forty-four years of age, discovering [discovered] Swamiji, whose life she is reading, and 'What a Romance—his coming to Chicago Parliament of Religions in 1893!' she writes. So now she and I will have new and old contacts. Life is so amazing, isn't it?" (December 27, 1940)

Josephine referred to many sayings of Swamiji in her letters; for instance: "'Whatever exists has a reason; find that reason' is really the basis of Swamiji's teachings, I think" (September 14, 1922). "I do think that 'the constitutional belief in freedom is the basis of all reasoning'—as Swamiji fundamentally puts it" (October 4, 1923). "'Always free on the spiritual plane; never free on the mental and physical—hence the struggle,' said our Swamiji" (March 25, 1925). "'Tell me what you've suffered, and I'll tell you how great you are,' said Swamiji" (February 16, 1916). "As Swamiji put it, 'Don't fight your faults; fill yourself with something else; then they will drop off, not being nourished'" (March 27, 1939). "Swamiji says, 'The heart is the river of your life; the head is the bridge over the river—always follow your heart'" (December 5, 1923). "Get your Post (God) as Swamiji says, and then play any game you like: nothing matters but the Post" (January 29, 1925). "'Wherever there is filth, or degradation, or ignorance, there I identify myself', says Swamiji" (February 26, 1913). "I don't think anyone can go far who hasn't faith in the people. That is what Swamiji had, pre-eminently. He knew that each one of us was a child of God—so he told it broadcast: 'Make every man a Brahmin, a twice-born. Do it by thousands, by nations, and the people will rise en masse'" (April 6, 1928). "The day before Swamiji died he told them how great this place, Belur Math, was to be! They smiled incredulously. He said, 'The power of this place will last nine hundred years. Nothing can withstand it'" (June 29, 1922).

Josephine was not an all-renouncing type of woman like Sister Nivedita. Nor had she the single-minded devotion to an ideal which we find in Sister Christine. But in her own way she took the propagation and realization of Swamiji's ideas as the mission of her life. Her sense of responsibility in this respect becomes evident as we read her letters.

Rejoicing when certain happenings augured well for the prospects of the Belur Math she wrote: "It's such fun to see the pattern being woven, and only be responsible for one's own little thread and keep it straight and unknotted so that it can be used" (March 3, 1926). On another occasion she wrote: "You can see that a great Prophet, as Swamiji was, saw in vast expanses of time, coming world-issues and changes. He was true. To me, this is a great satisfaction. It does not lessen our today's responsibility, but gives further scope for solution" (July 2, 1941).

Josephine came into contact with all sorts of people during her long life, and she tried to inspire many of them with Swamiji's ideals. Some instances of this, scattered through her letters, are as follows:

"I've poured out all my heart of all the wealth that Swamiji poured into me—on him (Dhan Gopal Mukherjee)—and now my work is done and I feel a curious lightness" (June 17, 1922). "When on Bernard Shaw's eighty-eighth birthday, there was in New York Times a picture of him sawing wood, I wrote to him saying we were both in the category of the eighties, he taking much exercise and I none, and at once I got a p.c. (postcard) from him in his beautiful writing: 'My dear Josephine, how very jolly to hear from you. I have been a widower since 12th September last. A little before that we were talking about you and wondering what had become of you. You were and are a special friend; and we always hoped that we should foregather again at Hallscroft.[11] But I am better out of sight now. I'm dreadfully

---

11. A well-known house at Stratford-on-Avon, England.

old. G. Bernard Shaw.' Of course, I answered at once, saying, in this new world there would be much for us to do. Then I told him of the Willcock's[12] Irrigation of Bengal, etc. etc." (September 18, 1944). "Lord Lytton[3] wrote on February 26th: 'We were delighted with our visit to Belur (Math), and I shall long cherish grateful recollections of that haven of peace. The little Lalique statuette of Vivekananda now stands upon my writing table and every afternoon as it catches the rays of the setting sun, it shines as if lit up by a sacred flame from within'" (March 5, 1924). "Lady Wavell has written to Isabel [Margesson], thanking her for the Lalique crystal of Swamiji, and to me for the four little Swamiji books. It is such fun to be used at eighty-five, to scatter these truths!" (June 19, 1944). "Isabel Margesson has written a page of her glowing memories of Swamiji to the February [1939] Prabuddha Bharata. Perhaps some day you'll do so?" (February 10, 1939). "Have you Shankara's Chudamani?[13] If not ask—for one. I had sent her four. You know, Swamiji said he was Shankara! He came back after 800 years" (April 10, 1944).

"Last evening at 6-30 two brothers came to see me after I was tucked away behind my mosquito net, to tell me that the younger, twenty-eight (since nine months a member of the Ramakrishna Math at Dacca), had been one of seventy-two new prisoners taken by the eighteenth century ordinance and had been to Dacca jail since October 24th. Today he must give himself up to the Superintendent of Police of 24 Parganas, to be interned in the village of Haroa, Bengal, till further orders.... So I had my chance of telling him what it really meant! And what he might do for India and Swamiji, whose ideal was that each village of India (over 700,000) should have a centre, one man of education, to recreate the village. So I gave him five volumes of Swamiji and told him that

---

12. Sir Alfred Willcox, a retired engineer. persuaded by Miss MacLeod to take up the work of renovating the irrigation system in Bengal.

13. The Vivekachudamani, a treatise on Vedanta by Acharya Shankara.

'Mother' had chosen him, by the Governor and Council to do Her work.... Darling, to have seen those two brothers' faces change from despair to hope! Eager to begin! And saying they 'were ignorant and didn't know "Mother God" worked that way.' Simple children! Then I told them that Swamiji's definition of his own religion is 'to learn' and with that spirit go into this new village of Haroa, to learn the village's needs, to teach sanitation, English and Swamiji's ideals, and to live them, and lift India!" (November 27, 1927).

Josephine considered the propagation of Swamiji's message in the West as her special responsibility. After the outbreak of World War II, she wrote: "I am not at all inclined to go to the War zone, in India or Europe. and as Swamiji says, 'My work will be more in the West: thence it will react on India.' I may help more in U.S.A. than in India. Now there are hundreds interested in Indian spirituality in U.S.A.; they will grow to thousands, then millions, and as America is becoming the leading country, its influence will react on the world" (March 6, 1940).

Whenever there was some celebration, the opening of a centre or some special worship, Josephine strove to be present there, believing sincerely that her presence lent a touch of Swamiji to the occasion. She writes: "Little by little new openings are coming here for Swamiji's message. Yesterday three of us met to consecrate a little meditation room in the basement of Miss Spencer's house. It may mean something, or nothing. The real thing is that we keep His message ever before us that all men are Divine" (March 16, 1914). "Today I had one hour of Kali Puja—at Nikhilananda's centre, about twenty of us; they do so like my going to them, since I knew Swamiji" (October 8, 1940). "It seems I am the last living person who knew Swamiji well, personally. This year being the fiftieth anniversary of Swamiji's coming to U.S.A., Chicago, July 1893, each Vedanta Centre is to celebrate this, and Nikhilananda wants me to give a little talk at his Centre, 17 E. 94th St., and Swami Virajananda, the Abbot of the Math, wrote in his last letter 'that Tantine [Josephine] has kept alive all these forty-eight years the vividness of Swamiji shows His spirituality'" (October 6, 1943).

Josephine spared no troubles and expenses for the publication of Swamiji's works in Western languages. She writes: "Edgar Lee Masters has written to MacMillan (Publishers who refused to publish Swamiji's four Yogas): 'I believe that the spiritual solution of the world depends upon the assimilation of these works.' So without telling me the reason they have asked me to return Swamiji's books for further consideration which I have done today. But isn't life thrilling! And aren't we to play a big part?" (June 9, 1919).

"Today airmail I've sent to Toni Sussman the written manuscript of Inspired Talks that I want her to read—oversee—and change anything she wishes to, have typed, and sent where she sent her translation of Jnana Yoga. I've already paid Jean Herbert to have this printed in German, thus completing the four small [books] of Swamiji. I don't know how it was to be done, nor where, but I paid Jean Herbert the 1,600 dollars he asked, to be responsible and publish all these works of Swamiji in German. Toni has asked me what further work can she do for Swamiji. This I should like her to do, as soon as possible. Mrs. Berliner has made this translation, but she thinks Toni's Jnana Yoga much finer, so go ahead, please" (April 4, 1941). "Today you go to Hallscroft and on July 25 Toni goes there for the weekend. I am writing you today, to send you her last fine letter to me, as I am also writing her airmail and send the American pocket edition of Inspired Talks to her, for it is this edition I want her to put into German, every word and picture and poem! It sums up Swamiji in a synthetic way" (July 21, 1941).

Naturally, advancement of the cause of women, especially Indian women, was something dear to Josephine's heart: "You see it is women teachers who are so rare to find in India... and the girls (Sister) Christine trains will be long in coming to maturity, and though the method is right that she is using, the experience and prestige is not acquired except by responsibility... In twenty years from now there ought to be several centres for women under women in India, and we'll have to help to choose the right women; all depends upon them" (March 20, 1916). "Sister Gayatri...is splendid; has been sixteen years in U.S.A., knows Sanskrit, has been lecturing thirteen years, and wants to continue Paramananda's work in California and here, together with Sister Daya, daughter of Senator Jones of California. So now we have women capable and consecrated to found the Women's Math—a thing Swamiji always wanted. 1 am rejoiced!" (September 10, 1940).

Whenever there was any expansion in the Ramakrishna -Vivekananda movement, any new activity, Josephine was delighted. Her sense of involvement in the movement becomes evident from the following extracts: "These little glimpses into the lives and purposes of these young monks show the lines along which the Order will grow. One of their great achievements now is that they are starting Agriculture. The Govt expert comes today from 3 to 5 and all are gradually to be trained so as to carry scientific food growing as part of the outside centres' work. It's all slow, but it is true; solid! There is no good in attacking a big problem till the home one is solved, and these men have been lighted by the torch that Swamiji carried round the world... Remember Swamiji said, 'No fact in your life can equal your imagination, Alberta'" (June 2, 1926). "You remember Swamiji saying Belur Math will be a great University with religious foundation, so perhaps in yours and my lifetime, we will see his prophecy come true" (February 22, 1939). "I'm begging them here at the Math to send the young out, to beg, as Swamiji did, his own food, on foot, walking, learning by actual experience. Swamiji didn't come full-fledged from the sky; he grew! And his monks must do the same, or else they will be soft, no fibre or resilience, power of adaptation" (February 16, 1927). "Thrift gives me the joy of spiritually helping, for that is what money does when it saves courage in those I love" (October 23, 1939). "Thousands are below (on the Belur Math grounds)! Just to pay their tribute to that one life—Swamiji's

Birthday Celebration! I sit and wonder. Boshi Sen comes to cook the things Swamiji loved tonight. I furnish chocolate ice-cream—which they all eat. It is so childish, yet because of that very thing perhaps, his life is kept young and fresh and vital" (January 25, 1927).

What glimpses of Josephine's mind do we get from these letters? The things which strike us most are her enthusiasm and her receptivity; for instance, she writes: "I seldom return anywhere. 'Life is beautiful, the future sacred', so I'm out for new experiences and friends. It was because Swamiji was new and fresh every day that he held one! So if we learn every day, as he did, we will not grow old, or stale or flat! Life is expectancy, wonder! So is the Lord, isn't He?" (December 7, 1938). "Life always seems to me to be just beginning— no five-year-old ever felt it more than I do—and as at five, I had the dream in Detroit that if I'd dig in the garden I'd find gold, (and did find the gold drop of an ear-ring), —so now I'm looking, digging into and finding wonders everywhere, now especially that my body has stopped worrying me.... There is no asceticism in me; that I see plainly; but recognition of the good, I find everywhere, including the Best occasionally. When I see what others put up with, I am filled with amazement and admiration, and it is only when one gets at the heart, the confidence of people, one learns: that is the reason I like confidence—friendships that only grow in intimacy....If I go to New York, it is for the Unknown! The Unknown God, that takes such myriad of shapes and forms, always keeping us guessing—wondering!" (March 21, 1939). "It is this wonder that keeps me alive; what the other man has to give me—not what I give to him. I like people to be different to me, and to take and use (not exploit) them as they are, thus broadening my horizon. It would be difficult to deepen it, since I lived with Swamiji" (September 7, 1946). "I live mostly in others. I expand, with fresh ideas and culture" (November 27, 1938). "'The readiness is all' shall be put on my tombstone if I ever have one!...I stumbled into a family that gave freedom! Then Swamiji at thirty-five, gave spiritual freedom; no wonder I'm happy—learning!" (February 28, 1939). "Life, here on earth, is a grand opportunity; learn, learn, day and night, knowing that all one can learn on earth one can use, any and everywhere, since Spirit never dies" (December 22,1939). "When I joined the Town Hall Club last Monday, they asked my occupation and I wrote: 'To Learn'" (October 30, 1940). "Well, my Religion is to learn from any and everybody, for this is the Lord's world and He has put me here to learn, as well as to worship!" (May 14, 1941).

Josephine herself declared: "I haven't any Renunciation! But I've freedom, to see and help India grow. That's my job, and now I love it. To see this group of fiery idealists, burning new paths and outlets from this jungle called life" (March 12, 1923).

But this enthusiasm and involvement were based on deep knowledge and conviction and were imbued with a sense of detachment: "I'm beginning to see that when the present is deepened it does become Eternity. A sort of new dimension, as Einstein puts it" (October 4, 1923). "It's all a pretty pageant, life just now, and I do enjoy it all—but deep down knowing that empires pass away—and only God remains!" (January 29, 1925). "You ask if I am utterly secure in my grasp on the Ultimate. Yes—utterly. It seems to be part and parcel of me. It is the 'Truth' (that I saw in Swamiji) that has set me free. One's faults seem so insignificant. Why remember them, when one has the Ocean of Truth to be one's playground?" (March 12, 1923). "But do remember that Life is fluid, like water, takes on different shapes, colours, tastes, constantly; so if we can take on this fluidity, instead of the shape, colour, taste, we will watch—be the witness, instead of the victim" (December 30, 1938). "We know so little of ourselves, don't we? Our needs? Only a tiny window is opened of ourselves, and we are so surprised at the depths, heights, widths, that have never been fathomed, only apprehended. We are really much finer, nobler than we know, and are so often surprised at our own capacity!" (August 11, 1928).

The following extracts sum up her philosophy of life: "I find that when they say we must get rid of our Ego, I don't agree, for the basis of every life is the Spirit—Ego, only covered up! Get rid of the covering, and let the Ego shine in all its glory" (December 22, 1939). "I do not feel called upon to adjust the world's problems, but my own little intimate one, a narrow one, limited by my physical strength first, then the moral and spiritual values as I see them. This is the reason I said to Swamiji, 'I've never done an unselfish act in my life'—and he answered, 'True, but there is a larger or a smaller self'—to which I agreed. If I can expand, like loving others, it is I that expand, isn't it? And the more I expand and love others, the more represent the Lord, the one, unique" (March 22, 1940).

Does weakness ever take hold of her?: "What is this crouching fear of death that possesses one? Instead of making the occasion for a great achievement, a glory. The fact is hidden, as if it were a curse, instead of a blessing, an opportunity, to show that the spirit is triumphant over the flesh" (September 4, 1923). "Bless you darling, you and yours. Try to keep alive till I go out of the body; but the Soul is Eternal so why trouble too much about the body?" (August 29, 1943).

But through all her robustness, at times we can see the devotee in her: "I am rejoiced to see—keeps her heart so full of kindness towards—. I see so much anger and criticism everywhere, not changing the world, but shutting out the Lord, as if two things can be in the heart at once!" (December 7, 1939). "I'd like Incarnation to come each generation to revive and re-inspire humanity in its own divine birthright and outlook; wouldn't you? Perhaps they do come. Certainly I've known one, and it is they that keep us 'floating on the warm heart of the Mother', as Swamiji put it. If we could learn to float, instead of gripping so hard, we'd have more time and strength for watching and learning. However, I'm not managing this world" (September 21, 1922).

(*Prabuddha Bharata*, January 1979)

Abbreviations used in the References

Life	*The Life of Swami Vivekandna,* by His Eastern and Western Disciples, 2 vols., 5th ed., 1979-1981 (unless otherwise specified)
New Discoveries	*Swami Vivekananda in the West: New Discoveries,* 6 vols.
Monastic Disciples	*The Monastic Disciples of Swami Vivekananda,* 2003.

About the Authors

Shivananda, Swami (Taraknath Ghosal; 1854–1934): One of Ramakrishna's sixteen monastic disciples. From 1922 to 1934 he served as the second president of the Ramakrishna Order.

Turiyananda, Swami (Harinath Chattopadhyay; 1863–1922): One of the sixteen monastic disciples of Ramakrishna. He established Shanti Ashrama in California and taught Vedanta there from 1899 to 1902.

Saradananda, Swami (Sharat Chandra Chakrabarty; 1865–1927): One of the sixteen monastic disciples of Ramakrishna; the first General Secretary of the Ramakrishna Order; the author of Sri Sri Ramakrishna Lilaprasanga.

Akhandananda, Swami: (Gangadhar Gangopadhyay; 1864–1937): One of the sixteen monastic disciples of Ramakrishna. He served as the third president of the Ramakrishna Order, from 1934 to 1937.

Vijnanananda, Swami (Hari Prasanna Chattopadhyay; 1868–1938): One of the sixteen monastic disciples of Ramakrishna. Hewas an engineer, and he supervised construction of the buildings and temples at BelurMath. Heserved as the fourth president of the Ramakrishna Order from 1937 to 1938.

Achalananda, Swami (Kedar Baba; 1876-1947): Last monastic disciple of Swamiji; pre-monastic name Kedarnath Moulik. He accompanied Swami Shivananda to Varanasi in June 1902 to assist the latter in setting up an ashrama there. He became the Vice-President of the Math and the Mission in 1938 Severe austerities caused his health to break down and he passed away at the Varanasi Sevashrama.

725

Atulananda, Swami (1869-1966): Pre-monastic name Cornelius J. Heijblom. Was a disciple of Holy Mother and was initiated into sannyasa by Swami Abhedananda in 1923. He is the author of the book Atman Alone Abides.

Virajananda, Swami (1873–1951): Pre-monastic name Kalikrishna Bose. He was a disciple of Holy Mother and the sixth President of the Order. Is the author of Paramartha Prasanga, translated into English as Towards the Goal of Supreme.

Sadananda, Swami: (Gupta Maharaj, 1865–1911): Pre-monastic name, Sharatchandra Gupta. Was perhaps Swamiji's first disciple.

Shuddhananda, Swami: (1872-1938): began visiting the monastic disciples of Sri Ramakrishna at their monastery and then met Swamiji in 1897 on the latter's return from the West. Soon after, he joined the monastery at Alambazar. He was a very scholarly monk, and succeeded Swami Saradananda as the General Secretary of the Order after the latter's death in 1927. Swami Shuddhananda became President of the Order in May 1938, but died in October of the same year.

Bodhananda, Swami (1870–1950): A monastic disciple of Swami Vivekananda. In 1891, when he was a student at Ripon College, he and some of his friends began visiting the Baranagore Math, where the monastic disciples of Sri Ramakrishna lived. Soon after Swamiji's return from the West in 1897, he joined the monastery, which was then at Alambazar, and received sannyasa vows from Swamiji. He was sent to New York in 1906 to assist Swami Abhedananda, and eventually took charge of the centre there. In 1922 he established a permanent home for the centre at 34 W. 71 st Street.

Vimalananda, Swami (1872–1908): A monastic disciple of Swamiji and was also among the group of young men who began visiting Baranagore Math in 1891. After Swamiji returned from the West in 1897, he joined the monastery at Alambazar and was initiated into sannyasa by Swamiji. In 1899 he was sent from Belur Math to Advaita Ashrama in Mayavati and became joint-editor of the monthly English journal Prabuddha Bharata. In 1908 he passed away at Mayavati.

Sadashivananda, Swami: He was among a group of young men living in Varanasi who became greatly inspired by Swamiji's message of service. They started a society in the city to serve the poor and ailing people that eventually became the Ramakrishna Mission Home of Service. When Swamiji visited Varanasi in February 1902 he was extremely pleased with their work and gave initiation to them. Later some of them were given sannyasa vows by Swami Brahmananda.

Brajendranath Seal (1864–1938): A famed scholar-philosopher and intellectual and was college mate of Narendranath at Calcutta General Assemblies Institution, being senior to him by two years. He presided over the inaugural session of the week-long Parliament of the World's Religions at the Town Hall, Calcutta, in March 1937 on the occasion of the birth-centenary of the Master.

Nagendranath Gupta: A publicist and literary man of distinction. During his student days he attended the same college as Swami Vivekananda. He also saw Sri Ramakrishna in 1881 when he was among a party headed by Keshab Chandra Sen on board a steamer. In August 1886 he took part in the funeral procession that brought Sri Ramakrishna's body to the cremation ground. Later he moved to Lahore and became the editor of Tribune. He came in contact with many distinguished people in the later part of the 19th century.

B.G. Tilak (Lokmanya Bal Gangadhar Tilak; (1856–1920): Renowned scholar and one of the foremost leaders of the freedom movement of India. He brought forth evidence to prove that the Vedas existed in the present form at least 5000 years before Christ. He also laid the foundation for India's freedom movement that later national leaders built on. In 1905 he suggested that Hindi be adopted as the national language of India. Swami Vivekananda stayed with him at his home in Pune for eight or ten days, probably in 1892.

Haripada Mitra: A subdivisional Forest Officer in Belgaum in whose home Swamiji stayed for 9 days in October 1892. He and his wife were initiated by Swamiji. He met Swamiji again in 1899 and 1902.

G. S. Bhate: Maharashtrian professor, son of Sadashiv B. Bhate, whose guest Swamiji had been for a few days at Belgaum.

K. Sundararama Iyer: A professor with whom Swamiji stayed for 9 days in Trivandrum in 1892. Mr. Iyer again met Swamiji in Madras in 1897, just after Swamiji's return from his first visit to the West. Mr. Iyer was the tutor to the First Prince of Travancore, Martanda Varma, the nephew of the Maharaja of Travancore.

K.S. Ramaswami Shastri: The elder son of K. Sundararama Iyer, who later became the acting District Judge of Trichinopally and a Subordinate Judge of Chittor. He was a young college student when Swamiji stayed at their home. He also spent much time with Swamiji when both of them were in Madras in 1897.

A. Srinivasa Pai: First met Swamiji in Madras in 1893 when he was a college student. He and his friends often came to listen to Swamiji's informal talks there. Later he also spent time with Swamiji when the latter came to Madras in 1897.

Sarah Ellen Waldo, Miss (1845–1926): She was a member of the Brooklyn Ethical Association when Swamiji started giving classes in New York in 1894. After attending his classes for some time, she became his disciple and was given the name Haridasi. She was among those given brahmacharya vows at Thousand Island Park. Most of Swamiji's Raja Yoga was dictated by him to her and also edited by her. In addition, she took down notes of the classes given by Swamiji at Thousand Island Park, and these were later published as Inspired Talks.

Sister Devamata (Laura Franklin Glenn): Saw Swamiji's in New York in 1896 and attended his classes. She graduated from Vassar and then lived in Europe for ten years, studying at the Sorbonne and other academies there. In 1907 she was initiated by Swami Paramananda, who had started a Vedanta centre in Boston. Soon afterwards she went to India where she associated with Swami Ramakrishnananda in Madras for two years and also with Sri Sarada Devi in Calcutta for some time.

Cornelia Conger: Was the granddaughter of Mr. and Mrs. John B. Lyons, in whose home Swamiji stayed in Chicago in 1893 during the days of the Parliament of Religions and also several weeks afterwards. Many years later she came to India and shared her reminiscences of Swamiji at Belur Math.

Martha Brown Fincke: She was a student at Smith College in Northampton, Massachusetts, when she met Swami Vivekananda in November 1893. He had come to deliver a lecture at the college, and he stayed as a guest for a couple of days at the house where she was boarding. She also came to India years later and shared her reminiscences at Belur Math.

Henry J. Van Haagen: Dutch draughtsman and printer of New York,. He made Swamiji's sketch of the emblem of the Ramakrishna Math and Mission into a finished drawing. After attending Swamiji's classes for some time, he became his disciple and received brahmacharya vows from him.

Sister Christine (Christine Greenstidel: 1866–930): She was born in Germany, but came to the U.S. at the age of three when her parents settled in Detroit. She was a school teacher when she heard Swamiji lecture in Detroit in 1894. In July 1895 she came with her friend Mrs. Mary Funke to Thousand Island Park, where Swamiji was then staying, and they both became his disciples. Christine also received brahmacharya vows from Swamiji at that time. A few years later she came to India and dedicated her life to the education of Indian women.

Josephine MacLeod (Tantine; 1860–1949): A a devoted follower of Swami Vivekananda who did much to serve the Ramakrishna Movement. Her sister and brother-in-law, Betty and Frank Leggett, had their country home at Ridgely Manor, where Swamiji stayed for about 10 weeks in 1899. Swamiji wrote many inspiring letters to Miss MacLeod over the years, and he had a high opinion of her for her strength, commonsense, and kindness.

Constance Towne: American Roman Catholic lady, lived with her mother in New York. Met Swamiji at a dinner hosted in his honour by Dr. Egbert Guernsey on 29 April 1894. Swamiji impressed her deeply with the catholicity of his outlook. Their friendship began then. She later saw him at other social gatherings.

Mary C. Funke: A a friend of Sister Christine who attended Swamiji's lectures with her in Detroit in 1894. Later the two of them went to Thousand Island Park to attend Swamiji's classes there, and her reminiscences of those days are especially inspiring and informative. Like Sister Christine, she was initiated by Swamiji there. Passed away in 1927.

Madame E. Calve (Rosa Emma Calve: 1858–1942): A well-known French opera singer, noted especially for her role as Carmen in Bizet's opera of that name. She met Swamiji in Chicago when she was at the peak of her career, and later wrote about his great influence on her life in her autobiography. She also came to India after his passing away to pay respects to his memory.

Maud Stumm: An American artist, studying in Paris, when she met Swamiji there in 1895. Later, in 1899, she was a guest at Ridgely Manor when Swamiji was staying there. She was recognized for her portraitures and other works of art. She did a series of studies in pastel of Sarah Bernhardt, a world-famous actress who was also an admirer of Swami Vivekananda. Miss Stumm also drew a portrait of Swamiji at the Ridgely Manor.

Sister Nivedita (Margaret Noble; 1867–1911): was an Irish woman who first met Swamiji in London in November 1895, when she was working as the principal of a school. She was then deeply interested in educational work. At his request, she came to India to set up a school for Indian women. Swamiji gave her the vows of brahmacharya then, and she dedicated the rest of her life to serving India in various ways. She was a powerful lecturer and also wrote several books on Swamiji and on various aspects of Indian life. In later days she immersed herself in India's freedom movement. She passed away in 1911 in Darjeeling.

Eric Hammond: An English journalist and poet who lived in a suburb of Wimbledon with his wife, Nell. He was well known in that area for his annual lectures on poets and poetry. The couple met Swamiji in England in 1896 through their friend Margaret Noble, and became very devoted to him. Eric later did much to help S wamiji's work in England.

E.T. Sturdy (Edward Sturdy): An English disciple of Swami Vivekananda. Before meeting Swamiji he was a member of the Theosophical Society, and travelled to America and India to meet the leading Theosophists. After some time he left the organization and began wandering in the Himalayas, where he met Swami Shivananda and learned about Swamiji. Soon after, he returned to England and married. In 1895 he wrote to Swamiji when the latter was in the U.S. and invited him to be his guest in England. Swamiji came a few months later and stayed for about six weeks in his home, helping him with his Sanskrit studies and with his translation of the Narada Bhakti Sutras. Mr. Sturdy did much to help Swamiji's work get started in England.

T.J. Desai: Met Swamiji in England in 1895. Soon after, he became a member of the Royal Asiatic Society of Great

Britain and Ireland. When Swamiji was in England in 1895 and 1896, Desai often associated with him and also dined with him on occasion.

Kamakhyanath Mitra: (1873–1948): Distinguished educationist. Saw Swamiji a couple of times at Balaram Bose's house in 1897, and again at the Star Theatre in 1898. After serving as Professor of English at several colleges, Kamakhyanath retired as Principal of Rajendra College, Faridpore. He was an original thinker and bold writer.

Manmathanath Ganguli: Was a clerk in a government office in Allahabad when he heard about Swami Vivekananda's return to India from the West. Taking leave from his work, he went to Calcutta to meet Swamiji. After that he would often come to Calcutta to see him, and was eventually given spiritual initiation by Swamiji.

S. K. Blodgett, Mrs.: American devotee of Swamiji, resident of Los Angeles, had heard him speak at the Parliament of Religions at Chicago. Swamiji was her guest from mid-December 1899 to the second week of January 1900, at her house in Los Angeles.

Ida Ansell: American lady devotee of Swami Vivekananda whose notes of his classes in Northern California, along with those of Mr. Rhodehamel, are the only records of Swamiji's lectures and classes in San Francisco and Alameda, when he spoke "to large audiences and small, at least sixty-one times" within a period of forty-six days. Swami Turiyananda imparted initiation to her naming her Ujvala. Spent her last seven years in Vivekananda House of Hollywood Centre and died there on 31 January 1955.

Christina Albers: She met Swamiji at a lecture in San Francisco in 1900.

Isabel Margesson (Lady Margesson): Sister of Seventh Earl of Buckinghamshire, Hon. Secretary of Sesame Club, ardent feminist, elite, intellectual member of society. Heard Swamiji speak at Prince's Hall, London on 22 October 1895. Deeply impressed, invited him to give a talk at her residence on 10 November 1895 at a gathering of intellectuals. Margaret Noble (later Sister Nivedita), first saw and heard Swamiji that day.

Viraja Devi (Edith Allan): First met Swamiji at a lecture in San Francisco in March 1900, and he invited her to come and see him privately the next day at his Turk Street flat. After that she came to see him every day for the month that he was there, and also went to Alameda when he gave talks there. She sometimes helped him cook after his classes. Later, she and her husband, Thomas Allan, were initiated by Swami Trigunatitananda, and both were active in the work of the Vedanta Society of Northern California. Mr. Allen was President of the Society in later years.

C. Ramanujachari: Disciple of Swami Brahmananda, Executive Secretary of Students' Home, Chennai. In their youth he and his brother Ramaswamy Iyengar had come in touch with Swami Ramakrishnananda and been inspired by the Ramakrishna Vivekananda ideology. Their tireless efforts led to the founding of the Students' Home in 1905. An accomplished singer and actor. Passed away on 4 November 1956 at the age of 81.

K. S. Ghosh: He was a young student of Deoghar High School in 1898 when Swamiji came to Deoghar to recuperate his health. He later became a professor of philosophy at Hazaribagh College.

Frank Rhodehamel: Admirer of Swamiji, students of Vedanta. First heard his lecture at the Unitarian Church Oakland. Deeply interested, became a close follower, attending all his lectures at Oakland and in San Francisco as well as the classes at his residence (February–April, 1900). Rhodehamel came in contact with Swami Turiyananda in California and joined Brahmachari Gurudas in development activities. Said to have been the disciple of Swami Turiyananda.

Kate Sanborn: American lady, a lecturer, a writer and also an enthusiastic hostess. Owner of a farm, "Breezy

Meadows", at Metcalf near Boston, Swamiji's first home in America. He had met her on the train to Chicago from Vancouver. She introduced Swamiji to John Henry Wright, a professor of Greek classics at Harvard University, who was instrumental in enabling Swamiji to be a delegate at the Parliament.

Kumudbandhu Sen: Disciple of Swami Brahmananda, a lifelong bachelor and a scholar. First saw Swamiji in 1897 in a rented house on that Sarkarbari Lane. The Udbodhan published numerous articles written by him. Died on 14 February 1962 at the age of 82 in Calcutta.

Lillian Montgomary: Attended Vivekananda's New York lectures in 1900.

Mohanlal Shah: Closely connected with Advaita Ashrama, Mayavati, since its very inception. Stayed in the ashrama itself for about thirty-six years. He was the printer of Prabuddha Bharata for a number of years.

Mary Tapan Wright: Wife of Prof. John Henry Wright, professor of Greek History at Harvard University, who was instrumental in enabling Swamiji to represent Hinduism at the Parliament of Religions, Chicago. She heard Swamiji speak when he delivered his first public lecture in the Western world at a little village church in Annisquam.

Sacchindranath Bose: Was employed by the Raja of Mahisadal as a Manage and was a boyhood friend of Swami Shubhananda, a disciple of Swami Vivekananda. His reminiscences were collected from his letters to Subhananda.

Manmathanath Chowdhury: In his itinerant days Swamiji, with Swami Akhandananda, spent a week at his house in Bhagalpur (August 1890). A staunch Brahmo, reconverted to Hinduism under the influence of Swamiji who elucidated to him the various aspects of Hindu religion.

Harbilas Sardar: President of the Arya Samaj at Ajmer during Swamiji's time. Met Swamiji for the first time at Mount Abu on 24 June 1891. Swamiji stayed at his house for three or four days when he visited Ajmer in 1891. Later distinguished himself as a historian of Rajputana, and as a member of the Central Legislative Assembly of India.

G. G. Narasimhachari: Resident of Bangalore, also known as Narasimha or Narasimhacharya. First met Swamiji at the house of Manmathanath Bhattacharya, Deputy-Accountant General of Madras in early 1893. Impressed by his personality and speech, marshalled his friends and with their co-operation took steps to help Swamiji's cause, in particular to send him abroad. Played vital role in the publication of the Brahmavadin, a fortnightly journal, published from Madras at the behest of Swamiji.

Ella Wheeler Wilcox: Well-known, popular poetess from New York, and a devout pupil of Swamiji. In 1895 she and her husband chanced to attend a lecture of Swamiji "out of curiosity". At the end of the lecture they went out "with new courage, new hope, new strength, new faith, to meet life's vicissitudes".

Shailendranath Bandopadhyay: Swamiji's disciple. As a young boy had met Swamiji and Sister Nivedita. His parents were initiated by Swamiji and he loved them greatly for their devout disposition. Swamiji stayed with his family when he came to Darjeeling. Later did his schooling and college studies staying at Belur Math as a residential student. Later became a well-known lawyer in Calcutta High Court.

Alice M. Hansbrough: One of the three Mead sisters. First saw and heard Swamiji at Blanchard Hall in Los Angeles on 8.12.1899. After a few days met Swamiji at Mrs. Blodgett's house and invited him to be her guest. Following an initial visit Swamiji was the guest of the Mead sisters for about six weeks. Went to Northern California as Swamiji's secretary and for three months served him tirelessly, attending to every aspect of his work.

Reeves Calkins: was a young Christian minister when he heard Swami Vivekananda speak at the Parliament of

Religions in Chicago in 1893. In 1900 he was on a ship to India as a missionary when he met Swamiji on board and had many discussions with him.